Lisp in Small Pieces

Lisp in Small Pieces

Christian Queinnec
Ecole Polytechnique

Translated by Kathleen Callaway

CAMBRIDGE
UNIVERSITY PRESS

PUBLISHED BY THE PRESS SYNDICATE OF THE UNIVERSITY OF CAMBRIDGE
The Pitt Building, Trumpington Street, Cambridge, United Kingdom

CAMBRIDGE UNIVERSITY PRESS
The Edinburgh Building, Cambridge CB2 2RU, UK
40 West 20th Street, New York NY 10011–4211, USA
477 Williamstown Road, Port Melbourne, VIC 3207, Australia
Ruiz de Alarcón 13, 28014 Madrid, Spain
Dock House, The Waterfront, Cape Town 8001, South Africa

http://www.cambridge.org

First published in French as *Les Langages Lisp* by Interéditions 1994

First published in English 1996
First paperback edition 2003

Translated by
Kathleen Callaway, 9 allée des Bois du Stade, 33700 Merignac, France

A catalogue record for this book is available from the British Library

ISBN 0 521 56247 3 hardback
ISBN 0 521 54566 8 paperback

Table of Contents

To the Reader

EVEN though the literature about Lisp is abundant and already accessible to the reading public, nevertheless, this book still fills a need. The logical substratum where Lisp and Scheme are founded demand that modern users must read programs that use (and even abuse) advanced technology, that is, higher-order functions, objects, continuations, and so forth. Tomorrow's concepts will be built on these bases, so not knowing them blocks your path to the future.

To explain these entities, their origin, their variations, this book will go into great detail. Folklore tells us that even if a Lisp user knows the value of every construction in use, he or she generally does not know its cost. This work also intends to fill that mythical hole with an in-depth study of the semantics and implementation of various features of Lisp, made more solid by more than thirty years of history.

Lisp is an enjoyable language in which numerous fundamental and non-trivial problems can be studied simply. Along with ML, which is strongly typed and suffers few side effects, Lisp is the most representative of the applicative languages. The concepts that illustrate this class of languages absolutely must be mastered by students and computer scientists of today and tomorrow. Based on the idea of "function," an idea that has matured over several centuries of mathematical research, applicative languages are omnipresent in computing; they appear in various forms, such as the composition of Un⋆x byte streams, the extension language for the Emacs editor, as well as other scripting languages. If you fail to recognize these models, you will misunderstand how to combine their primitive elements and thus limit yourself to writing programs painfully, word by word, without a real architecture.

Audience

This book is for a wide, if specialized audience:

- to graduate students and advanced undergraduates who are studying the implementation of languages, whether applicative or not, whether interpreted, compiled, or both.
- to programmers in Lisp or Scheme who want to understand more clearly the costs and nuances of constructions they're using so they can enlarge their expertise and produce more efficient, more portable programs.

- to the lovers of applicative languages everywhere; in this book, they'll find many reasons for satisfying reflection on their favorite language.

Philosophy

This book was developed in courses offered in two areas: in the graduate research program (DEA ITCP: Diplôme d'Études Approfondies en Informatique Théorique, Calcul et Programmation) at the University of Pierre and Marie Curie of Paris VI; some chapters are also taught at the École Polytechnique.

A book like this would normally follow an introductory course about an applicative language, such as Lisp, Scheme, or ML, since such a course typically ends with a description of the language itself. The aim of this book is to cover, in the widest possible scope, the semantics and implementation of interpreters and compilers for applicative languages. In practical terms, it presents no less than twelve interpreters and two compilers (one into byte-code and the other into the C programming language) without neglecting an object-oriented system (one derived from the popular MEROON). In contrast to many books that omit some of the essential phenomena in the family of Lisp dialects, this one treats such important topics as reflection, introspection, dynamic evaluation, and, of course, macros.

This book was inspired partly by two earlier works: *Anatomy of Lisp* [All78], which surveyed the implementation of Lisp in the seventies, and *Operating System Design: the Xinu Approach* [Com84], which gave all the necessary code without hiding any details on how an operating system works and thereby gained the reader's complete confidence.

In the same spirit, we want to produce a precise (rather than concise) book where the central theme is the semantics of applicative languages generally and of Scheme in particular. By surveying many implementations that explore widely divergent aspects, we'll explain in complete detail how any such system is built. Most of the schisms that split the community of applicative languages will be analyzed, taken apart, implemented, and compared, revealing all the implementation details. We'll "tell all" so that you, the reader, will never be stumped for lack of information, and standing on such solid ground, you'll be able to experiment with these concepts yourself.

Incidentally, all the programs in this book can be picked up, intact, electronically (details on page xix).

Structure

This book is organized into two parts. The first takes off from the implementation of a naive Lisp interpreter and progresses toward the semantics of Scheme. The line of development in this part is motivated by our need to be more specific, so we successively refine and redefine a series of name spaces (Lisp$_1$, Lisp$_2$, and so forth), the idea of continuations (and multiple associated control forms), assignment, and writing in data structures. As we slowly augment the language that we're defining, we'll see that we inevitably pare back its defining language so that it is reduced to

Chapter	Signature
1	`(eval exp env)`
2	`(eval exp env fenv)`
	`(eval exp env fenv denv)`
	`(eval exp env denv)`
3	`(eval exp env cont)`
4	`(eval e r s k)`
5	`((meaning e) r s k)`
6	`((meaning e sr) r k)`
	`((meaning e sr tail?) k)`
	`((meaning e sr tail?))`
7	`(run (meaning e sr tail?))`
10	`(->C (meaning e sr))`

Figure 1 Approximate signatures of interpreters and compilers

a kind of λ-calculus. We then convert the description we've gotten this way into its denotational equivalent.

More than six years of teaching experience convinced us that this approach of making the language more and more precise not only initiates the reader gradually into authentic language-research, but it is also a good introduction to denotational semantics, a topic that we really can't afford to leap over.

The second part of the book goes in the other direction. Starting from denotational semantics and searching for efficiency, we'll broach the topic of fast interpretation (by pretreating static parts), and then we'll implement that preconditioning (by precompilation) for a byte-code compiler. This part clearly separates program preparation from program execution and thus handles a number of topics: dynamic evaluation (**eval**); reflective aspects (first class environments, auto-interpretable interpretation, reflective tower of interpreters); and the semantics of macros. Then we introduce a second compiler, one compiling to the C programming language.

We'll close the book with the implementation of an object-oriented system, where objects make it possible to define the implementation of certain interpreters and compilers more precisely.

Good teaching demands a certain amount of repetition. In that context, the number of interpreters that we examine, all deliberately written in different styles—naive, object-oriented, closure-based, denotational, etc.—cover the essential techniques used to implement applicative languages. They should also make you think about the differences among them. Recognizing these differences, as they are sketched in Figure 1, will give you an intimate knowledge of a language and its implementation. Lisp is not just one of these implementations; it is, in fact, a *family* of dialects, each one made up of its own particular mix of the characteristics we'll be looking at.

In general, the chapters are more or less independent units of about forty pages or so; each is accompanied by exercises, and the solutions to those exercises are found at the end of the book. The bibliography contains not only historically important references, so you can see the evolution of Lisp since 1960, but also references to current, on-going research.

Prerequisites

Though we hope this book is both entertaining and informative, it may not necessarily be easy to read. There are subjects treated here that can be appreciated
only if you make an effort proportional to their innate difficulty. To harken back
to something like the language of courtly love in medieval France, there are certain
objects of our affection that reveal their beauty and charm only when we make a
chivalrous but determined assault on their defences; they remain impregnable if we
don't lay seige to the fortress of their inherent complexity.

In that respect, the study of programming languages is a discipline that demands the mastery of tools, such as the λ-calculus and denotational semantics.
While the design of this book will gradually take you from one topic to another in
an orderly and logical way, it can't eliminate all effort on your part.

You'll need certain prerequisite knowledge about Lisp or Scheme; in particular,
you'll need to know roughly thirty basic functions to get started and to understand
recursive programs without undue labor. This book has adopted Scheme as the
presentation language; (there's a summary of it, beginning on page xviii) and it's
been extended with an object layer, known as MEROON. That extension will come
into play when we want to consider problems of representation and implementation.

All the programs have been tested and actually run successfully in Scheme.
For readers that have assimilated this book, those programs will pose no problem
whatsoever to port!

Thanks and Acknowledgments

I must thank the organizations that procured the hardware (Apple Mac SE30
then Sony News 3260) and the means that enabled me to write this book: the
École Polytechnique, the Institut National de Recherche en Informatique et Automatique (INRIA-Rocquencourt, the national institute for research in computing
and automation at Rocquencourt), and Greco-PRC de Programmation du Cen-
tre National de la Recherche Scientifique (CNRS, the national center for scientific
research, special group for coordinated research on computer science).

I also want to thank those who actually participated in the creation of this book
by all the means available to them. I owe particular thanks to Sophie Anglade,
Josy Baron, Kathleen Callaway, Jérôme Chailloux, Jean-Marie Geffroy, Christian
Jullien, Jean-Jacques Lacrampe, Michel Lemaître, Luc Moreau, Jean-François Perrot, Daniel Ribbens, Bernard Serpette, Manuel Serrano, Pierre Weis, as well as my
muse, Claire N.

Of course, any errors that still remain in the text are surely my own.

Notation

Extracts from programs appear in **this type face**, no doubt making you think unavoidably of an old-fashioned typewriter. At the same time, certain parts will appear in *italic* to draw attention to variations within this context.

The sign → indicates the relation "has this for its value" while the sign ≡ indicates equivalence, that is, "has the same value as." When we evaluate a form in detail, we'll use a vertical bar to indicate the environment in which the expression must be considered. Here's an example illustrating these conventions in notation:

```
(let ((a (+ b 1)))
  (let ((f (lambda () a)))
    (foo (f) a) ) )|           ; the value of foo is the function for creating dotted
                  | b→ 3  ; pairs that is, the value of the global variable cons.
                  | foo≡ cons
≡ (let ((f (lambda () a))) (foo (f) a))|
                                       | a→ 4
                                       | b→ 3
                                       | foo≡ cons
                                       | f≡ (lambda () a)|
                                                         | a→ 4
≡ (foo (f) a)|
             | a→ 4
             | b→ 3
             | foo≡ cons
             | f≡ (lambda () a)|
                               | a→ 4
→ (4 . 4)
```

We'll use a few functions that are non-standard in Scheme, such as **gensym** that creates symbols guaranteed to be new, that is, different from any symbol seen before. In Chapter 10, we'll also use **format** and **pp** to display or "pretty-print." These functions exist in most implementations of Lisp or Scheme.

Certain expressions make sense only in the context of a particular dialect, such as COMMON LISP, Dylan, EuLisp, IS-Lisp, Le-Lisp[1], Scheme, etc. In such a case, the name of the dialect appears next to the example, like this:

```
(defdynamic fooncall                                    IS-Lisp
  (lambda (one :rest others)
    (funcall one others) ) )
```

To make it easier for you to get around in this book, we'll use this sign [see p.] to indicate a cross-reference to another page. When we suggest variations detailed in the exercises, we'll also use that sign, like this [see Ex.]. You'll also find a complete index of the function definitions that we mention. [see p. 495]

---

1. Le-Lisp is a trademark of INRIA.

Short Summary of Scheme

There are excellent books for learning Scheme, such as [AS85, Dyb87, SF89]. For reference, the standard document is the *Revised revised revised revised Report on Scheme*, informally known as R⁴RS.

This summary merely outlines the important characteristics of that dialect, that is, the characteristics that we'll be using later to dissect the dialect as we lead you to a better understanding of it.

Scheme lets you handle symbols, characters, character strings, lists, numbers, Boolean values, vectors, ports, and functions (or procedures in Scheme parlance).

Each of those data types has its own associated predicate: **symbol?**, **char?**, **string?**, **pair?**, **number?**, **boolean?**, **vector?**, and **procedure?**.

There are also the corresponding selectors and modifiers, where appropriate, such as: **string-ref**, **string-set!**, **vector-ref**, and **vector-set!**.

For lists, there are: **car**, **cdr**, **set-car!**, and **set-cdr!**.

The selectors, **car** and **cdr**, can be composed (and pronounced), so, for example, to designate the second term in a list, we use **cadr** and pronounce it something like *kadder*.

These values can be implicitly named and created simply by mentioning them, as we do with symbols and identifiers. For characters, we prefix them by **#** as in **#\Z** or **#\space**. We enclose character strings within quotation marks (that is, **"**) and lists within parentheses (that is, **()**). We use numbers are they are. We can also make use of Boolean values, namely, **#t** and **#f**. For vectors, we use this syntax: **#(do re mi)**, for example. Such values can be constructed dynamically with **cons**, **list**, **string**, **make-string**, **vector**, and **make-vector**. They can also be converted from one to another, by using **string->symbol** and **int->char**.

We manage input and output by means of these functions: **read**, of course, reads an expression; **display** shows an expression; **newline** goes to the next line.

Programs are represented by Scheme values known as *forms*.

The form **begin** lets you group forms to evaluate them sequentially; for example, **(begin (display 1) (display 2) (newline))**.

There are many conditional forms. The simplest is the form *if—then—else—* conventionally written in Scheme this way: **(if** *condition then otherwise***)**. To handle choices that entail more than two options, Scheme offers **cond** and **case**. The form **cond** contains a group of *clauses* beginning with a Boolean form and ending by a series of forms; one by one the Boolean forms of the clauses are evaluated until one returns true (or more precisely, not false, that is, not **#f**); the forms that follow the Boolean form that succeeded will then be evaluated, and their result becomes the value of the entire **cond** form. Here's an example of the form **cond** where you can see the default behavior of the keyword **else**.

```
(cond ((eq? x 'flip) 'flop)
      ((eq? x 'flop) 'flip)
      (else (list x "neither flip nor flop")) )
```

The form **case** has a form as its first parameter, and that parameter provides a key that we'll look for in all the clauses that follow; each of those clauses specifies which key or keys will set it off. Once an appropriate key is found, the associated forms will be evaluated and their result will become the result of the entire **case** form. Here's how we would convert the preceding example using **cond** into one using **case**.

```
(case x
  ((flip) 'flop)
  ((flop) 'flip)
  (else (list x "neither flip nor flop")) )
```

Functions are defined by a **lambda** form. Just after the keyword **lambda**, you'll find the variables of the function, followed by the expressions that indicate how to calculate the function. These variables can be modified by assignment, indicated by **set!**. Literal constants are introduced by **quote**. The forms **let**, **let***, and **letrec** introduce local variables; the initial value of such a local variable may be calculated in various ways.

With the form **define**, you can define named values of any kind. We'll exploit the internal writing facilities that **define** forms provide, as well as the non-essential syntax where the name of the function to define is indicated by the way it's called. Here is an example of what we mean.

```
(define (rev l)
  (define nil '())
  (define (reverse l r)
    (if (pair? l) (reverse (cdr l) (cons (car l) r)) r) )
  (reverse l nil) )
```

That example could also be rewritten without inessential syntax, like this:

```
(define rev
  (lambda (l)
    (letrec ((reverse (lambda (l r)
                        (if (pair? l) (reverse (cdr l)
                                               (cons (car l) r))
                            r ) )))
      (reverse l '()) ) ) )
```

That example completes our brief summary of Scheme.

Programs and More Information

The programs (both interpreted and compiled) that appear in this book, the object system, and the associated tests are all available on-line by anonymous **ftp** at:

(IP 128.93.2.54) `ftp.inria.fr:INRIA/Projects/icsla/Books/LiSP.tar.gz`

At the same site, you'll also find articles about Scheme and other implementations of Scheme.

The electronic mail address of the author of this book is:

`Christian.Queinnec@polytechnique.fr`

Recommended Reading

Since we assume that you already know Scheme, we'll refer to the standard reference [AS85, SF89].

To gain even greater advantage from this book, you might also want to prepare yourself with other reference manuals, such as COMMON LISP [Ste90], Dylan [App92b], EuLISP[PE92], IS-Lisp [ISO94], Le-Lisp [CDD+91], OakLisp [LP88], Scheme [CR91b], T [RAM84] and, Talk [ILO94].

Then, for a wider perspective about programming languages in general, you might want to consult [BG94].

1
The Basics of Interpretation

*T*HIS chapter introduces a basic interpreter that will serve as the foundation for most of this book. Deliberately simple, it's more closely related to Scheme than to Lisp, so we'll be able to explain Lisp in terms of Scheme that way. In this preliminary chapter, we'll broach a number of topics in succession: the articulations of this interpreter; the well known pair of functions, **eval** and **apply**; the qualities expected in environments and in functions. In short, we'll start various explorations here to pursue in later chapters, hoping that the intrepid reader will not be frightened away by the gaping abyss on either side of the trail.

The interpreter and its variations are written in native Scheme without any particular linguistic restrictions.

Literature about Lisp rarely resists that narcissistic pleasure of describing Lisp in Lisp. This habit began with the first reference manual for Lisp 1.5 [MAE+62] and has been widely imitated ever since. We'll mention only the following examples of that practice: (There are many others.) [Rib69], [Gre77], [Que82], [Cay83], [Cha80], [SJ93], [Rey72], [Gor75], [SS75], [All78], [McC78b], [Lak80], [Hen80], [BM82], [Cli84], [FW84], [dRS84], [AS85], [R3R86], [Mas86], [Dyb87], [WH88], [Kes88], [LF88], [Dil88], [Kam90].

Those evaluators are quite varied, both in the languages that they define and in what they use to do so, but most of all in the goals they pursue. The evaluator defined in [Lak80], for example, shows how graphic objects and concepts can emerge naturally from Lisp, while the evaluator in [BM82] focuses on the size of evaluation.

The language used for the *definition* is important as well. If assignment and surgical tools (such as **set-car!**, **set-cdr!**, and so forth) are allowed in the definition language, they enrich it and thus minimize the size (in number of lines) of descriptions; indeed, with them, we can precisely simulate the language *being defined* in terms that remind us of the lowest level machine instructions. Conversely, the description uses more concepts. Restricting the definition language in that way complicates our task, but lowers the risk of semantic divergence. Even if the size of the description grows, the language being defined will be more precise and, to that degree, better understood.

Figure 1.1 shows a few representative interpreters in terms of the complexity

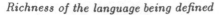

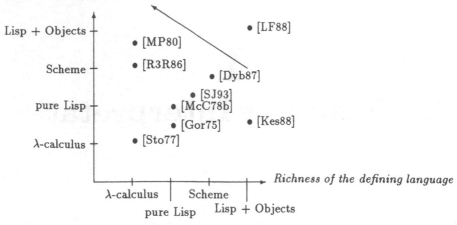

Figure 1.1

of their definition language (along the x-axis) and the complexity of the language being defined (along the y-axis). The knowledge progression shows up very well in that graph: more and more complicated problems are attacked by more and more restricted means. This book corresponds to the vector taking off from a very rich version of Lisp to implement Scheme in order to arrive at the λ-calculus implementing a very rich Lisp.

1.1 Evaluation

The most essential part of a Lisp interpreter is concentrated in a single function around which more useful functions are organized. That function, known as `eval`, takes a program as its argument and returns the value as output. The presence of an explicit evaluator is a characteristic trait of Lisp, not an accident, but actually the result of deliberate design.

We say that a language is *universal* if it is as powerful as a Turing machine. Since a Turing machine is fairly rudimentary (with its mobile read-write head and its memory composed of binary cells), it's not too difficult to design a language that powerful; indeed, it's probably more difficult to design a useful language that is not universal.

Church's thesis says that any function that can be computed can be written in any universal language. A Lisp system can be compared to a function taking programs as input and returning their value as output. The very existence of such systems proves that they are computable: thus a Lisp system can be written in a universal language. Consequently, the function `eval` itself can be written in Lisp, and more generally, the behavior of Fortran can be described in Fortran, and so forth.

What makes Lisp unique—and thus what makes an explication of `eval` non-trivial—is its reasonable size, normally from one to twenty pages, depending on the level of detail.[1] This property is the result of a significant effort in design to make the language more regular, to suppress special cases, and above all to establish a syntax that's both simple and abstract.

Many interesting properties result from the existence of **eval** and from the fact that it can be defined in Lisp itself.

- You can learn Lisp by reading a reference manual (one that explains functions thematically) or by studying the **eval** function itself. The difficulty with that second approach is that you have to know Lisp in order to read the definition of **eval**—though knowing Lisp, of course, is the *result* we're hoping for, rather than the *prerequisite*. In fact, it's sufficient for you to know only the subset of Lisp used by **eval**. The language that defines **eval** is a pared-down one in the sense that it procures only the essence of the language, reduced to special forms and primitive functions.

  It's an undeniable advantage of Lisp that it brings you these two intertwined approaches for learning it.

- The fact that the definition of **eval** is available in Lisp means that the programming environment is part of the language, too, and costs little. By programming environment, we mean such things as a tracer, a debugger, or even a reversible evaluator [Lie87]. In practice, writing these tools to control evaluation is just a matter of elaborating the code for **eval**, for example, to print function calls, to store intermediate results, to ask the end-user whether he or she wants to go on with the evaluation, and so forth.

  For a long time, these qualities have insured that Lisp offers a superior programming environment. Even today, the fact that **eval** can be defined in Lisp means that it's easy to experiment with new models of implementation and debugging.

- Finally, **eval** itself is a programming tool. This tool is controversial since it implies that an application written in Lisp and using **eval** must include an entire interpreter or compiler, but more seriously, it must give up the possibility of many optimizations. In other words, using **eval** is not without consequences. In certain cases, its use is justified, notably when Lisp serves as the definition and the implementation of an incremental programming language.

  Even apart from that important cost, the semantics of **eval** is not clear, a fact that justifies its being separated from the official definition of Scheme in [CR91b]. [see p. 271]

1.2 Basic Evaluator

Within a program, we distinguish *free variables* from *bound variables*. A variable is free as long as no binding form (such as **lambda**, **let**, and so forth) qualifies it; otherwise, we say that a variable is bound. As the term indicates, a free variable is unbound by any constraint; its value could be anything. Consequently, in order

---

1. In this chapter, we define a Lisp of about 150 lines.

to know the value of a fragment of a program containing free variables, we must know the values of those free variables themselves. The data structure associating variables and values is known as an *environment*. The function **evaluate**[2] is thus binary; it takes a program accompanied by an environment and returns a value.

```
(define (evaluate exp env) ...)
```

1.3   Evaluating Atoms

An important characteristic of Lisp is that programs are represented by expressions of the language. However, since any representation assumes a degree of encoding, we have to explain more about how programs are represented. The principal conventions of representation are that a variable is represented by a symbol (its name) and that a functional application is represented by a list where the first term of the list represents the function to apply and the other terms represent arguments submitted to that function.

Like any other compiler, **evaluate** begins its work by syntactically analyzing the expression to evaluate in order to deduce what it represents. In that sense, the title of this section is inappropriate since this section does not literally involve evaluating atoms but rather evaluating programs where the representation is atomic. It's important, in this context, to distinguish the program from its representation (or, the message from its medium, if you will). The function **evaluate** works on the representation; from the representation, it deduces the expected intention; finally, it executes what's requested.

```
(define (evaluate exp env)
  (if (atom? exp)   ; (atom?  exp) ≡ (not (pair?  exp))
      ...
      (case (car exp)
        ...
        (else ...) ) ) )
```

If an expression is not a list, perhaps it's a symbol or actual data, such as a number or a character string. When the expression is a symbol, the expression represents a *variable* and its value is the one attributed by the environment.

```
(define (evaluate exp env)
  (if (atom? exp)
      (if (symbol? exp) (lookup exp env) exp)
      (case (car exp)
        ...
        (else ...) ) ) )
```

The function **lookup** (which we'll explain later on page 13) knows how to find the value of a variable in an environment. Here's the signature of **lookup**:

```
(lookup variable environment) → value
```

---

2. There is a possibility of confusion here. We've already mentioned the evaluator defined by the function **eval**; it's widely present in any implementation of Scheme, even if not standardized; it's often unary—accepting only one argument. To avoid confusion, we'll call the function **eval** that we are defining by the name **evaluate** and the associated function **apply** by the name **invoke**. These new names will also make your life easier if you want to experiment with these programs.

In consequence, an implicit conversion takes place between a symbol and a variable. If we were more meticulous about how we write, then in place of (`lookup exp env`), we should have written:

... (`lookup (symbol->variable exp) env`) ...

That more scrupulous way of writing emphasizes that the symbol—the value of `exp`—must be changed into a variable. It also underscores the fact that the function `symbol->variable`[3] is not at all an identity; rather, it converts a syntactic entity (the symbol) into a semantic entity (the variable). In practice, then, a variable is nothing other than an imaginary object to which the language and the programmer attach a certain sense but which, for practical reasons, is handled only by means of its representation. The representation was chosen for its convenience: `symbol->variable` works like the identity because Lisp exploits the idea of a symbol as one of its basic types. In fact, other representations could have been adopted; for example, a variable could have appeared in the form of a group of characters, prefixed by a dollar sign. In that case, the conversion function `symbol->variable` would have been less simple.

If a variable were an imaginary concept, the function `lookup` would not know how to accept it as a first argument, since `lookup` knows how to work only on tangible objects. For that reason, once again, we have to encode the variable in a representation, this time, a key, to enable `lookup` to find its value in the environment. A precise way of writing it would thus be:

... (`lookup (variable->key (symbol->variable exp)) env`) ...

But the natural laziness of Lisp-users inclines them to use the symbol of the same name as the key associated with a variable. In that context, then, `variable->key` is merely the inverse of `symbol->variable` and the composition of those two functions is simply the identity.

When an expression is atomic (that is, when it does not involve a dotted pair) and when that expression is not a symbol, we have the habit of considering it as the representation of a constant that is its own value. This idempotence is known as the *autoquote* facility. An autoquoted object does not need to be quoted, and it is its own value. See [Cha94] for an example.

Here again, this choice is not obvious for several reasons. Not all atomic objects naturally denote themselves. The value of the character string `"a?b:c"` might be to call the C compiler for this string, then to execute the resulting program, and to insert the results back in Lisp.

Other types of objects (functions, for example) seem stubbornly resistant to the idea of evaluation. Consider the variable `car`, one that we all know the utility of; its value is the function that extracts the left child from a pair; but that function *car* itself—what is its value? Evaluating a function usually proves to be an error that should have been detected and prevented earlier.

Another example of a problematic value is the empty list (). From the way it is written, it might suggest that it is an empty application, that is, a functional application without any arguments where we've even forgotten to mention the

---

3. Personally, I don't like names formed like this x->y to indicate a conversion because this order makes it difficult to understand compositions; for example, $(y$->$z(x$->$y...))$ is less straightforward than $(z$<-$y(y$<-$x...))$. In contrast, x->y is much easier to read than y<-x. You can see here one of the many difficulties that language designers come up against.

function. That syntax is forbidden in Scheme and consequently is not defined as
having a value.

For those kinds of reasons, we have to analyze expressions very carefully, and
we should *autoquote* only those data that deserve it, namely, numbers, characters,
and strings of characters. [see p. 7] We could thus write:

```
(define (evaluate e env)
  (if (atom? e)
      (cond ((symbol? e) (lookup e env))
            ((or (number? e)(string? e)(char? e)(boolean? e)(vector? e))
             e )
            (else (wrong "Cannot evaluate" e)) )
      ... ) )
```

In that fragment of code, you can see the first case of possible errors. Most
Lisp systems have their own exception mechanism; it, too, is difficult to write
in portable code. In an error situation, we could call **wrong**[4] with a character
string as its first argument. That character string would describe the kind of error,
and the following arguments could be the objects explaining the reason for the
anomaly. We should mention, however, that more rudimentary systems send out
cryptic messages, like **Bus error: core dump** when errors occur. Others stop the
current computation and return to the basic interaction loop. Still others associate
an exception handler with a computation, and that exception handler catches the
object representing the error or exception and decides how to behave from there.
[see p. 255] Some systems even offer exception handlers that are quasi-expert
systems themselves, analyzing the error and the corresponding code to offer the
end-user choices about appropriate corrections. In short, there is wide variation in
this area.

1.4   Evaluating Forms

Every language has a number of syntactic forms that are "untouchable": they
cannot be redefined adequately, and they must not be tampered with. In Lisp,
such a form is known as a *special form*.   It is represented by a list where the first
term is a particular symbol belonging to the set of *special operators*.[5]

A dialect of Lisp is characterized by its set of special forms and by its library
of primitive functions (those functions that cannot be written in the language
itself and that have profound semantic repercussions, as, for example, **call/cc** in
Scheme).

In some respects, Lisp is simply an ordinary version of applied λ-calculus, augmented by a set of special forms. However, the special genius of a given Lisp is
expressed in just this set. Scheme has chosen to minimize the number of special
operators (**quote, if, set!**, and **lambda**). In contrast, COMMON LISP (CLtL2

---

4. Notice that we did not say "the function **wrong**." We'll see more about error recovery on
page 255.
5. We will follow the usual lax habit of considering a special operator, say **if**, as being a "special
form," although **if** is not even a form. Scheme treats them as "syntactic keywords" whereas
COMMON LISP recognizes them with the **special-form-p** predicate.

[Ste90]) has more than thirty or so, thus circumscribing the number of cases where it's possible to generate highly efficient code.

Because special forms are coded as they are, their syntactic analysis is simple: it is based on the first term of each such form, so one `case` statement suffices. When a special form does not begin with a keyword, we say that is it is a *functional application* or more simply an application. For the moment, we're looking at only a small subset of the general special forms: `quote`, `if`, `begin`, `set!`, and `lambda`. (Later chapters introduce new, more specialized forms.)

```
(define (evaluate e env)
  (if (atom? e)
      (cond ((symbol? e) (lookup e env))
            ((or (number? e)(string? e)(char? e)(boolean? e)(vector? e))
             e )
            (else (wrong "Cannot evaluate" e)) )
      (case (car e)
        ((quote)  (cadr e))
        ((if)     (if (evaluate (cadr e) env)
                      (evaluate (caddr e) env)
                      (evaluate (cadddr e) env) ))
        ((begin)  (eprogn (cdr e) env))
        ((set!)   (update! (cadr e) env (evaluate (caddr e) env)))
        ((lambda) (make-function (cadr e) (cddr e) env))
        (else     (invoke (evaluate (car e) env)
                          (evlis (cdr e) env) )) ) ) )
```

In order to lighten that definition, we've reduced the syntactic analysis to its minimum, and we haven't bothered to verify whether the quotations are well formed, whether `if` is really ternary[6] (accepting three parameters) each time, and so forth. We'll assume that the programs that we're analyzing are syntactically correct.

1.4.1 Quoting

The special form `quote` makes it possible to introduce a value that, without its quotation, would have been confused with a legal expression. The decision to represent a program as a value of the language makes it necessary, when we want to speak about a particular value, to find a means for discriminating between data and programs that usurp the same space. A different syntactic choice could have avoided that problem. For example, M-expressions, originally planned in [McC60] as the normal syntax for programs written in Lisp, would have eliminated this particular problem, but they would have forbidden macros—a marvelously useful tool for extending syntax; however, M-expressions disappeared rapidly [McC78a]. The special form `quote` is consequently the principal discriminator between program and data.

---

6. As a form, `if` is not necessarily ternary. That is, it does not have to have three parameters. Scheme and COMMON LISP, for example, support both binary and ternary `if`, whereas EuLisp and IS-Lisp accept only ternary `if`; Le-Lisp supports at least binary `if` with a `progn` implicit in the alternative. (`progn` corresponds to Scheme `begin`.)

Quotation consists of returning, as a value, that term following the keyword. That practice is clearly articulated in this fragment of code:

```
... (case (car e)
         ((quote) (cadr e)) ...) ...
```

You might well ask whether there is a difference between implicit and explicit quotation, for example, between 33 and '33 or even between #(fa do sol) and '#(fa do sol).[7] The first comparison—between 33 and '33—impinges on immediate objects although the second one—between #(fa do sol) and '#(fa do sol)—impinges on composite objects (though they are atomic objects in Lisp terminology). It is possible to imagine divergent meanings for those two fragments. Explicit quotation simply returns its quotation as its value whereas #(fa do sol) could return a new instance of the vector for every evaluation—a new instance of a vector of three components initialized by three particular symbols. In other words, #(fa do sol) may be nothing other than the abbreviation of (vector 'fa 'do 'sol) (that's one of the possibilities in Scheme, though not the right one), and its behavior is quite different from '#(fa do sol) and from (vector fa do sol), for that matter. We'll be returning later [see p. 140] to the question of what meaning to give to quotation, since, as you can see, the subject is far from simple.

1.4.2   Alternatives

As we look at *alternatives*, we'll consider the special form if as ternary, a control structure that evaluates its first argument (the *condition*), then according to the value it gets from that evaluation, chooses to return the value of its second argument (the *consequence*) or its third argument (the *alternate*). That idea is expressed in this fragment of code:

```
... (case (car e) ...
       ((if) (if (evaluate (cadr e) env)
                 (evaluate (caddr e) env)
                 (evaluate (cadddr e) env) )) ... ) ...
```

This program does not do full justice to the representation of Booleans.   As you have no doubt noticed, we're mixing two languages here: the first is Scheme (or at least, a close enough approximation that it's indistinguishable from Scheme) whereas the second is also Scheme (or at least something quite close). The first language implements the second. As a consequence, there is the same relation between them as, for example, between Pascal (the language of the first implementation of TeX) and TeX itself [Knu84]. Consequently, there is no reason to identify the representation of Booleans of these two languages.

The function **evaluate** returns a value belonging to the language that is being defined. That value maintains no *a priori* relation to the Boolean values of the defining language. Since we follow the convention that any object different from the Boolean *false* must be considered as Boolean *true*, a more carefully written program would look like this:

```
... (case (car e) ...
```

---

7. In Scheme, the notation #(...) represents a quoted vector.

```
((if) (if (not (eq? (evaluate (cadr e) env) the-false-value))
           (evaluate (caddr e) env)
           (evaluate (cadddr e) env) )) ... ) ...
```

Of course, we assume that the variable `the-false-value` has as its value the representation in the defining language of the Boolean *false* in the language being defined. There's a wide choice available to us for this value; for example,

```
(define the-false-value (cons "false" "boolean"))
```

The comparison of any value to the Boolean *false* is carried out by the physical comparer `eq?`, so a dotted pair handles the issue very well and can't be confused with any other possible value in the language being defined.

This discussion is not really trivial. In fact, Lisp chronicles are full of disputes about the differences between the Boolean value *false*, the empty list (), and the symbol `NIL`. The cleanest position to take in this controversy, quite independent of whether or not to preserve existing practice, is that *false* is different from ()—which is, after all, simply an empty list—and that those two have nothing to do with the symbol spelled `N, I, L`.

That is, in fact, the position that Scheme takes; the position was adopted several weeks before being standardized by IEEE (the Institute of Electrical and Electronic Engineers) [IEE91].

Where things get worse is that () is pronounced *nil*! In "traditional" Lisp, *false*, (), and `NIL` are all one and same symbol. In Le-Lisp, `NIL` is a variable, its value is (), and the empty list has been assimilated with the Boolean *false* and with the empty symbol ||.

1.4.3 Sequence

A *sequence* makes it possible to use a single syntactic form for a group of forms to evaluate sequentially. Like the well known `begin` ... `end` of the family of languages related to Algol, Scheme prefixes this special form by `begin` whereas other Lisps use `progn`, a generalization of `prog1`, `prog2`, etc. The sequential evaluation of a group of forms is "subcontracted" to a particular function: `eprogn`.

```
... (case (car e) ...
      ((begin) (eprogn (cdr e) env)) ... ) ...

(define (eprogn exps env)
  (if (pair? exps)
      (if (pair? (cdr exps))
          (begin (evaluate (car exps) env)
                 (eprogn (cdr exps) env) )
          (evaluate (car exps) env) )
      '() ) )
```

With that definition, the meaning of the sequence is now canonical. Nevertheless, we should note that in the middle of the definition of `eprogn`, there is a tail recursive call to `evaluate` to handle the final term of the sequence. That computation of the final term of a sequence is carried out as though it, and it alone, replaced the entire sequence. (We'll talk more about tail recursion later. [see p. 104])

We should also note the meaning we have to attribute to (begin). Here, we've defined (begin) to return the empty list (), but why should we choose the empty list? Why not something else, anything else, like **bruce** or **brian**[8]? This choice is part of our heritage from Lisp, where the prevailing custom returns **nil** when nothing better seems to be obligatory. However, in a world where *false*, (), and **nil** are distinct, what should we return? We're going to specialize our language as it's defined in this chapter so that (begin) returns the value **empty-begin**, which will be the (almost) arbitrary number 813[9] [Leb05].

```
(define (eprogn exps env)
  (if (pair? exps)
      (if (pair? (cdr exps))
          (begin (evaluate (car exps) env)
                 (eprogn (cdr exps) env) )
          (evaluate (car exps) env) )
      empty-begin ) )
(define empty-begin 813)
```

Our problem comes from the fact that the implementation that we are defining must necessarily return a value. Like Scheme, the language could attribute no particular meaning to (begin); that choice could be interpreted in at least two different ways: either this way of writing is permitted within a particular implementation, in which case it is an extension that must return a value freely chosen by the implementation in question; or this way of writing is not allowed and thus an error. In light of the consequences, it's better to avoid using this form when no guarantee exists about its value. Some implementations have an object, #<unspecified>, that lends itself to this use, as well as more generally to any situation where we don't know what we should return because nothing seems appropriate. That object is usually printable; it should not be confused with the undefined pseudo-value. [see p. 60]

Sequences are of no particular interest if a language is purely functional (that is, if it has no side effects). What is the point of evaluating a program if we don't care about the results? Well, in fact there are situations in which we use a computation simply for its side effects. Consider, for example, a video game programmed in a purely functional language; computations take time, whether we are interested in their results or not; it may be just this very side effect—slowing things down— rather than the result that interests us. Provided that the compiler is not smart enough to notice and remove any useless computation, we can use such side effects to slow the program down sufficiently to accomodate a player's reflexes, say.

In the presence of conventional read or write operations, which have side effects on data flow, sequencing becomes very interesting because it is obviously clearer to pose a question (by means of **display**), then wait for the response (by means of **read**) than to do the reverse. Sequencing is, in that sense, the explicit form for putting a series of evaluations in order. Other special forms could also introduce a certain kind of order. For example, alternatives could do so, like this:

$$(\text{if } \alpha \; \beta \; \beta) \equiv (\text{begin } \alpha \; \beta)$$

---

8. For the Monty Python fans in the audience
9. Fans of the gentleman thief Arsene Lupin will recognize the appropriateness of this choice.

That rule,[10] however, could also be simulated by this:

(begin α β) ≡ ((lambda (*void*) β) α)

That last rule shows—in case you weren't convinced yet—that **begin** is not really a necessary special form in Scheme since it can be simulated by the functional application that forces arguments to be computed before the body of the invoked function (the *call by value* evaluation rule).

1.4.4 Assignment

As in many other languages, the value of a variable can be modified; we say then that we assign the variable. Since this assignment involves modifying the value in the environment of the variable, we leave this problem to the function **update!**.[11] We'll explain that function later, on page 129.

```
... (case (car e)
        ((set!) (update! (cadr e) env (evaluate (caddr e) env))) ...) ...
```

Assignment is carried out in two steps: first, the new value is calculated; then it becomes the value of the variable. Notice that the variable is not the result of a calculation. Many semantic variations exist for assignment, and we'll discuss them later. [see p. 11] For the moment, it's important to bear in mind that the value of an assignment is not specified in Scheme.

1.4.5 Abstraction

Functions (also known as *procedures* in the jargon of Scheme) are the result of evaluating the special form, **lambda**, a name that refers to λ-calculus and indicates an *abstraction*. We delegate the chore of actually creating the function to **make-function**, and we furnish all the available parameters that **make-function** might need, namely, the list of variables, the body of the function, and the current environment.

```
... (case (car e) ...
        ((lambda) (make-function (cadr e) (cddr e) env)) ...) ...
```

1.4.6 Functional Application

When a list has no special operator as its first term, it's known as a *functional application*, or, referring to λ-calculus again, a *combination*. The function we get by evaluating the first term is applied to its arguments, which we get by evaluating the following terms. The following code reflects that very idea.

```
... (case (car e) ...
        (else (invoke (evaluate (car e) env)
                      (evlis (cdr e) env) )) ) ...
```

---

10. The variable *void* must not be free in β. That condition is trivially satisfied if *void* does not appear in β. For that reason, we usually use **gensym** to create new variables that are certain to have not yet been used. See Exercise 1.11.

11. According to current practice in Scheme, functions with side effects have a name suffixed by an exclamation point.

The utility function **evlis** takes a list of expressions and returns the corresponding list of values of those expressions. It is defined like this:

```
(define (evlis exps env)
  (if (pair? exps)
      (cons (evaluate (car exps) env)
            (evlis (cdr exps) env) )
      '() ) )
```

The function **invoke** is in charge of applying its first argument (a function, unless an error occurs) to its second argument (the list of arguments of the function indicated by the first argument); it then returns the value of that application as its result. In order to clarify the various uses of the word "argument" in that sentence, notice that **invoke** is similar to the more conventional **apply**, outside the explicit eruption of the environment. (We'll return later in Section 1.6 [see p. 15] to the exact representation of functions and environments.)

More about evaluate

The explanation we just walked through is more or less precise. A few utility functions, such as **lookup** and **update!** (that handle environments) or **make-function** and **invoke** (that handle functions) have not yet been fully explained. Even so, we can already answer many questions about **evaluate**. For example, it is already apparent that the dialect we are defining has only one unique name-space; that it is mono-valued (like Lisp$_1$) [see p. 31]; and that there are functional objects present in the dialect. However, we don't yet know the order of evaluation of arguments.

The order in which arguments are evaluated in the Lisp that we are defining is similar to the order of evaluation of arguments to **cons** as it appears in **evlis**. We could, however, impose any order that we want (for example, left to right) by using an explicit sequence, like this:

```
(define (evlis exps env)
  (if (pair? exps)
      (let ((argument1 (evaluate (car exps) env)))
        (cons argument1 (evlis (cdr exps) env)) )
      '() ) )
```

Without enlarging the arsenal[12] that we're using in the defining language, we have increased the precision of the description of the Lisp we've defined. This first part of this book tends to define a certain dialect more and more precisely, all the while restricting more and more the dialect serving for the definition.

1.5   Representing the Environment

The environment associates values with variables. The conventional data structure in Lisp for representing such associations is the *association list*, also known as the *A-list*. We're going to represent the environment as an A-list associating values

---

12. As you know, **let** is a macro that expands into a functional application: $(\text{let } ((x\ \pi_1))\pi_2) \equiv ((\text{lambda } (x)\ \pi_2)\ \pi_1)$.

and variables. To simplify, we'll represent the variables by symbols of the same name.

In this way, we can define the functions **lookup** and **update!** very easily, like this:

```
(define (lookup id env)
  (if (pair? env)
      (if (eq? (caar env) id)
          (cdar env)
          (lookup id (cdr env)) )
      (wrong "No such binding" id) ) )
```

We see a second[13] kind of error appear when we want to know the value of an unknown variable. Here again, we'll just use a call to **wrong** to express the problem that the interpreter confronts.

Back in the dark ages, when interpreters had very little memory[14] to work with, implementors often favored a generalized mode of *autoquote*. A variable without a value still had one, and that value was the symbol of the same name. It's disheartening to see things that we attached so much importance to separating— like symbol and variable—already getting back together and re-introducing so much confusion.

Even if it were practical for implementers never to provoke an error and thus to provide an idyllic world from which error had been banished, that design would still have a major drawback because the goal of a program is not so much to avoid committing errors but rather to fulfil its duty. In that sense, an error is a kind of crude guard rail: when we encounter it, it shows us that the program is not going as we intended. Errors and erroneous contexts need to be pointed out as early as possible so that their source can be corrected as soon as possible. The *autoquote* mode is consequently a poor design-choice because it lets certain situations worsen without our being able to see them in time to repair them.

The function **update!** modifies the environment and is thus likely to provoke the same error: the value of an unknown variable can't be modified. We'll come back to this point when we talk about the global environment.

```
(define (update! id env value)
  (if (pair? env)
      (if (eq? (caar env) id)
          (begin (set-cdr! (car env) value)
                 value )
          (update! id (cdr env) value) )
      (wrong "No such binding" id) ) )
```

The contract that the function **update!** abides by foresees that the function returns a value which will become that final special form of assignment. The value of an assignment is not defined in Scheme. That fact means that a portable program cannot expect a precise value, so there are many possible return values. For example,

---

13. The first kind of error appeared on page 6.
14. Memory, along with input/output facilities, still remains the most expensive part of a computer, even though the price keeps falling.

1. the value that has just been assigned; (That's what we saw earlier with
   update!.)

2. the former contents of the variable; (This possibility poses a slight problem
   with respect to initialization when we give the first value to a variable.)

3. an object representing whatever has not been specified, with which we can
   do very little—something like #<UFO>;

4. the value of a form with a non-specified value, such as the form set-cdr! in
   Scheme.

The environment can be seen as a composite abstract type. We can then extract
or modify subparts of the environment with selection and modification functions.
We then still have to define how to construct and enrich an environment.

Let's start with an empty initial environment. We can represent that idea
simply, like this:

```
(define env.init '())
```

(Later, in Section 1.6, we'll make the effort to produce a standard environment
a little richer than that.)

When a function is applied, a new environment is built, and that new environment binds variables of that function to their values. The function **extend** extends
an environment **env** with a list of **variables** and a list of **values**.

```
(define (extend env variables values)
   (cond ((pair? variables)
          (if (pair? values)
              (cons (cons (car variables) (car values))
                    (extend env (cdr variables) (cdr values)) )
              (wrong "Too less values") ) )
         ((null? variables)
          (if (null? values)
              env
              (wrong "Too much values") ) )
         ((symbol? variables) (cons (cons variables values) env)) ) ) )
```

The main difficulty is that we have to analyze syntactically all the possible
forms that a *<list-of-variables>* can have within an abstraction in Scheme.[15] A
list of variables is represented by a list of symbols, possibly a dotted list, that
is, terminated not by () but by a symbol, which we call a *dotted variable*. More
formally, a list of variables corresponds to the following pseudo-grammar:

$$\begin{array}{rcl}
\textit{<list-of-variables>} & := & () \\
& | & \textit{<variable>} \\
& | & (\ \textit{<variable>}\ .\ \textit{<list-of-variables>}\ ) \\
\textit{<variable>} & \in & \textbf{Symbol}
\end{array}$$

When we extend an environment, there must be agreement between the names
and values. Usually, there must be as many values as there are variables, unless

---

15. Certain Lisp sytems, such as COMMON LISP, have succombed to the temptation to enrich the
list of variables with various keywords, such as &aux, &key, &rest, and so forth. This practice
greatly complicates the binding mechanism. Other systems generalize the binding of variables
with pattern matching [SJ93].

the list of variables ends with a dotted variable or an *n-ary variable* that can take all the superfluous values in a list. Two errors can thus be raised, depending on whether there are too many or too few values.

1.6 Representing Functions

Perhaps the easiest way to represent functions is to use functions. Of course, the two instances of the word "function" in that sentence refer to different entities. More precisely, we should say, "The way to represent functions in the language that is being defined is to use functions of the defining language, that is, functions of the implementation language." The representation that we've chosen here minimizes the calling protocol in this way: the function `invoke` will have to verify only that its first argument really is a function, that is, an object that can be applied.

```
(define (invoke fn args)
  (if (procedure? fn)
      (fn args)
      (wrong "Not a function" fn) ) )
```

We really can't get any simpler than that. You might ask why we have specialized the function `invoke`, already a simple definition and merely called once from `evaluate`. The reason is that here we're setting the general structure of the interpreters that we're going to stuff you with later, and we will see other ways of coding that are simpler but more efficient and that require a more complicated form of `invoke`. You could also tackle Exercises 1.7 and 1.8 now.

A new kind of error appears here when we try to apply an object that is not a function. This kind of error can be detected at the moment of application, that is, after the evaluation of all the arguments. Other strategies would also be possible; for example, to attempt to warn the user as early as possible. In that case, we could impose an order in the evaluation of function applications, like this:

1. evaluate the term in the functional position;
2. if that value is not applicable, then raise an error;
3. evaluate the arguments from left to right;
4. compare the number of arguments to the arity of the function to apply and raise an error if they do not agree.

Evaluating arguments in order from left to right is useful for those who read left to right. It is also easy to implement since the order of evaluation is then obvious, but it complicates the task of the compiler. If the compiler tries to evaluate the arguments in a different order (for example, to improve register allocations), the compiler must prove that the new order of expressions does not change the semantics of the program.

Of course, we could attempt to do even better, by checking the arity sooner, like this:

1. evaluate the term in the functional position;
2. if that value is not applicable, then raise an error; otherwise, check its arity;

3. evaluate the arguments from left to right as long as their number still agrees with the arity; otherwise, raise an error;

4. apply the function to its arguments.[16]

Common Lisp insists that arguments must be evaluated from left to right, but for reasons of efficiency, it allows the term in the function position to be evaluated either before or after the others.

Scheme, in contrast, does not impose an order of evaluation for the terms of a functional application, and Scheme does not distinguish the function position in any particular way. Since there is no imposed order, the evaluator is free to choose whatever order it prefers; the compiler can then re-order terms without worrying. **[see p. 164]** The user no longer knows which order will be chosen, and so must use **begin** when certain effects must be kept in sequence.

As a matter of style, it's not very elegant to use a functional application to put side effects in sequence. For that reason, you should avoid writing such things as (f (set! f π) (set! f π')) where the function that will actually be applied can't be seen. Errors arising from that kind of practice, that is, errors due to the fact that the order of evaluation cannot be known, are extremely hard to detect.

The Execution Environment of the Body of a Function

Applying a function comes down to evaluating its body in an environment where its variables are bound to values that they have assumed during the application. Remember that during the call to **make-function**, we provided it with the parameters that were made available by **evaluate**. Throughout the rest of this section, we'll highlight the various environments that come into play by mentioning them in *italic*.

Minimal Environment

Let's first try a definition of a stripped down, minimal environment.

```
(define (make-function variables body env)
  (lambda (values)
    (eprogn body (extend env.init variables values)) ) )
```

In conformity with the contract that we explained earlier, the body of the function is evaluated in an environment where the variables are bound to their values. For example, the combinator K defined as (lambda (a b) a) can be applied like this:

(K 1 2) → 1

The nuisance here is that the means available to a function are rather minimal. The body of a function can utilize nothing other than its own variables since the initial environment, *env.init*, is empty. It does not even have access to the global environment where the usual functions, such as **car**, **cons**, and so forth, are defined.

---

16. The function could then examine the types of its arguments, but that task does not have to do with the function call protocol.

Patched Environment

Let's try again with an enriched environment patched like this:

```
(define (make-function variables body env)
  (lambda (values)
    (eprogn body (extend env.global variables values)) ) )
```

This new version lets the body of the function use the global environment and all its usual functions. Now how do we globally define two functions that are mutually recursive? Also, what is the value of the expression on the left (macroexpanded on the right)?

```
(let ((a 1))                 ((lambda (a)
  (let ((b (+ 2 a)))  ≡        ((lambda (b)
    (list a b) ) )              (list a b) )
                               (+ 2 a) ) )
                             1 )
```

Let's look in detail at how that expression is evaluated:

```
((lambda (a) ((lambda (b) (list a b)) (+ 2 a))) 1)|
                                                   |  env.global

= ((lambda (b) (list a b)) (+ 2 a))|
                                   |  a→ 1
                                   |  env.global

= (list a b)|
            |  b→ 3
            |  env.global
```

The body of the internal function (lambda (b) (list a b)) is evaluated in an environment that we get by extending the global environment with the variable b. That environment lacks the variable a because it is not visible, so this try fails, too!

Improving the Patch

Since we need to see the variable a within the internal function, it suffices to provide the current environment to **invoke**, which in turn will transmit that environment to the functions that are called. In consequence, we now have an idea of a current environment kept up to date by **evaluate** and **invoke**, so let's modify these functions. However, let's modify them in such a way that we don't confuse these new definitions with the previous ones; we'll use a prefix, **d.** to avoid confusion, like this:

```
(define (d.evaluate e env)
  (if (atom? e) ...
      (case (car e)
        ...
        ((lambda) (d.make-function (cadr e) (cddr e) env))
        (else (d.invoke (d.evaluate (car e) env)
                        (evlis (cdr e) env)
                        env )) ) ) )
(define (d.invoke fn args env)
```

```
    (if (procedure? fn)
        (fn args env)
        (wrong "Not a function" fn) ) )

(define (d.make-function variables body def.env)
  (lambda (values current.env)
    (eprogn body (extend current.env variables values)) ) )
```

Here we notice that in the definition of **d.invoke**, it is no longer really useful to provide the definition environment **env** to the *def.env* variable since only the current environment, *current.env*, is being used.

Now if we look at the same expression, highlighted with the name of the environment being used, we see that our example works like this:

```
((lambda (a) ((lambda (b) (list a b)) (+ 2 a))) 1)|
                                                    |  env.global

= ((lambda (b) (list a b)) (+ 2 a))|
                                    |  a→ 1
                                    |  env.global

= (list a b)|
            |  b→ 3
            |  a→ 1
            |  env.global
```

Of course, in this example, we clearly see the stack discipline that the bindings are following. Every binding form pushes its new bindings onto the current environment and pops them off after execution.

Fixing the Problem

There is still a problem, though. To see it, look at this variation:

```
(((lambda (a)
     (lambda (b) (list a b)) )
   1 )
   2 )
```

The function (**lambda (b) (list a b)**) is created in an environment where a is bound to 1, but at the time the function is applied, the current environment is extended by the sole binding to b, and once again, a is absent from that environment. As a consequence, the function (**lambda (b) (list a b)**) once again forgets or loses its variable a.

No doubt you noticed in the previous definition of **d.make-function** that two environments were present: the definition environment for the function, *def.env*, and the calling environment of the function, *current.env*. Two moments are important in the life of a function: its creation and its application(s). Granted, there is only one moment when the function is created, but there can very well be many times when the function is applied; or indeed, there may be no moment when it is applied! As a consequence, the only[17] environment that we can associate with a function with any certainty is the environment when it was created. Let's go back

---

17. True, we could leave it up to the program to choose explicitly which environment the function should end up in. See the form **closure** on page 113.

to the original definitions of the functions **evaluate** and **invoke**, and this time, let's write **make-function** this way:

```
(define (make-function variables body env)
  (lambda (values)
    (eprogn body (extend env variables values)) ) )
```

All the examples now behave well, and in particular, the preceding example now has the following evaluation trace:

```
(((lambda (a) (lambda (b) (list a b))) 1) 2)|
                                            | env.global
= ( (lambda (b) (list a b))|
                           | a→ 1
                           | env.global
    2 )|
       | env.global
= (list a b)|
            | b→ 2
            | a→ 1
            | env.global
```

The form (**lambda (b) (list a b)**) is created in the global environment extended by the variable **a**. When the function is applied in the global environment, it extends its own environment of definition by **b**, and thus permits the body of the function to be evaluated in an environment where both **a** and **b** are known. When the function returns its result, the evaluation continues in the global environment. We often refer to the value of an abstraction as its *closure* because the value closes its definition environment.

Notice that the present definition of **make-function** itself uses closure within the definition language. That use is not obligatory, as we'll see later in Chapter 3. [see p. 92] The function **make-function** has a closure for its value, and that fact is a distinctive trait of higher-order functional languages.

1.6.1 Dynamic and Lexical Binding

There are at least two important points in that discussion about environments. First, it demonstrates clearly how complicated the issues about environments are. Any evaluation is always carried out within a certain environment, and the management of the environment is a major point that evaluators must resolve efficiently. In Chapter 3, we will see more complicated structures, such as escapes and the form **unwind-protect**, that oblige us to define very precisely which environments are under consideration.

The second point concerns the last two variations in the previous section which are characteristic of *dynamic*[18] and *lexical* binding. In a *lexical* Lisp, a function evaluates its body in its own definition environment extended by its variables, whereas in a *dynamic* Lisp, a function extends the current environment, that is, the environment of the application.

---

18. In the context of object-oriented languages, the term *dynamic binding* usually refers to the fact that the method associated with a message is determined by the dynamic type of the object to which the message is sent, rather than by its static type.

Current fashion favors lexical Lisps, but you mustn't conclude from that fact that dynamic languages have no future. For one thing, very useful dynamic languages are still widely in use, such languages as TEX [Knu84], GNU EMACS LISP [LLSt93], or Perl [WS90].

For another, the idea of dynamic binding is an important concept in programming. It corresponds to establishing a valid binding when beginning a computation and that binding is undone automatically in a guaranteed way as soon as that computation is complete.

This programming strategy can be employed effectively in forward-looking computations, such as, for example, those in artificial intelligence. In those situations, we pose a hypothesis, and we develop consequences from it. When we discover an incoherence or inconsistency, we must abandon that hypothesis in order to explore another; this technique is known as backtracking. If the consequences have been carried out with no side-effects, for example in such structures as A-lists, then abandoning the hypothesis will automatically recycle the consequences, but if, in contrast, we had used physical modifications such as global assignments of variables, modifications of arrays, and so forth, then abandoning a hypothesis would entail restoring the entire environment where the hypothesis was first formulated. One oversight in such a situation would be fatal! Dynamic binding makes it possible to insure that a dynamic variable is present and correctly assigned during a computation and only during that computation regardless of the outcome. This property is heavily used for exception handling.

Variables are programming entities that have their own *scope*. The scope of a variable is essentially a geographic idea corresponding to the region in the programming text where the variable is visible and thus is accessible. In pure Scheme (that is, unburdened with superfluous but useful syntax, such as `let`), only one binding form exists: `lambda`. It is the only form that introduces variables and confers on them a scope limited strictly to the body of the function. In contrast, the scope of a variable in a dynamic Lisp has no such limitation *a priori*. Consider this, for example:

```
(define (foo x) (list x y))
(define (bar y) (foo 1991))
```

In a lexical Lisp, the variable `y` in `foo`[19] is a reference to the global variable `y`, which in no way can be confused with the variable `y` in `bar`. In dynamic Lisp, the variable `y` in `bar` is visible (indeed, it is seen) from the body of the function `foo` because when `foo` is invoked, the current environment contains that variable `y`. Consequently, if we give the value 0 to the global variable `y`, we get these results:

```
(define y 0)
(list (bar 100) (foo 3))      →  ((1991 0) (3 0))      in lexical Lisp
(list (bar 100) (foo 3))      →  ((1991 100) (3 0))    in dynamic Lisp
```

Notice that in dynamic Lisp, `bar` has no means of knowing that the function `foo` that `bar` calls references its own variable `y`. Conversely, the function `foo` doesn't know where to find the variable `y` that it references. For this reason, `bar` must put `y` into the current environment so that `foo` can find it there. Just before `bar` returns, `y` has to be removed from the current environment.

---

19. For the etymology of foo, see [Ray91].

Of course, in the absence of free variables, there is no noticeable difference between dynamically scoped and lexically scoped Lisp.

Lexical binding is known by that name because we can always start simply from the text of the function and, for any variable, either find the form that bound the variable or know with certainty that it is a global variable. The method is so simple that we can point with a pencil (or a mouse) at the variable and go right along from right to left, from bottom to top, until we find the first binding form around this variable. The name dynamic binding plays on another concept, that of the *dynamic extent*, which we'll get to later. [see p. 77]

Scheme supports only lexical variables. COMMON LISP supports both kinds of binding with the same syntax. EULISP and IS-Lisp clearly distinguish the two kinds syntactically in two separate name spaces. [see p. 43]

Scope may be obscured locally by *shadowing*. Shadowing occurs when one variable hides another because they both have the same name. Lexical binding forms are nested or disjoint from one another. This well known "block" discipline is inherited from Algol 60.

Under the inspiration of λ-calculus, which loaned its name to the special form `lambda` [Per79], Lisp 1.0 was defined as a dynamic Lisp, but early on, John McCarthy recognized that he expected the following expression to return (2 3) rather than (1 3).

```
(let ((a 1))
  ((let ((a 2)) (lambda (b) (list a b)))
   3 ) )
```

That anomaly (dare we call it a bug?) was corrected by introducing a new special form, known as `function`. Its argument was a `lambda` form, and it created a *closure*, that is, a function associated with its definition environment. When that closure was applied, instead of extending the current environment, it extended its own definition environment that it had closed (in the sense of preserved) within itself. In programming terms, the special form `function`[20] is defined accordingly with `d.evaluate` and `d.invoke`, like this:

```
(define (d.evaluate e env)
  (if (atom? e) ...
    (case (car e)
      ...
      ((function)    ;Syntax: (function (lambda variables body))
       (let* ((f   (cadr e))
              (fun (d.make-function (cadr f) (cddr f) env)) )
         (d.make-closure fun env) ) )
      ((lambda) (d.make-function (cadr e) (cddr e) env))
      (else     (d.invoke (d.evaluate (car e) env)
                          (evlis (cdr e) env)
                          env )) ) ) )
```

---

20. This simulation is not exactly correct in the sense that there are many dialects (such as CLtL1 in [Ste84]) where `lambda` is not a special operator, but a keyword, a kind of syntactic marker similar to `else` that can appear in Scheme in a `cond` or a `case`. `lambda` does not require `d.evaluate` for it to be handled correctly. `lambda` forms may also be restricted to appear exclusively in the first term of functional applications, accompanied by `function`, or in function definitions.

```
(define (d.invoke fn args env)
   (if (procedure? fn)
        (fn args env)
        (wrong "Not a function" fn) ) )
(define (d.make-function variables body env)
   (lambda (values current.env)
       (eprogn body (extend current.env variables values)) ) )
(define (d.make-closure fun env)
   (lambda (values current.env)
        (fun values env) ) )
```

That's not the end of the story, however. That function was regarded as a
convenience that the end-user had to rely on because of an inadequate implementation. The early compilers very quickly caught on to the fact that, in terms of
performance, lexical environments have a great advantage—as one might expect in
compilation—and that in any case, wherever the variables were during execution,
the compiler could generate a more or less direct access rather than searching dynamically for the value. By default, then, all the variables of compiled functions
were treated as lexical, except those that were explicitly declared as dynamic, or
in the jargon of the time, *special*. The declaration (declare (special *x*)) solely
for the use of the compiler in Lisp 1.5, MacLisp, COMMON LISP, and so forth,
designated the variable *x* as having special behavior.

Efficiency was not the only reason for this turn of events. There was also a loss of
referential transparency. Referential transparency is the property that a language
has when substituting an expression in a program for an equivalent expression does
not change the behavior of the program; that is, they both calculate the same thing;
either they return the same value, or neither of the two terminates. For example,
consider this:

(let ((x (lambda () 1))) (x)) $\equiv$ ((let ((x (lambda () 1))) x)) $\equiv$ 1

Referential transparency is lost once a language has side effects. In such a case,
we need new, more precise definitions for equivalence as a relation in order to talk
about referential transparency. Scheme—without assignment, without side effects,
without continuations—is referentially transparent. [see **Ex. 3.10**] This property
is also a goal that we work toward when we are trying to write programs that are
genuinely re-usable, in the sense of depending as little as possible on the context
where they are used.

The variables of a function such as (lambda (u) (+ u u)) are what we conventionally call *silent*. Their names have no particular importance and can be
replaced by any other name. The function (lambda (n347) (+ n347 n347)) is
nothing more nor less[21] than the function (lambda (u) (+ u u)).

We're still waiting for the language that respects this invariant. There's nothing
like that in dynamic Lisp. Just consider this:

```
(define (map fn l)            ; mapcar in Lisp
   (if (pair? l)
        (cons (fn (car l)) (map fn (cdr l)))
```

---

21. In the technical terms of λ-calculus, this change of names for variables is known as an α-
conversion.

```
          '() ) )
   (let ((l '(a b c)))
     (map (lambda (x) (list-ref l x))
          '(2 1 0) ) )
```

(The function `list-ref` extracts the element at index *n* from a list.)

In Scheme, the result would be (c b a), but in a dynamic Lisp, the result would be (0 0 0). The reason: the variable l is free in the body of (`lambda (x)` (`list-ref l x`)) but that variable is captured by the variable l in `map`.

We could resolve that problem simply by changing the names that are in conflict. For example, it suffices to rename one of those two variables, l. We might perhaps choose to rename the variable in `map` since it is probably the more useful, but what name could we choose that would guarantee that the problem would not crop up again? If we prefix the names of variables by the social security number of the programmer and suffix them by the standardized time (indicated, say, by the number of hundredths of seconds elapsed since noon, 1 January 1901), we obviously lower the risk of name-collisions, but we lose something in readability in our programs.

The situation at the beginning of the eighties was particularly sensitive. We taught Lisp to students by observing its interpreter, which differed from its compiler in this fundamental point about the value of a variable. From 1975 on, Scheme [SS75] had shown that we could reconcile an interpreter and compiler and then live in a completely lexical world. COMMON LISP buried the problem by postulating that *good* semantics were compiler semantics, so everything should be lexical by default. An interpreter just had to conform to these new canonical laws. The increasing success of Scheme, of functional languages such as ML, and of their spin-offs first spread and then imposed this new view.

1.6.2 Deep or Shallow Implementation

Things are not so simple, however, and implementers have found ways of increasing how fast the value of a dynamic variable is determined. When the environment is represented as an association-list, the cost of searching[22] for the value of a variable (that is, the cost of the function `lookup`) is linear with respect to the length of the list. This mechanism is known as *deep binding*.

Another technique, known as *shallow binding*, also exists. Shallow binding occurs when each variable is associated with a place where its value is always stored independently of the current environment. The simplest implementation of this idea is that the location should be a field in the symbol associated with the variable; it's known as Cval, or the *value cell*. The cost of `lookup` is constant in that case since the cost is based on an indirection, possibly followed by an additional offset. Since there's rarely a gain without a loss, we have to admit here that a function call is more costly in this model since it has to save the values of variables that are going to be bound and modify the symbols associated with those variables

---

22. Fortunately, statistics show that we search more often for the first variables than for those that are buried more deeply. Besides, it's worth noting that lexical environments are smaller than dynamic environments, since dynamic environments have to carry around all the bindings that are being computed [Bak92a].

so that the symbols contain the new values. When the function returns, moreover, it must restore the old values in the symbols that they came from—a practice that can compromise tail recursion. (But see [SJ93] for alternatives.)

We can partially simulate[23] shallow binding by changing the representation of the environment. In what follows, we'll assume that lists of variables are not dotted. This assumption will make it easier to decode lists of variables. We'll also assume that we don't need to verify the arity of functions. These new functions will be prefixed by **s.** to make them easier to recognize.

```
(define (s.make-function variables body env)
  (lambda (values current.env)
    (let ((old-bindings
           (map (lambda (var val)
                    (let ((old-value (getprop var 'apval)))
                      (putprop var 'apval val)
                      (cons var old-value) ) )
                variables
                values ) ))
      (let ((result (eprogn body current.env)))
        (for-each (lambda (b) (putprop (car b) 'apval (cdr b)))
                  old-bindings )
        result ) ) ) )
(define (s.lookup id env)
  (getprop id 'apval) )
(define (s.update! id env value)
  (putprop id 'apval value) )
```

In Scheme, the functions **putprop** and **getprop** are not standard because they cause highly inefficient global side effects, but they resemble the functions **put** and **get** in [AS85]. [see **Ex. 2.6**]

Here, the functions **putprop** and **getprop** simulate that field[24] where a symbol stores the value of a variable of the same name. Independently[25] of their actual implementation, these functions should be regarded as though they have constant cost.

Notice that in the preceding simulation, the environment **env** has completely disappeared because it no longer serves any purpose. This disappearance means that we have to modify the implementation of closures since they can no longer close the environment (since it doesn't exist any longer). The technique for doing so (which we'll see later) consists of analyzing the body of the function to identify free variables and then treating them in the appropriate way.

Deep binding favors changing the environment and programming by multi-tasking, to the detriment of searching for values of variables. Shallow binding favors searching for the values of variables to the detriment of function calls. Henry Baker

---

23. However, we are not treating the assignment of a closed variable here. For that topic, see [BCSJ86].

24. The name of the property being used, apval [see p. **31**], was chosen in honor of the name used in [MAE+62] when these values really were stored in P-lists.

25. The functions sweep down a symbol's list of properties (its P-list) until they find the right property. The cost of this search is linear with respect to the length of the P-list, unless the implementation associates symbols with properties by means of a hash table.

[Bak78] combined the two in the technique of *rerooting*.

Remember, finally, that deep binding and shallow binding are merely implementation techniques that have nothing to do with the semantics of binding.

1.7 Global Environment

An empty global environment is a poor thing, so most Lisp systems supply *libraries* to fill it up. There are, for example, more than 700 functions in the global environment of COMMON LISP (CLtL1); more than 1,500 in Le-Lisp; more than 10,000 in ZetaLisp, etc. Without its library, Lisp would be only a kind of λ-calculus in which we couldn't even print the results of calculations. The idea of a library is important for the end-user. Whereas the special forms are the essence of the language from the point of view of any one producing the evaluator, it's the libraries that make a real difference for the end-user. Lisp folk history insists that it was the lack of such banalities as a library of trigonometric functions that made number crunchers drop Lisp early on. Their feeling, according to [Sla61], was that it might be a good thing to know how to integrate or differentiate symbolically but without sine or tangent, what could anyone really do with the language?

We expect to find all the usual functions, such as car, cons, etc., in the global environment. We may also find simple variables whose values are well known data, such as Boolean values and the empty list.

Now we are going to define two macros—just for convenience at this point, since we haven't even talked about macros yet,[26] important as they are. In fact, macros are such a significant and complicated phenomenon that we will devote an entire chapter to them later. [see p. 311]

The two macros that we'll define here will make it easier to elaborate the global environment. We'll define the global environment as an extension of the empty initial environment, env.init.

```
(define env.global env.init)
(define-syntax definitial
  (syntax-rules ()
    ((definitial name)
     (begin (set! env.global (cons (cons 'name 'void) env.global))
            'name ) )
    ((definitial name value)
     (begin (set! env.global (cons (cons 'name value) env.global))
            'name ) ) ) )
(define-syntax defprimitive
  (syntax-rules ()
    ((defprimitive name value arity)
     (definitial name
       (lambda (values)
         (if (= arity (length values))
             (apply value values)          ; The real apply of Scheme
             (wrong "Incorrect arity"
```

---

26. It is not our intention to put the whole book in its first chapter.

```
(list 'name values) ) ) ) ) ) ) )
```

Now we'll define a few very useful constants, though none of these three appears in standard Scheme. We note here that t is a variable in the Lisp that is being defined, while #t is a value in the Lisp that we are using as the definition language. Any value other than that of the-false-value is true.

```
(definitial t #t)
(definitial f the-false-value)
(definitial nil '())
```

Though it's useful to have a few global variables that let us get the real objects that represent Booleans or the empty list, another solution is to develop a syntax appropriate for doing that. Scheme uses the syntax #t and #f, and the values of those are the Booleans true and false. The point of those two is that they are always visible and that they cannot be corrupted.

1. They are always visible because we can write #t for *true* in any context, even if a local variable is named t.

2. They are incorruptible, an important fact, since many evaluators authorize alterations in the value of the variable t.

Such alterations lead to puzzles like this one: (if t 1 2) will have the value 2 in (let ((t #f)) (if t 1 2)).

Many solutions to that problem are possible. The simplest is to lock the immutability of these constants into the evaluator, like this:

```
(define (evaluate e env)
  (if (atom? e)
      (cond ((eq? e 't) #t)
            ((eq? e 'f) #f)
            ...
            ((symbol? e) (lookup e env))
            ...
            (else (wrong "Cannot evaluate" e)) )
      ... ) )
```

We could also introduce the idea of *mutable* and *immutable* binding. An immutable binding could not be the object of an assignment. Nothing could ever change the value of a variable that has been immutably bound. That concept exists, even if it is somewhat obscured, in many systems. The idea of *inline* functions designates those functions (also known as *integrable* or *open coded*) [see p. 199] where the body, appropriately instantiated, can replace the call.

To replace (car x) by the code that extracts the contents of the car field from the value of the dotted pair x implies the important hypothesis that nothing ever alters, has never altered, will never alter the value of the global variable car. Imagine the misfortune that the following fragment of a session illustrates.

```
(set! my-global (cons 'c 'd))
   → (c . d)
(set! my-test (lambda () (car my-global)))
   → #<MY-TEST procedure>
(begin (set! car cdr)
       (set! my-global (cons 'a 'b))
```

```
(my-test) )
```
$\rightarrow$ *?????*

Fortunately again, the response can only be a or b. If my-test uses the value of car current at the time my-test was defined, the response would be a. If my-test uses the current value of car, the response would be b. It's helpful to compare the behavior of my-test and my-global, knowing that we'll usually see the first kind of behavior for my-test when the evaluator is a compiler, and usually the second kind of behavior for my-global. [see p. 54]

We'll also add a few working variables[27] to the global environment that we've been building because there is no dynamic creation of global variables in the present evaluator. The names that we suggest here cover roughly 96.037% of the names of functions that Lispers testing a new evaluator usually come up with spontaneously.

```
(definitial foo)
(definitial bar)
(definitial fib)
(definitial fact)
```

Finally, we'll define a few functions, but not all of them, because listing all of them would put you to sleep. Our main difficulty now is to adapt the primitives of Lisp to the calling protocol of the Lisp that is being defined. Knowing that the arguments are all brought together into one list by the interpreter, we simply have to use apply.[28] Note that the arity of the primitive will be respected because of the way defprimitive expands it.

```
(defprimitive cons cons 2)
(defprimitive car car 1)
(defprimitive set-cdr! set-cdr! 2)
(defprimitive + + 2)
(defprimitive eq? eq? 2)
(defprimitive < < 2)
```

1.8 Starting the Interpreter

The only thing left to tell you is how to get into this new world that we've defined.

```
(define (chapter1-scheme)
  (define (toplevel)
    (display (evaluate (read) env.global))
    (toplevel) )
  (toplevel) )
```

Since our interpreter is still open to innovation, we suggest an exercise in which you implement a function for exiting.

---

27. These variables are, unfortunately, initialized here. This fault will be corrected later.
28. Once again, we congratulate ourselves that we did not call invoke "apply."

1.9   Conclusions

Have we really defined a language at this point?

No one could doubt that the function **evaluate** can be started, that we can submit expressions to it, and that it will return their values, once its computations are complete. However, the function **evaluate** itself makes no sense apart from its definition language, and, in the absence of a definition of the definition language, nothing is sure. Since every true Lisper has an in-born reflex for bootstrapping, it's probably sufficient to identify the definition language as the language that we've defined. In consequence, we now have a language L defined by a function **evaluate**, written in the language L. The language defined that way is thus a solution to this equation in L:

$$\forall \pi \in \textbf{Program}, L(\texttt{evaluate (quote } \pi) \texttt{ env.global}) \equiv L\pi$$

For any program π, the evaluation of π in L (denoted $L\pi$) must behave the same way (and thus have the same value if π terminates) as the evaluation of the expression (**evaluate (quote** π) **env.global**), all still in L. One amusing consequence of this equation is that the function **evaluate**[29] is capable of auto-interpretation. The following expressions are thus equivalent:

```
(evaluate (quote π) env.global) ≡
  (evaluate (quote (evaluate (quote π) env.global)) env.global)
```

Are there any solutions to that equation? The answer is yes; in fact, there are many solutions. As we saw earlier, the order of evaluation is not necessarily apparent from the definition of **evaluate**, and many other properties of the definition language are unconsciously *inherited* by the language being defined. We can say next to nothing about them, in fact, because there are also a great many trivial solutions to the equation. Take, for example, the language L_{2001}; its semantics is that every program written in it has, as its value, the number 2001. That language trivially satisfies our equation. We have to depend on other methods, then, if we want to define a real language, and those other methods will be the subject of later chapters.

1.10   Exercises

Exercise 1.1 : Modify the function **evaluate** so that it becomes a tracer. All function calls should display their arguments and their results. You can well imagine extending such a rudimentary tracer to make a step-by-step debugger that could modify the execution path of the program under its control.

Exercise 1.2 : When **evlis** evaluates a list containing only one expression, it has to carry out a useless recursion. Find a way to eliminate that recursion.

---

29. It is necessary to clean all syntactic abbreviations and macros out of **evaluate**—such things as **define**, **case**, and so forth. Then we still have to provide a global environment containing the variables **evaluate**, **evlis**, etc.

Exercise 1.3 : Suppose we now define the function **extend** like this:

```
(define (extend env names values)
   (cons (cons names values) env) )
```

Define the associated functions, **lookup** and **update!**. Compare them with their earlier definitions.

Exercise 1.4 : Another way of implementing shallow binding was suggested by the idea of a *rack* in [SS80]. Instead of each symbol being associated with a field to contain the value of the variable of the same name, there is a stack for that purpose. At any given time, the value of the variable is the value found on top of that stack of associated values. Rewrite the functions **s.make-function**, **s.lookup**, and **s.update!** to take advantage of this new representation.

Exercise 1.5 : The definition of the primitive **<** is false! In practice, it returns a Boolean value of the implementation language instead of a Boolean value of the language being defined. Correct this fault.

Exercise 1.6 : Define the function **list**.

Exercise 1.7 : For those who are fond of continuations, define **call/cc**.

Exercise 1.8 : Define **apply**.

Exercise 1.9 : Define a function **end** so that you can exit cleanly from the interpreter we developed in this chapter.

Exercise 1.10 : Compare the speed of Scheme and **evaluate**. Then compare the speed of **evaluate** and **evaluate** interpreted by **evaluate**.

Exercise 1.11 : The sequence **begin** was defined by means of **lambda** [see p. 9] but it used **gensym** to avoid any possible captures. Redefine **begin** in the same spirit but do not use **gensym** to do so.

Recommended Reading

All the references to interpreters mentioned at the beginning of this chapter make interesting reading, but if you can read only a little, the most rewarding are probably these:

- among the λ-papers, [SS78a];
- the shortest article ever written that still presents an evaluator, [McC78b];

- to get a taste of non-pedantic formalism, [Rey72];
- to get to know the origins and beginnings, [MAE+62].

2
Lisp, 1, 2, ... ω

SINCE functions occupy a central place in Lisp, and because their efficiency is so crucial, there have been many experiments and a great deal of research about functions. Indeed, some of those experiments continue today. This chapter explains various ways of thinking about functions and functional applications. It will carry us up to what we'll call Lisp$_1$ or Lisp$_2$, their differences depending on the concept of separate name spaces. The chapter closes with a look at recursion and its implementation in these various contexts.

Among all the objects that an evaluator can handle, a function represents a very special case. This basic type has a special creator, `lambda`, and at least one legal operation: application. We could hardly constrain a type less without stripping away all its utility. Incidentally, this fact—that it has few qualities—makes a function particularly attractive for specifications or encapsulations because it is opaque and thus allows only what it is programmed for. We can, for example, use functions to represent objects that have fields and methods (that is, data members and member functions) as in [AR88]. Scheme-users are particularly appreciative of functions.

Attempts to increase the efficiency of functions have motivated many, often incompatible, variations. Historically, Lisp 1.5 [MAE$^+$62] did not recognize the idea of a functional object. Its internals were such, by the way, that a variable, a function, a macro—all three—could co-exist with the same name, and at the same time, the three were represented with different properties (`APVAL`, `EXPR`, or `MACRO`[1]) on the P-list of the associated symbol.

MacLisp privileged named functions, and only recently, its descendant, COMMON LISP(CLtL2) [Ste90] introduced first class functional objects. In COMMON LISP, `lambda` is a syntactic keyword declaring something like, "Warning: we are defining an anonymous function." `lambda` forms have no value and can appear only in syntactically special places: in the first term of an application or as the first parameter of the special form `function`.

In contrast, Scheme, since its inception in 1975, has spread the ideas of a functional object and of a unique space of values by conferring the status of *first class*

---

1. `APVAL`, *A Permanent VALue*, stores the global value of a variable; `EXPR`, *an EXPRession*, stores a global definition of a function; `MACRO` stores a macro.

on practically everything. A first class object can be an argument or the value of
a function; it can be stored in a variable, a list, an array, etc. The philosophy of
Scheme is compatible with functional languages in the same class as ML, and we'll
adopt the same philosophy here.

2.1 Lisp$_1$

The main activity in the previous chapter was to conform to that philosophy:
the idea of a functional object prevailed there (**make-function** creates functional
objects); and the process of evaluating terms in an application did not distinguish
the function from its arguments; that is, the expression in the *function position*
was not treated differently from the expressions in the following positions, those
in the *parametric* positions. Let's look again at the most interesting fragments of
that preceding interpreter.

```
(define (evaluate e env)
  (if (atom? e) ...
      (case (car e)
        ...
        ((lambda) (make-function (cadr e) (cddr e) env))
        (else (invoke (evaluate (car e) env)
                      (evlis (cdr e) env) )) ) ) )
```

The salient points in it are these:

1. **lambda** is a special form creating first class objects; closures capture their
   definition environment.

2. All the terms in an application are evaluated by the same evaluator, namely,
   evaluate; **evlis** is simply **evaluate** mapped over a list of expressions.

That second characteristic makes Scheme into Lisp$_1$.

2.2 Lisp$_2$

Programs in Lisp are generally such that most functional applications have the
name of a global function in their function position. That's certainly the case of
all the programs in the preceding chapter. We could restrict the grammar of Lisp
to impose a symbol in the **car** of every form. Doing so would not noticeably alter
the look of the language, but it would imply that the evaluation that occurs for
the term in the function position no longer needs all the complexity of **evaluate**
and could get along with a mini-evaluator for those expressions—a mini-evaluator
that knows how to handle only names of functions. Implementing this idea entails
modifying the last clause in the preceding interpreter, like this:

```
...
(else (invoke (lookup (car e) env)
              (evlis (cdr e) env) )) ...
```

We now have two different evaluators, one for each of the two positions where a
variable may occur (that is, in functional or parametric position). Many different

kinds of behavior can correspond to one identifier, depending on its position; in this
case, its position could be the position of a function or a parameter. If we specialize
the function position, that specialization may be accompanied by the presence of
a supplementary environment uniquely dedicated to functions. As a result, *a
priori* it will be easier to look for the function associated with a name since this
dedicated environment won't contain normal variables. The basic interpreter can
then be rewritten to take into account these details. A function environment, **fenv**,
and an evaluator specific to forms, **evaluate-application**, are clearly identified.
We'll have two environments and two evaluators then, and so we'll adopt the name
Lisp₂ [SG93].

```
(define (f.evaluate e env fenv)
  (if (atom? e)
      (cond ((symbol? e) (lookup e env))
            ((or (number? e)(string? e)(char? e)(boolean? e)(vector? e))
             e )
            (else (wrong "Cannot evaluate" e)) )
      (case (car e)
        ((quote) (cadr e))
        ((if)    (if (f.evaluate (cadr e) env fenv)
                     (f.evaluate (caddr e) env fenv)
                     (f.evaluate (cadddr e) env fenv) ))
        ((begin) (f.eprogn (cdr e) env fenv))
        ((set!)  (update! (cadr e)
                          env
                          (f.evaluate (caddr e) env fenv) ))
        ((lambda) (f.make-function (cadr e) (cddr e) env fenv))
        (else    (evaluate-application (car e)
                                       (f.evlis (cdr e) env fenv)
                                       env
                                       fenv )) ) ) )
```

The evaluator dedicated to forms is **evaluate-application**; it receives the
unevaluated function term, the evaluated arguments, and the two current envi
ronments. Notice that creating the function (by means of **lambda**) closes the two
environments, both **end** and **fenv**, in a way that sets the values of free variables
that occur in the body of functions, whether they appear in the position of a function or parameter. In other respects, this new version differs from the preceding
one only by the fact that **fenv** accompanies **env**, the environment for variables,
like a shadow. The functions **eprogn** and **evlis**, of course, have to be updated to
propagate **fenv**, so they become this:

```
(define (f.evlis exps env fenv)
  (if (pair? exps)
      (cons (f.evaluate (car exps) env fenv)
            (f.evlis (cdr exps) env fenv) )
      '() ) )
(define (f.eprogn exps env fenv)
  (if (pair? exps)
      (if (pair? (cdr exps))
          (begin (f.evaluate (car exps) env fenv)
                 (f.eprogn (cdr exps) env fenv) )
```

```
        (f.evaluate (car exps) env fenv) )
     empty-begin ) )
```

When those functions are invoked, they bind their variables in the environment for variables, but only the way functions are created has been modified; the way they are invoked (by means of **invoke**) has not changed.

```
(define (f.make-function variables body env fenv)
  (lambda (values)
    (f.eprogn body (extend env variables values) fenv) ) )
```

The task of the function evaluator is to analyze the function term in order to prepare the final invocation. If we keep the grammar of COMMON LISP, then only a symbol or a **lambda** form can appear in the function position.

```
(define (evaluate-application fn args env fenv)
  (cond ((symbol? fn)
         (invoke (lookup fn fenv) args) )
        ((and (pair? fn) (eq? (car fn) 'lambda))
         (f.eprogn (cddr fn)
                   (extend env (cadr fn) args)
                   fenv ) )
        (else (wrong "Incorrect functional term" fn)) ) )
```

What have we gained and lost by doing this? The first advantage is that searching for a function associated with a name is much easier than before because the search requires only a simple call to **lookup** now, and we thus eliminate a call to **f.evaluate** followed by determining syntactically that this is a reference. Moreover, since the function environment has been freed from all variables, it is certainly more compact, so searches can proceed more quickly there. A second advantage is that handling forms where there is a **lambda** form in the function position is greatly improved. Consider this example:

```
(let ((state-tax 1.186))
  ((lambda (x) (* state-tax x)) (read)) )
```

In that example, you can see that the closure corresponding to (**lambda (x)** (*** state-tax x)**) will not be created; its body will be evaluated directly in the right environment.

The problem, though, is that the two advantages are not real gains since a simple analysis could produce the same effects in Lisp$_1$. The only real difference is in the implementation. Lisp$_2$ is a little bit more efficient because in it we can be sure that any name present in **fenv** is bound to a function. Each time that a binding enriches the function environment, we simply have to verify that the value present in the binding is really a function. Then we never again have to verify during use that it is really a function. Since every name has to belong to the initial function environment, we will bind it to a function calling **wrong** if it is invoked by accident.

Moreover, since every name is bound in **fenv** to a function, we can simplify the call to **invoke** to avoid the test in (**procedure? fn**). We do that by keeping in mind that our implementation language is really Scheme (since what we are about to do is not legal in COMMON LISP because of the presence of a function

calculated in the form ((`lookup fn fenv`) `args`)). We will define the function
`evaluate-application` more precisely, like this:

```
(define (evaluate-application fn args env fenv)
  (cond ((symbol? fn) ((lookup fn fenv) args))
        ... ) )
```

In Lisp, the number of function calls is such that any sort of improvement in function calls is always for the good and can greatly influence overall performance. However, this particular gain is not particularly great since it comes into play only on *calculated* functional applications, that is, those that are not known statically, of which there are very few.

In contrast, on the down side, we have just lost the possibility of calculating the function to apply. The expression (`if` *condition* (`+ 3 4`) (`* 3 4`)) can be factored in Scheme because of its common arguments 3 and 4, and thus we can rewrite the expression as ((`if` *condition* `+ *`) `3 4`). The rule for doing that is simple and highly algebraic. In fact, it is practically an identity, but in Lisp₂, that program is not even legal since the first term is neither a symbol nor a `lambda` form.

2.2.1   Evaluating a Function Term

The function environment introduced thus far is a long way from offering us the facilities of the environment for variables (the parametric environment). Particularly, as you saw in the preceding example, it does not let us calculate the function to apply. The traditional trick, prevailing at least as far back as MacLisp, was to enrich the function evaluator in order to send off any expressions that it did not understand to `f.evaluate`, so we have this:

```
(define (evaluate-application2 fn args env fenv)
  (cond ((symbol? fn)
         ((lookup fn fenv) args) )
        ((and (pair? fn) (eq? (car fn) 'lambda))
         (f.eprogn (cddr fn)
                   (extend env (cadr fn) args)
                   fenv ) )
        (else (evaluate-application2              ; ** Modified **
               (f.evaluate fn env fenv) args env fenv )) ) )
```

Now we can solve our problem and write this:

(`if` *condition* (`+ 3 4`) (`* 3 4`)) ≡ ((`if` *condition* `'+ '*`) `3 4`)

That transformation is far from elegant since we have to add those disgraceful quotation marks to it, but at least it works. Yes, it works, but perhaps it works too well since the evaluator can now get into a loop.

(' ' ' ' ' ' '1789 *arguments*)

The expression ' ' ' ' ' ' '1789 is evaluated as many times as there are quotation marks; then it loops on the number 1789, with the number always equal to itself, never to a function. In short, the subcontracting we get from `f.evaluate` is a bit too well done and demands a bit more control. A variation on this problem exists as well when `evaluate-application` looks like this:

```
(define (evaluate-application3 fn args env fenv)
  (cond
    ((symbol? fn)
     (let ((fun (lookup fn fenv)))
       (if fun (fun args)
           (evaluate-application3 (lookup fn env) args env fenv)) ) )
    ... ) )
```

In that variation, not all the symbols have been predefined in the initial function environment, **fenv.global**, and when a symbol has not been defined in the function environment, we search for its value in the environment for variables. Oops! Even if we assume that no such function **foo** exists, then we still get programs that can loop on the value of a variable, like this:

```
(let ((foo 'foo))
  (foo arguments) )
```

And it's a good idea to add a feature to **evaluate-application** to detect variables that have, as their value, the symbol that bears their name. Then we can again trick the function evaluator into looping even more viciously on lines like these:

```
(let ((flip 'flop)
      (flop 'flip) )
  (flip) )
```

The only clean solution is that first definition that we gave for the function evaluator, **evaluate-application** [see p. 34], and we have to search for a new method that will accept the calculation of the function term.

2.2.2   Duality of the Two Worlds

To summarize these problems, we should say that there are calculations belonging to the parametric world that we want to carry out in the function world, and vice versa. More precisely, we may want to pass a function as an argument or as a result, or we may even want the function that will be applied to be the result of a lengthy calculation.

If it is necessary to indicate a function in the function term, and if we want to calculate the function to apply, then it is sufficient to have a predefined function that knows how to apply functions, so let's introduce the function **funcall** (that is, *function call*). It applies its first argument (which ought to be a function) to its other arguments. Let's try to write our first program using **funcall**, like this:

(if *condition* (+ 3 4) (* 3 4)) ≡ (funcall (if *condition* + *) 3 4) *WRONG*

The arguments, especially the first one, are evaluated by the normal evaluator **f.evaluate**. The function **funcall** takes everything and carries out the application. We could easily define **funcall** like this:

```
(lambda (args)
  (if (> (length args) 1)
      (invoke (car args) (cdr args))
      (wrong "Incorrect arity" 'funcall) ) )
```

In Lisp₂, the function **funcall** represents the calculated call. In all other cases, the function is known, and the verification of the fact that it is a function is no longer necessary.

In the definition of **funcall**, notice the call to **invoke**. It carries out that verification, in contrast to **evaluate-application**, where the verification has been suppressed. The function **funcall** resembles **apply** somewhat. Both take a function as the first argument and other arguments follow. The difference between them is that in a **funcall** form, we statically know the number of arguments that will be provided to the final function that is being invoked.

Unfortunately, there is still one more problem. When we write (**if** *condition* + *), we want to get the addition or multiplication function as the result. But what we get right now is the value of the variable + or *! In COMMON LISP these variables have nothing to do with any arithmetic operations whatsoever, but they are bound by the interaction mechanism to the last expression read and to the last result returned by the basic interaction loop (that is, *toplevel*)!

We introduced **funcall** because we wanted normal evaluation to lead to a result before behaving like a function. The reverse exists (which is really what we would like to have available) in a normal interpreter, of a result coming from the function evaluator. We want the value of the function variable +, such as **evaluate-application** would get, so we will introduce once again a new linguistic device: **function**. As a special form, **function** takes the name of a function and returns its functional value. In that way, we can jump between the two spaces and safely write the following:

(**if** *condition* (+ 3 4) (* 3 4)) ≡
        (**funcall** (**if** *condition* (**function** +) (**function** *)) 3 4)

To define **function**, we will add a supplementary clause to our interpreter, **f.evaluate**. The definition of **function** that follows has nothing to do with the similarly named one [see **p. 21**] that defined the syntax (**function** (**lambda** *variable body*)) to mark the creation of a closure. Here, we'll define (**function** *name-of-function*) to convert the name of a function into a functional value.

```
...
((function)
 (cond ((symbol? (cadr e))
        (lookup (cadr e) fenv) )
       (else (wrong "Incorrect function" (cadr e))) ) ) ...
```

The definition of **function** could be extended, as it is in COMMON LISP, to handle forms like (**function** (**lambda** ...)), similar to what we say on page 21, but that is superfluous in the language that we've just defined because we have **lambda** available directly to do that. In COMMON LISP, that tactic is indispensable because there **lambda** is not really a special form, but rather a marker or syntactic keyword announcing that the definition of a function will follow. A special form prefixed by **lambda** can appear only in the function position or as an argument of the special form **function**.

The function **funcall** lets us take the result of a calculation coming from the parametric world and put it into the function world as a value. Conversely, the special form **function** lets us get the value of a variable from the function world.

There is a striking parallel between the functional application and `funcall` (a function) and between the reference to a variable and `function` (a special form). In short, the simultaneous existence of the two worlds and the necessity of interacting between them demand these bridges.

Notice that now it is no longer possible to modify the function environment; there is no assignment form to do so. This property makes it possible for compilers to *inline* function calls in a way that is semantically clean. One of the attractions of multiple name spaces is to be able to give them specific virtues.

2.2.3   Using Lisp$_2$

To make our definition of Lisp$_2$ autonomous, we have to indicate what is the global function environment, and how to start the interpreter, `f.evaluate`. The global function environment is coded in a similar way to the environment for variables. We'll change only the macro `defprimitive` to extend one environment but not the other.

```
(define fenv.global '())
(define-syntax definitial-function
  (syntax-rules ()
    ((definitial-function name)
     (begin (set! fenv.global (cons (cons 'name 'void) fenv.global))
            'name ) )
    ((definitial-function name value)
     (begin (set! fenv.global (cons (cons 'name value) fenv.global))
            'name ) ) ) )
(define-syntax defprimitive
  (syntax-rules ()
    ((defprimitive name value arity)
     (definitial-function name
       (lambda (values)
         (if (= arity (length values))
             (apply value values)
             (wrong "Incorrect arity" (list 'name values)) ) ) ) ) ) )
(defprimitive car car 1)
(defprimitive cons cons 2)
```

Now we actually get into that world by this means:

```
(define ( │ a certain Lisp₂ │ )
  (define (toplevel)
    (display (f.evaluate (read) env.global fenv.global))
    (toplevel) )
  (toplevel) )
```

2.2.4   Enriching the Function Environment

Environments of any kind are instances of an abstract type. What do we expect from an environment? We expect that it will contain bindings, that we can look there for the binding associated with a name, and that we can also extend it. We want to have local functions available, and to do so, we want to be able to extend the function environment locally. just as a functional application or the form `let` can extend the environment of variables, At this point, the function environment is frozen, so we would gain a lot by extending it. A new special form, `flet` for *functional let*, will be useful to this purpose. Here's its syntax:

> (flet ((*name*₁ *list-of-variables*₁ *body*₁)
>   (*name*₂ *list-of-variables*₂ *body*₂)
>   ...
>   (*name*ₙ *list-of-variables*ₙ *body*ₙ))
>   *expressions* ...)

Since the form `flet` knows how to create only local functions, there is no need to indicate the keyword `lambda` which is implicit. The special form `flet` evaluates the various forms (`lambda` *list-of-variables*ᵢ *body*ᵢ) corresponding to the local functions indicated. Then it binds them to the *name*ᵢ in the function environment. The *expressions* forming the body of the `flet` are evaluated in this enriched function environment. All those *name*ᵢ can be used in the function position and can be subjected to `function` if the associated closure is needed in some calculation.

Adding `flet` to `f.evaluate` is straightforward:

```
...
((flet)
 (f.eprogn
  (cddr e)
  env
  (extend fenv
          (map car (cadr e))
          (map (lambda (def)
                 (f.make-function (cadr def) (cddr def) env fenv) )
               (cadr e) ) ) )) ...
```

Because of `flet`, the possibilities in the function environment increase greatly, and the closure of `fenv` and `env` by the `lambda` form can be explained. For example, consider this:

> (flet ((square (x) (* x x)))
>   (lambda (x) (square (square x))))

The value of that expression is an anonymous function raising a number to the fourth power. The closure that is created there closes the local function, `square`, and that local function is useful to the closure in its calculations.

2.3 Other Extensions

Once the evaluator has been specialized to handle function terms, new variations come immediately to mind. For example, integers could have a function value assimilating them with list accessors, like this:

> (2 '(foo bar hux wok)) → hux
> (-2 '(foo bar hux wok)) → (hux wok)

The integer n is assimilated with the $cad^n r$ if it is positive and with $cd^n r$ if it is negative. The basic accessors, `car` and `cdr`, are 1 and −1. Then we can imagine algebraically rewriting (-1 (-2 π)) as (-3 π) and (2 (-3 π)) as (5 π).

Another variation could confer a meaning on lists in the function position with the stipulation that they must be lists of functions, like this:

```
((list + - *) 5 3)        → (8 2 15)
```

Applying a list of functions comes down to returning the list of values that each of those functions returns for its arguments. The preceding extract is thus equivalent to this:

```
(map (lambda (f) (f 5 3))
     (list + - *) )
```

Finally, we could even allow the function to be in the second position in order to simulate infix notation. In that case, (1 + 2) should return 3. DWIM (that is, Do What I Mean) in [Tei74, Tei76] knows how to recover from that kind of situation.

All these innovations are dangerous because they reduce the number of erroneous forms and thus hide the occurrence of errors that would otherwise be easily detected. Furthermore, they do not lead to any appreciable savings in code, and when everything is taken into account, these innovations are actually rarely used. They also remove that affinity between functions and applicable functional objects, that is, the objects that could appear in the function position. With these innovations, a list or a number would be applicable without so much as becoming a function itself. As a consequence, we could add applicable objects without raising an error, like this:

```
(apply (list 2 (list 0 (+ 1 2)))
       '(foo bar hux wok) )
  → (hux (foo wok))
```

For all those reasons, then, we do not recommend incorporating these innovations into a language such as Lisp. [see **Ex. 2.3**]

2.4   Comparing Lisp₁ and Lisp₂

Now that we are coming to the end of our explorations of Lisp$_1$ and Lisp$_2$, what exactly can we say about these two philosophies?

Scheme is a kind of Lisp$_1$, nice to program and pleasant to teach because the evaluation process is simple and consistent. By comparison, Lisp$_2$ is more difficult because the existence of the two worlds obliges us to exploit forms that cross over from one world to the other. COMMON LISP is not exactly a Lisp$_2$ because other binding spaces exist, such as the environment of lexical escapes, the labels of `tagbody` forms, etc. For that reason, we sometimes speak of Lisp$_n$ because we can associate many kinds of behavior with the same name depending on its syntactic position. Languages with strong syntax (indeed, some people would say overwhelming syntax) often have multiple name spaces or multiple environments (environments for variables, for functions, for types, etc.). These multiple environments have specialized properties. If, for example, there are no modifications possible (that is, no assignments) in the local function environment, then it is easy to optimize the call to local functions.

A program written in Lisp$_2$ clearly separates the world of functions from the rest of its computations. This is a profitable distinction that all good Scheme compilers exploit, according to [Sén89]. Internally, these compilers rewrite Scheme programs into a kind of Lisp$_2$ that they can then compile better. They make clear every place where **funcall** has to be inserted, that is, all the calculated calls. A user of Lisp$_2$ has to do much of the work of the compiler in that way and thus understands better what it's worth.

Since we've walked through so many possible variations in the preceding pages, we think it may be useful to give a definition here—the simplest possible—of another instance of Lisp$_2$ inspired by COMMON LISP. The only modification that we're going to include here is to introduce the function **f.lookup** to search for a name in the function environment. If the name cannot be found, a function calling **wrong** will be returned. This device makes it possible to insure that **f.lookup** always returns a function in finite time. Of course, this device also introduces a kind of deferred error since such an error does not occur in the reference to the non-existing function, but rather it occurs in the application of the function, which could occur later or perhaps not at all.

```
(define (f.evaluate e env fenv)
  (if (atom? e)
      (cond ((symbol? e) (lookup e env))
            ((or (number? e)(string? e)(char? e)(boolean? e)(vector? e))
             e )
            (else (wrong "Cannot evaluate" e)) )
      (case (car e)
        ((quote)  (cadr e))
        ((if)     (if (f.evaluate (cadr e) env fenv)
                      (f.evaluate (caddr e) env fenv)
                      (f.evaluate (cadddr e) env fenv) ))
        ((begin)  (f.eprogn (cdr e) env fenv))
        ((set!)   (update! (cadr e)
                           env
                           (f.evaluate (caddr e) env fenv) ))
        ((lambda) (f.make-function (cadr e) (cddr e) env fenv))
        ((function)
         (cond ((symbol? (cadr e))
                (f.lookup (cadr e) fenv) )
               ((and (pair? (cadr e)) (eq? (car (cadr e)) 'lambda))
                (f.make-function
                  (cadr (cadr e)) (cddr (cadr e)) env fenv ) )
               (else (wrong "Incorrect function" (cadr e))) ) )
        ((flet)
         (f.eprogn (cddr e)
                   env
                   (extend fenv
                           (map car (cadr e))
                           (map (lambda (def)
                                  (f.make-function (cadr def) (cddr def)
                                                   env fenv ) )
                                (cadr e) ) ) ) )
```

```
       ((labels)
        (let ((new-fenv (extend fenv
                            (map car (cadr e))
                            (map (lambda (def) 'void) (cadr e)) )))
           (for-each (lambda (def)
                        (update! (car def)
                                 new-fenv
                                 (f.make-function (cadr def) (cddr def)
                                                  env new-fenv ) ) )
                     (cadr e) )
           (f.eprogn (cddr e) env new-fenv ) ) )
        (else    (f.evaluate-application (car e)
                                         (f.evlis (cdr e) env fenv)
                                         env
                                         fenv )) ) ) )
  (define (f.evaluate-application fn args env fenv)
    (cond ((symbol? fn)
           ((f.lookup fn fenv) args) )
          ((and (pair? fn) (eq? (car fn) 'lambda))
           (f.eprogn (cddr fn)
                     (extend env (cadr fn) args)
                     fenv ) )
          (else (wrong "Incorrect functional term" fn)) ) )
  (define (f.lookup id fenv)
    (if (pair? fenv)
        (if (eq? (caar fenv) id)
            (cdar fenv)
            (f.lookup id (cdr fenv)) )
        (lambda (values)
          (wrong "No such functional binding" id) ) ) )
```

Other more pragmatic considerations comparing $Lisp_1$ and $Lisp_2$ are connected to readability, according to [GP88]. Surely experienced Lisp programmers avoid writing this kind of code:

```
(defun foo (list)
  (list list) )
```

From the point of view of $Lisp_1$, (list list) is a legal auto-application[2] and its meaning is very different in $Lisp_2$. In COMMON LISP those two names are evaluated in two different environments, and thus there is no conflict between them. Even so, it is still good programming style to avoid naming local variables with the names of well known global functions; macro-writers will thank you, and your programs will be less dependent on which Lisp or Scheme you happen to use.

Another difference between $Lisp_1$ and $Lisp_2$ concerns macros themselves. A macro that expands into a lambda form, for example, to implement a system of objects, is highly problematic in COMMON LISP because of the grammatical restrictions that COMMON LISP imposes on the places where lambda can appear. A lambda form can appear only in the function position, so an expression like this

---

2. Other auto-applications that make sense do exist, though they are not numerous. Here's another (number? number?).

(... (`lambda` ...) ...) is erroneous. A `lambda` form can also appear in the special form `function`, but that form itself can appear only in the position of a parameter, so this expression ((`function` (`lambda` ...)) ...) is erroneous, too. A macro that is going to be expanded never knows where—in which function context or parametric context—it will be inserted; consequently, a macro cannot be written without inducing a transformation of a program into something more complicated and more global. For that system of objects that we mentioned, we could adopt an expansion toward (`function` (`lambda` ...)) and add `funcall` to the head of all the forms likely to contain an object in the function position.

Finally, we should mention a means that many languages adopt. We can limit the risk of confusion, even with multiple value spaces, by forbidding the same name to appear in more than one space at a time. In the example we looked at earlier, `list` could not be used as a variable because it already appears in the global function environment. Almost all Lisp or Scheme systems also forbid a name to serve simultaneously as the name of a function and of a macro. This kind of rule certainly makes some aspects of life easier.

2.5 Name Spaces

An *environment* associates entities with names. We've already seen two kinds of environments: `env`, the normal environment, and `fenv`, the function environment associating names with functions. The reason we separated those two spaces of values was to improve the way function calls were handled and to distinguish the function world clearly from the variable world. That distinction, however, obliged us to introduce two different evaluators as well as some way of getting from one world to the other—changes that complicate the semantics of the language. When we discussed dynamic variables, we mentioned that recent dialects of Lisp (such as ILOG TALK, EULISP, IS-Lisp) put dynamic variables in a separate name space as well. We're going to look more closely at that variation here. In doing so, we'll illustrate the idea of a *name space*.

An environment is a kind of abstract type. An environment contains *bindings* between names and the *entities* referenced by these names. These entities can be either values (that is, objects that the user can manipulate like any other first class object) or real entities (that is, second class objects that can be handled only by means of their name and generally only across an appropriate set of syntactic elements and special forms). For the moment, the only entities that we recognize are bindings. For us, these entities exist because they can be captured within closures. We'll have more to say about the qualities of these bindings when we study side effects later.

There are many things that we might search for in an environment. We might search to see whether a given name appears in a given environment; we might search for the entity associated with a name; we might search in order to modify that association. We can also extend an environment with new associations (or new bindings) whether that environment is current, local, or global. Of course, not all these operations are necessarily relevant to every environment. In fact, many environments are useful only because they limit such operations. The following chart, for example, lists the qualities of the environment for variables in Scheme.

Reference	x
Value	x
Modification	(set! x . . .)
Extension	(lambda (. . . x . . .) . . .)
Definition	(define x . . .)

We'll be using the ideas in that chart quite frequently to discuss properties of environments, so we'll say a bit more about it now. That first line indicates the syntax we use to reference a variable in a closure. The second line corresponds to the syntax that lets us get the value of a variable. In the case of variables, the syntax for both the value and the closure is the same, but that is not always the case. The third line shows how the binding associated with the variable can be modified. The fourth line shows a way to extend the environment of lexical variables: by a lambda form, or of course, by macros such as let or let* since they expand into lambda forms. Finally, the last line of the chart shows how to define a global binding. In case these distinctions seem obscure or feel like overkill to you, we should point out here that the next charts in this chapter will clarify the various intentions behind the ways that variables are used.

In Lisp$_2$, examined at the beginning of this chapter, the space for functions could be characterized by this chart.

Reference	(f . . .)
Value	(function f)
Modification	that's not possible here
Extension	(flet (. . . (f . . .) . . .) . . .)
Definition	not treated before (cf. defun)

2.5.1   Dynamic Variables

Dynamic variables, as a concept, are so different from lexical variables that we're going to treat them separately. The following chart shows the qualities that we want to have in our new environment, the environment for dynamic variables.

Reference	can not be captured
Value	(dynamic d)
Modification	(dynamic-set! d . . .)
Extension	(dynamic-let (. . . (d . . .) . . .) . . .)
Definition	not treated here.

This new name space takes into account many facts: that dynamic variables[3] can be bound locally by dynamic-let with syntax comparable to that of let or flet; that we can get the value of a dynamic variable by dynamic; that we can modify one with dynamic-set!.

Those three are special forms that we'll see again later in another implementation. For now, we're going to take the interpreter f.evaluate and add a new

---

3. In this context, "dynamic variable" is a poor choice of name since, in some ways, this is not a specialization of (lexical) variables.

environment to it: **denv**. That new environment will contain only dynamic variables. This new interpreter, which we'll call Lisp₃, will use functions that prefix their names by **df.** to minimize confusion. Here's the new evaluator. (We've removed **flet** to avoid overloading it.)

```
(define (df.evaluate e env fenv denv)
  (if (atom? e)
      (cond ((symbol? e) (lookup e env))
            ((or (number? e)(string? e)(char? e)(boolean? e)(vector? e))
             e )
            (else (wrong "Cannot evaluate" e)) )
      (case (car e)
        ((quote) (cadr e))
        ((if) (if (df.evaluate (cadr e) env fenv denv)
                  (df.evaluate (caddr e) env fenv denv)
                  (df.evaluate (cadddr e) env fenv denv) ))
        ((begin) (df.eprogn (cdr e) env fenv denv))
        ((set!) (update! (cadr e)
                         env
                         (df.evaluate (caddr e) env fenv denv) ))
        ((function)
         (cond ((symbol? (cadr e))
                (f.lookup (cadr e) fenv) )
               ((and (pair? (cadr e)) (eq? (car (cadr e)) 'lambda))
                (df.make-function
                  (cadr (cadr e)) (cddr (cadr e)) env fenv ) )
               (else (wrong "Incorrect function" (cadr e))) ) )
        ((dynamic) (lookup (cadr e) denv))
        ((dynamic-set!)
         (update! (cadr e)
                  denv
                  (df.evaluate (caddr e) env fenv denv) ) )
        ((dynamic-let)
         (df.eprogn (cddr e)
                    env
                    fenv
                    (extend denv
                            (map car (cadr e))
                            (map (lambda (e)
                                   (df.evaluate e env fenv denv) )
                                 (map cadr (cadr e)) ) ) ) )
        (else (df.evaluate-application (car e)
                                       (df.evlis (cdr e) env fenv denv)
                                       env
                                       fenv
                                       denv )) ) ) )
(define (df.evaluate-application fn args env fenv denv)
  (cond ((symbol? fn) ((f.lookup fn fenv) args denv) )
        ((and (pair? fn) (eq? (car fn) 'lambda))
         (df.eprogn (cddr fn)
                    (extend env (cadr fn) args)
```

```
                        fenv
                        denv ) )
              (else (wrong "Incorrect functional term" fn)) ) )
    (define (df.make-function variables body env fenv)
      (lambda (values denv)
        (df.eprogn body (extend env variables values) fenv denv) ) )
    (define (df.eprogn e* env fenv denv)
      (if (pair? e*)
          (if (pair? (cdr e*))
              (begin (df.evaluate (car e*) env fenv denv)
                     (df.eprogn (cdr e*) env fenv denv) )
              (df.evaluate (car e*) env fenv denv)  )
          empty-begin ) )
```

Since we introduced the new environment **denv**, we have to augment the signatures of **df.evaluate** and **df.eprogn** to convey that information. In addition,
df.evaluate introduces three new special forms to handle **denv**, the *dynamic environment*. There's a more subtle modification in **df.evaluate-application**: now
a function is applied not only to its arguments but also to the current dynamic
environment. You've already seen this situation [see p. 19] when we had to pass
the current environment to the invoked function.

With respect to a functional application, there are several environments in play
at once. There's the environment for variables and functions that have been captured by the definition of the function. There's also the environment for dynamic
variables current at the time of the application. That environment for dynamic
variables cannot be captured, and every reference to a dynamic variable involves
a search for its value in the current dynamic environment. This search may prove
unfruitful; in such a case, we raise an error. Other choices could be possible: for
example, to have a unique dynamic global environment, as provided by IS-Lisp; or
to have many global dynamic environments, in fact, one per module, as in EuLisp;
or even to have the global environment of lexical variables, as in Common Lisp.
[see p. 48]

One of the advantages of this new space is that it shows clearly what is dynamic
and what isn't. Any time we intervene in the dynamic environment, we do so by
means of a special form prefixed by **dynamic**. This eye-catching notation lets us
see the interface to a function right away. In practice in this version of Lisp₃, the
behavior of a function is stipulated not only by the value of its variables but also
by the dynamic environment.

Among the conventional ways of using a dynamic environment, the most important concerns error handling. When an error or some other exceptional situation
occurs during a computation, an object defining the exception is formed, and to
that object, we apply the current function for handling exceptions (and possibly
for recovering from errors). That exception handler could be a global function,
but in that case it would require undesirable assignments in order to specify which
handler monitors which computation. The "airtightness" of lexical environments
hardly lends itself to specifying functions to handle errors. In contrast, a computation has an extent perfectly enclosed by a form like **let** or **dynamic-let**.
dynamic-let even has several advantages:

1. the bindings that it introduces cannot be captured;

2. those bindings are accessible only during the extent of the computation of its body;

3. those bindings are automatically undone at the end of the computation.

For those reasons, `dynamic-let` is ideal for temporarily establishing a function to handle errors.

Here's another example of how we use dynamic variables. The print functions in COMMON LISP are governed by various dynamic variables such as `*print-base*`, `*print-circle*`, etc. Those dynamic variables specify such things as the numeric base for printing numbers, whether the data to print entails cycles, and so forth. Of course, it would be possible for every print function to take all this information as arguments. In that case, instead of simply writing (`print` *expression*), we would have to write (`print` *expression print-escape print-radix print-base print-circle print-pretty print-level print-length print-case print-gensym print-array*) each time. That is, dynamic variables are a way of setting parameters for a computation and avoiding exhaustive enumeration of parameters that usually have an acceptable default value.

Scheme, uses a similar mechanism for specifying input and output ports. We can write (`display` *expression*) or[4] (`display` *expression port*). That first form, with only one argument, prints the value of *expression* to the current output port. The second form, with two arguments, specifies explicitly which output port to use. The function `with-output-to-file` lets you specify the current output port during the duration of a computation. You can find out the current output port by means of the function `current-output-port`. We could write a function[5] to print cyclic lists, independent of the print port, in this way:

```
(define (display-cyclic-spine list)
  (define (scan l1 l2 flip)
    (cond ((atom? l1)  (unless (null? l1) (display " . ")
                                          (display l1) )
                       (display ")") )
          ((eq? l1 l2) (display "...)") )
          (else        (display (car l1))
                       (when (pair? (cdr l1)) (display " "))
                       (scan (cdr l1)
                             (if (and flip (pair? l2)) (cdr l2) l2)
                             (not flip) ) ) ) )
  (display "(")
  (scan list (cons 123 list) #f) )
(display-cyclic-spine                      ;prints (1 2 3 4 1 ...)
  (let ((l (list 1 2 3 4)))
    (set-cdr! (cdddr l) l)
    l ) )
```

---

4. One of the democratic principles of Lisp is "Let others do what you allow yourself to do." Notice that the function `display` can take either one or two arguments, but no linguistic mechanism would allow that in Scheme. Lisp, in contrast to Scheme, supports the idea of optional arguments.
5. See also the function `list-length` in COMMON LISP.

If we go back to our chart, we can adapt it to the space for output ports in Scheme, like this:

Reference	referenced every time that it's not mentioned in a print function
Value	`(current-output-port)`
Modification	not modifiable
Extension	`(with-output-to-file` *file-name thunk*`)`
Definition	—not applicable—

In COMMON LISP, this mechanism explicitly uses dynamic variables. By default, the functions `print`, `write`, etc., use the output port with the value of the dynamic variable `*standard-output*`.[6] We could thus simulate[7] `with-output-to-file` by:

```
(define (with-output-to-file filename thunk)
  (dynamic-let ((*standard-output* (open-input-file filename)))
    (thunk) ) )
```

2.5.2 Dynamic Variables in COMMON LISP

Even though COMMON LISP keeps the concepts of lexical and dynamic variables quite separate, it still tries to unify them syntactically. The form `dynamic-let` doesn't really exist but it could be simulated like this:

```
(dynamic-let ((x α))   ≡ (let ((x α))
   β )                          (declare (special x))
                                β )
```

However, the innovation is that to get the value of the dynamic variable `x` into β, we won't pass by the **dynamic** form, but we'll simply write `x`. The reason: the declaration (`declare (special x)`) stipulates two things at once: that the binding that `let` establishes must be dynamic, and that any reference to the name `x` in the body of `let` must be considered equivalent to what we've named (`dynamic x`).

That strategy is inconvenient because it no longer lets us refer to the lexical variable named `x` inside β; we can only refer to its homonym, the dynamic variable. Going the other direction, we can refer to the dynamic variable `x` in any context by writing (`locally (declare (special x)) x`). That corresponds to our special form, **dynamic**.

The strategy of COMMON LISP thus lexically specifies the nature of a reference. We can make that mechanism explicit by modifying our interpreter, like this:

```
(define (df.evaluate e env fenv denv)
  (if (atom? e)
      (cond ((symbol? e) (cl.lookup e env denv))
            ((or (number? e)(string? e)(char? e)(boolean? e)(vector? e))
             e )
            (else (wrong "Cannot evaluate" e)) )
      (case (car e)
```

---

6. It's conventional to put stars around the names of dynamic variables to highlight them.
7. That's not COMMON LISP nor IS-Lisp; it's Lisp3, as we defined it a little earlier.

```
            ((quote) (cadr e))
            ((if) (if (df.evaluate (cadr e) env fenv denv)
                      (df.evaluate (caddr e) env fenv denv)
                      (df.evaluate (cadddr e) env fenv denv) ))
            ((begin) (df.eprogn (cdr e) env fenv denv))
            ((set!) (cl.update! (cadr e)
                                env
                                denv
                                (df.evaluate (caddr e) env fenv denv) ))
            ((function)
             (cond ((symbol? (cadr e))
                    (f.lookup (cadr e) fenv) )
                   ((and (pair? (cadr e)) (eq? (car (cadr e)) 'lambda))
                    (df.make-function
                     (cadr (cadr e)) (cddr (cadr e)) env fenv ) )
                   (else (wrong "Incorrect function" (cadr e))) ) )
            ((dynamic) (lookup (cadr e) denv))
            ((dynamic-let)
             (df.eprogn (cddr e)
                        (special-extend env              ;** Modified **
                                        (map car (cadr e)) )
                        fenv
                        (extend denv
                                (map car (cadr e))
                                (map (lambda (e)
                                       (df.evaluate e env fenv denv) )
                                     (map cadr (cadr e)) ) ) ) )
            (else (df.evaluate-application (car e)
                                           (df.evlis (cdr e) env fenv denv)
                                           env
                                           fenv
                                           denv )) ) ) )
(define (special-extend env variables)
  (append variables env) )
(define (cl.lookup var env denv)
  (let look ((env env))
    (if (pair? env)
        (if (pair? (car env))
            (if (eq? (caar env) var)
                (cdar env)
                (look (cdr env)) )
            (if (eq? (car env) var)
                ;;lookup in the current dynamic environment
                (let lookup-in-denv ((denv denv))
                  (if (pair? denv)
                      (if (eq? (caar denv) var)
                          (cdar denv)
                          (lookup-in-denv (cdr denv)) )
                      ;; default to the global lexical environment
                      (lookup var env.global) ) )
                (look (cdr env)) ) ) ) )
```

```
            (wrong "No such binding" var) ) ) )
```

Here's how that mechanism works: when we bind dynamic variables by **dyna-mic-let**, we bind them normally in the dynamic environment, but we also mark them as being dynamic in the lexical environment. We code that information by pushing their name into the lexical environment. The process that associates a reference with its value (see function **cl.lookup**) is thus modified, first of all, to achieve the syntactic analysis in order to determine the nature of the reference (whether it is lexical or dynamic); then we search for the associated value in the right environment. In addition, if we do not find the dynamic value, then we go back to the global lexical environment, since it also serves as the global dynamic environment in COMMON LISP.

To give a quick example of how Lisp₃ imitates COMMON LISP in this respect, we could evaluate this:

```
(dynamic-let ((x 2))
   (+ x                              ; dynamic
      (let ((x (+                    ; lexical
                  x x )))            ; dynamic
         (+ x                        ; lexical
            (dynamic x) ) ) ) )     ; dynamic
→ 8
```

2.5.3 Dynamic Variables without a Special Form

The way of dealing with dynamic variables that we've presented so far uses three special forms. Since Scheme makes an effort to limit the number of special forms, we might want to consider some other mechanism. Without looking at every conceivable variation that has ever been studied for Scheme, we propose the following because it uses only two functions. The first function associates two values; the second function finds the second of those two values when we hand it the first one. We'll use symbols to name dynamic variables. Finally, if we want to modify those associations, we have to use mutable data, such as a dotted pair. In these ways, we can respect the austerity of Scheme.

As we study this variation, we'll introduce a new interpreter with two environments, **env** and **denv**. This new interpreter is like the previous one except that we have removed a few things from it: all superfluous special forms, the space for functions, and the references to variables, as in COMMON LISP. As a consequence, only the essence of the dynamic environment remains, and that hardly seems useful anymore since it is not modified anywhere. It is, however, always provided to functions, and that provision will enable us to do what we intend. To distinguish this variation from the others, we'll prefix the functions by **dd**.

```
(define (dd.evaluate e env denv)
   (if (atom? e)
       (cond ((symbol? e) (lookup e env))
             ((or (number? e)(string? e)(char? e)(boolean? e)(vector? e))
              e )
             (else (wrong "Cannot evaluate" e)) )
       (case (car e)
```

```
            ((quote) (cadr e))
            ((if) (if (dd.evaluate (cadr e) env denv)
                     (dd.evaluate (caddr e) env denv)
                     (dd.evaluate (cadddr e) env denv) ))
            ((begin) (dd.eprogn (cdr e) env denv))
            ((set!) (update! (cadr e)
                            env
                            (dd.evaluate (caddr e) env denv)))
            ((lambda) (dd.make-function (cadr e) (cddr e) env))
            (else (invoke (dd.evaluate (car e) env denv)
                          (dd.evlis (cdr e) env denv)
                          denv )) ) ) )
(define (dd.make-function variables body env)
   (lambda (values denv)
      (dd.eprogn body (extend env variables values) denv) ) )
(define (dd.evlis e* env denv)
   (if (pair? e*)
       (if (pair? (cdr e*))
           (cons (dd.evaluate (car e*) env denv)
                 (dd.evlis (cdr e*) env denv) )
           (list (dd.evaluate (car e*) env denv)) )
       '() ) )
(define (dd.eprogn e* env denv)
   (if (pair? e*)
       (if (pair? (cdr e*))
           (begin (dd.evaluate (car e*) env denv)
                  (dd.eprogn (cdr e*) env denv) )
           (dd.evaluate (car e*) env denv) )
       empty-begin ) )
```

As we promised, we're going to introduce two functions. We'll name the first of the two **bind-with-dynamic-extent**, and we'll abbreviate that as **bind/de**. As its first parameter, it takes a key, **tag**; as its second, it takes **value** which will be associated with that key; and finally, it takes a **thunk**, that is, a calculation represented by a 0-ary function (that is, a function without variables). The function **bind/de** invokes the thunk after it has enriched the dynamic environment.

```
(definitial bind/de
   (lambda (values denv)
      (if (= 3 (length values))
          (let ((tag (car values))
                (value (cadr values))
                (thunk (caddr values)) )
             (invoke thunk '() (extend denv (list tag) (list value))) )
          (wrong "Incorrect arity" 'bind/de) ) ) )
```

The second function that we'll introduce exploits the dynamic environment. Since we have to make provisions for the case where we do not find what we're looking for in the dynamic environment, the function **assoc/de** takes a key as its first argument, and a function as its second. It will invoke that function on the key if the key is not present in the dynamic environment.

```
(definitial assoc/de
```

```
(lambda (values current.denv)
  (if (= 2 (length values))
      (let ((tag      (car values))
            (default (cadr values)) )
        (let look ((denv current.denv))
          (if (pair? denv)
              (if (eqv? tag (caar denv))
                  (cdar denv)
                  (look (cdr denv)) )
              (invoke default (list tag) current.denv) ) ) )
      (wrong "Incorrect arity" 'assoc/de) ) ) )
```

Many variations on this are possible, depending on whether we use **eqv?** or **equal?** for the comparison. [see **Ex. 2.4**]

To take an earlier example again, we will evaluate this:

```
(bind/de 'x 2
  (lambda () (+ (assoc/de 'x error)
                (let ((x (+
                          (assoc/de 'x error) (assoc/de 'x error) )))
                  (+ x (assoc/de 'x error)) ) )) )
→ 8
```

In that way, we've shown that there is really no need for special forms to get the equivalent of dynamic variables. In doing so, we have actually gained something since we can now associate anything with anything else. Of course, that advantage can be offset by inconvenience since there are efficient implementations of dynamic variables (even without parallelism). For example, shallow binding demands that the value of the key[8] must be a symbol. On the positive side, for this variation, we can count on transparence. Accessing a dynamic variable will surely be expensive because it entails calls to specialized functions. We're rather far from the fusion that COMMON LISP introduced.

Along with all the other inconveniences, we have to mention the syntax that using **bind/de** requires: a thunk and **assoc/de** to handle those associations. Of course, judicious use of macros can hide that problem. Another inconvenience comes when we try to compile calls to these functions correctly. The compiler must know them intimately; it has to know their exact behavior and all their properties. True, the fact that we rarely access this kind of variable and the fact that we have a functional interface to do so both simplify naive compilers.

2.5.4   Conclusions about Name Spaces

At the end of this digression about dynamic variables, it is important to keep in mind the idea of a name space that corresponds to a specialized environment to manipulate certain types of objects. We've seen Lisp₃ at work, and we've looked closely at the method that COMMON LISP uses for dynamic variables.

Nevertheless, that last variation—the one that used only two functions rather than three special forms for the same effects—raises a new problem. If this is a Lisp$_n$, which n is it? We started off from Scheme, and in the implementation that

---

8. Many implementations of Lisp forbid the use of keys like **nil** or **if** as the names of variables.

we've given, there are clearly two environments, **env** and **denv**. However, there is only one rule for all evaluations, and that's always consistent with Scheme, and thus it must be a Lisp$_1$. Yet things are not so clear-cut because we had to modify the definition (just compare the definition of **evaluate** and **dd.evaluate**) in order to implement the functions **bind/de** and **assoc/de**. At that point, we're facing primitive functions that we cannot recreate in pure Scheme if they don't already exist, and moreover the very existence of those two functions in the library of available functions profoundly changes the semantics of the language. In the next chapter, we'll see a similar case with **call/cc**.

In short, we seem to have made a Lisp$_1$ if we count the number of evaluation rules, but we appear to have a Lisp$_2$ if we focus on the number of name spaces. A generalization of this observation is that some authorities claim that the existence of a property list is the sign of a Lisp$_n$, where n is unbounded. Since our definition involves a global name space implemented by non-primitive functions, [see **Ex. 2.6**], we'll settle for that name: Lisp$_2$.

We can draw another lesson from this study of lexical and dynamic variables. COMMON LISP tries to unify the access to two different spaces by using a uniform syntax, and as a consequence, it has to promulgate rules to determine which name space to use. In COMMON LISP, the dynamic global space is confused with the lexical global space. In Lisp 1.5, there was a concept of constant defined by the special form **csetq** where **c** indicated constant.

Reference	x
Value	x
Modification	(csetq x *form*)
Extension	not possible
Definition	(csetq x *form*)

The introduction of constants makes the syntax ambiguous. When we write **foo**, it could be a constant or a variable. The rule in Lisp 1.5 was this: if **foo** is a constant, then return its value; otherwise, search for the value of the lexical variable of the same name. However, constants can be modified (yes! imagine that) by the form that creates them, **csetq**. In that sense, constants belong to the world of global variables in Scheme where the order is the reverse since in Scheme the lexical value is considered first, and the global value is considered only in default of it.

This problem is fairly general. When several different spaces can be referred to by an ambiguous syntax, the rules have to be spelled out in order to eliminate the ambiguity.

2.6 Recursion

Recursion is essential to Lisp, though nothing we've seen yet explains how it is implemented. Now we're going to analyze various kinds of recursion and the different problems that each of them poses.

2.6.1 Simple Recursion

The most widely known simply recursive function is probably the factorial, defined like this:

```
(define (fact n)
  (if (= n 0) 1
      (* n (fact (- n 1))) ) )
```

The language that we defined in the previous chapter does not know the meaning of **define**, so let's assume for the moment that this macro expands like this:

```
(set! fact (lambda (n)
             (if (= n 1) 1
                 (* n (fact (- n 1))) ) ))
```

This prompts us to consider an assignment, that is, a modification impinging on the variable **fact**. Such a modification would make no sense unless the variable exists already. We can characterize the global environment as the place where all variables already exist. That's certainly a kind of *virtual reality* where the effective implementation (and more precisely, the mechanism for reading programs) has to hurry, once a variable is named, in order to create the binding associated with that named variable in the global environment and to pretend that it had always been there. Every variable is thus reputed to be pre-existing: defining a variable is merely a question of modifying its value. This position, however, poses a problem about what can be the value of a variable that has not yet been assigned. The implementation has to make arrangements to trap this new kind of error corresponding to a binding that exists but has not been initialized. Here you can see that the idea of a binding is complicated, so we'll analyze it in greater detail in Chapter 4. [see p. 111]

We can get rid of this problem connected to the troublesome existence of a binding that exists but has not been initialized, if we adopt another point of view. Either assignment can modify only existing bindings, or bindings do not "pre-exist." In that case, it would be necessary to create bindings when we want them, and for that task, **define** could therefore be considered as a new special form with this role. Thus we could not refer to a variable nor modify its value unless it had already been created. Consider the other side of the coin for a moment in the following example.

```
(define (display-pi)
  (display pi) )
(define pi 2.7182818285)                                      ;MISTAKE
(define (print-pi)
  (display pi) )
(define pi 3.1415926536)
```

Is that definition of **display-pi** legal? Its body refers to the variable **pi** even though that variable does not yet exist. The fourth definition modifies the second one (to correct it) but even if the meaning of **define** is to create a new binding, does it still have the right to create a new one with the same name?

There is more than one possible response to that rhetorical question. In fact, at least two different positions confront each other here: the first extends the principle of lexicality to global definitions (ML takes this one); the second, used by Lisp, takes a more dynamic stance.

In a *global* world that is *purely lexical*—which we'll call *hyperstatic*—we cannot talk about a variable (that is, we can't refer to it, nor evaluate it, nor modify it) unless it already exists. In that context, the function `display-pi` is erroneous since it refers to the variable `pi` even though that variable does not yet exist. Any call to the function `display-pi` should surely raise the error "unknown variable: `pi`" if even the system allowed the definition of the `display-pi` function. Such would not be the case of the function `print-pi`; it would display the value that was valid at the time of its definition (in our example, 2.7182818285), and it would do so indefinitely. In this world, "redefinition" of `pi` is entirely legal, and doing so creates a new variable of the same name having the rest of these interactions as its scope. An imaginative way of seeing this mechanism is to consider the preceding sequence as equivalent to this:

```
(let ((display-pi (lambda () (display pi))))
  (let ((pi 2.7182818285))
    (let ((print-pi (lambda () (display pi))))
      (let ((pi 3.1415926536))
        ...
```

The three dots mark the rest of the interactions or the remaining global definitions.

Lisp, as we said, takes a more dynamic view. It assumes that at most only one global variable can exist with a given name, and that this global variable is visible everywhere, and, in particular, Lisp supports forward references to such a variable without the forward reference being highlighted in any syntactic way. (By syntactically highlighted, we mean such conventions as we see in Pascal with `forward` or in ISO C with prototypes as in [ISO90].)

That discussion is non-trivial. When we choose the environment in which the function is evaluated, we have to ask ourselves, "What will be the value of `fact`?" If the evaluation occurs in the global environment, before the binding of `fact` is created, then `fact` cannot be recursive. The reason for that is simple: the reference to `fact` in the body of the function must be looked for in the environment captured by the closure (the one enriched by the closure that has been created), but that environment does not contain the variable `fact`. As a consequence, it is necessary that the environment which will be closed contain not only the global environment but also the variable `fact`. This observation tends to favor a global environment where all the variables pre-exist because then we would not even have to ask that question we began with. However, if we adhere to the second possibility—the hyperstatic vision of a global environment—then we have to be sure that `define` binds `fact` before evaluating the closure that will become the value of this binding. In short, simple recursion demands a global environment.

2.6.2 Mutual Recursion

Now let's suppose that we want to define two mutually recursive functions. Let's say `odd?` and `even?` test (very inefficiently, by the way) the parity of a natural number. Those two are simply defined like this:

```
(define (even? n)
  (if (= n 0) #t (odd? (- n 1))) )
(define (odd? n)
  (if (= n 0) #f (even? (- n 1))) )
```

Regardless of the order in which we put these two definitions, the first one cannot be aware of the second; in this case, for example, **even?** knows nothing about **odd?**. Here again, the global environment, where all variables pre-exist, seems a winner because then the two closures capture the global environment, and thus capture all variables, and thus, in particular, capture **odd?** and **even?**. Of course, we're leaving the details of how to represent a global environment that contains an enumerable number of variables to the implementor.

It is more difficult to adopt the point of view of purely lexical global definitions because the first definition necessarily knows nothing about the second. One solution would be to introduce the two definitions together, at the same time. Doing so would insure their mutual acquaintance with each other. (We'll come back to this point once we have studied local recursion.) For example, if we dig out that old version of **define** from Lisp 1.5, we would write this:

```
(define ((even? (lambda (n) (if (= n 0) #t (odd? (- n 1)))))
         (odd? (lambda (n) (if (= n 0) #f (even? (- n 1)))))
))
```

Mutual recursion can in that way be expressed by the global environment on condition that it's blessed with *ad hoc* qualities.

What happens now if we want functions that are locally recursive?

2.6.3 Local Recursion in Lisp$_2$

Some of the problems we encountered when we were defining **fact** in a global environment come up again when we want to define **fact** locally. We have to do something so that the call to **fact** in the body of **fact** will be recursive. That is, we need for the function associated with this name to be the factorial value of **fact** in the function environment. However, a major difference exists here: when a binding does not exist in a local environment, an error occurs. Consider what happens if we write this in Lisp$_2$:

```
(flet ((fact (n) (if (= n 0) 1
                     (* n (fact (- n 1))) )))
  (fact 6) )
```

The function **fact** is bound in the current function environment. This closure captures both the function environment and the parametric environment current in the locality where the form **flet** is evaluated. In consequence, the function **fact** that appears in the body of **fact** refers to the function **fact** valid outside of the form **flet**. There's no reason for that function to be the factorial, and as a consequence, we don't really get recursion here.

That problem had already been recognized in Lisp 1.5 where a special form named **label** made it possible to define a locally recursive function. In that case, we would have written this:

```
(label fact (lambda (n) (if (= n 0) 1
```

```
                    (* n (fact (- n 1))) ) ))
```

That form returns an anonymous function that computes the factorial. Moreover, this anonymous function is the value of the function **fact** that appears in its body.

We cannot guarantee, however, that Lisp 1.5 was an authentic Lisp$_2$, and as interesting as it is, the form **label**, unfortunately, is not able to handle the case of mutual recursion simply. For that reason, an n-ary version was invented much later, according to [HS75]: the special form **labels**. This later form has the same syntax as the form **flet**, but it insures that the closures that are created will be in a function environment where all the local functions are aware of each other. Thus we can also locally define the recursive function **fact** as well as the mutually recursive functions **even?** and **odd?**, as we show in this:

```
(labels ((fact (n) (if (= n 0) 1
                       (* n (fact (- n 1))) ) ))
   (fact 6) )        → 720
(funcall (labels ((even? (n) (if (= n 0) #t (odd? (- n 1))))
                  (odd? (n) (if (= n 0) #f (even? (- n 1)))) )
            (function even?) )
      4 )      → #t
```

In Lisp$_2$, then we have two forms available, **flet** and **labels**, to enrich the local function environment.

2.6.4 Local Recursion in Lisp$_1$

The problem of defining locally recursive functions occurs in Lisp$_1$ as well, and we solve that problem in a similar way. A particular form, known as **letrec** for "let recursive," has much the same effect as **labels**.

In Scheme, **let** has the following syntax:

```
(let ((variable₁ expression₁)
      (variable₂ expression₂)
      ...
      (variableₙ expressionₙ) )
   expressions... )
```

Its effect is equivalent to this expression:

```
((lambda (variable₁ variable₂ ... variableₙ) expressions...)
   expression₁ expression₂ ... expressionₙ )
```

Here's a more discursive explanation of what's going on. First, the expressions, $expression_1$, $expression_2$, ... $expression_n$, are evaluated; then the variables, $variable_1$, $variable_2$, ... $variable_n$, are bound to the values that have already been gotten; finally, in the extended environment, the body of **let** is evaluated (within an implicit **begin**), and its value becomes the value of the entire **let** form.

A priori, the form **let** does not seem useful since it can be simulated by **lambda** and thus can be only a simple macro. (By the way, this is not a special form in Scheme, but primitive syntax.) Nevertheless, the form **let** becomes very useful on the stylistic level because it allows us to put a variable just next to its initial value, like a block in Algol. This idea leads us to remark that the variables in a **let** form are initialized by values computed in the current environment; only the body of `let` is evaluated in the enriched environment.

For the same reasons that we encountered in Lisp$_2$, this way of doing things means that we cannot write mutually recursive functions in a simple way, so we'll use `letrec` again here for the same purpose.

The syntax of the form `letrec` is similar to that of the form `let`. For example, we would write:

```
(letrec ((even? (lambda (n) (if (= n 0) #t (odd? (- n 1)))))
         (odd? (lambda (n) (if (= n 0) #f (even? (- n 1)))))) )
   (even? 4) )
```

The difference between `letrec` and `let` is that the expressions initializing the variables are evaluated in the same environment where the body of the `letrec` form is evaluated. The operations carried out by `letrec` are comparable to those of `let`, but they are not done in the same order. First, the current environment is extended by the variables of `letrec`. Then, in that extended environment, the initializing expressions of those same variables are evaluated. Finally, the body is evaluated, still in that enriched environment. This description of what's going on suggests clearly how to implement `letrec`. To get the same effect, we simply have to write this:

```
(let ((even? 'void)
      (odd? 'void) )
   (set! even? (lambda (n) (or (= n 0) (odd? (- n 1)))))
   (set! odd? (lambda (n) (or (= n 1) (even? (- n 1)))))
   (even? 4) )
```

The bindings for **even?** and **odd?** are created. (By the way, the variables are bound to values of no particular importance because `let` or `lambda` do not allow uninitialized bindings to be created.) Then those two variables are initialized with values computed in an environment that is aware of the variables **even?** and **odd?**. We've used the phrase "aware of" because, even though the bindings of the variables **even?** and **odd?** exist, their values have no relation to what we expect from them inasmuch as they have not been initialized. The bindings of **even?** and **odd?** exist enough to be captured but not enough to be evaluated validly.

However, the transformation is not quite correct because of the issue of order: a `let` form is equivalent to a functional application, and its initialization forms become the arguments of the functional application that's being generated; if indeed a `let` form is equivalent to a functional application, then the order of evaluating the initialization forms should not be specified. Unfortunately, the expansion we just used forces a particular order: left to right. [see **Ex. 2.9**]

Equations and `letrec`

A major problem of `letrec` is that its syntax is not very strict; in fact, it allows anything as initialization forms, and not solely functions. In contrast, the syntax of **labels** in COMMON LISP forbids the definition of anything other than functions. In Scheme, it's possible to write this:

```
(letrec ((x (/ (+ x 1) 2))) x)
```

Notice that the variable x is defined in terms of itself according to the semantics of letrec. That's a veritable equation written like this:

$$x = \frac{x+1}{2}$$

It seems logical to bind x to the solution of this equation, so the final value of that letrec form would be 1.

But what happens according to this interpretation when an equation has no solution or has multiple solutions?

```
(letrec ((x (+ x 1))) x)              ;x = x + 1
(letrec ((x (+ 1 (power x 37)))) x)   ;x = x^37 + 1
```

There are many other domains (all familiar in Lisp) like S-expressions, where we can sometimes insure that there will always be a unique solution, according to [MS80]. For example, we can build an infinite list without apparent side effects, rather like a language with lazy evaluation, by writing this:

```
(letrec ((foo (cons 'bar foo))) foo)
```

The value of that form would then be either the infinite list (bar bar bar ...) calculated the lazy way, as in [FW76, PJ87], or the circular structure (less expensive) that we get from this:

```
(let ((foo (cons 'bar 'wait)))
  (set-cdr! foo foo)
  foo )
```

For that reason, we have to adopt a more pragmatic rule for letrec to forbid the use of the value of a variable of letrec during the initialization of the same variable. Accordingly, the two preceding examples demand that the value of x must already be known in order to initialize x. That situation raises an error and will be punished. However, we should note that the order of initialization is not specified in Scheme, so certain programs can be error-prone in certain implementations and not so in others. That's the case, for example, with this:

```
(letrec ((x (+ y 1))
         (y 2) ) )
    x )
```

If the initialization form of y is evaluated before the one for x, then everything turns out fine. In the opposite case, there will be an error because we have to try to increment y which is bound but which does not yet have a value. Some Scheme or ML compilers analyze initialization expressions and sort them topologically to determine the order in which to evaluate them. This kind of sorting is not always feasible when we introduce mutual dependence[9] like this:

```
(letrec ((x y)(y x)) (list x y))
```

That example reminds us strongly about that discussion of the global environment and the semantics of define. There we had a problem of the same kind: how to know about the existence of an uninitialized binding.

---

9. Again, returning the list (42 42) does not violate the statement of this form.

2.6.5   Creating Uninitialized Bindings

The official semantics of Scheme makes `letrec` derived syntax, that is, a useful abbreviation but not really necessary. Accordingly, every `letrec` form is equivalent to a form that could have been written directly in Scheme. We tried that approach earlier when we bound the variables of `letrec` temporarily to `void`. Unfortunately, doing so initialized the bindings and made it impossible to detect the error we mentioned before. Our misfortune is actually even worse than that because none of the four special forms in Scheme allows the creation of uninitialized bindings.

A first attempt at a solution might use the object `#<UFO>` [see p. 14] in place of `void`. Of course, we can't do much with `#<UFO>`: we can't add it, nor take its `car`, but since it is a first class object, we can make it appear in a `cons`, so the following program would not be false and would return `#<UFO>`:

```
(letrec ((foo (cons 'foo foo))) (cdr foo))
```

The underlying reason for that is that the lack of initialization of a binding is a property of the binding itself, not of its contents. Consequently, using a first class value, `#<UFO>`, is not a solution to our problem.

If we think about implementations, then we notice that often a binding is uninitialized if it has a very particular value. Let's call that very special value `#<uninitialized>`, and let's suppose for the moment that this value is first class. When it appears as the value of a variable, then the variable has to be regarded as uninitialized. We will thus replace `void` by `#<uninitialized>` and get the error detection that we wanted. However, this mechanism is too powerful because anybody can provide `#<uninitialized>` as an argument to any function, and we thus lose an important property that every variable of a function has a value. According to those terms, our old reliable factorial function cannot even assume any longer that its variable n is bound and thus it must test explicitly whether n has a value, like this:

```
(define (fact n)
  (if (eq? n '#<uninitialized>)
      (wrong "Uninitialized n")
      (if (= n 0) 1
          (* n (fact (- n 1))) ) ) )
```

This surcharge is too costly and, consequently, `#<uninitialized>` can't be a first class value; it can be only an internal flag reserved to the implementor, one that the end-user can't touch. This second path is consequently closed to us, as far as a solution to our problem goes.

A third solution is to introduce a new special form, capable of creating uninitialized bindings. Let's take advantage of a syntactic variation of `let`, one that exists in COMMON LISP but not in Scheme, to do that, like this:

```
(let ( variable ... )
    ... )
```

When a variable appears alone, without an initialization form, in the list of local variables in a `let` form, then the binding will be created uninitialized. Any evaluation, or even any attempt at evaluation, of this variable must verify whether it is really initialized. The expansion of a `letrec` now no longer calls anything foreign to it. In what follows, the variables $temp_i$ are *hygienic*; that is, they cannot provoke conflicts with the *variables$_i$* nor with those that are free in π.

$$
\begin{array}{ll}
\texttt{(letrec ((}variable_1\ expression_1\texttt{)} & \texttt{(let (\ }variable_1 \ldots variable_n\ \texttt{)} \\
\qquad \ldots & \quad \texttt{(let ((\ }temp_1\ expression_1\ \texttt{)} \\
\qquad \texttt{(}variable_n\ expression_n\texttt{))} \quad \equiv & \qquad \ldots \\
\quad body\ \texttt{)} & \qquad \texttt{(\ }temp_n\ expression_n\ \texttt{))} \\
& \quad \texttt{(set! }variable_1\ temp_1\texttt{)} \\
& \qquad \ldots \\
& \quad \texttt{(set! }variable_n\ temp_n\texttt{)} \\
& \quad body\ \texttt{))}
\end{array}
$$

In that way, we've resolved the problem in a satisfactory way because only the uninitialized variables pay the surcharge due to uninitialization. However, the form `let` is no longer just syntax; rather, it is a primitive special form that must thus appear in the basic interpreter. For that reason, we'll add the following clause to `evaluate`.

```
  ...
  ((let)
   (eprogn (cddr e)
           (extend env
                   (map (lambda (binding)
                          (if (symbol? binding) binding
                              (car binding) ) )
                        (cadr e) )
                   (map (lambda (binding)
                          (if (symbol? binding) the-uninitialized-marker
                              (evaluate (cadr binding) env) ) )
                        (cadr e) ) ) ) ) ...
```

The variable `the-uninitialized-marker` belongs to the definition language. It could be defined like this:

```
(define the-non-initialized-marker (cons 'non 'initialized))
```

Of course, the internal flag is exploited by the function `lookup` which must be adapted for it. The function `update!` is not affected by this change. In the following function, the two different calls to `wrong` characterize two different situations: non-existing binding and uninitialized binding.

```
(define (lookup id env)
  (if (pair? env)
      (if (eq? (caar env) id)
          (let ((value (cdar env)))
            (if (eq? value the-non-initialized-marker)
                (wrong "Uninitialized binding" id)
                value ) )
          (lookup id (cdr env)) )
      (wrong "No such binding" id) ) )
```

After these syntactic-semantic ramblings, we have a form of `letrec` that allows us to co-define local functions that are mutually recursive.

2.6.6   Recursion without Assignment

The form `letrec` that we've been analyzing uses assignments to insure that initialization forms are evaluated. Languages that are known as *purely functional* don't have this resource available to them; side effects are unknown among them, and what is assignment if not a side effect on the value of a variable?

As a philosophy, forbidding assignment offers great advantages: it preserves the referential integrity of the language and thus leaves an open field for many transformations of programs, such as moving code, using parallel evaluation, using lazy evaluation, etc. However, if side effects are not available, certain algorithms are no longer so clear, and the introspection of a real machine is impeded, since real machines work only because of the side effects of their instructions.

The first solution that comes to mind is to make `letrec` another special form, as it is in most languages in the same class as ML. We would enrich `evaluate` so that it could handle the case of `letrec`, like this:

```
 ...
((letrec)
 (let ((new-env (extend env
                        (map car (cadr e))
                        (map (lambda (binding) the-uninitialized-marker)
                             (cadr e) ) )))
     (map (lambda (binding)          ;map to preserve chaos !
              (update! (car binding)
                       new-env
                       (evaluate (cadr binding) new-env) ) )
          (cadr e) )
     (eprogn (cddr e) new-env) ) ) ...
```

In that way, we regain side effects, formerly attributed to assignments, now carried out by **update!**. We also note that the order of evaluation is still not significant because **map** (in contrast to **for-each**) does not guarantee anything about the order in which it handles terms in a list.[10]

letrec and the Purely Lexical Global Environment

A purely lexical global environment allows the use of a variable only if the variable has already been defined. The problem with that rule is that we cannot define simply recursive functions nor groups of mutually recursive functions. With `letrec`, we can suggest how to resolve that problem by making it possible to define more than one function at a time by indicating whether the definition is recursive or not. We would thus write this:

```
(letrec ((fact (lambda (n)
                (if (= n 0) 1 (* n (fact (- n 1)))) )))
    (letrec ((odd? (lambda (n) (if (= n 0) #f (even? (- n 1)))))
             (even? (lambda (n) (if (= n 0) #t (odd? (- n 1)))))) )
     ...
```

Those dots represent the rest of the interactions or definitions.

---

10. The cost here is that we have to build a useless list—useless since it is forgotten as soon as it is built.

Paradoxical Combinator

If you have experience with λ-calculus, then you probably remember how to write *fixed-point combinators* and among them, the famous *paradoxical combinator*, **Y**. A function f has a fixed point if there exists an element x in its domain such that $x = f(x)$. The combinator **Y** can take any function of λ-calculus and return a fixed point for it. This idea is expressed in one of the loveliest and most profound theorems of λ-calculus:

Fixed Point Theorem: $\exists Y, \forall F, \; YF = F(YF)$

In Lisp terminology, **Y** is the value of this:

```
(let ((W (lambda (w)
           (lambda (f)
             (f ((w w) f)) ) )))
  (W W) )
```

Our demonstration of that assertion is quite short. If we assume that **Y** is equal to **(WW)**, then how should we choose **W** so that **(WW)F** will be equal to **F((WW)F)**? Obviously, **W** is no other than $\lambda W.\lambda F.F((WW)F)$. That Lisp expression is nothing other than a transcription of these ideas.

The problem here is that the strategy of call by value in Scheme is not compatible with this kind of programming. We are obliged to add a superfluous η-conversion (superfluous from the point of view of pure λ-calculus) to block any premature evaluation of the term `((w w) f)`. We'll cut across then to the following fixed-point combinator in which `lambda (x) ( ... x))` marks the η-conversion.

```
(define fix
  (let ((d (lambda (w)
             (lambda (f)
               (f (lambda (x) (((w w) f) x))) ) )))
    (d d) ) )
```

The most troubling aspect of that definition is how it works. (We're going to show you that right away.) Let's define the function **meta-fact** like this:

```
(define (meta-fact f)
  (lambda (n)
    (if (= n 0) 1
        (* n (f (- n 1))) ) ) )
```

That function has a disconcerting relation to factorial. We will verify by example that the expression **(meta-fact fact)** calculates the factorial of a number just as well as **fact**, though more slowly. More precisely, let's suppose that we know a fixed point f of **meta-fact**; in other words, $f =$ **(meta-fact** f**)**. That fixed point has, by definition, the property of being a solution to the functional equation in f:

```
f = (lambda (n)
      (if (= n 1) 1
          (* n (f (- n 1))) ) )
```

So what is f? It can't be anything other than our well known factorial.

Actually, nothing guarantees that the preceding functional equation has a solution, nor that it is unique. (All those terms, of course, must be mathematically well defined, though that is beyond the purpose of this book.) Indeed, the equation has many solutions, for example:

```
(define (another-fact n)
  (cond ((< n 1) (- n))
        ((= n 1) 1)
        (else (* n (another-fact (- n 1)))) ) )
```

We urge you to verify that the function **another-fact** is yet another fixed point of **meta-fact**. Analyzing all these fixed points shows us that there is a set of answers on which they all agree: they all compute the factorial of natural numbers. They diverge from one another only where **fact** diverges in infinite calculations. For negative integers, **another-fact** returns one result where many might be possible since the functional equation says nothing[11] about those cases. Therefore, there must exist a least fixed point which is the least determined of the solution functions of the functional equation.

The meaning to attribute to a definition like the one for **fact** in the global environment is that it defines a function equal to the least fixed point of the associated functional equation, so when we write this:

```
(define (fact n)
  (if (= n 0) 1
      (* n (fact (- n 1))) ) )
```

we should realize that we have just written an equation where the variable is named **fact**. As for the form **define**, it resolves the equation and binds the variable **fact** to that solution of the functional equation. This way of looking at things takes us far from discussions about initialization of global variables [**see p. 54**] and turns **define** into an equation-solver. Actually, **define** is implemented as we suggested before. Recursion across the global environment coupled with normal evaluation rules does, indeed, compute the least fixed point.

Now let's get back to **fix**, our fixed-point combinator, and trace the execution of ((**fix meta-fact**) 3). In the following trace, remember that no side effects occur, so we'll substitute their values for certain variables directly from time to time.

```
    ((fix meta-fact) 3)
  = (((d d)|
             |  d≡ (lambda (w)
                     (lambda (f)
                        (f (lambda (x)
                             (((w w) f) x) )) ) )
        meta-fact )
      3 )
  = (((lambda (f)                              ; (i)
         (f (lambda (x)
              (((w w) f) x) )) )|
                                 | w≡ (lambda (w)
                                         (lambda (f)
                                            (f (lambda (x)
                                                 (((w w) f) x) )) ) )
```

---

11. See [Man74] for more thorough explanations.

```
         meta-fact )
      3 )
 = ((meta-fact (lambda (x)
               (((w w) meta-fact) x) ))|
                                        | w≡ (lambda (w)
                                              (lambda (f)
                                                (f (lambda (x)
                                                     (((w w) f) x) )) ) )
      3 )
 =((lambda (n)
     (if (= n 0) 1
        (* n (f (- n 1))) ) )|
                             | f≡ (lambda (x)
                                    (((w w) meta-fact) x))|
                                                          | w≡
                                                 (lambda (w)          ⋮
                                                   (lambda (f)        ↵
                                                     (f (lambda (x)
                                                          (((w w) f) x) )) ) )
      3 )
 = (* 3 (f 2))|
              | f≡ (lambda (x)
                     (((w w) meta-fact) x))|
                                           | w≡
                                  (lambda (w)          ⋮
                                    (lambda (f)        ↵
                                      (f (lambda (x)
                                           (((w w) f) x) )) ) )
 = (* 3 (((w w) meta-fact) 2))|
                              | w≡ (lambda (w)
                                     (lambda (f)
                                       (f (lambda (x)
                                            (((w w) f) x) )) ) )

 = (* 3 (((lambda (f)                          ; (ii)
            (f (lambda (x)
                 (((w w) f) x) )) )|
                                   | w≡ (lambda (w)
                                          (lambda (f)
                                            (f (lambda (x)
                                                 (((w w) f) x) )) ) )
         meta-fact )
      2 ) )
```

We'll pause there to note that, in gross terms, the expression at step *i* occurs again at step *ii*, and, like the thread in a needle, it leads to this:

```
(* 3 (* 2 (((lambda (f)
              (f (lambda (x)
                   (((w w) f) x) )) )|
                                     | w≡ (lambda (w)
                                            (lambda (f)
```

```
                                             (f (lambda (x)
                                                  (((w w) f) x) )) ) )
                meta-fact )
              1 )))
  = (* 3 (* 2 ((meta-fact (lambda (x)
                           (((w w) meta-fact) x) ))|
                                                    |  w≡
                          (lambda (w)               |   ⋮
                            (lambda (f)             |   ↩
                              (f (lambda (x)
                                   (((w w) f) x) )) ) )
              1 )))
  = (* 3 (* 2 ((lambda (n)
                 (if (= n 0) 1
                   (* n (f (- n 1))) ) )|
                                        |  f→ ...
              1 )))
  = (* 3 (* 2 (if (= n 0) 1 (* n (f (- n 1))))))|
                                                |  n→ 1
                                                |  f→ ...
  = (* 3 (* 2 1))
  = 6
```

Notice that as the computation winds its way along, an object corresponding
to the factorial has, indeed, been constructed. It's this value:

```
(lambda (x)
  (((w w) f) x) )|
                 |  f≡ meta-fact
                 |  w→(lambda (w)
                         (lambda (f)
                           (f (lambda (x)
                                (((w w) f) x) )) ) )
```

The cleverness lies in the way we recompose a new instance of this factorial
every time a recursive call needs it.

That's the way that we could get simple recursion, without side effects, by
means of **fix**, a fixed-point combinator. Thanks to **Y** (or to **fix** in Lisp), it is
possible to define **define** as a solver of recursive equations; it takes an equation as
its argument, and it binds the solution to a name. Thus the equation defining the
factorial leads to binding the variable **fact** to this value:

```
(fix (lambda (fact)
       (lambda (n)
         (if (= n 0) 1
           (* n (fact (- n 1))) ) ) ))
```

We can extend this technique to the case of multiple functions that are mutually
recursive by regrouping them. The functions **odd?** and **even?** can be fused, like
this:

```
(define odd-and-even
  (fix (lambda (f)
```

```
        (lambda (which)
          (case which
            ((odd) (lambda (n) (if (= n 0) #f
                                   ((f 'even) (- n 1)) )))
            ((even) (lambda (n) (if (= n 0) #t
                                   ((f 'odd) (- n 1)) ))) ) ) )) ) )
(define odd? (odd-and-even 'odd))
(define even? (odd-and-even 'even))
```

The problem with this method, however, is that it is not very efficient in terms of performance, compared to even an imperfect compilation of a `letrec` form. (Yet see [Roz92, Ser93].) Nevertheless, this method has its own practitioners, especially when it's time to write books. Functional languages do not adopt this method either, according to [PJ87], because of its inefficiency and because the definition of `fix` is not susceptible to typing. In effect, its nature is to take a functional[12] that takes, as its argument, the function typed $\alpha \rightarrow \beta$ and that returns a fixed point of that functional. The type is consequently this:

$$\text{fix:} \ ((\alpha \rightarrow \beta) \ \rightarrow \ (\alpha \rightarrow \beta)) \ \rightarrow \ (\alpha \rightarrow \beta)$$

But in the definition of `fix`, we have the auto-application (`d d`) that has γ for its type, like this:

$$\gamma = \gamma \ \rightarrow \ (\alpha \rightarrow \beta)$$

We need a system of non-trivial types to contain this recursive type, or we have to consider `fix` a primitive function that (fortunately) already exists because we don't know how to define it within the language, if it's missing.

2.7 Conclusions

This chapter has crossed several of the great chasms that split the Lisp world in the past thirty years. When we examine the points where these divergences begin, though, we see that they are not so grand. They generally have to do with the meaning of `lambda` and the way that a functional application is calculated. Even though the idea of a function seems like a well founded mathematical concept, its incarnation within a functional language (that is, a language that actually uses functions) like Lisp is quite often the source of many controversies. Being aware of and appreciating these points of divergence is part of Lisp culture. When we analyze the traces of our elders in this culture, we not only build up a basis for mutual understanding, but we also improve our programming style.

Paradoxically, this chapter has shown the importance of the idea of binding. In Lisp$_1$, a variable (that is, a name) is associated with a unique binding (possibly global) and thus with a unique value. For that reason, we talk about the value of a variable rather than the value associated with the binding of that variable. If we look at a binding as an abstract type, we can say that a binding is created by a binding form, and that it is read or written by evaluation of the variable or by

---

12. McCarthy in [MAE+62] defines a functional as a function that can have functions as arguments.

assignment, and finally, that it can be captured when a closure is created in which the body refers to the variable associated with that binding.

Bindings are not first class objects. They are handled only indirectly by the variables with which they are associated. Nevertheless, they have an indefinite extent; in fact, they are so useful because they endure.

A binding form introduces the idea of scope. The scope of a variable or of a binding is the textual space where that variable is visible. The scope of a variable bound by `lambda` is restricted to the body of that `lambda` form. For that reason, we talk about its textual or lexical scope.

The idea of binding is complicated by the fact of assignment, and we'll study it in greater detail in the next chapter.

2.8   Exercises

Exercise 2.1 : The following expression is written in COMMON LISP. How would you translate it into Scheme?

```
(funcall (function funcall) (function funcall) (function cons) 1 2)
```

Exercise 2.2 : In the pseudo-COMMON LISP you saw in this chapter, what is the value of this program? What does it make you think of?

```
(defun test (p)
  (function bar) )
(let ((f (test #f)))
  (defun bar (x) (cdr x))
  (funcall f '(1 . 2)) )
```

Exercise 2.3 : Incorporate the first two innovations presented in Section 2.3 [see p. 39] into the Scheme interpreter. Those innovations concern numbers and lists in the function position.

Exercise 2.4 : The function `assoc/de` could be improved to take a comparer (such as `eq?`, `equal?`, or others) as an argument. Write this new version.

Exercise 2.5 : With the aid of `bind/de` and `assoc/de`, write macros that simulate the special forms `dynamic-let`, `dynamic`, and `dynamic-set!`.

Exercise 2.6 : Write the functions `getprop` and `putprop` to simulate lists of properties. We could associate a value with the key in the list of properties of a symbol with `putprop`; we could search the list of properties for the value associated with a key with `getprop`. Of course, we have the following property:

```
(begin (putprop 'symbol 'key 'value)
       (getprop 'symbol 'key) )              → value
```

Exercise 2.7 : Define the special form `label` in Lisp$_1$.

Exercise 2.8 : Define the special form `labels` in Lisp$_2$.

Exercise 2.9 : Think of a way to expand `letrec` in terms of `let` and `set!` so that the order does not matter when initializations of expressions are evaluated.

Exercise 2.10 : The fixed-point combinator in Scheme has a weakness: it works only for unary functions. Give a new version, `fix2`, that works correctly for binary functions. Then write a version, `fixN`, that works correctly for functions of any arity.

Exercise 2.11 : Now write a function, `NfixN`, that returns a fixed point from a list of functionals of any arity. We would use such a thing, for example, to define this:

```
(let ((odd-and-even
       (NfixN (list (lambda (odd? even?)     ;odd?
                     (lambda (n)
                      (if (= n 0) #f (even? (- n 1)))) ) )
                    (lambda (odd? even?)     ;even?
                     (lambda (n)
                      (if (= n 0) #t (odd? (- n 1)))) ) ) )) ))
  (set! odd? (car odd-and-even))
  (set! even? (cadr odd-and-even)) )
```

Exercise 2.12 : Here's the function `klop`. Is it a fixed-point combinator? Try to show whether or not (`klop` f) returns a fixed-point of f, the way `fix` would do.

```
(define klop
  (let ((r (lambda (s c h e m)
             (lambda (f)
               (f (lambda (n)
                   (((m e c h e s) f) n) )) ) )))
   (r r r r r) ) )
```

Exercise 2.13 : If the function `hyper-fact` is defined like this:

```
(define (hyper-fact f)
  (lambda (n)
    (if (= n 0) 1
        (* n ((f f) (- n 1))) ) ) )
```

then what is the value of ((`hyper-fact` `hyper-fact`) 5)?

Recommended Reading

In addition to the paper about λ-calculus [SS78a] that we mentioned earlier, you could also consider the analysis of functions in [Mos70] and the comparative study of Lisp$_1$ and Lisp$_2$ in [GP88].

There is an interesting introduction to λ-calculus in [Gor88].

The combinator **Y** is also discussed in [Gab88].

3
Escape & Return: Continuations

EVERY computation has the goal of returning a value to a certain entity that we call a *continuation*. This chapter explains that idea and its historic roots. We'll also define a new interpreter, one that makes continuations explicit. In doing so, we'll present various implementations in Lisp and Scheme and we'll go into greater depth about the programming style known as "Continuation Passing Style." Lisp is distinctive among programming languages because of its elaborate forms for manipulating execution control. In some respects, that richness in Lisp will make this chapter seem like an enormous catalogue [Moz87] where you'll probably feel like you've seen a thousand and three control forms one by one. In other respects, however, we'll keep a veil over continuations, at least over how they are physically carried out. Our new interpreter will use objects to show the relatives of continuations and its control blocks in the *evaluation stack*.

The interpreters that we built in earlier chapters took an expression and an environment in order to determine the value of the expression. However, those interpreters were not capable of defining computations that included *escapes*, useful control structures that involve getting out of one context in order to get into another, more preferable one. In conventional programming, we use escapes principally to master the behavior of programs in case of unexpected errors, or to program by exceptions when we define a general behavior where the occurrence of a particular event interrupts the current calculation and sends it back to an appropriate place.

The historic roots of escapes go all the way back to Lisp 1.5 to the form **prog**. Though that form is now obsolete, it was originally introduced in the vain hope of attracting Algol users to Lisp since it was widely believed that they knew how to program only with **goto**. Instead, it seems that the form distracted otherwise healthy Lisp programmers away from the precepts[1] of tail-recursive functional programming. Nevertheless, as a form, **prog** merits attention because it embodies several interesting traits. Here, for example, is factorial written with **prog**.

---

1. As an example, consider the stylistic differences between the first and third editions of [WH88].

```
(defun fact (n)                               COMMON LISP
  (prog (r)
            (setq r 1)
     loop  (cond ((= n 1) (return r)))
            (setq r (* n r))
            (setq n (- n 1))
            (go loop) ) )
```

The special form **prog** first declares the local variables that it uses (here, only the variable r). The expressions that follow are instructions (represented as lists) or labels (represented by symbols). The instructions are evaluated sequentially like in **progn**; and normally the value of a **prog** form is **nil**. Multiple special instructions can be used in one **prog**. Unconditional jumps are specified by **go** (with a label which is not computed) whereas **return** imposes the final value of the **prog** form. There was one restriction in Lisp 1.5: **go** forms and **return** forms could appear only in the first level of a **prog** or in a **cond** at the first level.

The form **return** made it possible to get out of the **prog** form by imposing its result. The restriction in Lisp 1.5 allowed only an escape from a simple context; successive versions improved this point by allowing **return** to be used with no restrictions. Escapes then became the normal way of taking care of errors. When an error occurred, the calculation tried to escape from the error context in order to regain a safer context. With that point in mind, we could rewrite the previous example in the following equivalent code, where the form **return** no longer occurs on the first level.

```
(defun fact2 (n)                              COMMON LISP
  (prog (r)
            (setq r 1)
     loop  (setq r (* (cond ((= n 1) (return r))
                            ('else n) )
                      r ))
            (setq n (- n 1))
            (go loop) ) )
```

If we reduce the forms **return** and **prog** to nothing more than their control effects, we see clearly that they handle the calling point (and the return point) of the form **prog** exactly like in the case of a functional application where the invoked function returns its value precisely to the place where it was called. In some sense, then, we can say that **prog** binds **return** to the precise point that it must come back to with a value. Escape, then, consists of not knowing the place from which we take off while specifying the place where we want to arrive. Additionally, we hope that such a *jump* will be implemented efficiently: escape then becomes a programming method with its own disciples. You can see it in the following example of searching for a symbol in a binary tree. A naive programming style for this algorithm in Scheme would look like this:

```
(define (find-symbol id tree)
  (if (pair? tree)
      (or (find-symbol id (car tree))
          (find-symbol id (cdr tree)) )
      (eq? tree id) ) )
```

Let's assume that we're looking for the symbol **foo** in the expression **(((a . b) . (foo . c)) . (d . e))**. Since the search takes place from left to right and depth-first, once the symbol has been found, then the value **#t** must be passed across several embedded **or** forms before it becomes the final value (the whole point of the search, after all). The following shows the details of the preceding calculation in equivalent forms.

```
(find-symbol 'foo '(((a . b) . (foo . c)) . (d . e)))
≡ (or (find-symbol 'foo '((a . b) . (foo . c)))
      (find-symbol 'foo '(d . e)) )
≡ (or (or (find-symbol 'foo '(a . b))
          (find-symbol 'foo '(foo . c)) )
      (find-symbol 'foo '(d . e)) )
≡ (or (or (or (find-symbol 'foo 'a)
              (find-symbol 'foo 'b) )
          (find-symbol 'foo '(foo . c)) )
      (find-symbol 'foo '(d . e)) )
≡ (or (or (find-symbol 'foo 'b)
          (find-symbol 'foo '(foo . c)) )
      (find-symbol 'foo '(d . e)) )
≡ (or (find-symbol 'foo '(foo . c))
      (find-symbol 'foo '(d . e)) )
≡ (or (or (find-symbol 'foo 'foo)
          (find-symbol 'foo 'c) )
      (find-symbol 'foo '(d . e)) )
≡ (or (or #t
          (find-symbol 'foo 'c) )
      (find-symbol 'foo '(d . e)) )
≡ (or #t
      (find-symbol 'foo '(d . e)) )
→ #t
```

An efficient escape seems appropriate there. As soon as the symbol that is being searched for has been found, an efficient escape has to support the return of the very same value without considering any remaining branches of the search tree.

Another example comes from programming by exception where repetitive treatment is applied over and over again until an exceptional situation is detected in which case an escape is carried out in order to *escape* from the repetitive treatment that would otherwise continue more or less perpetually. We'll see an example of this later with the function **better-map**. [see p. 80]

If we want to characterize the entity corresponding to a calling point better, we note that a calculation specifies not only the expression to compute and the environment of variables in which to compute it, but also where we must return the value obtained. This "where" is known as a *continuation*. It represents all that remains to compute.

Every computation has a continuation. For example, in the expression **(+ 3 (* 2 4))**, the continuation of the subexpression **(* 2 4)** is the computation of an addition where the first argument is **3** and the second is expected. At this point, theory comes to our rescue: this continuation can be represented in a form that's easier to see—as a function. A continuation represents a computation, and it doesn't take place unless we get a value for it. This protocol strongly resembles the one for a function and is thus in that guise that continuations will be represented. For the preceding example, the continuation of the subexpression (* 2 4) will thus be equivalent to (lambda (x) (+ 3 x)), thus faithfully underlining the fact that the calculation waits for the second argument in the addition.

Another representation also exists; it specifies continuations by contexts inspired from λ-calculus. In that representation, we would denote the preceding continuation as (+ 3 []), where [] stands for the place where the value is expected.

Truly everything has a continuation. The evaluation of the condition of an alternative is carried out by means of a continuation that exploits the value that will be returned in order to decide whether to take the true or false branch of the alternative. In the expression (if (foo) 1 2), the continuation of the functional application (foo) is thus (lambda (x) (if x 1 2)) or (if [] 1 2).

Escapes, programming by exception, and so forth are merely particular forms for manipulating continuations. With that idea in mind, now we'll detail the diverse forms and great variety of continuations observed over the past twenty years or so.

3.1 Forms for Handling Continuations

Capturing a continuation makes it possible to handle the control thread in a program. The form **prog** already makes it possible to do that, but carries with it other effects, like those of a **let** for its local variables. Paring down **prog** so that it concerns only control was the first goal of the forms **catch** and **throw**.

3.1.1 The Pair catch/throw

The special form **catch** has the following syntax:

> (catch *label forms...*)

The first argument, *label*, is evaluated, and its value is associated with the current continuation. This facts makes us suppose that there must be a new space, the *dynamic escape space*, binding values and continuations. If we can't think of labels which are not identifiers, we actually can't talk anymore about a name space; this, however, really is one, if we accept the fact that every value can be a valid label for that space. Yet that condition poses the problem of equality within this space: how can we recognize that one value names what another has associated with a continuation?

The other *forms* make up the body of the form **catch** and are themselves evaluated sequentially, like in a **progn** or in a **begin**. If nothing happens, the value of the form **catch** is that of the last of the forms in its body. However, what can intervene is the evaluation of a **throw**.

The form **throw** has the following syntax.

> (throw *label form*)

The first argument is evaluated and must lead to a value that a dynamically embedding **catch** has associated with a continuation. If such is the case, then the

evaluation of the body of this `catch` form will be interrupted, and the value of the
form will become the value of the entire `catch` form.

Let's go back to our example of searching for a symbol in a binary tree, and
let's put into it the forms `catch` and `throw`. The variation that you are about to
see has factored out the search process in order not to transmit the variable `id`
pointlessly, since it is lexically visible in the entire search. We will thus use a local
function to do that.

```
(define (find-symbol id tree)
  (define (find tree)
    (if (pair? tree)
        (or (find (car tree))
            (find (cdr tree)) )
        (if (eq? tree id) (throw 'find #t) #f) ) )
  (catch 'find (find tree)) )
```

As its name indicates, `catch` traps the value that `throw` sends it. An escape
is consequently a direct transmission of the value associated with a control ma-
nipulation. In other words, the form `catch` is a binding form that associates the
current continuation with a label. The form `throw` actually makes the reference to
this binding. That form also changes the thread of control as well; `throw` does not
really have a value because it returns no result by itself, but it organizes things in
such a way that `catch` can return a value. Here, the form `catch` captures the continuation of the call to `find-symbol`, while `throw` accomplishes the direct return
to the caller of `find-symbol`.

The dynamic escape space can be characterized by a chart listing its various
properties.

Reference	(throw *label* ...)
Value	no because it's a second class continuation
Modification	no
Extension	(catch *label* ...)
Definition	no

As we said earlier, `catch` is not really a function, but a special form that
successively evaluates its first argument (the label), binds its own continuation to
this latter value in the dynamic escape environment, and then begins the evaluation
of its other arguments. Not all of them will necessarily be evaluated. When `catch`
returns a value or when we escape from it, `catch` dissociates the label from the
continuation.

The effect of `throw` can be accomplished either by a function or by a special
form. When it is a special form, as it is in COMMON LISP, it calculates the label, it
verifies the existence of an associated `catch`, then it evaluates the value to transmit,
and finally it jumps. When `throw` is a function, it does things in a different order:
it first calculates the two arguments, then verifies the existence of an associated
`catch`, and then it jumps.

These semantic differences clearly show how unreliably a text might describe
the behavior of these control forms. A lot of questions remain unanswered. What
happens, for example, when there is no associated `catch`? Which equality is used
to compare labels? What does this expression do (throw α (throw β π))? We'll
find answers to those kinds of questions a little later.

3.1.2   The Pair `block`/`return-from`

The escapes that `catch` and `throw` perform are dynamic. When `throw` requests an
escape, it must verify during execution whether an associated `catch` exists, and it
must also determine which continuation it refers to. In terms of implementation,
there is a non-negligible cost here that we might hope to reduce by means of *lexical*
escapes, as they are known in the terminology of COMMON LISP. The special forms
`block` and `return-from` superficially resemble `catch` and `throw`.

Here's the syntax of the special form `block`:

(block *label forms...*)

The first argument is not evaluated and must be a name suitable for the escape: an
identifier. The form `block` binds the current continuation to the name *label* within
the *lexical escape environment*. The body of `block` is evaluated then in an implicit
`progn` with the value of this `progn` becoming the value of `block`. This sequential
evaluation can be interrupted by `return-from`.

Here's the syntax of the special form `return-from`:

(return-from *label form*)

That first argument is not evaluated and must mention the name of an escape that
is lexically visible; that is, a `return-from` form can appear only in the body of an
associated `block`, just as a variable can appear only in the body of an associated
`lambda` form. When a `return-from` form is evaluated, it makes the associated
`block` return the value of *form*.

Lexical escapes generate a new name space, and we'll summarize its properties
in the following chart.

Reference	(return-from *label* ...)
Value	no because it's a second class continuation
Modification	no
Extension	(block *label* ...)
Definition	no

Let's look again at the preceding example, this time, writing[2] it like this:

```
(define (find-symbol id tree)
  (block find
    (letrec ((find (lambda (tree)
                     (if (pair? tree)
                         (or (find (car tree))
                             (find (cdr tree)) )
                         (if (eq? id tree) (return-from find #t)
                             #f ) ) )))
      (find tree) ) ) )
```

Notice that this is not an ordinary translation of the previous example where
"`catch 'find`" simply turns into "`block find`" nor likewise for `throw`. Without the migration of "`block find`," the form `return-from` would not have been
bound to the appropriate `block`.

---

2. Warning to Scheme-users: `define` is translated internally into a `letrec` because `(let ()`
`(define ...) ...)` is not valid in Scheme because of the `()`.

The generated code corresponding to that form is highly efficient. In gross, general terms, **block** stores the height of the execution stack under the name of the escape **find**. The form **return-from** consists solely of putting **#t** where a value is expected (for example, in a register) and re-adjusting the stack pointer to the height that **block** associated with **find**. This represents only a few instructions, in contrast to the dynamic behavior of **catch**. **catch** would work through the entire list of valid escapes, little by little, until it found one with the right label. You can see that difference clearly if you consider this simulation of **catch**[3] by **block**.

```
(define *active-catchers* '())
(define-syntax throw
  (syntax-rules ()
    ((throw tag value)
     (let* ((label tag)                                      ; compute once
            (escape (assv label *active-catchers*)) )        ; compare with eqv?
       (if (pair? escape)
           ((cdr escape) value)
           (wrong "No associated catch to" label) ) ) ) ) )
(define-syntax catch
  (syntax-rules ()
    ((catch tag . body)
     (let* ((saved-catchers *active-catchers*)
            (result (block label
                      (set! *active-catchers*
                            (cons (cons tag
                                        (lambda (x)
                                          (return-from label x) ) )
                                  *active-catchers* ) )
                      . body )) )
       (set! *active-catchers* saved-catchers)
       result ) ) ))
```

In that simulation, the cost of the pair **catch/throw** is practically entirely concentrated in the call to **assv**[4] in the expansion of **throw**. But first, let's explain how the simulation works. A global variable (here, named *active-catchers*) keeps track of all the active **catch** forms, that is, those whose execution has not yet been completed. That variable is updated at the exit from **catch** and consequently at the exit from **throw**. The value of *active-catchers* is an A-list, where the keys are the labels of **catch** and the values are the associated continuations. This A-list embodies the dynamic escape environment for which **catch** was the binding form and for which **throw** was the referencing form, as you can easily see in that simulation code.

3.1.3 Escapes with a Dynamic Extent

That simulation, however, is imperfect in the sense that it prohibits simultaneous uses of **block**; doing so would perturb the value of the variable *active-catchers*.

---

3. The definition of **catch** uses a **block** with the name **label**. The rules for hygienic naming of variables, of course, should be extended to the name space.
4. In passing, you see that the labels are compared by eqv?.

The art of simulation or syntactic extension of a dialect is a difficult one, as [Fel90, Bak92c] observe, because frequently adding new traits requires a complicated architecture that prohibits direct access to resources mobilized for the simulation or extension. Later, we'll show you an authentic simulation of catch by block, but it will require yet another linguistic means: unwind-protect.[5]

Like all entities in Lisp, continuations have a certain extent. In the simulation of catch by block, you saw that the extent of a continuation caught by catch is limited to the duration of the calculation in the body of the catch in question. We refer to this extent as *dynamic*. When we use that term, we are also thinking of dynamic binding since it insures only that the value of a dynamic variable lasts as long as the evaluation of the body of the corresponding binding form. We could take advantage of this property to offer a new definition of catch and throw in terms of block and return-from; this time, the list of catchers that can be activated is easily maintained in the dynamic variable *active-catchers*. This program reconciles block and catch so that they can be used simultaneously now.

```
(define-syntax throw
  (syntax-rules()
    ((throw tag value)
     (let* ((label tag)                              ; compute once
            (escape (assv label (dynamic *active-catchers*))) )
       (if (pair? escape)
           ((cdr escape) value)
           (wrong "No associated catch to" label) ) ) ) ) )
(define-syntax catch
  (syntax-rules ()
    ((catch tag . body)
     (block label
       (dynamic-let ((*active-catchers*
                       (cons (cons tag (lambda (x)
                                         (return-from label x) ))
                             (dynamic *active-catchers*) ) ))
         . body ) ) ) ) )
```

The extent of an escape caught by block is dynamic in COMMON LISP, so the escape can be used only during the calculation of the body of the block. Likewise, the extent of an escape caught by catch is also dynamic in COMMON LISP, so again, the escape can be used only during the calculation of the body of the catch. This fact poses an interesting problem with block, a problem that does not occur with catch: if throw and return-from make it possible to abbreviate computations, then some computation must exist to be escaped from. Consider the following program.

```
((block foo (lambda (x) (return-from foo x)))
 33 )
```

The value of the first term is an escape to foo, but this escape is obsolete when it is applied, and in consequence, we get an execution error. When the closure

---

5. Another solution would be to redefine the new forms block and return-from, with the help of the old ones, so that they would be compatible with catch and throw. That solution is difficult to implement directly, but it can be done by adding a new level of interpretation.

is created, it closes the lexical escape environment, especially the binding of **foo**. That closure is then returned as the value of the form **block**, but that return occurs when we exit from **block**, and consequently, it is out of the question to exit yet again, since that has already happened. When that closure is applied, we verify whether the continuation associated with **foo** is still valid, and we jump if that is the case. The following example shows that closures around lexical escapes do not mix bindings.

```
(block foo
   (let ((f1 (lambda (x) (return-from foo x))))
      (* 2 (block foo
            (f1 1) )) ) ) → 1
```

Compare those results with what we would get by replacing "**block foo**" by "**catch 'foo**" like this:

```
(catch 'foo
   (let ((f1 (lambda (x) (throw 'foo x))))
      (* 2 (catch 'foo
            (f1 1) )) ) ) → 2
```

The catcher invoked by the function **f1** is the more recent one, having bound the label **foo**; the result of **catch** is consequently multiplied by 2 and returns 2 finally.

3.1.4 Comparing catch and block

The forms **catch** and **block** have many points of comparison. The continuations that they capture have a dynamic extent: they last only as long as an evaluation. In contrast, **return-from** can refer an indefinitely long time to a continuation, whereas **throw** is more limited. In terms of efficiency, **block** is better in most cases because it never has to verify during a **return-from** whether the corresponding **block** exists, since that existence is guaranteed by the syntax. However, it is necessary to verify that the escape is not obsolete, though that fact is often syntactically visible. You can see a parallel between dynamic and lexical escapes, on one side, and dynamic and lexical variables, on the other: many problems are common to both groups.

Dynamic escapes allow conflicts that are completely unknown to lexical escapes. For one thing, dynamic escapes can be used anywhere, so one function can put an escape in place, and another function may unwittingly intercept it. For example,

```
(define (foo)
   (catch 'foo (* 2 (bar))) )
(define (bar)
   (+ 1 (throw 'foo 5)) )
(foo)   → 5
```

Independently of the extent of the escape, **block** limits its reference to its body whereas **catch** authorizes that as long as it lives. As a consequence, it is possible to use the escape bound to **foo** all the time that (* 2 (bar)) is being evaluated. In the preceding example, you cannot replace "**catch 'foo**" by "**block foo**" and expect the same results. An even more dangerous collision would be this:

```
(catch 'not-a-pair
       (better-map (lambda (x)
                     (or (pair? x)
                         (throw 'not-a-pair x) ) )
              (hack-and-return-list) ) )
```

Let's assume that we heard, next to the coffee-machine, that the function **better-map** is much better than **map**; and let's also suppose that we'll risk using it to test whether the result of (**hack-and-return-list**) is really a list made up of pairs; and furthermore, we'll assume that we don't know the definition of **better-map**, which happens to be this:

```
(define (better-map f l)
  (define (loop l1 l2 flag)
    (if (pair? l1)
        (if (eq? l1 l2)
            (throw 'not-a-pair l)
            (cons (f (car l1))
                  (loop (cdr l1)
                        (if flag (cdr l2) l2)
                        (not flag) ) ) ) ) )
  (loop l (cons 'ignore l) #t) )
```

In fact, the function **better-map** is quite interesting because it halts even if the list in the second argument is cyclic. Yet if (**hack-and-return-list**) returns the infinite list #1=((foo . hack) . #1#)[6] then **better-map** would try to escape. If that fact is not specified in its user interface, there might be a name conflict and a collision of escapes comparable to a twenty-car pile-up at rush hour. Here again we could change the names to limit such conflicts; doing so is simple with **catch** because it allows its label to be any possible Lisp value; in particular, the value could be a dotted pair that we construct ourselves. We could rewrite it more certainly this way then:

```
(let ((tag (list 'not-a-pair)))
  (catch tag
         (better-map (lambda (x)
                       (or (pair? x)
                           (throw tag x) ) )
                (foo-hack) ) )
```

It is possible to simulate **block** by **catch** but there is no gain in efficiency in doing so. It suffices to convert the lexical escapes into dynamic ones, like this:

```
(define-syntax block
  (syntax-rules ()
    ((block label . body)
     (let ((label (list 'label)))
       (catch label . body) ) ) ) )
(define-syntax return-from
  (syntax-rules ()
    ((return-from label value)
```

---

6. Here, we've used COMMON LISP notation for cyclic data. We could also have built such a list by (**let** ((p (**list** (**cons** 'foo hack)))) (**set-cdr!** p p) p).

```
(throw label value) ) ) )
```

The macro **block** creates a unique label and binds it lexically to the variable of the same name. Doing so insures that only the **return-from**(s) present in its body will see that label. Of course, by doing that, we pollute the variable space with the name **label**. To offset that fault, we can try to use a name that doesn't conflict or even a name created by **gensym**, but once we do that, we have to make arrangements for the same name to appear in both **catch** and **throw**.

3.1.5 Escapes with Indefinite Extent

As part of its massive overhaul of Lisp around 1975, Scheme proposed that continuations caught by **catch** or **block** should have an indefinite extent. This property gave them new and very interesting characteristics. Later, in an attempt to reduce the number of special forms in Scheme, there was an effort to capture continuations by means of a function as well as to represent a continuation as a function, that is, as a first class citizen. In [Lan65], Landin suggested the operator J to capture continuations, and the function **call/cc** in Scheme is its direct descendant.

We'll try to explain its syntax as simply as possible at this first encounter. First of all, it involves the capture of a continuation, so we need a form that captures the continuation of its caller, k, like this:

$$k (\dots)$$

Now since we want it to be a function, we'll name it **call/cc**, like this:

$$k (\text{call/cc} \dots)$$

Once we have captured k, we have to furnish it to the user, but how do we do that? We really can't return it as the value of the form **call/cc** because then we would render k to k. If the user is waiting for this value in order to use it in a calculation, it's so that he or she can turn this calculation into a unary function[7] since it is only an object that is waiting for a value to be used in a calculation. Accordingly, we could furnish this function as an argument to **call/cc**, like this:

$$k (\text{call/cc (lambda (k)} \dots))$$

In that way, the continuation k is turned into a first class value, and the function-argument of **call/cc** is invoked on it. The last choice due to Scheme is to not create a new type of object and thus to represent continuations by unary functions, indistinguishable from functions created by **lambda**. The continuation k is thus *reified*, that is, turned into an object that becomes the value of **k**, and it then suffices to invoke the function **k** to transmit its argument to the caller of **call/cc**, like this:

$$k (\text{call/cc (lambda (k) (+ 1 (k 2))))} \quad \rightarrow 2$$

Another solution would be to create another type of object, namely, continuations themselves. This type would be distinct from functions, and would necessitate a special invoker, namely, **continue**. The preceding example would then be rewritten like this:

$$k (\text{call/cc (lambda (k) (+ 1 (continue k 2))))} \quad \rightarrow 2$$

---

7. Warning to Scheme users: it is sufficient that the argument of **call/cc** should accept being called with only one argument. Then we could also write (**call/cc list**).

It is still possible to transform a continuation into a function by enclosing it in an abstraction (`lambda (v) (continue k v)`). Some people like calls to continuations that are syntactically eye-opening because they make alteration of the thread of control more evident.

The ultimate difficulty with `call/cc` is that its real name is `call-with-current-continuation`, a fact that does not improve the situation, so let's rewrite our example to use `call/cc`, like this:

```
(define (find-symbol id tree)
  (call/cc
   (lambda (exit)
     (define (find tree)
       (if (pair? tree)
           (or (find (car tree))
               (find (cdr tree)) )
           (if (eq? tree id) (exit #t) #f) ) )
     (find tree) ) ) )
```

The call continuation of the function `find-symbol` is captured by `call/cc`, reified as a unary function bound to the variable `exit`. When the symbol is found, the escape is triggered by a call to the function `exit` (which never returns).

The indefinite extent of continuations is not obvious in that example since the continuation is used only during the invocation of the argument of `call/cc`, that is, during its dynamic extent. The following program illustrates indefinite extent.

```
(define (fact n)
  (let ((r 1)(k 'void))
    (call/cc (lambda (c) (set! k c) 'void))
    (set! r (* r n))
    (set! n ( - n 1))
    (if (= n 1) r (k 'recurse)) ) )
```

The continuation reified in `c` and stored in `k` corresponds to this:

k = (lambda (u)
  (set! r (* r n))
  (set! n (- n 1))
  (if (= n 1) r (k 'recurse)))$\Big|$
        r$\rightarrow$ 1
        k$\equiv$ k
        n

This continuation k appears as the value of the variable `k` that it encloses. Recursion, as we know, always implies something cyclic somewhere, and in this case, it is assured by the call to `k`, re-invoked until n reaches the threshold that we want. That whole effort, of course, computes the factorial.

In that example, you see that the continuation k is used outside it dynamic extent, which is equal to the time during which the body of the argument of `call/cc` is being evaluated. On that basis, you can imagine many other variations, for example, to submit the identity to `call/cc`, like this:

```
(define (fact n)
```

```
(let ((r 1))
  (let ((k (call/cc (lambda (c) c))))
    (set! r (* r n))
    (set! n ( - n 1))
    (if (= n 1) r (k k)) ) ) )
```

Now it's necessary for the recursive call to be the auto-application (k k) because, at every call of the continuation, the variable k is bound again to the argument provided to it. The continuation can be represented by this:

```
(lambda (u)
  (let ((k u))
    (set! r (* r n))
    (set! n ( - n 1))
    (if (= n 1) r (k k)) ) )
```
$$r \rightarrow 1$$
$$n$$

When we confer an indefinite extent on continuations, we make their implementation more problematic and generally more expensive. (Nevertheless, see [CHO88, HDB90, Mat92].) Why? Because we must abandon the model of evaluation as a stack and adopt a tree instead. In effect, when continuations have a dynamic extent, we can qualify them as escapes since their only goal is to escape from a computation. Escaping is the same as getting away from any remaining computations in order to impose a final value on a form that is still being evaluated. A computation begins when the evaluation of a form starts, and it seems simple enough to determine when it ends. In the presence of continuations with a dynamic extent, a computation always has a detectable end.

However, with continuations of indefinite extent, things are not so simple. Consider, for example, the expression (call/cc ...) in the preceding factorial. That expression returns a result many times. That fact (that a form can return values many[8] times) implies that the ultimate boundary of its computation is not necessarily the moment when it returns a result.

The function call/cc is very powerful and makes it possible in some ways to handle time. Escaping is like speeding up time until we provoke an event that we can foresee but that we foresee a long way off. Once it has escaped, a continuation with indefinite extent makes it possible to come back to that state. It's not just a means of convoluted looping because the values of the variables will generally have changed in the meantime, so coming back to a point already seen in the program forces the computation to take a new path.

We might compare call/cc to the "harmful" goto instruction of imperative languages. However, call/cc is more restricted since it is only possible to jump to places where we once passed through (after capture of that continuation) but not to places where we never went.

In the beginning, the function call/cc is sufficiently subtle to handle because the continuation is unary like the argument of call/cc. The following rewrite rule shows the effect of call/cc from another angle.

$$_k(\text{call/cc } \phi) \quad \rightarrow \quad _k(\phi \quad k)$$

---

8. Returning values multiple times is not the same as returning multiple values, as in COMMON LISP.

In that rule, k represents the call continuation of `call/cc` and ϕ is some unary function. `call/cc` proceeds to reify the continuation k, an implementation entity, turning it into a value in the language that can appear as the second term of an application. Notice that the current continuation when ϕ is invoked is still k. Thus we are not compelled to use the continuation provided as an argument, and we implicitly depend on the same continuation, as you see in the following extract:

```
(call/cc (lambda (k) 1515)) → 1515
```

Some people might regret this fact, and like a strict authority figure, they might impose the rule that when we take the continuation, we remove it then from the underlying evaluator. In consequence, we would have to use that continuation to return a value, like this:

```
(call/cc (lambda (k) (k 1615))) → 1615
```

In that hypothetical world, (k 1615) would be evaluated with a continuation something like a black hole, say, $(\lambda u.\bullet)$. That continuation would absorb the value which would be rendered to it without further dissemination of information. Then there would be no posterior computation; your keyboard would dissolve into thin air; you would no longer exist, and neither would this book. In such a world, you certainly must not forget to invoke your continuation!

3.1.6 Protection

We need to look at one last effect linked to continuations. It has to do with the special form **unwind-protect**. That name comes from the period when the implementation of a trait determined its name[9] and indicated how to use it. Here's the syntax of the special form **unwind-protect**.

```
(unwind-protect form
       cleanup-forms )
```

The term *form* is evaluated first; its value becomes the value of the entire form **unwind-protect**. Once this value has been obtained, the *cleanup-forms* are evaluated for their effect before this value is finally returned. The effect is almost that of **prog1** in COMMON LISP or of **begin0** in some versions of Scheme, that is, evaluating a series of forms (like **progn** or **begin**) but returning the value of the first of those forms. The special form **unwind-protect** guarantees that the cleanup forms will always be evaluated regardless of the way that computation of *form* occurs, even if it is by an escape. Thus:

```
(let ((a 'on))                                        COMMON LISP
  (cons (unwind-protect (list a)
          (setq a 'off) )
        a ) )    → ((on) . off)
(block foo
  (unwind-protect (return-from foo 1)
      (print 2) ) )   → 1  ; and prints 2
```

---

9. The names `car` and `cdr` come from that same period; they are closely connected to the implementation of Lisp 1.5. They are acronyms for "contents of the address register" and "contents of the decrement register."

That form is interesting in the case of a subsystem where we want to insure that a certain property will be restored, regardless of the outcome in the subsystem. The conventional example is that of handling a file: we want to be sure that it will be closed even if an error occurs. Another more interesting example concerns a simulation of `catch` by `block`. Using `block` simultaneously would de-synchronize the variable `*active-catchers*`. We could correct that fault by means of a judicious, well placed `unwind-protect`, like this:

```
(define-syntax catch
  (syntax-rules
    ((catch tag . body)
     (let ((saved-catchers *active-catchers*))
       (unwind-protect
         (block label
           (set! *active-catchers*
                 (cons (cons tag (lambda (x) (return-from label x)))
                       *active-catchers* ) )
           . body )
         (set! *active-catchers* saved-catchers) ) ) ) ) )
```

Whatever the outcome of the computation carried out in the body, the list of active `catch` forms will always be up to date at the end of the computation. The `block` forms can thus be used freely along with the `catch` forms. The simulation is still not perfect because the variable `*active-catchers*` must be private to `catch` and `throw` (or, more accurately, private to their expansions). In the current state, we might alter it, either accidentally or intentionally, and thus destroy the order among these macros.

The form `unwind-protect` protects the computation of a form by insuring that a certain treatment will happen once the computation has been completed. Thus the form `unwind-protect` is inevitably tied to detecting when a computation is complete, and from there, to continuations with dynamic extent. For the reasons that we discussed earlier, `unwind-protect`[10] does not get along well with `call/cc` nor with continuations that have an indefinite extent.

As we have often emphasized before, the meaning of these constructions is not at all precise. Let's just consider a few questions about the values of the following forms:

```
(block foo
  (unwind-protect (return-from foo 1)
    (return-from foo 2) ) )                              → ?
```

```
(catch 'bar
  (block foo
    (unwind-protect (return-from foo (throw 'bar 1))
      (throw 'no-associated-catch (return-from foo 2)) ) ) ) → ?
```

This kind of vagueness tends to make us want more careful and precise formality in these concepts. Nevertheless, we have to observe the equivocal status of cleanup forms and especially their continuations. We qualify the continuation as *floating*

---

10. An operational description of `unwind-protect` for Scheme, known as `dynamic-wind`, appears in [FWH92]; see also [Que93c].

because it cannot be known statically and may correspond to an escape that is
already underway. Consider this, for example:

```
(block bar
    (unwind-protect (return-from bar 1)
        (block foo π₂ ) ) )
```

The cleanup form captures the continuation corresponding to the lexical escape
to **bar**. If the cleanup form returns a value, then this escape to **bar** will be taken
back. If the cleanup form itself escapes, then its own continuation will be abandoned. (We'll discuss these phenomena later when we explain the implementation
in greater detail.)

Other control forms also exist, and notably in COMMON LISP, where the old-
fashioned form of **prog** metamorphoses into **tagbody** and **go**; they can be simulated
by **labels** and **block**. [see **Ex. 3.3**] We'll come back to the fact that in a world
of continuations with dynamic extent, **block**, **return-from**, and **unwind-protect**
together provide the base of special forms that we usually find there. Similarly, in
the world of Scheme, **call/cc** is all we need. It's clear that we cannot simulate
call/cc directly with continuations with a dynamic extent. The inverse is feasible,
but to do so, we have to tone down **call/cc**, which proves a little too powerful in
that situation. The method for doing so will be clearer once we've explicated the
interpreter with explicit continuations.

Protection and Dynamic Variables

Certain implementations of Scheme get their dynamic variables a little differently
from the variations that we've looked at so far. They depend on the presence of
the form **unwind-protect** or something similar. The idea involves a sort of lexical
borrow and something of a theft. These dynamic variables are introduced by the
form **fluid-let**, like this:

```
(fluid-let ((x α))   ≡ (let ((tmp x))
    β ... )                 (set! x α)
                            (unwind-protect
                            (begin β ...)
                            (set! x tmp) ) )
```

During the calculation of β, the variable **x** has the value α as its value; the preceding value of **x** is saved in a local variable, *tmp*, and it's restored at the end of the
calculation. This form implies the existence of a lexical binding to borrow, usually
a global binding, thus making the variable visible everywhere. If, in contrast, a
local binding is borrowed, then (differing greatly from dynamic variables in COM-
MON LISP) this will be accessible in the body of the form **fluid-let** and only in
it, with possibly pernicious effects on the co-owners of this variable. Moreover, the
form **unwind-protect** and indefinite extent continuations don't get along together
very well. Indeed, this form is even more subtle to use than dynamic variables in
COMMON LISP.

3.2 Actors in a Computation

Now, from our current point of view, a computation is made up of three elements: an expression, an environment, and a continuation. While the immediate goal is to evaluate the expression in the environment, the long term goal is to return a value to the continuation.

Here we're going to define a new interpreter to highlight all the continuations needed at every level. Since continuations are usually represented as blocks or activation records in a stack or heap, we will use objects to represent them within the interpreter that we're undertaking.

3.2.1 A Brief Review about Objects

This section will not present an entire system of objects in all its glory; that task remains for Chapter 11. Here our goal is simply to present a set of three macros associated with a few naming rules. This set is merely the essence of a system of objects, and it's independent of any implementation of such a system. We chose to use objects in this chapter in order to suggest how to implement continuations. Objects with their fields conveniently evoke activation records that implement languages. The idea of inheritance, put to work here in a very elementary way, will let us factor out certain common effects and thus reduce the size of the interpreter that we're presenting.

We'll assume that you're familiar with the philosophy, terminology, and customary practice about objects, and we'll simply go over a few linguistic conventions that we'll be exploiting.

Objects are grouped into *classes*; objects in the same class respond to the same *methods*; messages are sent by means of *generic functions*, popularized by Common Loops [BKK+86], CLOS [BDG+88], and ΤΕΛΟΣ[PNB93]. For our purposes, the interesting aspect of object-oriented programming is that we can organize various special forms or primitive functions for control around a kernel evaluator. The drawback of this style for us is that the dissemination of methods makes it harder to see the big picture.

Defining a Class

A class is defined by **define-class**, like this:

```
(define-class class superclass
    ( fields... ) )
```

This form defines a class with the name *class*, inheriting the fields and methods of its *superclass*, plus its own fields, indicated by *fields*. Once a class has been created, we can use a multitude of associated functions. The function known as **make-***class* creates objects belonging to *class*; that function has as many arguments as the class has fields, and those arguments occur in the same order as the fields. The read-accessors for fields in these objects have a name prefixed by the name of the class, suffixed by the name of the field, separated by a hyphen. The write-accessors prefix the name of the read-accessor by **set-** and suffix it by an exclamation point.

Write-accessors do not have a specific return value. The predicate *class?* tests whether or not an object belongs to *class*.

The root of the inheritance hierarchy is the class `Object` having no fields.

The following definition:

```
(define-class continuation Object (k))     ; example
```

makes the following functions available:

```
(make-continuation k)          ; creator
(continuation-k c)             ; read-accessor
(set-continuation-k! c k)      ; write-accessor
(continuation? o)              ; membership predicate
```

Defining a Generic Function

Here's how we define a generic function:

```
(define-generic (function variables)
   [ default-treatment ... ] )
```

That form defines a generic function named *function*; *default-treatment* specifies what it does when no other appropriate method can be found. The list of variables is a normal list of variables except that it specifies as well the variable that serves as the *discriminator*; the discriminator is enclosed in parentheses.

```
(define-generic (invoke (f) v* r k)
   (wrong "not a function" f r k) )
```

That form defines the generic function `invoke`, which could be enriched with methods eventually. The function has four variables; the first is the discriminator: `f`. If there is a call to `invoke` and no appropriate method is defined for the class of the discriminator, then the default treatment, `wrong`, will be invoked.

Defining a Method

We use `define-method` to stuff a generic function with specific methods.

```
(define-method (function variables)
   treatment ...   )
```

Just like the form `define-generic`, this form uses the list of variables to specify the class for which the method is defined. This class appears with the discriminator between parentheses. For example, the following form defines a method for the class `primitive`:

```
(define-method (invoke (ff primitive) vv* rr kk)
  ((primitive-address ff) vv* rr kk) )
```

That completes the set of characteristics that we'll be using. Chapter 11 will show you an implementation of this system of objects, but regardless of the implementation, for now, we'll only use the most widely known characteristics of objects and those least subject to hazards.

3.2.2 The Interpreter for Continuations

Now the function **evaluate** has three arguments: the expression, the environment, and the continuation. The function **evaluate** begins by syntactically analyzing the expression to determine appropriate treatment for it. Each of these treatments is individualized in a particular function. Before we get into the new interpreter, we should indicate the rules that we'll follow in naming our variables. The first convention is that a variable suffixed by a star represents a list of whatever the same variable without the star would represent.

$$
\begin{array}{rl}
\texttt{e, et, ec, ef} \ldots & \text{expression, form} \\
\texttt{r} \ldots & \text{environment} \\
\texttt{k, kk} \ldots & \text{continuation} \\
\texttt{v} \ldots & \text{value (integer, pair, closure, etc.)} \\
\texttt{f} \ldots & \text{function} \\
\texttt{n} \ldots & \text{identifier}
\end{array}
$$

Now here's the interpreter. It assumes that anything that is atomic and unknown to it as a variable must be an implicit quotation.

```
(define (evaluate e r k)
  (if (atom? e)
      (cond ((symbol? e) (evaluate-variable e r k))
            (else        (evaluate-quote e r k)) )
      (case (car e)
        ((quote)  (evaluate-quote (cadr e) r k))
        ((if)     (evaluate-if (cadr e) (caddr e) (cadddr e) r k))
        ((begin)  (evaluate-begin (cdr e) r k))
        ((set!)   (evaluate-set! (cadr e) (caddr e) r k))
        ((lambda) (evaluate-lambda (cadr e) (cddr e) r k))
        (else     (evaluate-application (car e) (cdr e) r k)) ) ) )
```

That interpreter is actually built from three functions: **evaluate**, **invoke**, and **resume**. Only those last two are generic and know how to invoke applicable objects or handle continuations, whatever their nature. The entire interpreter will be little more than a series of hand-offs among these three functions. Nevertheless, two other generic functions will prove useful to determine or to modify the value of a variable; they are **lookup** and **update!**.

```
(define-generic (invoke (f) v* r k)
  (wrong "not a function" f r k) )
(define-generic (resume (k continuation) v)
  (wrong "Unknown continuation" k) )
(define-generic (lookup (r environment) n k)
  (wrong "not an environment" r n k) )
(define-generic (update! (r environment) n k v)
  (wrong "not an environment" r n k) )
```

All the entities that we'll manipulate will derive from three virtual classes:

```
(define-class value Object ())
(define-class environment Object ())
(define-class continuation Object (k))
```

The classes of values manipulated by the language that we are defining will inherit from **value**; the environments inherit from **environment**; and of course, the continuations inherit from **continuation**.

3.2.3   Quoting

The special form for quoting is still the simplest and consists of rendering the quoted term to the current continuation, like this:

```
(define (evaluate-quote v r k)
  (resume k v) )
```

3.2.4   Alternatives

An alternative brings two continuations into play: the current one and the one that consists of waiting for the value of the condition in order to determine which branch of the alternative to choose. To represent that continuation, we will define an appropriate class. When the condition of an alternative is evaluated, the alternative will choose between the true and false branch; consequently, those two branches must be stored along with the environment needed for their evaluation. The result of one or the other of those branches must be returned to the original continuation of the alternative, which must then be stored as well. Thus we get this:

```
(define-class if-cont continuation (et ef r))
(define (evaluate-if ec et ef r k)
  (evaluate ec r (make-if-cont k
                               et
                               ef
                               r )) )
(define-method (resume (k if-cont) v)
  (evaluate (if v (if-cont-et k) (if-cont-ef k))
            (if-cont-r k)
            (if-cont-k k) ) )
```

Then the alternative decides to evaluate its condition **ec** in the current environment **r**, but with a new continuation, made from all the ingredients needed for the computation. Once the computation of the condition has been completed by a call to **resume**, the computation of the alternative will get underway again and ask for the value of the condition **v** to determine which branch to choose, but in any case, it will evaluate it in the environment that was saved and with the initial continuation of the alternative.[11]

3.2.5   Sequence

A sequence also calls two continuations into play, like this:

```
(define-class begin-cont continuation (e* r))
(define (evaluate-begin e* r k)
```

---

11. Those who are implementation buffs should note that **make-if-cont** can be seen as a form pushing **et** and then **ef** and finally r onto the execution stack, the lower part of which is represented by k. Reciprocally, (**if-cont-et** k) and the others pop those same values.

```
      (if (pair? e*)
        (if (pair? (cdr e*))
          (evaluate (car e*) r (make-begin-cont k e* r))
          (evaluate (car e*) r k) )
        (resume k empty-begin-value) ) )
    (define-method (resume (k begin-cont) v)
      (evaluate-begin (cdr (begin-cont-e* k))
                      (begin-cont-r k)
                      (begin-cont-k k) ) )
```

The cases of (**begin**) and (**begin** π) are simple. When the form **begin** involves several terms, the first one must be evaluated by providing it a new continuation, (**make-begin-cont k e* r**). When that new continuation receives a value by **resume**, it will trigger the method for **begin-cont**. That continuation will discard the value returned, **v**, and will restart the computation of the other forms present in **begin**.[12]

3.2.6 Variable Environment

The values of variables are recorded in an environment. That, too, will be represented as an object, like this:

```
(define-class null-env environment ())
(define-class full-env environment (others name))
(define-class variable-env full-env (value))
```

Two kinds of environments are needed: an empty environment to initialize computations, and instances of **variable-env** corresponding to non-empty environments. Those non-empty environments store a binding, that is, a name and a value; the rest of the environment is linked via the field **others**. Even though this way of organizing things uses objects, it is functionally similar to the A-list except that it consumes only an object of three fields rather than two dotted pairs.

Thus to search for the value of a variable, we do this:

```
(define (evaluate-variable n r k)
  (lookup r n k) )
(define-method (lookup (r null-env) n k)
  (wrong "Unknown variable" n r k) )
(define-method (lookup (r full-env) n k)
  (lookup (full-env-others r) n k) )
(define-method (lookup (r variable-env) n k)
  (if (eqv? n (variable-env-name r))
    (resume k (variable-env-value r))
    (lookup (variable-env-others r) n k) ) )
```

The generic function **lookup** scrutinizes the environment until it finds the right binding. The value determined that way is sent to the continuation by means of the generic function **resume**.

---

12. As an attentive reader, you will have noticed the form (cdr (begin-cont-e* k)) presented in the method resume. Equivalently, we could have directly built it in evaluate-begin, like this: (make-begin-cont k (cdr e*) r). The reason is that in case of error, analyzing the continuation will make it possible to know which expression was underway.

Modifying a variable entails the same process:

```
(define-class set!-cont continuation (n r))
(define (evaluate-set! n e r k)
  (evaluate e r (make-set!-cont k n r)) )
(define-method (resume (k set!-cont) v)
  (update! (set!-cont-r k) (set!-cont-n k) (set!-cont-k k) v) )
(define-method (update! (r null-env) n k v)
  (wrong "Unknown variable" n r k) )
(define-method (update! (r full-env) n k v)
  (update! (full-env-others r) n k v) )
(define-method (update! (r variable-env) n k v)
  (if (eqv? n (variable-env-name r))
      (begin (set-variable-env-value! r v)
             (resume k v) )
      (update! (variable-env-others r) n k v) ) )
```

It's necessary to introduce a particular continuation because the evaluation of an assignment is carried out in two phases: computing the value to assign and then modifying the variable involved. The class **set-cont!** implements this new kind of continuation; the adapted method **resume** merely calls the environment in order to update it.

3.2.7 Functions

Creating a function is a simple process, left to **make-function**.

```
(define-class function value (variables body env))
(define (evaluate-lambda n* e* r k)
  (resume k (make-function n* e* r)) )
```

What's a little more complicated is how to invoke functions. Notice the implicit **progn** or **begin** in the function bodies.

```
(define-method (invoke (f function) v* r k)
  (let ((env (extend-env (function-env f)
                         (function-variables f)
                         v* )))
    (evaluate-begin (function-body f) env k) ) )
```

It might seem unusual to you that the functions take the current environment r as an argument, even though they don't apparently use it. We've left it there for two reasons. One, there is often a register dedicated to the environment in implementations, and like any register, it's available. Two, certain functions (we'll see more of them later when we discuss reflexivity) can influence the current lexical environment, such as, for example, debugging functions.

The following function extends an environment. There is no need to test whether there are enough values or names because the functions have already verified that.

```
(define (extend-env env names values)
  (cond ((and (pair? names) (pair? values))
         (make-variable-env
```

```
                (extend-env env (cdr names) (cdr values))
                (car names)
                (car values) ) )
          ((and (null? names) (null? values)) env)
          ((symbol? names) (make-variable-env env names values))
          (else (wrong "Arity mismatch")) ) )
```

All that remains is to indicate how to define a functional application. In doing
so, we should keep in mind that functions are invoked on arguments organized into
a list.

```
(define-class evfun-cont continuation (e* r))
(define-class apply-cont continuation (f r))
(define-class argument-cont continuation (e* r))
(define-class gather-cont continuation (v))
(define (evaluate-application e e* r k)
  (evaluate e r (make-evfun-cont k e* r)) )
(define-method (resume (k evfun-cont) f)
  (evaluate-arguments (evfun-cont-e* k)
                      (evfun-cont-r k)
                      (make-apply-cont (evfun-cont-k k)
                                       f
                                       (evfun-cont-r k) ) ) )
(define (evaluate-arguments e* r k)
  (if (pair? e*)
      (evaluate (car e*) r (make-argument-cont k e* r))
      (resume k no-more-arguments) ) )
(define no-more-arguments '())
(define-method (resume (k argument-cont) v)
  (evaluate-arguments (cdr (argument-cont-e* k))
                      (argument-cont-r k)
                      (make-gather-cont (argument-cont-k k) v)) )
(define-method (resume (k gather-cont) v*)
  (resume (gather-cont-k k) (cons (gather-cont-v k) v*)) )
(define-method (resume (k apply-cont) v)
  (invoke (apply-cont-f k)
          v
          (apply-cont-r k)
          (apply-cont-k k) ) )
```

The technique is a little disconcerting at first glance. Evaluation takes place
from left to right; the function term is thus evaluated first with a continuation of
the class **evfun-cont**. When that continuation takes control, it proceeds to the
evaluation of the arguments, leaving a continuation which will apply the function to
them, once they have all been computed. During the evaluation of the arguments,
continuations of the class **gather-cont** are left; their role is to gather the arguments
into a list.

Let's take an example to see the various continuations that appear during the
computation of (**cons foo bar**). We'll assume that **foo** has the value 33 and **bar**,
−77. To illustrate this computation, we'll draw the continuations as horizontal

stacks; k will be the continuation; r will be the current environment. We'll use *cons* to denote the global value of **cons**, that is, the allocation function for dotted pairs.

```
evaluate (cons foo bar) r                                                      k
evaluate cons r                                    evfun-cont (foo bar) r  k
resume cons                                        evfun-cont (foo bar) r  k
evaluate-arguments (foo bar) r                              apply-cont cons k
evaluate foo r                    argument-cont (foo bar) r apply-cont cons k
resume 33                         argument-cont (foo bar) r apply-cont cons k
evaluate-arguments (bar) r              gather-cont 33 apply-cont cons k
evaluate bar r          argument-cont () r gather-cont 33 apply-cont cons k
resume -77              argument-cont () r gather-cont 33 apply-cont cons k
evaluate-arguments () r  gather-cont -77 gather-cont 33 apply-cont cons k
resume ()                gather-cont -77 gather-cont 33 apply-cont cons k
resume (-77)                             gather-cont 33 apply-cont cons k
resume (33 -77)                                        apply-cont cons k
invoke cons (33 -77)                                                    k
```

3.3   Initializing the Interpreter

Before we plunge into the arcane mysteries of control forms, let's sketch a few details about how to authorize execution of this interpreter. This section greatly resembles Section 1.7. [see p. 25] We first have to deck out the interpreter with a few well chosen variables, and to do so, we'll define some macros to enrich the global environment.

```
(define-syntax definitial
  (syntax-rules ()
    ((definitial name)
     (definitial name 'void) )
    ((definitial name value)
     (begin (set! r.init (make-variable-env r.init 'name value))
            'name ) ) ) )
(define-class primitive value (name address))
(define-syntax defprimitive
  (syntax-rules ()
    ((defprimitive name value arity)
     (definitial name
       (make-primitive
        'name (lambda (v* r k)
                (if (= arity (length v*))
                    (resume k (apply value v*))
                    (wrong "Incorrect arity" 'name v*) ) ) ) ) ) ) )
(define r.init (make-null-env))
(defprimitive cons cons 2)
(defprimitive car car 1)
```

The primitives created have to be able to be invoked, like any other user-function, by **invoke**. These primitives each have two fields. The first makes debugging easier because it indicates the original name of the primitive. Of course, that's only a hint because you can bind the primitive to other global names if you want.[13] The second field in any of those primitives contains the "address" of the primitive, that is, something executable by the underlying machine. A primitive is thus triggered like this:

```
(define-method (invoke (f primitive) v* r k)
  ((primitive-address f) v* r k) )
```

Then to start the interpreter, and begin to enjoy its facilities, we will define an initial continuation in a way similar to **null-env**. That initial continuation will print the results that we provide it.

```
(define-class bottom-cont continuation (f))
(define-method (resume (k bottom-cont) v)
  ((bottom-cont-f k) v) )
(define (chapter3-interpreter)
  (define (toplevel)
    (evaluate (read)
              r.init
              (make-bottom-cont 'void display) )
    (toplevel) )
  (toplevel) )
```

Notice that the entire interpreter could easily be written in a real object-language, like Smalltalk [GR83], so we could take advantage of its famous browser and debugger. The only thing left to do is to add whatever is needed to open a lot of little windows everywhere.

3.4 Implementing Control Forms

Let's begin with the most powerful control form, **call/cc**. Paradoxically, it is the simplest to implement if we measure simplicity by the number of lines. The style of programming we've been following—by objects—and the fact that we've made continuations explicit will almost make this implementation a trivial task.

3.4.1 Implementation of `call/cc`

The function **call/cc** takes the current continuation **k**, transforms it into an object that we can submit to **invoke**, and then applies the first argument, a unary function, to it. The lines that follow here express that idea equally strongly.

```
(definitial call/cc
  (make-primitive
   'call/cc
   (lambda (v* r k)
     (if (= 1 (length v*))
         (invoke (car v*) (list k) r k)
```

---

13. This same hint makes it possible in many systems to get the following effect: (begin (set! foo car)(set! car 3) foo) has a result that is printed as #<car> where the name of the primitive follows the functional object and not the binding through which it was found.

```
(wrong "Incorrect arity" 'call/cc v*) ) ) ) )
```

Even though there are few lines there, we should explain them a little. Although it is a function, `call/cc` is defined by `definitial` because it needs access to its continuation so badly. The variable `call/cc` (now here we are in a Lisp₁) is thus bound to an object of the class **primitive**. The call protocol for these objects associates them with an "address" represented in the defining Lisp by a function with the signature (`lambda (v* r k) ...`). Eventually, the first argument is applied to the continuation. That continuation has been delivered just as it is. Since the continuation might possibly be submitted to **invoke**, we remind ourselves that way to confer the *ad hoc* method on **invoke**.

```
(define-method (invoke (f continuation) v* r k)
  (if (= 1 (length v*))
      (resume f (car v*))
      (wrong "Continuations expect one argument" v* r k) ) )
```

3.4.2 Implementation of `catch`

The form `catch` is interesting to implement because the mechanisms that it brings into play are quite different from those in `block`, which we will get to later. As usual, we'll add the necessary clauses to **evaluate** to analyze the forms `catch` and `throw`, like this:

```
    ...
    ((catch) (evaluate-catch (cadr e) (cddr e) r k))
    ((throw) (evaluate-throw (cadr e) (caddr e) r k)) ...
```

Here we've taken the option of making `throw` a special form, not a function taking a thunk. We did so to simulate COMMON LISP. As a special form, `catch` is defined like this:

```
(define-class catch-cont continuation (body r))
(define-class labeled-cont continuation (tag))
(define (evaluate-catch tag body r k)
  (evaluate tag r (make-catch-cont k body r)) )
(define-method (resume (k catch-cont) v)
  (evaluate-begin (catch-cont-body k)
                  (catch-cont-r k)
                  (make-labeled-cont (catch-cont-k k) v) ) )
```

Now it is apparent that `catch` evaluates its first argument, binds that argument to its continuation by creating a tagged block, and then goes on with its work of sequentially evaluating its body. When a value is returned to the tagged block, that block is removed and simply transmits the value. The form `throw` will make better use of that tagged block.

```
(define-class throw-cont continuation (form r))
(define-class throwing-cont continuation (tag cont))
(define (evaluate-throw tag form r k)
  (evaluate tag r (make-throw-cont k form r)) )
(define-method (resume (k throw-cont) tag)
  (catch-lookup k tag k) )
```

```
(define-method (resume (k throw-cont) tag)
  (catch-lookup k tag k) )
(define-generic (catch-lookup (k) tag kk)
  (wrong "Not a continuation" k tag kk) )
(define-method (catch-lookup (k continuation) tag kk)
  (catch-lookup (continuation-k k) tag kk) )
(define-method (catch-lookup (k bottom-cont) tag kk)
  (wrong "No associated catch" k tag kk) )
(define-method (catch-lookup (k labeled-cont) tag kk)
  (if (eqv? tag (labeled-cont-tag k)) ;comparator
      (evaluate (throw-cont-form kk)
                (throw-cont-r kk)
                (make-throwing-cont kk tag k) )
      (catch-lookup (labeled-cont-k k) tag kk) ) )
(define-method (resume (k throwing-cont) v)
  (resume (throwing-cont-cont k) v) )
```

The form **throw** first evaluates its first argument and then checks whether a continuation tagged that way exists. If not, it raises an error; otherwise, the value to transmit is then computed, and it will be transmitted to the continuation that's already been located. That continuation can not have changed. The evaluation of the value to transmit has a continuation that's a little special: an instance of **throwing-cont**. The reason: if by accident an error or control effect occurs in the computation of this value, the right context will be the current context, not the one that would have been adopted if everything had gone well. Thus we can write this:

```
(catch 2
  (* 7 (catch 1
         (* 3 (catch 2
                (throw 1 (throw 2 5)) )) )) )
```

The result is (* 7 3 5) and not 5. This definition of **throw** makes it possible to detect errors that could not have been caught if **throw** were a function.

```
(catch 2 (* 7 (throw 1 (throw 2 3))))
```

That form, for example, does not lead to 3 but to the error message, **"No associated catch"** since there is no **catch** form with tag 1.

3.4.3 Implementation of block

There are two problems to resolve in implementing lexical escapes. The first is to confer a dynamic extent on continuations. The second problem is to give lexical scope to the tags on lexical escapes. To do that, we'll use the lexical environment to confer the right scope. We'll define a new kind of environment to associate tags with continuations.

We'll add a clause to **evaluate**—a clause recognizing special **block** forms—and we'll define everything that follows.

```
(define-class block-cont continuation (label))
(define-class block-env full-env (cont))
```

```
(define (evaluate-block label body r k)
  (let ((k (make-block-cont k label)))
    (evaluate-begin body
                    (make-block-env r label k)
                    k ) ) )
(define-method (resume (k block-cont) v)
  (resume (block-cont-k k) v) )
```

Now everything is in place for `return-from`, so we will add a clause to analyze
`return-from` forms inside `evaluate`.

```
...
((block)       (evaluate-block (cadr e) (cddr e) r k))
((return-from) (evaluate-return-from (cadr e) (caddr e) r k)) ...
```

And we will also define this:

```
(define-class return-from-cont continuation (r label))
(define (evaluate-return-from label form r k)
  (evaluate form r (make-return-from-cont k r label)) )
(define-method (resume (k return-from-cont) v)
  (block-lookup (return-from-cont-r k)
                (return-from-cont-label k)
                (return-from-cont-k k)
                v ) )
(define-generic (block-lookup (r) n k v)
  (wrong "not an environment" r n k v) )
(define-method (block-lookup (r block-env) n k v)
  (if (eq? n (block-env-name r))
      (unwind k v (block-env-cont r))
      (block-lookup (block-env-others r) n k v) ) )
(define-method (block-lookup (r full-env) n k v)
  (block-lookup (variable-env-others r) n k v) )
(define-method (block-lookup (r null-env) n k v)
  (wrong "Unknown block label" n r k v) )
(define-method (resume (k return-from-cont) v)
  (block-lookup (return-from-cont-r k)
                (return-from-cont-label k)
                (return-from-cont-k k)
                v ) )
(define-generic (unwind (k) v ktarget))
(define-method (unwind (k continuation) v ktarget)
  (if (eq? k ktarget) (resume k v)
      (unwind (continuation-k k) v ktarget) ) )
(define-method (unwind (k bottom-cont) v ktarget)
  (wrong "Obsolete continuation" v) )
```

Once we've got the value to transmit, `block-lookup` searches for the continuation associated with the tag of the `return-from` in the lexical environment. If
`block-lookup` finds it, then we verify whether the associated continuation is still
valid by looking for it in the current continuation by means of the new function,
`unwind`.

The search for an ad hoc block in the lexical environment is carried out by the generic function, **block-lookup**. We've defined the necessary methods for it so that it can skip environments for variables that don't really interest it in order to look only at instances of **block-cont**. Reciprocally, we've extended the generic function, **lookup** so that it ignores instances of **block-cont**. These methods have been defined for the virtual class **full-env** so that they can be shared in case other classes of environments are created.

The generic function **unwind** tries to transmit a value to a certain continuation which must still be alive, that is, it can be found in the the current continuation.

3.4.4 Implementation of unwind-protect

The form **unwind-protect** is the most complicated to handle; it implies modifications in the preceding definitions of the forms **catch** and **block** because they must be adapted to the presence of **unwind-protect**. It's a good example of a feature whose introduction alters the definition of everything that exists up to this point. However, not making use of **unwind-protect** implies a certain cost, too. The lines that follow here define **unwind-protect**, apparently only slightly different from **prog1**.

```
(define-class unwind-protect-cont continuation (cleanup r))
(define-class protect-return-cont continuation (value))
(define (evaluate-unwind-protect form cleanup r k)
   (evaluate form
             r
             (make-unwind-protect-cont k cleanup r) ) )
(define-method (resume (k unwind-protect-cont) v)
   (evaluate-begin (unwind-protect-cont-cleanup k)
             (unwind-protect-cont-r k)
             (make-protect-return-cont
             (unwind-protect-cont-k k) v ) ) )
(define-method (resume (k protect-return-cont) v)
   (resume (protect-return-cont-k k) (protect-return-cont-value k)) )
```

Now, as we said, we have to modify **catch** and **block** to take into acount programmed cleanups when an **unwind-protect** form is breached by an escape. For **catch**, we'll modify the definition of **throwing-cont**, like this:

```
(define-method (resume (k throwing-cont) v)          ; ** Modified **
   (unwind (throwing-cont-k k) v (throwing-cont-cont k)) )
(define-class unwind-cont continuation (value target))
(define-method (unwind (k unwind-protect-cont) v target)
   (evaluate-begin (unwind-protect-cont-cleanup k)
             (unwind-protect-cont-r k)
             (make-unwind-cont
             (unwind-protect-cont-k k) v target ) ) )
(define-method (resume (k unwind-cont) v)
   (unwind (unwind-cont-k k)
             (unwind-cont-value k)
             (unwind-cont-target k) ) )
```

To transmit the escape value, we have to run back through the continuation a second time until we find the `target` continuation. During that rerun, if any `unwind-protects` are breached, the associated cleanup forms will be evaluated. The continuation of these cleanup forms is from the class `unwind-cont` so it is possible to capture any of them. They correspond to pursuing the examination of the continuation—the floating continuations that we mentioned earlier on page 86.

With respect to `block`, the modification is the same kind but involves only `block-lookup`.

```
(define-method (block-lookup (r block-env) n k v)  ; ** Modified **
  (if (eq? n (block-env-name r))
      (unwind k v (block-env-cont r))
      (block-lookup (block-env-others r) n k v) ) )
```

We look for the continuation of the associated `block` in the lexical environment, and then we unwind the continuation as far as this target block.

You might think that in the presence of `unwind-protect`, the form `block` is no faster than `catch` since they both share the heavy cost of `unwind`. Actually, since `unwind-protect` is a special form and thus its use can't be hidden, there are savings for all the `return-froms` that are not separated from their associated `block` by any `unwind-protect` or `lambda`.

Curiously enough, COMMON LISP (CLtL2 [Ste90]) introduced a restriction on escapes in cleanup forms. Those cleanup forms can't go *less far* than the escape currently underway. The intention of the restriction was to prevent any program being stuck in a situation where no escape could pull it out. [see **Ex. 3.9**] Consequently, the following program produces an error because the cleanup form wants to do less than the escape targeted toward 1.

```
(catch 1                                      COMMON LISP
  (catch 2
    (unwind-protect (throw 1 'foo)
      (throw 2 'bar) ) ) )          → error!
```

3.5 Comparing `call/cc` to `catch`

Thanks to objects, continuations look like linked lists of blocks. Some of these blocks are accessible from the lexical environment; others can be found only by running through the continuation, block by block. Still others give rise to various treatments when they are breached.

In a language such as Lisp, since it is blessed with continuations that have a dynamic extent, the idea of a stack is synonymous with the idea of continuation. When we write (`evaluate ec r (make-if-cont k et ef r)`) we signify that we are pushing another block onto the stack indicating what to do on the return of the value of the condition of an alternative. Reciprocally, the expression (`evaluate-begin (cdr (begin-cont-e* k)) (begin-cont-r k) (begin-cont-k k)`) says explicitly that the current block has been abandoned, popped in favor of the block just below: (`begin-cont-k k`). We could verify that in such a language, no data structure keeps obsolete parts of continuations, that is, those parts that have disappeared from the stack. For that reason, when we leave a block, the associated continuation (possibly captured elsewhere) is invalidated. In terms of implementation, continuations can be kept in a stack or even in several synchronized stacks and compiled into C primitives: `setjmp/longjmp`. [see p. 402]

In the dialect EuLISP[PE92], there is a special form named `let/cc` with the following syntax:

    `(let/cc` *variable forms*... `)`   EuLISP

In Dylan [App92b], we write the same thing like this:

    `(bind-exit (`*variable*`) ` *forms*... `)`   Dylan

This special form binds the current continuation to the *variable* with a scope equal to the body of the form `let/cc` in EuLISP or `bind-exit` in Dylan. That continuation is consequently a first class entity with a unary functional interface. However, its *useful* extent is dynamic, so its use is limited to the evaluation time of the body of the form binding `let/cc` or `bind-exit`. More precisely, the object value of *variable* has an indefinite extent but a limited interest for the duration of the dynamic extent. This characteristic is typical of EuLISP and Dylan, but it does not show up at all in Scheme (where continuations have an indefinite extent) nor in COMMON LISP (where continuations are not first class objects). However, we can simulate that behavior by writing this:

```
(define-syntax let/cc
  (syntax-rules ()
    ((let/cc variable . body)
     (block variable
       (let ((variable (lambda (x) (return-from variable x))))
         . body ) ) ) ) )
```

In the world of Scheme, continuations can no longer be put on the stack because they can be kept in external data structures. Thus we have to adopt another model: a hierarchic model, sometimes called a *cactus stack*. The most naive approach is to leave the stack and allocate blocks for continuations directly in the heap.

This technique makes allocations uniform, and it makes porting easier, according to [AS94]. However, it decreases the locality of references in memory, and it means that we have to maintain the links between blocks explicitly. ([MB93], nevertheless, proposes solutions to those problems.) Generally, implementers work very hard to keep as many things as possible on the stack, so in this case, the canonical implementation of `call/cc` copies the stack into the heap; the continuation is thus this very copy of the stack. Other techniques have been studied, of course, as in [CHO88, HDB90], for sharing copies, delaying copies, making partial copies, etc. Each one of them, however, introduces certain costs.

The forms `block` and `call/cc` are more similar than are `catch` and `call/cc`. They share the same lexical discipline; they are distinguished only by the extent of their continuation. There's a restricted variation of `call/cc` in certain dialects, as in [IM89]; the restriction is known as `call/ep` for *call with exit procedure*; it is quite apparent in `block/return-from` as well as in the preceding `let/cc`. The function `call/ep` has the same interface as `call/cc`, like this:

    `(call/ep (lambda (exit) ...))`

The variable **exit** in the unary function (the argument of **call/ep**) is bound
to the continuation of the form **call/ep** limited to its dynamic extent. The resemblance to **block** is quite clear here except that instead of using a disjoint name
space (the lexical escape environment), we borrow the name space for variables.
The main difference that **call/ep** brings in is that the continuation of an escape
becomes first class and can thus be handled like any other first class object. However, if we have to use **block**, then we must explicitly construct that first-class value
if we need it. To do so, we write (**lambda** (**x**) (**return-from** *label* **x**)). The expression is equally powerful, but all the calling sites (that is, the **return-from**
forms) are known statically in a **block** form. That's not always the case during a
call to **call/ep**: for example, (**call/ep foo**) doesn't say anything about the use
of an escape except after more refined analysis, an analysis not local to **foo**. Consequently, the function **call/ep** complicates the work of the compiler as compared
to what a special form like **block** requires.

When we compare **block** and **call/ep**, we thus see some differences. For one,
an efficient execution must not create the argument closure of **call/ep** if it is
an explicit **lambda** form. Thus at compilation, we must distinguish the case of
(**call/ep** (**lambda** ...)) since it can be compiled better. This particular case
is comparable to the way a special form is handled since both of them lead to
treatment that is distinct within the compiler. Functions are the favorite vehicles
for adepts of Scheme whereas special forms correspond more nearly to a kind of
declaration that makes life easier for the compiler. Both are often equally powerful,
though their complexity is different for both the user and the implementer.

In summary, if you're looking for power at low volume, then **call/cc** is for you
since in practice it lets you code every known control structure, namely, escape,
coroutine, partial continuation, and so forth. If you need only "normal" things
(and Lisp has already demonstrated that you can write many interesting applications without **call/cc**), then choose instead the forms of COMMON LISP where
compilation is simple and the generated code is efficient.

3.6   Programming by Continuations

There's a style of programming based on continuations. It entails explicitly telling a
computation where to send the result of that computation. Once the computation
has been achieved, the executor applies the receiver to the result, rather than
returning it as a normal value. What that boils down to is this: if we have the
computation (**foo** (**bar**)), we modify the function **bar** into **new-bar** in order to
take an argument; that argument will be exactly what we will call the continuation.
In the present case, that's **foo**. The modified computation will thus appear as
(**new-bar foo**). Let's look at an example with our familiar friend, the factorial;
let's assume that we want to compute $n(n!)$:

```
(define (fact n k)
  (if (= n 0) (k 1)
      (fact (- n 1) (lambda (r) (k (* n r)))) ) )
(fact n (lambda (r) (* n r)))   →  n(n!)
```

The factorial thus takes a new argument **k**, the receiver of the final result. When the result is 1, it is simple to apply **k** to it. However, when the result is not immediate, we recall recursively as expected. Now the problem is to do two things at once: to transmit the receiver and to multiply the factorial of n-1 by n. And furthermore, since we want multiplication to remain a commutative operation, we have to do these things in order! First, we'll multiply by n and then call the receiver. Since that receiver will be applied to 1 in the end, there's nothing left to do but compose the receiver and the supplementary handling and thus get (**lambda (r) (k (* n r))**).

The advantage this new factorial offers us is that the same definition makes it possible to calculate many results, namely, the factorial (**fact** *n* (**lambda (x) x**)), the double factorial (**fact** *n* (**lambda (x) (* 2 x)**)), etc.

3.6.1 Multiple Values

Using continuations is also the key to multiple values. When a computation has to return multiple results, continuations become an interesting technique for doing so. In COMMON LISP, division (i.e., **truncate**) returns a multiple value composed of the divisor and the remainder. We could get a similar operator—one that we'll call **divide**—to take two numbers and a continuation, compute the quotient and the Euclidean remainder of those two numbers, and apply the continuation of the third argument to them. Then, to verify whether a division is correct, we could just do this:

```
(let* ((p (read)) (q (read)))
  (divide p q (lambda (quotient remainder)
    (= p (+ (* quotient q) remainder)) )) )
```

An example with more depth involves calculating Bezout numbers.[14] The Bezout identity stipulates that if p and q are relatively prime, then there must exist numbers u and v such that $up + vq = 1$. To compute Bezout numbers, we first have to compute the gcd (greatest common divisor) verifying as we do so that p and q are relatively prime.

```
(define (bezout n p k)        ;assume n > p
  (divide
    n p (lambda (q r)
      (if (= r 0)
          (if (= p 1)
              (k 0 1)    ;since 0 × 1 − 1 × 0 = 1
              (error "not relatively prime" n p) )
          (bezout
            p r (lambda (u v)
              (k v (- u (* v q))) ) ) ) ) ) )
```

The **bezout** function uses **divide** to fill in q and r as the quotient and remainder of the division of n by p. If the numbers are really relatively prime, there's a trivial solution of 0 and 1. Otherwise, we keep increasing those values until we hit the initial n and p. We could verify the underlying mathematics; to do so, it suffices to know enough number theory to understand gcd or (proof by fire!) to verify that

---

14. Oof! I finally eventually succeed in publishing that function, first written in 1981!

(bezout 1991 1960 list) → (-569 578)

3.6.2   Tail Recursion

In the example of the factorial with continuations, a call to `fact` generally turned
out to be nothing other than a call to `fact`. If we trace the computation of (`fact`
`3` `list`), but skip the obvious steps, we get this:

```
(fact 3 list)
≡ (fact 2 (lambda (r) (k (* n r))))|
                                    | n→ 3
                                    | k≡ list
≡ (fact 1 (lambda (r) (k (* n r))))|
                                    | n→ 2
                                    | k→ (lambda (r) (k (* n r)))|
                                    |                            | n→ 3
                                    |                            | k≡ list
≡ (k (* n 1))|
             | n→ 2
             | k→ (lambda (r) (k (* n r)))|
             |                            | n→ 3
             |                            | k≡ list
≡ (k (* n 2))|
             | n→ 3
             | k≡ list
→ (6)
```

When the call to `fact` is translated directly into a call to `fact`, the new call is
carried out with the same continuation as the old call. This property is known as
tail recursion—recursion because it is recursive and tail because it's the last thing
remaining to do. Tail recursion is a special case of a tail call. A tail call occurs
when a computation is resolved by another one without the necessity of going back
to the computation that's been abandoned. A call in *tail position* is carried out by
a *constant continuation*.

In the example of the `bezout` function, `bezout` calls the function `divide` in tail
position. The function `divide` itself calls its continuation in tail position. That
continuation recursively calls `bezout` in tail position again.

In the "classic" factorial, the recursive call to `fact` within (`* n (fact (- n`
`1)))` is said to be *wrapped* since the value of (`fact (- n 1)`) is taken again in the
current environment to be multiplied by n.

A tail call makes it possible to abandon the current environment completely
when that environment is no longer necessary. That environment thus no longer
deserves to be saved, and as a consequence, it won't be restored, and thus we gain
considerable savings. These techniques have been studied in great detail by the
French Lisp community, as in [Gre77, Cha80, SJ87], who have thus produced some
of the fastest interpreters in the world; see also [Han90].

Tail recursion is a very desirable quality; the interpreter itself can make use of
it quite happily. Optimizations linked to tail recursion are based on a simple point:
on the definition of a sequence, of course. Up to now, we have written this:

```
(define (evaluate-begin e* r k)
  (if (pair? e*)
    (if (pair? (cdr e*))
      (evaluate (car e*) r (make-begin-cont k e* r))
      (evaluate (car e*) r k) )
    (resume k empty-begin-value) ) )
(define-method (resume (k begin-cont) v)
  (evaluate-begin (cdr (begin-cont-e* k))
                  (begin-cont-r k)
                  (begin-cont-k k) ) )
```

We could have also written it more simply like this:

```
(define (evaluate-begin e* r k)
  (if (pair? e*)
    (evaluate (car e*) r (make-begin-cont k e* r))
    (resume k empty-begin-value) ) )
(define-method (resume (k begin-cont) v)
  (let ((e* (cdr (begin-cont-e* k))))
    (if (pair? e*)
      (evaluate-begin e* (begin-cont-r k) (begin-cont-k k))
      (resume (begin-cont-k k) v) ) ) )
```

That first way of writing it is preferable because when we evaluate the last term of a sequence, with the first way, we don't have to build the continuation (`make-begin-cont k e* r`) to find out finally that it's equivalent to `k`, and building that continuation, of course, is costly in time and memory. In keeping with our usual operating principle of good economy in not keeping around useless objects unduly (notably the environment `r` in (`make-begin-cont k e* r`)), it's better to get rid of that superfluous continuation as soon as possible. This case is very important because every sequence has a last term!

The same effect can be applied to the evaluation of arguments, so we will write the following for all the same reasons we gave before about sequences:

```
(define-class no-more-argument-cont continuation ())
(define (evaluate-arguments e* r k)
  (if (pair? e*)
    (if (pair? (cdr e*))
      (evaluate (car e*) r (make-argument-cont k e* r))
      (evaluate (car e*) r (make-no-more-argument-cont k))) )
    (resume k no-more-arguments) ) )
(define-method (resume (k no-more-argument-cont) v)
  (resume (no-more-argument-cont-k k) (list v)) )
```

Here, we've written a new kind of continuation that lets us make a list out of the value of the last term of a list of arguments without having to keep the environment `r`. Friedman and Wise in [Wan80b] are credited with discovering this effect.

3.7   Partial Continuations

Among the questions that continuations raise, there's one about the following continuation: during an escape, what becomes of the part that disappears? In other
words, the portion of the continuation (or "execution stack") which is located between the place from which we escape and the place where we jump represents
a continuation slice. This slice takes an input value, and since it has an end, it
also provides a result on exit. Thus it is equivalent to a unary function. Many
researchers, such as [FFDM87, FF87, Fel88, DF90, HD90, QS91, MQ94], have
elaborated control forms to reify these slices, or *partial continuations*, as they are
known.

Consider for a moment the following simplified actions:

```
(+ 1 (call/cc (lambda (k) (set! foo k) 2)))    → 3
(foo 3)                                         → 4
```

In conformity with what we've already said, the continuation k, assigned to
foo, is $\lambda u.1 + u$. But then what is the value of (foo (foo 4))?

```
(foo (foo 4))                                   → 5
```

The result is 5, not 6 as composing the continuations might lead you to think.
In effect, calling a continuation corresponds to abandoning a computation that is
underway and thus at most only one call can be carried out. Thus the call inside
foo forces the computation of the continuation $\lambda u.1+u$ for 4; its mission is to return
the value that's gotten as the final value of the entire computation. Consequently,
we never get back from a continuation! More specifically, the continuation k has to
wait for a value, add 1 to it, and return the result as the *final and definitive* result.

The same example is even more vivid with contexts. The continuation of the
example was (+ 1 []). Since we are in a call by value, (foo (foo 4)) corresponds
to eliminating the context (foo []) around (foo 4) so that we rewrite it as (+ 1
4), and its final value is 5.

Partial continuations represent the followup of computations that remain to be
carried out up to a certain well identified point. In [FWFD88, DF90, HD90, QS91],
there are proposals about how to make continuations partial and thus composable.
Let's assume that the continuation bound to foo is now [(+ 1 [])], where the
external square brackets indicate that it must return a value. Then (foo (foo 4))
is really (foo [(+ 1 [4])]) since (+ 1 5) eventually results in 6. The captured
continuation [(+ 1 [])] does not define all the rest of the computation but only
what remains up to but not including the return to the toplevel loop. Thus the
continuation has an end, and it's thus a function and composable.

Another way of looking at this effect is to take the example again that we saw
earlier—the one that has the side effect on the global variable foo—as well as an
interaction with the toplevel loop. Let's condense the two expressions into one and
write this:

```
(begin (+ 1 (call/cc (lambda (k) (set! foo k) 2)))
       (foo 3) )
```

Kaboom! That loops indefinitely because foo is now bound to the context (begin
(+ 1 []) (foo 3)) which calls itself recursively. From this experiment, we can
conclude that gathering together the forms that we've just created is not a neutral

activity with respect to continuations nor with respect to the toplevel loop. If we really want to simulate the effect of the toplevel loop better, then we could write this:

```
(let (foo sequel print?)
  (define-syntax toplevel
    (syntax-rules ()
      ((toplevel e) (toplevel-eval (lambda () e))) ) )
  (define (toplevel-eval thunk)
    (call/cc (lambda (k)
               (set! print? #t)
               (set! sequel k)
               (let ((v (thunk)))
                 (when print? (display v)(set! print? #f))
                 (sequel v) ) )) )
  (toplevel (+ 1 (call/cc (lambda (k) (set! foo k) 2))))
  (toplevel (foo 3))
  (toplevel (foo (foo 4))) )
```

Every time that `toplevel` gets a form to evaluate, we store a continuation in the variable `sequel`—the continuation leading to the next form to evaluate. Every continuation gotten during evaluation is thus by this fact limited to the current form. As you've observed, when `call/cc` is used outside its dynamic extent, there must be either one of two things: either a side effect, or an analysis of the received value to avoid looping.

Partial continuations specify up to what point to take a continuation. That specification insures that we don't go too far and that we get interesting effects. We can thus rewrite the preceding example to redefine `call/cc` so that it captures continuations only up to `toplevel` and no further. The idea of escape is also necessary here to eliminate a slice of the continuation. Even so, for us, partial continuations are still not really attractive because we're not aware of any programs using them in a truly profitable way and yet being any simpler than if rewritten more directly. In contrast, what's essential is that all the operators suggested for partial continuations can be simulated in Scheme with `call/cc` and assignments.

3.8 Conclusions

Continuations are omnipresent. If you understand them, then you've simultaneously gained a new programming style, mastered the intricacies of control forms, and learned how to estimate the cost of using them. Continuations are closely bound to execution control because at any given moment, they dynamically represent the work that remains to do. For that reason, they are highly useful for handling exceptions.

The interpreter presented in this chapter is quite precise yet still locally readable. In the usual style of object programming, there are a great many small pieces of code that make understanding of the big picture more subtle and more challenging. This interpreter is quite modular and easily supports experiments with new linguistic features. It's not particularly fast because it uses up a great many objects, usually only to abandon them right away. Of course, one of the roles of a compiler is to determine just which entities would be useful to build anyway.

3.9   Exercises

Exercise 3.1 : What is the value of (call/cc call/cc)? Does the evaluation order influence your answer?

Exercise 3.2 : What's the value of ((call/cc call/cc) (call/cc call/cc))?

Exercise 3.3 : Write the pair **tagbody/go** with **block**, **catch**, **labels**. Remember the syntax of **tagbody**, as defined in COMMON LISP:

```
(tagbody
        expressions₀...
   label₁ expressions₁...
        ...
   labelᵢ expressionsᵢ...
        ... )
```

All the expressions $expressions_i$ but only the expressions $expressions_i$ may contain unconditional branching forms (**go** *label*) or escapes (**return** *value*). If no **return** is encountered, then the final value of **tagbody** is **nil**.

Exercise 3.4 : You might have noticed that, during the invocation of functions, they verify their actual arity, that is, the number of arguments submitted to them. Modify the way functions are created to precompute their arity so that we can speed up this verification process. You only have to handle functions with fixed arity for this exercise.

Exercise 3.5 : Define the function **apply** so that it is appropriate for the interpreter in this chapter.

Exercise 3.6 : Extend the functions recognized by the interpreter in this chapter so that the interpreter accepts functions with variable arity.

Exercise 3.7 : Modify the way the interpreter is started so that it calls the function **evaluate** only once.

Exercise 3.8 : The way continuations are presented in Section 3.4.1 means that the code mixes continuations and values. Since instances of the class **continuation** may appear as values, we were obliged there to define a method of **invoke** for **continuation**. Redefine call/cc to create a new subclass of **value** corresponding to reified continuations.

Exercise 3.9 : In COMMON LISP, write a function `eternal-return` to take a thunk as its argument, to call it without stopping, and to make sure that no escape attempted by the thunk will succeed in getting out of the function `eternal-return`.

Exercise 3.10 : Consider the following function, due to Alan Bawden:

```
(define (make-box value)
  (let ((box
          (call/cc
            (lambda (exit)
              (letrec
                ((behavior
                   (call/cc
                     (lambda (store)
                       (exit (lambda (msg . new)
                               (call/cc
                                 (lambda (caller)
                                   (case msg
                                     ((get) (store (cons (car behavior)
                                                         caller )))
                                     ((set)
                                      (store
                                        (cons (car new)
                                              caller ) ) ) ) ) ) ) )) ) ) ))
                ((cdr behavior) (car behavior)) ) ) ) ) )
         (box 'set value)
         box ) )
```

If we assume that `box1` has, as its value, the result of `(make-box 33)`, then what is the value of the following expressions?

```
(box1 'get)
(begin (box1 'set 44) (box1 'get))
```

Exercise 3.11 : The function `evaluate` is the only one that is not generic. If we want to create a class of programs with as many subclasses as there are different syntactic forms, then the reader would no longer have recourse to an S-expression but to an object corresponding to a program. The function `evaluate` would thus be generic, and we could add new special forms easily and even incrementally. Redesign the interpreter to make that possible.

Exercise 3.12 : Define `throw` as a function instead of a special form.

Exercise 3.13 : Compare the execution speed of normal code and that translated into CPS.

Exercise 3.14 : Program `call/cc` by means of `the-current-continuation`. Assume that `the-current-continuation` is defined like this:

```
(define (the-current-continuation)
  (call/cc (lambda (k) k)) )
```

Recommended Reading

A good, non-trivial example of the use of continuations appears in [Wan80a]. You should also read [HFW84] about the simulation of messy control structures. In the historical perspective in [dR87], the rise of reflection in control forms is clearly stressed.

4
Assignment and Side Effects

IN the previous chapters, with their spiraling build-up of repetition and variations, you may have felt like you were being subjected to the Lisp-equivalent of Ravel's *Bolero*. Even so, no doubt you noticed two motifs were missing: assignment and side effects. Some languages abhor both because of their nasty characteristics, but since Lisp dialects procure them, we really have to study them here. This chapter examines assignment in detail, along with other side effects that can be perpetrated. During these discussions, we'll necessarily digress to other topics, notably, equality and the semantics of quotations.

Coming from conventional algorithmic languages, assignment makes it more or less possible to modify the value associated with a variable. It induces a modification of the state of the program that must record, in one way or another, that such and such a variable has a value other than its preceding one. For those who have a taste for imperative languages, the meaning we could attribute to assignment seems simple enough. Nevertheless, this chapter will show that the presence of closures as well as the heritage of λ-calculus complicates the ideas of binding and variables.

The major problem in defining assignment (and side effects, too) is choosing a formalism independent of the traits that we want to define. As a consequence, neither assignment nor side effects can appear in the definition. Not that we have used them excessively before; the only side effects that appeared in our earlier interpreters were localized in the function **update!** (when it involved defining assignment, of course) and in the definition of "surgical tools" like **set-car!** (in the Lisp being defined) which was only an encapsulation of **set-car!** (in the defining Lisp).

4.1 Assignment

Assignment, as we mentioned, makes it possible to modify the value of a variable. We can, for example, program the search for the minimum and maximum of a binary tree of natural integers by maintaining two variables containing the largest and smallest values seen so far. We could write that this way:

```
(define (min-max tree)
```

```
(define (first-number tree)
  (if (pair? tree)
      (first-number (car tree))
      tree ) )
(let* ((min (first-number tree))
       (max min) )
  (define (scan! tree)
    (cond ((pair? tree)
           (scan! (car tree))
           (scan! (cdr tree)) )
          (else (if (> tree max) (set! max tree)
                    (if (< tree min) (set! min tree)) )) ) )
  (scan! tree)
  (list min max) ) )
```

The function **min-max** is easy to understand and has the advantage that it uses only two dotted pairs to return the result we want. The algorithm is very much like one we could write in Pascal, and it's no less representative of the conventional use for variables. Notice, too, that the side effects it perpetrates on these local variables are completely invisible from outside the function **min-max** and thus do no damage to the general quality of the surrounding program. This is an example of a healthy side effect; it's clear and efficient, compared to purely functional versions of the same program. [see **Ex. 4.1**]

The assignment of an unshared local variable poses hardly any problems. For example, the following function enumerates the natural numbers, starting from zero. It's obvious there that asking for the value of the variable n immediately after assigning it is sure to return the new value that it's taken.

```
(define enumerate
  (let ((n -1))
    (lambda () (set! n (+ n 1))
               n ) ) )
```

Every call to **enumerate** returns a number. The function **enumerate** has an internal state, represented by the number **n**, which is modified progressively each time **enumerate** is called. Altering a closed variable is a problem in itself. λ-calculus is silent about this effect that exists only because we want to offer assignment within the language. To apply a function in mathematics, like in λ-calculus, we substitute for its variables the values or expressions that they take during the application. Assignment forces us to abandon this semantics, and it makes programs that use it lose their referential transparency.

If, for example, we replace all the occurrences of the variable n by its initial value in **enumerate**, then there would be no question of that function generating all the natural numbers, and **enumerate** would return the value **-1** eternally. Thus assignment forces us to abandon instantaneous substitution of variables by their values as a mode of computation. Substitution is now deferred in time, and it's carried out only when we want a specific value for a variable. Consequently, there are ways of interpolating assignments to modify substitutions that have not occurred yet.

Another example will highlight that problem more clearly. Consider this program:

```
(let ((name "Nemo"))
  (set! winner (lambda () name))
  (set! set-winner! (lambda (new-name) (set! name new-name)
                                       name ))
  (set-winner! "Me")
  (winner) )
```

Will the call to (winner) return "Nemo" or "Me"? In other words, are the modifications belonging to set-winner! perceived by winner?

Once more, λ-calculus is silent about this subject, and there's a good reason for its reticence: the idea of assignment is completely foreign to λ-calculus. Even so, we have said that the creation of a function should capture its definition environment; that is, the functions winner and set-winner! should store the fact that the variable name has the value "Nemo" at the time of their creation. It seems obvious that the form (set-winner! "Me") is going to return "Me" since the text of the function declares that we assign the variable name and then we return its value. The problem is to determine whether (winner) sees this new value, since it sees the same variable name.

A literal way of looking at the fact that a closure is defined in the environment where the free variables in its body have values that they had when it was created works in favor of isolation. In consequence, we could not distinguish the preceding program from the following one:

```
(let ((name "Nemo"))
  (set! winner (lambda () name))
  (winner) )
```

[Sam79] proposed that assignment should be visible only to the one who makes the assignment. In that case, the function set-winner! would return the modified value while winner always continued to return only "Nemo". In that world, the idea of binding doesn't even exist. There is a connection between a variable and a value, but that connection is direct. The reference to a variable thus consults the current environment and returns the associated value. Assignment creates a new environment equivalent to the old one except that the assigned variable now has the assigned value; this new environment is provided as the current one to the continuation.

This way of looking at things recalls the traditional way of implementing closure in old dynamic Lisps. A closure was created explicitly by the special form closure; it took a list of variables to close as its first term, and as its second term, it took a function. For example, the form (closure (x) (lambda (y) (+ x y))) leads to (lambda (y) (let ((x 'value-of-x)) (+ x y))). There's capture of the value associated with the variable x, and that seems like it conforms to the philosophy inherited from λ-calculus.

However, that model does not support assignment very well. It also makes the idea of a shared variable problematic. Other solutions have also been suggested; [SJ87] recommends a form of closure that analyzes the body of the function to close so that it automatically extracts the free variables to capture. We could also modify assignments found in the body of the function to close in such a way as to fix the difficult problem of updating close variables, as suggested in [BCSJ86, SJ93].

Scheme tackles the problem differently by introducing the idea of *binding* and achieves a number of interesting programming effects that way. The form `let` introduces a new binding between the variable `name` and the value `"Nemo"`. Functions created in the body of `let` capture, not the value of the variable, but its binding. The reference to the variable `name` is thus interpreted as a search for the binding associated with the variable `name` and then the extraction of the value associated with the binding that has already been discovered.

Assignment proceeds in the same way: assignment searches for the binding associated with the variable `name` and then alters the associated value inside this binding. The binding is thus a second class entity; a variable references a binding; a binding designates a value. Assigning a variable does not change the binding associated with it but modifies the contents of this binding to designate a new value.

4.1.1   Boxes

To flesh out the idea of binding, let's look again at A-lists. In the preceding interpreters, an A-list served us as the environment for variables, simply acting like a backbone to organize the set of variable-value pairs. A variable-value pair is represented by a dotted pair there. We search for that dotted pair when the variable is read- or write-referenced. That dotted pair (or, more precisely, its `cdr`) is modified by assignment. For this representation, then, we can identify the binding with this dotted pair. Other kinds of encoding are also possible; in fact, bindings can be represented by *boxes*. This transformation is significant because it lets us free ourselves entirely from assignments strictly in favor of side effects.

A box is created by the function `make-box`, conferring its initial value. A box can be read and written by the functions `box-ref` and `box-set!`. If we try a first draft of the function in message passing style, it would look like this:

```
(define (make-box value)
  (lambda (msg)
    (case msg
      ((get) value)
      ((set!) (lambda (new-value) (set! value new-value))) ) ) )
(define (box-ref box)
  (box 'get) )
(define (box-set! box new-value)
  ((box 'set!) new-value) )
```

A way of implementing it without closure would use dotted pairs directly, like this:

```
(define (other-make-box value)
  (cons 'box value) )
(define (other-box-ref box)
  (cdr box) )
(define (other-box-set! box new-value)
  (set-cdr! box new-value) )
```

More briefly, we could simply use `define-class` and just write this:

```
(define-class box Object (content))
```

In those three ways (and you can see a fourth way in Exercise 3.10), we highlight the indeterminism of the value that `box-set!` returns. Every variable that submits to one or more assignments can be transcribed in a box which can be implemented conveniently. It is easy then to determine whether a variable is mutable; we do so by looking at the body of the form which binds it to see whether the variable is the object of an assignment. (One of the attractive features of lexical languages is that all the places where a local variable might be used are visible.)

We will specify how to box a variable by rewrite rules, where π will be transformed into $\overline{\pi}^v$ and v is the name of the variable to box.

$$\overline{x}^v = \text{if } x = v \text{ then (box-ref } v) \text{ else } x$$
$$\overline{(\text{quote } \epsilon)}^v = (\text{quote } \epsilon)$$
$$\overline{(\text{if } \pi_c \ \pi_t \ \pi_f)}^v = (\text{if } \overline{\pi_c}^v \ \overline{\pi_t}^v \ \overline{\pi_f}^v)$$
$$\overline{(\text{begin } \pi_1 \ ... \pi_n)}^v = (\text{begin } \overline{\pi_1}^v \ ... \overline{\pi_n}^v)$$
$$\overline{(\text{set! } x \ \pi)}^v = \text{if } x = v \text{ then (box-set! } v \ \overline{\pi}^v)$$
$$\text{else (set! } x \ \overline{\pi}^v)$$
$$\overline{(\text{lambda } (...x...) \ \pi)}^v = \text{if } v \in \{...x...\} \text{ then (lambda } (...x...) \ \pi)$$
$$\text{else (lambda } (...x...) \ \overline{\pi}^v)$$
$$\overline{(\pi_0 \ \pi_1 \ ... \pi_n)}^v = (\ \overline{\pi_0}^v \ \overline{\pi_1}^v \ ... \overline{\pi_n}^v)$$

As usual, we must be careful in correctly handling local variables that have the same name as the variable that we want to rewrite in a box. By re-iterating the process on all the variables that are the object of an assignment that is all mutable variables, we completely suppress assignments in preference to boxes where the contents can be revised by side effects. We'll thus add the following rule:

$$(\text{lambda } (...x...) \ \pi) \quad \wedge \quad (\text{set! } x \ ...) \in \pi$$
$$\rightarrow \quad (\text{lambda } (...x...) \ (\text{let } ((x \ (\text{make-box } x))) \ \overline{\pi}^x)$$

Let's look at the preceding example again and rewrite it in terms of boxes to get this:

```
(let ((name (make-box "Nemo")))
   (set! winner (lambda () (box-ref name)))
   (set! set-winner! (lambda (new-name) (box-set! name new-name)
                                        (box-ref name) ))
   (set-winner! "Me")
   (winner) )
```

Using boxes in place of mutable variables (that is, assignable ones) is conventional and corresponds to "references" in dialects of ML. Boxes offer the advantage of (apparently) suppressing assignments and the problems connected with them. They also make it possible to avoid introducing special cases in the search for the value of a variable since no variables can be modified under those circumstances. Since they are pure side effects, they make us lose referential transparency, but they lend themselves to typing. On the other hand, boxes introduce two problems.

The first is that a binding, now represented by a box, becomes a first class object and can be manipulated as such. In other words, `box-ref` and `box-set!` are not the only operations that can be applied to boxes. Two people aware of the same box create an alias effect that can be used to implement modules.

The second problem is that the future of a box is usually indeterminate. Like a dotted pair that can be subjected to a disastrous `set-car!` by just about anybody, the places where boxes are used are generally unknown. In contrast, lexical assignment has this going for it that all the sites where a binding can be altered are statically known. Compilations can take advantage of such knowledge when, for example, an assigned variable is neither closed nor shared; such is the case for the variables **min** and **max** in the function **min-max**.

Each assignable variable is associated with a place in memory (that is, its address) containing the value of the binding. That location in memory will be modified when the variable is assigned.

4.1.2   Assignment of Free Variables

Another problem involving assignment is the meaning to impute to it for a free variable. Consider this example:

```
(let ((passwd "timhukiTrolrk"))     ; That's a real password!
  (set! can-access? (lambda (pw) (string=? passwd (crypt pw)))) )
```

The variable **can-access?** is free in the body of **let**. Moreover, it is also assigned. When we follow the rules of Scheme, the variable **can-access?** must be global since it is not claimed locally. But the fact that the environment should be global does not necessarily signify that it contains the variable **can-access?**! We debated a similar topic earlier [see p. 54] where we saw several different possible solutions.

What can we do with a global variable, other than assign it? Like any other variable, we can reference it, close it, get its value, and in general define it before any other operation. The global environment itself is a name space, and we're going to see many different ways of producing it.

Universal Global Environment

The global environment can be defined as the place where all variables pre-exist. In fact, every time a new variable name appears, the implementation manages to make sure that the variable by that name is present in the global environment as though it had always been there, according to [Que95]. In that world, for every name, there exists one and only one variable with that name. The idea of defining a global variable makes no sense since all variables pre-exist there. Modifying a variable poses no problem since its existence cannot be in doubt. Consequently, we can reduce the operator **define** to a mere **set!** and, as a corollary, multiple definitions of the same variable are possible.

Only one problem crops up when we want to get the value of a variable which has not yet been assigned. That variable exists, but does not yet have a value. This type of error often goes under the name of an *unbound variable* message, even though in the strictest sense, the variable does indeed have a binding: its associated box. In other words, the variable exists but is uninitialized.

We can summarize the properties of this environment in the following chart.

Reference	x
Value	x
Modification	(set! x ...)
Extension	no
Definition	no, define≡set!

This definition environment is more interesting than it might appear at first glance. For one thing, it does not need many concepts because everything in it pre-exists. That makes it easy to write mutually recursive functions. In case of error, it lets us redefine global functions. That characteristic means that any reference to a global variable has to be handled with care since *(i)* it might not be initialized yet (but once initialized, it's permanent); *(ii)* it can change value—a fact that prohibits any hypothesis based on its current value. In particular, we must not even *inline* the primitive functions car and cons, but we can automatically recompile anything that depends on a hypothesis which has just been trashed.

To illustrate this environment, consider the following fragment, showing various properties.

```
g                          ; error: g uninitialized
(define (P m) (* m g))
(define g 10)
(define g 9.81)            ; ≡ (set! g 9.81)
(P 10)            → 98.1
(set! e 2.78)              ; definition of e
```

In summary, you can think of the global environment as one giant let form, defining all variables, something like this:

```
(let (... a aa  ... ab  ... ac ... )
   ... )
```

Frozen Global Environment

Now imagine that for every name there is at most one global variable by that name and that the set of defined names is immutable. This is the situation of a compiled, autonomous application without dynamically created code (that is, no calls to eval). That was also the situation of the preceding interpreters that did not authorize the creation of new global variables. They had to be created explicitly by the form definitial in the implementation language.

In such an environment, a global variable exists only after having been created by define. We can get or modify its value only if it has been defined beforehand. Yet, since there can be only one variable by any given name, we can reference such a variable even before it is defined. (That's the feature that allows mutual recursion.) However, we cannot define a global variable more than once. We'll summarize those properties in our familiar chart.

Reference	x
Value	x but x must exist
Modification	(set! x ...) but x must exist
Extension	define (only one time)
Definition	no

Now for this environment, let's look again at the preceding fragment to see where it leads this time.

```
g                          ; error: no variable g
(define (P m) (* m g))     ; forward reference to g
(define g 10)
(define g 9.81)            ; error: redefinition of g
(set! g 9.81)              ; modification of g
(P 10)              → 98.1
(set! e 2.78)              ; error: no variable e
```

This environment is beginning to suggest the idea of a program. A program is defined by a set of expressions $\pi_1 \ldots \pi_n$ that we can organize into a single expression built like this: we put the forms $\pi_1 \ldots \pi_n$ into a unique **let** form introducing all the free variables present in $\pi_1 \ldots \pi_n$ as non-initialized local variables; and then we modify all the **define** forms by changing them into the equivalent **set!** forms.

To clarify those ideas, here's a little application written in Scheme:

```
(define (crypt pw) ...)
(let ((passwd "timhukiTrolrk"))
  (set! can-access? (lambda (pw) (string=? passwd (crypt pw)))) )
(define (gatekeeper)
  (until (can-access? (read)) (gatekeeper)) )
```

That little application asks the user for a password and won't let the user through unless he or she supplies the right one. That computerized version of Cerberus is equivalent to this:

```
(let (crypt make-can-access? can-access? gatekeeper)
  (set! crypt (lambda (pw) ...))
  (set! make-can-access?
        (lambda (passwd)
          (lambda (pw) (string=? passwd (crypt pw))) ) )
  (set! can-access? (make-can-access? "timhukiTrolrk"))
  (set! gatekeeper
        (lambda () (until (can-access? (read)) (gatekeeper))) )
  (gatekeeper) )|
                 |  car≡ car
                 |  cons≡ cons
                 |  ...
```

Global definitions are transformed into local definitions assigning the free variables of the application, re-organized and still non-initialized, in an all-encompassing **let**.[1] Of course, the usual functions, like **read**, **string=?**, **string-reverse**, or **string-append**, are visible. In this world, the global environment is finite and restricted to predefined variables (like **car** and **cons**) and to free variables of the program. However, it is not possible to assign a free variable not present in the global environment since that very environment was designed to avoid such a possibility. The only way to provoke that error would be to have a form of **eval** that allowed dynamic evaluation of code.

---

1. That definition of a program inadvertently makes multiple definitions of the same variable meaningful; for that reason, we have to add a few syntactic constraints.

Automatically Extendable Global Environment

If a toplevel loop is present, then we need to be able to augment the global environment dynamically. We just saw that the form **define** could help augment the set of global variables. You might also think that assignment would suffice for the same task; that is, that assigning a free variable would be equivalent to defining that variable in the global environment if it had not appeared there before. Thus we could directly write this:

```
(let ((name "Nemo"))
  (set! winner (lambda () name))
  (set! set-winner! (lambda (new-name) (set! name new-name)
                        name )) )
```

With the preceding variation, we would have had to prefix this expression by two absurd definitions, like these:

```
(define winner      'without-tail)
(define set-winner! 'nor-head)
```

Those expressions would have created the two variables, initialized them in any old way, then would have modified them immediately so that they would take on their real value. That technique is annoying because it explicitly makes the defined variables mutable since they have been the object of at least one assignment. For that reason, quite a long time ago, in Scheme [SS78b] there was a **static** form enabling us to write something[2] like this:

```
(let ((name "Nemo"))
  (define (static winner) (lambda () name))
  (define (static set-winner!)
    (lambda (new-name) (set! name new-name)
              name ) ) )
```

That way, the two global variables would have been co-defined together in a local lexical context without the intervention of assignment.

While assignment makes it possible to create global variables, we risk polluting the global environment by doing so. You might also think that it would be more clever to create the variable only locally; perhaps lexically at the level of the last **let** or, as in [Nor72], at the last dynamically enveloping[3] **prog**. Unfortunately, these ideas spoil referential transparency and forbid the preceding co-definitions.

Hyperstatic Global Environment

There is one more kind of global environment: one where several global variables can be associated with a name but where only forms located after a definition can see it. Let's look again at our favorite example:

```
g                     ; error: no variable g
(define (P m) (* m g)) ; error: no variable g
```

---

2. Nevertheless, we have to change the syntax of internal **define** forms so that they recognize the local presence of global definitions. That is, (**static** *variable*) is the reference to a global variable, rather than a call to the unary **static** function.

3. TEX does this: a definition made by \def disappears when we exit from the current group with \endgroup.

```
(define g 10)
(define (P m) (* m g))
(P 10)              → 100
(define g 9.81)
(P 10)              → 100   ; P sees the old g
(define (P m) (* m g))
(P 10)              → 98.1
(set! e 2.78)              ; error: no variable e
```

Here, faithful to the spirit that prefers to close functions in the environment where they are created, the first definition of P is statically an error since it references g which does not exist at that moment. Another solution would be to allow the definition of P but to make any call to P an error since g had no value a the moment when P was created. However, this solution should not be adopted since it delays warning the user and the sooner errors are caught, the better.

The second definition of P encloses the fact that g has the value 10, and that fact lasts as long as the function P. If we want a better approximation of g for some reason, we must redefine the function P to take account of that new value. The global environment here is managed in a completely lexical way; we call that mode *hyperstatic*, and it's the mode that ML chose. We'll summarize its characteristics in our usual chart.

Reference	x but x must exist
Value	x but x must exist
Modification	(set! x ...) but x must exist
Extension	define
Definition	no

However, that mode causes problems for recursive definitions. We have to be able to define both functions that are simply recursive and groups of functions that are mutually recursive. ML has a keyword—rec—to indicate that first kind, and another keyword—and—to indicate co-definitions. Those keywords correspond to letrec and let in Scheme, where those forms already authorize multiple definitions. To make that idea visible, consider the preceding example rewritten this time as a series of nested instances of let or letrec:

```
g                                    ; error: no variable g
(let ((P (lambda (m) (* m g))))      ; error: no variable g
  (let ((g 10))
    (let ((P (lambda (m) (* m g))))
      (P 10)
      (let ((g 9.81))
        ... ) ) ) )
```

And here's another example, this time in ML, of mutually recursive functions:

```
let rec odd n = if n = 0 then false else even (n - 1)
    and even n = if n = 0 then true else odd (n - 1)
```

That example obviously corresponds to this:

```
(letrec ((odd? (lambda (n) (if (= n 0) #f (even? (- n 1)))))
         (even? (lambda (n) (if (= n 0) #t (odd? (- n 1)))))  )
    ... )
```

Hyperstatic global environments have the obvious advantage of being able to detect undefined variables statically. Furthermore, if bindings are known to be immutable, these environments also compile very efficiently because they may take advantage of the fact that they know the value. When an error occurs, however, they have the disadvantage that they require a redefinition of everything that follows the erroneous definition.

4.1.3   Assignment of a Predefined Variable

Among the free variables appearing in a program, there are the predefined ones like **car** or **read**. Assigning them is thus our inalienable right, but just what does it mean to assign one? The speed of an implementation frequently depends on hypotheses that are rarely made explicit. In Lisp, we often talk about *inline* functions, that is, compiled and integrated functions; accessors such as **car** or **cdr** are usually inline. Redefining any of them thus causes problems because, once an assignment impinging on **car** is perceived, then all the calls to **car** have to use the current value of **car** rather than its primitive value.

In a hyperstatic interaction loop, that's not a real problem because only future expressions will see this modified **car** function. However, if the interaction loop is dynamic, then to be accurate, we have to recompile every inline call to **car**. That would lead us logically to redefining the function **cadr** since it's probably defined as the composition of **car** and **cdr**. This work would never actually get done since it introduces too much disorder and probably does not correspond to the real intentions of the users.

By the way, Scheme forbids the modification of a global binding from changing the values or the behavior of other predefined functions. In that context, modifying **car** would not be allowed, but defining a new **car** variable would be permitted, though it would probably not change the meaning of **cadr**. Since **map** (comparable to **mapcar** in Lisp) appears in the standard definition of Scheme, a modification of **car** would not perturb it, but since **mapc** is not part of the standard definition, modifying **car** would probably disturb it.

Modifying a global variable often looks like a way to trace or analyze calls to the function that is the value of that global variable. It also seems like a means to correct erroneous or aberrant behavior. However, we advise the impetuous and inexperienced to resist such temptations. Our advice is "Don't touch predefined variables!"

In summary, a hyperstatic global environment behaves logically but it is not as practical as a dynamic global environment for debugging.

4.2   Side Effects

So far, we've seen how a computation in Lisp is represented by an ordered triple of expression, environment, and continuation. As attractive as that triple is, it does not express the meaning of assignment nor of physical modification of data in memory. *Side effects* correspond to alterations in the state of the world and in particular to changes in memory.

The most familiar changes come from physically modifying data in memory, as `set-car!` and input/output functions do. Reading or writing in a stream makes a mark move along to show where the most recent read or write occurred. (That's a side effect!) Writing to a screen leaves an irreparable mark on it—a long lasting side effect—and writing to paper is even more indelible—yet another long term side effect. Requiring a user to type on a keyboard is likewise irreversible. In short, side effects are unfortunately omnipresent in computing. They correspond to sets of instructions for computers operating on registers, to file systems saving information (for example, the marvelous texts and programs that we concoct ourselves) between sessions. Of course, it is possible to imagine living in an ideal world with no side effects, but we would suffer from a kind of computer-autism there since we would not be able to communicate the results of computations. This nightmare won't keep us awake, however, since there is no computer in the world that actually works with no side effects.

We've already seen that assignments can be simulated by boxes. Inversely, can we simulate dotted pairs without dotted pairs? The response is yes, but we do so by using assignment! A dotted pair can be simulated by a function responding to the messages `car`, `cdr`, `set-car!`, and `set-cdr!`[4] like this:

```
(define (kons a d)
  (lambda (msg)
    (case msg
      ((car) a)
      ((cdr) d)
      ((set-car!) (lambda (new) (set! a new)))
      ((set-cdr!) (lambda (new) (set! d new))) ) ) )
(define (kar pair)
  (pair 'car) )
(define (set-kdr! pair value)
  ((pair 'set-cdr!) value) )
```

Once again, the simulation is not quite perfect, as [Fel90] points out, because we can no longer distinguish the dotted pairs from normal functions. With that programming practice, we can no longer write the predicate `pair?`. Except for this slight reduction in means (in fact, equivalent to being able to write new types of data), we see clearly that side effects and assignment maintain uneasy relations and that one is easily simulated by the other. Consequently, we have to ban both of them or accept them and their more or less uncontrollable fallout. Whether we choose assignment or physical modification then depends on the context and the properties that we are trying to preserve.

4.2.1 Equality

One inconvenience of physical modifiers is that they induce an alteration in equality. When can we say that two objects are equal? In the sense that Leibnitz used it, two objects are equal if we can substitute one for the other without damage. In programming terms, we say that two objects are equal if we have no means of distinguishing one from the other. The equality tautology says that an object is

---

4. To avoid confusion with the usual primitives, we'll spell their names with k.

equal to itself since we can always replace it by itself without changing anything. This is a weak notion of equality if we take it literally, but it's the same idea that we apply to integers. Things get more complicated when we consider two objects between which we don't know any relation (for example, when they derive from two different computations, like (* 2 2) and (+ 2 2)) and when we ask whether they can substitute for each other or whether they resemble each other.

In the presence of physical modifiers, two objects are different if an alteration of one does not provoke any change in the other. Admittedly, we're talking about *difference* here, not equality, but in this context, we'll classify objects in two groups: those that can change and those that are unchanging.

Kronecker said that the integers were a gift from God, so on that logical basis, we'll consider them unchanging: 3 will be 3 in all contexts. Also it's simple for us to decide that a non-composite object (that is, one without constituent parts) will be unchanging, so in addition to integers, we also have characters, Booleans, and the empty list. There aren't any other unchanging, non-composite objects.

For composite objects, such as lists, vectors, and character strings, it seems logical to consider two of them equal if they have the same constituents. That's the idea we generally find underlying the name **equal?** with different variations[5] whether recursive or not. Unfortunately, in the presence of physical modifiers, equality of components at a given moment hardly insures the persistence of equality in the future. For that reason, we'll introduce a new predicate for physical equality, **eq?**, and we'll say that two objects are **eq?** when it is, in fact, the same.[6] This predicate is often implemented in an extremely efficient way by comparing pointers; in that way, it tests whether two pointers designate the same location in memory.

In fact, we have two predicates available: **eq?**, testing the physical identity, and **equal?**, testing the structural equivalence. However, these two extreme predicates overlook the changeability of objects. Two immutable objects are equal if their components are equal. To be sure that two immutable objects are equal at some moment in time insures that they will always be so because they don't vary. Inversely, two mutable objects are eternally equal only if they are one and the same object. In practice, a single idea is emerging here as the definition of equality: whether one object can be substituted for the other. Two objects are equal if no program can distinguish between them.

The predicate **eq?** compares only entities comparable with respect to the implementation: addresses in memory[7] or immediate constants. The conventional techniques of representing objects in the dialects that we're considering do not insure[8] that two equal objects have comparable representations for **eq?**. It follows that **eq?** does not even implement tautology.

A new predicate, known as **eqv?** in Scheme and as **eql** in COMMON LISP, improves **eq?** in this respect. In general terms, it behaves like **eq?** but a little more slowly to insure that two equal immutable objects are recognized as such. The predicate **eqv?** insures that two equal numbers, even gigantic ones represented by

---

5. See, for example, the functions **equalp** or **tree-equal** in COMMON LISP.
6. This grammatical weirdness expresses the idea that there are not two objects, but only one.
7. For a distributed Scheme on a network of computers, **eq?** has to be able to compare objects located at different sites. In such a case, **eq?** is not necessarily immediate.
8. For example, (**eq?** 33 33) is not guaranteed to return **#t** in Scheme, hence the need for **eqv?**.

bignums, will be compared successfully regardless of their representation in memory.

If we look back at the interpreters that we've given so far, we notice how little mutable data are found in them. With the exception of bindings, everything there was unchanging. In fact, mutable structures are few, and the majority of allocated dotted pairs never submit to physical modifiers such as set-car! and set-cdr!. In some implementations of ML, but also in COMMON LISP, it's possible to indicate the mutability of fields in an object. We can thus create a constant dotted pair, like this:

```
(defstruct immutable-pair                              COMMON LISP
   (car '() :read-only t)
   (cdr '() :read-only t) )
```

Physically, constant dotted pairs could be allocated in a zone apart, and constants cited in programs could use this type of dotted pair.

In [Bak93], Henry Baker suggested unifying all the equality predicates in a sole **egal** defined like this: if the objects to compare are mutable, then **egal** behaves like **eq?**; otherwise, it behaves like **equal?**. This new predicate insures that two objects can be substituted for each other when they are recognized as equal by **egal**. It's easy to see the utility of this predicate in a parallel world involving the migration of data, as in [QD93, Que94].

Cyclic data present another problem. Comparing them is possible but expensive. If we don't know that the data being compared may be cyclic, then we may fall into a looping **equal?**. And if that problem were not bad enough, how to compare these structures is not obvious either. Consider this case, for example:

```
(define o1 (let ((pair (cons 1 2)))
             (set-car! pair pair)
             (set-cdr! pair pair)
             pair ))
(define o2 (let ((pair (cons (cons 1 2) 3)))
             (set-car! (car pair) pair)
             (set-cdr! (car pair) pair)
             (set-cdr! pair pair)
             pair ))
```

Let's suppose first of all that we have to evaluate (equal? o1 o1). If the implementation of **equal?** begins by testing whether the objects are **eq?** before it begins the structural comparison of their respective fields, then the answer is immediate and positive. In the opposite case, **equal?** will loop forever.[9]

Granted that (equal? o1 o1) is a suspicious case, what do you think of (equal? o1 o2)? The reply depends once again on knowing whether the dotted pairs composing o1 and o2 are mutable or not. If no one can modify them, then in the absence of **eq?**, no one can write a program that distinguishes them. This observation brings us back to the idea that it's better not to compare cyclic structures with **equal?**.

The preceding predicates cover the various kinds of data usually present, with the exception of symbols and functions. Symbols are complex data structures since they are often used by implementations to store information about global variables

---

9. As I wrote that, I checked four different implementations of Scheme, and two looped. I won't reveal their names since they are fully justified in doing so. [CR91b]

of the same name. Basically, a symbol is a data structure that we can retrieve by name and that is guaranteed unique for a given name.

Symbols often contain a property list—a dangerous addition because a property list is managed by side effects that are perceived globally. Moreover, a property list is usually burdensome, both in storage (since it takes two dotted pairs per property) and in use (since it requires a linear search). For those reasons, *hash tables*[10] are preferable.

4.2.2 Equality between Functions

For functions, our situation may seem desperate. We can say that two functions are equal if their results are equal whenever their arguments are equal, that is, they are undistinguishable. More formally, we can put it this way:

$$f = g \Leftrightarrow \forall x, f(x) = g(x)$$

Unfortunately, comparing two functions that way is an undecidable problem. For that reason, we could refuse to compare functions at all, or we could adopt a more flexible attitude but restrict the problem. Large classes of functions are comparable, and in many cases, we can easily discover that two functions cannot be equal (for example, when they don't even have the same number of arguments).

With those thoughts in mind, we can get an approximate equality predicate for functions by admitting that sometimes its response may be imprecise or even erroneous. Of course, we can rely on such an approximate predicate only if we understand clearly where and how it is imprecise.

Scheme, for example, defines **eqv?** for functions in the following way: if we must compare the functions **f** and **g**, and if there exists an application of **f** and **g** to the same arguments (where "the same arguments" is determined by **eqv?**) such that the results are different, then the functions **f** and **g** are not **eqv?**. Once again, we find ourselves considering difference rather than defining equality.

Let's look at a few examples now. The comparison (**eqv? car cdr**) should return false since their results are manifestly different, especially on an example like (**a . b**).

It should also be obvious that (**eqv? car car**) returns true since equality must surely handle tautology correctly. However, it's false in certain dialects where that form is equivalent to (**eqv? (lambda (x) (car x)) (lambda (x) (car x))**) because the function **car** can be inline. In fact, R^4RS does not specify what **eqv?** should return when it is used to compare predefined functions like **car**.

How can we compare **cons** and **cons** without invoking tautology? The function **cons** is an allocator of mutable data, and thus, even if the arguments seem comparable, the results are not necessarily equal since they are allocated in different places. Thus we're right to demand that **cons** should not be equal to **cons** and thus (**eqv? cons cons**) should return false since it is false that (**eqv? (cons 1 2) (cons 1 2)**)!

Now is it really true that **car** should be equal to **car** as we argued in the previous paragraphs? In a language without types, (**car 'foo**) raises an error and signals an exception, but then it's left up to the care of the local error handler, a

---

10. In my humble opinion, their invention was one of the greatest discoveries of computer science.

mechanism with unpredictable behavior that may vary wildly. For that reason, we cannot be sure that that call always returns favorably comparable results. The same observations hold for any partial function used outside its domain of definition.

How do we get out of this situation? Different languages try different means. Because of their typing which lets them detect all the places where comparisons between functions might be made, some dialects of ML forbid such situations purely and simply since we cannot and should not compare functions. In its semantics, Scheme makes `lambda` a closure constructor. Thus each `lambda` form allocates a new closure somewhere in memory. That closure has a certain address, so functions can be compared by a comparison of addresses, and the only case where two functions are the same (in the sense of `eqv?`) is when they are one and the same closure.

This behavior prevents certain improvements known in λ-calculus. Let's consider the function cleverly named `make-named-box`. It takes only one argument (a message), analyzes it, and responds in an appropriate way. This is one possible way of producing objects, and it's the one that we adopt for coding the interpreter in this chapter.

```
(define (make-named-box name value)
  (lambda (msg)
    (case msg
      ((type) (lambda () 'named-box))
      ((name) (lambda () name))
      ((ref)  (lambda () value))
      ((set!) (lambda (new-value) (set! value new-value))) ) ) )
```

That function creates an anonymous box and then gives it a name. The closure gotten by means of the message `type` does not depend on any of the local variables. Consequently, we could rewrite the entire function like this:

```
(define other-make-named-box
  (let ((type-closure (lambda () 'named-box)))
    (lambda (name value)
      (let ((name-closure  (lambda () name))
            (value-closure (lambda () value))
            (set-closure   (lambda (new-value)
                             (set! value new-value) )) )
        (lambda (msg)
          (case msg
            ((type) type-closure)
            ((name) name-closure)
            ((ref)  value-closure)
            ((set!) set-closure) ) ) ) ) ) )
```

This one differs from the preceding version because the closure `(lambda () 'named-box)`, for example, is allocated only once whereas earlier, it was allocated every time it was needed.

But then what's the value of the following comparison?

```
(let ((nb (make-named-box 'foo 33)))
  (compare? (nb 'type) (nb 'type)) )
```

Actually the question is badly phrased because it has meaning only if we specify the predicate for comparison. If we use **eq?**, then the exact number of allocations of **(lambda () 'named-box)** will play a role, whereas if we use **egal**, then the question is meaningless, and the final value is always true. From this, you can see that if a language includes a physical comparer, that comparer will make it possible to discern whether objects might possibly be equal.

When **lambda** is an allocator, we associate an address in memory with all the closures that it creates. Two closures having the same address are merely one and the same object and thus equal. Accordingly, in Scheme, we have this:

```
(let ((f (lambda (x y) (cons x y))))
  (eqv? f f) )        → #t
```

Since it compares the same object in memory, the predicate **eqv?** will return true even if it is false that **(eqv? (f 1 2) (f 1 2))**.

As you see, comparing functions is an activity beset by obstacles for which multiple points of view might be adopted, depending on the properties that we want to preserve. Keeping the mathematical aspect of equality of functions is practically out of the question. Depending on the implementation, many ways of using comparisons may be proscribed. Even though this very book contains such a comparison in the implementation of MEROONET, [see p. 447] we still offer the advice that, as far as possible, it is better to avoid comparing functions at all.

4.3 Implementation

For once, the interpreter that we'll explain in this chapter uses closures only for its data structures. Everything will be coded by **lambda** forms and by sending messages. All the objects are thus closures based on code functions similar to **(lambda (msg) (case msg ...))** like we saw in a few of the preceding examples. Some messages will be standard, like **boolify** or **type**. **boolify** associates a value with its equivalent truth value (that is, **#t** or **#f** for the purposes of conditionals). **type**, of course, returns its type.

Our chief problem is to find a method to define side effects. Formally, we say that a variable references a binding which is associated with a value. More prosaically, we say that a variable points to a box (an address) that contains a value. Memory is merely a function associating addresses with the values contained in those addresses. The environment is another function associating these addresses with variables. Those conventions all seem natural until you try to simulate their implementation.

Memory must be visible everywhere. We could make it a global variable, but that is not a very elegant solution, and we have already seen all the problems that a global environment entails. Another solution is to make all the functions see the memory. It would then suffice for all the functions to receive the memory as an argument and pass it along to others, possibly after modifying it. We'll actually adopt this way of doing it, and that choice forces us to consider a computation now as a quadruple: *expression, environment, continuation*, and *memory*. Those four components are named **e**, **r**, **k**, and **s**. To make sure that memory circulates freely, continuations will receive not only the value to transmit but also the resulting memory state.

As usual, the function `evaluate` will syntactically analyze its argument and call the appropriate function. We'll keep the conventions for naming variables from the previous chapters, and we'll add the following:

$$
\begin{array}{rl}
\text{e, et, ec, ef} \dots & \text{expression, form} \\
\text{r} \dots & \text{environment} \\
\text{k, kk} \dots & \text{continuation} \\
\text{v, void} \dots & \text{value (integer, pair, closure etc.)} \\
\text{f} \dots & \text{function} \\
\text{n} \dots & \text{identifier} \\
\text{s, ss, sss} \dots & \text{memory} \\
\text{a, aa} & \text{address (box)}
\end{array}
$$

Since the number of variables has increased, we'll adopt the discipline of always mentioning them in the same order: **e**, **r**, **s**, and then **k**.

Here's the interpreter:

```
(define (evaluate e r s k)
  (if (atom? e)
      (if (symbol? e) (evaluate-variable e r s k)
          (evaluate-quote e r s k) )
      (case (car e)
        ((quote)  (evaluate-quote (cadr e) r s k))
        ((if)     (evaluate-if (cadr e) (caddr e) (cadddr e) r s k))
        ((begin)  (evaluate-begin (cdr e) r s k))
        ((set!)   (evaluate-set! (cadr e) (caddr e) r s k))
        ((lambda) (evaluate-lambda (cadr e) (cddr e) r s k))
        (else     (evaluate-application (car e) (cdr e) r s k)) ) ) )
```

4.3.1 Conditional

A conditional introduces an auxiliary continuation that waits for the value of the condition.

```
(define (evaluate-if ec et ef r s k)
  (evaluate ec r s
    (lambda (v ss)
      (evaluate ((v 'boolify) et ef) r ss k) ) ) )
```

The auxiliary continuation takes into consideration not only the Boolean value **v** but also the memory state **ss** resulting from the evaluation of the condition. In effect, it is legal to have side effects in the condition, as the following expression shows:

```
(if (begin (set-car! pair 'foo)
           (cdr pair) )
    (car pair) 2 )
```

Any modification that occurs in the condition has to be visible in the two branches of the conditional. The situation would be quite different if we defined the conditional like this:

```
(define (evaluate-amnesic-if ec et ef r s k)
  (evaluate ec r s
    (lambda (v ss)
      (evaluate ((v 'boolify) et ef) r s    ;s ≠ ss!
               k ) ) ) )
```

In that latter case, the memory state present at the beginning of the evaluation of the condition would be restored. That would be characteristic of a language that supports backtracking in the style of Prolog. [see **Ex. 4.4**]

To take into account the fact that every object is coded by a function, True and False must not be the **#t** and **#f** of the implementation language. Since every object can also be considered as a truth value, we will assume that every object can receive the message **boolify** and will then return one of the λ-calculus style combinators, (lambda (x y) x) or (lambda (x y) y).

4.3.2 Sequence

Though it's not essential to us, the definition of a sequence shows clearly just how sequencing is treated in the language. It also highlights an intermediate continuation. For simplicity, we'll assume that sequences include at least one term.

```
(define (evaluate-begin e* r s k)
  (if (pair? (cdr e*))
      (evaluate (car e*) r s
        (lambda (void ss)
          (evaluate-begin (cdr e*) r ss k) ) )
      (evaluate (car e*) r s k) ) )
```

In such a bare form, you can see how little regard there is for the value of **void** and the final call to **evaluate** when there is only one form in a sequence.

4.3.3 Environment

The environment has to be coded as a function and must transform variables into addresses. Similarly, the memory is represented as a function, but one that transforms addresses into values. Initially, the environment contains nothing at all:

```
(define (r.init id)
  (wrong "No binding for" id) )
```

Now how do we modify an environment or even memory without a physical modifier and without assignment? To modify a memory state is to change the value associated with an address. We could thus define the function **update** so that it modifies memory when we offer it an address and a value, like this:

```
(define (update s a v)
  (lambda (aa)
    (if (eqv? a aa) v (s aa)) ) )
```

The meaning is apparent if we remember that a memory state is represented, as we said, by a function that transforms addresses into values. The form (**update**

s a v) returns a new memory state that faithfully resembles the s except that
at the address a the associated value is now v; for everything else, we see s. We
generalize update to take multiple addresses and multiple values, like this:

```
(define (update* s a* v*)
  ;; (assume (= (length a*) (length v*)))
  (if (pair? a*)
      (update* (update s (car a*) (car v*)) (cdr a*) (cdr v*))
      s ) )
```

The function update can also be applied to extending environments. In ML,
that would be a polymorphic function. Keeping in mind the kind of comparison that
update carries out, we'll code addresses as objects that are eminently comparable:
integers. To compare variables, we'll compare their names. In Scheme, the function
eqv? will thus be convenient in both cases.

4.3.4   Reference to a Variable

Consequently, the value of a variable is expressed simply, like this:

```
(define (evaluate-variable n r s k)
  (k (s (r n)) s) )
```

The form (r n) returns the address where the value of the variable is located
(that is, the value of n). The contents of this address is searched for in memory
and given to the continuation. Since searching for the value of a variable is a non-
destructive process, memory will not be modified that way and will be transmitted
as such to the continuation.

4.3.5   Assignment

Assignment requires an intermediate continuation.

```
(define (evaluate-set! n e r s k)
  (evaluate e r s
    (lambda (v ss)
      (k v (update ss (r n) v)) ) ) )
```

After the evaluation of the second term, its value and the resulting memory
are provided to the continuation to update the contents of the address associated
with the variable. That is, a new memory state is constructed, and that new state
will be provided to the original continuation of the assignment. By the way, this
assignment returns the assigned value.

Here you can see why making memory a function was a good idea. Doing so
lets us represent modifications without any side effects. In more Lispian terms,
this way of representing memory turns it into the list of all modifications that
it has undergone. Compared to real memory, this representation is manifestly
superfluous, but it enables us to handle various instances of memory simultaneously.
[see **Ex. 4.5**]

4.3.6 Functional Application

A functional application consists of evaluating all terms. Here we'll choose left to right order.

```
(define (evaluate-application e e* r s k)
  (define (evaluate-arguments e* r s k)
    (if (pair? e*)
        (evaluate (car e*) r s
          (lambda (v ss)
            (evaluate-arguments (cdr e*) r ss
              (lambda (v* sss)
                (k (cons v v*) sss) ) ) ) )
        (k '() s) ) )
  (evaluate e r s
    (lambda (f ss)
      (evaluate-arguments e* r ss
        (lambda (v* sss)
          (if (eq? (f 'type) 'function)
              ((f 'behavior) v* sss k)
              (wrong "Not a function" (car v*)) ) ) ) ) ) )
```

Here, the function usually named **evlis** becomes local, known under the name **evaluate-arguments**. It evaluates its arguments in order and organizes their values into a list. The function (the value of the first term of the functional application) is then applied to its arguments accompanied by the memory and the continuation of the call. There again, you can see how concise the program is.

Since the function is represented by a closure that responds at least to the message **boolify**, a new message—**behavior**—will extract its functional behavior, that is, the way it calculates.

4.3.7 Abstraction

To simplify things, let's assume for the moment that the special form **lambda** creates only functions with fixed arity. Two effects come together here—an allocation in memory and the construction of a first class value—as a closure. Creating a function involves constructing an object that, as you might expect, has to be allocated somewhere in memory. In other words, it is necessary for memory to be modified when a function is created. To that end, we furnish two things to the utility **create-function**: an address and the behavior of the function to create. The behavior we furnish is the same that the message **behavior** extracted before, during the functional application.

```
(define (evaluate-lambda n* e* r s k)
  (allocate 1 s
    (lambda (a* ss)
      (k (create-function
          (car a*)
          (lambda (v* s k)
            (if (= (length n*) (length v*))
                (allocate (length n*) s
                  (lambda (a* ss)
```

```
            (evaluate-begin e*
                           (update* r n* a*)
                           (update* ss a* v*)
                           k ) ) )
          (wrong "Incorrect arity") ) ) )
     ss ) ) ) )
```

When a function constructed by the special form `lambda` is called on one of its arguments, its behavior stipulates that, in current memory at the moment of the call, it must allocate as many new addresses as it has variables to bind; then it must initialize these addresses with the associated values and finally pursue the rest of its computations.

```
(define (evaluate-ftn-lambda n* e* r s k)
  (allocate (+ 1 (length n*)) s
    (lambda (a* ss)
      (k (create-function
        (car a*)
        (lambda (v* s k)
          (if (= (length n*) (length v*))
            (evaluate-begin e*
                           (update* r n* (cdr a*))
                           (update* s (cdr a*) v*)
                           k )
          (wrong "Incorrect arity") ) ) )
     ss ) ) ) )
```

If the addresses were allocated at another time, for example, at the time the function was created, we would get behavior more like that of Fortran, forbidding recursion. In effect, every recursive call to the function uses those same addresses to store the values of variables, thus making only the last such values accessible. The purpose for this variation is that there is no dynamic creation of functions in Fortran, and consequently these addresses can be allocated during compilation, thus making function calls faster but thereby forbidding recursion, the real strength of functional languages.

4.3.8 Memory

Memory is represented by a function that takes addresses and returns values. It must also be possible to allocate new addresses there, new addresses that are guaranteed free; that's the purpose of the function `allocate`. As arguments, it takes a memory and the number of addresses that it must reserve there; it also takes a third argument: a function (a continuation) to which it will give the list of addresses that it has selected in memory plus the new memory where these addresses have been initialized to the "uninitialized" state. The function `allocate` handles all the details of memory management and notably the recovery of cells that is, garbage collection. Fortunately, it's simple to characterize this function if we assume that memory is infinitely large; that is, if we assume that it's always possible to allocate new objects.

```
(define (allocate n s q)
  (if (> n 0)
```

```
(let ((a (new-location s)))
  (allocate (- n 1)
            (expand-store a s)
            (lambda (a* ss)
              (q (cons a a*) ss) ) ) )
(q '() s) ) )
```

The form **new-location** searches for a free address in memory. This is a real
function in the sense that the form (**eqv?** (**new-location** s) (**new-location**
s)) always returns True. We associate the highest address used so far with each
memory; that address will be used when we search for a free address by means of
new-location. To mark that an address has been reserved, we extend memory by
expand-store.

```
(define (expand-store high-location s)
  (update s 0 high-location) )
(define (new-location s)
  (+ 1 (s 0)) )
```

Initial memory doesn't contain anything, but it defines the first free address.
Memory is thus a closure responding to a certain message when it involves determining a free address or responding to messages coded as integers (that is, addresses)
when we want to know the contents of memory. We'll unify these two kinds of
messages by assuming that the address 0 contains the address most recently used.

```
(define s.init
  (expand-store 0 (lambda (a) (wrong "No such address" a))) )
```

4.3.9 Representing Values

We've decided to represent all values that the interpreter handles by functions
that send messages. These values are the empty list, Booleans, symbols, numbers,
dotted pairs, and functions. We'll look at each of these kinds of data in turn.

All values will thus be created on a skeleton function that responds to at least
two messages: *(i)* **type** for requesting its type; *(ii)* **boolify** for converting it to
a truth value. Other messages exist for specific types of data. The skeleton that
serves as the backbone of all these values will thus be this:

```
(lambda (msg)
  (case msg
    ((type) ...)
    ((boolify) ...)
    ... ) )
```

There is only one unique empty list, and according to R⁴RS, it is a legal representation of True, so we use this:

```
(define the-empty-list
  (lambda (msg)
    (case msg
      ((type)    'null)
      ((boolify) (lambda (x y) x)) ) ) )
```

The two Boolean values are created by **create-boolean**, like this:

```
(define (create-boolean value)
  (let ((combinator (if value (lambda (x y) x) (lambda (x y) y))))
    (lambda (msg)
      (case msg
        ((type)    'boolean)
        ((boolify) combinator) ) ) ) )
```

Symbols should respond to the specific message **name** that extracts their name represented as a symbol in the defining Scheme.

```
(define (create-symbol v)
  (lambda (msg)
    (case msg
      ((type)    'symbol)
      ((name)    v)
      ((boolify) (lambda (x y) x)) ) ) )
```

Numbers will have **value** as their specific message, like this:

```
(define (create-number v)
  (lambda (msg)
    (case msg
      ((type)    'number)
      ((value)   v)
      ((boolify) (lambda (x y) x)) ) ) )
```

Functions will respond to the messages **behavior** and **tag**. Of course, **behavior** extracts their behavior; **tag** indicates the address to which they have been allocated.

```
(define (create-function tag behavior)
  (lambda (msg)
    (case msg
      ((type)     'function)
      ((boolify)  (lambda (x y) x))
      ((tag)      tag)
      ((behavior) behavior) ) ) )
```

The last case we have to cover is that of dotted pairs. A dotted pair indicates two values that are both susceptible to modification by physical modifiers. For that reason, we're going to represent dotted pairs by a pair of addresses: one will contain the **car** of the dotted pair while the other will contain its **cdr**. This choice of representation may seem strange since a dotted pair is conventionally represented by a box of two contiguous values.[11] Thus only one address is needed to indicate the pair. This way of coding does not do justice to that implementation technique consisting of storing the **car** and **cdr** in two different arrays but at the same index in each array; a dotted pair is thus represented by such an index. According to that way of coding, two different addresses are thus associated with each dotted pair.

---

11. Very serious studies, such as [Cla79, CG77], have shown that it's better for cdr (rather than car) to be directly accessible without a supplementary displacement. Another reason to place cdr first is that pairs implement lists and thus inherit from the class of linked objects which define only one field: cdr.

To simplify the allocation of lists, we'll use the following two functions that take a list and memory, and then allocate the list in that memory. Since that allocation modifies the memory, a third argument (a continuation) will be called finally with the resulting memory and the allocated list.

```
(define (allocate-list v* s q)
  (define (consify v* q)
    (if (pair? v*)
        (consify (cdr v*) (lambda (v ss)
                            (allocate-pair (car v*) v ss q) ))
        (q the-empty-list s) ) )
  (consify v* q) )
(define (allocate-pair a d s q)
  (allocate 2 s
   (lambda (a* ss)
     (q (create-pair (car a*) (cadr a*))
        (update (update ss (car a*) a) (cadr a*) d) ) ) ) )
(define (create-pair a d)
  (lambda (msg)
    (case msg
      ((type)    'pair)
      ((boolify) (lambda (x y) x))
      ((set-car) (lambda (s v) (update s a v)))
      ((set-cdr) (lambda (s v) (update s d v)))
      ((car)     a)
      ((cdr)     d) ) ) )
```

4.3.10 A Comparison to Object Programming

The skeleton closure that we chose to represent values for this interpreter enables those values to respond to multiple messages, and in that sense, those values resemble the objects we used in the preceding chapter. Nevertheless there are several important differences between these objects coded by closures and those of ME-ROONET. The objects coded by closures contain their methods inside themselves; it is not possible to add new methods to them. The ideas of class and subclass remain virtual concepts since they are not implemented by these values. However, generic functions make it possible to add behavior to objects from the exterior without even requiring their cooperation; generic functions support not only methods, but also multimethods. Finally, the idea of a subclass makes it possible to share the structure of objects without useless repetition of their common characteristics. These various qualities shouldn't make you think of objects as *poor man's closures*, like some Scheme users suggest. In fact, the objects of the previous chapter have many more qualities than those of this chapter, but you can see an interesting defense of these latter in [AR88].

4.3.11 Initial Environment

As usual, we'll introduce two different kinds of syntax to put predefined variables into the initial environment (here, into the initial memory). With every global

variable, we'll associate an address containing its value. The syntax of `definitial`
will thus allocate a new address and fill it with the appropriate value.

```
(define s.global s.init)
(define r.global r.init)
(define-syntax definitial
  (syntax-rules ()
    ((definitial name value)
     (allocate 1 s.global
       (lambda (a* ss)
         (set! r.global (update r.global 'name (car a*)))
         (set! s.global (update ss (car a*) value)) ) ) ) ) )
```

The syntax of `defprimitive` will be built on top of `definitial`; it will define
a function of which the arity will be checked.

```
(define-syntax defprimitive
  (syntax-rules ()
    ((defprimitive name value arity)
     (definitial name
       (allocate 1 s.global
         (lambda (a* ss)
           (set! s.global (expand-store (car a*) ss))
           (create-function
            (car a*)
            (lambda (v* s k)
              (if (= arity (length v*))
                  (value v* s k)
                  (wrong "Incorrect arity" 'name) ) ) ) ) ) ) ) ) )
```

As we've become accustomed to doing, we will enrich the initial environment
with the Boolean variables `t` and `f` and with the empty list `nil`, like this:

```
(definitial t (create-boolean #t))
(definitial f (create-boolean #f))
(definitial nil the-empty-list)
```

We'll give two examples of predefined functions, one a predicate and the other
arithmetic. Their arguments are extracted from their representation, and then the
final result is repackaged as it should be, like this:

```
(defprimitive <=
  (lambda (v* s k)
    (if (and (eq? ((car v*) 'type) 'number)
             (eq? ((cadr v*) 'type) 'number) )
        (k (create-boolean (<= ((car v*) 'value) ((cadr v*) 'value))) s)
        (wrong "<= require numbers") ) )
  2 )
(defprimitive *
  (lambda (v* s k)
    (if (and (eq? ((car v*) 'type) 'number)
             (eq? ((cadr v*) 'type) 'number) )
        (k (create-number (* ((car v*) 'value) ((cadr v*) 'value))) s)
        (wrong "* require numbers") ) )
  2 )
```

4.3.12 Dotted Pairs

For the first time among all the interpreters that we've shown so far, the dotted pairs of the Scheme we are defining will not be represented by the dotted pairs of the definition Scheme.

Because of the function `allocate-pair`, constructing a dotted pair is simple enough.

```
(defprimitive cons
  (lambda (v* s k)
    (allocate-pair (car v*) (cadr v*) s k) )
  2 )
```

Reading or modifying fields is also simple, like this:

```
(defprimitive car
  (lambda (v* s k)
    (if (eq? ((car v*) 'type) 'pair)
        (k (s ((car v*) 'car)) s)
        (wrong "Not a pair" (car v*)) ) )
  1 )
(defprimitive set-cdr!
  (lambda (v* s k)
    (if (eq? ((car v*) 'type) 'pair)
        (let ((pair (car v*)))
          (k pair ((pair 'set-cdr) s (cadr v*))) )
        (wrong "Not a pair" (car v*)) ) )
  2 )
```

All values that can be manipulated are coded so that their type can be inspected. Since all objects know how to answer the message **type**, it is simple to write the predicate **pair?**. We'll use **create-boolean** to convert a Boolean from the definition Scheme into a Boolean of the Scheme being defined, like this:

```
(defprimitive pair?
  (lambda (v* s k)
    (k (create-boolean (eq? ((car v*) 'type) 'pair)) s) )
  1 )
```

4.3.13 Comparisons

One of the goals of this interpreter is to specify the predicate for physical comparisons: **eqv?**. That predicate physically compares two objects as well as numbers. That predicate first compares the types of the two objects, then, if they agree, it specifically compares the two objects. Symbols must have the same name to pass the comparison. Booleans and numbers must be the same. Dotted pairs or functions must be allocated to the same address(es).

```
(defprimitive eqv?
  (lambda (v* s k)
    (k (create-boolean
         (if (eq? ((car v*) 'type) ((cadr v*) 'type))
             (case ((car v*) 'type)
               ((null) #t)
```

```
       ((boolean)
        (((car v*) 'boolify)
         (((cadr v*) 'boolify) #t #f)
         (((cadr v*) 'boolify) #f #t) ) )
       ((symbol)
        (eq? ((car v*) 'name) ((cadr v*) 'name)) )
       ((number)
        (= ((car v*) 'value) ((cadr v*) 'value)) )
       ((pair)
        (and (= ((car v*) 'car) ((cadr v*) 'car))
             (= ((car v*) 'cdr) ((cadr v*) 'cdr)) ) )
       ((function)
        (= ((car v*) 'tag) ((cadr v*) 'tag)) )
       (else #f) )
     #f ) )
  s ) )
2 )
```

In fact, the only reason for giving a function an address (other than the one we just mentioned that functions—or more precisely, their closures—are data structures allocated in memory) is that we can then compare functions by means of **eqv?**. Functions are projected onto their addresses, which are entities that are easy to compare since they are merely integers. Notice that comparing dotted pairs does not necessitate any inspection of their contents but only the addresses associated with them. In consequence, comparison is a function with constant cost compared to **equal?**.

The definition of **eqv?** might seem generic since we have defined it as a set of methods for disparate classes. In fact, a clever representation of data let's us cut through type-testing and go directly to comparing the implementation address of objects; we can often reduce that activity to a simple instruction, except possibly for *bignums*.

4.3.14 Starting the Interpreter

Now we'll get right to the interpreter. The toplevel loop is re-invoked in the continuation that it gives to **evaluate**, still insuring the diffusion of the memory state acquired during the most recent interaction.

```
(define (chapter4-interpreter)
  (define (toplevel s)
    (evaluate (read)
              r.global
              s
              (lambda (v ss)
                (display (transcode-back v ss))
                (toplevel ss) ) ) )
  (toplevel s.global) )
```

The basic problem with this interpreter is that for the first time in this book, the data of the Scheme being interpreted are quite different from the underlying Scheme. This difference is particularly noticeable for dotted pairs, that is, for lists that serve internally, for example, to organize arguments submitted to a function. Since the dotted pairs of the two levels (defining and defined languages) are no longer equivalent, we resort to `transcode-back` for decoding the final value that we get. That function runs the value through certain memory state and transforms it into a value of the definition Scheme so that we can then print it. We could equally well have chosen to print it directly without passing by the `display` function of the underlying Scheme.

```
(define (transcode-back v s)
  (case (v 'type)
    ((null)     '())
    ((boolean)  ((v 'boolify) #t #f))
    ((symbol)   (v 'name))
    ((string)   (v 'chars))
    ((number)   (v 'value))
    ((pair)     (cons (transcode-back (s (v 'car)) s)
                      (transcode-back (s (v 'cdr)) s) ) )
    ((function) v) ; why not ?
    (else       (wrong "Unknown type" (v 'type))) ) )
```

4.4 Input/Output and Memory

We haven't yet talked about input/output functions. If we limit ourselves to a single input stream and a single output stream (that is, to the two functions `read` and `display`), then the problem could be treated precisely by adding two supplementary arguments to the interpreter to represent these two streams. The input stream would contain all that would be read, while the output stream would be made up of all that would be written there. We could even assume that the output stream would be the only observable response from the interpreter.

The output stream could be represented by a list of pairs (memory, value)—the ones that we provided one-by-one to the function `transcode-back`. But then what would the input stream be? The question is a subtle one because the values that will be read might contain dotted pairs that could be modified physically themselves. We could, indeed, write (`set-car!` (`read`) `'foo`) and then read (`bar hux`). That observation indicates that the expression read must be installed in the memory current at the moment that `read` is called. The function `transcode` will thus take a value of the underlying Scheme, a memory, and a continuation, and then will call this continuation on the transcoded value and the new memory state in which it has been installed.

```
(define (transcode v s q)
  (cond
    ((null? c)    (q the-empty-list s))
    ((boolean? c) (q (create-boolean c) s))
    ((symbol? c)  (q (create-symbol c) s))
    ((string? c)  (q (create-string c) s))
    ((number? c)  (q (create-number c) s))
    ((pair? c)
     (transcode (car c)
```

```
            s
          (lambda (a ss)
            (transcode (cdr c)
                 ss
              (lambda (d sss)
                (allocate-pair a d sss q) ) ) ) ) ) ) ) )
```

We won't go any further with this variation because it necessitates two more
arguments (to indicate the input and output streams) in all the functions we've
presented in this chapter.

4.5   Semantics of Quotations

Perhaps you've noticed the omission of quotations from the current interpreter.
The form **quote** was always "biblically" simple in the preceding chapters because
the values of the definition Scheme and the Scheme being defined were identical.
Since that identity no longer holds, we can no longer write things like this:

```
(define (evaluate-quote v r s k)                           WRONG
  (k v s) )
```

We would commit an error there by confusing **v** as an element of the program
(the element which *defines* the value to quote) with the value of the form. In other
words, **v** is not the value to return but rather the definition of it. That distinction
was not apparent in the previous interpreters because of their transparent coding.
We must thus make use of **transcode** to transform **v** into a value in the Scheme
being defined, like this:

```
(define (evaluate-quote c r s k)
  (transcode c s k) )
```

This definition is *compositional* because computing the value returned by the
quotation depends only on the arguments provided to **evaluate-quote**. At the
same time, it introduces a breach between the current program in Lisp or Scheme.
Consider only the expression (**quote** (a . b)). By definition, as we have given
it, it is *exactly* equivalent to (**cons** 'a 'b).[12] When we quote a composite object,
like the dotted pair here (a . b), we induce the construction of such an object
in current memory. Thus quotation is a shortcut conveniently expressing the idea
that a value is being constructed. That fact excludes the possibility of the following
expression returning True:

```
(let ((foo (lambda () '(f o o))))
  (eq? (foo) (foo)) )
```

In that example, the local function **foo** synthesizes new values at each call; the
futures of those values are independent of one another; those values are different in
the sense of **eq?**. If we always want True from that computation, then we need to
hack **evaluate-quote** so that it always returns the same value once such a value
has been chosen; that is, we need to make a memo-function. One reason for wanting
such a device is that, in the absence of side effects, (that is, in absence of **eq?**), it is

---

12. In more concise terms, '(a . b)≡'(,'a . ,'b).

not necessary to construct the same value over and over again, and besides, doing
so would be quite costly. Indeed, we can do without that completely.

Of course, in the presence of side effects, the situation is completely different,
as you can see from the following:

```
(define *shared-memo-quotations* '())
(define evaluate-memo-quote
  (lambda (c r s k)
    (let ((couple (assoc c *shared-memo-quotations*)))
      (if (pair? couple)
          (k (cdr couple) s)
          (transcode c s (lambda (v ss)
                           (set! *shared-memo-quotations*
                             (cons (cons c v)
                                   *shared-memo-quotations* ) )
                           (k v ss) )) ) ) ) )
```

However, the preceding memo-function has re-introduced an assignment, starting from a side effect, something for which we would like to reduce the need.
Another solution is to transform the initial program in such a way to regroup all
the quotations into one place where they will be evaluated only once: in the header
of the program. Then every time that a quotation appears, it will be replaced by
a reference to a variable which has already been correctly initialized. Accordingly,
we'll transform the program like this:

```
(let ((foo (lambda () '(f o o))))        (define quote35 '(f o o))
  (eq? (foo) (foo)) )          ⤳       (let ((foo (lambda () quote35)))
                                          (eq? (foo) (foo)) )
```

The program transformed that way will regain the usual semantics of Lisp
without our necessarily touching the definition of **evaluate-quote**.

If we want to get rid of quoting composite objects totally, we could follow up the
transformation we explained earlier and make explicit all the successive allocations
for constructing quoted values. In that way, we get this:

```
(define quote36 (cons 'o '()))
(define quote37 (cons 'o quote36))
(define quote38 (cons 'f quote37))
(let ((foo (lambda () quote38)))
  (eq? (foo) (foo)) )
```

However, that's not the end of this issue since we must also insure that quoted
symbols of the same name still correspond to the same value. For that reason, we'll
continue the transformation like this:

```
(define symbol40 (string->symbol "f"))
(define symbol39 (string->symbol "o"))
(define quote36 (cons symbol39 '()))
(define quote37 (cons symbol39 quote36))
(define quote38 (cons symbol40 quote37))
(let ((foo (lambda () quote38)))
  (eq? (foo) (foo)) )
```

We'll stop there since we can consider strings as primitive objects. We can
translate them as such in assembly language or in C, and it would be too costly to

translate them into their ultimate components: characters!

In the end, we can accept a compositional definition of quoting since, by transforming the program, we can revert to our usual habits. However, we might scrutinize these bad habits that depend on the fact that programs are often read with the function **read** and that thus the expression that appears in a **quote** and that specifies the immediate data to return is coded with the same conventions: same dotted pairs, same symbols, etc. Natural laziness thus impinges on the interpreter to use this same value and thus to return it every time it's needed. In doing so, we share it with all the receivers of the quotation which leads to the misunderstandings that have long been the delight of Lispers of the old school. Consider, for example, the following expressions:

```
(define vowel<=
  (let ((vowels '(#\a #\e #\i #\o #\u)))
    (lambda (c1 c2)
      (memq c2 (memq c1 vowels)) ) ) )

(set-cdr! (vowel<= #\a #\e) '())
(vowel<= #\o #\u)    → ?
```

When those expressions are interpreted, there's a strong possibility that the return value will not be **#t**, and they will provoke an error. Besides, if we print the definition of the function (or if we had made the closed variable **vowels** a global variable instead) then we would see that it changes into this:

```
(define vowel1<=
  (let ((vowels '(#\a #\e)))
    (lambda (c1 c2)
      (memq c2 (memq c1 vowels)) ) ) )
```

By doing so, we make part of the program disappear! The same technique could inversely make the value of the variable **vowels** grow instead of diminishing it. This "memo-visceral" effect happens only with the interpreter; it has no meaning if we compile the preceding program. In effect, if the global variable **vowel<=** is immutable, a call to (**vowel<= #\o #\u**) where the function and all its arguments are known, can be replaced by **#t**. That phenomenon is known as *constant folding*, a technique generalized by partial evaluation, as in [JGS93].

The compiler might also decide to transform the preceding definition after analyzing the possible cases for c_1, like this:

```
(define vowel2<=
  (lambda (c1 c2)
    (case c1
      ((#\a) (memq c2 '(#\a #\e #\i #\o #\u)))
      ((#\e) (memq c2 '(#\e #\i #\o #\u)))
      ((#\i) (memq c2 '(#\i #\o #\u)))
      ((#\o) (memq c2 '(#\o #\u)))
      ((#\u) (eq? c2 #\u))
      (else #f) ) ) )
```

This new equivalent form does not guarantee that (**eq? (cdr (vowel<= #\a #\e)) (vowel<= #\e #\i)**)) since the results do not come from the same quotation. In Lisp, it is not even guaranteed that the value of (**eq? (cdr (vowel<=**

#\a #\e)) (vowel<= #\e #\i)) will always be False because compilers usually retain the right to coalesce constants (that is, to fuse quotations) in order to make them take less space. Compilers might thus transform the preceding definition into this:

```
(define quote82 (cons #\u '()))
(define quote81 (cons #\o quote82))
(define quote80 (cons #\i quote81))
(define quote79 (cons #\e quote80))
(define quote78 (cons #\a quote79))
(define vowel3<=
  (lambda (c1 c2)
    (case c1
      ((#\a) (memq c2 quote78))
      ((#\e) (memq c2 quote79))
      ((#\i) (memq c2 quote80))
      ((#\o) (memq c2 quote81))
      ((#\u) (eq? c2 #\u))
      (else #f) ) ) )
```

This kind of transformation has an impact on shared quotations, and you can see the impact when you use eq?. One simple solution to all these problems is to forbid the modification of the values of quotations. Scheme and COMMON LISP take that approach. To modify the value of a quotation has unknown consequences there.

We could also insist that the value of a quotation must really be immutable, and to do so, we would define quotation like this:

```
(define (evaluate-immutable-quote c r s k)
  (immutable-transcode c s k) )
(define (immutable-transcode c s q)
  (cond
    ((null? c)   (q the-empty-list s))
    ((pair? c)
     (immutable-transcode
      (car c) s (lambda (a ss)
                  (immutable-transcode
                   (cdr c) ss (lambda (d sss)
                                (allocate-immutable-pair
                                 a d sss q ) ) ) ) ) )
    ((boolean? c) (q (create-boolean c) s))
    ((symbol? c)  (q (create-symbol c) s))
    ((string? c)  (q (create-string c) s))
    ((number? c)  (q (create-number c) s)) ) )
(define (allocate-immutable-pair a d s q)
  (allocate 2 s
    (lambda (a* ss)
      (q (create-immutable-pair (car a*) (cadr a*))
         (update (update ss (car a*) a) (cadr a*) d) ) ) ) )
(define (create-immutable-pair a d)
  (lambda (msg)
```

```
(case msg
  ((type)    'pair)
  ((boolify) (lambda (x y) x))
  ((set-car) (lambda (s v) (wrong "Immutable pair")))
  ((set-cdr) (lambda (s v) (wrong "Immutable pair")))
  ((car)     a)
  ((cdr)     d) ) ) )
```

With that definition, any attempt to corrupt a quotation will be detected. This way of distinguishing mutable from immutable dotted pairs can be extended to character strings, and (as in Mesa) we could distinguish modifiable *strings* from unmodifiable *ropes*.

In partial conclusion, it would be better not to attempt to modify values returned by quotations. Both Scheme and COMMON LISP make that recommendation. Even so, we're not yet at the end of the problems posed by quoting. We've already mentioned the technique of coalescing quotations and indicated how that technique can insure equal quotations constructing values that are physically equal according to **eq?**. Conversely, it could happen that we have physical equalities in quotations that we would like to sustain in their values. There are at least two ways to specify such physical equalities: macros and special handling in the reader.

In COMMON LISP, macro-characters carry out special programmable treatments when certain characters are read. For example, **#.**expression "reads" the value of *expression*. In other words, *expression* is read and evaluated[13] on the fly, and its value is reputed to be whatever was read. Accordingly, we can write this:

```
(define bar (quote #.(let ((list '(0 1)))          COMMON LISP
                (set-cdr! (cdr list) list)
                list )))
```

That expression initializes the variable **bar** with a circular list of 0 and 1, alternately. The quotation created that way defines a value that is physically equal to its **cddr**. CLtL2 [Ste90] insures that it will be equal to its **cddr** at execution. You can imagine that this practice makes the transformation of quotations we explained earlier somewhat more complicated because we now have to take into account the cycles for reconstructing them.

The preceding cycle cannot be constructed in Scheme because there we do not have character-macros. Nevertheless, we have macros that serve the same purpose. The following macros cannot be written with **define-syntax** so we use **define-abbreviation**, a macro for defining macros that we'll analyze in Chapter 9. [see p. 311]

```
(define-abbreviation (cycle n)
  (let ((c (iota 0 n)))
    (set-cdr! (last-pair c) c)
    '(quote ,c) ) )
(define bar (cycle 2))
```

In that way, we construct a circular list by means of a number that is known during macro-expansion and that appears in a quotation. We could not have written that quotation by hand because it is not possible to make Scheme read

---

13. We can't say how. That is, we don't know in which environment nor with which continuation.

cyclic data. That's possible in COMMON LISP with the aid of the character-macros #*n*= and #*n*#[14]:

```
(define bar #1=(0 1 . #1#))
```

The current semantics of Scheme seem to exclude such cycles because they correspond to definitions of values that we could not have written by hand. The only legal quotations are, in fact, those that we can write.

In Chapter 9, we'll go more deeply into the many problems posed by macros. [see p. 311]

4.6 Conclusions

Following this chapter, we could give a prodigious amount of advice to Schemers and other Lispers. The precise nature of global variables is complicated, even more so if we consider the problems of modules. Various ideas of equality are subtle and far from widely shared. Finally, quotation is not as simple as it first appears; we should abstain from convoluted quotations.

4.7 Exercises

Exercise 4.1 : Give a functional definition (without side effects) of the function min-max.

Exercise 4.2 : The dotted pairs that we simulated with closures use symbols as messages. Disallow the operations set-car! and set-cdr!, and rewrite the simulation by using only λ-forms.

Exercise 4.3 : Write a definition of eq? comparing dotted pairs with the help of set-car! or set-cdr!.

Exercise 4.4 : Define a new special form of syntax (or α β) to return the value of α if it's True; otherwise, undo all the side effects of the evaluation of α and return what β returns.

Exercise 4.5 : Assignment as we defined it in this chapter returns the value that has just been assigned. Redefine assignment so that its value is the value of the variable before assignment.

Exercise 4.6 : Define the functions apply and call/cc for the interpreter in this chapter.

---

14. In the example, it's necessary to read an object that is part of itself. Consequently, the function **read** must be intelligent enough to allocate a dotted pair and then fill it. You see there the usual paradoxes involving self-referential objects, like #1=#1#.

Exercise 4.7 : Modify the interpreter of this chapter to introduce n-ary functions (that is, functions with a dotted variable).

5
Denotational Semantics

FTER a brief review of λ-calculus, this chapter unveils denotational semantics in much of its glory. It introduces a new definition of Lisp—this time a denotational one—differing little from that of the preceding interpreter but this time associating each program with its meaning in the form of a respectable mathematical object: a term from λ-calculus.

What exactly is a program? A *program* is the description of a computing procedure that aims at a particular result or effect.

We often confuse a program with its executable incarnations on this or that machine; likewise, we sometimes treat the file containing the physical form of a program as its definition, though strictly speaking, we should keep these distinct.

A program is expressed in a *language*; the definition of a language gives a *meaning* to every program that can be expressed by means of that language. The meaning of a program is not merely the value that the program produces during execution since execution may entail reading or interacting with the exterior world in ways that we cannot know in advance. In fact, the meaning of a program is a much more fundamental property, its very essence.

The meaning of a program should be a mathematical object that can be manipulated. We'll judge as sound any transformation of a program, such as, for example, the transformation by boxes that we looked at earlier [see p. 115], if such a transformation is based on a demonstration that it preserves the meaning of every program to which it is applied. The meaning of a program must be a respectable mathematical object in that the meaning must not be ambiguous and it must be susceptible to the tools that have developed over centuries, even millenia, of mathematical practice. To give a meaning to a program is to associate it with an object from another space, a space more obviously mathematical. For example, it would be judicious, even clever, for the the program defining factorial [see p. 27] to be exactly the usual mathematical factorial because then we would know that this definition does, indeed, compute the factorial, and we would also know whether it variants like meta-fact [see p. 63] were really equivalent.

If we want to associate meaning with a program, then we have to search for a mathematical equivalent, but this search forces us to know the properties of the programming language that we're using. The problem is thus to associate a programming language with a method that gives meaning to every program written

in that language. In that sense, we speak of the *semantics* of a programming
language. The semantics of a programming language has more than one use: the
semantics enables us to understand a language so that we can implement it, so
that we can prove the validity of transformations in it, so that we can compare its
characteristics with other languages, and so forth. Indeed, the uses of semantics
are numerous, but semantics are not unique, and diverse methods exist.

The most venerable method of defining a language is surely to choose a *reference
implementation*. Then when we have a question about the language, such questions
as, for example, the value or the effects of such and such a program, then we submit
the issue to the reference implementation, and we accept its answer as if it were
an oracle. The difficulty here, though, is that we can hardly build a theory on
the reference implementation, certainly not if we have to treat it like a black box.
In contrast, if we're really interested in the implementation and consequently try
to open the black box, as it were, we'll find ourselves face to face with a program
written in a certain language, and our ignorance of that language or any ambiguities
in it put us squarely back in the problem of meaning again.

Another approach exploits the idea of a *virtual machine*. With it, we don't
escape entirely from the problem we just mentioned, but we divide it into two
distinct parts. In one part, the language is defined in terms of a virtual machine
having a certain architecture and instruction set. All instructions of the language
are defined by a certain group of instructions in the virtual machine. If we know
how the virtual machine works, then we understand the language. In the other
part, the virtual machine itself is written in an *ad hoc* formalism making it possible
to implement the virtual machine on any reasonable computer.

Many languages have been defined in that way, from PL1 (with VDM) to Le-Lisp
(and LLM3 [Cha80]), PSL [GBM82] or even Gambit above PVM [FM90].

The main difficulty is how to elaborate the virtual machine since it has to be
simultaneously clear in its intention, easy to use, and trivial to implement. To do
all that, we have the choice of machines with stack(s), register(s), driven by trees or
graphs, etc. (This scenario corresponds to an idealized version of programming in
assembly language where the designer would have the freedom to define his or her
own machine.) This technique makes it possible to compare programs by looking
at their translations into the virtual assembler or by examining the trace of their
execution. Since we have recourse here to a machine, even if it is virtual, we call
this technique *operational semantics*.

That strategy has a defect: it requires a non-standard machine, or more precisely, it requires a computing formalism. If, for that formalism, we used a theory
already known to everybody, then we could spare ourselves that machine. A program is above all a function that transforms its input into output. "To execute"
such a function does not require a complicated machine: only a few centuries of
mathematical practice and culture are sufficient "to apply" it. The idea is thus to
transform a program into a function (from an appropriate space of functions). We
call that function its *denotation*. The remaining problem is then to understand the
space of denotations.

For this purpose, λ-calculus is a good choice. Its basis is so simple that everybody agrees about how it works. The semantics of a language then becomes the
process by which we associate a program with its denotation. That process is, in

fact, a function, too. The denotation of a program is the λ-term representing its meaning. Provided by these denotations, the theory of standard λ-calculus makes it possible to determine what a given program computes, whether two programs are equal, and so forth. There are, of course, many variations depending on the nature of the denotations, the type of λ-calculus chosen, the way of constructing the semantic function to associate programs and their denotations, but the structure that we've just explained is what we conventionally call *denotational semantics*.

We should also mention another approach based on the proof of programs by Floyd and Hoare. This approach is known as *axiomatic semantics*. The idea is to define each elementary form of a language by a logical formula, like this: $\{P\}form\{Q\}$. That formula indicates that if P is true before the execution of *form*, and if the execution of *form* terminates, then Q will be true. We can thus specify all the elementary forms of a language and define it axiomatically. You can clearly see the advantage of such a description for the techniques to prove correctness in that language. In contrast, this is a non-constructive procedure so it reveals nothing about the implementation of a language. It doesn't even indicate whether an implementation exists.

Even so, we have not yet exhausted the arsenal of semantics currently in use. We should also mention *natural semantics* as in [Kah87]. It favors the idea of relations (over functions) in a context derived from denotational semantics. There is also *algebraic semantics*, as in [FF89], which reasons in terms of equivalent programs by means of rewrite rules.

5.1 A Brief Review of λ-Calculus

Denotational semantics consists of defining (for a given language) a function, called the *valuation*, that associates each valid program of the language with a term in the denotation space. As the denotation space, we'll choose λ-calculus because of its structural simplicity and its proximity to Scheme, described as an efficient interpreter of λ-calculus in [SS75, Wan84].

Here we'll very briefly cover λ-calculus.[1] Its syntax is simple: the terms of λ-calculus are variables, abstractions, or applications (or combinations since in Lispian terms, functions in λ-calculus are monadic). We'll use **Variable** to indicate the set of possible, usable variables and Λ for the set of terms of λ-calculus. Λ can be defined recursively like this:

$$
\begin{array}{lll}
variable: & \forall x \in \textbf{Variable}, & x \in \Lambda \\
abstraction: & \forall x \in \textbf{Variable}, \forall M \in \Lambda, & \lambda x.M \in \Lambda \\
combination & \forall M, N \in \Lambda, & (MN) \in \Lambda
\end{array}
$$

As usual in Lisp, the syntax is not terribly important, and we could equally well write the terms of λ-calculus in parenthesized form.[2] The set of terms of λ-calculus is thus syntactically a subset of the terms of Scheme reduced to the sole special form `lambda`, like this:

---

1. There's a good introduction to λ-calculus in [Sto77, Gor88]. The "bible" of λ-calculus begins with [Bar84].
2. By the way, that's what McCarthy did in 1960 at MIT.

$$x \qquad \text{(lambda } (x) \; M) \qquad (M \; N)$$

With λ-calculus, we can write functions. There is even a rule for applying them: the β-*reduction*. It simply stipulates that when we apply a function with body M and variable x to a term N, we get a new term which is the body M of the function with the variable x replaced by the term N. We indicate that by this notation: $M[x \rightarrow N]$. That's the usual model for substitution, always used in mathematics without ever being formalized. It's also the rule used in the preceding subset of Scheme (without side effects, with `lambda` as the sole special form) when we apply a function to its argument.

$$\beta\text{-réduction} : \qquad (\lambda x.M \; N) \xrightarrow{\beta} M[x \rightarrow N]$$

The substitution $M[x \rightarrow N]$ is a subtle operation defined by taking care not to capture unrelated variables. Such captures occur only when we make substitutions in the body of abstractions: there we again encounter the problem linked to free variables in the body of functions. The free variables of N must not be captured by the surrounding variables in M as was the case for dynamic binding. In Lispian terms, we should rather say that λ-calculus involves lexical binding. In the following definition of a substitution, we've added a few superfluous parentheses to isolate terms that are substituted.

$$x[x \rightarrow N] = N$$
$$y[x \rightarrow N] = y \qquad \text{with } x \neq y$$
$$(\lambda x.M)[x \rightarrow N] = \lambda x.M$$
$$(\lambda y.M)[x \rightarrow N] = \lambda z.(M[y \rightarrow z][x \rightarrow N]) \text{ with } x \neq y \text{ and } z \text{ not free in } (M \; N)$$
$$(M_1 \; M_2)[x \rightarrow N] = (M_1[x \rightarrow N] \; M_2[x \rightarrow N])$$

A *redex* is a reducible expression, or more precisely, an application in which the first term (that is, the term in the function position) is an abstraction. A β-reduction suppresses a redex. When a term contains no redex (in other words, it cannot be reduced further), we say that the term is in *normal form*. Terms in λ-calculus do not necessarily have a normal form, but when they have one, it is unique because of the Church-Rosser property.

When a term has a normal form, there exists a finite series of β-reductions that convert the original term into the normal form. An *evaluation rule* is a procedure that indicates which redex (if there is more than one) ought to be β-reduced. Unfortunately, there are both good and bad evaluation rules. One good evaluation rule is always to evaluate the redex for which the opening parenthesis is the leftmost. That rule does not necessarily minimize the computation, but it always terminates at the normal form if such a normal form exists. For that reason, we call it *normal order* or *call by name*. A bad evaluation rule—the one that Scheme follows, in fact—is known as *call by value*. In call by value, we apply the function only after having evaluated its arguments. Let's look at a few examples. Here's an example of a term without a normal form:

$$(\omega \; \omega) \quad \text{with } \omega = \lambda x.(x \; x) \qquad \text{since} \quad (\omega \; \omega) \xrightarrow{\beta} (\omega \; \omega) \xrightarrow{\beta} (\omega \; \omega) \xrightarrow{\beta} \ldots$$

In Scheme, that program loops and consequently leads to no term at all, thus certainly not to a normal form.

Here's a term that has a normal form, but the evaluation rule in Scheme prevents us from finding it:

$$((\lambda x.\lambda y.y \; (\omega\omega)) \; z) \quad \xrightarrow{\beta} (\lambda y.y \; z) \quad \xrightarrow{\beta} z$$

In Scheme, that first argument (ω ω) would be computed and loop infinitely, so the normal form would never be found.

Conversely, and also unfortunately, in Scheme we can evaluate a term without a normal form. The reason is that in Scheme we do not reduce terms in the body of `lambda` forms even if there is a redex. For example,

$\lambda x.(\omega\ \omega)$

So why do we cling to that evaluation rule in Scheme if it's not a good one? One reason is that computing by means of call by value is much more efficient than the "good rule," *call by name*, even if that one can be improved to *call by need*. Another reason is that every time Scheme achieves a value in normal form, it's the same value that would have been achieved by the "good rule" anyway since the normal form is after all unique. There is thus a frequent and fortunate coincidence between values produced by both good and bad evaluation rules.

A practical convention in λ-calculus syntactically supports functions with multiple variables by positing that $\lambda xy.M$ is the same as $\lambda x.\lambda y.M$. Reciprocally, to make it easier to apply these functions, we posit that (MN_1N_2) is in fact $((MN_1)N_2)$. That next to last example then becomes even easier to write and to understand as this simply: $(\lambda xy.y\ (\omega\ \omega)\ z)$

There you can see why it's pointless to compute the value bound to the variable x which will not even appear in the final answer.

There's great deal more we could say about the pleasures of λ-calculus, but for them, we'll direct you to fine works on the subject by [Bar84, Gor88, Dil88]. Among other things, we could enrich λ-calculus by supplementary terms, such as integers. When enlarged in that way, it's known as *applied* λ-calculus. We could also add new rules among such terms; for example, $2+2=4$ is known as a δ-*rule*. However, this kind of elaboration is not logically necessary since integers and Booleans can be encoded as λ-terms, and their arithmetic and logical operations can be as well. Even the structure of a list, with `cons`, `car`, `cdr`, can be built up that way, as in [Gor88]. [see **Ex. 4.2**]

In conclusion, we should say that λ-calculus is a highly refined theory that provides us simultaneously a simple but powerful framework for computing. In fact, β-reduction is as powerful though not so complicated as a Turing machine. Equally important, λ-calculus furnishes a basis for equality (two terms are equal if they reduce to the same third term) so we can compare terms. For all those reasons, λ-calculus is an excellent denotation space for our purposes.

5.2 Semantics of Scheme

As we've argued, then, λ-calculus is a great candidate to represent denotation. The preceding interpreter was written in a Scheme without side effects. It defined an evaluation function, `evaluate`, with the following signature:

evaluate : Program × Environment × Continuation × Memory → Value

With a slight effort, we can imagine modifying that signature by currying the first argument (the program) and thus getting this:

Program → (Environment × Continuation × Memory → Value)

We could associate each fragment of a program with a function that expects us to provide only an environment, a continuation, and memory to indicate which value it should return. We'll stop there, that is, with the semantics of Scheme as well as the exact nature of our denotations.

valuation : **Program** → **Denotation**
Denotation : **Environment** × **Continuation** × **Memory** → **Value**

However, the people who practice denotational semantics don't really like parentheses, and they even have strong preferences about the style for elaborating denotations. First of all, they use (and abuse) Greek letters and notation shortened to the point of being elliptic and even cryptic. The reason for such habits is that after much practice, they can keep the semantics of an entire language short enough to fit on one page where anyone can see the whole of it at a glance. This advantage[3] is incompatible, of course, with long identifiers or verbose keywords. The choice of Greek letters is also motivated by the fact that denotations are written in a language that must not be confused with the language that is being defined. Since most of the languages that denotational semanticists are defining are computing languages and thus use only that limited set of characters known as ASCII, Greek letters keep things short and limit confusion. Finally, for greater security, denotations are typed, and the names of variables indicate their type.

We, too, will follow those tenacious conventions. By long and customary usage, functions are indicated by φ. Other entities are usually indicated by the Greek initial of their English name, for example, κ for continuation, α for address, ν for identifier (that is, name), π for program, σ for memory (that is, *store*). But who knows why environments are indicated by ρ?

π	**Program**	ρ	**Environment**
ν	**Identifier**	α	**Address**
σ	**Memory**	ε	**Value**
κ	**Continuation**	φ	**Function**

Each word in boldface in that chart names a *domain* representing objects handled by denotations. You see there all the objects that the preceding chapters introduced. The following chart defines those domains.

$$\begin{aligned} \textbf{Environment} &= \textbf{Identifier} \rightarrow \textbf{Address} \\ \textbf{Memory} &= \textbf{Address} \rightarrow \textbf{Value} \\ \textbf{Value} &= \textbf{Function} + \textbf{Boolean} + \textbf{Integer} + \textbf{Pair} + \dots \\ \textbf{Continuation} &= \textbf{Value} \times \textbf{Memory} \rightarrow \textbf{Value} \\ \textbf{Function} &= \textbf{Value}^* \times \textbf{Continuation} \times \textbf{Memory} \rightarrow \textbf{Value} \end{aligned}$$

As usual, the asterisk indicates repetition. The domain **Value*** is the domain of sequences of **Value**. The sign × indicates a Cartesian product. The sign + represents the disjoint sum of domains; that is, an element of **Value** is an element of **Function** or of **Boolean** or of **Integer**, etc. All types of values are represented by a domain appearing in that sum. The disjoint sum of domains has the property that, when we take an element of **Value**, we know the exact domain that it comes from. Since we've accepted the rule that entities must be typed, we have to declare

---

3. This advantage is even more conspicuous if you recall that the average length of a typical scientific communication is about ten pages.

how and where these changes of domain occur. The expression ε *in***Value** means that we inject the term ϵ in the domain **Value** while $\varepsilon \mid_{\text{Integer}}$ projects the value ϵ in the domain from which it comes (assuming, of course, that ϵ is an integer).

These domains are defined recursively (a mathematically sensitive issue). Moreover, they are known as domains, rather than sets. Without going into detail, we should say that λ-calculus was developed by Alonzo Church in the thirties, but that this construction did not have a mathematical model until after work by Dana Scott around 1970. In short, λ-calculus had proved its usefulness already, but once it had a mathematical model, it was around for good. Since then, properties have been extended in several different ways, producing several different models: D^∞ or $\mathcal{P}_\omega$ in [Sco76, Sto77].

Extensionality is the property that $(\forall x, f(x) = g(x)) \Rightarrow (f = g)$. It is linked to the η-*conversion* that we often take as a supplementary rule of λ-calculus.

$$\eta\text{-conversion}: \quad \lambda x.(M\ x) \xrightarrow{\eta} M \qquad \text{with } x \text{ not free in } M$$

Strangely enough, $\mathcal{P}_\omega$ is extensional because two functions that compute the same thing at every point are equal, whereas D^∞ is not extensional. Is Mother Nature extensional?

Scott has shown that any system of domains recursively defined by means of only $\rightarrow$, $\times$, $+$, *, has a unique solution. In that sense, domains really exist.

An important principle of denotational semantics is *compositionality*: that the meaning of a fragment of a program depends only on the meaning of its components. This principle is the basis of inductive proof that we can carry out within the framework of a language defined in that way. It's also a useful principle from the point of view of the language itself: we can understand a fragment of a program independently of whatever surrounds it.

The valuation function associated with a language usually is indicated by $\mathcal{E}$. To re-enforce the distinction between a program and its semantics, we will enclose fragments of programs within semantic brackets, $[\![$ and $]\!]$. Finally, we'll present valuation case by case, that is, elementary form by elementary form.

5.2.1 References to a Variable

The simplest denotation concerns the value of a variable.

$$\mathcal{E}[\![\nu]\!] = \lambda\rho\kappa\sigma.(\kappa\ (\sigma\ (\rho\ \nu))\ \sigma)$$

The denotation of a reference to a variable (here, ν) is a λ-term that, given an environment ρ, a continuation κ, a memory σ, will determine the address associated with the variable in the environment ($\rho\ \nu$), will submit this address to memory to get the associated value ($\sigma\ (\rho\ \nu)$), will finally return this value to the continuation accompanied by the unmodified memory (since reading memory is non-destructive).

We've used a syntactic convention to write functions with multiple arguments. Nevertheless, if we want, we can write something more exact but less legible, like this:

$$\mathcal{E}[\![\nu]\!] = \lambda\rho.\lambda\kappa.\lambda\sigma.(\kappa\ (\sigma\ (\rho\ \nu))\ \sigma)$$

No need to show off our formalism, so we will abandon this painful and obscure way of writing. In passing, to simplify things even further, we'll adopt the following writing convention, similar to the style of **define** in Scheme. It will remove a few more layers of λ.

$$\mathcal{E}[\![\nu]\!]\rho\kappa\sigma = (\kappa \ (\sigma \ (\rho \ \nu)) \ \sigma)$$

There's a possible error in the denotation of references where the variable does not appear in the environment. That erroneous situation is handled by the initial environment, ρ_0, which is:

$$(\rho_0 \ \nu) = wrong \ \text{``No such variable''}$$

When a variable is not defined in the environment, the searcher will invoke the function *wrong* which, in turn, produces a value generally indicated by $\perp$. This value is absorbent; that is, $\forall f, f\perp = \perp$. Consequently, when an erroneous situation occurs, the entire computation results in $\perp$, a clear indication that an error has occurred. In fact, it is not so much $\perp$ that has this quality of absorbency; it's more the functions that we manipulate that we call *strict*. Specifically, f is strict if and only if $f\perp = \perp$. This convention relieves us to a degree from handling errors and leaves only the most significant part of the denotation.

5.2.2   Sequence

The denotation of a sequence will use an auxiliary valuation that will be the equivalent of the function **eprogn** that you saw in earlier interpreters. We will indicate it by $\mathcal{E}^+$. We chose that name because there is necessarily at least one term in the sequence of forms that it denotes. Still conforming to that tradition, we'll indicate a succession of non-empty forms as π^+. The valuation $\mathcal{E}^+$ will convert a succession of non-empty forms π^+ into a denotation evaluating all the terms in left to right order and returning the value of the last of these forms. Its purpose is that two cases define the sequence, depending on whether it contains only one or more than one form. In Scheme, the meaning of the empty sequence (**begin**) is not specified, a point highlighted by its absence from the following cases:

$$\mathcal{E}[\![(\text{begin } \pi^+)]\!]\rho\kappa\sigma = (\mathcal{E}^+[\![\pi^+]\!] \ \rho \ \kappa \ \sigma)$$

$$\mathcal{E}^+[\![\pi]\!]\rho\kappa\sigma = (\mathcal{E}[\![\pi]\!] \ \rho \ \kappa \ \sigma)$$

$$\mathcal{E}^+[\![\pi \ \pi^+]\!]\rho\kappa\sigma = (\mathcal{E}[\![\pi]\!] \ \rho \ \lambda\varepsilon\sigma_1.(\mathcal{E}^+[\![\pi^+]\!] \ \rho \ \kappa \ \sigma_1) \ \sigma)$$

When the sequence contains only one unique term, then the sequence is equivalent to that term. We may indicate that idea more directly, simply saying this:

$$\mathcal{E}^+[\![\pi]\!] = \mathcal{E}[\![\pi]\!]$$

In terms of λ-calculus, what we just wrote is an η-simplification. We'll avoid such ruffles and flourishes because they make code (or denotations) harder to read by completely masking the natural arity of functions; according to [WL93], they're often there only to look more intelligent anyway.

When the sequence contains more than one term, the denotation calculates the value of the first of these terms and forgets it in order to calculate the other terms. That's the usual definition that we see popping up once more with all the details that you've now become accustomed to. You see clearly here, in just one line, that the memory state resulting from the evaluation of the first term is the one that serves for the evaluation of the following terms. Continuations put the evaluations in sequence, each of them passing the memory they received and used to the next one.

5.2.3 Conditional

The denotation of a conditional is highly conventional and poses hardly any difficulties if we know how to get Booleans into λ-calculus. In fact, Booleans are easy to simulate in λ-calculus. We will define the values True and False as combinators (that is, functions without free variables), like this:

$$\mathbf{T} = \lambda xy.x \qquad \text{et} \qquad \mathbf{F} = \lambda xy.y$$

Intuitively, these definitions both take two values as arguments and return the first or the second. This strategy resembles that of the logical connector **If** which corresponds to the equations:

$$\mathbf{If}(true, p, q) = p \qquad \text{and} \qquad \mathbf{If}(false, p, q) = q$$

Careful: this logical connector has nothing to do with the special form `if` in Scheme. Here, we're not talking about the order of evaluation, but only about the fact that **If** is a *function* which could be defined by a truth table but which is written more simply like this:

$$\mathbf{If}(c, p, q) = (\neg c \vee p) \wedge (c \vee q)$$

If we take into account the code we choose for Booleans, there is a simple way to simulate **If** in λ-calculus: we write this new combinator **IF**, like this:

$$\mathbf{IF}\ c\ p\ q = (c\ p\ q)$$

Just as in ordinary logic, this definition says nothing about the order of the computation but states only a relation among three values. Seen as a function, **If** returns its second argument if the first value is True; it returns the third argument otherwise. Like [FW84], we'll call this function **ef**. In more Lispian terms, we can approximate this function like this:

```
(define (ef v v1 v2)
  (v v1 v2) )
```

To make the notation for a conditional more legible, for the moment, we'll adopt the following syntax from [Sch86]:

$\epsilon_0 \rightarrow \epsilon_1 [] \epsilon_2$

As for R^{4}RS, it uses this:

$\varepsilon_1 \rightarrow \varepsilon_2, \varepsilon_3$.

With these ideas in mind, we articulate the denotation of a conditional like this:

$\mathcal{E}[\![(\text{if } \pi\ \pi_1\ \pi_2)]\!]\rho\kappa\sigma =$
$(\mathcal{E}[\![\pi]\!]\ \rho\ \lambda\varepsilon\sigma_1.\ (boolify\ \varepsilon)$
$\qquad\qquad \rightarrow\ (\mathcal{E}[\![\pi_1]\!]\ \rho\ \kappa\ \sigma_1)$
$\qquad\qquad []\ (\mathcal{E}[\![\pi_2]\!]\ \rho\ \kappa\ \sigma_1)\ \sigma)$

The function *boolify* converts a value into a Boolean since every value in Scheme is implicitly a truth value. A conditional thus starts by evaluating its condition with a new continuation that decides which branch of the conditional to follow according to the value of the condition. Careful: the conditional in λ-calculus looks as though it behaves like our old friend `if-then-else`, but they differ in a significant respect: nothing, absolutely nothing, indicates the order of evaluation. Inside λ-calculus, we could very well evaluate the condition and two branches of a conditional in parallel in order to choose among them once all the computations are complete.

The consequences of that fact are important because we cannot look at λ-calculus (in some ways, the language in which we are defining a new interpreter) as we used to look at Scheme: there is no idea in λ-calculus of any order in evaluation. To articulate the denotation defining a conditional, we could say that the value of a conditional is (among the two possible values) the one indicated by the value of the condition.

There is no unfair competition nor hidden side effects if we evaluate the two branches of a conditional in parallel since each has its own set of parameters defining the computation, and besides, we're in a pure language completely stripped of side effects. For example, there's no problem with the following expression, even though you might think that if we don't evaluate the components in the "right" order, we're courting disaster:

```
(if (= 0 q) 1 (/ p q))
```

That expression tests whether the divisor is null before the division, and in that case, it returns the value 1. Its denotation simply states that the choice between the value 1 and the quotient of p divided by q will be made according to whether or not q is null.

The difficulty of this operator comes from the habit we might have acquired from Scheme and from the fact that we see λ-calculus through the evaluation rule for Scheme. To a degree, we diminish the distance between Scheme and λ-calculus by rewriting the denotation of a conditional like this:

$$\mathcal{E}[\![(\text{if } \pi \; \pi_1 \; \pi_2)]\!]\rho\kappa\sigma = (\mathcal{E}[\![\pi]\!] \; \rho \; \lambda\varepsilon\sigma_1.((boolify \; \varepsilon) \rightarrow \; \mathcal{E}[\![\pi_1]\!][\!] \; \mathcal{E}[\![\pi_2]\!]\rho \; \kappa \; \sigma_1) \; \sigma)$$

We've introduced a little sequentiality here since the redices have been ordered. The value of the conditional serves only to choose the denotation of the elected branch, the one invoked independently.

The problem with this new definition is knowing whether it is still equivalent to the preceding one. It entails proving whether the two denotations are the same for a given program. To do so, it suffices to show this:

$$(boolify \; \varepsilon) \rightarrow \; (\mathcal{E}[\![\pi_1]\!] \; \rho \; \kappa \; \sigma)[\!] \; (\mathcal{E}[\![\pi_2]\!] \; \rho \; \kappa \; \sigma) = ((boolify \; \varepsilon) \rightarrow \; \mathcal{E}[\![\pi_1]\!][\!] \; \mathcal{E}[\![\pi_2]\!]\rho \; \kappa \; \sigma)$$

That equivalence is obviously false in Scheme because of the fact that evaluation is ordered. To convince ourselves, all we have to do is make π_2 an expression that loops. However, denotations are terms from λ-calculus and thus have to be compared according to the laws of λ-calculus. Consequently, we simply distribute the application of a conditional.

When we see how cryptic that syntax is, we're prompted to adopt a more eloquent notation for denotational `if-then-else`:

$\mathcal{E}[\![(\texttt{if }\ \pi\ \pi_1\ \pi_2)]\!]\rho\kappa\sigma =$
$(\mathcal{E}[\![\pi]\!]\ \rho\ \lambda\varepsilon\sigma_1.(\ \textbf{if}\ (\textit{boolify}\ \varepsilon)$
$\qquad\qquad\qquad \textbf{then}\ \mathcal{E}[\![\pi_1]\!]$
$\qquad\qquad\qquad \textbf{else}\ \mathcal{E}[\![\pi_2]\!]$
$\qquad\qquad\qquad \textbf{endif}\ \rho\ \kappa\ \sigma_1)\ \sigma)$

5.2.4 Assignment

The denotation for assignment is simple. The version we present here has the newly
assigned value for its value.

$\mathcal{E}[\![(\texttt{set!}\quad \nu\ \pi)]\!]\rho\kappa\sigma = (\mathcal{E}[\![\pi]\!]\ \rho\ \lambda\varepsilon\sigma_1.(\kappa\ \varepsilon\ \sigma_1[(\rho\ \nu) \to \varepsilon])\ \sigma)$

$f[y \to z] = \lambda x.\ \textbf{if}\ y = x\ \textbf{then}\ z\ \textbf{else}\ (f\ x)\ \textbf{endif}$

Memory is extended to reflect the assignment that's carried out, so the value
ε is associated with the address of the variable ν. We produce this extension by
using suggestive *ad hoc* notation: $\sigma[\alpha \to \varepsilon]$. There is other, similar notation, like
$[\alpha \to \varepsilon]\sigma$ in [Sch86] or $[\varepsilon/\alpha]\sigma$ in [Sto77] or even $\sigma[\varepsilon/\alpha]$ in [Gor88, CR91b].

Let's enrich our λ-calculus with a few supplementary functions. We'll write
sequences between these delimiters: $\langle$ and $\rangle$. We'll indicate the concatenation of
sequences by this sign: §. To extract terms from a sequence, we'll indicate the
extraction of the ith term of a sequence by $\langle\varepsilon_1, \varepsilon_2, \dots, \varepsilon_n\rangle \downarrow i$. To indicate the
truncation of the first i terms from a sequence, (that is, to get this: $\langle\varepsilon_{i+1}, \dots, \varepsilon_n\rangle$),
we'll write: $\langle\varepsilon_1, \dots, \varepsilon_n\rangle \dagger i$. The notation $\#\varepsilon^*$ indicates the length of the sequence
ε^*. All this notation can be defined in pure λ-calculus, but doing so obscures the
presentation a bit, so without sacrilege, we'll use $\downarrow_1$, $\dagger 1$, $\#$, and § as the denotational
equivalent of **car**, **cdr**, **length**, and **append**.

We'll extend the extension of the environment itself to a group of points and
images. In what follows, we'll assume that the two sequences, x^* and y^*, have the
same length.

$f[y^* \overset{*}{\to} z^*] =\ \textbf{if}\ \#y^* > 0\ \textbf{then}\ f[y^* \dagger 1 \overset{*}{\to} z^* \dagger 1][y^* \downarrow_1 \to z^* \downarrow_1]\ \textbf{else}\ f\ \textbf{endif}$

5.2.5 Abstraction

As a first effort, we'll denote only functions with fixed arity, that is, those lacking
a dotted variable.

$\mathcal{E}[\![(\texttt{lambda }(\nu^*)\ \pi^+)]\!]\rho\kappa\sigma =$
$(\kappa\ \textit{in}\textbf{Value}(\lambda\ \varepsilon^*\kappa_1\sigma_1.$
$\qquad\qquad\qquad \textbf{if}\ \#\varepsilon^* = \#\nu^*$
$\qquad\qquad\qquad \textbf{then}\ \textit{allocate}\ \sigma_1\ \#\nu^*$
$\qquad\qquad\qquad\qquad \lambda\ \sigma_2\alpha^*.$
$\qquad\qquad\qquad\qquad\quad (\mathcal{E}^+[\![\pi^+]\!]\ \rho[\nu^* \overset{*}{\to} \alpha^*]\ \kappa_1\ \sigma_2[\alpha^* \overset{*}{\to} \varepsilon^*])$
$\qquad\qquad\qquad \textbf{else}\ \textit{wrong}\ \text{``}\textbf{Incorrect arity''}$
$\qquad\qquad\qquad \textbf{endif}\ )\ \sigma)$

The injection *in***Value** takes a λ-term representing a function and converts it to
a value. The inverse operation will appear in the functional application.

When a function is invoked and after its arity has been verified, new addresses are allocated to be associated with variables of the function and to contain the values that they take for this invocation. Allocation of addresses in memory is carried out by the function *allocate*; it takes memory, the addresses to allocate, and a kind of "continuation" that it will invoke on the allocated addresses and the new memory where these addresses have been allocated. *allocate* is a real function, so when its arguments are equal, it makes corresponding equal results, but its exact definition is generally left vague in order not to overburden denotations. Besides, its definition is so low-level technically that it is not very interesting.

The function *allocate* is polymorphic; α can represent any type. Here's it signature:

$$\textbf{Memory} \times \textbf{NaturalInteger} \times (\textbf{Memory} \times \textbf{Address}^* \to \alpha) \to \alpha$$

(A precise definition of *allocate* appeared in the previous chapter. [see p. 132])

5.2.6 Functional Application

Functions are meant to be applied, so here's the denotation of application. Once again, we'll use a new auxiliary valuation: $\mathcal{E}^*$, a kind of denotational `evlis`.

$$\mathcal{E}[\![(\pi\ \pi^*)]\!]\rho\kappa\sigma = (\mathcal{E}[\![\pi]\!]\ \rho\ \lambda\varphi\sigma_1.(\mathcal{E}^*[\![\pi^*]\!]\ \rho\ \lambda\varepsilon^*\sigma_2.(\varphi\mid_{\textbf{Function}}\ \varepsilon^*\ \kappa\ \sigma_2)\ \sigma_1)\ \sigma)$$

$$\mathcal{E}^*[\![\ ]\!]\rho\kappa\sigma = (\kappa\ \langle\rangle\ \sigma)$$

$$\mathcal{E}^*[\![\pi\ \pi^*]\!]\rho\kappa\sigma = (\mathcal{E}[\![\pi]\!]\ \rho\ \lambda\varepsilon\sigma_1.(\mathcal{E}^*[\![\pi^*]\!]\ \rho\ \lambda\varepsilon^*\sigma_2.(\kappa\ \langle\varepsilon\rangle\S\varepsilon^*\ \sigma_2)\ \sigma_1)\ \sigma)$$

Continuations that use $\mathcal{E}^*$ don't wait for a value but for a sequence of values. That was not the case for the valuation $\mathcal{E}^+$. The values of κ in these definitions thus have the following type:

$$\textbf{Value}^* \times \textbf{Memory} \to \textbf{Value}$$

5.2.7 call/cc

Our fast trip through denotations would not be complete without a definition of a function essential to the semantics of Scheme: `call/cc`. We define it like this:

$$(\sigma_0(\rho_0[\![\texttt{call/cc}]\!])) =$$
$in\textbf{Value}(\lambda\ \varepsilon^*\kappa\sigma.$
    if $1 = \#\varepsilon^*$
    then $(\ \varepsilon^*\downarrow_1\mid_{\textbf{Function}}$
        $\langle in\textbf{Value}(\lambda\ \varepsilon^*_1\kappa_1\sigma_1.$
            if $1 = \#\varepsilon^*_1$
            then $(\kappa\ \varepsilon^*_1\downarrow_1\ \sigma_1)$
            else *wrong* "Incorrect arity"
            endif $)\rangle\ \kappa\ \sigma)$
    else *wrong* "Incorrect arity"
    endif $)$

Notice that there are the successive injections and projections between the various domains of **Value** and **Function**. The denotation itself is not really any more complicated than the other ways of programming `call/cc` that you've already seen in Chapter 3. [see p. 95]

5.2.8 Tentative Conclusions

We've just managed, case by case, to define a function that associates a λ-term with every program. There's no doubt about the existence of this function because we have used the principle of composition to construct it. If we allow syntactically recursive programs as in [Que92a], then we need a little more theory to prove that we have a well defined function.

For now, we can show that the semantics of primitive special forms in Scheme can be seen at a glance: Table 5.1.

Of course, the special form `quote` is missing (quotation poses problems, as you remember [see p. 140]), and we won't see functions with variable arity until later. We're also missing `eq?` for comparing functions and a number of other predefined functions. We have, however, gotten `call/cc`, appearing in its simplest guise. Other functions of the predefined library, like `cons`, `car`, `set-cdr!` can be simulated in this subset by closures without adding any hidden features. On that basis, we can talk about the essentials independently of any additional functions that we might add. The basis of the language, that is, its special forms and primitive functions like `call/cc`, are enough to anchor our understanding.

Still, we insist that being able to see the essentials of Scheme in a single table with this degree of detail is well worth such austere coding practices. In this way, we're bringing to an end our progress since taking off from using an entire Scheme to define an approximate Scheme in the first chapter. Now we've arrived at using λ-calculus to define an entire Scheme.

5.3 Semantics of λ-calcul

Defining the essentials of a language in so few signs is one of the attractions of Scheme. Indeed, for just that reason, functional languages generally become veritable experimental linguistic laboratories for introducing new constructions and for studying them in terms of basic, fundamental, and common traits. Depending on the characteristics that we want to analyze, we could, of course, start from a more restricted linguistic basis, such as λ-calculus itself. That assertion is not really tautologic; it provides a second example of the denotation of a language that is different but related: the semantics of λ-calculus itself.

Let's focus first on the syntax. Since syntax has no importance for us here other than clarifying our ideas, we'll deliberately choose a Scheme-like syntax:

$$x \qquad (\text{lambda } (x) \ M) \qquad (M \ N)$$

Now let's determine the domains to manipulate. λ-calculus has no idea of assignment nor continuation, and we'll take advantage of those facts. While we're at it, we'll limit ourselves to a non-applied λ-calculus with closures as the only values. Here, then, are the domains. You can see that they are a restricted set of the domains of Scheme.

$$\mathcal{E}[\![\nu]\!] = \lambda\rho\kappa\sigma.(\kappa\ (\sigma\ (\rho\ \nu))\ \sigma)$$

$$\mathcal{E}[\![(\texttt{set!}\quad \nu\ \pi)]\!]\rho\kappa\sigma = (\mathcal{E}[\![\pi]\!]\ \rho\ \lambda\varepsilon\sigma_1.(\kappa\ \varepsilon\ \sigma_1[(\rho\ \nu)\to\varepsilon])\ \sigma)$$

$$\mathcal{E}[\![(\texttt{if}\ \pi\ \pi_1\ \pi_2)]\!]\rho\kappa\sigma =$$
$$(\mathcal{E}[\![\pi]\!]\ \rho\ \lambda\varepsilon\sigma_1.\ \textbf{if}\ (boolify\ \varepsilon)$$
$$\textbf{then}\ (\mathcal{E}[\![\pi_1]\!]\ \rho\ \kappa\ \sigma_1)$$
$$\textbf{else}\ (\mathcal{E}[\![\pi_2]\!]\ \rho\ \kappa\ \sigma_1)$$
$$\textbf{endif}\quad \sigma)$$

$$\mathcal{E}[\![(\texttt{lambda}\ (\nu^*)\ \pi^+)]\!]\rho\kappa\sigma =$$
$$(\kappa\ in\text{Value}(\lambda\ \varepsilon^*\kappa_1\sigma_1.$$
$$\textbf{if}\ \#\varepsilon^* = \#\nu^*$$
$$\textbf{then}\quad allocate\ \sigma_1\ \#\nu^*$$
$$\lambda\ \sigma_2\alpha^*.$$
$$(\mathcal{E}^+[\![\pi^+]\!]\ \rho[\nu^*\xrightarrow{*}\alpha^*]\ \kappa_1\ \sigma_2[\alpha^*\xrightarrow{*}\varepsilon^*])$$
$$\textbf{else}\ wrong\ \text{``Incorrect arity"}$$
$$\textbf{endif}\quad)\ \sigma)$$

$$\mathcal{E}[\![(\pi\ \pi^*)]\!]\rho\kappa\sigma = (\mathcal{E}[\![\pi]\!]\ \rho\ \lambda\varphi\sigma_1.(\mathcal{E}^*[\![\pi^*]\!]\ \rho\ \lambda\varepsilon^*\sigma_2.(\varphi\ |_{\texttt{Function}}\ \varepsilon^*\ \kappa\ \sigma_2)\ \sigma_1)\ \sigma)$$

$$\mathcal{E}^*[\![\pi\ \pi^*]\!]\rho\kappa\sigma = (\mathcal{E}[\![\pi]\!]\ \rho\ \lambda\varepsilon\sigma_1.(\mathcal{E}^*[\![\pi^*]\!]\ \rho\ \lambda\varepsilon^*\sigma_2.(\kappa\ \langle\varepsilon\rangle\S\varepsilon^*\ \sigma_2)\ \sigma_1)\ \sigma)$$

$$\mathcal{E}^*[\![\ ]\!]\rho\kappa\sigma = (\kappa\ \langle\rangle\ \sigma)$$

$$\mathcal{E}[\![(\texttt{begin}\ \pi^+)]\!]\rho\kappa\sigma = (\mathcal{E}^+[\![\pi^+]\!]\ \rho\ \kappa\ \sigma)$$

$$\mathcal{E}^+[\![\pi]\!]\rho\kappa\sigma = (\mathcal{E}[\![\pi]\!]\ \rho\ \kappa\ \sigma)$$

$$\mathcal{E}^+[\![\pi\ \pi^+]\!]\rho\kappa\sigma = (\mathcal{E}[\![\pi]\!]\ \rho\ \lambda\varepsilon\sigma_1.(\mathcal{E}^+[\![\pi^+]\!]\ \rho\ \kappa\ \sigma_1)\ \sigma)$$

$$(\sigma_0(\rho_0[\![\texttt{call/cc}]\!])) =$$
$$in\text{Value}(\lambda\ \varepsilon^*\kappa\sigma.$$
$$\textbf{if}\ 1 = \#\varepsilon^*$$
$$\textbf{then}\ (\ \varepsilon^*\downarrow_1|_{\texttt{Function}}$$
$$(in\text{Value}(\lambda\ \varepsilon^*_1\kappa_1\sigma_1.$$
$$\textbf{if}\ 1 = \#\varepsilon^*_1$$
$$\textbf{then}\ (\kappa\ \varepsilon^*_1\downarrow_1\ \sigma_1)$$
$$\textbf{else}\ wrong\ \text{``Incorrect arity"}$$
$$\textbf{endif}\quad)\rangle\ \kappa\ \sigma)$$
$$\textbf{else}\ wrong\ \text{``Incorrect arity"}$$
$$\textbf{endif}\quad)$$

Table 5.1 Essential Scheme

π **Program**
ν **Identifier**
ρ **Environment**   = **Identifier** $\rightarrow$ **Value**
ε **Value**   = **Function**
φ **Function**   = **Value** $\rightarrow$ **Value**

We'll call the valuation function $\mathcal{L}$. It will associate a λ-term with a denotation, that is, another λ-term. Consequently, the valuation has this signature:

$\mathcal{L}$: **Program** $\rightarrow$ (**Environment** $\rightarrow$ **Value**)

The only task left to do is to define that function, case by case, by analyzing the various syntactic possibilities, as in Table 5.2.

$$\mathcal{L}[\![\nu]\!]\rho = (\rho\ \nu)$$
$$\mathcal{L}[\![(\text{lambda } (\nu)\ \pi)]\!]\rho = \lambda\varepsilon.(\mathcal{L}[\![\pi]\!]\ \rho[\nu \rightarrow \varepsilon])$$
$$\mathcal{L}[\![(\pi\ \pi')]\!]\rho = ((\mathcal{L}[\![\pi]\!]\ \rho)(\mathcal{L}[\![\pi']\!]\ \rho))$$

Table 5.2 Semantics of λ-calculus

This denotation is scrupulous with respect to the order of evaluation of terms in a functional application (or combination). In effect, the combination is transformed into a combination and nothing is said about the order.

The valuation $\mathcal{L}$ is defined recursively. There's no problem in doing that here because of compositionality: all the recursive calls are carried out in smaller programs, and the terminal case is provided by reference to the variables.

λ-calculus is a special case for us because we already have a very clear idea of the semantics of its terms. We can prove (see [Sto77, page 158]) that the change to denotations preserves all its necessary properties and, notably, β-reduction.

Denotation from λ-calculus is the basis of denotation in functional languages with no side effects nor continuations. When side effects and continuations are introduced, it's generally necessary to introduce an explicit order of evaluation to handle them correctly. If we also want to add assignment, then we have to split the environment by introducing addresses, the famous boxes of Chapter 4 or references as in ML. [see p. 114]

5.4   Functions with Variable Arity

In this section, we'll show how to incorporate functions with variable arity into Scheme. These functions are special in that they handle excess arguments that they receive as a list. Consequently, at every invocation, there is an allocation disguised as dotted pairs, which, by the way, can be very expensive if these functions are used frequently. In a certain way, the antidote to functions with a list of dotted variables is the primitive function **apply**; it converts a list of values into the missing arguments. Functions of variable arity are thus inevitably associated in Scheme with lists, so we must define the denotations of the usual functions (like **cons**, **car**, **set-cdr!**) on lists.

Dotted pairs are represented by the domain **Pair**. It appears as one of the components of the disjoint sum defining **Value**. The domain **Pair** itself will be defined as in the preceding chapter, by the Cartesian product of two addresses.

$$\textbf{Value} = \quad \textbf{Function} + \textbf{Boolean} + \textbf{Integer} + \textbf{Pair} + \dots$$
$$\textbf{Pair} = \quad \textbf{Address} \times \textbf{Address}$$

The denotations of **cons**, **car**, and **set-cdr!** (we need to show at least one side effect on dotted pairs) are highly conventional; they hardly differ at all from the programming style we used in the preceding chapter. The only difficulties now are in notation because, for example, we have to interpret $\varepsilon^* \downarrow_1|_{\textbf{Pair}}\downarrow_2$ in this way: $\varepsilon^* \downarrow_1$ is the first argument of the function, a value, which is then projected on the domain of dotted pairs, $|_{\textbf{Pair}}$; if it is not a dotted pair, we get $\bot$; finally, we extract the address of its **cdr** from this dotted pair, that is, its second component, $\downarrow_2$.

$(\sigma_0(\rho_0\llbracket\textbf{cons}\rrbracket)) =$
$in\textbf{Value}(\lambda\varepsilon^*\kappa\sigma.$ **if** $2 = \#\varepsilon^*$
$\qquad\qquad$ **then** $allocate\ \sigma\ 2\ \lambda\sigma_1\alpha^*.(\kappa\ in\textbf{Value}(\langle\alpha^* \downarrow_1, \alpha^* \downarrow_2\rangle))\ \sigma_1[\alpha^* \overset{*}{\to} \varepsilon^*])$
$\qquad\qquad$ **else** *wrong* "**incorrect arity**"
$\qquad\qquad$ **endif** $)$

$(\sigma_0(\rho_0\llbracket\textbf{car}\rrbracket)) =$
$in\textbf{Value}(\lambda\varepsilon^*\kappa\sigma.$ **if** $1 = \#\varepsilon^*$
$\qquad\qquad$ **then** $(\kappa\ (\sigma\ \varepsilon^* \downarrow_1|_{\textbf{Pair}}\downarrow_1)\ \sigma)$
$\qquad\qquad$ **else** *wrong* "**incorrect arity**"
$\qquad\qquad$ **endif** $)$

$(\sigma_0(\rho_0\llbracket\textbf{set-cdr!}\rrbracket)) =$
$in\textbf{Value}(\lambda\varepsilon^*\kappa\sigma.$ **if** $2 = \#\varepsilon^*$
$\qquad\qquad$ **then** $(\kappa\ \varepsilon^* \downarrow_1\ \sigma[\varepsilon^* \downarrow_1|_{\textbf{Pair}}\downarrow_2\to \varepsilon^* \downarrow_2])$
$\qquad\qquad$ **else** *wrong* "**incorrect arity**"
$\qquad\qquad$ **endif** $)$

Once the structure of lists is known, **apply** is simple to specify. We gather the arguments from the second (since the first argument is the function to invoke) to the last, excluded. This gathering must be a list that we flatten. We then gather the successive terms into a sequence of arguments to which we apply the specified function.

$(\sigma_0(\rho_0\llbracket\textbf{apply}\rrbracket)) =$
$in\textbf{Value}(\lambda\varepsilon^*\kappa\sigma.$ **if** $\#\varepsilon^* \geq 2$
$\qquad\qquad$ **then** $(\varepsilon^* \downarrow_1|_{\textbf{Function}}\ (collect\ \varepsilon^* \dagger 1)\ \kappa\ \sigma)$
$\qquad\qquad\qquad$ **whererec** $collect = \lambda\varepsilon^*_1.$ **if** $\varepsilon^*_1 \dagger 1 = \langle\rangle$
$\qquad\qquad\qquad\qquad\qquad$ **then** $(flat\ \varepsilon^*_1 \downarrow_1)$
$\qquad\qquad\qquad\qquad\qquad$ **else** $\langle\varepsilon^*_1 \downarrow_1\rangle\S(collect\ \varepsilon^*_1 \dagger 1)$
$\qquad\qquad\qquad\qquad\qquad$ **endif**
$\qquad\qquad$ **and** $flat = \lambda\varepsilon.$ **if** $\varepsilon \in \textbf{Pair}$
$\qquad\qquad\qquad\qquad$ **then** $\langle(\sigma\ \varepsilon\ |_{\textbf{Pair}}\downarrow_1)\rangle\S(flat\ (\sigma\ \varepsilon\ |_{\textbf{Pair}}\downarrow_2))$

$$\textbf{else } \langle\rangle$$
$$\textbf{endif}$$
$$\textbf{else } wrong \text{ ``Incorrect arity''}$$
$$\textbf{endif })$$

Now we can actually get to functions with variable arity. For them, we'll change the denotation of the special form **lambda** and introduce a particular valuation function. Its only role will be to create bindings between variables and values. We'll call this new valuation $\mathcal{B}$ for *binding*. Its signature is related to the signature of denotations, the signature of $\mathcal{E}$. More precisely, we'll use an abbreviation τ as a shortcut and write this:

$$\tau \quad \equiv \quad \textbf{Value}^* \times \textbf{Environment} \times \textbf{Continuation} \times \textbf{Memory}$$
$$\mathcal{E}: \quad \textbf{Program} \rightarrow \tau \rightarrow \textbf{Value}$$
$$\mathcal{B}: \quad \textbf{ListofVariables} \rightarrow (\tau \rightarrow \textbf{Value}) \times \tau \rightarrow \textbf{Value}$$

$\mathcal{B}$, the binding valuation, binds a variable to the address that contains its value only after the arity has been verified by **lambda**. When that succeeds, it runs through the list of variables, and the corresponding locations are allocated one by one. The lexical environment where the function was defined is progressively enlarged. Finally, the body of the function is evaluated. Here, then, is the new way of presenting functions of fixed arity:

$$\mathcal{E}[\![(\textbf{lambda } (\nu^*) \ \pi^+)]\!]\rho\kappa\sigma =$$
$$(\kappa \ in\textbf{Value}(\lambda\varepsilon^*\kappa_1\sigma_1. \ \textbf{if } \#\varepsilon^* = \#\nu^*$$
$$\textbf{then } ((\mathcal{B}[\![\nu^*]\!] \ \lambda\varepsilon^*_1\rho_1\kappa_2\sigma_2.(\mathcal{E}^+[\![\pi^+]\!] \ \rho_1 \ \kappa_2 \ \sigma_2))\varepsilon^* \ \rho \ \kappa_1 \ \sigma_1)$$
$$\textbf{else } wrong \text{ ``Incorrect arity''}$$
$$\textbf{endif }) \ \sigma)$$

$$\mathcal{B}[\![\nu \ \nu^*]\!]\mu = (\mathcal{B}[\![\nu]\!] \ (\mathcal{B}[\![\nu^*]\!] \ \mu))$$

$$\mathcal{B}[\![\ ]\!]\mu = \mu$$

$$\mathcal{B}[\![\nu]\!]\mu =$$
$$\lambda\varepsilon^*\rho\kappa\sigma.allocate \ \sigma \ 1 \ \lambda\sigma_1\alpha^*. \ \textbf{let } \alpha = \alpha^* \!\downarrow_1$$
$$\textbf{in } (\mu \ \varepsilon^* \dagger 1 \ \rho[\nu \rightarrow \alpha] \ \kappa \ \sigma_1[\alpha \rightarrow \varepsilon^* \!\downarrow_1])$$

To handle functions of variable arity, we will introduce a new case in the denotation of **lambda** with a dotted list of variables as well as the appropriate binding clause. That clause takes a sequence of values, converts it into a list of values (a real list made up of real dotted pairs) and binds it to the dotted variable. The co-existence of functions with multiple arity, of the function **apply**, and of side effects (as specified in Scheme) means that fresh dotted pairs have to be allocated. So the following expression should return False:

```
(let ((arguments (list 1 2 3)))
  (apply (lambda args (eq? args arguments)) arguments) )
```

An evaluator that wants to share dotted pairs has to prove beforehand that doing so does not alter the semantics of the program.

Here, finally, are the denotations of functions with multiple arity:

$$\mathcal{E}[\![(\textbf{lambda } (\nu^* \ . \ \nu) \ \pi^+)]\!]\rho\kappa\sigma =$$
$$(\kappa \ in\textbf{Value}(\lambda \ \varepsilon^*\kappa_1\sigma_1.$$

if $\#\varepsilon^* \geq \#\nu^*$
then $(\;(\mathcal{B}[\![\nu^*]\!]\;(\mathcal{B}[\![.\quad\nu]\!]\;\lambda\,\varepsilon^*_1\rho_1\kappa_2\sigma_2.$
$$(\mathcal{E}^+[\![\pi^+]\!]\;\rho_1\;\kappa_2\;\sigma_2)\;))$$
$$\varepsilon^*\;\rho\;\kappa_1\;\sigma_1)$$
else *wrong* "Incorrect arity"
endif $)\;\sigma)$

$\mathcal{B}[\![.\quad\nu]\!]\mu =$
$\lambda\,\varepsilon^*\rho\kappa\sigma.$
$\quad(\textit{listify}\;\varepsilon^*\;\sigma\;\lambda\,\varepsilon\sigma_1.$
$$\textit{allocate}\;\sigma_1\;1$$
$$\lambda\,\sigma_2\alpha^*.$$
$$\textbf{let}\;\alpha = \alpha^*\downarrow_1$$
$$\textbf{in}\;(\mu\;\langle\rangle\;\rho[\nu\to\alpha]\;\kappa\;\sigma_2[\alpha\to\varepsilon])\quad)$$
$\textbf{whererec}\;\textit{listify} = \lambda\,\varepsilon^*_1\sigma_1\kappa_1.$
$$\textbf{if}\;\#\varepsilon^*_1 > 0$$
$$\textbf{then}\quad\textit{allocate}\;\sigma_1\;2$$
$$\lambda\,\sigma_2\alpha^*.$$
$$\textbf{let}\;\kappa_2 = \lambda\,\varepsilon\sigma_3.$$
$$(\kappa_1\;\textit{in}\textbf{Value}(\alpha^*)\;\sigma_3[\alpha^*\downarrow_2\to\varepsilon])$$
$$\textbf{in}\;(\textit{listify}\;\varepsilon^*_1\dagger 1\;\sigma_2[\alpha^*\downarrow_1\to\varepsilon^*_1\downarrow_1]\;\kappa_2)$$
$$\textbf{else}\;(\kappa_1\;\textit{in}\textbf{Value}(\langle\rangle)\;\sigma_1)$$
$$\textbf{endif}$$

Here you can see that the denotation of non-trivial characteristics of Scheme, such as functions of variable arity, necessitates a non-negligible denotational programming effort. In fact, we've written a veritable interpreter. When you compare the elegance of the description of the kernel with the preceding lines, you see that adding an interesting but minor trait nearly doubles the size of the definition; we won't mention how cryptic the addition makes the definition.

5.5   Evaluation Order for Applications

Occasionally in electronic news groups, there are violent, almost religious flames about this characteristic in the various standards for Scheme. Up to now, this point has been unchanging: that the order for evaluating terms of a functional application is not specified. Not specifying the evaluation order discourages everyone from writing programs that depend on evaluation order, but it also makes searching for errors in this area particularly difficult. A great many programs, even some written by recognized authorities, depend obscurely on the order of evaluation, especially when continuations are mixed in. For our part, we favor left to right order; it corresponds to the conventional direction for reading many languages, and it makes searching for errors at least more systematic.

Two objections from the opposing party are interesting in this context. The first is that many languages do not impose this order. Among them, the C programming language does not. Thus if we directly compile (foo (f x) (g x y)) in C as foo(f(x),g(x,y)), then nothing is sure about the order produced, and it can be expensive to impose order here.

The second argument is more subtle. In a world without order, we can impose one by using **begin** to impose a sequence explicitly. In contrast, if an order is imposed, then there is no longer a way to write a program where the order is left unspecified. We're reduced in such a case to something like using a random order generator that prescribes a particular order to follow at execution time—an expensive solution at best. [see **Ex. 5.4**]

Order is not imposed in C so that the compiler can consider the terms of an application in whatever order it needs or finds most efficient, notably with respect to allocating registers.

Explicit order simplifies program debugging by eliminating one source of indeterminism. If the order is not prescribed, two executions of the same program can turn out differently, not leading to the same result. Consider this example[4]:

```
(define (dynamically-changing-evaluation-order?)
  (define (amb)
    (call/cc (lambda (k) ((k #t) (k #f)))) )
  (if (eq? (amb) (amb))
      (dynamically-changing-evaluation-order?)
      #t ) )
```

The internal function **amb** returns True or False according to the evaluation order. If the order changes dynamically, then the function **dynamically-changing-evaluation-order?** halts; otherwise, it loops indefinitely. R^4RS does not stipulate anything that would necessarily make this program loop or halt. If order were imposed, then obviously this program loops forever.

In this discussion, we have to distinguish the implementation language clearly. An implementation absolutely must choose an evaluation order when it evaluates an application. It might decide to adopt left to right order for all applications, or right to left, like MacScheme, or some other order, depending on its whim of the moment. I know of no implementation that, having chosen an order for a particular application, changes that order dynamically. In practice, order is usually chosen at compile time and it's not questioned afterwards. The language may not impose an order, but the implementation is free to choose one and publish the choice; that's legal.

The problem that interests us now is how to specify that no order is prescribed. The solution we propose is to change the structure of denotation subtly. A denotation has been a λ-term waiting for an environment, a continuation, and memory to return a value. Our choice about returning a value has been somewhat limiting because in fact the result of an evaluation is twofold: it includes a value and, in addition, the resulting state of memory. For that reason, we could equally well take the pair (value, memory) as the image of a denotation. We'll actually transcend this question altogether by naming a codomain of denotations, **Result**, and we'll leave its definition a little vague for the moment.

Since more than one evaluation order is possible, then rather than returning a unique response, a denotation could return a set of possible responses among which one would be chosen according to obscure criteria left to the discretion of the implementation. We'll modify the preceding valuation $\mathcal{E}$ to return the set of all

---

4. This program was implemented in collaboration with Matthias Felleisen.

possible responses now, and we'll introduce $\mathcal{N}$ to choose one among them. We'll indicate the set of parts of Q as $\mathcal{P}(Q)$. The signatures then become these:

$$\mathcal{E}: \quad \textbf{Program} \to \textbf{Value}^* \times \textbf{Environment} \times \textbf{Continuation} \times \textbf{Memory}$$
$$\to \mathcal{P}(\textbf{Result})$$
$$\mathcal{N}: \quad \textbf{Program} \to \textbf{Value}^* \times \textbf{Environment} \times \textbf{Continuation} \times \textbf{Memory}$$
$$\to \textbf{Result}$$

The valuation $\mathcal{N}$ is defined straightforwardly as calling the function *oneof*; the definition of *oneof* is left to the implementation; it chooses the one it wants among all the possible results.

$$\mathcal{N}[\![\pi]\!]\rho\kappa\sigma = (oneof \ (\mathcal{E}[\![\pi]\!] \ \rho \ \kappa \ \sigma))$$

Now we have to modify the denotation of a functional application to return all possible values. Semantics inspires the technique we'll use. To say that there is no evaluation order is to say that when confronted with an application, the evaluator chooses one of the terms, say, π_{i_0}, evaluates it to get its value, ε_{i_0}, then chooses a second term, say, π_{i_1}, evaluates it in turn and gets ε_{i_1}, and continues that way to the last term. The values $\varepsilon_{i_0}, \varepsilon_{i_1}, \ldots$ are then re-ordered into $\varepsilon_0, \varepsilon_1 \ldots$, and the first among them is applied to the others. Notice the order of choices as it's been described. It would be quite different to fix the order of evaluation of all terms before the evaluation of the first one, as was done in R[3,4]RS. Let's take an example. Not only will this function print an undetermined digit when called, but the returned continuation when invoked will also print another undetermined digit.

```
(define (one-two-three)
   (call/cc (lambda (k)
              ((begin (display 1)(call/cc k))
               (begin (display 2)(call/cc k))
               (begin (display 3)(call/cc k)) ) )) )
```

The denotation of the application without order will "implement" exactly what we articulated earlier. It will consider all the possible choices of terms, aided by the function *forall* which applies its first argument (a ternary function) to all the possible cuts of its second argument (a list). The function *cut* chops a list into two segments; the first contains the first i terms of the list; all the other terms occur in the second. The continuation (the third argument of *cut*) is finally applied to these two segments. The programming is quite subtle, a good example of the continuation passing style. Sophie Anglade and Jean-Jacques Lacrampe, in [ALQ95], collaborated on the following definitions.

$$\mathcal{E}[\![(\pi_0 \ \pi_1 \ \ldots \ \pi_n)]\!]\rho\kappa\sigma =$$
$$((\textit{possible-paths} \ \langle \mathcal{E}[\![\pi_0]\!], \mathcal{E}[\![\pi_1]\!], \ldots \mathcal{E}[\![\pi_n]\!]\rangle)\rho \ \lambda\varepsilon^*\sigma_1.(\varepsilon^* \downarrow_1|_{\textbf{Function}} \ \varepsilon^* \dagger 1 \ \kappa \ \sigma_1) \ \sigma)$$

$$(\textit{possible-paths} \ \mu^+) =$$
$$\lambda \ \rho\kappa\sigma.$$
$$\quad \textbf{if} \ \#\mu^+ \dagger 1 > 0$$
$$\quad \textbf{then} \ (\textit{forall} \ \lambda \ \mu^+{}_1\mu\mu^+{}_2.$$
$$\qquad\qquad (\mu \ \rho \ \lambda \ \varepsilon\sigma_1.$$
$$\qquad\qquad\qquad (\ (\textit{possible-paths} \ \mu^+{}_1\S\mu^+{}_2)$$
$$\qquad\qquad\qquad \rho \ \lambda \ \varepsilon^*\sigma_2.$$
$$\qquad\qquad\qquad\qquad \textbf{let} \ \kappa_1 = \lambda \ \varepsilon^*{}_1\varepsilon^*{}_2.$$

$$(\kappa\ \varepsilon^*{}_1\S\langle\varepsilon\rangle\S\varepsilon^*{}_2\ \sigma_2)$$
$$\mathbf{in}\ (cut\ \#\mu^+{}_1\ \varepsilon^*\ \kappa_1)\ \ \sigma_1)\ \ \sigma)\ \ \mu^+)$$

$\quad\quad\mathbf{else}\ (\ \mu^+\downarrow_1$
$\quad\quad\quad\quad\rho\ \lambda\ \varepsilon\sigma_1.$
$\quad\quad\quad\quad\quad\quad(\kappa\ \langle\varepsilon\rangle\ \sigma_1)\ \ \sigma)$
$\quad\quad\mathbf{endif}$

$(forall\ \varphi\ l) =$
$(loop\ \langle\rangle\ l\downarrow_1\ \ l\dagger 1)$
$\quad\mathbf{whererec}\ loop = \lambda l_1\varepsilon l_2.(\varphi\ l_1\ \varepsilon\ l_2)\ \cup\ \mathbf{if}\ \#l_2 > 0$
$\quad\quad\quad\quad\quad\quad\quad\quad\quad\quad\quad\quad\quad\mathbf{then}\ (loop\ l_1\S\langle\varepsilon\rangle\ l_2\downarrow_1\ \ l_2\dagger 1)$
$\quad\quad\quad\quad\quad\quad\quad\quad\quad\quad\quad\quad\quad\mathbf{else}\ \emptyset$
$\quad\quad\quad\quad\quad\quad\quad\quad\quad\quad\quad\quad\quad\mathbf{endif}$

$(cut\ \iota\ \varepsilon^*\ \kappa) =$
$(accumulate\ \langle\rangle\ \iota\ \varepsilon^*)$
$\quad\mathbf{whererec}\ accumulate = \lambda l\iota_1 l_1.\ \ \mathbf{if}\ \iota_1 > 0$
$\quad\quad\quad\quad\quad\quad\quad\quad\quad\quad\quad\quad\mathbf{then}\ (accumulate\ \langle l_1\downarrow_1\rangle\S l\ \iota_1{-}1\ l_1\dagger 1)$
$\quad\quad\quad\quad\quad\quad\quad\quad\quad\quad\quad\quad\mathbf{else}\ (\kappa\ (reverse\ l)\ l_1)$
$\quad\quad\quad\quad\quad\quad\quad\quad\quad\quad\quad\quad\mathbf{endif}$

For all these variations about the order of evaluation, all were sequential—a point imposed by Scheme. The terms might not be evaluated in a particular order (they are "disordered," as it were), but they still have to be evaluated one after another. In that light, the only possible responses to the following program are (3 5) or (4 3), but in no case is (3 3) possible.

```
(let ((x 1)(y 2))
   (list (begin (set! x (+ x y)) x)
         (begin (set! y (+ x y)) y) ) )
```

In contrast, the new valuation $\mathcal{E}$ applied to the following program allows two possible responses: 1 or 2. A given implementation will compute only one, but it will be one of those foreseen.

```
(call/cc (lambda (k) ((k 1) (k 2))))   → 1 or 2
```

5.6 Dynamic Binding

The idea of dynamic binding is not only important but also useful, and it has prevailed so long in Lisp interpreters that we really have to give it one of its possible denotations. To do so, we'll extend the denotation of the Scheme we've already explained so far, and we'll add to that a few special forms for handling this new type of binding. There are, in fact, many kinds of dynamic binding using special forms or specialized functions. [see p. 50] Traditionally, Scheme exploits this latter solution to avoid tampering with the denotation of its kernel. Unfortunately, certain functions, though they respect the function calling protocol, perturb this ideal. Just think about `call/cc`: it requires continuations. The denotation of dynamic binding implies the existence of an environment for storing these bindings. For that reason, we'll introduce a new environment wherever needed. The kernel of a Scheme without embellishments appears in Table 5.3.

$\mathcal{E}[\![\nu]\!]\rho\delta\kappa\sigma = (\kappa\ (\sigma\ (\rho\ \nu))\ \sigma)$

$\mathcal{E}[\![(\text{if } \pi\ \pi_1\ \pi_2)]\!]\rho\delta\kappa\sigma =$
$(\mathcal{E}[\![\pi]\!]\ \rho\ \delta\ \lambda\varepsilon\sigma_1.(\ \textbf{if } (boolify\ \varepsilon)$
$\qquad\qquad\qquad \textbf{then } \mathcal{E}[\![\pi_1]\!]$
$\qquad\qquad\qquad \textbf{else } \mathcal{E}[\![\pi_2]\!]$
$\qquad\qquad\qquad \textbf{endif }\ \rho\ \delta\ \kappa\ \sigma_1)\ \sigma)$

$\mathcal{E}[\![(\text{set! }\ \nu\ \pi)]\!]\rho\delta\kappa\sigma = (\mathcal{E}[\![\pi]\!]\ \rho\ \delta\ \lambda\varepsilon\sigma_1.(\kappa\ \varepsilon\ \sigma_1[(\rho\ \nu) \to \varepsilon])\ \sigma)$

$\mathcal{E}[\![(\text{lambda } (\nu^*)\ \pi^+)]\!]\rho\delta\kappa\sigma =$
$(\kappa\ in\text{Value}(\lambda\ \varepsilon^*\delta_1\kappa_1\sigma_1.$
$\qquad\qquad\qquad \textbf{if } \#\varepsilon^* = \#\nu^*$
$\qquad\qquad\qquad \textbf{then }\ allocate\ \sigma_1\ \#\nu^*$
$\qquad\qquad\qquad\qquad \lambda\ \sigma_2\alpha^*.$
$\qquad\qquad\qquad\qquad\qquad (\mathcal{E}^+[\![\pi^+]\!]\ \rho[\nu^* \xrightarrow{*} \alpha^*]\ \delta_1\ \kappa_1\ \sigma_2[\alpha^* \xrightarrow{*} \varepsilon^*])$
$\qquad\qquad\qquad \textbf{else } wrong \text{ "Incorrect arity"}$
$\qquad\qquad\qquad \textbf{endif }\ )\ \sigma)$

$\mathcal{E}[\![(\pi\ \pi^*)]\!]\rho\delta\kappa\sigma =$
$(\mathcal{E}[\![\pi]\!]\ \rho\ \delta\ \lambda\ \varphi\sigma_1.$
$\qquad\qquad (\mathcal{E}^*[\![\pi^*]\!]\ \rho\ \delta\ \lambda\ \varepsilon^*\sigma_2.$
$\qquad\qquad\qquad (\ \varphi\ |_{\textbf{Function}}$
$\qquad\qquad\qquad\qquad \varepsilon^*\ \delta\ \kappa\ \sigma_2)\quad \sigma_1)\ \sigma)$

$\mathcal{E}^*[\![\pi\ \pi^*]\!]\rho\delta\kappa\sigma = (\mathcal{E}[\![\pi]\!]\ \rho\ \delta\ \lambda\varepsilon\sigma_1.(\mathcal{E}^*[\![\pi^*]\!]\ \rho\ \delta\ \lambda\varepsilon^*\sigma_2.(\kappa\ \langle\varepsilon\rangle\S\varepsilon^*\ \sigma_2)\ \sigma_1)\ \sigma)$

$\mathcal{E}^*[\![\ ]\!]\rho\delta\kappa\sigma = (\kappa\ \langle\rangle\ \sigma)$

$\mathcal{E}[\![(\text{begin } \pi^+)]\!] = \mathcal{E}^+[\![\pi^+]\!]$

$\mathcal{E}^+[\![\pi]\!]\rho\delta\kappa\sigma = (\mathcal{E}[\![\pi]\!]\ \rho\ \delta\ \kappa\ \sigma)$

$\mathcal{E}^+[\![\pi\ \pi^+]\!]\rho\delta\kappa\sigma = (\mathcal{E}[\![\pi]\!]\ \rho\ \delta\ \lambda\varepsilon\sigma_1.(\mathcal{E}^+[\![\pi^+]\!]\ \rho\ \delta\ \kappa\ \sigma_1)\ \sigma)$

$(\sigma_0(\rho_0[\![\text{call/cc}]\!])) =$
$in\text{Value}(\lambda\ \varepsilon^*\delta\kappa\sigma.$
$\qquad\qquad \textbf{if } 1 = \#\varepsilon^*$
$\qquad\qquad \textbf{then } (\ \varepsilon^* \downarrow_1 |_{\textbf{Function}}$
$\qquad\qquad\qquad \langle in\text{Value}(\lambda\ \varepsilon^*_1\delta_1\kappa_1\sigma_1.$
$\qquad\qquad\qquad\qquad\qquad \textbf{if } 1 = \#\varepsilon^*_1$
$\qquad\qquad\qquad\qquad\qquad \textbf{then } (\kappa\ \varepsilon^*_1\downarrow_1\ \sigma_1)$
$\qquad\qquad\qquad\qquad\qquad \textbf{else } wrong \text{ "Incorrect arity"}$
$\qquad\qquad\qquad\qquad\qquad \textbf{endif }\ )\rangle\ \delta\ \kappa\ \sigma)$
$\qquad\qquad \textbf{else } wrong \text{ "Incorrect arity"}$
$\qquad\qquad \textbf{endif }\ )$

Table 5.3 Scheme and dynamic binding

The dynamic environment, identified by δ, follows a very different path from the lexical environment ρ because it is passed as an argument to functions that can exploit the current dynamic environment that way. It is also different from memory, indicated by σ, which is *single-threaded*: every step of a computation takes the current memory as input, consults it or modifies it, and passes it to the next step. Memory is thus unique since we never need the preceding version of it. The dynamic environment is not like memory because, for example, it is common to all the terms of a functional application that share it.

The dynamic environment is defined by the domain **DynEnv** like this:

$$\delta \quad \textbf{DynEnv} \quad = \textbf{Identifier} \rightarrow \textbf{Value}$$

There are two special forms for handling dynamic bindings: `dynamic-let` and `dynamic`. `dynamic-let` establishes a dynamic binding between a *variable* and a *value* while its *body* is being computed. `dynamic-let` knows how to handle only one unique variable, but that fact does not lessen the power of the language, nor even its ease of use. `dynamic` returns the value of a dynamic variable; it raises an error if the variable has not yet been defined. Since we have not defined any way of modifying such a binding, the dynamic environment directly associates the name of variables with their values without any intermediate addresses. You can see the semantics of these two special forms in Table 5.4. Here's their syntax:

```
(dynamic-let (variable value) body ...)
(dynamic variable)
```

$(\delta_0 \ \nu) = wrong$ "`No such dynamic variable`"

$\mathcal{E}[\![(\texttt{dynamic} \ \nu)]\!] \rho \delta \kappa \sigma = (\kappa \ (\delta \ \nu) \ \sigma)$

$\mathcal{E}[\![(\texttt{dynamic-let} \ (\nu \ \pi) \ \pi^+)]\!] \rho \delta \kappa \sigma =$
$(\mathcal{E}[\![\pi]\!] \ \rho \ \delta \ \lambda \varepsilon \sigma_1.(\mathcal{E}^+[\![\pi^+]\!] \ \rho \ \delta[\nu \rightarrow \varepsilon] \ \kappa \ \sigma_1) \ \sigma)$

Table 5.4 Special forms of dynamic binding

Those two denotations are straightforward. They enlarge or search the dynamic environment and thus provide a new name space, one for dynamic variables—those that must not be confused with truly lexical variables. Once again, you can see from a short example using only a few Greek letters how powerful denotations are. They lend their aptitude to anyone who can decypher them.

The idea of a dynamic environment is very important. Not only does it serve dynamic variables; it also works for functions that handle errors, for escapes with dynamic extent, or for concepts that control computations, as in [HD90, QD93]. Here, for example, is a simplistic (and not very good) protocol for trapping errors: every time an anomaly occurs, the implementation constructs an object describing the anomaly and applies the value of the dynamic variable `*error*` to it. In that way, we protect ourselves from any possible error by means of the form `dynamic-let` binding `*error*` to an *ad hoc* function. As an example of this protocol, Scheme specifies that an attempt to open a non-existing file raises an error but provides no function to know whether the file exists. We could then program a predicate indicating whether a file exists at the exact moment that the predicate is called, like this:

```
(define (probe-file filename)
  (dynamic-let (*error* (lambda (anomaly) #f))
    (call-with-input-file filename
      (lambda (port) #t) ) ) )
```

That's just an approximate definition because, in fact, we have to test whether the anomaly really has to do with the error "absent file" and not, for example, with the error "no more input ports available." To handle such errors correctly, an evaluation must cooperate by constructing the right objects to represent anomalies.

5.7   Global Environment

In this section, we'll study the global environment, denoting it in several different ways. Just as we did when we introduced dynamic bindings, we'll denote the essence of Scheme by adding a global environment. Like the local environment ρ, this global environment γ transforms identifiers (names) into addresses. The global environment will faithfully accompany memory: every step of a computation will return memory and a global environment, possibly one that has been modified. Table 5.5 defines an essential Scheme with an explicit global environment. However, we've removed denotations involved with reference to a variable and to assignment from this definition.

5.7.1   Global Environment in Scheme

On this basis, we'll be able to construct many possible definitions of the global environment. Scheme stipulates that   *(i)* we can get the value of a variable only if it exists and is initialized; *(ii)* we can modify a variable only if it exists; *(iii)* redefining a variable is comparable to assignment.

To express those first two rules denotationally, we have to be able to test whether or not a variable appears in an environment. Thus instead of the codomain of environments being the address space, we'll enlarge this codomain with a point that differs from addresses. That point will denote the absence of a variable. In denotational terms, we'll do this:

$$\textbf{LocalEnvironment}:\quad \textbf{Identifier} \rightarrow \textbf{Address} + \{\textit{no-such-binding}\}$$
$$\textbf{GlobalEnvironment}:\quad \textbf{Identifier} \rightarrow \textbf{Address} + \{\textit{no-such-global-binding}\}$$

As a consequence now, the denotations for referring to a variable and for assigning a variable are straightforward: first, we check whether the variable is local, then whether it is global. This check produces an address which we then use to read the value of the variable. Of course, the initial environments have to match this coding.

$$(\rho_0 \; \nu) = \textit{no-such-binding}$$

$$(\gamma_0 \; \nu) = \textit{no-such-global-binding}$$

$\mathcal{E}[\![(\text{if } \pi \ \pi_1 \ \pi_2)]\!]\rho\gamma\kappa\sigma =$
$(\mathcal{E}[\![\pi]\!] \ \rho \ \gamma \ \lambda\varepsilon\gamma_1\sigma_1. \ \textbf{if } (boolify \ \varepsilon)$
$\qquad\qquad\qquad \textbf{then } (\mathcal{E}[\![\pi_1]\!] \ \rho \ \gamma_1 \ \kappa \ \sigma_1)$
$\qquad\qquad\qquad \textbf{else } (\mathcal{E}[\![\pi_2]\!] \ \rho \ \gamma_1 \ \kappa \ \sigma_1)$
$\qquad\qquad\qquad \textbf{endif } \ \sigma)$

$\mathcal{E}[\![(\text{lambda } (\nu^*) \ \pi^+)]\!]\rho\gamma\kappa\sigma =$
$(\kappa \ in\text{Value}(\lambda \ \varepsilon^*\gamma_1\kappa_1\sigma_1.$
$\qquad\qquad\qquad \textbf{if } \#\varepsilon^* = \#\nu^*$
$\qquad\qquad\qquad \textbf{then } allocate \ \sigma_1 \ \#\nu^*$
$\qquad\qquad\qquad\qquad \lambda \ \sigma_2\alpha^*.$
$\qquad\qquad\qquad\qquad\quad (\mathcal{E}^+[\![\pi^+]\!] \ \rho[\nu^* \xrightarrow{*} \alpha^*] \ \gamma_1 \ \kappa_1 \ \sigma_2[\alpha^* \xrightarrow{*} \varepsilon^*])$
$\qquad\qquad\qquad \textbf{else } wrong \ \text{``Incorrect arity''}$
$\qquad\qquad\qquad \textbf{endif }) \ \gamma \ \sigma)$

$\mathcal{E}[\![(\pi \ \pi^*)]\!]\rho\gamma\kappa\sigma =$
$(\mathcal{E}[\![\pi]\!] \ \rho \ \gamma \ \lambda\varphi\gamma_1\sigma_1.(\mathcal{E}^*[\![\pi^*]\!] \ \rho \ \gamma_1 \ \lambda\varepsilon^*\gamma_2\sigma_2.(\varphi \ |_{\textbf{Function}} \ \varepsilon^* \ \gamma_2 \ \kappa \ \sigma_2) \ \sigma_1) \ \sigma)$

$\mathcal{E}^*[\![\pi \ \pi^*]\!]\rho\gamma\kappa\sigma =$
$(\mathcal{E}[\![\pi]\!] \ \rho \ \gamma \ \lambda\varepsilon\gamma_1\sigma_1.(\mathcal{E}^*[\![\pi^*]\!] \ \rho \ \gamma \ \lambda\varepsilon^*\gamma_2\sigma_2.(\kappa \ \langle\varepsilon\rangle\S\varepsilon^* \ \gamma_2 \ \sigma_2) \ \sigma_1) \ \sigma)$

$\mathcal{E}^*[\![\,]\!]\rho\gamma\kappa\sigma = (\kappa \ \langle\rangle \ \gamma \ \sigma)$

$\mathcal{E}[\![(\text{begin } \pi^+)]\!]\rho\gamma\kappa\sigma = (\mathcal{E}^+[\![\pi^+]\!] \ \rho \ \gamma \ \kappa \ \sigma)$

$\mathcal{E}^+[\![\pi]\!]\rho\gamma\kappa\sigma = (\mathcal{E}[\![\pi]\!] \ \rho \ \gamma \ \kappa \ \sigma)$

$\mathcal{E}^+[\![\pi \ \pi^+]\!]\rho\gamma\kappa\sigma = (\mathcal{E}[\![\pi]\!] \ \rho \ \gamma \ \lambda\varepsilon\gamma_1\sigma_1.(\mathcal{E}^+[\![\pi^+]\!] \ \rho \ \gamma_1 \ \kappa \ \sigma_1) \ \sigma)$

$(\sigma_0(\rho_0[\![\text{call/cc}]\!])) =$
$in\text{Value}(\lambda \ \varepsilon^*\gamma\kappa\sigma.$
$\qquad\qquad \textbf{if } 1 = \#\varepsilon^*$
$\qquad\qquad \textbf{then } (\ \varepsilon^* \downarrow_1 |_{\textbf{Function}}$
$\qquad\qquad\qquad\qquad \langle in\text{Value}(\lambda \ \varepsilon^*_1\gamma_1\kappa_1\sigma_1.$
$\qquad\qquad\qquad\qquad\qquad\qquad \textbf{if } 1 = \#\varepsilon^*_1$
$\qquad\qquad\qquad\qquad\qquad\qquad \textbf{then } (\kappa \ \varepsilon^*_1\downarrow_1 \ \gamma_1 \ \sigma_1)$
$\qquad\qquad\qquad\qquad\qquad\qquad \textbf{else } wrong \ \text{``Incorrect arity''}$
$\qquad\qquad\qquad\qquad\qquad\qquad \textbf{endif })\rangle \ \gamma \ \kappa \ \sigma)$
$\qquad\qquad \textbf{else } wrong \ \text{``Incorrect arity''}$
$\qquad\qquad \textbf{endif })$

Table 5.5 Scheme and a global environment

$\mathcal{E}[\![\nu]\!] =$

$\lambda\rho\gamma\kappa\sigma.$ **let** $\alpha = (\rho\ \nu)$

in **if** $\alpha = no\text{-}such\text{-}binding$

then **let** $\alpha_1 = (\gamma\ \nu)$

in **if** $\alpha_1 = no\text{-}such\text{-}global\text{-}binding$

then *wrong* "No such variable"

else $(\kappa\ (\sigma\ \alpha_1)\ \gamma\ \sigma)$

endif

else $(\kappa\ (\sigma\ \alpha)\ \gamma\ \sigma)$

endif

$\mathcal{E}[\![(\texttt{set!}\quad \nu\ \pi)]\!]\rho\gamma\kappa\sigma =$

$(\mathcal{E}[\![\pi]\!]\ \rho\ \gamma\ \lambda\varepsilon\gamma_1\sigma_1.$ **let** $\alpha = (\rho\ \nu)$

in **if** $\alpha = no\text{-}such\text{-}binding$

then **let** $\alpha_1 = (\gamma_1\ \nu)$

in **if** $\alpha_1 = no\text{-}such\text{-}global\text{-}binding$

then *wrong* "No such variable"

else $(\kappa\ \varepsilon\ \gamma_1\ \sigma_1[\alpha_1 \to \varepsilon])$

endif

else $(\kappa\ \varepsilon\ \gamma_1\ \sigma_1[\alpha \to \varepsilon])$

endif $\sigma)$

We assume that the definition of global variables is carried out by the special operator **define**; also we assume that the special form (**define** ν π) defines (or redefines) the *global* variable ν. For the moment, we'll ignore internal definitions (introduced by the internal forms (**define** ...)); they are purely syntactic; for that reason, we'll appoint **define-global** for external definitions. Here, then, is the denotation of a definition, whether the effect of introducing a new variable or the effect of modifying an existing one.

$\mathcal{E}[\![(\texttt{define-global}\ \nu\ \pi)]\!]\rho\gamma\kappa\sigma =$

$(\mathcal{E}[\![\pi]\!]\ \rho\ \gamma\ \lambda\varepsilon\gamma_1\sigma_1.$ **let** $\alpha = (\gamma\ \nu)$

in **if** $\alpha = no\text{-}such\text{-}global\text{-}binding$

then *allocate* σ_1 1 $\lambda\sigma_2\alpha^*.(\kappa\ \varepsilon\ \gamma_1[\nu \to \alpha^* \downarrow_1]\ \sigma_2[\alpha^* \downarrow_1 \to \varepsilon])$

else $(\kappa\ \varepsilon\ \gamma_1\ \sigma_1[\alpha \to \varepsilon])$

endif $\sigma)$

These definitions characterize the behavior specified in Scheme except for the definition of the initial global environment γ_0, which we've left a little vague; it could contain only standard variables, or it could add a few additional ones, or it might even contain every imaginable variable that we might ever need. In that latter case, it would not know about non-existing variables, but we might encounter uninitialized variables.

5.7.2 Automatically Extendable Environment

Certain Lisp systems let the first assignment of a free variable be equivalent to its definition. It's easy to modify the semantics of assignment to incorporate the effect of a definition if the variable does not yet exist.

$\mathcal{E}[\![(\text{set}! \quad \nu \ \pi)]\!]\rho\gamma\kappa\sigma =$
$(\mathcal{E}[\![\pi]\!] \ \rho \ \gamma \ \lambda \ \varepsilon\gamma_1\sigma_1.$

$\qquad\qquad \textbf{let } \alpha = (\rho \ \nu)$
$\qquad\qquad \textbf{in } \textbf{if } \alpha = \textit{no-such-binding}$
$\qquad\qquad\qquad \textbf{then } \textbf{let } \alpha_1 = (\gamma_1 \ \nu)$
$\qquad\qquad\qquad\qquad \textbf{in } \textbf{if } \alpha_1 = \textit{no-such-global-binding}$
$\qquad\qquad\qquad\qquad\qquad \textbf{then } \textit{allocate } \sigma_1 \ 1$
$\qquad\qquad\qquad\qquad\qquad\qquad \lambda \ \sigma_2\alpha^*.$
$\qquad\qquad\qquad\qquad\qquad\qquad\quad (\kappa \ \varepsilon \ \gamma_1[\nu \to \alpha^* \downarrow_1] \ \sigma_2[\alpha^* \downarrow_1 \to \varepsilon])$
$\qquad\qquad\qquad\qquad\qquad \textbf{else } (\kappa \ \varepsilon \ \gamma_1 \ \sigma_1[\alpha_1 \to \varepsilon])$
$\qquad\qquad\qquad\qquad\qquad \textbf{endif}$
$\qquad\qquad\qquad \textbf{else } (\kappa \ \varepsilon \ \gamma_1 \ \sigma_1[\alpha \to \varepsilon])$
$\qquad\qquad\qquad \textbf{endif} \qquad \sigma)$

Such a variation is useful because the form **define** is no longer necessary and can be conflated with **set!**. The disadvantage is that a misspelling of the name of a variable can be hard to find since it does not automatically lead to an error at its first use.

5.7.3 Hyperstatic Environment

Inside a hyperstatic global environment, functions enclose not only the local definition environment but also the current global environment. We express that idea straightforwardly by a simple change in the denotation of an abstraction as it appeared in Table 5.5.

$\mathcal{E}[\![(\text{lambda} \ (\nu^*)\pi^+)]\!]\rho\gamma\kappa\sigma =$
$(\kappa \ in\text{Value}(\lambda \ \varepsilon^*\gamma_1\kappa_1\sigma_1.$
$\qquad\qquad \textbf{if } \#\varepsilon^* = \#\nu^*$
$\qquad\qquad \textbf{then } \textit{allocate } \sigma_1 \ \#\nu^*$
$\qquad\qquad\qquad \lambda \ \sigma_2\alpha^*.$
$\qquad\qquad\qquad (\mathcal{E}^+[\![\pi^+]\!] \ \rho[\nu^* \xrightarrow{*} \alpha^*] \ \gamma \ \kappa_1 \ \sigma_2[\alpha^* \xrightarrow{*} \varepsilon^*])$
$\qquad\qquad \textbf{else } \textit{wrong} \text{ "Incorrect arity"}$
$\qquad\qquad \textbf{endif} \ ) \ \gamma \ \sigma)$

That semantics is compatible with assignment in Scheme, where assignment can modify only existing variables. However, defining new variables on the fly by assignment leads to confusion. Just consider this:

```
(define (weird v)
  (set! a-new-variable v) )
```

The assignment inside the function **weird** extends the global environment that it closes, and it does so at every invocation since that extended global environment is not stored by **weird**.

As we've already mentioned, the problem with hyperstatic global environments is that non-local mutually recursive functions cannot be defined there straightforwardly. We could introduce a new form for codefinitions, authorizing the cojoint definition of a multitude of bindings, but we would rather introduce the possibility of referencing the global environment by means of a new special form (**global** ν).

That will make it possible to reference the global variable ν in *any* context, even
if a local variable ν exists. As a consequence, we can write the codefinition of the
functions odd? and even? like this:

```
(letrec ((odd? (lambda (n) (if (= n 0) #f (even? (- n 1)))))
         (even? (lambda (n) (if (= n 0) #t (odd? (- n 1)))))  )
   (define-global odd? odd?)
   (define-global even? even?) )
```

$\mathcal{E}[\![(\texttt{global }\nu)]\!]\rho\gamma\kappa\sigma =$
  let $\alpha = (\gamma\ \nu)$
  in if $\alpha = $ *no-such-global-binding*
      then *wrong* "No such variable"
      else $(\kappa\ (\sigma\ \alpha)\ \gamma\ \sigma)$
      endif

$\mathcal{E}[\![(\texttt{define-global }\nu\ \pi)]\!]\rho\gamma\kappa\sigma =$
$(\mathcal{E}[\![\pi]\!]\ \rho\ \gamma\ \lambda\varepsilon\gamma_1\sigma_1.$ let $\alpha = (\gamma\ \nu)$
                in if $\alpha = $ *no-such-global-binding*
                    then *allocate* σ_1 1 $\lambda\sigma_2\alpha^*.(\kappa\ \varepsilon\ \gamma_1[\nu \to \alpha^* \downarrow_1]\ \sigma_2[\alpha^* \downarrow_1 \to \varepsilon])$
                    else $(\kappa\ \varepsilon\ \gamma_1\ \sigma_1[\alpha \to \varepsilon])$
                    endif $\sigma)$

There we see again that denotational semantics enables us to specify many
diverse environments of a language very elegantly. Of course, we can combine the
various environments explicated here so that we could offer multiple name spaces
in all their specificity, like COMMON LISP does.

5.8   Beneath This Chapter

The main purpose of this chapter was to demystify denotational semantics. We've
gone about this in an informal way (some might say in a sacrilegious way) because
that seemed to us the likeliest means of stimulating wider use of denotational semantics. As we have progressively enriched the linguistic characteristics specified
by our various interpreters and no less progressively reduced the definition language, we've been able gradually to move toward the denotations in this chapter,
or perhaps we should say toward a denotational interpreter. Even though Scheme
and λ-calculus hardly seem alike, they are not so very dissimilar. In fact, it is
generally possible to get an executable denotation to correct errors that infiltrate
these semantic equations. The fact that it's executable is highly important: that's
what makes it possible for the defined language to behave like the designer wants it
to. The designer can exercise the language, experiment with it, test it to insure its
conformity with the equations of his or her dreams. Since the denotation is immediately executable as it appears in the equations, we can skip the implementation
phase where we would ordinarily have to prove rigorously that no distortions have
crept into the implementation.

Having to write a denotational interpreter is thus a gratifying and reassuring
activity. It doesn't cost us any advantages of λ-calculus, but it adds a supplementary constraint: a denotational interpreter has to be executable for a call by value

(that "bad" evaluation method that Scheme uses). This constraint can often be satisfied; to witness: all the denotations in this chapter correspond to code written in Scheme and in fact they have passed through a little converter (LiSP2TEX) to print them in Greek [Que93d]. Just imagine what it would be like to write the denotation of the application preserving the quality that evaluation order makes no difference if we were not using an applicative language in which we can test such functions!

Here's an example of the denotation of a simple abstraction (without variable arity) so you can compare its "Greek" portrait on page 160.

```
(define ((meaning-abstraction n* e+) r k s)
  (k (inValue (lambda (v* k1 s1)
                (if (= (length v*) (length n*))
                    (allocate s1 (length n*)
                      (lambda (s2 a*)
                        ((meaning*-sequence e+)
                         (extend* r n* a*)
                         k1
                         (extend* s2 a* v*) ) ) )
                    (wrong "Incorrect arity") ) ))
     s ) )
```

Here we've used the outmoded form **define** that allowed a first argument in the call position. The form (**define** (ν . *variables*) π*) is recursively equivalent to (**define** ν (**lambda** *variables* π*)) where ν can still be a form of calling.

We've articulated denotations case by case, automatically carried out by an appropriate function which produces the syntactic analysis. By now you're familiar with its structure:

```
(define (meaning e)
  (if (atom? e)
      (if (symbol? e) (meaning-reference e)
                      (meaning-quotation e) )
      (case (car e)
        ((quote)  (meaning-quotation (cadr e)))
        ((lambda) (meaning-abstraction (cadr e) (cddr e)))
        ((if)     (meaning-alternative (cadr e) (caddr e) (cadddr e)))
        ((begin)  (meaning-sequence (cdr e)))
        ((set!)   (meaning-assignment (cadr e) (caddr e)))
        (else     (meaning-application (car e) (cdr e))) ) ) )
```

5.9   λ-calculus and Scheme

Since we are concerned about whether denotations can be executed, we have a problem about the difference between Scheme and λ-calculus. (Of course, we're considering only that subset of "pure" Scheme with no assignment, no side effects.) The difference rests mainly in the evaluation strategy. There is no fixed strategy for λ-calculus, so we have to be careful not to take a bad one. In contrast, there is an evaluation strategy for Scheme, and it's different. Scheme uses call by value.

That is, the arguments of an application are evaluated before they are submitted to the function. Moreover, Scheme does not evaluate bodies of **lambda** forms.

We can simulate call by name in Scheme by using thunks. A thunk is a function without variables that we also call a "promise" according to some terminologies. In Scheme, there is the syntax **delay** to construct a promise, that is, an object representing a certain computation to start (or **force**) once the time for it arrives. We define **delay** and **force** like this:

```
(define-syntax delay
  (syntax-rules ()
    ((delay expression) (lambda () expression)) ) )
(define (force promise) (promise))
```

The form **delay** closes an expression in its lexical context in a thunk that we invoke on demand by **force**. We simulate a call by value with this mechanism if we transform the program like this: every application $(f\ a\ \dots\ z)$ is rewritten as $(f\ (\text{delay}\ a)\ \dots\ (\text{delay}\ z))$, and every variable in the body of a function is unfrozen by means of **force**. Here's an example. This calculation used to be problematic in Scheme:

```
(((lambda (x) (lambda (y) y))              ;((λx.λy.y  (ωω)) z)
  ((lambda (x) (x x)) (lambda (x) (x x))) )
 z )
```

We rewrite that computation in the following way to suspend the computation indefinitely without changing it and to return the value of the free variable **z**, like this:

```
(((lambda (x) (lambda (y) (force y)))
  (delay ((lambda (x) ((force x) (delay (force x))))
          (lambda (x) ((force x) (delay (force x)))) )) )
 (delay z) )
```

Although it's correct according to [DH92], this rewrite introduces some inefficiency. Putting aside the double promise in **(delay (force x))** (which is, in fact, equivalent to **x** which is already a promise) every time we need the value of a variable, we are obliged to force the computation even though it would suffice to do it only once and store the result. This technique is known as call by need. It corresponds to modifying **delay** to store the value that it leads to. Fortunately, Scheme is an excellent language for implementing languages, so we can program this technique by calling an assignment to the rescue, like this:

```
(define-syntax memo-delay
  (syntax-rules ()
    ((memo-delay expression)
     (let ((already-computed? #f)
           (value 'wait) )
       (lambda ()
         (if (not already-computed?)
             (begin
               (set! value expression)
               (set! already-computed? #t) ) )
         value ) ) ) ) )
```

Of course, we could refrain from carrying out these transformations by hand and design macros to do them, as in [DFH86]. If we really wanted to be efficient, we could go on with a *strictness* analysis to determine the cases where variables are always forced. That analysis would let us avoid constructing promises for those variables, as in [BHY87]. Finally, we could adopt clever code for the promises to eliminate the cost at execution time of the test (`if (not already-computed?)` ...). In Scheme, promises let us behave as if we were working in a lazy language where transformations announced earlier will be carried out automatically. However, this programming style poses problems during debugging because the computation is distributed. Moreover, this style does not go well with assignments and continuations. Just compare these two programs from [KW90, Mor92]. They differ only by one sole **delay** but they compute very different results.

```
(pair? (call/cc (lambda (k) (list (k 33)))))
(pair? (call/cc (lambda (k) (list (delay (k 33))))))
```

5.9.1 Passing Continuations

Even a quick look at denotations makes us realize that they are written in the programming style known as *programming by continuations* or CPS for *Continuation Passing Style*. Realizing that all of Scheme, including **call/cc** can be denoted by λ-calculus, which can itself be seen as a certain subset of Scheme excluding **call/cc**, we might validly ask about the possibility of transforming programs automatically from Scheme to Scheme, just to get rid of **call/cc**.

The chief interest of this style is thus to make continuations appear explicitly. Realizing that these same continuations can be represented by **lambda** forms, we ask, *"Can we get along without the primitive **call/cc**?"* The answer is yes, and we can thus develop a transformation that converts a program with **call/cc** into another equivalent program without it. Some compilers even use this latter form as a quasi-intermediate language, as in [App92a], because it contains only the simplest syntactic constructions. Others don't like it because this form in CPS is no longer readable, and it fixes the order of evaluation too soon. Nevertheless, it is equivalent, as [SF92] shows. The version of this transformation that we'll show soon is strongly inspired by [DF90]. We'll use yet another version in Section 10.11.2. [see p. 404]

Let's look at the technique. We'll assume that every function will be called with a supplementary argument,[5] the continuation. Thus $_k$(foo bar ... hux) will be transformed into (**foo** k **bar** ... **hux**). Consequently, we must have a representation of the continuation, we must also know how to handle special forms, so we'll go directly to an analysis of the text to translate, just as all the preceding interpreters have done. Like its denotational equivalent, the continuation waits for a value and returns the final result of the computation. The continuation thus closes the rest of the computations to carry out.

```
(define (cps e)
  (if (atom? e)
      (lambda (k) (k ',e))
      (case (car e)
```

---

5. We'll put it first to simplify the management of functions with variable arity.

```
((quote)  (cps-quote (cadr e)))
((if)     (cps-if (cadr e) (caddr e) (cadddr e)))
((begin)  (cps-begin (cdr e)))
((set!)   (cps-set! (cadr e) (caddr e)))
((lambda) (cps-abstraction (cadr e) (caddr e)))
(else     (cps-application e)) ) ) )
```

By passing a continuation, the transformation takes a program and returns a closure that converts one program into another. In other words, the type of the cps function is this:

```
Program → (( Program → Program ) → Program )
```

Quoting is now easy to handle, too:

```
(define (cps-quote data)
  (lambda (k)
    (k `(quote ,data)) ) )
```

Assignment becomes this:

```
(define (cps-set! variable form)
  (lambda (k)
    ((cps form)
     (lambda (a)
       (k `(set! ,variable ,a)) ) ) ) )
```

It converts the form for which the value will serve as the assignment to the variable and inserts it in its place in the assignment which must be generated.

Conditional is handled similarly:

```
(define (cps-if bool form1 form2)
  (lambda (k)
    ((cps bool)
     (lambda (b)
       `(if ,b ,((cps form1) k)
             ,((cps form2) k) ) ) ) ) )
```

Sequence is comparable:

```
(define (cps-begin e)
  (if (pair? e)
      (if (pair? (cdr e))
          (let ((void (gensym "void")))
            (lambda (k)
              ((cps-begin (cdr e))
               (lambda (b)
                 ((cps (car e))
                  (lambda (a)
                    (k `((lambda (,void) ,b) ,a)) ) ) ) ) ) )
          (cps (car e)) )
      (cps '()) ) )
```

Notice that **begin** forms have been suppressed in favor of closures.

The complicated part is how to handle the form **lambda**. It must be converted into a new function that takes a supplementary variable, and the functional application must provide the continuation as a supplementary argument to the invoked function. A slight improvement has been introduced here when the called function is trivial; that is, when it carries out a simple computation, a short one that always terminates. These functions have been organized into lists[6] of `primitives`.

```
(define (cps-application e)
  (lambda (k)
    (if (memq (car e) primitives)
        ((cps-terms (cdr e))
         (lambda (t*)
           (k '(,(car e) ,@t*)) ) )
        ((cps-terms e)
         (lambda (t*)
           (let ((d (gensym)))
             '(,(car t*) (lambda (,d) ,(k d))
               . ,(cdr t*) ) ) ) ) ) ) )
(define primitives '( cons car cdr list * + - = pair? eq? ))
(define (cps-terms e*)
  (if (pair? e*)
      (lambda (k)
        ((cps (car e*))
         (lambda (a)
           ((cps-terms (cdr e*))
            (lambda (a*)
              (k (cons a a*)) ) ) ) ) )
      (lambda (k) (k '())) ) )
(define (cps-abstraction variables body)
  (lambda (k)
    (k (let ((c (gensym "cont")))
         '(lambda (,c . ,variables)
           ,((cps body)
             (lambda (a) '(,c ,a)) ) )) ) ) )
```

That transformation is complete now, and we can use it to experiment with the factorial, like this:

```
(set! fact (lambda (n)
             (if (= n 1) 1
                 (* n (fact (- n 1))) ) ))
→ (set! fact
     (lambda (cont112 n)
       (if (= n 1)
           (cont112 1)
           (fact (lambda (g113) (cont112 (* n g113)))
                 (- n 1) ) ) ) )
```

Here we automatically get what we had to write by hand earlier. Notice that there are no complicated calculations after the transformation, only trivial applications like comparisons or simple arithmetic operations or applications with continuations. The rest is made up of only variables or closures.

In this world, a form $_k$(`call/cc f`) becomes (`call/cc k f`). The function `call/cc` is no more than (`lambda (k f) (f k k)`) and can be simplified directly so it does not show up anymore. Nevertheless, we must bind the global variable

---

6. Correct treatment of these calls to predefined primitive functions will be covered in Section 6.1.8.

call/cc to `(lambda (k f) (f k k))` in such a way that we can write, for example, `(procedure?  (apply call/cc (list call/cc)))`.

One virtue of a program written in CPS is that since we have put everything totally in sequence by explicitly indicating when terms should be evaluated and to whom their values should be returned, it is completely insensitive to the evaluation strategy. We could evaluate with call by value or call by name; we would get the same results. Thus by combining promises and CPS we can patch up the differences between Scheme and λ-calculus as in [DH92].

5.9.2   Dynamic Environment

The preceding section showed how the denotation of `call/cc` enables us to invent a program transformation that eliminates this very `call/cc`. With the denotation of the dynamic environment, we can imagine applying the same technique to get rid of the special forms **dynamic** and **dynamic-let**. To do so, we simply have to introduce the dynamic environment explicitly everywhere it's needed.

Let's assume we have an identifier that shows up nowhere else. Let's call it δ. The dynamic environment will be the value of δ everywhere, and it will be represented by a function transforming symbols that name dynamic variables into values. Let's also assume that the function **update** extends an environment functionally [see **p. 129**], that it's available everywhere, and that it cannot be hidden. The transformation known as $\mathcal{D}$ and the utility $\mathcal{D}^*$ appear in Table 5.6.

$$\mathcal{D}^*[\![\,]\!] \qquad\qquad\qquad\qquad \rightarrow$$
$$\mathcal{D}^*[\![\pi\ \pi^*]\!] \qquad\qquad\qquad \rightarrow\ \mathcal{D}[\![\pi]\!]\ \mathcal{D}^*[\![\pi^*]\!]$$
$$\mathcal{D}[\![(\text{if }\pi_0\ \pi_1\ \pi_2)]\!] \qquad\quad \rightarrow\ (\text{if } \mathcal{D}[\![\pi_0]\!]\ \mathcal{D}[\![\pi_1]\!]\ \mathcal{D}[\![\pi_2]\!])$$
$$\mathcal{D}[\![(\text{begin }\pi^*)]\!] \qquad\qquad \rightarrow\ (\text{begin } \mathcal{D}^*[\![\pi^*]\!])$$
$$\mathcal{D}[\![(\pi\ \pi^*)]\!] \qquad\qquad\quad \rightarrow\ (\mathcal{D}[\![\pi]\!]\ \delta\ \mathcal{D}^*[\![\pi^*]\!])$$
$$\mathcal{D}[\![(\text{lambda }(\nu^*)\ \pi^*)]\!] \qquad \rightarrow\ (\text{lambda }(\delta\ \nu^*)\ \mathcal{D}^*[\![\pi^*]\!])$$
$$\mathcal{D}[\![(\text{dynamic }\nu)]\!] \qquad\qquad \rightarrow\ (\delta\ (\text{quote }\nu))$$
$$\mathcal{D}[\![(\text{dynamic-let }(\nu\ \pi)\ \pi^+)]\!]\ \ \rightarrow\ (\text{let }((\delta\ (\text{update }\delta\ (\text{quote }\nu)\ \pi)))\ \mathcal{D}^*[\![\pi^+]\!])$$

Table 5.6 Transformation suppressing the dynamic environment

That transformation simply simulates dynamic bindings if we have no other means. The ultimate detail is to specify the initial dynamic environment. The program π to transform it will thus be:

`(let ((`δ` (lambda (n) (error "No such dynamic variable" n)))) `$\mathcal{D}[\![\pi]\!]$`)`

We can sum up our efforts this way: many denotations lead to program transformations that eliminate the forms that they define.

5.10   Conclusions

This chapter culminates a series of interpreters that more and more precisely define a language in the same class as Scheme; they do so with more and more restricted means. Denotational semantics, at least as we have explored it in this chapter, is a remarkably concise way of defining the *kernel* of a functional language. It often seems maladapted and unduly complicated to define an entire language in all its least details. The way we have presented Scheme here rules out the comparison of functions, the denotation of constants, and all sorts of characteristics that strain a definition with minutiae that are useful only rarely. Denotational semantics appears at its best when it outlines the general shape of a language, but it is quite boring for describing every single detail.

The range of things that we can define denotationally is quite vast. We can introduce parallelism with the technique of step calculations as in [Que90c]. We can define the effects of distributed data as in [Que92b]. There are also limitations, as indicated in [McD93]. For example, there is no easy way to define type inference denotationally, and that is one of the reasons for natural semantics [Kah87].

5.11 Exercises

Exercise 5.1 : Here is another way of writing the denotation of a functional application. Show that it is still equivalent to the one in Section 5.2.6.

$$\mathcal{E}[\![(\pi \; \pi^*)]\!]\rho\kappa\sigma = (\mathcal{E}[\![\pi]\!] \; \rho \; \lambda\varphi\sigma_1.(\overline{\mathcal{E}}[\![\; \pi^*]\!] \; \langle\rangle \; \rho \; \lambda\varepsilon^*\sigma_2.(\varphi \mid_{\text{Function}} \varepsilon^* \; \kappa \; \sigma_2) \; \sigma_1) \; \sigma)$$

$$\overline{\mathcal{E}}[\![\;]\!]\varepsilon^*\rho\kappa\sigma = (\kappa \; (\textit{reverse} \; \varepsilon^*) \; \sigma)$$

$$\overline{\mathcal{E}}[\![\pi \; \pi^*]\!]\varepsilon^*\rho\kappa\sigma = (\mathcal{E}[\![\pi]\!] \; \rho \; \lambda\varepsilon\sigma_1.(\overline{\mathcal{E}}[\![\; \pi^*]\!] \; \langle\varepsilon\rangle\S\varepsilon^* \; \rho \; \kappa \; \sigma_1) \; \sigma)$$

Exercise 5.2 : It is not very efficient to define recursive functions within λ-calculus the way we did in Section 5.3. Instead, we could enrich the language with the special form **label**, like in Lisp 1.5. In terms of Scheme, the form (**label** ν (**lambda** ...)) is equivalent to (**letrec** ((ν (**lambda** ...))) ν). Define the semantics of this **label** operator.

Exercise 5.3 : Modify the denotation of the special form **dynamic** so that if the dynamic variable is not found, its value in the global environment will be returned.

Exercise 5.4 : Write a macro to simulate a non-prescribed evaluation order in an implementation of Scheme that evaluates from left to right. You may assume that there is a unary function **random-permutation** that takes an integer n and returns a random permutation of $1, \ldots , n$.

Recommended Reading

The readings that you mustn't miss are [Sto77] and [Sch86]. Both are mines of information about denotational semantics and present examples of denotations of the language.

Serious fans of λ-calculus should also read [Bar84].

6
Fast Interpretation

I N the preceding chapter, there was a denotational interpreter that worked with extreme precision but remarkably slowly. This chapter analyzes the reasons for that slowness and offers a few new interpreters to correct that fault by pretreating programs. In short, we'll see a rudimentary compiler in this chapter. We'll successively analyze: the representation of lexical environments, the protocol for calling functions, and the reification of continuations. The pretreatment will identify and then eliminate computations that it judges static; it will produce a result that includes only those operations that it thinks necessary for execution. Specialized combinators are introduced for that purpose. They play the role of an intermediate language like a set of instructions for a hypothetical virtual machine.

The denotational interpreter of the preceding chapter culminated a series of interpreters leading to inexorably increasing precision. Now we'll have to correct that unbearable slowness. Still adhering to our technique of incremental modifications, particularly because the preceding denotational interpreter is the linguistic standard we have to conform to, we will present three successive interpreters, gradually relaxing some of the preliminary descriptive concerns for the benefit of the habits and customs of implementers.

6.1 A Fast Interpreter

To produce an efficient interpreter now, we'll assume that the implementation language contains a minimal number of concepts, notably, memory. We'll get rid of the one we added in Chapter 4 [see p. 111] since we added it just to explain the idea of memory. The only part we will keep has to do with binding variables. That activity delegates the management of dotted pairs to **cons**, the management of vectors to **vector**, the management of closures to **lambda**, and so on down the line. Memory will no longer be a huge mixture of function arguments, data structures, and even labels on closures. In fact, memory will now contain only bindings or activation records.

6.1.1   Migration of Denotations

The main source of inefficiency in our denotational interpreter is that programs
are ceaselessly denoted, denoted again, and again and again. The repair is simple:
we need to move the computations into positions where they will be calculated as
soon as possible, as in [Deu89]. Moving this way is known as *migrating* code and
as λ-*hoisting* in [Tak88] or as λ-*drifting* in [Roz92]. We must be careful in applying
it to Scheme because of side effects that might occur at an inappropriate time or
even the wrong number of times. A related problem is that migrating code can also
change the termination of an entire program if the computation being migrated is
one that loops indefinitely. Indeed, the expression (lambda (x) (ω ω)) where (ω
ω) is a non-terminating computation, is not equivalent to (let ((tmp (ω ω)))
(lambda (x) tmp)). However, these reasons don't hold for denotations because
denotations are exempt from side effects. Moreover, the denotations that migrate
always terminate because denotations are compositional, and the programs being
treated are always finite trees.

As an example of migration, here's a new version of abstraction. Here you can
see that the denotation of the body of the abstraction (meaning*-sequence e+) is
calculated only once, as is (length n*), the number of variables in the abstraction.

```
(define (meaning-abstraction n* e+)
  (let ((m (meaning*-sequence e+))
        (arity (length n*)) )
    (lambda (r k s)
      (k (inValue (lambda (v* k1 s1)
                    (if (= (length v*) arity)
                        (allocate s1 arity
                                  (lambda (s2 a*)
                                    (m (extend* r n* a*)
                                       k1
                                       (extend* s2 a* v*) ) ) )
                        (wrong "Incorrect arity") ) ))
         s ) ) ) )
```

6.1.2   Activation Record

If we decrease memory consumption, then in large measure we will also improve interpretation speed, too. One major reason for memory consumption is the function
calling protocol as expressed in the denotational interpreter. Invoking a function
there means providing it values that will become its arguments, that is, the values
of its variables. The denotational interpreter provided these values as a list; these
same values were then concatenated to the environment, which was also represented as a list. Since it is easy to write this way, the fact that we were specifying
and prototyping could justify our use of so many lists, but any serious pursuit of
speed rules out this way of working.

While some of these allocations are superfluous, others cannot be avoided. It's
a natural reflex of every implementer to exploit these latter to produce the effects of
the former as well. Since providing values to a function is the same act as invoking

it, we can't really eliminate it, and besides, those values have to appear somewhere: in registers, in a stack, or even in an *activation record*. An activation record will be represented by an object that contains the values provided to a function, so temporarily, we can do this:

```
(define-class activation-frame Object         TEMPORARY
  ( (* argument) ) )
```

That definition exploits a new characteristic of our object system that we haven't mentioned before: the star '*' specifies that a field is *indexed*; that is, it is not reduced to a single value but instead contains an ordered sequence of a size determined at creation time. (See Section 11.2 for more details about that idea.)

That representation is more advantageous than representation as a list once the number of arguments is greater than two. Moreover, it supports direct access to arguments, rather than sequential, linear access as in lists. An activation record must allow a lexical environment to be extended. Of course, we could even do something so that an environment would be a list of activation records, as in Figure 6.1

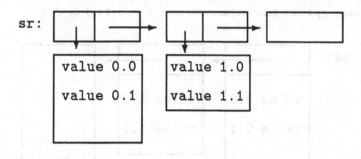

Figure 6.1 Environment and lists of activation records

Even more happily, we could reserve a supplementary field in activation records to link them together. Since the time needed to allocate activation records hardly depends on their size (as long as we overlook the memory management problems of initializing fields), we exchange two allocations for one enlarged only by a pointer. For those reasons, we'll adopt the following definition for activation records where we insert the field for linking in first position so we can follow it or modify it by an offset without disturbing any of the arguments that follow it, as in Figure 6.2.

```
(define-class environment Object
  ( next ) )
(define-class activation-frame environment
  ( (* argument) ) )
```

The values present in lexical environments are thus linked together in a chain of activation records. The function **sr-extend*** does this linking, like this:

```
(define (sr-extend* sr v*)
  (set-environment-next! v* sr)
  v* )
```

Activation records are physically modified. For that reason, they cannot be re-used since the functional invocation must allocate fresh bindings.

If we think again about the presentation of lexical environments in the denotational interpreter, we recall that they were composed of two distinct parts, ρ and σ. The environment ρ associates the name of a variable with an address so we can determine its value in the memory σ. But here we've saved little from memory except management of activation records. Any value can be retrieved from the chain of activation records by an "address" made up of two numbers: the first indicates in which activation record to look; the second then tells the index of the argument to look for. Figure 6.2 and the following two functions for reading and writing illustrate that idea.

```
(define (deep-fetch sr i j)
  (if (= i 0)
      (activation-frame-argument sr j)
      (deep-fetch (environment-next sr) (- i 1) j) ) )
(define (deep-update! sr i j v)
  (if (= i 0)
      (set-activation-frame-argument! sr j v)
      (deep-update! (environment-next sr) (- i 1) j v) ) )
```

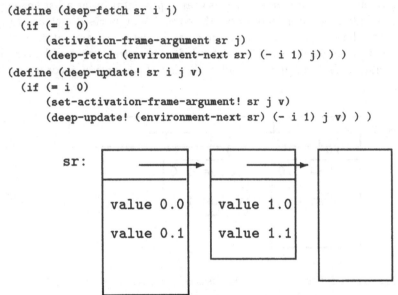

Figure 6.2 Environment and linked activation records

Thus the environment associating an identifier with an address enables us to retrieve the associated value. Memory (which we are trying to get out of our new interpreter) now exists for the sole purpose of representing activation records. Consequently, we'll still use r as the name for lexical environments, but we'll adopt sr for the *store* associated with the environment r, that is, the representation at execution of values in this environment. Although this latter should be represented by a linked list of activation records, we'll adopt a "ribcage" representation for the environment. That is, we'll use the list of lists of variables from abstractions. [see **Ex. 1.3**] We'll extend the environment by r-extend* (not to be confused with sr-extend*), and we'll use a semi-predicate local-variable? to search for the *lexical indices* of a value.

```
(define (r-extend* r n*)
  (cons n* r) )
(define (local-variable? r i n)
```

```
(and (pair? r)
     (let scan ((names (car r))
                (j 0) )
       (cond ((pair? names)
              (if (eq? n (car names))
                  `(local ,i . ,j)
                  (scan (cdr names) (+ 1 j)) ) )
             ((null? names)
              (local-variable? (cdr r) (+ i 1) n) )
             ((eq? n names) `(local ,i . ,j)) ) ) ) )
```

The purpose of doing things this way is to get a strong block structure from activation records. The strong block structure means that the address associated with an identifier is no longer an absolute address, but rather a pair of numbers interpreted relative to the linked activation records. As a consequence, computations with addresses become static calculations that can migrate during pretreatment of expressions to evaluate.

Cutting the lexical environment this way into static and dynamic parts does not depend on the representation that we have just chosen. It's actually a deeper property that only now becomes apparent. With the representation we chose for the denotational interpreter, it was already possible to predict the "position" (where position is counted in number of comparisons by **eq?**) of any variable inside the environment since the environment itself was merely a chain of the closures of bodies (lambda (u) (if (eq? u *x*) *y* (*f* u))).

6.1.3   The Interpreter: the Beginning

We know enough now to show the skeleton of the interpreter and a few of its special forms. As you might expect, we begin with the function **meaning**. It will now have the following signature:

$$\text{meaning}: \underbrace{\textbf{Program} \times \textbf{Environment}}_{static} \rightarrow$$

$$\underbrace{(\textbf{Activation-Record} \times \textbf{Continuation} \rightarrow \textbf{Value})}_{dynamic}$$

This signature clearly shows how the environment is cut into its static and dynamic components, **Environment** and **Activation-Record**. When a program is pretreated, the result is a binary function waiting for a list of linked activation records (that is, memory) and a continuation to calculate a value. This is a nonstandard way of representing programs, far removed from the original S-expression, but fundamentally the same structurally.

To simplify syntactic analysis, we'll assume as usual that the expressions submitted are syntactically legitimate programs. Here are the rules we'll use to name variables when we define the functions for syntactic analysis:

```
            e ...    expression, form
            r ...    environment
  sr, ... , v* ...   activation record
            v ...    value (integer, pair, closure, etc.)
            k ...    continuation
            f ...    function
            n ...    identifier
```

Here, then, are the functions for analyzing syntax:

```
(define (meaning e r)
  (if (atom? e)
      (if (symbol? e) (meaning-reference e r)
                      (meaning-quotation e r) )
      (case (car e)
        ((quote)  (meaning-quotation (cadr e) r))
        ((lambda) (meaning-abstraction (cadr e) (cddr e) r))
        ((if)     (meaning-alternative (cadr e) (caddr e) (cadddr e) r))
        ((begin)  (meaning-sequence (cdr e) r))
        ((set!)   (meaning-assignment (cadr e) (caddr e) r))
        (else     (meaning-application (car e) (cdr e) r)) ) ) )
```

Once again, quoting becomes trivial, like this:

```
(define (meaning-quotation v r)
  (lambda (sr k)
    (k v) ) )
```

Here's the conditional, a good example of code migration. We pretreat the two branches of the conditional, regardless of which of them will be the choice that might be made.

```
(define (meaning-alternative e1 e2 e3 r)
  (let ((m1 (meaning e1 r))
        (m2 (meaning e2 r))
        (m3 (meaning e3 r)) )
    (lambda (sr k)
      (m1 sr (lambda (v)
               ((if v m2 m3) sr k) )) ) ) )
```

We decompose a sequence into two conventional subcases, like this:

```
(define (meaning-sequence e+ r)
  (if (pair? e+)
      (if (pair? (cdr e+))
          (meaning*-multiple-sequence (car e+) (cdr e+) r)
          (meaning*-single-sequence (car e+) r) )
      (static-wrong "Illegal syntax: (begin)") ) )
(define (meaning*-single-sequence e r)
  (meaning e r) )
(define (meaning*-multiple-sequence e e+ r)
  (let ((m1 (meaning e r))
        (m+ (meaning-sequence e+ r)) )
    (lambda (sr k)
      (m1 sr (lambda (v)
```

```
              (m+ sr k) )) ) ) )
```

Things get a little stickier with an application. For an application, we have to define the invocation protocol more precisely.

Application

To pretreat an application, we must make several things explicit: how it's created, how it's filled in, the way it's passed—in short, how activation records handle it. While the pretreatment of the function term is conventional enough, how the arguments are handled is less so. For that purpose, we'll use the function **meaning***. For simplicity, functions will be represented by their closures.

```
(define (meaning-regular-application e e* r)
  (let* ((m (meaning e r))
         (m* (meaning* e* r (length e*))) )
    (lambda (sr k)
      (m sr (lambda (f)
              (if (procedure? f)
                  (m* sr (lambda (v*)
                           (f v* k) ))
                  (wrong "Not a function" f) ) )) ) ) )
```

Since we've been looking for computations that we can do statically,[1] we've seen that the size of an activation record to allocate is easily predicted since it can be deduced directly from the number of terms in the application. In contrast, it's much harder to know *when* to allocate the record. There are two potential moments: [see **Ex. 6.4**]

1. We could allocate the record before evaluating its arguments. In that case, each argument calculated there is immediately put into place.

2. We could allocate the record after evaluating its arguments. In that case, however, we consume twice as much memory since we have to store the values in the continuation—the same values that will all be organized into the newly allocated record.

The first of those two strategies seems more efficient since it consumes less memory. Unfortunately, the presence of **call/cc** in Scheme totally ruins that possibility. It's feasible only for Lisp. The reason: in Scheme it's possible to call a continuation more than once. [see **p. 82**] If the record is allocated first, before the arguments are computed, then, if one of those computations captures its continuation, it will also capture the record that appears in the continuation. The record will thus be shared by all the invocations of the function term—a sharing that is contrary to the abstraction which must allocate new addresses for its local variables at every invocation. The following program should return (2 1). Sharing activation records would incorrectly force a return of (2 2).[2] In effect, the

---

1. By the way, that's a major activity among language designers; they actually favor characteristics that are static.
2. Manuel Serrano discovered that a previous version of this example was depending subtly on the order of evaluation. The form cons should be evaluated from left to right. The form (let ((g ...))...) does that.

form `call/cc` captures the application ((lambda (a) ...) ...) and notably
the activation record if it has been pre-allocated. Since that continuation is used
twice, the two thunks created by (lambda () a) share the closed variable a by
conferring on it the last of the values that k received.

```
(let ((k 'wait)
      (f '()) )
  (set! f (let ((g ((lambda (a) (lambda () a))
                    (call/cc (lambda (nk) (set! k nk) (nk 1))) )))
            (cons g f) ))
  ;; f ≈(list (lambda () 1))
  (if (null? (cdr f)) (k 2))
  ;; f ≈(list (lambda () 2) (lambda () 1))
  (list ((car f)) ((cadr f))) )
```

But in fact, all is not lost in Scheme. It suffices in the implementation of
`call/cc` to duplicate the activation records captured when the continuations were
invoked. We can't program that here because continuations are represented by
closures, from which we cannot extract the enclosed activation records. In that
example, you can clearly see the impact of `call/cc`.

The function `meaning*` will thus take a supplementary argument corresponding
to the size of the activation record that must be allocated afer the evaluation of all
arguments. For reasons that will be clear when we discuss the implementation of
functions with variable arity in Section 6.1.6, [see p. 196], activation records will
contain one more field than necessary, but we will not initialize this excess field, so
it won't penalize these functions.

```
(define (meaning* e* r size)
  (if (pair? e*)
      (meaning-some-arguments (car e*) (cdr e*) r size)
      (meaning-no-argument r size) ) )
(define (meaning-no-argument r size)
  (let ((size+1 (+ size 1)))
    (lambda (sr k)
      (let ((v* (allocate-activation-frame size+1)))
        (k v*) ) ) ) )
```

Notice that `size+1` is precalculated since it would be too bad to leave that
computation until execution! Also notice the "non-migration" of the allocation
form that has to allocate a new activation record at every invocation.

Each term of the application is put into the right place, just after allocation of
the activation record. The right place is easily calculated in terms of the variables
`size` and `e*`.

```
(define (meaning-some-arguments e e* r size)
  (let ((m (meaning e r))
        (m* (meaning* e* r size))
        (rank (- size (+ (length e*) 1))) )
    (lambda (sr k)
      (m sr (lambda (v)
              (m* sr (lambda (v*)
                       (set-activation-frame-argument! v* rank v)
                       (k v*) )) )) ) ) )
```

We can finally define abstractions since they appear so clear now. Verification of the arity is carried out by inspection of the size of the activation record. There again, we've precalculated everything we can so we leave as little as possible until execution.

```
(define (meaning-fix-abstraction n* e+ r)
   (let* ((arity (length n*))
          (arity+1 (+ arity 1))
          (r2 (r-extend* r n*))
          (m+ (meaning-sequence e+ r2)) )
      (lambda (sr k)
       (k (lambda (v* k1)
           (if (= (activation-frame-argument-length v*) arity+1)
               (m+ (sr-extend* sr v*) k1)
               (wrong "Incorrect arity") ) )) ) ) )
```

6.1.4 Classifying Variables

Those preceding definitions handle only the case of local variables, that is, only variables in **lambda** forms. There are, of course, global variables, and among them, predefined variables and/or immutable ones, like **cons** or **car**. In our current state, the only way of accessing them would be to follow the links between activation records, but that technique makes access to global variables particularly slow since they are located in the ultimate activation record. For that reason, we'll treat these statically classified variables differently.

We'll assume that the global variable **g.current** contains the list of mutable global variables, while **g.init** contains the list of predefined, immutable ones, such as **cons**, **car**, etc. The function **compute-kind** classifies variables and returns a descriptor characterizing variables.

```
(define (compute-kind r n)
   (or (local-variable? r 0 n)
       (global-variable? g.current n)
       (global-variable? g.init n) ) )
(define (global-variable? g n)
   (let ((var (assq n g)))
      (and (pair? var) (cdr var)) ) )
```

We test **g.current** before **g.init** so that we can mask predefined variables, if need be. Considering primitives as values of immutable global variables is a safe practice. However, certain implementations of Scheme allow a program to redefine such a global variable (**car** for example) on condition that the redefinition modifies only this variable and not any other predefined function (not even those, like **map**, for example, that seem to use **car**). Only the functions explicitly in the program will see the new value of **car**. You can get this effect simply by **compute-kind**, but there is still a problem of knowing how to insert such a variable in the mutable environment. We could also invent a new special form, **redefine**, say, for this purpose. [see **Ex. 6.5**]

We'll add global variables to these environments by means of two functions, **g.current-extend!** and **g.init-extend!**.

```
(define (g.current-extend! n)
  (let ((level (length g.current)))
    (set! g.current (cons (cons n '(global . ,level)) g.current))
    level ) )
(define (g.init-extend! n)
  (let ((level (length g.init)))
    (set! g.init (cons (cons n '(predefined . ,level)) g.init))
    level ) )
```

The environments **g.current** and **g.init** return only addresses of variables, so
we have to search for their values in the appropriate place. The containers where we
search are simple vectors, values of the variables **sg.current** and **sg.init**. There's
an initial **s** because these vectors represent memory, conventionally prefixed by **s** for
store. Here[3] are the containers and the associated access functions. (However, we're
not giving **predefined-update!** since it makes no sense for immutable variables.)

```
(define sg.current (make-vector 100))
(define sg.init (make-vector 100))
(define (global-fetch i)
  (vector-ref sg.current i) )
(define (global-update! i v)
  (vector-set! sg.current i v) )
(define (predefined-fetch i)
  (vector-ref sg.init i) )
```

To help define global environments, we'll provide two functions, **g.current-
initialize!** and **g.init-initialize!**, to enrich (or modify) the static and dynamic environments synchronously.

```
(define (g.current-initialize! name)
  (let ((kind (compute-kind r.init name)))
    (if kind
        (case (car kind)
          ((global)
           (vector-set! sg.current (cdr kind) undefined-value) )
          (else (static-wrong "Wrong redefinition" name)) )
        (let ((index (g.current-extend! name)))
          (vector-set! sg.current index undefined-value) ) ) )
    name )
(define (g.init-initialize! name value)
  (let ((kind (compute-kind r.init name)))
    (if kind
        (case (car kind)
          ((predefined)
           (vector-set! sg.init (cdr kind) value) )
          (else (static-wrong "Wrong redefinition" name)) )
        (let ((index (g.init-extend! name)))
          (vector-set! sg.init index value) ) ) )
    name )
```

---

3. For simplicity, we've limited the number of mutable global variables to 100, but that limitation
will be lifted in Section 6.1.9.

Now we have an adequate arsenal to handle the pretreatment of variables and assignments. Those two have a similar structure: they analyze the classification returned by **compute-kind** and associate it with the correct access function. Notice that we don't use the functions **deep-fetch** nor **deep-update!** but the equivalent direct accessors when the variable we are searching for appears in the first activation record. Another clever trick (but one that some people would argue against) is that for predefined variables, we search for their value to read right away (like a quotation) rather than at execution. In that way, we gain an access indexed to the vector of constant global variables.

```
(define (meaning-reference n r)
  (let ((kind (compute-kind r n)))
    (if kind
        (case (car kind)
          ((local)
           (let ((i (cadr kind))
                 (j (cddr kind)) )
             (if (= i 0)
                 (lambda (sr k)
                   (k (activation-frame-argument sr j)) )
                 (lambda (sr k)
                   (k (deep-fetch sr i j)) ) ) ) )
          ((global)
           (let ((i (cdr kind)))
             (if (eq? (global-fetch i) undefined-value)
                 (lambda (sr k)
                   (let ((v (global-fetch i)))
                     (if (eq? v undefined-value)
                         (wrong "Uninitialized variable" n)
                         (k v) ) ) )
                 (lambda (sr k)
                   (k (global-fetch i)) ) ) ) )
          ((predefined)
           (let* ((i (cdr kind))
                  (value (predefined-fetch i)) )
             (lambda (sr k)
               (k value) ) ) ) )
        (static-wrong "No such variable" n) ) ) )
```

Assignment is similar in every way:

```
(define (meaning-assignment n e r)
  (let ((m (meaning e r))
        (kind (compute-kind r n)) )
    (if kind
        (case (car kind)
          ((local)
           (let ((i (cadr kind))
                 (j (cddr kind)) )
             (if (= i 0)
                 (lambda (sr k)
                   (m sr (lambda (v)
                           (k (set-activation-frame-argument!
```

```
                             sr j v )) )) )
                  (lambda (sr k)
                    (m sr (lambda (v)
                            (k (deep-update! sr i j v)) )) )) )) )) )
            ((global)
             (let ((i (cdr kind)))
                (lambda (sr k)
                  (m sr (lambda (v)
                          (k (global-update! i v)) )) )) )) )
            ((predefined)
             (static-wrong "Immutable predefined variable" n) ) )
          (static-wrong "No such variable" n) ) ) )
```

Static Errors

The purpose of this pretreatment is so that such errors as an attempt to modify
an immutable variable or to read a non-existing variable will be noticed during
pretreatment rather than during execution. Those kinds of errors may even remain
unnoticed if the erroneous forms are not evaluated. Such errors are signaled by the
function static-wrong rather than by wrong, which we reserve for unforeseeable
situations that occur during execution. The idea of a static error is useful but it
clearly marks the difference between a free-handed language like Lisp and most
others. If a program is valid in ML, then all its possible executions are exempt
from type errors. Conversely, if we do not know how to prove that all evaluations
of a program lead to errors, then we would have the tendency to think that the
program is legal in Lisp. For example, consider the following definition:

```
(define (statically-strange n)
  (if (integer? n)
      (if (= n 0) 1 (* n (statically-strange (- n 1))))
      (cons) ) )
```

Even though it is statically wrong, this function provides a real service when
applied to (positive!) integers. Whether we allow such a function or not depends
on the spirit of the language; there's a compromise between the security we're
looking for and the freedom we're ready to sacrifice for it. It is very important to
be warned about errors as soon as possible—that's the position of ML—but, if we
want no limits on our programming arsenal, if we want a little ease and a little
taste of danger, then we'll prefer Lisp.

The function static-wrong should thus be understood as delivering a message
about an anomaly but generating a result, valid for pretreatment; the pretreatment
itself will raise the error if by chance its evaluation is needed. That is, the warning
is tied to pretreatment; the error to execution. We make these ideas explicit in the
way we define static-wrong.

```
(set! static-wrong
      (lambda (message . culprits)
        (display '(*static-error* ,message . ,culprits))(newline)
        (lambda (sr k)
          (apply wrong message culprits) ) ) )
```

In that way, we ascend to a nirvana for implementers where we can have our cake and eat it, too.

Remember that for mutable global variables, we have to verify that they've been initialized when we access them, in contrast both to local variables and to immutable global variables. Thus there is a cost for accessing mutable global variables. In the case of incremental compilation (as, for example, in a compiling interaction loop like (display (compile-then-run (read)))), we could slightly improve the pretreatment of mutable global variables that have already been initialized. In fact, that's what we did[4] earlier in **meaning-reference**. [see Ex. 7.6]

6.1.5 Starting the Interpreter

The interpreter reads an expression, pretreats it, and then evaluates it. In that way, it produces a compiling interaction loop.

```
(define r.init '())
(define sr.init '())
(define (chapter61-interpreter)
  (define (compile e) (meaning e r.init))
  (define (run c) (c sr.init display))
  (define (toplevel)
    (run (compile (read)))
    (toplevel) )
  (toplevel) )
```

However, before we start this interpreter, we must enrich its initial environment a little. We'll assume again that we have some macros available to hide the implementation details so that the following definitions will resemble what they've always been. Here are a few of them, to which we've added, of course, the indispensible **call/cc**:

```
(definitial t #t)
(definitial f #f)
(definitial nil '())
(defprimitive cons cons 2)
(defprimitive car car 1)
(definitial call/cc
  (let* ((arity 1)
         (arity+1 (+ arity 1)) )
    (lambda (v* k)
      (if (= arity+1 (activation-frame-argument-length v*))
          ((activation-frame-argument v* 0)
           (let ((frame (allocate-activation-frame (+ 1 1))))
             (set-activation-frame-argument!
              frame 0
              (lambda (values kk)
```

---

4. If it were possible to modify code in place, we could also imagine patching the instruction that verifies the initialization of a global variable so that it no longer does so if that's really the case. Bigloo interpreter [Ser94] adopted that solution.

```
            (if (= (activation-frame-argument-length values)
                   arity+1 )
                (k (activation-frame-argument values 0))
                (wrong "Incorrect arity" 'continuation) ) ) )
        frame )
      k )
  (wrong "Incorrect arity" 'call/cc) ) ) ) )
```

6.1.6   Functions with Variable Arity

Our interpreter still lacks functions with variable arity. As always, those functions pose a few difficulties for us. As we have used them, activation records contain the values of arguments, but they also serve as the receptacles for bindings that will be created. In the case of functions with variable arity, the correspondence between these two effects is not reliable because there is no inevitable relation between the number of arguments passed to a function and its arity. For example, a function having (a b . c) as the list of variables could accept two, three, or more arguments without error, but it would bind only those three variables. For that reason, an activation record must always contain at least three fields. Simply put, for an application (f a b), the activation record that's allocated must have a superfluous field (and that makes three fields in all) to authorize the invocation of any function capable of accepting at least two values, that is, those functions with a list of variables congruent to (x y) or (x y . z) or (x . y) or even x.

Functions with variable arity thus handle the activation record they receive in such a way as to put "excess" arguments into a list. The function listify! will be used for that purpose and indeed only for that purpose. Programming it is not complicated, but doing so obliges us to juggle various indices numbering the terms of the application, the variables to bind, and the fields of the activation record. The value of the variable arity represents the minimal number of arguments expected.

```
(define (meaning-dotted-abstraction n* n e+ r)
  (let* ((arity (length n*))
         (arity+1 (+ arity 1))
         (r2 (r-extend* r (append n* (list n))))
         (m+ (meaning-sequence e+ r2)) )
    (lambda (sr k)
      (k (lambda (v* k1)
           (if (>= (activation-frame-argument-length v*) arity+1)
               (begin (listify! v* arity)
                      (m+ (sr-extend* sr v*) k1) )
               (wrong "Incorrect arity") ) )) ) ) )
(define (listify! v* arity)
  (let loop ((index (- (activation-frame-argument-length v*) 1))
             (result '()) )
    (if (= arity index)
        (set-activation-frame-argument! v* arity result)
        (loop (- index 1)
              (cons (activation-frame-argument v* (- index 1))
```

```
                          result ) ) ) ) )
```

Now we can pretreat all possible **lambda** forms by means of the following static analysis:

```
(define (meaning-abstraction nn* e+ r)
  (let parse ((n* nn*)
              (regular '()) )
    (cond
      ((pair? n*) (parse (cdr n*) (cons (car n*) regular)))
      ((null? n*) (meaning-fix-abstraction nn* e+ r))
      (else (meaning-dotted-abstraction (reverse regular) n* e+ r)) ) ) ) )
```

6.1.7   Reducible Forms

Our interpreter could take advantage of a conventional way of improving compilers with respect to reducible forms, that is, applications where the function term is a **lambda** form. In such a case, there's no point in creating a closure to apply later; it's sufficient to assimilate the form to a block with local variables, in the style of Algol. By the way, ((lambda ... ...) ...) is nothing other than a disguised **let**; it opens a block furnished with local variables. The case of functions with fixed arity is thus simplicity itself, but once again[5] that's not so for functions with variable arity. Not providing the right number of arguments to a function is now a static error that can be raised in pretreatment.

```
(define (meaning-closed-application e ee* r)
  (let ((nn* (cadr e)))
    (let parse ((n* nn*)
                (e* ee*)
                (regular '()) )
      (cond ((pair? n*)
             (if (pair? e*)
                 (parse (cdr n*) (cdr e*) (cons (car n*) regular))
                 (static-wrong "Too less arguments" e ee*) ) )
            ((null? n*)
             (if (null? e*)
                 (meaning-fix-closed-application
                  nn* (cddr e) ee* r )
                 (static-wrong "Too much arguments" e ee*) ) )
            (else (meaning-dotted-closed-application
                   (reverse regular) n* (cddr e) ee* r )) ) ) ) )
(define (meaning-fix-closed-application n* body e* r)
  (let* ((m* (meaning* e* r (length e*)))
         (r2 (r-extend* r n*))
         (m+ (meaning-sequence body r2)) )
    (lambda (sr k)
      (m* sr (lambda (v*)
               (m+ (sr-extend* sr v*) k) )) ) ) )
```

---

5. You can see by now why so many languages do not support functions with variable arity in spite of their usefulness.

For functions with variable arity, we can avoid using `listify!` since here
the arity of the function and the number of arguments are both known statically. The solution uses a variation on **meaning***. Here we call that variation
meaning-dotted*. It behaves like **meaning*** for obligatory arguments, but it builds
a list of "excess" arguments on the fly by inserting the necessary calls to **cons**.
Doing that entails a lot of code for a case that's fairly rare. However, we must
explicitly use () to initialize the superfluous field in the activation records; the
function **meaning-no-dotted-argument** does that. All that comes down to making a change on the fly, like this:

```
((lambda (a b . c) ...)        ≡    ((lambda (a b c) ...)
 α β γ δ ...)                         α β (cons γ (cons δ ...)) )
```

So here are those functions:

```
(define (meaning-dotted-closed-application n* n body e* r)
  (let* ((m* (meaning-dotted* e* r (length e*) (length n*)))
         (r2 (r-extend* r (append n* (list n))))
         (m+ (meaning-sequence body r2)) )
    (lambda (sr k)
      (m* sr (lambda (v*)
               (m+ (sr-extend* sr v*) k) )) ) ) )
(define (meaning-dotted* e* r size arity)
  (if (pair? e*)
      (meaning-some-dotted-arguments (car e*) (cdr e*) r size arity)
      (meaning-no-dotted-argument r size arity) ) )
(define (meaning-some-dotted-arguments e e* r size arity)
  (let ((m (meaning e r))
        (m* (meaning-dotted* e* r size arity))
        (rank (- size (+ (length e*) 1))) )
    (if (< rank arity)
        (lambda (sr k)
          (m sr (lambda (v)
                  (m* sr (lambda (v*)
                           (set-activation-frame-argument! v* rank v)
                           (k v*) )) )) )
        (lambda (sr k)
          (m sr (lambda (v)
                  (m* sr (lambda (v*)
                           (set-activation-frame-argument!
                            v* arity
                            (cons v (activation-frame-argument
                                     v* arity )) )
                           (k v*) )) )) ) ) ) )
(define (meaning-no-dotted-argument r size arity)
  (let ((arity+1 (+ arity 1)))
    (lambda (sr k)
      (let ((v* (allocate-activation-frame arity+1)))
        (set-activation-frame-argument! v* arity '())
        (k v*) ) ) ) )
```

6.1.8 Integrating Primitives

We can gain efficiency from another important source by cleverly pretreating calls to the predefined functions of the immutable global environment. An application, such as (car α), currently imposes the following incredible and painful sequence of steps:

1. Dereference the global variable car.

2. Evaluate α.

3. Allocate an activation record with two fields.

4. Fill that first field with the value of α.

5. Verify that the value of car really is a function.

6. Verify whether the value of car actually accepts one argument.

7. Apply the value of car to the argument. This step leads additionally to testing whether the argument really is a dotted pair for which it is legal to take the car.

We eliminate several of those steps if we're working in a strongly typed language, and that's what makes such languages so fast. In contrast, some of these verifications can be eliminated in a language like Lisp by pretreatments if such things can be verified statically. Since car is a global variable that cannot be modified, we can verify beforehand that it's a function that accepts one argument. In that way, we save step 5 (verify whether it's a function) and step 6 (verifying its arity). We can save even more by not allocating the activation record (steps 3 and 4), but inserting the code itself into the primitive being called (step 1).

This kind of integration—calling the primitive directly without going through a complete and consequently burdensome protocol—is known as *inlining*. In such circumstances, the only remaining steps are 2 and 7. A good compiler could still save a little in step 7 by factoring type tests so they would never be duplicated. For example, in the program (if (pair? e) (car e) ...) there is no point in car verifying whether its argument is a dotted pair because that is obviously and surely true. One method for doing so anyway is to consider (car x) as a macro equivalent to (let ((v x))(if (pair? v) (unsafe-car v) (error ...))) where unsafe-car[6] extracts the car of its argument if that argument is a pair but leads to unforeseeable side effects when that is not the case. All we have to do is to transform the code in order to migrate type-checks as far upstream as possible and to eliminate redundant tests. Here again, there is no problem in migrating computations because type-checks are immediate computations without possible errors.

A real compiler does not access values of immutable global variables since such variables belong to the realm of execution rather than to pretreatment. Besides, we don't have much need of these values; we only need to know whether they are functions and whether their arity is compatible with the function that we are

---

6. Primitives analogous to unsafe-car exist in most implementations in order to serve as targets for transformations of programs. These transformations should guarantee that unsafe-car is always used in safe contexts. In contrast, it is essential for an efficient compiler to be able to resort to these shortcut primitives and thus get rid of useless type-checking.

trying to pretreat. We'll add a new environment. Its role will be to describe the value of immutable global variables. That environment will be named `desc.init`, and it will associate a descriptor with a variable whose value is a function. The descriptor of a function will be a list; the first term of that list will be the symbol `function`; the second term will be the "address" of the primitive (which must really be invoked); the succeeding terms indicate the arity. We'll put the management of these descriptions inside the macro `defprimitive`, accompanied here by only one of its submacros, `defprimitive3`, to give you an idea of its siblings.

```
(define-syntax defprimitive
  (syntax-rules ()
    ((defprimitive name value 0) (defprimitive0 name value))
    ((defprimitive name value 1) (defprimitive1 name value))
    ((defprimitive name value 2) (defprimitive2 name value))
    ((defprimitive name value 3) (defprimitive3 name value)) ) )
(define-syntax defprimitive3
  (syntax-rules ()
    ((defprimitive3 name value)
     (definitial name
       (letrec ((arity+1 (+ 3 1))
                (behavior
                 (lambda (v* k)
                   (if (= (activation-frame-argument-length v*)
                          arity+1 )
                       (k (value (activation-frame-argument v* 0)
                                 (activation-frame-argument v* 1)
                                 (activation-frame-argument v* 2) ))
                       (wrong "Incorrect arity" 'name) ) ) ) )
         (description-extend!                    ; ** Modified **
          'name '(function ,value a b c))
         behavior ) ) ) ) )
```

The functions to manage this environment look like this:

```
(define desc.init '())
(define (description-extend! name description)
  (set! desc.init (cons (cons name description) desc.init))
  name )
(define (get-description name)
  (let ((p (assq name desc.init)))
    (and (pair? p) (cdr p)) ) )
```

We can explicate completely how applications are pretreated; that is, how they are analyzed so that they can be handed off to the right pretreatment. Notice that if a primitive appears in an application with the wrong arity, that anomaly will be indicated statically.

```
(define (meaning-application e e* r)
  (cond
    ((and (symbol? e)
          (let ((kind (compute-kind r e)))
            (and (pair? kind)
                 (eq? 'predefined (car kind))
```

```
                        (let ((desc (get-description e)))
                          (and desc
                               (eq? 'function (car desc))
                               (if (= (length (cddr desc)) (length e*))
                                   (meaning-primitive-application e e* r)
                                   (static-wrong "Incorrect arity for" e) ) )
                     ) ) ) ))
        ((and (pair? e)
              (eq? 'lambda (car e)) )
         (meaning-closed-application e e* r) )
        (else (meaning-regular-application e e* r)) ) )
```

Applications implicating known primitive functions are handled like this:

```
(define (meaning-primitive-application e e* r)
  (let* ((desc (get-description e)) ;desc = (function address . variables-list)
         (address (cadr desc))
         (size (length e*)) )
    (case size
      ((0) (lambda (sr k) (k (address))))
      ((1)
       (let ((m1 (meaning (car e*) r)))
         (lambda (sr k)
           (m1 sr (lambda (v)
                    (k (address v)) )) ) ) )
      ((2)
       (let ((m1 (meaning (car e*) r))
             (m2 (meaning (cadr e*) r)) )
         (lambda (sr k)
           (m1 sr (lambda (v1)
                    (m2 sr (lambda (v2)
                             (k (address v1 v2)) )) )) ) ) )
      ((3)
       (let ((m1 (meaning (car e*) r))
             (m2 (meaning (cadr e*) r))
             (m3 (meaning (caddr e*) r)) )
         (lambda (sr k)
           (m1 sr (lambda (v1)
                    (m2 sr (lambda (v2)
                             (m3 sr (lambda (v3)
                                      (k (address v1 v2 v3))
                                      )) )) )) ) ) )
      (else (meaning-regular-application e e* r)) ) ) )
```

The preceding integration involves only primitives with fixed arity. Primitives with variable arity, like append, for-each, list, map, *, +, and several others (except apply) in general can be considered as macros for which the expansion reduces to cases we've already studied. For example, (append π_1 π_2 π_3) can be rewritten as (append π_1 (append π_2 π_3)). That transformation lets us integrate forms with variable arity but does not imply that these functions have fixed arity. (apply append π) is an example where append will be called with a variable arity.

We have integrated only calls with three or fewer arguments. The reason for this limitation is simple: in Scheme, there are no essential functions of fixed arity that have more than three arguments anyway!

6.1.9   Variations on Environments

Accessing deep local variables (that is, those that do not belong to the first activation record) have a linearly increasing cost because we have to run through the linked records to find them. There is a simple technique—known as *display*—to access such variables in constant time. To do so, every deep activation record has to be accessible from the first one, as in Figure 6.3. In that way, every deep variable can be read or written by one indirection (to determine which record) and one offset (inside that record). However, even if accessing deep variables is faster in this way, the cost of allocating linked records is greater than before because every activation record must refer to all the deep records. Of course, it's possible to set up only the links really used, but doing so requires analyzing which variables are consulted. Additionally, this technique ruins our interpreter since with it, we will no longer know how large an activation record to create before the function to invoke checks the depth of its closed environment. For those reasons, we have to allocate the *display* somewhere else or even limit the maximal authorized depth (though such a limit is not very Lispian).

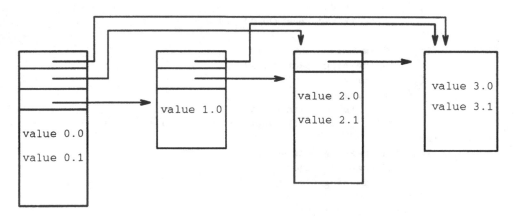

Figure 6.3 *Display* technique

Flat Environment

Another technique would be to adopt flat environments. When a closure is created, instead of closing the entire environment, we could build a new environment containing only the variables that are really closed. The cost of building the closures is thus higher, but in contrast the environment has at most only two activation records: the one that contains arguments and the one that contains closed variables. Then in order to make sure we can still share variables if need be, it's a good idea to transform things by a box. [see p. 115]

Finally, it's feasible to mix all these possibilities in order to adapt them to the cases where they excell. To carry out this adaptation, we must analyze programs more precisely. In short, we need a real compiler, not just an interpreter with pretreatments like ours.

Defining Global Variables

When it encounters a global variable, the current interpreter recognizes it by the fact that it belongs to the global predefined or mutable environment. Consequently, we must declare all the global variables that we're going to use. We do so in the definition of the interpreter by means of the macro `defvariable`:

```
(define-syntax defvariable
  (syntax-rules ()
    ((defvariable name) (g.current-initialize! 'name)) ) )
```

Regardless of the practices for declaring variables in other languages, this way of doing things is considered quite out of place in Lisp dialects. Consequently, when an identifier is used as a global variable, we want it to be created automatically. One easy solution is to improve the function `compute-kind` so that it detects such cases, like this:

```
(define (compute-kind r n)
  (or (local-variable? r 0 n)
      (global-variable? g.current n)
      (global-variable? g.init n)
      (adjoin-global-variable! n) ) )
(define (adjoin-global-variable! name)
  (let ((index (g.current-extend! name)))
    (vector-set! sg.current index undefined-value)
    (cdr (car g.current)) ) )
```

The problem is that in doing so, we've slightly violated the pretreatment discipline that we've adopted. In effect, the global variable is created during pretreatment rather than during execution. Let's analyze what goes on before the process of creating a variable. When a new variable is taken into account, two different results occur:

1. Its name is added to the environment of mutable global variables (known as **g.current**) and in passing, a number is assigned to it.

2. An address is allocated to the variable; the address contains its value, conforming to the number assigned to it.

In that light, consider the following program:

```
(begin (define foo (lambda () (bar)))
       (define bar (lambda () (if #t 33 hux))) )
```

Pretreating that program turns up three new variables: **foo**, **bar**, and **hux**. As soon as they are encountered, these variables are added by pretreatment to the global environment and receive a number. So after pretreatment, would you say that they have been created or merely exist potentially? Would you say that the variable **foo** appearing in the **define** form was only semi-created, or that **hux** is only semi-semi-created?

To execute a pretreated program, we assume that the mutable global execution environment contains the values of these new variables. Consequently, we must extend it at just the right moment: the beginning of the execution phase is, in fact, the only possible instant. Before the execution of a pretreated program, the size of the global execution environment is adapted to the number of mutable global variables present. The function `stand-alone-producer` illustrates that idea. It pretreats a program in a closure (`lambda (sr k)` ...), and the first act of that closure is to allocate the *ad hoc* global environment.

```
(define (stand-alone-producer e)
  (set! g.current (original.g.current))
  (let* ((m (meaning e r.init))
         (size (length g.current)) )
    (lambda (sr k)
      (set! sg.current (make-vector size undefined-value))
      (m sr k) ) ) )
```

There may be predefined variables in the mutable global environment so that environment can serve as the communication point between the system and a program, as for example the base used to read or write numbers. For that reason, we'll assume that these variables appear in the environment returned by (`original.g.current`).

With this style of programming, all variables exist as soon as they are mentioned. In a way closer to Scheme, we can also allow variables to be introduced only by the form **define**. In this latter case, and for the previous example, pretreatment must indicate a static error. There, **hux** is an undefined variable even it it is neither read nor written. That's not the case of **bar**: it isn't defined at its first use, but it is defined later.

To show the details of how **define** works, we'll add it as a new special form to the **meaning** pretreater:

```
... ((define) (meaning-define (cadr e) (caddr e) r)) ...
```

When definitions are analyzed, there is a test to see whether the variable exists already; if it does, the definition behaves like an assignment.

```
(define (meaning-define n e r)
  (let ((b (memq n *defined*)))
    (if (pair? b)
        (static-wrong "Already defined variable" n)
        (set! *defined* (cons n *defined*)) ) )
  (meaning-assignment n e r) )
```

Now the program pretreater has the responsibility of verifying whether any global variables have suddenly appeared without yet being explicitly defined. The list of defined global variables is thus put together at the beginning of pretreatment.

```
(define (stand-alone-producer e)
  (set! g.current (original.g.current))
  (let ((originally-defined (append (map car g.current)
                                    (map car g.init) )))
    (set! *defined* originally-defined)
    (let* ((m (meaning e r.init))
           (size (length g.current))
```

```
                   (anormals (set-difference (map car g.current) *defined*)) )
         (if (null? anormals)
             (lambda (sr k)
               (set! sg.current (make-vector size undefined-value))
               (m sr k) )
             (static-wrong "Not explicitly defined variables"
                           anormals ) ) ) ) )
   (define (set-difference set1 set2)
     (if (pair? set1)
         (if (memq (car set1) set2)
             (set-difference (cdr set1) set2)
             (cons (car set1) (set-difference (cdr set1) set2)) )
         '() ) )
```

In summary, we must distinguish what's within the jurisdiction of pretreatment
and what belongs to execution. A definition at execution is rigorously like assignment. In contrast, its pretreatment induces verifications, either instantaneous or
deferred until the end of pretreatment. The usual special forms (other than **define**)
have an effect only at execution. They have dynamic semantics. Definition belongs
to static semantics (implemented by pretreatment) since it will not be aware of
any global variable that is not accompanied by a definition. Moreover, it's a static
error to violate this rule.

As we said before about local variables of **letrec** [see p. 60], for variables, we
must distinguish the idea of existence from initialization. The fact that a variable
exists does not mean that it has been initialized. Here's an example to clarify that
point:

```
(begin (define foo bar)
       (define bar (lambda () 33)) )
```

In the case of a compiling interaction loop (a kind of incremental compiler immediately evaluating whatever it just compiled), all these problems are simplified
because the end of pretreatment coincides with the beginning of execution of pretreated code, and these two phases occur in the same memory space. Thus we
can adopt the first variation of **adjoin-global-variable!** as well as the present
improvement in **meaning-reference** which consisted of suppressing the test about
initialization for variables that have already been initialized.

6.1.10 Conclusions: Interpreter with Migrated Computa-
tions

It's hard to measure the improvements of this interpreter, but the gain is on the
order of 10 to 50. Pretreatment is fast enough even if still improvable (mainly that
compute-kind may use hashtables rather than lists for environments). In addition to these non-negligible gains, we've also taken advantage of the ideas of static
computations (what is pretreated) and dynamic computation (what is left until execution). In a certain way, then, the role of a good compiler is to leave the minimal
amount of work to do at execution. To invent the best pretreatments, there have
been many analyses carried out to identify which properties are valid at execution.
We'll mention only a few: abstract interpretation in [CC77], partial evaluation in

[JGS93], and flow control analysis in [Shi91]. Another area for improvement is how to choose good data structures, as you can see from the discussion about activation records.

Pretreatment reveals certain errors sooner and independently of their possible execution. It paves the way for a safer and more efficient programming style since fewer verifications are left until execution. The kind of pretreatment we looked at here is quite rudimentary, but it could certainly be extended to check types, as in ML.

The interpreter we finally got strongly resembles the one from Chapter 3 except that we've replaced closures by objects. Even though closures and objects have very similar internal representations, closures are poor man's objects: they are opaque; they can only be invoked; and we don't even know how to confer new behavior on them, for example, to introduce a little reflection.

6.2   Rejecting the Environment

Every expression is evaluated in a unique residual environment; its value is `sr`. Since that environment changes only during the invocation of functions that re-install and then extend their definition environment, you might ask whether it would be more useful to introduce the idea of the current environment, the value of which is the global variable (or even the register) `*env*`. Making that environment global lets us avoid explicitly passing environments as arguments to all the closures resulting from pretreatment. In other words, the result of pretreatment will no longer be an abstraction like (`lambda` (`sr k`) ...) but rather simply (`lambda` (`k`) ...).

To carry out this transformation, which will suppress local variables `sr` in favor of one global variable `*env*`, all we have to modify is the function **meaning** to introduce management of this variable there. *A priori* the modification seems simple:

1. We search for local variables in `*env*` now, not in `sr` anymore.

2. When a function is invoked, it assigns its own definition environment, conveniently extended already, to `*env*`.

However, on closer examination, we see that those steps are not sufficient because if `*env*` is assigned, then from time to time it will be necessary to restore its earlier value, if only to return to a computation that was interrupted during an invocation. Here's a trivial solution: when a function assigns an environment to `*env*`, the function stores the preceding value and restores that value at the moment that the function returns its final value. The problem with this solution is that it does not conform to Scheme, which demands that tail calls must be evaluated with a constant continuation.

This problem resembles the well known problem of defining a function-calling protocol in terms of machine registers. The registers have to be saved during the computation of the invoked function, but who should do it?

- The one being called knows exactly which registers it uses and as a consequence, it can limit its efforts to preserving only those that concern it. The difficulty here is that the one being called then begins by saving registers, evaluating its body, saving the value produced, restoring the registers, and then returning the final value. The body of the called function is thus evaluated with a continuation which is that of the caller plus that fact that the registers must be restored.

- The caller knows exactly which registers it will need after the invocation and can thus save just those itself. Then the one being called has only to evaluate its body and return the value produced. If the caller does not have to restore the registers itself, you see that the one being called does not add any constraints. However, this technique is obviously too punctilious since the one being called may need only a few registers and could get along with registers not used by the caller without requiring the caller to save anything at all.

[SS80] proposed the caller should mark registers in one of two ways: "must be saved if used" or "can be overwritten without harm." The one being called can then save only what is really needed and change the mark to "must be restored" or "has not changed." This technique boils down to making each register a stack where only the top is accessible and the depths store values that must be restored. During a return, a special machine instruction restores the registers according to their marks.

It is very important for tail calls to be executed with a constant continuation (that is, without increasing the size of the recursion stack) so that iterations can be efficient and not hampered by the size of the recursion stack. For those reasons, we'll adopt the second strategy, so the caller will be responsible for preserving the environment.

Fortunately, whether or not an evaluation is in tail position is a static property, so we will add a supplementary argument to the function **meaning**. That supplementary argument is a Boolean, **tail?**, indicating whether or not the expression is in the tail position. If the expression is in the tail position, it is not necessary to restore the environment. (It's superfluous to save that environment, but it is not forbidden to do so.)

How do we determine the expressions in tail position? It's sufficient to look at the denotations of Scheme: every subform evaluated with a continuation different from the continuation of the form containing it is not in tail position. In an assignment (**set!** x π), the subform π has a continuation different from that of the assignment since its value must be written in the variable x. Therefore, it is not in tail position. Likewise, in a conditional (**if** π_0 π_1 π_2), the condition π_0 is not in tail position. In a sequence (**begin** π_0 ... π_{n-1} π_n), the forms π_0 ... π_{n-1} are not in tail position so we must save the environment between the computation of various terms of the sequence. In an application (π_0 ... π_n), none of the terms are in tail position since the invocation still remains to be done. In contrast, the body of a function is in tail position as well as the evaluation of the entire program since neither the one nor the other will need to restore the previous environment.

Here is a new version of the function **meaning** followed by the function that starts this new interpreter.

```
(define (meaning e r tail?)
```

```
      (if (atom? e)
          (if (symbol? e) (meaning-reference e r tail?)
                          (meaning-quotation e r tail?) )
          (case (car e)
            ((quote)  (meaning-quotation (cadr e) r tail?))
            ((lambda) (meaning-abstraction (cadr e) (cddr e) r tail?))
            ((if)     (meaning-alternative (cadr e) (caddr e) (cadddr e)
                                           r tail? ))
            ((begin)  (meaning-sequence (cdr e) r tail?))
            ((set!)   (meaning-assignment (cadr e) (caddr e) r tail?))
            (else     (meaning-application (car e) (cdr e) r tail?)) ) ) )
(define *env* sr.init)
(define (chapter62-interpreter)
  (define (toplevel)
    (set! *env* sr.init)
    ((meaning (read) r.init #t) display)
    (toplevel) )
  (toplevel) )
```

6.2.1 References to Variables

A reference to a variable now uses the register ***env***. We won't give a new version
of **meaning-assignment** since you can deduce it easily enough.

```
    (define (meaning-reference n r tail?)
      (let ((kind (compute-kind r n)))
        (if kind
            (case (car kind)
              ((local)
               (let ((i (cadr kind))
                     (j (cddr kind)) )
                 (if (= i 0)
                     (lambda (k)
                       (k (activation-frame-argument *env* j)) )
                     (lambda (k)
                       (k (deep-fetch *env* i j)) ) ) ) )
              ((global)
               (let ((i (cdr kind)))
                 (if (eq? (global-fetch i) undefined-value)
                     (lambda (k)
                       (let ((v (global-fetch i)))
                         (if (eq? v undefined-value)
                             (wrong "Uninitialized variable" n)
                             (k v) ) ) )
                     (lambda (k)
                       (k (global-fetch i)) ) ) ) )
              ((predefined)
               (let* ((i (cdr kind))
                      (value (predefined-fetch i)) )
                 (lambda (k)
                   (k value) ) ) ) )
```

```
(static-wrong "No such variable" n) ) ) )
```

6.2.2 Alternatives

We'll skip over quoting; it only has to be (or not be) in tail position. We'll go on to the conditional. Since the condition is not in tail position, you see this:

```
(define (meaning-alternative e1 e2 e3 r tail?)
  (let ((m1 (meaning e1 r #f))          ;restore environment!
        (m2 (meaning e2 r tail?))
        (m3 (meaning e3 r tail?)) )
    (lambda (k)
      (m1 (lambda (v)
            ((if v m2 m3) k) )) ) ) )
```

6.2.3 Sequence

The last expression of a sequence saves the environment if the sequence must do so. Notice that the current environment is restored only if there have been applications that might have modified it. In particular, a sequence like (begin a (car x) ...) does not require that the environment be preserved during the computation of a nor (car x) because it won't be modified.

```
(define (meaning-sequence e+ r tail?)
  (if (pair? e+)
      (if (pair? (cdr e+))
          (meaning*-multiple-sequence (car e+) (cdr e+) r tail?)
          (meaning*-single-sequence (car e+) r tail?) )
      (static-wrong "Illegal syntax: (begin)") ) )
(define (meaning*-single-sequence e r tail?)
  (meaning e r tail?) )
(define (meaning*-multiple-sequence e e+ r tail?)
  (let ((m1 (meaning e r #f))
        (m+ (meaning-sequence e+ r tail?)) )
    (lambda (k)
      (m1 (lambda (v)
            (m+ k) )) ) ) )
```

6.2.4 Abstraction

An abstraction must capture the current environment, which is the "birth" environment of the closure being created. The abstraction must restore the environment to extend it to other invocation instances. The case of functions with variable arity is similar to that of functions with fixed arity.

```
(define (meaning-fix-abstraction n* e+ r tail?)
  (let* ((arity (length n*))
         (arity+1 (+ arity 1))
         (r2 (r-extend* r n*))
         (m+ (meaning-sequence e+ r2 #t)) )
    (lambda (k)
```

```
(let ((sr *env*))
  (k (lambda (v* k1)
       (if (= (activation-frame-argument-length v*) arity+1)
           (begin (set! *env* (sr-extend* sr v*))
                  (m+ k1) )
           (wrong "Incorrect arity") ) )) ) ) ) )
```

6.2.5 Applications

The only really complicated case is that of an application since an application has
to manage whether or not the environment must be restored after the invocation.

```
(define (meaning-regular-application e e* r tail?)
  (let* ((m (meaning e r #f))
         (m* (meaning* e* r (length e) #f)) )
    (if tail?
        (lambda (k)
          (m (lambda (f)
               (if (procedure? f)
                   (m* (lambda (v*)
                         (f v* k) ))
                   (wrong "Not a function" f) ) )) )
        (lambda (k)
          (m (lambda (f)
               (if (procedure? f)
                   (m* (lambda (v*)
                         (let ((sr *env*))         ; save environment
                           (f v* (lambda (v)
                                   (set! *env* sr) ; restore environment
                                   (k v) )) ) ))
                   (wrong "Not a function" f) ) )) ) ) ) )
(define (meaning* e* r size tail?)
  (if (pair? e*)
      (meaning-some-arguments (car e*) (cdr e*) r size tail?)
      (meaning-no-argument r size tail?) ) )
(define (meaning-some-arguments e e* r size tail?)
  (let ((m (meaning e r #f))
        (m* (meaning* e* r size tail?))
        (rank (- size (+ (length e*) 1))) )
    (lambda (k)
      (m (lambda (v)
           (m* (lambda (v*)
                 (set-activation-frame-argument! v* rank v)
                 (k v*) ) )) )) ) )
(define (meaning-no-argument r size tail?)
  (let ((size+1 (+ size 1)))
    (lambda (k)
      (let ((v* (allocate-activation-frame size+1)))
        (k v*) ) ) ) )
```

In this way, we've produced a new interpreter with the environment put into a register. The initial global environments are the same as before.

6.2.6 Conclusions: Interpreter with Environment in a Register

This transformation is not always helpful. If we want to add parallelism to the language, the global variable ***env*** would be a unique resource shared by all tasks. Moreover it would have to be saved in the context of every task. However, the fact that the environment is always available is advantageous if we want to add reflection to the language because we can then imagine primitives accessing it.

This new interpreter is no faster than the preceding one. Of course invocations now have only one variable instead of two, but they do so at the expense of a reference to a global variable that can change every time the environment has to be checked. On the positive side, the idea of tail position is clearer now, and we are gently getting closer to the next interpreter.

6.3 Diluting Continuations

It is not rare for the implementation language to provide sorts of continuations that we can use directly (rather than handle them explicitly as in the preceding interpreter). That situation is not as crazy as it sounds. If we have a compiler available for Scheme, we usually get an interpreter for it by writing one in Scheme and compiling it. The interpreter we get that way then uses the execution library, especially the **call/cc** it finds there. However, if we compile only Lisp, the only continuations we'll ever need are equivalent to **setjmp/longjmp** from the C language library. In these two cases, **call/cc** can be considered as a magic operator, and it is therefore totally pointless to reify continuations everywhere. Always having them on hand requires an extraordinary rate of allocation, allocations that we give up if we are trying to increase the interpretation speed.

The next interpreter will thus return to a direct style without explicit continuations. We'll take advantage of it to make two new modifications:

1. functions will now be represented explicitly as *ad hoc* objects;

2. the results of pretreatment will appear as combinators (written as capital letters) reminding us of the instructions of a hypothetical virtual machine.

We'll take up all the improvements in the first interpreter (calls to primitives, reducible forms, etc.) again and then give them all definitions again.

6.3.1 Closures

As usual, closures will be represented by objects with two fields, one for their code and another for their definition environment. The invocation protocol will be adapted to this representation by the function **invoke**, like this:

```
(define-class closure Object
  ( code
    closed-environment
    ) )
```

```
(define (invoke f v*)
  (if (closure? f)
      ((closure-code f) v* (closure-closed-environment f))
      (wrong "Not a function" f) ) )
```

The code of interpreted closures will thus be represented by a closure with two
variables, one for the activation record, and the other for the definition environment. In that way, the definition environment will be available for extensions.
Every invocation of a closure must thus pass by the invocation function, named
(reasonably enough) **invoke**.

6.3.2 The Pretreater

Pretreatment of programs is handled by the function **meaning**. Instead of returning
a closure (**lambda (k)** ...), now it returns (**lambda ()** ...), an object that we
can interpret as a address to which we simply jump to execute it. (This practice
descends directly from Forth.) By suppressing all variables, we get thunks. Moreover, it won't be hard to have an invocation protocol slightly more elaborate than
the current one to produce a simple but effective **GOTO** [see **Ex. 6.6**] to invoke
thunks.

You can see the function **meaning** on page 207.

6.3.3 Quoting

Quoting is still quoting, but it appears even easier to read because of the combinator
CONSTANT, like this:

```
(define (meaning-quotation v r tail?)
  (CONSTANT v) )
(define (CONSTANT value)
  (lambda () value) )
```

6.3.4 References

Pretreating variables always involves categorizing them and then associating them
with the right reader. These readers will be generated by appropriate combinators.
Since we use combinators, this definition is lighter and consequently easier to read.

```
(define (meaning-reference n r tail?)
  (let ((kind (compute-kind r n)))
    (if kind
        (case (car kind)
          ((local)
           (let ((i (cadr kind))
                 (j (cddr kind)) )
             (if (= i 0)
                 (SHALLOW-ARGUMENT-REF j)
                 (DEEP-ARGUMENT-REF i j) ) ) ) )
          ((global)
           (let ((i (cdr kind)))
             (CHECKED-GLOBAL-REF i) ) )
```

```
              ((predefined)
               (let ((i (cdr kind)))
                 (PREDEFINED i) ) ) )
            (static-wrong "No such variable" n) ) ) )
  (define (SHALLOW-ARGUMENT-REF j)
    (lambda () (activation-frame-argument *env* j)) )
  (define (PREDEFINED i)
    (lambda () (predefined-fetch i)) )
  (define (DEEP-ARGUMENT-REF i j)
    (lambda () (deep-fetch *env* i j)) )
  (define (GLOBAL-REF i)
    (lambda () (global-fetch i)) )
  (define (CHECKED-GLOBAL-REF i)
    (lambda ()
      (let ((v (global-fetch i)))
        (if (eq? v undefined-value)
            (wrong "Uninitialized variable")
            v ) ) ) )
```

Nevertheless, notice that in the combinator CHECKED-GLOBAL-REF, when the variable is not initialized, since we have available only the index of the variable in the vector sg.current, it is no longer possible simply to indicate the name of the erroneous variable. To do that, we have to keep what we conventionally call a "symbol table" (here, the list g.current) indicating the names of variables and the locations where they are stored. [see **Ex. 6.1**] With that device, if we know the index of a faulty variable, then we can retrieve its name.

6.3.5 Conditional

Conditionals are clearer here, too, because of the combinator ALTERNATIVE, which takes as arguments the results of the pretreatment of its three subforms.

```
  (define (meaning-alternative e1 e2 e3 r tail?)
    (let ((m1 (meaning e1 r #f))
          (m2 (meaning e2 r tail?))
          (m3 (meaning e3 r tail?)) )
      (ALTERNATIVE m1 m2 m3) ) )
  (define (ALTERNATIVE m1 m2 m3)
    (lambda () (if (m1) (m2) (m3))) )
```

6.3.6 Assignment

The structure of assignment resembles the structure of referencing except that there is a subform to evaluate, a subform provided as an argument to all the write-combinators.

```
  (define (meaning-assignment n e r tail?)
    (let ((m (meaning e r #f))
          (kind (compute-kind r n)) )
      (if kind
          (case (car kind)
```

```
          ((local)
           (let ((i (cadr kind))
                 (j (cddr kind)) )
             (if (= i 0)
                 (SHALLOW-ARGUMENT-SET! j m)
                 (DEEP-ARGUMENT-SET! i j m) ) ) )
          ((global)
           (let ((i (cdr kind)))
             (GLOBAL-SET! i m) ) )
          ((predefined)
           (static-wrong "Immutable predefined variable" n) ) )
        (static-wrong "No such variable" n) ) ) )
(define (SHALLOW-ARGUMENT-SET! j m)
  (lambda () (set-activation-frame-argument! *env* j (m))) )
(define (DEEP-ARGUMENT-SET! i j m)
  (lambda () (deep-update! *env* i j (m))) )
(define (GLOBAL-SET! i m)
  (lambda () (global-update! i (m))) )
```

6.3.7 Sequence

We express a sequence clearly in terms of the combinator SEQUENCE corresponding
to a binary begin.

```
(define (meaning-sequence e+ r tail?)
  (if (pair? e+)
      (if (pair? (cdr e+))
          (meaning*-multiple-sequence (car e+) (cdr e+) r tail?)
          (meaning*-single-sequence (car e+) r tail?) )
      (static-wrong "Illegal syntax: (begin)") ) )
(define (meaning*-single-sequence e r tail?)
  (meaning e r tail?) )
(define (meaning*-multiple-sequence e e+ r tail?)
  (let ((m1 (meaning e r #f))
        (m+ (meaning-sequence e+ r tail?)) )
    (SEQUENCE m1 m+) ) )
(define (SEQUENCE m m+)
  (lambda () (m) (m+)) )
```

6.3.8 Abstraction

Closures are created by the combinators FIX-CLOSURE or NARY-CLOSURE. Their
differences involve verifying the arity and putting the excess arguments into a list.

```
(define (meaning-abstraction nn* e+ r tail?)
  (let parse ((n* nn*)
              (regular '()) )
    (cond
      ((pair? n*) (parse (cdr n*) (cons (car n*) regular)))
      ((null? n*) (meaning-fix-abstraction nn* e+ r tail?))
```

```
            (else        (meaning-dotted-abstraction
                           (reverse regular) n* e+ r tail? )) ) ) )
     (define (meaning-fix-abstraction n* e+ r tail?)
       (let* ((arity (length n*))
              (r2 (r-extend* r n*))
              (m+ (meaning-sequence e+ r2 #t)) )
         (FIX-CLOSURE m+ arity) ) )
     (define (meaning-dotted-abstraction n* n e+ r tail?)
       (let* ((arity (length n*))
              (r2 (r-extend* r (append n* (list n))))
              (m+ (meaning-sequence e+ r2 #t)) )
         (NARY-CLOSURE m+ arity) ) )
     (define (FIX-CLOSURE m+ arity)
       (let ((arity+1 (+ arity 1)))
         (lambda ()
           (define (the-function v* sr)
             (if (= (activation-frame-argument-length v*) arity+1)
                 (begin (set! *env* (sr-extend* sr v*))
                        (m+) )
                 (wrong "Incorrect arity") ) )
           (make-closure the-function *env*) ) ) )
     (define (NARY-CLOSURE m+ arity)
       (let ((arity+1 (+ arity 1)))
         (lambda ()
           (define (the-function v* sr)
             (if (>= (activation-frame-argument-length v*) arity+1)
                 (begin
                   (listify! v* arity)
                   (set! *env* (sr-extend* sr v*))
                   (m+) )
                 (wrong "Incorrect arity") ) )
           (make-closure the-function *env*) ) ) )
```

6.3.9 Application

The only thing left to handle is applications. **meaning-application** analyzes their
nature. It recognizes reducible forms, calls to primitives, and any applications.

```
     (define (meaning-application e e* r tail?)
       (cond ((and (symbol? e)
                   (let ((kind (compute-kind r e)))
                     (and (pair? kind)
                          (eq? 'predefined (car kind))
                          (let ((desc (get-description e)))
                            (and desc
                                 (eq? 'function (car desc))
                                 (or (= (length (cddr desc)) (length e*))
                                     (static-wrong
                                      "Incorrect arity for primitive" e )
                                     ) ) ) ) ) )
              (meaning-primitive-application e e* r tail?) )
```

```
((and (pair? e)
      (eq? 'lambda (car e)) )
 (meaning-closed-application e e* r tail?) )
(else (meaning-regular-application e e* r tail?)) ) )
```

All applications are subject to only four combinators. In the combinator TR-REGULAR-CALL, the computations of the function term and the arguments are put into sequence. As usual, the evaluation order is left to right.

```
(define (meaning-regular-application e e* r tail?)
  (let* ((m (meaning e r #f))
         (m* (meaning* e* r (length e*) #f)) )
    (if tail? (TR-REGULAR-CALL m m*) (REGULAR-CALL m m*)) ) )
(define (meaning* e* r size tail?)
  (if (pair? e*)
      (meaning-some-arguments (car e*) (cdr e*) r size tail?)
      (meaning-no-argument r size tail?) ) )
(define (meaning-some-arguments e e* r size tail?)
  (let ((m (meaning e r #f))
        (m* (meaning* e* r size tail?))
        (rank (- size (+ (length e*) 1))) )
    (STORE-ARGUMENT m m* rank) ) )
(define (meaning-no-argument r size tail?)
  (ALLOCATE-FRAME size) )
(define (TR-REGULAR-CALL m m*)
  (lambda ()
    (let ((f (m)))
      (invoke f (m*)) ) ) )
(define (REGULAR-CALL m m*)
  (lambda ()
    (let* ((f (m))
           (v* (m*))
           (sr *env*)
           (result (invoke f v*)) )
      (set! *env* sr)
      result ) ) )
(define (STORE-ARGUMENT m m* rank)
  (lambda ()
    (let* ((v (m))
           (v* (m*)) )
      (set-activation-frame-argument! v* rank v)
      v* ) ) )
(define (ALLOCATE-FRAME size)
  (let ((size+1 (+ size 1)))
    (lambda ()
      (allocate-activation-frame size+1) ) ) )
```

6.3.10 Reducible Forms

Since reducible forms include an explicit lambda form in the function position, their pretreatment adds four new combinators. CONS-ARGUMENT creates the list of excess arguments. `ALLOCATE-DOTTED-FRAME` creates an activation record, very much like `ALLOCATE-FRAME` except that the supplementary field is explicitly initialized by () (an initialization we avoided in `ALLOCATE-FRAME` for performance reasons).

```
(define (meaning-dotted-closed-application n* n body e* r tail?)
  (let* ((m* (meaning-dotted* e* r (length e*) (length n*) #f))
         (r2 (r-extend* r (append n* (list n))))
         (m+ (meaning-sequence body r2 tail?)) )
    (if tail? (TR-FIX-LET m* m+)
        (FIX-LET m* m+) ) ) ) )
(define (meaning-dotted* e* r size arity tail?)
  (if (pair? e*)
      (meaning-some-dotted-arguments (car e*) (cdr e*)
                                     r size arity tail? )
      (meaning-no-dotted-argument r size arity tail?) ) )
(define (meaning-some-dotted-arguments e e* r size arity tail?)
  (let ((m (meaning e r #f))
        (m* (meaning-dotted* e* r size arity tail?))
        (rank (- size (+ (length e*) 1))) )
    (if (< rank arity) (STORE-ARGUMENT m m* rank)
        (CONS-ARGUMENT m m* arity) ) ) )
(define (meaning-no-dotted-argument r size arity tail?)
  (ALLOCATE-DOTTED-FRAME arity) )
(define (FIX-LET m* m+)
  (lambda ()
    (set! *env* (sr-extend* *env* (m*)))
    (let ((result (m+)))
      (set! *env* (environment-next *env*))
      result ) ) )
(define (TR-FIX-LET m* m+)
  (lambda ()
    (set! *env* (sr-extend* *env* (m*)))
    (m+) ) )
(define (CONS-ARGUMENT m m* arity)
  (lambda ()
    (let* ((v (m))
           (v* (m*)) )
      (set-activation-frame-argument!
       v* arity (cons v (activation-frame-argument v* arity)) )
      v* ) ) )
(define (ALLOCATE-DOTTED-FRAME arity)
  (let ((arity+1 (+ arity 1)))
    (lambda ()
      (let ((v* (allocate-activation-frame arity+1)))
        (set-activation-frame-argument! v* arity '())
        v* ) ) ) )
```

The combinator `FIX-LET` must restore the current environment—implying that it must have been stored somewhere earlier so that it could be restored eventually. There is an elegant solution here: since it appears in the linked activation records, we simply have to go look for it there.

6.3.11 Calling Primitives

The last type (and not the least important in number) is the case of forms where we have an immutable global variable in the function position. In that case, we will call the right invoker, using the arity as a parameter, so that we no longer need to re-verify the arity.

```
(define (meaning-primitive-application e e* r tail?)
  (let* ((desc (get-description e))
         ;; desc = (function address . variables-list)
         (address (cadr desc))
         (size (length e*)) )
    (case size
      ((0) (CALL0 address))
      ((1)
       (let ((m1 (meaning (car e*) r #f)))
         (CALL1 address m1) ) )
      ((2)
       (let ((m1 (meaning (car e*) r #f))
             (m2 (meaning (cadr e*) r #f)) )
         (CALL2 address m1 m2) ) )
      ((3)
       (let ((m1 (meaning (car e*) r #f))
             (m2 (meaning (cadr e*) r #f))
             (m3 (meaning (caddr e*) r #f)) )
         (CALL3 address m1 m2 m3) ) )
      (else (meaning-regular-application e e* r tail?)) ) ) ) )
(define (CALL0 address)
  (lambda () (address)) )
(define (CALL3 address m1 m2 m3)
  (lambda () (let* ((v1 (m1))
                    (v2 (m2)) )
               (address v1 v2 (m3)) )) )
```

CALL3 explicitly puts the arguments in sequence to respect the left to right order.

6.3.12 Starting the Interpreter

Since continuations are no longer explicit in this interpreter, we must look again at the macros that enrich the global environment. Their structure has changed little, so we'll show you only **defprimitive2** by way of example:

```
(define-syntax defprimitive2
  (syntax-rules ()
    ((defprimitive2 name value)
     (definitial name
       (letrec ((arity+1 (+ 2 1))
                (behavior
                 (lambda (v* sr)
                   (if (= arity+1 (activation-frame-argument-length v*))
                       (value (activation-frame-argument v* 0)
```

```
                          (activation-frame-argument v* 1) )
                  (wrong "Incorrect arity" 'name) ) ) ) )
        (description-extend! 'name '(function ,value a b))
        (make-closure behavior sr.init) ) ) ) ) )
```

We start the interpreter by this:

```
(define (chapter63-interpreter)
  (define (toplevel)
    (set! *env* sr.init)
    (display ((meaning (read) r.init #t)))
    (toplevel) )
  (toplevel) )
```

6.3.13 The Function `call/cc`

Now since the function `call/cc` is magic, for its own definition, it needs the function `call/cc` from the library on which the interpreter is built, so here we have the tautologic definitions of the first interpreters.

```
(definitial call/cc
  (let* ((arity 1)
         (arity+1 (+ arity 1)) )
    (make-closure
     (lambda (v* sr)
       (if (= arity+1 (activation-frame-argument-length v*))
           (call/cc
            (lambda (k)
              (invoke
               (activation-frame-argument v* 0)
               (let ((frame (allocate-activation-frame (+ 1 1))))
                 (set-activation-frame-argument!
                  frame 0
                  (make-closure
                   (lambda (values r)
                     (if (= (activation-frame-argument-length values)
                            arity+1 )
                         (k (activation-frame-argument values 0))
                         (wrong "Incorrect arity" 'continuation) ) )
                   sr.init ) )
                 frame ) ) ) )
           (wrong "Incorrect arity" 'call/cc) ) )
     sr.init ) ) )
```

6.3.14 The Function `apply`

To look beyond our usual horizon, here's the function `apply`. It is always difficult to write because it strongly depends on how functions themselves are coded and on which calling protocol has been chosen, but here it is in all its detail and complexity.

```
(definitial apply
  (let* ((arity 2)
```

```
                    (arity+1 (+ arity 1)) )
      (make-closure
       (lambda (v* sr)
         (if (>= (activation-frame-argument-length v*) arity+1)
             (let* ((proc (activation-frame-argument v* 0))
                    (last-arg-index
                     (- (activation-frame-argument-length v*) 2) )
                    (last-arg
                     (activation-frame-argument v* last-arg-index) )
                    (size (+ last-arg-index (length last-arg)))
                    (frame (allocate-activation-frame size)) )
               (do ((i 1 (+ i 1)))
                   ((= i last-arg-index))
                 (set-activation-frame-argument!
                  frame (- i 1) (activation-frame-argument v* i) ) )
               (do ((i (- last-arg-index 1) (+ i 1))
                    (last-arg last-arg (cdr last-arg)) )
                   ((null? last-arg))
                 (set-activation-frame-argument! frame i (car last-arg)) )
               (invoke proc frame) )
             (wrong "Incorrect arity" 'apply) ) )
      sr.init ) ) )
```

That primitive verifies that it has at least two arguments and then runs through the activation record to find the exact number of arguments to which the function in the first argument applies. To do so, it must compute the length of the list in the last argument. Once it has this number, we can then allocate an activation record of the correct size. We copy into that record all the arguments in their correct position; the first ones we copy directly from the activation record furnished to apply; the following ones, by exploring the list of "superfluous" arguments. That exploration stops when that list is empty, as determined by the test null?. It might seem more robust to use atom? but that would make the program (apply list '(a b . c)) correct—contrary to the norms of Scheme.

As you can see, apply is not an inexpensive operation because it allocates a new activation record, and it must run through the list in the last argument.

6.3.15 Conclusions: Interpreter without Continuations

This new interpreter is two to four times faster than the previous one, mainly because we don't reify continuations in it. In effect, representing continuations by closures mixes them up with other, more ordinary values. Doing that disregards an important property of continuations: that they habitually have a very short extent. For that reason, allocating continuations on a stack is usually a winner because it is a low-cost strategy. That's also the case for de-allocations, usually just one instruction popping the pointer from the top of the stack. Just so we don't make a mistake here, we should repeat that the mass of data allocated to represent a continuation is the same order of magnitude whether on a stack or in a heap, but managing it on a stack is less costly than managing it in a heap. (See also [App87] for a different opinion that does not take locality into account.) This observation holds even if we imagine specializing the heap in several zones with one adapted to continuations, as described in [MB93].

The thunks that this most recent interpreter uses belong to the technique of *threaded code* as in [Bel73] and common in Forth [Hon93]. This interpreter is also strongly inspired by that of Marc Feeley and Guy Lapalme in [FL87].

Combinators actually play the role of code generators. We introduced them in this interpreter because they offer a simple interface that makes it easy to change the representation of pretreated programs. With them, we can easily imagine building objects rather than closures. In fact, there's an exercise [**see Ex. 6.3**] in preparation for the next chapter, where we'll see their use in compilation.

6.4 Conclusions

At first glance, this chapter and its three interpreters might seem like a giant step backward, wiping out all the progress we had made in the first four chapters. Indeed, we have practically suppressed memory (except for managing activation records), and continuations have disappeared. On the positive side, we've presented the idea of pretreatment as a preliminary to compilation. We've also separated static from dynamic and made various improvements to increase execution speed. We actually achieved that last goal: we've improved speed by roughly two orders of magnitude in comparison with the denotational interpreter.

The third interpreter of this chapter actually implements all the special forms of Scheme and represents the essence of any language. All that's left to do is endow the interpreter with a memory manager and *ad hoc* libraries specialized for editing text, industrial drafting and design, Scheme as a language, materials testing, virtual reality, etc. Of course, when we say "all that's left," we're glossing over the incredible complexity of choosing representation schema for primitive objects in memory where the chief goals are rapid type checking as in [Gud93] and no less efficient garbage collection.

Of course, we could improve these interpreters or even extend them to handle new special forms, but remember that our real purpose is to produce a set of interpreters modified incrementally to reduce the mass of detail composing them and to highlight new goals that they illustrate.

6.5 Exercises

Exercise 6.1 : [see p. 213] Modify the combinator `CHECKED-GLOBAL-REF` so that the error message about an uninitialized variable is more meaningful.

Exercise 6.2 : Define the primitive `list` for the third interpreter of this chapter. You will, of course, do so elegantly and with little effort.

Exercise 6.3 : Instead of pretreating a program, we could display the way it would be pretreated. Here's what we mean for factorial:

```
? (disassemble '(lambda (n) (if (= n 0) 1 (* n (fact (- n 1))))))
```

```
= (FIX-CLOSURE
    (ALTERNATIVE
      (CALL2 #<=> (SHALLOW-ARGUMENT-REF 0) (CONSTANT 0))
      (CONSTANT 1)
      (CALL2 #<*> (SHALLOW-ARGUMENT-REF 0)
                  (REGULAR-CALL
                    (CHECKED-GLOBAL-REF 10)  ;← fact
                    (STORE-ARGUMENT
                      (CALL2 #<-> (SHALLOW-ARGUMENT-REF 0) (CONSTANT 1))
                      (ALLOCATE-FRAME 1)
                      0 ) ) ) )
    1 )
```

Write such a disassembler to display pretreatment.

Exercise 6.4 :   Modify the last interpreter of this chapter so that activation records are allocated before arguments are computed. Then arguments could be put directly into the right place. [**see p. 189**]

Exercise 6.5 : Define a special form, **redefine**, to take a variable in the immutable global environment and insert it in the mutable global environment, as we discussed on page 191. The initial value of this new global variable is the value that it had before.

Exercise 6.6 : Improve the pretreatment of functions without variables. [**see p. 212**]

Recommended Reading

The last interpreter in this chapter is inspired by [FL87]. The method of getting from the denotational interpreter to combinators comes from [Cli84]. If you really like fast interpretation, you'll enjoy meditating on [Cha80] and [SJ93].

7

Compilation

THE preceding chapter explicated a pretreatment procedure that transcribed a program written in Scheme into a tree-like language of about twenty-five instructions. This chapter exploits the results of that pretreatment to transform it into a set of bytes, an *ad hoc* machine language. We'll look at each of the following ideas in turn: defining a virtual machine, compiling into its own language, and implementing various extensions of Scheme, such as escapes, dynamic variables, and exceptions.

(SHALLOW-ARGUMENT-REF j)	(PREDEFINED i)
(DEEP-ARGUMENT-REF i j)	(SHALLOW-ARGUMENT-SET! j m)
(DEEP-ARGUMENT-SET! i j m)	(GLOBAL-REF i)
(CHECKED-GLOBAL-REF i)	(GLOBAL-SET! i m)
(CONSTANT v)	(ALTERNATIVE $m1$ $m2$ $m3$)
(SEQUENCE m $m+$)	(TR-FIX-LET $m*$ $m+$)
(FIX-LET $m*$ $m+$)	(CALL0 $address$)
(CALL1 $address$ $m1$)	(CALL2 $address$ $m1$ $m2$)
(CALL3 $address$ $m1$ $m2$ $m3$)	(FIX-CLOSURE $m+$ $arity$)
(NARY-CLOSURE $m+$ $arity$)	(TR-REGULAR-CALL m $m*$)
(REGULAR-CALL m $m*$)	(STORE-ARGUMENT m $m*$ $rank$)
(CONS-ARGUMENT m $m*$ $arity$)	(ALLOCATE-FRAME $size$)
(ALLOCATE-DOTTED-FRAME $arity$)	

Table 7.1 The intermediate language with 25 instructions: m, $m1$, $m2$, $m3$, $m+$, and v are values; $m*$ returns an activation record; *rank*, *arity*, *size*, i, and j are natural numbers (positive integers); *address* represents a predefined function (subr) that takes values and returns one of them.

Compilation often produces a set of fairly low-level instructions. That was not the case in the pretreatment from the previous chapter. In fact, it built the equivalent of a structured tree. For a more eloquent example, consider the following program:

```
((lambda (fact) (fact 5 fact (lambda (x) x)))
```

```
  (lambda (n f k) (if (= n 0) (k 1)
                      (f (- n 1) f (lambda (r) (k (* n r)))) )) )
```

After transcription, its pretreatment looks like this:

```
(TR-FIX-LET
 (STORE-ARGUMENT
  (FIX-CLOSURE
   (ALTERNATIVE
    (CALL2 #<=> (SHALLOW-ARGUMENT-REF 0) (CONSTANT 0))
    (TR-REGULAR-CALL (SHALLOW-ARGUMENT-REF 2)
                     (STORE-ARGUMENT (CONSTANT 1)
                                     (ALLOCATE-FRAME 1) 0) )
    (TR-REGULAR-CALL (SHALLOW-ARGUMENT-REF 1)
     (STORE-ARGUMENT (CALL2 #<-> (SHALLOW-ARGUMENT-REF 0) (CONSTANT 1))
      (STORE-ARGUMENT (SHALLOW-ARGUMENT-REF 1)
       (STORE-ARGUMENT (FIX-CLOSURE
                        (TR-REGULAR-CALL (DEEP-ARGUMENT-REF 1 2)
                         (STORE-ARGUMENT (CALL2 #<*>
                                         (DEEP-ARGUMENT-REF 1 0)
                                         (SHALLOW-ARGUMENT-REF 0) )
                          (ALLOCATE-FRAME 1)
                          0 ) )
                        1 )
         (ALLOCATE-FRAME 3)
         2 )
        1 )
       0 ) ) )
     3 )
   (ALLOCATE-FRAME 1)
   0)
 (TR-REGULAR-CALL (SHALLOW-ARGUMENT-REF 0)
  (STORE-ARGUMENT (CONSTANT 5)
   (STORE-ARGUMENT (SHALLOW-ARGUMENT-REF 0)
    (STORE-ARGUMENT (FIX-CLOSURE (SHALLOW-ARGUMENT-REF 0) 1)
     (ALLOCATE-FRAME 3)
     2 )
    1 )
   0 ) ) )
```

It's not easy to read, but it's accurate. The purpose of this chapter is to show that this form is far from final. Indeed, certain transformations, such as linearizing and byte-coding, can even transmute it into other languages. The language of the twenty-five instructions/generators in Table 7.1 will serve as our intermediate language, a kind of springboard for leaping into other realms.

We'll regard the pretreatment phase (that last interpreter in the preceding chapter, the one that produced the famous intermediate language) as the first pass of a compiler. Consequently, we'll be interested only in the twenty-five functions/generators. In fact, we'll adapt them to the characteristics of our final target language. By dividing the work in this way, we take advantage of the fact that the intermediate language is executable. We've already used that fact to test the pretreater. Now it will let us concentrate solely on the second pass.

First, we'll study compilation toward a virtual machine. It will be a simple one, but one that presents all the characteristics of any machine programmable in machine language. Its instruction set will be represented by bytes, in particular, integers from 0 to 255. This technique is known as *byte-coding*. It appeared sometime before 1980, according to [Deu80, Row90]. Since then, it has often been used to highlight the rudiments of compilation, as in [Hen80]. The code we get this way is particularly compact, a quality that justifies its use on machines with little memory or limited caching. It's the technique used by PC-Scheme [BJ86] and Caml Light [LW93].

There are several aspects to the entire technique. After pretreatment, a program is compiled into byte-code vectors. These byte-codes are then evaluated by an interpreter. That is, compilation and interpretation are both involved, but only interpreting byte-code is necessary for execution.

7.1 Compiling into Bytes

Our goal is little by little to bring up a machine specialized to interpret byte-code. We define this machine by defining the twenty-five instructions of the intermediate language. Some of these definitions are obvious, but others will require a little inventiveness on our part. To our advantage, we'll be designing both the machine and its instruction set at the same time. This flexibility will be indispensible when we want, say, to add new registers or introduce a stack.

To get the ultimate byte-code vector, we'll have to linearize the program expressed in intermediate language. For that reason, we must be sure that communication between instructions is limited to the common resources of the machine, that is, the registers and the stack. For the moment, our machine has only one register; it contains the current lexical environment, ***env***, but we'll soon fatten up this somewhat Spartan architecture.

7.1.1 Introducing the Register *val*

Among the twenty-five instructions in the intermediate language, some of them produce values, for example, like the instructions **SHALLOW-ARGUMENT-REF** or **CONSTANT**, whereas others, like **FIX-LET** or **ALTERNATIVE**, coordinate computations. In that light, let's look more closely at **GLOBAL-SET!**. It was defined like this:

```
(define (GLOBAL-SET! i m)
  (lambda () (global-update! i (m))) )
```

To break communication, we have to have another register. We'll call it ***val***. Instructions that produce values will put them there so that consumers can find them. Consequently, an instruction like **CONSTANT**—one that produces values—will be written like this:

```
(define (CONSTANT value)
  (lambda ()
    (set! *val* value) ) )
```

In contrast, a consumer of values, like **GLOBAL-SET!**, will become:

```
(define (GLOBAL-SET! i m)
```

```
(lambda ()
  (m)
  (global-update! i *val*) ) )
```

The form (m) will eventually produce a value in the register *val*, which will then be transferred by global-update! to the right address. Notice that global-update! does not disturb the register *val*. To disturb it would cost at least one instruction. As a consequence, the value of a form that assigns something to a global variable is the value found in the register *val*, that is, the assigned value.

It's easy enough to deduce the rest of the transformation of the two examples we gave earlier. For example, we linearize SEQUENCE automatically, like this:

```
(define (SEQUENCE m m+)
  (lambda () (m) (m+)) )
```

while FIX-LET becomes this:

```
(define (FIX-LET m* m+)
  (lambda ()
    (m*)
    (set! *env* (sr-extend* *env* *val*))
    (m+)
    (set! *env* (activation-frame-next *env*)) ) )
```

7.1.2   Inventing the Stack

We've already achieved part of the linearizing that we wanted to do, but for some instructions, the issues are more subtle. For example, STORE-ARGUMENT has become:

```
(define (STORE-ARGUMENT m m* rank)
  (lambda ()
    (m)
    (let ((v *val*))
      (m*)
      (set-activation-frame-argument! *val* rank v) ) ) )
```

That instruction uses the form let to save values and restore them later if needed. Here, the form let saves a value in an "anonymous register" v while (m*) is being calculated. We can't associate a real machine register with v because we might need more than one such v simultaneously, especially in the case of multiple forms of STORE-ARGUMENT nested inside the computation of (m*). Consequently, we need a place where we can save any number of values. A stack would be useful here, the more so because the pushes and pops seem equally balanced. We'll assume then that we have a well defined stack managed by the following functions:

```
(define *stack* (make-vector 1000))
(define *stack-index* 0)
(define (stack-push v)
  (vector-set! *stack* *stack-index* v)
  (set! *stack-index* (+ *stack-index* 1)) )
(define (stack-pop)
```

```
(set! *stack-index* (- *stack-index* 1))
(vector-ref *stack* *stack-index*) )
```

Endowed with this new technology, we can adapt the instruction STORE-ARGU-MENT to indulge immoderately in pushing and popping the stack. Instead of saving values in a register, we'll keep them on a stack, and we'll get them back from the stack when needed as well. This plan works only if we insure that the stack that (m*) takes is the same one that (m*) returns. Consequently, there is an invariant to respect as we write the instruction.

```
(define (STORE-ARGUMENT m m* rank)
  (lambda ()
    (m)
    (stack-push *val*)
    (m*)
    (let ((v (stack-pop)))
      (set-activation-frame-argument! *val* rank v) ) ) )
```

The case of REGULAR-CALL is clear except that we must simultaneously keep the function to invoke during the computation of its arguments and the current environment during the invocation itself. We had this:

```
(define (REGULAR-CALL m m*)
  (lambda ()
    (m)
    (let ((f *val*))
      (m*)
      (let ((sr *env*))
        (invoke f *val*)
        (set! *env* sr) ) ) ) )
```

After we invent a new register—*fun*—we can transform that definition into this one:

```
(define (REGULAR-CALL m m*)
  (lambda ()
    (m)
    (stack-push *val*)
    (m*)
    (set! *fun* (stack-pop))
    (stack-push *env*)
    (invoke *fun*)
    (set! *env* (stack-pop)) ) )
```

In passing, we notice that we have also redefined the calling protocol for functions. It no longer takes the activation record as an argument since that record is already in the register *val*. You can see this in the current version of FIX-CLOSURE:

```
(define (FIX-CLOSURE m+ arity)
  (let ((arity+1 (+ arity 1)))
    (lambda ()
      (define (the-function sr)
        (if (= (activation-frame-argument-length *val*) arity+1)
            (begin (set! *env* (sr-extend* sr *val*))
```

```
                  (m+) )
            (wrong "Incorrect arity") ) )
      (set! *val* (make-closure the-function *env*)) ) ) )
```

By adding registers, we can also linearize calls to primitives as well. We'll introduce the registers *arg1* and *arg2*. One of them is not necessarily different from *fun*, which is never used at the same time anyway. Consequently, we'll write CALL3 like this:

```
(define (CALL3 address m1 m2 m3)
  (lambda ()
    (m1)
    (stack-push *val*)
    (m2)
    (stack-push *val*)
    (m3)
    (set! *arg2* (stack-pop))
    (set! *arg1* (stack-pop))
    (set! *val* (address *arg1* *arg2* *val*)) ) )
```

7.1.3 Customizing Instructions

Currently the twenty-five instructions that we're redefining generate thunks where the body of a thunk is a sequence of register effects. To get the instructions we want, we need to transform these twenty-five instructions so that they generate sequences of thunks that have only one unique effect: to modify one register, to push one value onto the stack, etc. By inverting our point of view in this way, we'll introduce the idea of a program counter, that is, a specialized register designating the next instruction to execute. If we have a program counter, we will also be able to define the function calling protocol more precisely, and thus eventually we'll be able to describe the mysteries of implementing call/cc, too.

Linearizing Assignments

Let's take the case of SHALLOW-ARGUMENT-SET!. That instruction was defined like this:

```
(define (SHALLOW-ARGUMENT-SET! j m)
  (lambda ()
    (m)
    (set-activation-frame-argument! *env* j *val*) ) )
```

To transform it into a sequence of instructions, we'll rewrite it as the following two functions:

```
(define (SHALLOW-ARGUMENT-SET! j m)
  (append m (SET-SHALLOW-ARGUMENT! j)) )
(define (SET-SHALLOW-ARGUMENT! j)
  (list (lambda () (set-activation-frame-argument! *env* j *val*))) )
```

That first one, with the same name as before, composes various effects and returns the list of final instructions. The second function SET-SHALLOW-ARGUMENT! is specialized to write in an activation record.

Linearizing Invocations

REGULAR-CALL provides a good example of linearization. To customize all its components, we add the following instructions to the final machine: PUSH-VALUE, POP-FUNCTION, PRESERVE-ENV, FUNCTION-INVOKE, and RESTORE-ENV.

Here are those new definitions:

```
(define (REGULAR-CALL m m*)
  (append m (PUSH-VALUE)
         m* (POP-FUNCTION) (PRESERVE-ENV)
            (FUNCTION-INVOKE) (RESTORE-ENV)
         ) )
(define (PUSH-VALUE)
  (list (lambda () (stack-push *val*))) )
(define (POP-FUNCTION)
  (list (lambda () (set! *fun* (stack-pop)))) )
(define (PRESERVE-ENV)
  (list (lambda () (stack-push *env*))) )
(define (FUNCTION-INVOKE)
  (list (lambda () (invoke *fun*))) )
(define (RESTORE-ENV)
  (list (lambda () (set! *env* (stack-pop)))) )
```

Just as we wanted, now the result of compiling is a list of elementary instructions. However, this list is not directly executable, so we must provide an engine to evaluate this list of instructions. For that purpose, we define **run** like this:

```
(define (run)
  (let ((instruction (car *pc*)))
    (set! *pc* (cdr *pc*))
    (instruction)
    (run) ) )
```

Compiling now results in a list of instructions stored in the variable *pc* which plays the role of the program counter. The function **run** simulates a processor that reads an instruction, increments the program counter, executes the instruction, and then begins all over again. Incidentally, all the instructions here are represented by closures with the same signature (lambda () ...).

Linearizing the Conditional

Linearizing a conditional is always problematic because of the two possible exits. How should we linearize a fork like that? To handle that, we'll (re)invent two new jump instructions that affect the program counter: JUMP-FALSE and GOTO. GOTO, familiar from other languages, represents an unconditional jump. JUMP-FALSE tests the contents of the register *val* and jumps only if it contains False. Both these instructions affect only the register *pc* to the exclusion of any other.

```
(define (JUMP-FALSE i)
  (list (lambda () (if (not *val*) (set! *pc* (list-tail *pc* i))))) )
(define (GOTO i)
  (list (lambda () (set! *pc* (list-tail *pc* i)))) )
```

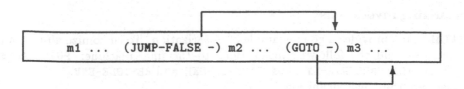

Figure 7.1 Linearizing the conditional

With those two new instructions, here's how we linearize the conditional. You can see it better in Figure 7.1.

```
(define (ALTERNATIVE m1 m2 m3)
   (append m1 (JUMP-FALSE (+ 1 (length m2))) m2 (GOTO (length m3)) m3) )
```

The condition is calculated and then tested by `JUMP-FALSE`. If the condition is true, we execute the instructions that follow it, and at the end of those computations, we jump over the corresponding instructions in the alternate. If the condition is false, we jump to the alternate that will be executed. Here you can see that we've just arrived at the level of an assembly language. Notice, however, that these jumps are relative to our current position, that is, they are program-counter relative.

Linearizing Abstractions

The last instruction that's hard to linearize is the one to create a closure. It's difficult because we have to splice together the code for the function with the code which creates it. Again, we'll use a jump to do this, as in Figure 7.2. Here's how we create a closure with variable arity:

```
(define (NARY-CLOSURE m+ arity)
   (define the-function
      (append (ARITY>=? (+ arity 1)) (PACK-FRAME! arity) (EXTEND-ENV)
              m+ (RETURN) ) )
   (append (CREATE-CLOSURE 1) (GOTO (length the-function))
           the-function ) )
(define (CREATE-CLOSURE offset)
   (list (lambda () (set! *val* (make-closure (list-tail *pc* offset)
                                              *env* )))) )
(define (PACK-FRAME! arity)
   (list (lambda () (listify! *val* arity))) )
```

The new instruction `CREATE-CLOSURE` builds a closure for which the code is found right after the following `GOTO` instruction. Once the closure has been created and put into the register `*val*`, its creator jumps over the code corresponding to its body in order to continue in sequence.

7.1.4   Calling Protocol for Functions

Functions are invoked by the instructions `TR-REGULAR-CALL` or `REGULAR-CALL`, which we covered a little earlier. [see p. 229] The function **invoke** condenses

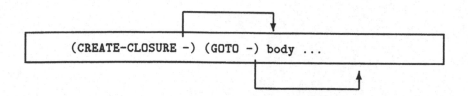

Figure 7.2 Linearizing an abstraction

that function calling protocol, like this:

```
(define (invoke f)
  (cond ((closure? f)
         (stack-push *pc*)
         (set! *env* (closure-closed-environment f))
         (set! *pc* (closure-code f)) )
        ... ) )
```

To invoke a function, we save the program counter that indicates the next instruction that follows the instruction (**FUNCTION-INVOKE**) in the caller. Then we take apart the closure to put its definition environment into the environment register ***env***. Eventually, we assign the address of the first instruction in its body to the program counter. We don't save the current environment because it has already been handled elsewhere according to whether the function was invoked by **TR-REGULAR-CALL** or **REGULAR-CALL**.

Then the function **run** takes over and executes the first instruction from the body of the invoked function to verify its arity, then, in case of successful verification, to extend the environment with its activation record. The activation record is in the register ***val***. By now, everything is in place for the function to evaluate its own body. A value is then computed and put into ***val***. Then that value has to be transmitted to the caller; that's the role of the **RETURN** instruction. It pops the program counter from the top of the stack and returns to the caller, like this:

```
(define (RETURN)
  (list (lambda () (set! *pc* (stack-pop)))) )
```

About Jumps

Assembly language programmers have probably noticed that we've been using only forward jumps. Moreover, the jumps as well as the construction of closures are all relative to the program counter. This relativity means that the code is independent of its actual place in memory. We call this phenomenon *pc-independent code* in the sense of independent of the program counter.

7.2 Language and Target Machine

Now we're going to define our target machine as well as the language for programming it. The machine will have five registers (***env***, ***val***, ***fun***, ***arg1***, and ***arg2***), a program counter (***pc***), and a stack, as you see in Figure 7.3.

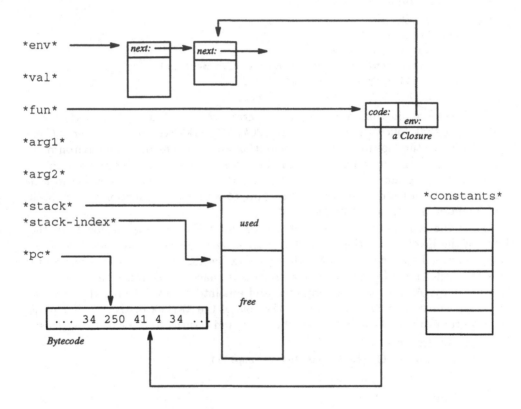

Figure 7.3 Byte machine

There are now thirty-four instructions. They appear in Table 7.2. In addition to the instructions you've already seen, we've added FINISH to complete calculations (or, more precisely, to get out of the function run) and to return control to the operating system or to its simulation in Lisp. [see p. 223]

The twenty-five instructions/generators of the intermediate language can be organized into two groups: leaf instructions and composite instructions. The nine leaf instructions are identified as such by the same name; they are marked by a star as a suffix in Table 7.2. In contrast, the sixteen composite instructions are defined explicitly in terms of the twenty-five new elementary instructions. We could have customized them more, for example, by decomposing CHECKED-GLOBAL-REF into a sequence of two instructions that carried out GLOBAL-REF and then verified that *val* actually contains an initialized value, but that would have slowed the interpreter. Conversely, we could have grouped some instructions together, as for CALL3: (POP-ARG2) is always followed by (POP-ARG1) so that particular sequence could be combined into one instruction.

(SHALLOW-ARGUMENT-REF *j*)∗	(PREDEFINED *i*)∗
(DEEP-ARGUMENT-REF *i j*)∗	(SET-SHALLOW-ARGUMENT! *j*)
(SET-DEEP-ARGUMENT! *i j*)	(GLOBAL-REF *i*)∗
(CHECKED-GLOBAL-REF *i*)∗	(SET-GLOBAL! *i*)
(CONSTANT *v*)∗	(JUMP-FALSE *offset*)
(GOTO *offset*)	(EXTEND-ENV)
(UNLINK-ENV)	(CALL0 *address*)∗
(INVOKE1 *address*)	(PUSH-VALUE)
(POP-ARG1)	(INVOKE2 *address*)
(POP-ARG2)	(INVOKE3 *address*)
(CREATE-CLOSURE *offset*)	(ARITY=? *arity* + 1)
(RETURN)	(PACK-FRAME! *arity*)
(ARITY>=? *arity* + 1)	(POP-FUNCTION)
(FUNCTION-INVOKE)	(PRESERVE-ENV)
(RESTORE-ENV)	(POP-FRAME! *rank*)
(POP-CONS-FRAME! *arity*)	(ALLOCATE-FRAME *size*)∗
(ALLOCATE-DOTTED-FRAME *arity*)∗	(FINISH)

Table 7.2 Symbolic instructions

A few of the sixteen composite instructions of the intermediate language haven't appeared before, so here are their unadorned definitions with no explanation. Later we'll get to the definition of the missing machine instructions that appeared in Table 7.2.

```
(define (DEEP-ARGUMENT-SET! i j m)
  (append m (SET-DEEP-ARGUMENT! i j)) )
(define (GLOBAL-SET! i m)
  (append m (SET-GLOBAL! i)) )
(define (SEQUENCE m m+)
  (append m m+) )
(define (TR-FIX-LET m* m+)
  (append m* (EXTEND-ENV) m+) )
```

```
(define (FIX-LET m* m+)
  (append m* (EXTEND-ENV) m+ (UNLINK-ENV)) )
(define (CALL1 address m1)
  (append m1 (INVOKE1 address) ) )
(define (CALL2 address m1 m2)
  (append m1 (PUSH-VALUE) m2 (POP-ARG1) (INVOKE2 address)) )
(define (CALL3 address m1 m2 m3)
  (append m1 (PUSH-VALUE)
          m2 (PUSH-VALUE)
          m3 (POP-ARG2) (POP-ARG1) (INVOKE3 address) ) )
(define (FIX-CLOSURE m+ arity)
  (define the-function
    (append (ARITY=? (+ arity 1)) (EXTEND-ENV) m+ (RETURN)) )
  (append (CREATE-CLOSURE 1) (GOTO (length the-function))
          the-function ) )
(define (TR-REGULAR-CALL m m*)
  (append m (PUSH-VALUE) m* (POP-FUNCTION) (FUNCTION-INVOKE)) )
(define (STORE-ARGUMENT m m* rank)
  (append m (PUSH-VALUE) m* (POP-FRAME! rank)) )
(define (CONS-ARGUMENT m m* arity)
  (append m (PUSH-VALUE) m* (POP-CONS-FRAME! arity)) )
```

The many **appends** that break up these definitions make pretreatment particularly costly and inefficient. A good solution is to build the final code in one pass. That's what we would do to compile into C. [see **p. 379**] To do that, we must linearize the code production; that's an activity that is independent of linearizing the code as we have done it in this chapter. To take just one example: for **CALL2**, we would do the following:

1. generate the code for **m1**;

2. produce the code for (**PUSH-VALUE**);

3. generate the code for **m2**;

4. produce the code for (**POP-ARG1**);

5. produce the code for (**INVOKE2 address**).

Carrying out those modifications is trivial everywhere except in the **GOTO**s and **JUMP-FALSE**s. We can no longer precompute them in **ALTERNATIVE**, **FIX-CLOSURE**, nor **NARY-CLOSURE**. To handle that chore, we must implement *backpatching*. For example, in **FIX-CLOSURE**, we must do the following:

1. produce the instruction **CREATE-CLOSURE**;

2. produce a **GOTO** instruction without specifying the offset but noting the current value of the program counter;

3. generate the code for the body of the function;

4. note the current value of the program counter to deduce the offset of the **GOTO** we generated earlier;

5. write that offset in the place[1] reserved for it in the **GOTO**.

_____
1. Things get a little complicated on a byte machine, depending on whether we reserve one or

The result will be a cleaner, more efficient process for producing code than the one we've come up with, but we kept ours around for its simplicity.

7.3 Disassembly

At the beginning of this chapter, [see **p. 223**] we showed the intermediate form of the following little program:

```
((lambda (fact) (fact 5 fact (lambda (x) x)))
 (lambda (n f k) (if (= n 0) (k 1)
                     (f (- n 1) f (lambda (r) (k (* n r)))) )) )
```

Now we can show the symbolic form that it elaborates in our machine language. The 78 instructions of Figure 7.4 are really beginning to look like machine language.

7.4 Coding Instructions

For pages and pages, we've talking about bytes, but we've not yet actually seen one. To bring them out of hiding, we simply have to look at the instructions in Table 7.2 differently: instead of seeing them as instructions, we should regard them as byte generators executed by a new, more highly adapted **run**. This change in our point of view will highlight important improvements in the generated code, namely its speed and compactness.

Coding instructions as bytes has to be done very carefully. We must simultaneously choose a byte and associate it with its behavior inside the **run** function as well as with various other information, such as the length of the instruction (for example, for a disassembly function). For all those reasons, instructions will be defined by means of special syntax: **define-instruction**. We'll assume that all the definitions of instructions appearing here and there in the text have actually been organized inside the macro **define-instruction-set** along with a few utilities, like this:

```
(define-syntax define-instruction-set
  (syntax-rules (define-instruction)
    ((define-instruction-set
       (define-instruction (name . args) n . body) ... )
     (begin
       (define (run)
         (let ((instruction (fetch-byte)))
           (case instruction
             ((n) (run-clause args body)) ... ) )
         (run) )
       (define (instruction-size code pc)
         (let ((instruction (vector-ref code pc)))
           (case instruction
             ((n) (size-clause args)) ... ) ) )
       (define (instruction-decode code pc)
```

---

two bytes for the offset, since it might be more or less than 256, once it's determined. There is some risk here of suboptimality.

```
(CREATE-CLOSURE 2)              (INVOKE2 *)
(GOTO 59)                       (PUSH-VALUE)
(ARITY=?  4)                    (ALLOCATE-FRAME 2)
(EXTEND-ENV)                    (POP-FRAME! 0)
(SHALLOW-ARGUMENT-REF 0)        (POP-FUNCTION)
(PUSH-VALUE)                    (FUNCTION-GOTO)
(CONSTANT 0)                    (RETURN)
(POP-ARG1)                      (PUSH-VALUE)
(INVOKE2 =)                     (ALLOCATE-FRAME 4)
(JUMP-FALSE 10)                 (POP-FRAME! 2)
(SHALLOW-ARGUMENT-REF 2)        (POP-FRAME! 1)
(PUSH-VALUE)                    (POP-FRAME! 0)
(CONSTANT 1)                    (POP-FUNCTION)
(PUSH-VALUE)                    (FUNCTION-GOTO)
(ALLOCATE-FRAME 2)             (RETURN)
(POP-FRAME! 0)                  (PUSH-VALUE)
(POP-FUNCTION)                  (ALLOCATE-FRAME 2)
(FUNCTION-GOTO)                 (POP-FRAME! 0)
(GOTO 39)                       (EXTEND-ENV)
(SHALLOW-ARGUMENT-REF 1)        (SHALLOW-ARGUMENT-REF 0)
(PUSH-VALUE)                    (PUSH-VALUE)
(SHALLOW-ARGUMENT-REF 0)        (CONSTANT 5)
(PUSH-VALUE)                    (PUSH-VALUE)
(CONSTANT 1)                    (SHALLOW-ARGUMENT-REF 0)
(POP-ARG1)                      (PUSH-VALUE)
(INVOKE2 -)                     (CREATE-CLOSURE 2)
(PUSH-VALUE)                    (GOTO 4)
(SHALLOW-ARGUMENT-REF 1)        (ARITY=?  2)
(PUSH-VALUE)                    (EXTEND-ENV)
(CREATE-CLOSURE 2)              (SHALLOW-ARGUMENT-REF 0)
(GOTO 19)                       (RETURN)
(ARITY=?  2)                    (PUSH-VALUE)
(EXTEND-ENV)                    (ALLOCATE-FRAME 4)
(DEEP-ARGUMENT-REF 1 2)         (POP-FRAME! 2)
(PUSH-VALUE)                    (POP-FRAME! 1)
(DEEP-ARGUMENT-REF 1 0)         (POP-FRAME! 0)
(PUSH-VALUE)                    (POP-FUNCTION)
(SHALLOW-ARGUMENT-REF 0)        (FUNCTION-GOTO)
(POP-ARG1)                      (RETURN)
```

Figure 7.4 Compilation

```
                  (define (fetch-byte)
                    (let ((byte (vector-ref code pc)))
                      (set! pc (+ pc 1))
                      byte ) )
                  (let-syntax
                    ((decode-clause
                       (syntax-rules ()
                         ((decode-clause iname ()) '(iname))
                         ((decode-clause iname (a))
                          (let ((a (fetch-byte))) (list 'iname a)) )
                         ((decode-clause iname (a b))
                          (let* ((a (fetch-byte))(b (fetch-byte)))
                                (list 'iname a b) ) ) )))
                       (let ((instruction (fetch-byte)))
                         (case instruction
                           ((n) (decode-clause name args)) ... ) ) ) ) ) ) ) )
         (define-syntax run-clause
           (syntax-rules ()
             ((run-clause () body) (begin . body))
             ((run-clause (a) body)
              (let ((a (fetch-byte))) . body) )
             ((run-clause (a b) body)
              (let* ((a (fetch-byte))(b (fetch-byte))) . body) ) ) )
         (define-syntax size-clause
           (syntax-rules ()
             ((size-clause ())    1)
             ((size-clause (a))   2)
             ((size-clause (a b)) 3) ) )
```

With **define-instruction**, we can generate three functions at once: the function **run** to interpret bytes; the function **instruction-size** to compute the size of an instruction; the function **instruction-decode** to disassemble bytes composing a given instruction. **instruction-decode** is particularly useful during debugging. Let's consider one of those functions:

```
(define-instruction (SHALLOW-ARGUMENT-REF j) 5
  (set! *val* (activation-frame-argument *env* j)) )
```

That definition participates in the definition of **run** by adding a clause triggered by byte 5, like this:

```
(define (run)
  (let ((instruction (fetch-byte)))
    (case instruction
      ...
      ((5) (let ((j (fetch-byte)))
             (set! *val* (activation-frame-argument *env* j)) ))
      ... ) )
  (run) )
```

The function **fetch-byte** reads the necessary argument or arguments. Simply defined, it has a secondary effect of incrementing the program counter, like this:

```
(define (fetch-byte)
```

```
(let ((byte (vector-ref *code* *pc*)))
  (set! *pc* (+ *pc* 1))
  byte ) )
```

The program counter itself is handled by the function **run**, which also uses **fetch-byte** to read the next instruction. By the way, that's also the case with certain other processors: during the execution of one instruction, the program counter indicates the *next* instruction to execute, not the one currently being executed.

If we want to increase the speed at which bytes are interpreted (in other words, if we want a fast **run**), we have to keep an eye on the execution speed of the form **case** appearing there. Since an instruction can be only one byte, that is, a number between 0 and 255, the best compilation of **case** uses a jump table indexed by bytes because in that way choosing a clause to carry out takes constant time. If instead we expanded **case** into a set of (**if** (**eq?** ...) ...), then we would be obliged to use a linear search, a tactic that would be lethal in terms of execution speed. Few compilers for Lisp (but among them are Sqil [Sén91] and Bigloo [Ser93]) are capable of the performance we've designed here.

define-instruction also participates in the function **instruction-size**; it adds the clause so that an instruction **SHALLOW-ARGUMENT-REF** has two-byte length. The instruction is indicated by its address (**pc**) in the byte-code vector where it appears. The **case** form here is equivalent to the vector of instruction sizes.

```
(define (instruction-size code pc)
  (let ((instruction (vector-ref code pc)))
    (case instruction
      ...
      ((5) 2)
      ... ) ) )
```

define-instruction also participates in the function **instruction-decode** by adding to it a specialized clause to recognize **SHALLOW-ARGUMENT-REF**. The function **instruction-decode** uses its own definition of **fetch-byte** so that it does not disturb the program counter but it still resembles **run**, like this:

```
(define (instruction-decode code pc)
  (define (fetch-byte)
    (let ((byte (vector-ref code pc)))
      (set! pc (+ pc 1))
      byte ) )
  (let ((instruction (fetch-byte)))
    (case instruction
      ...
      ((5) (let ((j (fetch-byte))) (list 'SHALLOW-ARGUMENT-REF j)))
      ... ) ) )
```

7.5   Instructions

There are 256 possibilities in our instruction set, leaving us plenty of room since we need only 34 instructions. We'll take advantage of this bounty to set aside a few bytes for coding the most useful combinations. For example, it's already clear that most of the functions have few variables, as [Cha80] observed. At the time I wrote these lines, I analyzed the arity of functions appearing in the programs associated with this book, and got the following results. Only 16 functions have variable arity; the 1,988 others are distributed as you see in Table 7.3.

arity	0	1	2	3	4	5	6	7	8
frequence (in %)	35	30	18	9	4	1	0	0	0
accumulation (in %)	35	66	84	93	97	99	99	99	100

Table 7.3 Distribution of functions by arity

A look at this table indicates that most functions have fewer than four variables. If we generalize these results, we have to admit that zero arity is over-represented here because of Chapter 6. With these observations in mind, we'll start looking for ways to improve the execution speed of functions having fewer than four variables. In consequence, all instructions involving arity will be specialized for arities less than four.

7.5.1 Local Variables

Among all the possibilities, let's first take the case of **SHALLOW-ARGUMENT-REF**. This instruction needs an argument, j, and it loads the register ***val*** with the argument j of the first activation record contained in the environment register ***env***. We can specialize it by dedicating five bytes to represent the cases $j = 0, 1, 2, 3$. We can also restrict our machine so that it does not accept functions of more than 256^2 variables. That limit will let us code the index of the argument to search for in only one byte. The function **check-byte**[3] verifies that. Here then is the function **SHALLOW-ARGUMENT-REF** as a generator of byte-code. It returns the list[4] of generated bytes. That list contains one or two bytes, depending on the case.

```
(define (SHALLOW-ARGUMENT-REF j)
  (check-byte j)
  (case j
    ((0 1 2 3) (list (+ 1 j)))
    (else      (list 5 j)) ) )
(define (check-byte j)
  (unless (and (<= 0 j) (<= j 255))
    (static-wrong "Cannot pack this number within a byte" j) ) )
```

---

2. COMMON LISP has the constant `lambda-parameters-limit`; its value is the maximal number of variables that a function can have; this number cannot be less than 50. Scheme says nothing about this issue, and that silence can be interpreted in various ways. How to represent an integer is an interesting problem anyway. Most systems with *bignums* limit them to integers less than $(256)^{2^{32}}$, rather short of infinity. One solution is to prefix the representation of such a number by the length of its representation. This eminently recursive strategy stops short, of course, at the representation of a small integer.

3. We won't mention `check-byte` again in the explanations that follow, simply to shorten the presentation.

4. Once again, we're using up our capital by a profusion of `lists` and `appends`.

Here are the five[5] associated physical instructions:

```
(define-instruction (SHALLOW-ARGUMENT-REF0) 1
  (set! *val* (activation-frame-argument *env* 0)) )
(define-instruction (SHALLOW-ARGUMENT-REF1) 2
  (set! *val* (activation-frame-argument *env* 1)) )
(define-instruction (SHALLOW-ARGUMENT-REF2) 3
  (set! *val* (activation-frame-argument *env* 2)) )
(define-instruction (SHALLOW-ARGUMENT-REF3) 4
  (set! *val* (activation-frame-argument *env* 3)) )
(define-instruction (SHALLOW-ARGUMENT-REF j) 5
  (set! *val* (activation-frame-argument *env* j)) )
```

SET-SHALLOW-ARGUMENT! operates on local variables. Modifying local variables involves the same treatment and leads to what follows. (You can easily deduce the missing definitions.)

```
(define (SET-SHALLOW-ARGUMENT! j)
  (case j
    ((0 1 2 3) (list (+ 21 j)))
    (else      (list 25 j)) ) )
```

```
(define-instruction (SET-SHALLOW-ARGUMENT!2) 23
  (set-activation-frame-argument! *env* 2 *val*) )
(define-instruction (SET-SHALLOW-ARGUMENT! j) 25
  (set-activation-frame-argument! *env* j *val*) )
```

As for deep variables, we'll assume that all cases[6] are equally probable, so we'll code them like this:

```
(define (DEEP-ARGUMENT-REF i j) (list 6 i j))
(define (SET-DEEP-ARGUMENT! i j) (list 26 i j))
```

```
(define-instruction (DEEP-ARGUMENT-REF i j) 6
  (set! *val* (deep-fetch *env* i j)) )
(define-instruction (SET-DEEP-ARGUMENT! i j) 26
  (deep-update! *env* i j *val*) )
```

7.5.2   Global Variables

We'll assume that all mutable global variables are equally probable and they can thus be coded directly. To simplify, we'll also assume that we can't have more than 256 such variables so that we can code each one in a unique byte. Thus we'll have this:

```
(define (GLOBAL-REF i) (list 7 i))
(define (CHECKED-GLOBAL-REF i) (list 8 i))
(define (SET-GLOBAL! i) (list 27 i))
```

---

5. There's no instruction for the code 0 because there are already too many zeroes at large in the world.
6. Well, in fact, that is a false assumption since the explanations we just offered at least show that the parameter j is generally less than four. However, deep variables are rare, and that fact justifies our not trying to improve access to them.

```
(define-instruction (GLOBAL-REF i) 7
  (set! *val* (global-fetch i)) )
(define-instruction (CHECKED-GLOBAL-REF i) 8
  (set! *val* (global-fetch i))
  (when (eq? *val* undefined-value)
    (signal-exception #t (list "Uninitialized global variable" i)) ) )
(define-instruction (SET-GLOBAL! i) 27
  (global-update! i *val*) )
```

The case of predefined variables that cannot be modified is more interesting because we can dedicate a few bytes to the statistically most significant cases. Here, we'll deliberately accelerate the evaluation of the variables T, F, NIL, CONS, CAR, and a few others, like this:

```
(define (PREDEFINED i)
  (check-byte i)
  (case i
    ;; 0=#t, 1=#f, 2=(), 3=cons, 4=car, 5=cdr, 6=pair?, 7=symbol?, 8=eq?
    ((0 1 2 3 4 5 6 7 8) (list (+ 10 i)))
    (else                (list 19 i)) ) )
(define-instruction (PREDEFINED0) 10    ; #T
  (set! *val* #t) )
(define-instruction (PREDEFINED i) 19
  (set! *val* (predefined-fetch i)) )
```

Since we've begun by special treatment for a few constants, we'll treat quoting in the same way. Let's assume that the machine has a register, *constants*, containing a vector that itself contains all the quotations in the program. Then the function quotation-fetch can search for a quotation there.

```
(define (quotation-fetch i)
  (vector-ref *constants* i) )
```

Quotations are collected inside the variable *quotations* by the combinator CONSTANT during the compilation phase. Those quotations will be saved during compilation and put into the register *constants* at execution. Once more, all quoted values are not equal; some are quoted more often than others, so we'll dedicate a few bytes to those. We'll reuse a few of the bytes we've already predefined, namely, PREDEFINED0 and those that follow it. Finally, we'll assume that we can quote as immediate integers only those between 0 and 255. Other integers will be quoted[7] like normal constants.

```
(define (CONSTANT value)
  (cond ((eq? value #t)      (list 10))
        ((eq? value #f)      (list 11))
        ((eq? value '())     (list 12))
        ((equal? value -1)   (list 80))
        ((equal? value 0)    (list 81))
        ((equal? value 1)    (list 82))
        ((equal? value 2)    (list 83))
        ((equal? value 4)    (list 84))
```

---

7. That's annoying, but it still lets us implement *bignums* as lists.

```
      ((and (integer? value)   ;immediate value
            (<= 0 value)
            (< value 255) )
       (list 79 value) )
      (else (EXPLICIT-CONSTANT value)) ) )
(define (EXPLICIT-CONSTANT value)
  (set! *quotations* (append *quotations* (list value)))
  (list 9 (- (length *quotations*) 1)) )

(define-instruction (CONSTANT-1)  80
  (set! *val* -1) )
(define-instruction (CONSTANT0) 81
  (set! *val* 0) )
(define-instruction (SHORT-NUMBER value) 79
  (set! *val* value) )
```

7.5.3   Jumps

If you think the restrictions we've imposed so far are too limiting, wait until you
see what we do about jumps. We must not limit GOTO and JUMP-FALSE to 256-byte
jumps[8] since the size of a jump depends on the size of the compiled code. We'll
distinguish two cases: whether the jump takes one byte or two. We'll thus have
two[9] physically different instructions: SHORT-GOTO and LONG-GOTO. This will, of
course, be a handicap for our compiler that it won't know how to leap further than
65,535 bytes.

```
(define (GOTO offset)
  (cond ((< offset 255) (list 30 offset))
        ((< offset (+ 255 (* 255 256)))
         (let ((offset1 (modulo offset 256))
               (offset2 (quotient offset 256)) )
           (list 28 offset1 offset2) ) )
        (else (static-wrong "too long jump" offset)) ) )
(define (JUMP-FALSE offset)
  (cond ((< offset 255) (list 31 offset))
        ((< offset (+ 255 (* 255 256)))
         (let ((offset1 (modulo offset 256))
               (offset2 (quotient offset 256)) )
           (list 29 offset1 offset2) ) )
        (else (static-wrong "too long jump" offset)) ) )

(define-instruction (SHORT-GOTO offset) 30
  (set! *pc* (+ *pc* offset)) )
(define-instruction (SHORT-JUMP-FALSE offset) 31
  (if (not *val*) (set! *pc* (+ *pc* offset))) )
(define-instruction (LONG-GOTO offset1 offset2) 28
```

---

8. Old machines like those based on the 8086 had that kind of limitation.
9. The same technique of doubling an instruction in SHORT- and LONG- could be applied to
GLOBAL-REF and its companions so that the number of mutable global variables would no longer
be limited to 256.

```
(let ((offset (+ offset1 (* 256 offset2)))  )
  (set! *pc* (+ *pc* offset))) ) )
```

7.5.4 Invocations

We need to analyze first general invocations and then inline calls. The reason we favored functions with low arity is still valid here. For a few bytes more, we can specialize the allocation of activation records for arities up to four variables.

```
(define (ALLOCATE-FRAME size)
  (case size
    ((0 1 2 3 4) (list (+ 50 size)))
    (else        (list 55 (+ size 1))) ) )

(define-instruction (ALLOCATE-FRAME1) 50
  (set! *val* (allocate-activation-frame 1)) )

(define-instruction (ALLOCATE-FRAME size+1) 55
  (set! *val* (allocate-activation-frame size+1)) )
```

How we put the values of arguments into activation records can also be improved for low arities, like this:

```
(define (POP-FRAME! rank)
  (case rank
    ((0 1 2 3) (list (+ 60 rank)))
    (else      (list 64 rank)) ) )

(define-instruction (POP-FRAME!0) 60
  (set-activation-frame-argument! *val* 0 (stack-pop)) )

(define-instruction (POP-FRAME! rank) 64
  (set-activation-frame-argument! *val* rank (stack-pop)) )
```

Inline calls are very frequent, so they warrant a few dedicated bytes themselves. For example, INVOKE1, the special invoker for predefined unary functions, is written like this:

```
(define (INVOKE1 address)
  (case address
    ((car)     (list 90))
    ((cdr)     (list 91))
    ((pair?)   (list 92))
    ((symbol?) (list 93))
    ((display) (list 94))
    (else (static-wrong "Cannot integrate" address)) ) )

(define-instruction (CALL1-car) 90
  (set! *val* (car *val*)) )

(define-instruction (CALL1-cdr) 91
  (set! *val* (cdr *val*)) )
```

Of course, we'll do the same thing for predefined functions of arity 0, 2, and 3. The reason that display appears in INVOKE1 is connected with debugging; it's actually a function that belongs in a library of non-primitives because of its size and the amount of time it requires when it's applied. It would be better to dedicate a few bytes to `cddr`, then to `cdddr`, and finally to `cadr` (in the order of their usefulness).

Verifying arity itself can be specialized for low arity, so we'll distinguish these cases:

```
(define (ARITY=? arity+1)
  (case arity+1
    ((1 2 3 4) (list (+ 70 arity+1)))
    (else      (list 75 arity+1)) ) )

(define-instruction (ARITY=?2) 72
  (unless (= (activation-frame-argument-length *val*) 2)
    (signal-exception
     #f (list "Incorrect arity for unary function") ) ) )
(define-instruction (ARITY=? arity+1) 75
  (unless (= (activation-frame-argument-length *val*) arity+1)
    (signal-exception #f (list "Incorrect arity")) ) )
```

Taking into account the low proportion of functions with variable arity, we'll reserve the previous treatments for functions of fixed arity. So far, the inline functions we've distinguished are very simple and their computation is quick. Since we still have some free bytes, we could inline more complicated functions, such as, for example, `memq` or `equal`. The risk in doing so is that the invocation of `memq` might never terminate (or just take a really long time) if the list to which it applies is cyclic. MacScheme [85M85] limits the length of lists that `memq` can search to a few thousand.

7.5.5   Miscellaneous

There's still a number of minor instructions that we will simply code as one byte because they have no arguments. Byte generators are all cut from the same cloth, so to speak, so here's one example:

```
(define (RESTORE-ENV) (list 38))
```

And here are their definitions in terms of instructions:

```
(define-instruction (EXTEND-ENV) 32
  (set! *env* (sr-extend* *env* *val*)) )
(define-instruction (UNLINK-ENV) 33
  (set! *env* (activation-frame-next *env*)) )
(define-instruction (PUSH-VALUE) 34
  (stack-push *val*) )
(define-instruction (POP-ARG1) 35
  (set! *arg1* (stack-pop)) )
(define-instruction (POP-ARG2) 36
  (set! *arg2* (stack-pop)) )
(define-instruction (CREATE-CLOSURE offset) 40
  (set! *val* (make-closure (+ *pc* offset) *env*)) )
(define-instruction (RETURN) 43
  (set! *pc* (stack-pop)) )
(define-instruction (FUNCTION-GOTO) 46
```

```
      (invoke *fun* #t) )
   (define-instruction (FUNCTION-INVOKE) 45
      (invoke *fun* #f) )
   (define-instruction (POP-FUNCTION) 39
      (set! *fun* (stack-pop)) )
   (define-instruction (PRESERVE-ENV) 37
      (preserve-environment) )
   (define-instruction (RESTORE-ENV) 38
      (restore-environment) )
```

The following functions define how to save and restore the environment:

```
(define (preserve-environment)
   (stack-push *env*) )
(define (restore-environment)
   (set! *env* (stack-pop)) )
```

There are two methods to invoke functions: **FUNCTION-GOTO** in tail position and **FUNCTION-INVOKE** for everything else. For tail position, the stack holds the return address on top. For a non-tail position and after a function has been called, the machine must get back to the instruction that follows (**FUNCTION-INVOKE**) to carry on with its work. For that reason, **FUNCTION-INVOKE** must save the return program counter. When the call is in tail position, the instruction **FUNCTION-GOTO** should have already been compiled into **FUNCTION-INVOKE** followed by **RETURN**, but there's no point in pushing the address of **RETURN** onto the stack; it's sufficient not to put it there in the first place. Accordingly, **FUNCTION-GOTO** invokes a function without saving the caller since the caller has finished its work and has nothing left to do. Here's the generic definition of **invoke**. We hope it clarifies this explanation.

```
(define-generic (invoke (f) tail?)
   (signal-exception #f (list "Not a function" f)) )
(define-method (invoke (f closure) tail?)
   (unless tail? (stack-push *pc*))
   (set! *env* (closure-closed-environment f))
   (set! *pc* (closure-code f)) )
```

The function **invoke** is generic so that it can be extended to new types of objects and, for example, to primitives that we represent as thunks.

```
(define-method (invoke (f primitive) tail?)
   (unless tail? (stack-push *pc*))
   ((primitive-address f)) )
```

There again, the value of the variable **tail?** determines whether or not we save the return address.

7.5.6 Starting the Compiler-Interpreter

To produce an interpretation loop (as we've done in all the preceding chapters) we need finely tuned cooperation between a compiler and an execution machine. The function **stand-alone-producer7d** takes a program and initializes the compiler. By "initializes the compiler," we mean in particular its environment of predefined mutable global variables and the list of quotations. The result of the function

meaning is now a list of bytes that we put into a vector preceded by the code for **FINISH** and followed by the code corresponding to **RETURN**. The initial program counter is computed to indicate the first byte that follows the prologue. (Here, that's the second byte, that is, the one with the address 1.) For reasons that you'll see later [see **Ex. 6.1**] but that have already been explained, we'll prepare the list of mutable global variables and the list of quotations. Eventually, the final product of the compilation is represented by a function waiting to evaluate what we provide as the size of the stack.

```
(define (chapter7d-interpreter)
  (define (toplevel)
    (display ((stand-alone-producer7d (read)) 100))
    (toplevel) )
  (toplevel) )
(define (stand-alone-producer7d e)
  (set! g.current (original.g.current))
  (set! *quotations* '())
  (let* ((code (make-code-segment (meaning e r.init #t)))
         (start-pc (length (code-prologue)))
         (global-names (map car (reverse g.current)))
         (constants (apply vector *quotations*)) )
    (lambda (stack-size)
      (run-machine stack-size start-pc code
                   constants global-names ) ) ) )
(define (make-code-segment m)
  (apply vector (append (code-prologue) m (RETURN))) )
(define (code-prologue)
  (set! finish-pc 0)
  (FINISH) )
```

The function **run-machine** initializes the machine and then starts it. It allocates a vector to store values of mutable global variables; it organizes the names of these same variables; it allocates a working stack, and it initializes all the registers. Now our only problem is stopping the machine! The program is compiled as if it were in tail position, that is, it will end by executing a **RETURN**. To get back, the stack must initially contain an address to which **RETURN** will jump. For that reason, the stack initially contains the address of the instruction **FINISH**. It's defined like this:

```
(define-instruction (FINISH) 20
  (*exit* *val*) )
```

When that instruction is executed, it stops the machine and returns the contents of its ***val*** register by means of a judicious escape set by **run-machine**.

```
(define (run-machine stack-size pc code constants global-names)
  (set! sg.current (make-vector (length global-names) undefined-value))
  (set! sg.current.names global-names)
  (set! *constants*    constants)
  (set! *code*         code)
  (set! *env*          sr.init)
  (set! *stack*        (make-vector stack-size))
  (set! *stack-index* 0)
  (set! *val*          'anything)
```

```
(set! *fun*          'anything)
(set! *arg1*         'anything)
(set! *arg2*         'anything)
(stack-push finish-pc)                    ; pc for FINISH
(set! *pc*           pc)
(call/cc (lambda (exit)
           (set! *exit* exit)
           (run) )) )
```

7.5.7 Catching Our Breath

To finish off this long section about instructions, we'll look at the final form of the program we saw at the beginning of the chapter, as byte code, once it has been disassembled to be more readable. See Figure 7.5.

7.6 Continuations

We've already shown that `call/cc` is a kind of magic operator that reifies the evaluation context, turning the context into an object that can be invoked. Now we'll demystify its implementation. The following implementation is canonical. You'll find more efficient but more complicated ones in [CHO88, HDB90, MB93].

The evaluation context is made up of the stack and nothing but the stack. In effect, the registers `*fun*`, `*arg1*`, and `*arg2*` play only temporary roles; in no case can they be captured. (You can't call[10] `call/cc` nor anything else while they are active.)

The register `*val*` transmits values submitted to continuations and thus is not anything to save. The register `*env*` need not be saved either because `call/cc` is not a function that we integrate there; in fact, the environment has already been saved because of the call to `call/cc`. Consequently, there is only the stack to save, and to do so, we'll use these functions:

```
(define (save-stack)
  (let ((copy (make-vector *stack-index*)))
    (vector-copy! *stack* copy 0 *stack-index*)
    copy ) )
(define (restore-stack copy)
  (set! *stack-index* (vector-length copy))
  (vector-copy! copy *stack* 0 *stack-index*) )
(define (vector-copy! old new start end)
  (let copy ((i start))
    (when (< i end)
          (vector-set! new i (vector-ref old i))
          (copy (+ i 1)) ) ) )
```

Continuations will have their own class and their own special calling protocol. When a continuation is invoked, it restores the stack, puts the value received into the register `*val*`, and then branches (by a RETURN) to the address contained on

---

10. That statement may be false if we have to respond to asynchronous calls, such as Un*x signals. In that case, it's better to set a flag that we test regularly from time to time as in [Dev85].

```
(CREATE-CLOSURE 2)              (CALL2-*)
(SHORT-GOTO 59)                 (PUSH-VALUE)
(ARITY=?4)                      (ALLOCATE-FRAME2)
(EXTEND-ENV)                    (POP-FRAME!0)
(SHALLOW-ARGUMENT-REF0)         (POP-FUNCTION)
(PUSH-VALUE)                    (FUNCTION-GOTO)
(CONSTANT0)                     (RETURN)
(POP-ARG1)                      (PUSH-VALUE)
(CALL2-=)                       (ALLOCATE-FRAME4)
(SHORT-JUMP-FALSE 10)           (POP-FRAME!2)
(SHALLOW-ARGUMENT-REF2)         (POP-FRAME!1)
(PUSH-VALUE)                    (POP-FRAME!0)
(CONSTANT1)                     (POP-FUNCTION)
(PUSH-VALUE)                    (FUNCTION-GOTO)
(ALLOCATE-FRAME2)               (RETURN)
(POP-FRAME!0)                   (PUSH-VALUE)
(POP-FUNCTION)                  (ALLOCATE-FRAME2)
(FUNCTION-GOTO)                 (POP-FRAME!0)
(SHORT-GOTO 39)                 (EXTEND-ENV)
(SHALLOW-ARGUMENT-REF1)         (SHALLOW-ARGUMENT-REF0)
(PUSH-VALUE)                    (PUSH-VALUE)
(SHALLOW-ARGUMENT-REF0)         (SHORT-NUMBER 5)
(PUSH-VALUE)                    (PUSH-VALUE)
(CONSTANT1)                     (SHALLOW-ARGUMENT-REF0)
(POP-ARG1)                      (PUSH-VALUE)
(CALL2--)                       (CREATE-CLOSURE 2)
(PUSH-VALUE)                    (SHORT-GOTO 4)
(SHALLOW-ARGUMENT-REF1)         (ARITY=?2)
(PUSH-VALUE)                    (EXTEND-ENV)
(CREATE-CLOSURE 2)              (SHALLOW-ARGUMENT-REF0)
(SHORT-GOTO 19)                 (RETURN)
(ARITY=?2)                      (PUSH-VALUE)
(EXTEND-ENV)                    (ALLOCATE-FRAME4)
(DEEP-ARGUMENT-REF 1 2)         (POP-FRAME!2)
(PUSH-VALUE)                    (POP-FRAME!1)
(DEEP-ARGUMENT-REF 1 0)         (POP-FRAME!0)
(PUSH-VALUE)                    (POP-FUNCTION)
(SHALLOW-ARGUMENT-REF0)         (FUNCTION-GOTO)
(POP-ARG1)                      (RETURN)
```

Figure 7.5 Compilation result

top of the stack. Since `call/cc` can be called only by (`FUNCTION-INVOKE`), the following instruction will necessarily be a (`RESTORE-ENV`). (You can verify that in the definition of `REGULAR-CALL`). [see p. 229]

```
(define-class continuation Object
  ( stack ) )
(define-method (invoke (f continuation) tail?)
  (if (= (+ 1 1) (activation-frame-argument-length *val*))
      (begin
        (restore-stack (continuation-stack f))
        (set! *val* (activation-frame-argument *val* 0))
        (set! *pc* (stack-pop)) )
      (signal-exception #f (list "Incorrect arity" 'continuation)) ) )
```

For the invocation of a continuation to succeed, the stack must have a special structure built by `call/cc`. Building that structure is a subtle task because the capture of the continuation must not consume the stack. That is, in the form (`call/cc` f), the function f must be called in tail[11] position. The following definition accomplishes that. It allocates an activation record, fills in the reified continuation, and calls its argument `f` with it.

```
(definitial call/cc
  (let* ((arity 1)
         (arity+1 (+ arity 1)) )
    (make-primitive
     (lambda ()
       (if (= arity+1 (activation-frame-argument-length *val*))
           (let ((f (activation-frame-argument *val* 0))
                 (frame (allocate-activation-frame (+ 1 1))) )
             (set-activation-frame-argument!
              frame 0 (make-continuation (save-stack)) )
             (set! *val* frame)
             (set! *fun* f)                ; useful for debug
             (invoke f #t) )
           (signal-exception #t (list "Incorrect arity"
                                      'call/cc )) ) ) ) ) )
```

In conclusion, the canonical implementation of `call/cc` costs one copy of the stack for each reification and another copy at every invocation of a continuation. Better strategies exist, but they are more complicated to implement. The main idea of most of these strategies is that when a continuation is reified, it stands a good chance of happening again, either in whole or in part, according to [Dan87], so strategies that allow captures to be shared should be favored.

7.7 Escapes

Even if the cost of `call/cc` can be reduced, it wouldn't be fair not to show how to implement simple escapes. We've decided to implement the special form `bind-exit`. [see p. 101] It's present in Dylan and analogous to `let/cc` in EU-LISP, to `block/return-from` in COMMON LISP, and to `escape` in Vlisp [Cha80].

---

11. That's not necessary in Scheme.

In contrast to the spirit of Scheme, we've opted for a new special form rather than a function for two main reasons: first, introducing a new special form is slightly more simple because in doing so, we don't have to conform to the structure of the stack as dictated by the function calling protocol; second, we can thus show the entire compiler in cross-section. If you need yet another reason, remember that a function and a special form are equally powerful here since we can write one in terms of the other.

The form **bind-exit** has the following syntax:

```
(bind-exit (variable) forms ...)                                    Dylan
```

The *variable* is bound to the continuation of the form **bind-exit**; then the body of the form is evaluated. The captured continuation can be used only during that evaluation. If **bind-exit** is available to us, we can define the function **call/ep** (for *call-with-exit-procedure*) and conversely.

```
(define (call/ep f)
  (bind-exit (k) (f k)) )
```

```
(bind-exit (k) body) ≡ (call/ep (lambda (k) body))
```

Escapes are represented by objects of the class **escape**. They have a unique field to designate the height of the stack where the evaluation of the form **bind-exit** begins.

```
(define-class escape Object
  ( stack-index ) )
```

To define a new special form, we must first add a clause to the function **meaning**, the lexical analyzer of forms to compile. That additional clause will recognize these new forms, so we'll add the following clause to **meaning**:

```
... ((bind-exit) (meaning-bind-exit (caadr e) (cddr e) r tail?)) ...
```

Then we'll define the pretreatment function for those forms, like this:

```
(define (meaning-bind-exit n e+ r tail?)
  (let* ((r2 (r-extend* r (list n)))
         (m+ (meaning-sequence e+ r2 #t)) )
    (ESCAPER m+) ) )
```

The pretreatment consists of making a sequence from the body of the form **bind-exit**; that sequence will be pretreated in a lexical environment extended by the local variable that introduces **bind-exit**. The function **ESCAPER** (all in upper case letters) takes care of generating the code. For that function, we invent two new instructions: **PUSH-ESCAPER** and **POP-ESCAPER**.

```
(define (ESCAPER m+)
  (append (PUSH-ESCAPER (+ 1 (length m+))) m+ (RETURN) (POP-ESCAPER)) )
(define (POP-ESCAPER) (list 250))
(define escape-tag (list '*ESCAPE*))
(define (PUSH-ESCAPER offset) (list 251 offset))
```

```
(define-instruction (POP-ESCAPER) 250
  (let* ((tag (stack-pop))
         (escape (stack-pop)) )
    (restore-environment) ) )
```

```
(define-instruction (PUSH-ESCAPER offset) 251
  (preserve-environment)
  (let* ((escape (make-escape (+ *stack-index* 3)))
         (frame (allocate-activation-frame 1)) )
    (set-activation-frame-argument! frame 0 escape)
    (set! *env* (sr-extend* *env* frame))
  (stack-push escape)
  (stack-push escape-tag)
  (stack-push (+ *pc* offset)) ) )
```

You can see how the instruction PUSH-ESCAPER works in Figure 7.6. Here's what it does:

1. it saves the current environment on the stack;

2. it allocates a valid escape indicating the third word above the current top of the stack;

3. it allocates an activation record to enrich the current lexical environment; (its unique field contains the escape);

4. pushes this escape on the stack finally and then puts on that strange flag (*ESCAPE*), followed by an address indicating the (POP-ESCAPER) instruction that follows.

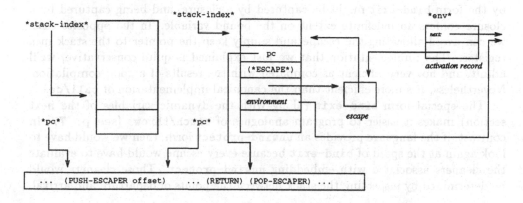

Figure 7.6 The stack before and after PUSH-ESCAPER

The method for invoking escapes is complicated by the fact that we have to check whether or not the escape is valid. An escape is valid if the height of the stack is greater than the height saved in the escape; if there really is an escape at that place in the stack; and if that escape really is the one we're interested in. All those conditions are verified in constant time by the function escape-valid?, like this:

```
(define-method (invoke (f escape) tail?)
  (if (= (+ 1 1) (activation-frame-argument-length *val*))
      (if (escape-valid? f)
          (begin (set! *stack-index* (escape-stack-index f))
                 (set! *val* (activation-frame-argument *val* 0))
```

```
                  (set! *pc* (stack-pop)) )
            (signal-exception #f (list "Escape out of extent" f)) )
         (signal-exception #f (list "Incorrect arity" 'escape)) ) )
(define (escape-valid? f)
  (let ((index (escape-stack-index f)))
    (and (>= *stack-index* index)
         (eq? f (vector-ref *stack* (- index 3)))
         (eq? escape-tag (vector-ref *stack* (- index 2)))) ) ) )
```

When an escape is invoked, it first verifies whether it is valid; then it takes the level of the stack back to the level prevailing at the beginning of the evaluation of the body of the form **bind-exit**; it puts the value provided into the register ***val***; then it carries out the equivalent of a **(RETURN)** resetting the program counter. The following instruction will thus be **(POP-ESCAPER)**, which pops the stack, restores the saved environment, and exits from the form **bind-exit**.

If no escape is called during the body of the form **bind-exit**, the same scenario applies: the **(RETURN)** that precedes **(POP-ESCAPER)** removes the address from the stack makes it possible to branch to the same instruction in the same configuration of the stack as during the call to the escape.

Getting into the form **bind-exit** costs two object allocations and four places on the stack. Invoking an escape costs one validity test and a few register moves. We explicitly allocated the escape because it may happen that the variable bound by the form **bind-exit** might be captured by a closure, and being captured by a closure confers an indefinite extent on the bound variable. In the opposite case, we can avoid allocating the escape and simply keep the pointer to the stack in a register. The implementation that we just explained is quite conservative, we'll admit, and not very efficient as compared with the results of a good compilation. Nevertheless, it's more efficient than the canonical implementation of **call/cc**.

The special form **bind-exit** (along with the dynamic variables of the next section) makes it easier to program analogues of **catch/throw**. [see **p. 77**] In contrast, if the language provides an **unwind-protect** form, then we would have to look again at the speed of **bind-exit** because every escape would have to evaluate the cleaners associated with embedding **unwind-protect**. Those cleaners would be determined by inspecting the stack between the points of departure and arrival.

7.8   Dynamic Variables

We've already often written that dynamic variables correspond to a significant idea. We implemented them using deep binding. Like before [see **p. 167**], we'll assume that we have two new special forms to create and refer to dynamic variables. Here's the syntax of those forms:

> (dynamic-let (*variable value*) *body*...)
> (dynamic *variable*)

The form **dynamic-let** binds a variable and value during the evaluation of its body. We can get the value of the variable by means of the form **dynamic**. Of course, it would be an error to ask for the value of a variable that has not been bound.

For those reasons, we'll add two new clauses to **meaning**, our syntactic analyzer:

```
... ((dynamic)     (meaning-dynamic-reference (cadr e) r tail?))
    ((dynamic-let) (meaning-dynamic-let (car (cadr e))
                                        (cadr (cadr e))
                                        (cddr e) r tail? )) ...
```

We'll also associate the necessary pretreatments with them, like this:

```
(define (meaning-dynamic-let n e e+ r tail?)
  (let ((index (get-dynamic-variable-index n))
        (m (meaning e r #f))
        (m+ (meaning-sequence e+ r #f)) )
    (append m (DYNAMIC-PUSH index) m+ (DYNAMIC-POP)) ) )
(define (meaning-dynamic-reference n r tail?)
  (let ((index (get-dynamic-variable-index n)))
    (DYNAMIC-REF index) ) )
```

Those pretreatments use these three new generators:

```
(define (DYNAMIC-PUSH index) (list 242 index))
(define (DYNAMIC-POP)        (list 241))
(define (DYNAMIC-REF index)  (list 240 index))
```

Those three generators correspond to three new instructions in our virtual machine, namely:

```
(define-instruction (DYNAMIC-PUSH index) 242
  (push-dynamic-binding index *val*) )
(define-instruction (DYNAMIC-POP) 241
  (pop-dynamic-binding) )
(define-instruction (DYNAMIC-REF index) 240
  (set! *val* (find-dynamic-value index)) )
```

Now how do we represent the environment for dynamic variables? The first idea that comes to mind is to invent a new register, say, ***dynenv***, that permanently points to an association list pairing dynamic variables with their values. Well, actually, this "list" is not a real list, but rather a few *frames*, that is, regions chained together in the stack. Unfortunately, with this idea we've augmented the machine state since the contents of the register ***dynenv*** now have to be saved, too, by **PRESERVE-ENV**, and of course they have to be restored by **RESTORE-ENV**. Since those two instructions occur quite frequently already, adding the register ***dynenv*** will be costly even if we never use it. An important rule for us is that only users should pay for services; as a corollary, those who never use a service shouldn't have to pay for it. From that point of view, adding another register looks like a bad idea.

Rather than maintain a register, we give the means of establishing information about dynamic variables only to those who use them and only if they need them. The cost will thus be greater, but at least this way of doing things will not penalize those who don't need it. The environment will be implemented as frames in the stack, but each of those frames will be preceded by a special label identifying it, as in Figure 7.7. The function **search-dynenv-index** provides information that we would have been able to find in that register we decided not to add.

```
(define dynenv-tag (list '*dynenv*))
```

```
(define (search-dynenv-index)
  (let search ((i (- *stack-index* 1)))
    (if (< i 0) i
        (if (eq? (vector-ref *stack* i) dynenv-tag)
            (- i 1)
            (search (- i 1)) ) ) ) )
(define (pop-dynamic-binding)
  (stack-pop)
  (stack-pop)
  (stack-pop)
  (stack-pop) )
(define (push-dynamic-binding index value)
  (stack-push (search-dynenv-index))
  (stack-push value)
  (stack-push index)
  (stack-push dynenv-tag) )
```

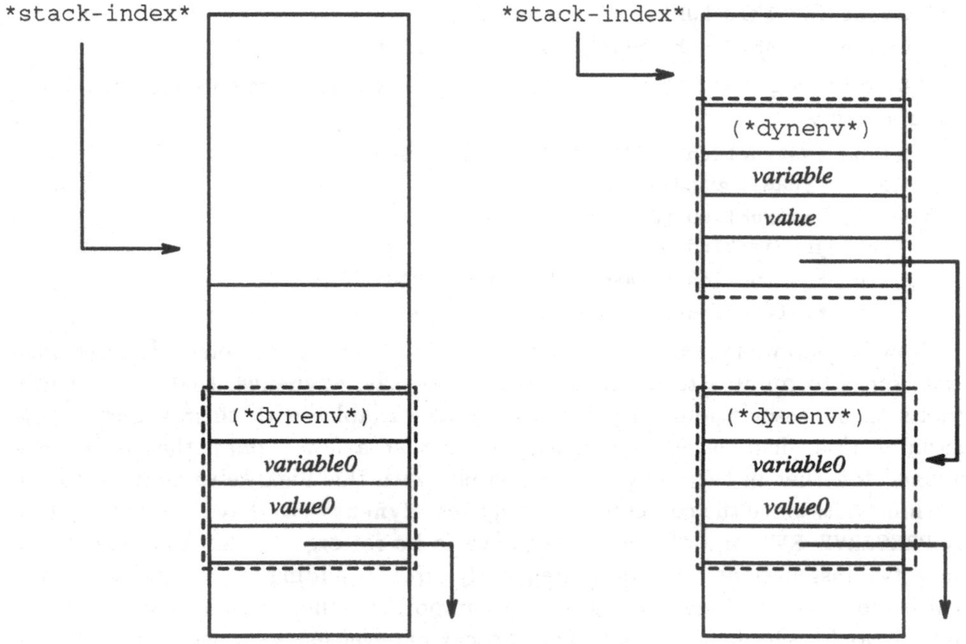

Figure 7.7 Stack before and after DYNAMIC-PUSH

The one obscure point that we still have to clear up is this: how do we refer to dynamic variables? A reference like (**dynamic foo**) must be compiled into bytes, so that rules out referring directly to the symbol **foo**. We've already numbered mutable global variables as they appeared, so in the same way, we'll number dynamic variables by means of **get-dynamic-variable-index**, like this:

```
(define *dynamic-variables* '())
(define (get-dynamic-variable-index n)
```

```
(let ((where (memq n *dynamic-variables*)))
  (if where (length where)
      (begin
        (set! *dynamic-variables* (cons n *dynamic-variables*))
        (length *dynamic-variables*) ) ) ) )
```

Every dynamic variable is given an index so we can retrieve it from the dynamic environment present in the stack. The variable `*dynamic-variables*` belongs to the realm of compilation so it is not essential to the virtual machine. Even so, it might be useful to establish error messages that report the name of a variable in case of anomalies.

We mentioned that we introduced dynamic variables by means of two special forms. To get them by means of functions would have been more faithful to the spirit of Scheme, but it would not have been equivalent. Since functions are invoked with computed arguments, the names of dynamic variables would have been computed, too, but that is not the case with special forms. Obviously, it would not have been possible to number dynamic variables if we had relied on functions to introduce them since any conceivable symbol (not to mention their values) would have been available. [see p. 50] In that case, we would then have had to arrange for another compilation, for example, by explicitly referring to symbols, which are afterall structures of considerable size that may pose problems in comparisons especially if we add packages or interning.

7.9 Exceptions

Every real language defines some way of handling errors. Error handling makes it possible to build robust, autonomous applications. There are, however, no specifications for error handling in Scheme, so we'll introduce error handling ourselves just to show what it is without much ado.

The idea of errors actually covers several different kinds in reality. First under this heading, we find unforeseen situations—situations we did not want but for which we can test. The underlying system may stumble, either because of problems with the type, `(car 33)`, or with the domain, `(quotient 111 0)`, or with arity `(cons)`. With appropriate predicates, we can test explicitly for those situations. However, other events can occur, such as an attempt to open a non-existing file. Handling that kind of error necessitates the following:

1. a way of reifying the error in a data structure that a user's programs can understand;

2. a call to the function that the user designates as the error handler.

Once this mechanism has been built into a language, users themselves want to exploit it. For that reason, errors take on the name *exceptions*, and thus is born *programming by exception* where the user programs only the right case and leaves the exiting (possibly even multiple exits) to the exception handler.

There are several models for exceptions. These models base practically all research about exception handlers on the idea of dynamic extent. When we want to protect a computation from the effects of exceptions, we associate a function for catching errors with the computation throughout its extent. If the computation

is completed without exception, then the error handler no longer has a purpose
and becomes inactive. In contrast, if an error occurs, the error handler must be
invoked. If the user invokes the exception system, it will provide the exception
object. In contrast, if the system discovers the situation, then it will be up to the
system to build the exception.

Among the models for exceptions, there are those with and without resumption.
When certain exceptions are signaled (in particular, those that the programmer
can signal, like `cerror` in COMMON LISP) it is sometimes possible to take up the
computation again in the same place where it was interrupted. In many other
cases, however, that's not feasible, and the only possible control operation is to
escape to a safe context.

The exception model in COMMON LISP is more than complete, but its size is
contrary to the design of this book, which is to show only the essentials. The
model of ML does not support recovery; when an exception is signaled, the stack is
unwound to the level it had when the exception handler was specified. It's possible
to restart the exception to take advantage of the preceding handler. That model is
not convenient for us because it loses the environment for dynamic variables that
was present when the exception occurred. So here's the model we propose. (It's
strongly inspired by the model of EULISP.) We'll first describe it informally and
then implement it, hoping all the while that the two coincide!

The special form `monitor` associates a function for handling exceptions with
the computation corresponding to its body. Its syntax is thus:

(monitor *handler forms* ...)

So we'll add the special form `monitor` to the syntactic analyzer `meaning`, like
this:

    ... ((monitor) (meaning-monitor (cadr e) (cddr e) r tail?)) ...

The handler is evaluated and becomes the current exception handler. The forms
in the body of `monitor` are consequently evaluated as if they were in a `begin` form.
If no exception is signaled during the computation, the form `monitor` returns the
value of the last form in its body and then reactivates the exception handler, which
was hidden by the form `monitor`.

If an exception is signaled, then we search for the current handler, that is, the
one associated by the dynamically closest `monitor`. (In implementation terms, we
search for the handler highest in the evaluation stack.) Changing neither the stack
nor its height nor its contents, we invoke the handler with two arguments: a Boolean
indicating whether the exception can be continued and the object representing
the exception. Since we have to foresee the possibility that the error handlers
themselves may be erroneous, the current handler is executed under the control
of the handler that it hides. The computation undertaken by the handler can
either escape or return a value. If the exception could be continued, that value
becomes the value expected in the place where the exception was signaled. If the
exception could not be continued, then an exception is signaled—one that cannot
be continued. When we exit from the handler by escaping, the computation is once
again controlled by the nearest handler. Finally, there is a basic handler at the
bottom of the stack. If it is ever invoked, it stops the program that is running and
returns to the operating system (or to whatever takes the place of an operating

system), as in Figure 7.8.

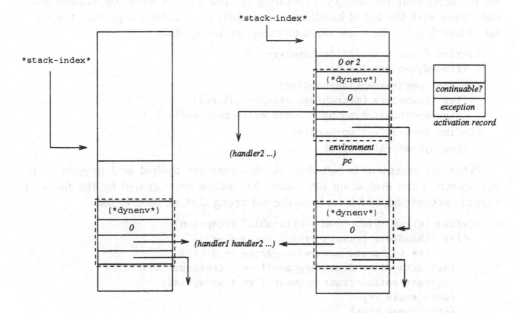

Figure 7.8 Signaling an exception

The pretreatment associated with the form **monitor** uses two new generators to manage the hierarchy of handlers.

```
(define (meaning-monitor e e+ r tail?)
  (let ((m (meaning e r #f))
        (m+ (meaning-sequence e+ r #f)) )
    (append m (PUSH-HANDLER) m+ (POP-HANDLER)) ) )
(define (PUSH-HANDLER) (list 246))
(define (POP-HANDLER)  (list 247))
```

To treat the case of exceptions that cannot be continued yet are continued anyway, we'll add the generator **NON-CONT-ERR**.

```
(define (NON-CONT-ERR) (list 245))
```

The instructions **PUSH-HANDLER** and **POP-HANDLER** just call the appropriate functions.

```
(define-instruction (PUSH-HANDLER) 246
  (push-exception-handler) )
(define-instruction (POP-HANDLER) 247
  (pop-exception-handler) )
```

Now we're ready to get to work. To determine which handler is closest to the top of the stack is easy. That's a task for dynamic binding, so we'll use dynamic binding. As a consequence, among other things, we won't have to create a new register containing the list of active handlers. For that reason, we will use the index 0 to store handlers because we realize that the index 0 can not have been attributed by the function **get-dynamic-variable-index**. The subtle point here

is that a handler should be invoked under the control of the preceding handler.
We'll resolve that problem by associating the index 0 not with the handler itself
but rather with the list of handlers, and make it responsible for putting the right
list of handlers on the stack when an exception is signaled.

```
(define (search-exception-handlers)
  (find-dynamic-value 0) )
(define (push-exception-handler)
  (let ((handlers (search-exception-handlers)))
    (push-dynamic-binding 0 (cons *val* handlers)) ) )
(define (pop-exception-handler)
  (pop-dynamic-binding) )
```

When no exception is signaled, the handlers are pushed and popped without upsetting the evaluation discipline. Exceptions are signaled by the function
signal-exception, which replaces the old **wrong** that we used to use.

```
(define (signal-exception continuable? exception)
  (let ((handlers (search-exception-handlers))
        (v* (allocate-activation-frame (+ 2 1))) )
    (set-activation-frame-argument! v* 0 continuable?)
    (set-activation-frame-argument! v* 1 exception)
    (set! *val* v*)
    (stack-push *pc*)
    (preserve-environment)
    (push-dynamic-binding 0 (if (null? (cdr handlers)) handlers
                                (cdr handlers) ))
    (if continuable?
        (stack-push 2)    ;pc for (POP-HANDLER) (RESTORE-ENV) (RETURN)
        (stack-push 0) )  ;pc for (NON-CONT-ERR)
    (invoke (car handlers) #t) ) )
```

The function **signal-exception** is called with two arguments: a Boolean that
indicates whether or not the function must call the handler in a way that can
be continued; and a value representing the exception. Any value is acceptable
here, and predefined exceptions are encoded here as lists where the first term
is a character string describing the anomaly. COMMON LISP and EULISP reify
exceptions as real objects whose class is significant. First, we search for the list of
active handlers; then we allocate an activation record and fill it in for the call to the
first among those active handlers. The subtle part here is that we must prepare the
stack, which is, after all, in an unknown state because we don't know yet where the
exception occurred. We begin by saving the program counter and the environment
(in case we need to return and restart there); then we save the list of handlers,
shortened by the first one. Since there must be at least one handler in the list,
we'll make sure that the program begins with a first (and last) handler, one that
we never remove. Of course, that handler must never commit an error; we're sure
of that since it sends an error message and returns control to the operating system.
Now how do we distinguish an error that can be continued from one that cannot?
One easy way is to assume that code in memory contains adequate instructions at
fixed addresses. We've already put the instruction (**FINISH**) in a well known place.
We can add others there, too.

```
(define (code-prologue)
  (set! finish-pc 1)
  (append (NON-CONT-ERR) (FINISH) (POP-HANDLER) (RESTORE-ENV) (RETURN)) )
```

Thus it's simple to make it possible to continue or not continue exception handling: that's represented by the address to return to, an address that was put onto the stack and that will be retrieved by (RETURN) which closes the handler. The address 0 leads to (NON-CONT-ERR) which indicates a new exception; the address 2 pops whatever signal-exception pushed onto the stack and returns to the place from which we left.

```
(define-instruction (NON-CONT-ERR) 245
  (signal-exception #f (list "Non continuable exception continued")) )
```

There's nothing left to do except show how to start the machine in spite of these additional constraints. We'll enrich the function run-machine so that it puts the ultimate handler in place. That ultimate handler could be programmed, for example, to print its final state and then stop. With no more ado, that gives us this:

```
(define (run-machine pc code constants global-names dynamics)
  (define base-error-handler-primitive
    (make-primitive base-error-handler) )
  (set! sg.current (make-vector (length global-names) undefined-value))
  (set! sg.current.names   global-names)
  (set! *constants*        constants)
  (set! *dynamic-variables* dynamics)
  (set! *code*             code)
  (set! *env*              sr.init)
  (set! *stack-index*      0)
  (set! *val*              'anything)
  (set! *fun*              'anything)
  (set! *arg1*             'anything)
  (set! *arg2*             'anything)
  (push-dynamic-binding 0 (list base-error-handler-primitive))
  (stack-push finish-pc)                    ;pc for FINISH
  (set! *pc*               pc)
  (call/cc (lambda (exit)
            (set! *exit* exit)
            (run) )) )
(define (base-error-handler)
  (show-registers "Panic error: content of registers:")
  (wrong "Abort") )
```

The function signal-exception could be made available to programs. That function (like error/cerror in COMMON LISP or EULISP) signals and traps its own exceptions. However, its cost should limit it to exceptional situations.

In this section, we've defined an exception handler. This model makes it possible to return and restart after an exception. It also invokes the handler in the dynamic environment where the exception occurred, thus providing more possibilities as far as precisely detecting the context of the anomaly without affecting it. For example, with this model, we can write an unusual version of the factorial, like this:

```
(monitor (lambda (c e) ((dynamic foo) 1))
```

```
(let fact ((n 5))
  (if (= n 0) (/ 11 0)
      (* n (bind-exit (k)
             (dynamic-let (foo k)
               (fact (- n 1)) ) )) ) ) )
```

To avoid losing too much information about the context of the anomaly, it's a good idea not to escape too soon.

Since we're using a virtual machine where the code is represented by bytes, we've simplified the implementation of exception handling since exceptions can occur only during the treatment of instructions, and instructions are highly individualized, so the resources of the machine are always consistent between two instructions. That's not the case for a real implementation, which might receive asynchronous signals in unforeseen states.

You might ask why some predefined exceptions can be continued whereas others cannot. A byte machine is so regular that all exceptions could be made to continue because they can always be associated with a well defined program counter. Once again, that's not the case for a real implementation where either the idea of a program counter is a little vague or an anomaly, such as division by zero, cannot be detected until after the faulty operation. It is likely that only exceptions signaled by the user can be continued in a way that's portable.

Along these lines, it is pertinent to ask whether it's necessary to signal pre-treatment errors by **signal-exception** and to ask among other things whether these errors can be continued or not. Since the handler is consequently the responsibility of the compiler, we can envisage the compiler using exceptions that can be continued to correct certain anomalies on the fly.

7.10   Compiling Separately

As it is practiced in languages like C or Pascal, compilation happens through files. This section takes up that theme and presents such a compiler with an autonomous executable launcher. We'll also look at linking in this section.

7.10.1   Compiling a File

Compiling files poses hardly any problems. The function `compile-file` which follows here easily meets the challenge. It initializes the compilation variables **g.current** to represent the mutable global environment, ***quotation*** to collect quotations, and ***dynamic-variables*** to gather dynamic variables, of course. It also compiles the contents of the file, considering that like a huge **begin**, and saves the outcome (that is, the new values of those three variables along with the code) in the resulting file.

```
(define (read-file filename)
  (call-with-input-file filename
    (lambda (in)
      (let gather ((e (read in))
                   (content '()) )
        (if (eof-object? e)
```

```
                     (reverse content)
                     (gather (read in) (cons e content)) ) ) ) ) )
    (define (compile-file filename)
      (set! g.current '())
      (set! *quotations* '())
      (set! *dynamic-variables* '())
      (let* ((complete-filename (string-append filename ".scm"))
             (e                 '(begin . ,(read-file complete-filename)))
             (code              (make-code-segment (meaning e r.init #t)))
             (global-names      (map car (reverse g.current)))
             (constants         (apply vector *quotations*))
             (dynamics          *dynamic-variables*)
             (ofilename         (string-append filename ".so")) )
        (write-result-file ofilename
                      (list ";;; Bytecode object file for "
                            complete-filename )
                      dynamics global-names constants code
                      (length (code-prologue)) ) ) )
    (define (write-result-file ofilename comments
                               dynamics global-names constants code entry )
      (call-with-output-file ofilename
        (lambda (out)
          (for-each (lambda (comment) (display comment out))
                    comments )(newline out)(newline out)
          (display ";;; Dynamic variables" out)(newline out)
          (write dynamics out)(newline out)(newline out)
          (display ";;; Global modifiable variables" out)(newline out)
          (write global-names out)(newline out)(newline out)
          (display ";;; Quotations" out)(newline out)
          (write constants out)(newline out)(newline out)
          (display ";;; Bytecode" out)(newline out)
          (write code out)(newline out)(newline out)
          (display ";;; Entry point" out)(newline out)
          (write entry out) (newline out) ) ) )
```

In order not to burden ourselves with problems tied to the file system and to the struture of file names, we'll assume (like in Scheme) that file names can be indicated by character strings. The compiler accepts such a string corresponding to the root of the file name. (By "root," we mean the name stripped of its usual suffix, here, ".scm".) The result of compilation will be stored in a file named by the same root suffixed by ".so". That result is made up of the code produced, the list of names of mutable global variables, the list of dynamic variables, the list of quotations, and the program counter for the first instruction to execute in the code. Always trying to simplify, we'll build the output file by means of write in its simplest style. We'll also add a few comments there to help a human read the result.

If the file to compile is this:

---

file si/example.scm

```
(set! fact
     ((lambda (fact) (lambda (n)
                        (if (< n 0)
                            "Toctoc la tete!"
                            (fact n fact (lambda (x) x)) ) ))
        (lambda (n f k)
          (if (= n 0)
              (k 1)
              (f (- n 1) f (lambda (r) (k (* n r)))) ) ) ) )
```

Then the result of compiling will be this:

---

file si/example.so

```
;;; Bytecode object file for si/example.scm

;;; Dynamic variables
()

;;; Global modifiable variables
(FACT)

;;; Quotations
#("Toctoc la tete!")

;;; Bytecode
#(245 20 247 38 43 40 30 59 74 32 1 34 81 35 106 31 10 3 34 82 34 51 60
   39 46 30 39 2 34 1 34 82 35 105 34 2 34 40 30 19 72 32 6 1 2 34 6 1 0
   34 1 35 109 34 51 60 39 46 43 34 53 62 61 60 39 46 43 34 51 60 32 40
   30 38 72 32 1 34 81 35 107 31 4 9 0 30 24 6 1 0 34 1 34 6 1 0 34 40
   30 4 72 32 1 43 34 53 62 61 60 39 46 43 33 27 0 43)

;;; Entry point
5
```

7.10.2   Building an Application

Compiling files is all well and good, but eventually we want to execute them!
The second utility we'll add corresponds to what we often call a *linker* (the ld
of UN⋆X). It organizes compiled files into a unique executable file. The function
build-application takes the name of a file to generate and then the names of
files to link.

```
(define (build-application application-name ofilename . ofilenames)
  (set! sg.current.names    '())
```

```
(set! *dynamic-variables* '())
(set! sg.current          (vector))
(set! *constants*         (vector))
(set! *code*              (vector))
(let install ((filenames (cons ofilename ofilenames))
              (entry-points '()) )
  (if (pair? filenames)
      (let ((ep (install-object-file! (car filenames))))
        (install (cdr filenames) (cons ep entry-points)) )
      (write-result-file application-name
                         (cons ";;; Bytecode application containing "
                               (cons ofilename ofilenames) )
                         *dynamic-variables*
                         sg.current.names
                         *constants*
                         *code*
                         entry-points ) ) ) )
```

Most of the work is carried out by `install-object-file!`, which installs a compiled file inside the five variables governing the machine:

- `sg.current.names` indicates the mutable global variables;
- `*dynamic-variables*` indicates the dynamic variables;
- `sg.current` contains the values of mutable global variables;
- `*constants*` contains the quotations;
- `*code*` is the byte vector of instructions.

After installing all these files, we only have to write the resulting executable file in a form that resembles the compiled files except for the entry point; it becomes a list of entry points.

The function `install-object-file!` installs a compiled file and returns the address of its first instruction. Putting the code of the file to install into the `*code*` vector is easy. What's harder is to make the files share what they have in common and to protect what each file has for its own use. That will be the purpose of the functions whose names begin with `relocate` in the following definition:

```
(define (install-object-file! filename)
  (let ((ofilename (string-append filename ".so")))
    (if (probe-file ofilename)
        (call-with-input-file ofilename
          (lambda (in)
            (let* ((dynamics     (read in))
                   (global-names (read in))
                   (constants    (read in))
                   (code         (read in))
                   (entry        (read in)) )
              (close-input-port in)
              (relocate-globals! code global-names)
              (relocate-constants! code constants)
              (relocate-dynamics! code dynamics)
              (+ entry (install-code! code)) ) ) )
        (signal #f (list "No such file" ofilename)) ) ) )
```

```
(define (install-code! code)
  (let ((start (vector-length *code*)))
    (set! *code* (vector-append *code* code))
    start ) )
```

Quotations, for example, belong privately to each file where they appear, and one should not be confused with another. In each file, then, they are numbered starting from zero and thus share the same numbers. Quotations will be concatenated in the variable *constants*, and numbers referring to them will be updated. Those numbers appear in the vector of instructions as arguments to the instruction CONSTANT, so it is there that we must update them. To do so, we examine the vector of code part by part sequentially, like this:

```
(define CONSTANT-code 9)
(define (relocate-constants! code constants)
  (define n (vector-length *constants*))
  (let ((code-size (vector-length code)))
    (let scan ((pc 0))
      (when (< pc code-size)
        (let ((instr (vector-ref code pc)))
          (when (= instr CONSTANT-code)
            (let* ((i (vector-ref code (+ pc 1)))
                   (quotation (vector-ref constants i)) )
              (vector-set! code (+ pc 1) (+ n i)) ) )
          (scan (+ pc (instruction-size code pc))) ) ) ) )
  (set! *constants* (vector-append *constants* constants)) )
```

For global variables, in contrast, we must make sure they are shared. Any two files that both use foo must share that variable. Variables are numbered with respect to a local list of names. The only places where these numbers appear are as arguments to the instructions GLOBAL-REF, CHECKED-GLOBAL-REF, and SET-GLOBAL!. Each number we find will be associated with its external name; that name is associated with a number belonging to the variable in the executable; the executable number will eventually replace the other number.

```
(define CHECKED-GLOBAL-REF-code 8)
(define GLOBAL-REF-code 7)
(define SET-GLOBAL!-code 27)
(define (relocate-globals! code global-names)
  (define (get-index name)
    (let ((where (memq name sg.current.names)))
      (if where (- (length where) 1)
          (begin (set! sg.current.names (cons name sg.current.names))
                 (get-index name) ) ) ) )
  (let ((code-size (vector-length code)))
    (let scan ((pc 0))
      (when (< pc code-size)
        (let ((instr (vector-ref code pc)))
          (when (or (= instr CHECKED-GLOBAL-REF-code)
                    (= instr GLOBAL-REF-code)
                    (= instr SET-GLOBAL!-code) )
            (let* ((i (vector-ref code (+ pc 1)))
```

```
                      (name (list-ref global-names i)) )
                 (vector-set! code (+ pc 1) (get-index name)) ) )
              (scan (+ pc (instruction-size code pc))) ) ) ) )
    (let ((v (make-vector (length sg.current.names) undefined-value)))
      (vector-copy! sg.current v 0 (vector-length sg.current))
      (set! sg.current v) ) )
```

The process is similar for dynamic variables.

```
(define DYNAMIC-REF-code 240)
(define DYNAMIC-PUSH-code 242)
(define (relocate-dynamics! code dynamics)
  (for-each get-dynamic-variable-index dynamics)
  (let ((dynamics (reverse! dynamics))
        (code-size (vector-length code)) )
    (let scan ((pc 0))
      (when (< pc code-size)
        (let ((instr (vector-ref code pc)))
          (when (or (= instr DYNAMIC-REF-code)
                    (= instr DYNAMIC-PUSH-code) )
            (let* ((i (vector-ref code (+ pc 1)))
                   (name (list-ref dynamics (- i 1))) )
              (vector-set! code (+ pc 1)
                           (get-dynamic-variable-index name) ) ) )
          (scan (+ pc (instruction-size code pc))) ) ) ) ) )
```

Notice that these functions use the function **instruction-size**. We should also note that examining the vector of code three times is a waste of effort; we should factor that work into a single pass.

The form we adopted for compiled files makes it easy to imagine new modes for combining files. The list of mutable global variables serves as a sort of interface to a file considered as a module. That module then exports all its mutable global variables under the name they had within the file. We could simply rename these variables or restrict them. We could even invent a language for linking that specifies how to group modules and manage the names of variables that they use. Let's explain a bit more about that language, inspired by the language proposed for modules of EuLisp in [QP91a]. As an example, the following directive defines what the module **mod** imports:

```
(ordered-union
   (only (fact) (expose "fact"))
   (union (except-pattern ("fib*") (expose "fib"))
          (rename ((call/cc call-with-current-continuation))
            (expose "scheme") )
          (expose "numeric") ) )
```

Let's assume that the notation **foo@mod** designates the variable named **foo** in the module **mod**. Let's also suppose that that the module **fact** defines the variables **fact** and **fact100** (containing the precalculated value of (**fact 100**), a value often in demand); that the module **fib** defines the variables **fib**, **fib20**, and **Fibonacci**. The module **numeric** procures functions like **fact** and **fib**, while **scheme** procures all the functions of R4RS. The module produced by that directive is thus formed this way: it contains the variable **fact@fact**; (the variable **fact20@fact**, although

exposed by the directive (**expose "fact"**), is excluded by the restrictive directive
only;) the sole variable **Fibonacci@fib**; (the other variables from the same module
are excluded by the clause **except-pattern**;). The variable **call/cc@scheme** renames the variable **call-with-current-continuation@scheme**. Since the union
creating **mod** is specified as ordered, the module **fact** will be evaluated before the
others (**fib**, **numeric**, and **scheme**) whose order is not specified but must be compatible with their definition. Since the module **numeric** very probably uses the
module **scheme**, it should be evaluated afterwards.

7.10.3   Executing an Application

The purpose of an executable is, of course, to be executed. Since we've prepared
everything in advance, the execution becomes simple even if it is long and tedious
as far as initializing all the registers.

```
(define (run-application stack-size filename)
  (if (probe-file filename)
      (call-with-input-file filename
        (lambda (in)
          (let* ((dynamics     (read in))
                 (global-names (read in))
                 (constants    (read in))
                 (code         (read in))
                 (entry-points (read in)) )
            (close-input-port in)
            (set! sg.current.names    global-names)
            (set! *dynamic-variables* dynamics)
            (set! sg.current (make-vector (length sg.current.names)
                                          undefined-value ))
            (set! *constants*         constants)
            (set! *code*              (vector))
            (install-code! code)
            (set! *env*               sr.init)
            (set! *stack*             (make-vector stack-size))
            (set! *stack-index*       0)
            (set! *val*               'anything)
            (set! *fun*               'anything)
            (set! *arg1*              'anything)
            (set! *arg2*              'anything)
            (push-dynamic-binding
             0 (list (make-primitive (lambda ()
                                       (show-exception)
                                       (*exit* 'aborted) ))) )
            (stack-push 1)                       ;pc for FINISH
            (if (pair? entry-points)
                (for-each stack-push entry-points)
                (stack-push entry-points) ) )
          (set! *pc* (stack-pop))
          (call/cc (lambda (exit)
                     (set! *exit* exit)
                     (run) )) ) ) )
```

```
(static-wrong "No such file" filename) ) )
```

We begin by reading the file containing the executable, and we close the input port as soon as it become useless. We initialize the global variables of the machine, like the function **run-machine** used to do. After reserving a place for the base exception handler, we push all the entry points for the compiled files participating in the executable. To be more general, we also consider a simple compiled file as an executable on its own. The default handler terminates execution if it is invoked; to do so, it captures the call continuation of **run-application** (the operating system) and then places it in the variable ***exit***. The function (**show-exception**) is responsible for printing a meaningful error message[12] on the basis of the exception present in the register ***val***. The only remaining task is to simulate a (**RETURN**) to evaluate the first file of the executable; that file will return to the second file, and so on down the line.

The function **run-application** takes the size of the evaluation stack to use as an argument. To keep the size of the stack within limits is a subtle but very important implementation point. It would be too costly to test whether we have overrun the stack at every **stack-push**. Sometimes, we could use the operating system or the properties of segmented memory to eliminate that test and increase the size of the stack in case of overrunning it. Here our simulation is particularly inefficient because we can never say often enough how expensive the form (**vector-ref** v i) is since it must verify that v is a vector and i is an positive integer less than the size of the vector.

The function **run-application** doesn't need much to execute a compiled file. It really needs only **run** and functions related to vectors, lists, and other classes like **primitive**, **continuation**, etc. It also needs a **read** function for quotations. Thus it's quite independent of the compiler that produced the application, (but it doesn't help us much with debugging the program) and that, of course, was the goal!

7.11 Conclusions

To get a real implementation of Scheme, we would have to add many missing functions as well as the corresponding data types. That presents hardly any problems except detecting errors in data types or domain.

The implementation we wrote earlier is general enough and certainly can be improved. It's interesting because it derives from the preceding efficient interpreter, the one that we reconfigured as a compiler. There is, in fact, a profound connection between an interpreter and compiler (explored in [Nei84]). An interpreter executes a program whereas a compiler transcribes a program as something that will be executed. Thus there is a simple difference in library—execution library or generation library—in question here. We've exploited that connection to derive the compiler from the interpreter.

However, we've inherited only the information that appears in the intermediate language, and that information is insufficient to insure a good compilation. We know nothing, for example, about the use of local variables; indeed that is the

---

12. For example, "**bus error; core not dumped.**"

principal analysis that we lack. We don't know whether these variables can be modified, whether they are closed, multiply closed, modified while closed, etc. In many cases, all those static properties make it possible to get rid of activation records and to use only the stack—thus improving allocation and speed. Activation records are useful only to save the values of closed variables, so it's not necessary to allocate such records when variables are not closed. Since their values are already on the stack, as long as we leave them there and search for them there, we'll speed things up a lot.

7.12   Exercises

Exercise 7.1 : Modify the compiler defined in this chapter to use a register ***dynenv*** to indicate the dynamic environment. [see p. 252]

Exercise 7.2 : Define a function **load** to load a compiled program at execution and execute the program. For example, if **fact.scm** is a file compiled as **fact.so**, we should be able to compile and execute the following file:

```
(begin (load "fact")
       (fact 5) )
```

Exercise 7.3 : Write a function **global-value** to take the name of a global variable and return its value.

Exercise 7.4 : Modify the instructions involved with dynamic variables to implement them by shallow binding. [see p. 23]

Exercise 7.5 : [see p. 265] Write a function to rename exported variables. If **fact.so** is a compiled file, then the following lines should create a new module, **nfact.so** where the variable **fact** has been renamed as **factorial**.

```
(build-application-renaming-variables
  "nfact.so" "fact.so" '((fact factorial)) )
```

Exercise 7.6 : [see p. 195] Modify the instruction **CHECKED-GLOBAL-REF** so it can modify itself into **GLOBAL-REF** once the variable being read has been initialized.

Project 7.7 : Gnu Emacs Lisp in [LLSt93] and xscheme in [Bet91], among other implementations of Lisp or Scheme, have byte-code compilers. Adapt the compiler from this chapter to interpret byte-code implemented by those virtual machines.

Recommended Reading

There are few works that explain the rudiments of compilation. In fact, that's one reason for this book. Nevertheless, you might consult [All78] and [Hen80].

For higher order compilation, see [Dil88]. These sources also contain interesting compilers with comments: [Ste78, AS85, FWH92].

8
Evaluation & Reflection

*U*NIQUELY characteristic of Lisp is its evaluation mechanism: **eval**. Although this book talks relentlessly about evaluation, we haven't said a word yet about the problem of making evaluation available to programmers. Evaluation poses a number of problems with respect to specification, integrity, and linguistics. Some people are thinking of all these problems when they say concisely, "**eval** is *evil.*" Catching its genius in a useful form is the first step toward programming reflection, a topic this chapter also covers.

For 271 pages now, we've been presenting various interpreters detailing the core of the evaluation mechanism. For most of them, making the evaluation mechanism accessible to programmers is trivial, a task requiring very little code. That's what implementers have been doing for ages. The existence of such a mechanism [see p. 2] was surely one of the goals in creating Lisp. From the very beginning of the sixties, in fact, making the **eval** function explicit showed up in the writings of the founders, such as [McC60, MAE+62].

Explicit evaluation is fundamental, supporting as it does so many effects, notably, a powerful system of macros, immersion of the programming environment within the language, and pronounced reflection. Of course, explicit evaluation also has some defects such as macros, a programming environment right inside the language, and invasive reflection. Like a magic djinn, explicit evaluation can be both useful and dangerous.

What sort of contract should explicit evaluation satisfy? Clearly, we would like to say that:

$$(\texttt{eval '}\pi) \quad \equiv \quad \pi \tag{1}$$

But right now we're going to show you the ambiguity of that formula.

8.1 Programs and Values

Let's actually try to put **eval** inside the first interpreter in this book. [see p. 3] That interpreter was written in pure Scheme, without any particular restrictions. Let's assume first that **eval** should be a special form. In consequence, it will appear in **evaluate** which then becomes this:

```
(define (evaluate e env)
```

```
(if (atom? e)
    (cond ((symbol? e) (lookup e env))
          ((or (number? e)(string? e)(char? e)(boolean? e)) e)
          (else (wrong "Cannot evaluate" e)) )
    (case (car e)
      ((quote)  (cadr e))
      ((if)     (if (not (eq? (evaluate (cadr e) env)
                              the-false-value ))
                    (evaluate (caddr e) env)
                    (evaluate (cadddr e) env) ))
      ((begin)  (eprogn (cdr e) env))
      ((set!)   (update! (cadr e) env (evaluate (caddr e) env)))
      ((lambda) (make-function (cadr e) (cddr e) env))
      ((eval)   (evaluate (evaluate (cadr e) env) env)) ; ** Modified **
      (else     (invoke (evaluate (car e) env)
                        (evlis (cdr e) env) )) ) ) )
```

As a special form, **eval** begins by evaluating the form that corresponds to its first argument (just like a function does); then it evaluates the resulting value in the current environment. This patently trivial description of what it does hides some gaping questions.

As we've emphasized time and again, the function **evaluate** entails a first stage of syntactic analysis and a second stage of evaluation. We separated those stages into **meaning** and **run** in the most recent interpreters. The first argument of **evaluate** corresponds to a program, whereas its result belongs to the domain of values. There's a problem, then, (let's call it a type-checking problem) with the form (**evaluate** (**evaluate** ...) ...) where the outermost **evaluate** is applied to a value and not to a program. Are programs values? Are values programs?

Programming languages are usually defined by a grammar specifying their syntactic form. The grammar of Scheme appears in [CR91b]. It specifies that certain arrangements of parentheses and letters are syntactically legal programs. The grammar also specifies the syntax of data, and we can check that any program conforms to that syntax for data. The **read** function, in fact, is universal in the sense that it can read both programs and data. However, nothing makes it obligatory for programs to be read by **read** in order to be evaluated, even if doing so is simpler. A Smalltalk evaluator, as in [GR83], for example, reads its programs in windows with a special reader that stores positions in terms of rows and columns in order to highlight portions of these programs that are syntactically incorrect. Since this usage prevails, of course, it is clear that any program respecting the grammar of Scheme is or can be associated with a legitimate value according to this same grammar.

Conversely and no less clear, there are many values that correspond to programs but even more that don't, for example, (**quote** . 1). Unfortunately, there remain values whose status is not so clear.

- Take a value more or less resembling a program apart from a few clinkers, for example, (**if #t 1** (**quote** . 2)). Is it a program? That expression poses no problem for the operational definition we just gave for **eval** since (**quote** . 2) is not evaluated, but this expression hardly conforms to the grammar of Scheme programs.

- Take a value such as the one constructed by the expression `'(',car '(a b))` and having in its function position a form quoting the value of the function `car`. Is it a program? That value is not a program according to the syntax of R^4RS because it has no external representation: it cannot be typed with a normal keyboard. Yet once again, it poses no problem for `eval` as we described it before.

- Let's consider the syntactic conventions of COMMON LISP where `#1=` is a name for the expression that follows it, and `#1#` represents the expression of name 1. With that in mind, let's consider the following expression, whose graphic representation is shown in Figure 8.1.

```
(let ((n 4))
  #1=(if (= n 1) 1
      (* n ((lambda (n) #1#) (- n 1))) ) )
```

This value has a cycle. In fact, we would say that the program involved is syntactically recursive, so it is not syntactically legal in Scheme. Once again, it poses no problem, however, for the `eval` form that we described earlier.

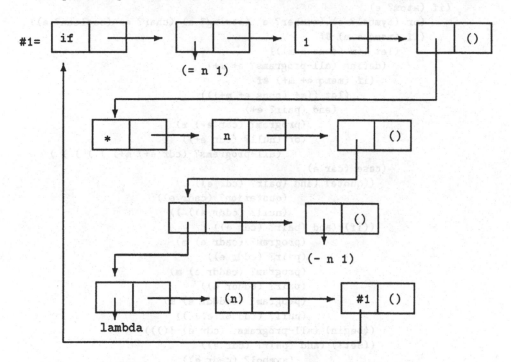

Figure 8.1 Syntactically recursive factorial

From the grammatical point of view, those expressions all look like they come from a careful study in how to produce monstrosities, but they clearly show that the idea of a program is subtle with respect to `eval`. The same problem arises about macros that carry out computations on representations of programs. Here again we find the distinction between static and dynamic errors that we discussed earlier. [see p. 194] Drawing the line is difficult, but we'll risk doing so! The most permissive hypothesis is to allow everything, so a syntactic anomaly like (quote . 3) is not detected until we're obliged to evaluate the program. The strictest hypothesis is to accept only those programs represented by finite acyclic graphs where all nodes are syntactically correct. That rule eliminates the syntactically recursive factorial—the one we offered as an example just before—even though it is syntactically correct. This hard line—the one taken by Scheme—is the one we'll take since it has been shown in [Que92a] that syntactically recursive programs can be rewritten purely as trees with no cycles. As for quotations, we'll authorize any finite value for which the atoms (the leaves of the tree) have an external representation. This rule excludes quotations that entail closures, continuations, or streams, as well as cyclic[1] structures.

Operationally, we'll use the following predicates to characterize the values that we allow as legitimate programs. These predicates test syntax and detect[2] cycles.

```
(define (program? e)
  (define (program? e m)
    (if (atom? e)
        (or (symbol? e) (number? e) (string? e) (char? e) (boolean? e))
        (if (memq e m) #f
            (let ((m (cons e m)))
              (define (all-programs? e+ m+)
                (if (memq e+ m+) #f
                    (let ((m+ (cons e+ m+)))
                      (and (pair? e+)
                           (program? (car e+) m)
                           (or (null? (cdr e+))
                               (all-programs? (cdr e+) m+) ) ) ) ) )
              (case (car e)
                ((quote) (and (pair? (cdr e))
                              (quotation? (cadr e))
                              (null? (cddr e)) ))
                ((if) (and (pair? (cdr e))
                           (program? (cadr e) m)
                           (pair? (cddr e))
                           (program? (caddr e) m)
                           (pair? (cdddr e))
                           (program? (cadddr e) m)
                           (null? (cddddr e)) ))
                ((begin) (all-programs? (cdr e) '()))
                ((set!) (and (pair? (cdr e))
                             (symbol? (cadr e))
                             (pair? (cddr e))
                             (program? (caddr e) m)
                             (null? (cdddr e)) ))
                ((lambda) (and (pair? (cdr e))
```

---

1. Allowing them is not too costly, and they may be useful, for example, in the implementation of MEROONET.
2. Note that the value (let ((e '(x))) '(lambda ,e ,e)) is a legitimate program.

```
                                    (variables-list? (cadr e))
                                    (all-programs? (cddr e) '()) ))
                    (else (all-programs? e '())) ) ) ) ) )
    (program? e '()) )
  (define (variables-list? v*)
    (define (variables-list? v* already-seen)
      (or (null? v*)
          (and (symbol? v*) (not (memq v* already-seen)))
          (and (pair? v*)
               (symbol? (car v*))
               (not (memq (car v*) already-seen))
               (variables-list? (cdr v*)
                                 (cons (car v*) already-seen) ) ) ) )
    (variables-list? v* '()) )
  (define (quotation? e)
    (define (quotation? e m)
      (if (memq e m) #f
          (let ((m (cons e m)))
            (or (null? e)(symbol? e)(number? e)
                (string? e)(char? e)(boolean? e)
                (and (vector? e)
                     (let loop ((i 0))
                       (or (>= i (vector-length e))
                           (and (quotation? (vector-ref e i) m)
                                (loop (+ i 1)) ) ) ) )
                (and (pair? e)
                     (quotation? (car e) m)
                     (quotation? (cdr e) m) ) ) ) ) )
    (quotation? e '()) )
```

Armed with the predicate **program?**, we can improve our formulation of the
special form **eval** in this way:

```
    ... ((eval) (let ((v (evaluate (cadr e) env)))
                  (if (program? v)
                      (evaluate v env)
                      (wrong "Illegal program" v) ) )) ...
```

Alas, that form is still clumsy because the preceding predicates do not test
whether a value *is* a program and a quotation *is* correct; they only test whether a
value is a *legitimate representation* of a program or quotation. That's a pledge of the
intelligibility of a value in a particular role. The value is neither the program itself
nor the quotation. Indeed, a program and a quotation are whatever the interpreter
needs for them to be. To refine these ideas, let's look now at the pre-denotational
interpreter of Chapter 4. [see p. 111] There memory and continuations were explicit, and inside them the data of interpreted Scheme were represented by closures
simulating objects. Here's that interpreter, but we've added the special form **eval**:

```
(define (evaluate e r s k)
  (if (atom? e)
      (if (symbol? e) (evaluate-variable e r s k)
          (evaluate-quote e r s k) )
      (case (car e)
```

```
        ((quote)  (evaluate-quote (cadr e) r s k))
        ((if)     (evaluate-if (cadr e) (caddr e) (cadddr e) r s k))
        ((begin)  (evaluate-begin (cdr e) r s k))
        ((set!)   (evaluate-set! (cadr e) (caddr e) r s k))
        ((lambda) (evaluate-lambda (cadr e) (cddr e) r s k))
        ((eval)   (evaluate-eval (cadr e) r s k))           ; ** Modified **
        (else     (evaluate-application (car e) (cdr e) r s k)) ) ) )
(define (evaluate-eval e r s k)
  (evaluate e r s
    (lambda (v ss)
      (let ((ee (transcode-back v ss)))
        (if (program? ee)
            (evaluate ee r ss k)
            (wrong "Illegal program" ee) ) ) ) ) )
```

In this interpreter, the value we get by evaluating the first argument of the **eval** form is first decoded as its external form (by **transcode-back**). Then the nature of the program is checked so that it is eventually evaluated. The variables **e** and **ee** have as their domain the descriptions of programs, while the variable **v** indicates the values. The role of **transcode-back** is to take a value and put it into such a form that it can be considered as a description of the program. This is just what gets the effect of **eval** in a Scheme, where there is no **load** function available: write the value to evaluate into a file; use **display** for **transcode-back**; then evaluate that file by **load** instead of **evaluate**. In that case, the program is "compiled"[3] in the name of the file.

Let's take a last example, this time, the fast compiling interpreter from Chapter 6. [see p. 183] It reveals a few more interesting points. There, values and descriptions of programs share the same support; thus it will not be necessary to introduce a conversion between them. In contrast, the goal of the fast interpreter was to suppress evaluation for any static calculation that could be carried out before hand.

```
(define (meaning e r tail?)
  (if (atom? e)
      (if (symbol? e) (meaning-reference e r tail?)
                      (meaning-quotation e r tail?) )
      (case (car e)
        ((quote)  (meaning-quotation (cadr e) r tail?))
        ((lambda) (meaning-abstraction (cadr e) (cddr e) r tail?))
        ((if)     (meaning-alternative (cadr e) (caddr e) (cadddr e)
                                       r tail? ))
        ((begin)  (meaning-sequence (cdr e) r tail?))
        ((set!)   (meaning-assignment (cadr e) (caddr e) r tail?))
        ((eval)   (meaning-eval (cadr e) r tail?))          ; ** Modified **
        (else     (meaning-application (car e) (cdr e) r tail?)) ) ) )
(define (meaning-eval e r tail?)
  (let ((m (meaning e r #f)))
    (lambda ()
      (let ((v (m)))
```

---

3. In fact, coding **eval** by **load** provides an **eval** only at *toplevel*. We'll get to that idea later.

```
(if (program? v)
    (let ((mm (meaning v r tail?)))
      (mm) )
    (wrong "Illegal program" v) ) ) ) ) )
```

Now it becomes clear that for this fast compiling interpreter, which converts a description of a program into a tree of thunks, that compiling the value **v** cannot be done statically. For the first time, a thunk will be generated which does not contain only simple calculations like allocations, conditionals, sequences, or read-access or write-access inside various data structures. Instead, (oh, horrors!) it entails a call to **meaning**. This call thus implies that we must keep the code for **meaning** and its affiliates at execution: not a slight cost!

We've tried here to eliminate the confusion between values and programs. This confusion is on the same order as that between quotations and values. There's a reason that **eval** and **quote** are often said to play reverse roles: for its argument, **quote** takes a description of a value to synthesize whereas **eval** starts from a value and converts it into a program to evaluate. Both perform conversions between signified and signifier, so it is important not to confuse them.

8.2 eval as a Special Form

When **eval** is a special form, we get close to the ideal that we advocated in equation (1); that is, we make (**eval** (**quote** π)) equivalent to π. That's just what we want if we adopt equational thinking, as in [FH89, Mul92]. In a well built theory, we can substitute two things that are mutually equal *in any context*. More precisely, that implies that (1) is an attenuated form of (2), where $C[]$ represents a context.

$$\forall C[], \quad C[(\texttt{eval } '\pi)] \equiv C[\pi] \tag{2}$$

Accordingly, the evaluation of a closed form (without free variables) like (**eval** '((lambda (x y) x) 1 2)) returns 1. Moreover, we can also take advantage of the current lexical environment, like this:

```
((lambda (x) (eval 'x))
 3 )                            → 3
((lambda (x y) (eval y))
 4 'x )                         → 4
((lambda (x y z) (eval y))
 5 (list 'eval 'z) 'x )         → 5
```

This effect is made possible only because the current lexical environment is available. About the fast compiling interpreter, we can even observe that it is not only necessary to have the compiler **meaning** in a working state at execution time, but it is also necessary to capture the current lexical environment in order to take up the compilation again in the same environment. For that reason the generated thunk encloses not only **meaning** but also **r** (and as an accessory, **tail?**): all of them must be present at execution.

This effect is even more pertinent if we show what has become of the byte-code compiler from Chapter 7. [see p. 223] The analyzing function **meaning-eval** calls the byte-code generator EVAL/CE (for *eval in the current environment*). This generator receives the argument to evaluate as well as the lexical environment for compilation, like this:

```
(define (meaning-eval e r tail?)
  (let ((m (meaning e r #f)))
    (EVAL/CE m r) ) )
(define (EVAL/CE m r)
  (append (PRESERVE-ENV) (CONSTANT r) (PUSH-VALUE)
          m (COMPILE-RUN) (RESTORE-ENV) ) )
```

The byte-code generator EVAL/CE systematically preserves the execution environment because we don't take account of the parameter tail?. A new intruction (COMPILE-RUN) condenses the whole compiler-evaluator. That instruction takes the expression to evaluate in the register *val* and the compilation environment on the top of the stack and delegates to compile-on-the-fly the task of compiling the program and installing its code in memory to execute as if it were the body of a function.

```
(define (COMPILE-RUN) (list 255))

(define-instruction (COMPILE-RUN) 255
  (let ((v *val*)
        (r (stack-pop)) )
    (if (program? v)
        (compile-and-run v r #f)
        (signal-exception #t (list "Illegal program" v)) ) ) )

(define (compile-and-run v r tail?)
  (unless tail? (stack-push *pc*))
  (set! *pc* (compile-on-the-fly v r)) )
(define (compile-on-the-fly v r)
  (set! g.current '())
  (for-each g.current-extend! sg.current.names)
  (set! *quotations* (vector->list *constants*))
  (set! *dynamic-variables* *dynamic-variables*)
  (let ((code (apply vector (append (meaning v r #f) (RETURN)))))
    (set! sg.current.names (map car (reverse g.current)))
    (let ((v (make-vector (length sg.current.names) undefined-value)))
      (vector-copy! sg.current v 0 (vector-length sg.current))
      (set! sg.current v) )
    (set! *constants* (apply vector *quotations*))
    (set! *dynamic-variables* *dynamic-variables*)
    (install-code! code) ) )
```

Compiling on the fly means that we have to update the global variables for compilation: g.current (the environment of mutable global variables), *quotations*, and *dynamic-variables*.[4] The compiled code is followed by a (RETURN) so that it can return to its caller. After the compilation, we enrich the execution environment in order to add new quotations, mutable global variables, or dynamic

---

4. An contrast to other variables, *dynamic-variables* is shared between the compiler and the executing machine. Also idempotent assignments to it are pointless, but those assignments indicate what must change if they were not shared.

variables created at that time. There's nothing left to do but to install the new code segment and then execute it.

This installation is analogous to dynamic linking. It shows that for a language like C, eval comes down to writing a character string in a file, then compiling that file by a call to cc, then loading that file by dynamic linking, and finally executing it. Code installed that way can't be eliminated in the current state of the machine and thus in the long term it will obstruct memory. Recuperating memory consumed by compiled code is always a touchy issue.

The cost of introducing this new special form is thus

- a new instruction (COMPILE-RUN) accompanied by the function meaning and a few other utilities, representing a great increase in size for small applications;

- and, at every call to eval, supplementary quotations to store the necessary compilation environments.

Fortunately, we have to save these compilation environments only in these places. The marginal cost is thus proportional to the number of eval forms.

As far as implementation and debugging, inserting an eval form makes it possible to program a local interaction loop to check or modify local variables by their own name. If a debugger were available and could be activated by a simple interruption (by an interruption from the keyboard, for example) at any stage of the program where we wanted, it would require us to keep the entire text of the program as well as saving all the compilation environments.

8.3 Creating Global Variables

Because of the explicit contract in equation (2), the expression (eval '(set! foo 33)) should be equivalent to (set! foo 33). We've already seen its various semantics [see p. 111] in Chapter 4. They were analyzed in Section 6.1.9 [see p. 203]. If simply mentioning the name of a variable makes it exist, then eval should behave likewise. In contrast, if variables must be declared before they are used, then eval should conform to that practice instead. The function compile-on-the-fly extends the global evaluation environment on its return in order to take into account new mutable global variables that have just appeared.

This point of that remark is to make you realize that equations (1) or (2) stipulate that not only the values of π and (eval 'π) but also their induced effects (such as any global variables created, any modifications of the global environment or the evaluation context) should be the same. This idea of "same" is taken into account by equation (2) which must remain valid regardless of the context. That means that π and (eval 'π) must be indistinguishable. In other words, there can be no program[5] that we can write that can tell them apart.

_____

5. This statement is somewhat theoretical since we might let the program check the clock to measure its own execution time and by that means, a program could deduce whether it had encountered an eval or not.

8.4   eval as a Function

The special form eval evaluates its argument as a function would do, so we might as well ask ourselves whether we could achieve the same evaluation as a function rather than a special form. To that end, let's take each of the various interpreters again and show how to introduce such a function in each one.

With the naive interpreter at the beginning of this book [see p. 3], we would write this:

```
(defprimitive eval
  (lambda (v)
    (if (program? v)
        (evaluate v env.global)
        (wrong "Illegal program" v) ))
  1 )
```

Right away, the major difference is apparent: we've lost the current lexical environment. Since we still have to give one to the evaluator, evaluate, we'll provide the only one that's visible: the global environment! As a consequence, we have here a function playing the role of a global evaluator equivalent to the one used by the toplevel loop. We'll name it eval/at for *eval at top-level* while we'll name the preceding special form eval/ce to distinguish it when we feel the need to do so. Using eval/at is not a complete loss because we save some effort with it: we no longer have to store the lexical environments present when eval/ce is called. We save a few quotations that way.

To clarify these ideas, we'll take up the preceding examples again: assuming that eval/at as a function leads to this:

```
(set! x 2)(set! z 1)
((lambda (x) (eval/at 'x))
 3 )                                → 2
((lambda (x y) (eval/at y))
 4 'x )                             → 2
((lambda (x y z) (eval/at y))
 5 (list 'eval/at 'z) 'x )          → 1
```

Even if eval/at seems like a step backward from eval/ce, we can still (almost) simulate one with the other by doing this:

```
(define (eval/at x) (eval/ce x))
```

Unfortunately, there is one variable too many in the environment that's been captured: the local variable named x hides the global variable of the same name. [see Ex. 8.3] This problem might make you think that a more refined way of handling the environment could solve the difficulty, so this definition suggests to us how we should define eval/at in the interpreter that compiles byte-code. The new definition again uses the function compile-and-run but without asking it to push the return address because the caller of eval/at has already done it. The compilation, however, is done here with r.init since we no longer have access to the current lexical environment.

```
(definitial eval
  (let* ((arity 1)
         (arity+1 (+ arity 1))) )
```

```
(make-primitive
 (lambda ()
   (if (= arity+1 (activation-frame-argument-length *val*))
       (let ((v (activation-frame-argument *val* 0)))
         (if (program? v)
             (compile-and-run v r.init #t)
             (signal-exception #t (list "Illegal program" v)) ) )
       (signal-exception #t (list "Incorrect arity" 'eval)) ) ) ) ) )
```

Evaluating as if we were at the toplevel loop should not be taken too literally because of the dynamic environment. For example, whether **eval** is a special form or a function, we should still observe this:

```
(dynamic-let (a 22)
  (eval '(dynamic a)) )    → 22
```

As far as the initial contract of **eval** with respect to equation (1), it begins in the empty context, that is, right at the fundamental level. In contrast, **eval/at** does not satisfy equation (2), as those earlier examples prove. To be more specific about the behavior of **eval/at**, we'll turn to equation (3) where v is a variable that cannot be captured:

$$C[(\text{eval/at } '\pi)] \equiv (\text{let } ((v \ (\text{lambda } () \ \pi))) \ C[(v)]) \tag{3}$$

The variation of **eval** that you'll encounter most commonly among Lisp systems is **eval/at**.

8.5 The Cost of eval

The overall cost of using **eval** is hard to grasp. Suppose first of all that the autonomous application that we are about to construct is none other than the famous (**display** "Hello world"). If the special form **eval/ce** does not occur in the application (and that's something we can simply check statically) then there's no cost! If it occurs, then we must at least add the compiler to the application, so its size changes by an order of magnitude; let's say roughly 50 to 500 kilobytes. If we get dynamic evaluation in the form of a function, and if it is not proved that the function will not be useless (in short, if we need the function) then we're back to the same case. To prove that **eval/at** is not needed, we must verify that it is never used. The language is helpful for this proof: in Scheme, for example, it suffices to prove that the global variable **eval/at** is not mentioned. In COMMON LISP, that's generally not possible since we must prove in addition (and among other things) that nobody has generated the character string "eval/at", converted it to a symbol by means of **find-symbol**, and (by means of **symbol-function**) extracted the function of the same name from that symbol. It's costly to detect even just the mention of **symbol-function** with an argument that we cannot foresee.

If by chance a call to **eval** occurs, can we limit the set of values to which **eval** is applied? In most cases, this analysis is hardly possible, and you might even think that any value is possible. Consequently, we can no longer remove a single function from the global environment since *anything* and *everything* might be called. The generation of an application thus must contain everything that the language defines, with no exceptions, and the size of the executable, especially in a language as rich as COMMON LISP, grows another order of magnitude.

We're not past the worst yet. Even if we are in the ideal case with a system of modules that limit where the global environment can be seen and whether it can be modified, as in [QP91b], the very presence of eval kills off the possibility of many ways of improving compilation. Look at the following definition:

```
(define (fib n)
  (if (< n 2) (eval (read))
      (+ (fib (- n 1)) (fib (- n 2))) ) )
```

Independently of the effects that eval might have on other global variables, eval can also modify the global variable fib. That fact obliges us, during the second recursive call, to search for the value of fib by the address associated with the global variable, rather than using a blind GOTO. Since eval can modify anything, we don't even have the usual advantages of global variables being invariable. In short, the presence of even one single eval in a module makes it possible to modify practically anything in that module.

For all those reasons, eval is considered an expensive characteristic. However, inside a large application (something like a few megabytes) and in development where everything is in a more or less unstable state, eval is a low-level, useful addition. True: if we have only a minor little calculation to program, it is simpler (in terms of how long it takes to program and how costly a programmer's time is) to call eval to compute arithmetic expressions, rather than to implement an interpreter in an *ad hoc* language. Lisp is a remarkable extension language, and making eval available in a library is a major advantage.

8.6   Interpreted eval

This book uses an immoderate number of interpreters. In case there were no eval in a system, you might ask whether a user couldn't supply one by his or her own means. After all, given the number of interpreters you've already seen, you would only have to choose one from the many available, pick up the code by FTP (or just type it in yourself), and put it into your application. Well, yes and no.

In pure Scheme, if you want to write an evaluator, it can only be a function since you can't define your own special forms there. Two problems then arise.

8.6.1   Can Representations Be Interchanged?

The first problem we alluded to is how to organize interactions between the underlying system and the interpreter that you want to write. This problem means that you can't impose new data types and that in fact you must conform to existing types. The pairs that the interpreter manages must be the same pairs as the implementation; Booleans must be the same; functions have to respect a similar calling protocol. Explicit evaluation, which appears in the following example, must necessarily return a function that can be invoked by the underlying system.

```
((eval '(lambda (x) (cons x x)))
  33 )    →  (33 . 33)
```

Conversely, the interpreter must also know how to invoke functions from the underlying system, like this:

```
(((eval '(lambda (f)
            (lambda (x) (f x)) ))
   list )
   44 )    → (44)
```

One possible common representation for functions is to use functions with multiple arity (`lambda values ...`) in a way that adapts to the two possible invocation modes. The modifications that this entails for the first interpreter in this book (the naive interpreter of the first chapter [see **p. 3**]) for example, are simple. You can easily deduce the others from this:

```
(define (invoke fn args)
   (if (procedure? fn)
       (apply fn args)
       (wrong "Not a function" fn) ) )
(define (make-function variables body env)
   (lambda values
       (eprogn body (extend env variables values)) ) )
```

A subtle point is to make sure that error handling (for example, errors about arity) is the same in `eval` and in the underlying system, but we'll skip that detail.

8.6.2 Global Environment

The second problem we alluded to concerns how to handle the global environment. The evaluators in this book all have their own definition of their global environment; they build it by means of such macros as `definitial`, `defprimitive`, and others. Here, the problem is to cooperate with the underlying system to insure that the global environment whether seen from the interpreter or from the system is the same. In other words, the following expression has to be evaluated without error:

```
(begin (set! foo 128)
       (eval '(set! bar (+ foo foo)))
       bar )    → 256
```

Compiler for Autonomous Applications

In a compiler that works on files, like Scheme→C in [Bar89] or Bigloo in [Ser94], the program is known in advance and by construction it does not know how to access variables that it does not mention. Thus the variables that `eval` creates can be handled only by `eval`. Consequently, all we have to do is connect the underlying global environment to the interpreter, and to do so, we define two functions known as `global-value` and `set-global-value!`. Their body is systematically formed after all the global variables of the program, and they are known statically. We can even imagine that these functions[6] are synthesized automatically. [see **Ex. 7.3**]

```
(define (global-value name)
```

---

6. In the function `set-global-value!`, the variable car does not occur in order to preserve its immutability.

```
    (case name
      ((car) car)
      ...
      ((foo) foo)
      (else (wrong "No such global variable" name)) ) )
  (define (set-global-value! name value)
    (case name
      ((foo) (set! foo value))
      ...
      (else (wrong "No such mutable global variable" name)) ) )
```

The interpreter can create as many global variables as it wants; none of them can be reached directly by the underlying system; only the interpreter can manipulate them. This is not a problem since the underlying system does not mention them so it may safely continue to ignore them.

Interactive System

In contrast, if we're in a system that has an interactive loop, then the system and the interpreter can both create new variables. The example we gave earlier can explode into a sequence of interactions where we see that we can ask the underlying system the value of a variable created by the interpreter and vice-versa, like this:

```
? (begin (set! foo 128)
         (eval '(set! bar (+ foo foo)))
         2001 )
= 2001
? bar
= 256
```

There are several solutions to this problem of cooperation.

Using Symbols

The most conventional of these solutions uses symbols, a practice that has for years undermined the semantic basis of Lisp because it regrettably confuses symbols with variables, a confusion made worse by the fact that variables are represented by symbols and that (as you will see) symbols can implement variables.

Symbols are data structures that need a unique field to associate the symbol with its name, a character string. Symbols are created explicitly in Scheme by the function **string->symbol**. Two symbols of the same name cannot exist simultaneously and still be different. We usually insure that point with a hash table associating character strings with their symbol. The function **string->symbol** begins by searching in the hash table to see whether a symbol by that name already exists and if so, the function returns it; otherwise, the function builds the symbol. To make searching for symbols by name faster, supplementary (hidden) fields are often added to connect symbols to each other.

We often add a property list to symbols. It is usually managed as a P-list, but you'll also encounter A-lists and hash tables in this role as well. How large they are and how fast you can access them depends on the implementation of property lists. Some Lisp systems, such as Le-Lisp have even added fields to symbols to serve as caches for properties that are widely used, such as, for example, how to pretty-print forms beginning with that symbol.

Since the structure of a symbol is nothing more than a few fields, why don't we add another field there to store the global value of the variable of the same name? In the case of Lisp$_2$, why don't we store the value of the global function of the same name as well? In fact, since time immemorial, that is exactly what is done under the names of Cval and Fval, as in [Cha80, GP88]. Functions exist to read and write these fields. In COMMON LISP, they are `symbol-value` and (`setf symbol-value`) as well as `symbol-function` and (`setf symbol-function`).

This technique is particularly attractive because it is exceedingly sure. Every symbol that might serve as the representation of a global variable necessarily has been built beforehand by `symbol->string` (generally by `read`) so an address to contain its global value exists already as a field in the symbol. Of course, this arrangement is wasteful since not every symbol necessarily supports the representation of a global variable of the same name; on the other hand, no global variable exists without being associated with an address to contain its global value.

Thus it suffices to provide two functions, `global-value` and `set-global-value!`, to get and assign the value of global variables, starting from their names. The explicit interpreter will handle the global environment through these functions, and the problem of extending this environment never comes up since it is resolved by the magical underlying mechanism connected to the idea of a symbol.

Let's indicate how to enrich the interpreter from the first chapter to take into account these magic functions. The environment, the value of the variable `env`, will contain only local variables to the exclusion of global variables which will be managed directly. Since we have adopted a common representation of functions between the interpreter and the system, we can drop the definition of the global environment entirely from the interpreter because the interpreter can now use the global environment of the system directly. Thus we have this:

```
(define (lookup id env)
  (if (pair? env)
      (if (eq? (caar env) id)
          (cdar env)
          (lookup id (cdr env)) )
      (global-value id) ) )
(define (update! id env value)
  (if (pair? env)
      (if (eq? (caar env) id)
          (begin (set-cdr! (car env) value)
                 value )
          (update! id (cdr env) value) )
      (set-global-value! id value) ) )
```

This solution seems elegant, but at an impressive cost since every global variable is thus accessible by name. An autonomous application containing a call to `global-value` cannot eliminate anything from the library of initial functions since *a priori* every name can be computed and thus everything is necessary. That's not too annoying in a programming environment since one of its properties is to make everything available to the programmer. However, it is a real problem for a small autonomous application. Even worse, the function `set-global-value!` can change the value of any global variable and thus break any optimization of the compilation since nothing is any longer *a priori* immutable.

The two functions, `global-value` and `set-global-value!`, can be considered as one specialized version of `eval`. By the way, we found it in old Lisp systems under the name `symeval`. You can also see those two functions as reflective functions that reify access to the global environment. Writing "`foo`" in order to know the value of the global variable `foo` is the same as writing and explicitly evaluating (`global-value 'foo`).

First Class Environment

Another technique is to define an `eval` function with two variables: the expression to compute and the environment in which to compute it. The binary `eval` of the naive evaluator in the first chapter has a signature like that, but the shortcoming in adopting that solution is that we must be able to provide values as the second argument and environments too, although no operation is available for getting them. Consequently, we must allow reification of environments as well as possibly other operations, such as extraction or modification of the value of variables. By means of these operations, we can connect the environments handled by the explicit evaluator with the environments of the implementation. This technique raises many problems that we'll address now.

8.7   Reifying Environments

The denotational interpreter clearly demonstrated that in Scheme, evaluation depends on a triple: environment, continuation, memory. Once again rejecting memory, we see that continuations can be handled via `call/cc` or `bind-exit` (which reifies them). That was not the case for lexical environments, which could not be accessed directly. The next section covers how to reify them in data structures that can be manipulated.

The implementations of first class environments are characterized and differentiated, according to [RA82, MR91], by their properties and their operations. The three fundamental operations of a first class environment are: searching for the value of a variable; modifying the value of a variable extending the environment. To reify the environment is to provide a means of capturing bindings but without the abstractions that capture them only in an opaque way or in a way that cannot be manipulated.

8.7.1   Special Form `export`

We'll introduce a special form, named `export`; we'll mention to it the names of variables to capture, and it will return an environment enclosing their bindings with the specified variables. The reified environment can be used as the second argument of the binary evaluation function; we'll distinguish that function from earlier ones by naming it `eval/b`. Let's take a few examples.

```
(let ((r (let ((x 3) (export x)))))
```

```
        (eval/b 'x r) )                              → 3
    (let ((f+r (let ((x 3))
                (cons (lambda () x) (export x)) )))
        (eval/b '(set! x (+ 1 x)) (cdr f+r))
        ((car f+r)) )                                → 4
    (let ((r (export car cons)))
        (let ((car cdr))
            (eval/b '(car (cons 1 2)) r) ) )         → 1
```

In the first example, the first class environment that's being created captures the variable **x** which can thus be used at leisure by **eval/b**. The second example shows that we can also modify the variable **x**, and that it really is the binding being captured since the modification is perceived from what encloses it by the normal means of abstraction. The third example shows that we can also capture global bindings.

The special form **export** lets us juggle environments, so to speak, by capturing the purposes of environments and using them elsewhere. Its implementation is not trivial, so we'll describe it. As we do for all special forms, we'll add a clause for it to **meaning**, the function that analyzes syntax, like this:

```
    ... ((export) (meaning-export (cdr e) r tail?)) ...
```

A reified environment must not only capture the list of activation records but also save the names and addresses of variables that are supposed to be captured. That aspect recalls the implementation of **eval/ce** which required us to save the same information. We'll represent a reified environment by an object with two fields: the list of activation records and a list of name-address pairs that serve as the "roadmap" to the activation records. You can see what we mean in Figure 8.2.

```
(define-class reified-environment Object
    ( sr r ) )
```

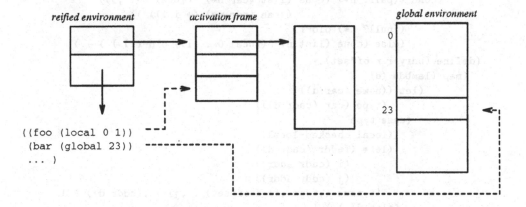

Figure 8.2 Reified environment

Without going into the details right away, we will compile an **export** form like this:

```
(define (meaning-export n* r tail?)
  (unless (every? symbol? n*)
          (static-wrong "Incorrect variables" n*) )
  (append (CONSTANT (extract-addresses n* r)) (CREATE-1ST-CLASS-ENV)) )
(define (CREATE-1ST-CLASS-ENV) (list 254))

(define-instruction (CREATE-1ST-CLASS-ENV) 254
  (create-first-class-environment *val* *env*) )

(define (create-first-class-environment r sr)
  (set! *val* (make-reified-environment sr r)) )
```

The list of name-address pairs will be represented by a quotation; the new
instruction CREATE-1ST-CLASS-ENV will take that quotation in the register *val*
to build the object that we want.

To simplify the evaluation, we will change the representation of static environments for compilation (the values of variables r). In place of the representation as a
rib cage, we'll adopt a more explicit representation as an association list of names-
addresses like the one in Figure 8.2. There is little to change, but by simplifying
compute-kind, we complicate r-extend*: every time we extend the environment,
it must bury the deep variables a little deeper.

```
(define (compute-kind r n)
  (or (let ((var (assq n r)))
        (and (pair? var) (cadr var)) )
      (global-variable? g.current n)
      (global-variable? g.init n)
      (adjoin-global-variable! n) ) )
(define r.init '())
(define (r-extend* r n*)
  (let ((old-r (bury-r r 1)))
    (let scan ((n* n*)(i 0))
      (cond ((pair? n*) (cons (list (car n*) '(local 0 . ,i))
                              (scan (cdr n*) (+ i 1)) ))
            ((null? n*) old-r)
            (else (cons (list n* '(local 0 . ,i)) old-r)) ) ) ) )
(define (bury-r r offset)
  (map (lambda (d)
         (let ((name (car d))
               (type (car (cadr d))) )
           (case type
             ((local checked-local)
              (let* ((addr (cadr d))
                     (i (cadr addr))
                     (j (cddr addr)) )
                '(,name (,type ,(+ i offset) . ,j) . ,(cddr d)) ) )
             (else d) ) ) )
       r ) )
```

Rather than reify an environment with only those variables that are mentioned,
we will make (export) equivalent to the form (export *variables* ...) where we
will already have specified all the variables of the ambient abstractions. With the

form (`export`), which is often called (`the-environment`), `eval/b` can be simulated entirely by `eval/ce` since:

$$(\texttt{eval/ce ' }\pi) \quad \equiv \quad (\texttt{eval/b ' }\pi \texttt{ (export))}$$

To achieve that improvement, all we have to do is capture every available environment (which now has the right structure) and write this:

```
(define (extract-addresses n* r)
  (if (null? n*) r
      (let scan ((n* n*))
        (if (pair? n*)
            (cons (list (car n*) (compute-kind r (car n*)))
                  (scan (cdr n*)) )
            '() ) ) ) )
```

8.7.2 The Function `eval/b`

There are still traces of `eval/ce` inside `eval/b`. Those two are similar as far as how they get evaluation parameters and with respect to the return protocol for evaluation. Indeed, it's useful to compare what follows with what went before. The function `eval/b` verifies the nature of its arguments, then delegates the function `compile-on-the-fly` (which you've already seen) to take care of first compiling the expression in the environment that's provided, then installing the code somewhere in memory, and executing it. The current environment doesn't need to be saved since that save has already been taken care of by the calling protocol for functions.

```
(definitial eval/b
  (let* ((arity 2)
         (arity+1 (+ arity 1)) )
    (make-primitive
     (lambda ()
       (if (= arity+1 (activation-frame-argument-length *val*))
           (let ((exp (activation-frame-argument *val* 0))
                 (env (activation-frame-argument *val* 1)) )
             (if (program? exp)
                 (if (reified-environment? env)
                     (compile-and-evaluate exp env)
                     (signal-exception
                      #t (list "Not an environment" env) ) )
                 (signal-exception #t (list "Illegal program" exp)) ) )
           (signal-exception
            #t (list "Incorrect arity" 'eval/b) ) ) ) ) ) )
(define (compile-and-evaluate v env)
  (let ((r (reified-environment-r env))
        (sr (reified-environment-sr env)) )
    (set! *env* sr)
    (set! *pc* (compile-on-the-fly v r)) ) )
```

8.7.3   Enriching Environments

Since environments are extended so often, it makes sense to get this operation for
ourselves, too. We will thus furnish a function, **enrich**, which takes an environment
and the names of variables to add to it. The return value will be a *new* enriched
environment. In fact, **enrich** is a functional modifier that does not disturb its
arguments. Let's look at an example of how it is used. We'll simulate **letrec** by
explicitly enriching the environment. A global binding[7] will be captured; two local
variables, **odd?** and **even?** will enrich it; two mutually recursive definitions will be
evaluated there; a computation will be carried out eventually.

```
((lambda (e)
   (set! e (enrich (export *) 'even? 'odd?))
   (eval/b '(set! even? (lambda (n) (if (= n 0) #t (odd? (- n 1))))) e)
   (eval/b '(set! odd? (lambda (n) (if (= n 0) #f (even? (- n 1))))) e)
   (eval/b '(even? 4) e) )
 'ee )                                  → #t
```

Figure 8.3 shows the results of this construction in detail. A new activation
record is allocated to contain the new variables. The reified environment associates
these new names with the appropriate addresses. The only difficulty is that these
new variables have no values, even though the variables exist. Here we find ourselves
back in the discussion about **letrec** or about non-initialized variables. [see p. 60]

We'll thus introduce a new type of local address, **checked-local**, which is
almost analogous to **checked-global**. Our definition of **enrich** brings us the possibility of non-initialized local variables—a situation that was not possible with
lambda. One fix would be to force environments to be enriched by variables accompanied by their values.

Programming **enrich** is simple now, if not short:

```
(definitial enrich
  (let* ((arity 1)
         (arity+1 (+ arity 1)) )
    (make-primitive
     (lambda ()
       (if (>= (activation-frame-argument-length *val*) arity+1)
           (let ((env (activation-frame-argument *val* 0)))
             (listify! *val* 1)
             (if (reified-environment? env)
                 (let* ((names (activation-frame-argument *val* 1))
                        (len (- (activation-frame-argument-length *val*)
                                2 ))
                        (r (reified-environment-r env))
                        (sr (reified-environment-sr env))
                        (frame (allocate-activation-frame
                                (length names) )) )
                   (set-activation-frame-next! frame sr)
                   (do ((i (- len 1) (- i 1)))
                       ((< i 0))
```

---

7. Ahem, there is a design error here: there is no means to create an empty environment with
export, so we capture just any old thing—in this case, multiplication—to create a little environment, as in [QD96].

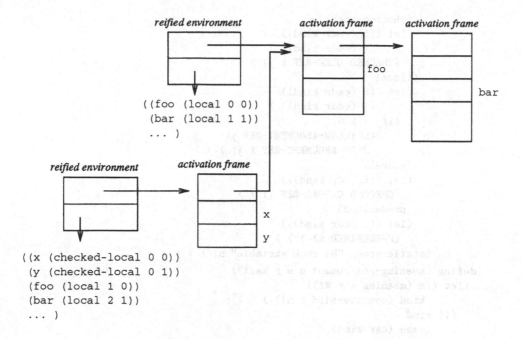

Figure 8.3 Enriched environment (**enrich** *env* **'x 'y**)

```
                    (set-activation-frame-argument! frame i
                                            undefined-value ) )
              (unless (every? symbol? names)
                (signal-exception
                  #f (list "Incorrect variable names" names ) ) )
              (set! *val* (make-reified-environment
                            frame
                            (checked-r-extend* r names) ))
              (set! *pc* (stack-pop)) )
            (signal-exception
                #t (list "Not an environment" env) ) ) )
          (signal-exception
              #t (list "Incorrect arity" 'enrich) ) ) ) ) ) )
(define (checked-r-extend* r n*)
  (let ((old-r (bury-r r 1)))
    (let scan ((n* n*)(i 0))
      (cond ((pair? n*) (cons (list (car n*) '(checked-local 0 . ,i))
                              (scan (cdr n*) (+ i 1)) ))
            ((null? n*) old-r) ) ) ) )
```

However, we must upate the two generators, **meaning-reference** and **meaning-assignment**, to take into account this new type of address (**checked-local**).

```
(define (meaning-reference n r tail?)
  (let ((kind (compute-kind r n)))
    (if kind
        (case (car kind)
```

```
      ((checked-local)
       (let ((i (cadr kind))
             (j (cddr kind)) )
         (CHECKED-DEEP-REF i j) ) )
      ((local)
       (let ((i (cadr kind))
             (j (cddr kind)) )
         (if (= i 0)
             (SHALLOW-ARGUMENT-REF j)
             (DEEP-ARGUMENT-REF i j) ) ) )
      ((global)
       (let ((i (cdr kind)))
         (CHECKED-GLOBAL-REF i) ) )
      ((predefined)
       (let ((i (cdr kind)))
         (PREDEFINED i) ) ) )
    (static-wrong "No such variable" n) ) ) )
(define (meaning-assignment n e r tail?)
  (let ((m (meaning e r #f))
        (kind (compute-kind r n)) )
    (if kind
        (case (car kind)
          ((local checked-local)
           (let ((i (cadr kind))
                 (j (cddr kind)) )
             (if (= i 0)
                 (SHALLOW-ARGUMENT-SET! j m)
                 (DEEP-ARGUMENT-SET! i j m) ) ) )
          ((global)
           (let ((i (cdr kind)))
             (GLOBAL-SET! i m) ) )
          ((predefined)
           (static-wrong "Immutable predefined variable" n) ) )
        (static-wrong "No such variable" n) ) ) )
```

We must not forget to add the instruction CHECKED-DEEP-REF to our byte-code machine, like this:

```
(define-instruction (CHECKED-DEEP-REF i j) 253
  (set! *val* (deep-fetch *env* i j))
  (when (eq? *val* undefined-value)
    (signal-exception #t (list "Uninitialized local variable")) ) )
```

8.7.4 Reifying a Closed Environment

Some interpreters make primitives available to extract an environment from a closure that contains it. Next to the function procedure->environment, these interpreters often add the function procedure->definition, which extracts the definition from a closure. These two functions are simple to implement in an interpreter, but in a compiler, they become more complicated and consume more memory. In effect, we have to do two things at once: one, store definitions (which adds to quotations) and two, reify closed environments (which necessitates saving their structure and adding new quotations). Moreover, the function `procedure->environment` is very indiscrete since we might modify a closed environment when we reify it—a change that prohibits any optimization of local variables because under these conditions even local things can be reached. In that sense, `procedure->environment` is much more costly than `export` because it strips the evaluator without putting any limitations on what can be done with it, whereas `export` restricts what can be (un)done to only those variables that are mentioned.

The function `procedure->definition` is useful for introspection. With it, we can provide a debugger that can dissect functions to apply. Here is an example of how to use those two functions. The function `trace-procedure1` takes a unary function, examines it, and rebuilds a new unary function, comparable to the first one but printing its argument on input and its result on output.

```
(define (trace-procedure1 f)
  (let* ((env (procedure->environment f))
         (definition (procedure->definition f))
         (variable (car (cadr definition)))
         (body (cddr definition)) )
    (lambda (value)
      (display (list 'entering f 'with value))
      (eval/b '(begin (set! ,variable ',value)
                      (let ((result (begin . ,body)))
                        (display (list 'result 'is result))
                        result ) )
              (enrich env variable) ) ) ) )
```

In fact, that program cheats a little. A unary function like `car` will upset `trace-procedure1`. The synthesized program for `eval/b` is not even a legal program because it quotes the value of `value`, which is not always a value that can be legitimately quoted. However, the function `trace-procedure1` produces an important effect for debugging. That effect results from combining introspection functions for closures, first class environments, and explicit evaluation.

If we suggest a way of implementing these functions, you can judge their cost for yourself. The function `procedure->definition` is the simpler: all it has to do is associate any closure with the expression that defines that closure, that is, a quotation. The problem: where to put that quotation since there may be many closures associated with the same definition. The salient characteristic of a closure is the address of its code. All the closures of a given abstraction share that same address, so we'll associate that address with the appropriate quotation. To do so, we'll use a technique well known to programmers in asssembly language: we'll insert data in the instructions. Since our machine forbids that, we'll actually insert quotations as in Figure 8.4.

Programming it is trivial. Once again we must change the code generators since now we must provide the definition and the static compilation environment to them because the functions `procedure->environment` and `procedure->definition` need that information. The version for an n-ary function is easy[8] to deduce:

---

8. Using `EXPLICIT-CONSTANT` means we do not get a (PREDEFINEDO) in place of a (CONSTANT '()).

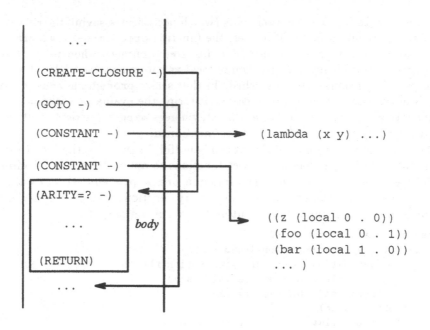

Figure 8.4 Abstraction that can be dissected

```
(define (meaning-fix-abstraction n* e+ r tail?)
  (let* ((arity (length n*))
         (r2 (r-extend* r n*))
         (m+ (meaning-sequence e+ r2 #t)) )
    (REFLECTIVE-FIX-CLOSURE m+ arity '(lambda ,n* . ,e+) r) ) )
(define (REFLECTIVE-FIX-CLOSURE m+ arity definition r)
  (let* ((the-function (append (ARITY=? (+ arity 1)) (EXTEND-ENV)
                               m+   (RETURN) ))
         (the-env (append (EXPLICIT-CONSTANT definition)
                          (EXPLICIT-CONSTANT r) ))
         (the-goto (GOTO (+ (length the-env) (length the-function)))) )
    (append (CREATE-CLOSURE (+ (length the-goto) (length the-env)))
            the-goto the-env the-function ) ) )
```

The function **procedure->definition** finds the definition of a closure by the quotation located two instructions before the code of its body.

```
(definitial procedure->definition
  (let* ((arity 1)
         (arity+1 (+ arity 1)) )
    (make-primitive
     (lambda ()
       (if (>= (activation-frame-argument-length *val*) arity+1)
           (let ((proc (activation-frame-argument *val* 0)))
             (if (closure? proc)
                 (let ((pc (closure-code proc)))
                   (set! *val* (vector-ref
```

```
                              *constants*
                      (vector-ref *code* (- pc 3)) ))
              (set! *pc* (stack-pop)) )
          (signal-exception #f (list "Not a procedure" proc)) ) )
      (signal-exception
        #t (list "Incorrect arity" 'enrich) ) ) ) ) ) )
```

The function `procedure->environment` extracts the closed environment from the closure and reifies it by adding the name-address mapping to it, making it intelligible. This mapping is found one instruction before the code for its body.

```
(definitial procedure->environment
  (let* ((arity 1)
         (arity+1 (+ arity 1)) )
    (make-primitive
      (lambda ()
        (if (>= (activation-frame-argument-length *val*) arity+1)
            (let ((proc (activation-frame-argument *val* 0)))
              (if (closure? proc)
                  (let* ((pc (closure-code proc))
                         (r (vector-ref
                              *constants*
                              (vector-ref *code* (- pc 1)) )) )
                    (set! *val* (make-reified-environment
                                  (closure-closed-environment proc)
                                  r ))
                    (set! *pc* (stack-pop)) )
                  (signal-exception #f (list "Not a procedure" proc)) ) )
            (signal-exception
              #t (list "Incorrect arity" 'enrich) ) ) ) ) ) )
```

In short, adding the functions `procedure->definition` and `procedure->environment` makes it possible for programs to understand their own code. They also make it possible to write introspective debugging tools. However, they both have a non-negligible cost because of the amount of information to save. Above all, they are both totally indiscrete since if all things can be reified, then nothing can be definitively hidden. You can no longer sell code that you want to keep secret, nor can you hide the implementation of certain types of data, nor even hope that certain local optimizations can take place since nothing can any longer be guaranteed constant.

Nevertheless, we can offset some of these faults by creating a new special form, say, `reflective-lambda`, with the following syntax:

```
(reflective-lambda (variables) (exportations)
  body )
```

Like the abstractions that they generalize, their variables are specified in the first parameter and their body in the last ones. Between those two, the exportation clause sets the only free variables in the body which will be available for inspection from the outside in the environment that this abstraction encloses. Accordingly, a normal abstraction (`lambda` (*variables*) *body*) is none other than (`reflective-lambda` (*variables*) () *body*); that is, it doesn't export anything.

By making only a few bindings visible, we can conceal others and thus protect ourselves from possible indiscretions.

There is yet another problem with the inquisitive function `procedure->environment`. Exactly which environment does the abstraction in the following example enclose anyway?

```
(let ((x 1)(y 2))
   (lambda (z) x) )
```

The enclosed environment certainly contains **x**, which is free in the body of the abstraction. Does it capture **y**, which is present in the surrounding lexical environment? The way of programming that we looked at earlier also captures **y** because we can assume that the contract from `procedure->environment` lets us evaluate any expression (even one containing **x** and **y**) as if it were found in the lexical environment where the closure was created. It's not so much the closed environment that `procedure->environment` returns as the entire lexical environment from the creation of the closure.

8.7.5   Special Form `import`

Quite often the form on which to call the evaluator has a static structure. That was the case, for example, in the procedure `trace-procedure1`. Rather than recompile on the fly, we might imagine a kind of precompilation that makes it possible to branch on an environment which would not be available until execution. The new special form **import** meets that contract. It looks like this:

```
(import (variables) environment forms )
```

The special form **import** evaluates the *forms* that make up its body in a rather special lexical environment. The names of free variables of the body appearing in the list[9] *variables* are the ones to take in the *environment*; the others are to take in the lexical environment of the call to **import**. The list of variables is static, not computed; *environment* is evaluated first, then the *forms*.

Here is an example, inspired by MEROONET where we had the problem of representing generic functions which are simultaneously objects and functions. If we allow access to enclosed variables, then a closure can be handled like an object where the fields are its free variables. This idea is the basis[10] for identifying closures with objects. In the implementation of MEROONET, to add a method to a generic function, we write this method in the right place in the vector of methods. Assuming that a generic function encloses this vector under the name **methods**, we can write it directly like this:

```
(define (add-method! generic class method)
   (import (methods) (procedure->environment generic)
      (vector-set! methods (Class-number class) method) ) )
```

In that example, you can see the usefulness of the special form **import** with respect to the function **eval/b**. The references to the variables **class** and **method** are static while only the variable **methods** still floats; it can be resolved only when the second parameter of **import** is known. Thus we've gained compilation on the

---

9. No variables could mean that all of them are captured as in [QD96].
10. Other facilities, like specializing the class of functions, are still missing.

fly like `eval/b` executed, and we see that we no longer synthesize programs to
compile: `import` is a kind of `eval` with its fat removed; it's more static since we
know statically the only references that still have to be resolved. In that sense,
`import` belongs to the kind of quasi-static binding proposed in [LF93] or in [NQ89].
Its very name suggests its close relation to its "cousin" `export`: one produces
the environments that the other branches to. We're getting nearer here to the
rudiments of first class modules.

How should we implement `import` as a special form? First, we'll add a line to
the syntactic analyzer, `meaning`, to recognize this new special form.

```
... ((import) (meaning-import (cadr e) (caddr e) (cdddr e) r tail?)) ...
```

The associated byte-code generator stores the list of floating variables on top
of the stack, evaluates the environment which will end up in the register `*val*`,
executes the new instruction `CREATE-PSEUDO-ENV`, and procedes to the evaluation
of the body of the `import` form, whether in tail position or not.

```
(define (meaning-import n* e e+ r tail?)
  (let* ((m (meaning e r #f))
         (r2 (shadow-extend* r n*))
         (m+ (meaning-sequence e+ r2 #f)) )
    (append (CONSTANT n*) (PUSH-VALUE) m (CREATE-PSEUDO-ENV)
            (if tail? m+ (append m+ (UNLINK-ENV))) ) ) )
```

The body of the special form `import` is evaluated by constructing of a pseudo-
activation record (an instance of the class `pseudo-activation-frame`); its size
is the number of floating variables mentioned in the form. It behaves like an
environment in the sense that we can connect them just like activation records,
but in fact it contains real addresses where to look for the floating variables as well
as the environment from which to extract them. During the creation of this pseudo-
activation-frame, we use `compute-kind` to compute where the floating variables are,
and we put its address (not its value) into the pseudo-frame.

```
(define-instruction (CREATE-PSEUDO-ENV) 252
  (create-pseudo-environment (stack-pop) *val* *env*) )

(define-class pseudo-activation-frame environment
  ( sr (* address) ) )

(define (create-pseudo-environment n* env sr)
  (unless (reified-environment? env)
    (signal-exception #f (list "not an environment" env)) )
  (let* ((len (length n*))
         (frame (allocate-pseudo-activation-frame len)) )
    (let setup ((n* n*)(i 0))
      (when (pair? n*)
        (set-pseudo-activation-frame-address!
         frame i (compute-kind (reified-environment-r env) (car n*)) )
        (setup (cdr n*) (+ i 1)) ) )
    (set-pseudo-activation-frame-sr! frame (reified-environment-sr env))
    (set-pseudo-activation-frame-next! frame sr)
    (set! *env* frame) ) )
```

The body of the special form `import` has to be specially compiled with respect
to floating variables. Those variables are scattered through the compilation envi-

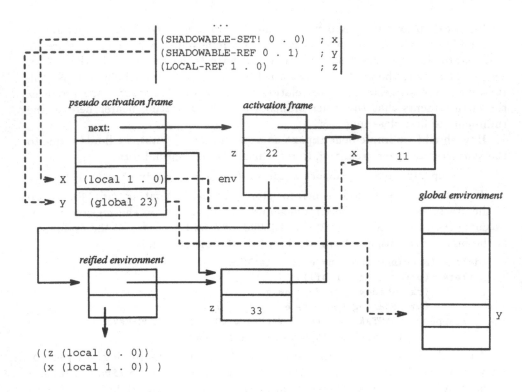

Figure 8.5 Environments in `import`

ronment **r** by the special extension function, **shadow-extend***. As the old saying goes, there's no computing problem that a well placed indirection can't solve: the address of the floating variables will be found by means of one indirection. We have to search for the value of a floating variable, we will find its address in the pseudo-activation record, and we'll use that address to extract the value from the environment provided explicitly for that. You can see those ideas in Figure 8.5 for the following program:

```
(let ((x 11))
  (let ((z 22)
        (env (let ((z 33)) (export))) )
    (import (x y) env
      (list (set! x y) z) ) ) ) )
```

Floating variables will be compiled in a special way, so they are specially marked by **shadow-extend*** in the compilation environment.

```
(define (shadow-extend* r n*)
  (let enum ((n* n*)(j 0))
    (if (pair? n*)
        (cons (list (car n*) '(shadowable 0 . ,j))
              (enum (cdr n*) (+ j 1)) )
        (bury-r r 1) ) ) )
```

We'll modify **meaning-reference** as well as **meaning-assignment** to accept these new types of variables, and we'll invent two new instructions, SHADOW-REF and SHADOW-SET!, to manage access to them.

```
(define (meaning-reference n r tail?)
  (let ((kind (compute-kind r n)))
    (if kind
        (case (car kind)
          ((checked-local)
           (let ((i (cadr kind))
                 (j (cddr kind)) )
             (CHECKED-DEEP-REF i j) ) )
          ((local)
           (let ((i (cadr kind))
                 (j (cddr kind)) )
             (if (= i 0)
                 (SHALLOW-ARGUMENT-REF j)
                 (DEEP-ARGUMENT-REF i j) ) ) )
          ((shadowable)
           (let ((i (cadr kind))
                 (j (cddr kind)) )
             (SHADOWABLE-REF i j) ) )
          ((global)
           (let ((i (cdr kind)))
             (CHECKED-GLOBAL-REF i) ) )
          ((predefined)
           (let ((i (cdr kind)))
             (PREDEFINED i) ) ) )
        (static-wrong "No such variable" n) ) ) )

(define-instruction (SHADOW-REF i j) 231
  (shadowable-fetch *env* i j) )

(define (shadowable-fetch sr i j)
  (if (= i 0)
      (let ((kind (pseudo-activation-frame-address sr j))
            (sr (pseudo-activation-frame-sr sr)) )
        (variable-value-lookup kind sr) )
      (shadowable-fetch (environment-next sr) (- i 1) j) ) )

(define (variable-value-lookup kind sr)
  (if (pair? kind)
      (case (car kind)
        ((checked-local)
         (let ((i (cadr kind))
               (j (cddr kind)) )
           (set! *val* (deep-fetch sr i j))
           (when (eq? *val* undefined-value)
             (signal-exception
              #t (list "Uninitialized local variable") ) ) ) )
        ((local)
         (let ((i (cadr kind))
               (j (cddr kind)) )
```

```
        (set! *val* (if (= i 0)
                        (activation-frame-argument sr j)
                        (deep-fetch sr i j) )) ) )
   ((shadowable)
    (let ((i (cadr kind))
          (j (cddr kind)) )
      (shadowable-fetch sr i j) ) )
   ((global)
    (let ((i (cdr kind)))
      (set! *val* (global-fetch i))
      (when (eq? *val* undefined-value)
        (signal-exception #t
          (list "Uninitialized global variable") ) ) ) ) )
   ((predefined)
    (let ((i (cdr kind)))
      (set! *val* (predefined-fetch i)) ) ) )
  (signal-exception #f (list "No such variable")) ) )
```

The function `shadowable-fetch` will use a statically known address to search
for a dynamic address indicating where the variable is actually located. For that
reason, we have to be able to decode all types of addresses, namely, `local` and
`checked-local`, `global` and `predefined`, and even `shadowable`, as it can occur
also. The function `variable-value-lookup` does that decoding. In a way, the
form `import` corresponds to a kind of syntax transforming references to floating
variables into calls to `eval/b`. Let's look again at our earlier example: the form[11]
`(import (x y) env (list (set! x y) z))` is none other than this:

```
(list ((eval/b '(lambda (v) (set! x v)) env)
       (eval/b 'y env) )
      z )
```

Let's summarize all the types of bindings we've seen.

Lexical binding—the type implemented by `lambda`—allocates boxes to put values into them. The bound names make it possible to retrieve these boxes. Their
extent is indefinite; that is, they go away only when they are no longer needed.
The scope of these bindings is restricted to the body of the `lambda` form.

Dynamic binding—the type implemented by `dynamic-let`—associates a name
with a value[12] throughout the duration of a given computation. The scope is
unlimited during that computation. The association disappears afterward.

Quasi-static binding puts names on bindings that already exist. Moreover,
since these are names of bindings that must be used again, introducing this kind of
binding upsets α-conversion. Why? Because even in the absence of `procedure-en-`
`vironment`, reifying[13] an environment captures the names of bindings and prohibits
us from knowing all the places where they might be used.

---

11. To avoid generating a program that includes a quotation that might not be legal, here we've
generated a closure taking the value to assign.
12. As we implemented it, `dynamic-let` won't let you modify this association; there is no
`dynamic-set!`. It's easy to get around this limitation by binding mutable data to this name.
13. We could improve `reflective-lambda` as explained earlier so that in addition it specified the
kind of operations allowed on exported bindings by limiting them, for example, to read-only. Like
[LF93], we could also allow free variables to be renamed for exportation.

8.7.6 Simplified Access to Environments

The preceding sections have shown that most ways of evaluation can be programmed explicitly except those that involve access to the global environment. The preceding digressions have given us an appreciation for first class environments and also lead us to generalize the functions global-value and set-global-value! into their counterparts variable-value, set-variable-value!, and variable-defined?.

The function variable-value takes a first class environment and looks for the value of a variable; set-variable-value! modifies it; variable-defined? tests whether it is present. They use the same functions to decode an address as the function shadowable-fetch: all take care not to use compute-kind directly as it "accepts" variables passed to it and creates them on the fly. We've left out set-variable-value!, but you can guess its definition easily enough.

```
(definitial variable-value
   (let* ((arity 2)
          (arity+1 (+ arity 1)) )
     (make-primitive
      (lambda ()
        (if (= (activation-frame-argument-length *val*) arity+1)
            (let ((name (activation-frame-argument *val* 0))
                  (env (activation-frame-argument *val* 1)) )
              (if (reified-environment? env)
                  (if (symbol? name)
                      (let* ((r (reified-environment-r env))
                             (sr (reified-environment-sr env))
                             (kind
                              (or (let ((var (assq name r)))
                                    (and (pair? var) (cadr var)) )
                                  (global-variable? g.current name)
                                  (global-variable? g.init name) ) ) )
                        (variable-value-lookup kind sr)
                        (set! *pc* (stack-pop)) )
                      (signal-exception
                       #f (list "Not a variable name" name) ) )
                  (signal-exception
                   #t (list "Not an environment" env) ) ) )
            (signal-exception #t (list "Incorrect arity"
                                       'variable-value )) ) ) ) ) )
(definitial variable-defined?
   (let* ((arity 2)
          (arity+1 (+ arity 1)) )
     (make-primitive
      (lambda ()
        (if (= (activation-frame-argument-length *val*) arity+1)
            (let ((name (activation-frame-argument *val* 0))
                  (env (activation-frame-argument *val* 1)) )
              (if (reified-environment? env)
                  (if (symbol? name)
                      (let* ((r (reified-environment-r env))
```

```
                    (sr (reified-environment-sr env)) )
          (set! *val*
                 (if (or (let ((var (assq name r)))
                             (and (pair? var) (cadr var)) )
                         (global-variable? g.current name)
                         (global-variable? g.init name) )
                     #t #f ) )
                 (set! *pc* (stack-pop)) )
            (signal-exception
             #f (list "Not a variable name" name) ) )
          (signal-exception
           #t (list "Not an environment" env) ) ) )
       (signal-exception #t (list "Incorrect arity"
                                  'variable-defined? )) ) ) ) ) )
```

The function **variable-defined?** is a function for inspecting first class environments. It determines whether or not a given variable occurs in a given environment. That question interests us since we can enrich such environments, but the question itself depends on the nature of the global environment: is it mutable or not? If the global environment is immutable, then **variable-defined?** is a function with a constant response: if a variable does not appear now in an immutable global environment, then it will never occur there. However, if the global environment can change, then it can be extended even while remaining equal to itself (as if we had an **enrich!** function) and thus **variable-defined?** might respond True at some point even after having responded False.

8.8 Reflective Interpreter

In the mid-eighties, there was a fashion for reflective interpreters, a fad that gave rise to a remarkable term: "reflective towers." Just imagine a marsh shrouded in mist and a rising tower with its summit lost in gray and cloudy skies—pure Rackham! In fact, the foundations of this mystical image are anchored in the experiments carried on around continuations, first class environments, and FEXPR of InterLisp (put to death by Kent Pitman in [Pit80]).

Well, who hasn't dreamed about inventing (or at least having available) a language where anything could be redefined, where our imagination could gallop unbridled, where we could play around in complete programming liberty without trammel nor hindrance? However, we pay for this dream with exasperatingly slow systems that are almost incompilable and plunge us into a world with few laws, hardly even any gravity.

At any rate, this section presents a small reflective interpreter in which few aspects are hidden or intangible. Many proposals for such an interpreter exist already, for example in [dRS84], [FW84], [Wan86], [DM88], [Baw88], [Que89], [IMY92], [JF92], and others. They are distinguished from each other by their particular aspects of reflection and by their implementations.

Reflective interpreters should support introspection, so they must offer the programmer a means of grabbing the computational context at any time. By "computational context," we mean the lexical environment and the continuation. To get the right continuation, we already have `call/cc`. To get the right lexical environment, we'll take the form (`export`), also known as (`the-environment`), to reify the current lexical environment. Reification is one of the imperatives of reflection, but there are many ways of reifying, and how we choose to do it will affect the operations that we can carry out later.

As [Chr95] once said, "Puisqu'une fois la borne franchie, il n'est plus de limite." That is, once we've crossed the boundary, there are no more limits, so we must also authorize programs to define new special forms. InterLisp experimented with a mechanism already present in Lisp 1.5 under the name FEXPR. When such an object is invoked, instead of passing arguments to it, we give it the text of its parameters as well as the current lexical environment. Then it can evaluate them whatever way it wants to, or even more generally, it can manipulate them at will. For that purpose, we'll introduce the new special form `flambda` with the following syntax:

(flambda (*variables...*) *forms ...*)

The first variable receives the lexical environment at invocation, while the following variables receive the text of the call parameters. With such a mechanism, we can trivially write quotation like this:

(set! quote (flambda (r quotation) quotation))

A reflective interpreter must also provide means to modify itself (a real thrill, no doubt), so we'll make sure that functions implementing the interpreter are accessible to interpreted programs. The form (`the-environment`) insures this effect since it gives us access to the variables of the implementation as if they belonged to interpreted programs.

So here's a reflective interpreter, one weighing in at only[14] 1362 bytes. Thus you can see that it is not costly in terms of memory to get such an interpreter for ourselves in a library. It is written in the language that the byte-code compiler compiles.

```
(apply
 (lambda (make-toplevel make-flambda flambda? flambda-apply)
   (set! make-toplevel
         (lambda (prompt-in prompt-out)
           (call/cc
            (lambda (exit)
              (monitor (lambda (c b) (exit b))
               ((lambda (it extend error global-env
                         toplevel eval evlis eprogn reference )
                  (set! extend
                        (lambda (env names values)
                          (if (pair? names)
                              (if (pair? values)
                                  ((lambda (newenv)
                                     (begin
                                       (set-variable-value!
                                        (car names) newenv (car values) )
```

---

14. Once it's compiled, that is, because its text is only about 120 lines, 6000 characters, and 583 pairs.

```
                        (extend newenv (cdr names)
                                (cdr values) ) ) )
                    (enrich env (car names)) )
                    (error "Too few arguments" names) )
              (if (symbol? names)
                  ((lambda (newenv)
                      (begin
                        (set-variable-value!
                          names newenv values )
                        newenv ) )
                    (enrich env names) )
                  (if (null? names)
                      (if (null? values)
                          env
                          (error "Too much arguments"
                                 values ) )
                      env ) ) ) ) )
(set! error (lambda (msg hint)
              (exit (list msg hint)) ))
(set! toplevel
      (lambda (genv)
        (set! global-env genv)
        (display prompt-in)
        ((lambda (result)
           (set! it result)
           (display prompt-out)
           (display result)
           (newline) )
         ((lambda (e)
            (if (eof-object? e)
                (exit e)
                (eval e global-env) ) )
          (read) ) )
        (toplevel global-env) ) )
(set! eval
      (lambda (e r)
        (if (pair? e)
            ((lambda (f)
               (if (flambda? f)
                   (flambda-apply f r (cdr e))
                   (apply f (evlis (cdr e) r)) ) )
             (eval (car e) r) )
            (if (symbol? e) (reference e r) e) ) ) )
(set! evlis
      (lambda (e* r)
        (if (pair? e*)
            ((lambda (v)
               (cons v (evlis (cdr e*) r)) )
             (eval (car e*) r) )
            '() ) ) )
(set! eprogn
```

```
                        (lambda (e+ r)
                          (if (pair? (cdr e+))
                              (begin (eval (car e+) r)
                                     (eprogn (cdr e+) r) )
                              (eval (car e+) r) ) ) )
                 (set! reference
                       (lambda (name r)
                         (if (variable-defined? name r)
                             (variable-value name r)
                             (if (variable-defined? name global-env)
                                 (variable-value name global-env)
                                 (error "No such variable" name) ) ) ) )
          ((lambda (quote if set! lambda flambda monitor)
             (toplevel (the-environment)) )
           (make-flambda
            (lambda (r quotation) quotation) )
           (make-flambda
            (lambda (r condition then else)
              (eval (if (eval condition r) then else) r) ) )
           (make-flambda
            (lambda (r name form)
              ((lambda (v)
                 (if (variable-defined? name r)
                     (set-variable-value! name r v)
                     (if (variable-defined? name global-env)
                         (set-variable-value! name global-env v)
                         (error "No such variable" name) ) ))
               (eval form r) ) ) )
           (make-flambda
            (lambda (r variables . body)
              (lambda values
                (eprogn body (extend r variables values)) ) ) )
           (make-flambda
            (lambda (r variables . body)
              (make-flambda
               (lambda (rr . parameters)
                 (eprogn body
                         (extend r variables
                                 (cons rr parameters) ) ) ) ) ) )
           (make-flambda
            (lambda (r handler . body)
              (monitor (eval handler r)
                       (eprogn body r) ) ) ) )
           'it 'extend 'error 'global-env
           'toplevel 'eval 'evlis 'eprogn 'reference ) ) ) ) )
     (make-toplevel "?? " "== ") )
 'make-toplevel
 ((lambda (flambda-tag)
    (list (lambda (behavior) (cons flambda-tag behavior))
          (lambda (o) (if (pair? o) (= (car o) flambda-tag) #f))
          (lambda (f r parms) (apply (cdr f) r parms)) ) )
```

```
98127634 ) )
```

As Julia Kristeva would say,[15] that definition is saturated with subtlety at least with respect to signs. You'll probably have to use this interpreter before you'll be able to believe in it.

The initial form (`apply ...`) creates four local variables. The last three all work on reflective abstractions or `flambda` forms; specifically, `make-flambda` encodes them; `flambda?` recognizes them; `flambda-apply` applies them. These objects have a very special call protocol, and for that reason, we must get acquainted with them. The first variable of the four, `make-toplevel` is initialized in the body so that it can make these four variables available to programmers. It starts an interaction loop with customizable prompts. In the beginning, these prompts are `??` and `==`.

This interaction loop captures its call continuation—the one where it will return in case of error or in case of a call to the function `exit`.[16] That continuation will also be accessible from programs. The interaction loop itself is protected by a form, `monitor`. [see p. 256] The loop then introduces and initializes an entire group of variables that will also be available for interpreted programs to share. The variable `it` is bound to the last value computed by the interaction loop. The function `extend`, of course, extends an environment with a list of variables and values; it also checks arity. The function `error` prints an error message and then terminates with a call to `exit`.

The function `toplevel` implements interaction in the usual way. The functions that accompany `eval` (namely, `evlis`, `eprogn`, and `reference`) are standard, too, except for the fact that they are accessible to programs. The function `eval` is simplicity itself. Either the expression to compute is a variable or an implicit quotation, or it's a form, in which case we evaluate the term in the function position. If that term is a reflective function, then we invoke it by passing it the current environment and the call parameters; if it's a normal function, we simply invoke it normally.

This flexibility is the characteristic that makes the language defined by this interpreter non-compilable. Let's assume that we've defined the following normal function:

```
(set! stammer (lambda (f x) (f f x)))
```

Now we can write two programs:

```
(stammer (lambda (ff yy) yy) 33)     → 33
(stammer (flambda (ff yy) yy) 33)    → x
```

According to their definitions, one executes its body; the other reifies one part of its body to provide that to its argument `f`. Consequently, we must compile every functional application twice to satisfy normal and reflective abstractions. However, since every program represented by a list is also possibly a functional application, we must also doubly compile forms beginning with the usual special forms, like `quote`, `if`, and others because they, too, could be redefined to do something else.

---

15. Well, she said something like that one Sunday morning on radio France Musique, 19 September 1993, while I was writing this.
16. Finally we have a Lisp from which we can exit! You can check for yourself that there is no such convenience in the definitions of COMMON LISP, Scheme, or even Dylan.

In short, there are practically no more invariants for the compiler to exploit to produce efficient code—thus leaving an open field for the joys of interpretation.

We define a few reflective functions just before starting the interaction loop because it is simpler to do so there than to program them. In that way, we define `quote`, `if`, `set!`, `lambda`, `flambda`, and `monitor`. Any others that are missing can be added explicitly, like this:

```
(set! global-env
      (enrich global-env 'begin 'the-environment) )
(set! the-environment
      (flambda (r) r) )
(set! begin
      (flambda (r . forms)
        (eprogn forms r) ) )
```

The variable `global-env` is bound to the reified environment containing all preceding functions and variables, including itself, and that's the strength of this procedure. Not only is the global environment provided to programers. but also they can modify it retroactively through the interpreter. The interpreter and the program share the same `global-env`. Assignment by either means leads to the same effect, to the same thrills and dangers. Because of this two-way binding, we can better express the earlier example, or even the following one, where we define a new special form: `when`.

```
(set! global-env (enrich global-env 'when))
(set! when
      (flambda (r condition . body)
        (if (eval condition r) (eprogn body r) #f) ) )
```

First of all, we extend the global environment with a new global variable, one that has not yet been initialized, of course. Immediately afterwards, we initialize it with an appropriate reflective function. Interestingly enough, this extension of the global environment is visible to the interpreter: assigning `when` with a reflective abstraction actually adds a new special form to the interpreter.

At this point, you're probably asking, "Just where is that mystical tower poking through the fog that was alluded to some time ago?" Programs can create new levels of interpretation with the function `make-toplevel`. They can also evaluate their own definition and thus achieve a truly astounding slowdown that way, speed that makes this possibility purely theoretical in fact. Auto-interpretation is a little different from reflection. We need to follow two hard rules to make this interpreter auto-interpretive. First, we must avoid using special forms when they have been redefined in order to avoid instability. That's why the body of the abstraction which binds `set!` and the others is reduced to (`toplevel` (`the-environment`)). Second, instances of `flambda` must be recognized by the two levels of interpretation. That's why we have used the label `flambda-tag`: it's unique, though it might be falsified.

A final possibility is that we can reify whatever we have just been doing (including the continuation and the environment), think about whatever we have just been doing, imagine what we should have done instead, and do it. According to the way of programming that we've adopted for reification, there may be new and exciting possibilities for introspection, like scutinizing the environment or control blocks in the continuation, as in [Que93a]. In fact, these kinds of introspection are the reason this type of interpreter is known as "reflective."

The Form `define`

Interestingly enough, the preceding reflective interpreter supports an operational definition of a highly complex form, `define` in Scheme. As we've already explained, `define` is a special, special form: it behaves like a declaration doubled by an assignment. It's like assignment because after execution, the variable will have a well defined value. It's like a declaration because it introduces a new variable as soon as the text mentioning `define` is prepared for execution. This declaration changes the global environment. All these aspects are highlighted in the following definition of the special form, `define`, but we've excluded syntactic aspects that `define` also has; those syntactic aspects let `define` accept variations like (`define` (`foo x`) (`define` (`bar`) ...) ...) and participate in various situations known as internal `defines`. (You can measure how complex a special form `define` is.)

```
(set! global-env (enrich global-env 'define))
(set! define (flambda (r name form)
                  (if (variable-defined? name r)
                      (set-variable-value! name r (eval form r))
                      ((lambda (rr)
                         (set! global-env rr)
                         (set-variable-value! name rr (eval form rr)) )
                       (enrich r name) ) ) ))
```

First of all, `define` tests whether the variable to define already belongs to the global environment. In that case, the definition is merely an assignment, according to R4RS §5.2.1. In the opposite case, a new binding is created inside the global environment, the global environment is updated to include this new binding, and the value to assign is computed in this new environment, in order to support recursions.

8.9   Conclusions

This chapter presented various aspects of explicit evaluation, aspects that appear as special forms or as functions. According to the qualities that we want to keep in a language, we might prefer forms stripped of all the "fat" of evaluation like first class environments or like quasi-static scope. You can clearly see here that the art of designing languages is quite subtle and offers an immense range of solutions.

This chapter also clearly shows how fortunate a choice Lisp made (or, more precisely, the choice its inspired designer, John McCarthy, made) by reducing how much coding and decoding would be needed and by mixing the usual levels of language and metalanguage to increase the field for experiment so greatly.

8.10   Exercises

Exercise 8.1 : Why doesn't the function **variables-list?** test whether the list of variables is non-cyclic?

Exercise 8.2 : The special form **eval/ce** compiles on the fly the expression given to it. That's too bad if you want to evaluate the same expression several times in succession. Think up a way to correct this problem.

Exercise 8.3 : Improve the definition of **eval/at** in terms of **eval/ce** in order to get rid of the inadvertantly captured variable. Hint: use **gensym** if you want.

Exercise 8.4 : Can a user define **variable-defined?** him- or herself? Why or why not?

Exercise 8.5 : Make the reflective interpreter run in pure Scheme.

Recommended Reading

The article [dR87] remarkably reveals just how reflective Lisp is. [Mul92] offers algebraic semantics for the reflective aspects of Lisp. For reflection in general, you should look at recent work by [JF92] and [IMY92].

9
Macros: Their Use & Abuse

*I*NORED, abused, unjustly criticized, insufficiently justified (theoretically), macros are no less than one of the fundamental bases of Lisp and have contributed significantly to the longevity of the language itself. While functions abstract computations and objects abstract data, macros abstract the structure of programs. This chapter presents macros and explores the problems they pose. By far one of the least studied topics in Lisp, there is enormous variation in macros in the implementation of Lisp or Scheme. Though this chapter contains few programs, it tries to sweep through the domain where these little known beings—macros—have evolved.

Invented by Timothy P. Hart [SG93] in 1963 shortly after the publication of the Lisp 1.5 reference manual, macros turned out to be one of the essential ingredients of Lisp. Macros authorize programmers to imagine and implement the language appropriate to their own problem. Like mathematics, where we continually invent new abbreviations appropriate for expressing new concepts, dialects of Lisp extend the language by means of new syntactic constructions. Don't get me wrong: I'm not talking about augmenting the language by means of a library of functions covering a particular domain. A Lisp with a library of graphic functions for drawing is still Lisp and no more than Lisp. The kind of extensions I'm talking about introduce new syntactic forms that actually increase the programmer's power.

Extending a language means introducing new notation that announces that we can write X when we want to signify Y. Then every time programmers write X, they could have written Y directly, if they were less lazy. However, they are intelligently lazy and thus use a simple form to eliminate senseless details so that those details no longer encumber their thoughts. Many mathematical concepts become usable only after someone invents a suitable notation to express them. To insure greater flexibility, the rule about abbreviations usually exploits parameters. In fact, when we write $X(t_1, \ldots, t_n)$, we intend $Y(t_1, \ldots, t_n)$. Macros are not just a hack, but a highly useful abstraction technique, working on programs by means of their representation.

Most imperative languages have only a fixed number of special forms. You can usually find a `while` loop in one, and perhaps an `until` loop, but if you need a new kind of loop, for example, it's generally not possible to add one. In Lisp, in contrast, all you have to do is introduce the new notation. Here's an example of what we mean: every time we write (repeat :while *p* :unless *q* :do *body*...), in fact we mean this:

```
(let loop ()
  (if p (begin (if (not q) (begin body...))
              (loop) )) )
```

This example is deliberately extravagant: it takes extra keywords (recognizable by the colon prefixing each one) although customary use in Scheme is rather to suppress such syntactic noise. [see Ex. 9.1] Also, the example introduces a local variable, loop, that might hide a variable of the same name that *p* or *q* or *body* might want to refer to. Real loop-lovers should also look at the Mount Everest of loops (the macro loop for which the popular implementation takes tens of pages) defined in [Ste90, Chapter 26].

Unfortunately, like many other concepts, especially the most advanced or the most subtle, macros can run amuck. The goal of this chapter is to unravel their problems and show off their beauties. To do so, we'll logically reconstruct macros so that we can survey their problems and the roots of their variations.

9.1   Preparation for Macros

The evaluators that evolved in the immediately preceding chapters distinguish two phases as they handle programs: *preparation* (the term used in IS-Lisp) followed by *execution*. Evaluation, as in fast interpretation, [see p. 183], can thus be seen as (run (prepare *expression*)). That way of looking at things was quite apparent not only in the fast interpreter but also in the byte-code compiler where prepared expressions were successively a tree of thunks [see p. 223] or a byte vector. At worst, in all the early interpreters we developed, we could assimilate preparation with the identity.

Preparation itself can be divided into many phases. For example, realizing that the expressions to evaluate are initially character strings, many Lisps offer the idea of macro-characters that influence the syntactic analysis of a string during its transformation into an S-expression. The outstanding example of a macro-character is the quote: when it is read, it reads the expression that follows and inserts that expression into a form prefixed by the symbol quote. We could reproduce that process as (list (quote quote) (read)).

So that the Lisp reader can be influenced, the read function to a certain degree makes it possible to adapt the language to special needs. That's the case for Bigloo [SW94]. When it compiles a program written in Caml Light, it chooses the appropriate read function; the only constraint is that a compilable S-expression will be returned. In fact, this read function is the front-end of the Caml Light compiler [LW93].

We won't dwell any longer, though, on the subject of macro-characters as they are highly dependent on the algorithm for reading S-expressions.

The preparation phase is often assimilated to a compilation phase of varying complexity. The important point is to maintain a strict separation between this phase and the following one (that is, execution) to clarify their relation, to minimize their common interface, and above all to insure that experiments can be repeated.

This imperative gives rise to two different ways of thinking about preparation: in terms of *multiple worlds* or in terms of a *unique world*.

9.1.1 Multiple Worlds

With multiple worlds, an expression is prepared by producing a result often stored in a file (conventionally, a `.o` or `.fasl` file). Such a file is executed by a distinct process which sometimes has a facility for gathering expressions prepared separately (that is, *linking*). Most conventional languages work in this mode, based on the idea of independent or separate compilation. In this way, it's possible to factor preparation and to manage name spaces better by means of import and export directives. We speak of this way of doing things as "multiple worlds" because the expression that is being prepared is the only means of communication between the expression-preparer and the ultimate evaluator. Those two processes live in distinct worlds. No effects in the first world is perceptible in the second.

$$
\begin{array}{l}
expression_0 \xrightarrow{\ \texttt{prepare}\ } prepared\text{-}expression_0 \\
expression_1 \xrightarrow{\ \texttt{prepare}\ } prepared\text{-}expression_1 \\
\quad \cdots \xrightarrow{\ \texttt{prepare}\ } \cdots \\
expression_n \xrightarrow{\ \texttt{prepare}\ } prepared\text{-}expression_n
\end{array} \left.\vphantom{\begin{array}{l} a \\ b \\ c \\ d \end{array}}\right\} \texttt{run}
$$

9.1.2 Unique World

In contrast to multiple worlds, the hypothesis of a unique world stipulates that the center of the universe is the toplevel loop and that thus all computations started from there cohabit in the same memory where we can neither limit nor control communication by altering globally visible resources (such as global variables, property lists, etc.). In the unique world, the interaction loop ties together the reading of an expression, its preparation, and then its evaluation. This interaction loop plays the role of a command interpreter (a veritable *shell*) but nevertheless makes it possible to prepare expressions without evaluating them immediately after. In many systems, that's exactly what the function `compile-file` does: it takes the name of a file containing a sequence of expressions, prepares them, and produces a file of prepared expressions. The evaluation of a prepared file can also occur from the interaction loop by means of the function `load` or one of its derivatives. You see then that you could factor the preparation of an expression and thus interlace preparation and evaluation.

The idea of a unique world is not so bad. In fact, it's only a reflection of the one-world mentality of an operating system like UN⋆X, where the user counts on a certain internal state depending simultaneously on the file system, local variables, global variables, aliases, and so forth that his or her favorite command interpreter (`sh`, `tcsh`, etc.) provides. But again, the point is to insure, as simply as possible, that experiments can be repeated.

When we build software, it's a good idea to have a reliable method for getting an executable from it. We want any two reconstructions starting from the same source to end up in the same result. That's just a basic intellectual premise. Without too much difficulty, it is insured by the idea of multiple worlds because there we can easily control the information submitted as input. It's a bit harder with the unique world hypothesis because we have difficulty mastering its internal state[1] and its hidden communications. Instead of being re-initialized for every preparation, the preparer (that is, the compiler) stays the same and is modified little by little since it works in a memory image that is constantly being enriched and always less under our control.

In short, the preparation of a program has to be a process that we control completely.

9.2   Macro Expansion

We need a way of abbreviating, but one that belongs strictly to preparation. For that reason, we might split preparation into two parts: first, *macro expansion*, followed by preparation itself. On this new ground, there are two warring factions: *exogenous* macro expansion and *endogenous* macro expansion. We can prepare an expression by this succession: (**really-prepare** (**macroexpand** *expression*)). We're interested only in the *macro expander*, that is, the function that implements the process of macro expansion: **macroexpand**. Where does it come from?

9.2.1   Exogenous Mode

The exogenous school of macro expansion, as defined in [QP91b, DPS94b], stipulates that the function **macroexpand** is provided *independently* of the expression to prepare, for example, by preparation directives.[2] Thus the function **prepare** looks something like this:

```
(define (prepare expression directives)
  (let ((macroexpand (generate-macroexpand directives)))
    (really-prepare (macroexpand expression)) ) )
```

Several implementations exist. We'll illustrate them with the byte-code compiler we presented earlier, [**see p. 262**]. We'll assume that the main functionalities of this compilation chain are: **run** to run an application and **build-application** to construct an application. We'll also assume that **compile.so** is the executable corresponding to the entire compiler. In the examples that follow, the macro expansion directive simply mentions the name of the executable in charge of the macro expansion.

A macro expansion might occur as a cascade, like the top of Figure 9.1. In that case, a command like "**compile file.scm expand.so**" (where the file to compile is specified in the first position and the macro expander in the second position) corresponds in pseudo-Un*x to this:

```
run expand.so < file.scm | run compile.so > file.so
```

A macro expansion might also occur through the synthesis of a new compiler (here, **tmp.so**), like the bottom of Figure 9.1. Then the command "**compile file.scm expand.so**" is analogous to this:

---

1. Who knows, for example, all the environment variables that printenv reveals or all the .*rc files on which our comfort depends?
2. These directives may, for instance, be found in the first S-expression of a file.

```
( build-application compile.so expand.so -o tmp.so ;
  run tmp.so ) < file.scm > file.so
```

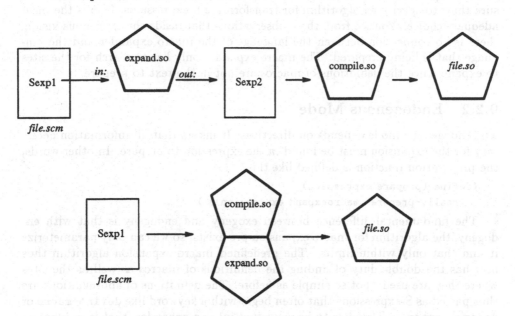

Figure 9.1 Two examples of exogenous mode (with the byte-code compiler); pentagons represent compiled modules.

Among the hidden problems, we still have to define a protocol for exchanging information between the preparer and the macro expander. The macro expander must receive the expression to expand; it might receive the expression as a value or as the name of a file to read; it must then return the result to its caller; at that point, it might return an S-expression or the name of a file in which the result has been written. Passing information by files is not absurd. In fact, it's the technique used by the C compiler (cc and cpp). As a technique, it prevents hidden communication; that is, every communication is evident. In contrast, passing information by S-expressions means that the preparer must know how to call the macro expander dynamically, either to evaluate or to load, by load, since they are both in the same memory space.

Rather than impose a monolithic macro expander, we might build it from smaller elements. We might thus want to compose it of various abbreviations. That comes down to extending the directive language so that we can specify all the abbreviations. Of course, doing that means that the macros must be composable, and that point in turn implies that we must define protocols to insure such things as the associativity and commutativity of macro definitions.

In consequence, the idea of exogeny associates an independently built macro expander with a program. If we organize things in this way, we can be sure that experiments can be repeated; we can also be sure that remains from macro expansions do not stay around in the prepared programs. Besides achieving the perfect separation we wanted between macro expansion and evaluation, this solution puts no limits on our imagination since any macro expander is legal as long as it leads to an S-expression. We can even use **cpp**, **m4**, or **perl** for the job! However, we're sure that to specify an algorithm for transforming S-expressions, Lisp is the most adequate choice. You see from these observations that inside the exogenous vision, there is no connection between the language of the macro expander and the language that is being prepared. The macro expander only has to search for the sites to expand since the definitions of macros are not in the text to prepare.

9.2.2 Endogenous Mode

The endogenous mode depends on directives. It insists that all information necessary for the expansion must be found *in* the expression to prepare. In other words, the preparation function is defined like this:

```
(define (prepare expression)
  (really-prepare (macroexpand expression)) )
```

The fundamental difference between exogeny and endogeny is that with endogeny, the algorithm for macro expansion pre-exists, so we can only parameterize it and that only within limits. The predefined macro expansion algorithm thus now has the double duty of finding the definitions of macros as well as the sites where they are used—not so simple as before. The definitions of abbreviations are thus passed as S-expressions that often begin with a keyword like **define-macro** or **define-syntax**.   That has to be converted into an expander, that is, a function whose role is to transform an abbreviation into the text that it represents. Thus the macro expander contains the equivalent of a function for converting a text into a program! There's the stroke of genius: rather than invent a special language for macros, we simply use the function **eval**. In other words, the definition language for macros is Lisp!

Of course, that stroke of genius is also the source of problems. Macros bring up again an old and subtle technique that was long ago assimilated as part of black magic: macrology. In fact, it's precisely this identification between the languages that fogs up our perception of what macros really are. For a long time, they were seen as real functions except that their calling protocol was a little strange because their arguments were not evaluated but their results were. That model, while it was convenient in an interpreted unique world, has been abandoned since we've made such progress in compiler design and for reasons cited in the article by Kent Pitman [Pit80]. Now we think of a macro as a process whose social role is to convert texts filled with abbreviations into new texts stripped of abbreviations.

Our choice of Lisp as the language for defining macros is resisted by those who restrict this language to filtering. Such are the macros proposed in the appendix of R^{4}RS. By doing that, they lose expressiveness since certain transformations can no longer be expressed, but they gain clarity in the simpler macros that are nevertheless the most common ones that we write. As an example, programs associated with this book at the time of publication contain 63 macro definitions using **define-syntax** as opposed to only 5 using the more liberal **define-abbreviation**.[3] The last three of those five uses define fundamental macros of ME-

---

3. We chose this exotic name to avoid conflict with various semantics conferred on **define-macro** by the different Lisp and Scheme evaluators.

ROONET (`define-class`, `define-generic`, and `define-method`); they couldn't be programmed with `define-syntax`.

In short, whether we impose a procedure for macro expansion or whether we decide to exploit parameters for an existing mechanism (at the price of incorporating a local evaluator for macro expansion), both models favor Lisp as the definition language for macros. In contrast to the exogenous mode, the endogenous mode requires an evaluator inside the macro expander; that's its characteristic trait. However, you must not confuse the language for writing macros with the language that is being prepared: they are related but not the same. When old fashioned manuals describe macros as things that work by double evaluation, they sin by omission since they don't mention that the two evaluations involve two different evaluators.

Figure 9.2 Exogenous (left) and endogenous (right) macroexpansions

9.3 Calling Macros

The macro expander has to find the places where the abbreviations to replace are located. Some languages, for example [Car93], already have elaborate syntactic analyzers that we can extend with new grammar productions for the syntactic extensions we want. That can be as simple as syntactic declarations indicating whether an operator is unary or binary, or prefix, postfix, infix. Sometimes we can also add an indication of precedence.

In Lisp, the representation of S-expressions favors the extraction of `car` from forms, so the following scheme is widely distributed: a list where the `car` is a keyword is a call to the macro of the same name. This scheme has many virtues: it is extendable, simple, and uniform. An abbreviation (that is, a macro) has a name associated with a function (an *expander*). The algorithm for macro expansion is thus quite simple: it runs recursively through the expression to handle, and when it identifies a call to a macro, it invokes the associated expander, providing the expander the S-expression that set things off. In the `cdr` of the S-expression, the expander can find whatever parameters for the expansion have been delivered to it.

The idea of a macro symbol comes in here, too, as in COMMON LISP, where we can connect the activation of an abbreviation with the ocurrence of a symbol. This offers us a lighter form, stripped of superfluous parentheses, when we want to associate some treatment with something that superficially resembles a variable.

A macro in that sense is thus just an association between an expansion function and a name matching a condition of activation. It's a kind of binding in what looks like a new name space reserved for macros. The macro is not exactly a binding, nor the expander, nor the activation condition, but everything all three imply inside

the macro expander. As we do in any conveniently managed name space, we want
to be able to define both global and local macros there: **define-abbreviation**
and **let-abbreviation** introduce such macros.

The purpose of the function for macro expansion is to convert an S-expression
into a program that can be assimilated. The consequence is that the search for sites
where macros are called occurs in an S-expression, not in a program. Of course,
this S-expression has some parts that are already programs. Equally certain, too,
a site of a call resembles a functional application but basically this is only an S-
expression, and nothing prevents a macro from showing bad taste. Accordingly,
the S-expression (**foo . 5**) could be defined in an ugly way as an abbreviation
for (**vector-ref foo 5**)!

The problem of the macro expander is thus to survey an S-expression, a gram-
matically soft structure with respect to the grammar of programs. That poses
certain problems of precedence between macros and lexical behavior. So if **bar**
is a macro and **lambda** is not one, then is the expression (**bar 34**) appearing in
((**lambda (bar) (bar 34)**) ...) a site where the macro **bar** is being used? The
problem arises because of the presence of the local variable, also named **bar**. Is it
hiding the macro **bar**? R^{4}RS takes a position favoring the respect for lexicality.
The same confusion also exists for quotations. Does (**quote (bar 34)**) contain a
site where the macro **bar** is being used?

It is unfortunately also necessary to look into the algorithm for expansion so
that we can see, when it scans an S-expression, how it finds the positions in which it
might find the sites where macros are called. For example, can we write (**let (foo)**
...) in a context where (**foo**) is a macro call generating a set of bindings? A great
many other examples exist, like (**cond (foo)** ...) or (**case key (foo)** ...).
In Lisp, good taste demands that we respect as much as possible the grammar of
forms in a way that confuses the difference between functions and macros. Without
more information, (**bar** ...) might be a call to the function **bar** or the site of a
call to the macro of the same name.

9.4   Expanders

What contract does an expander offer? At least two solutions co-exist.

In *classic* mode, the result delivered by the expander is considered as an S-
expression which can yet again include abbreviations. For that reason, the result
is re-expanded until it no longer contains any abbreviations. If **find-expander**
is the function which associates an expander with the name of a macro, then the
expansion of a macro call such as (**foo .   expr**) can be defined like this:

```
(macroexpand '(foo . expr)) ⤳
        (macroexpand ((find-expander 'foo) '(foo . expr)))
```

Another, more complicated, mode also exists. It's known as *Expansion Passing
Style* or EPS in [DFH88]. There the contract is that the expander must return the
expression completely stripped of abbreviations. Thus there is no **macroexpand**
waiting on the return of the call to the expander. The difficulty is that the expander
must recursively expand the subterms making up the expression that it generates.
It can do that only if it, too, knows the way of invoking macro expansion. One

solution is make sure that macro expanders have access to the global variable
macroexpand, whose value is the function for macro expansion. Another, more
clever solution, takes into account the need for local macros and modifies the calling
protocol for expanders so that they take as a second argument the current function
for macro expansion. In Lisp-like terms, we thus have this:

```
(macroexpand '(foo . expr)) ⤳
    ((find-expander 'foo) '(foo . expr) macroexpand)
```

Those two systems—classic versus EPS—are not equivalent. Indeed, EPS is
clearly superior in that it can program the former. A major difference in their
behavior concerns the need for local macros. Let's assume that we want to introduce an abbreviation locally. In EPS, we can extend the function **macroexpand**
to handle this abbreviation locally on subterms. In classic mode, for example in
COMMON LISP, the same request is treated this way: a special macro **macrolet**
modifies the internal state of the macro expander to add local macros there; then
it expands its body; then it remodifies the internal state to remove those macros
that it previously introduced there. The macro **macrolet** is primitive in the sense
that we cannot create it if by chance we don't have it. Likewise, in classic mode, it
is not possible to de-activate a macro external to **macrolet** (it is necessarily visible
or shadowed by a local macro) although in EPS, we can locally introduce syntax
arbitrarily different locally from the surrounding syntax. All we have to do is recursively use another function on the subterms—a function other than **macroexpand**.
In [DFH88], there are many examples of tracing and currying in this way.

Most abbreviations have local effects, that is, they lead only to a substitution of one particular text for another. It's important that EPS lets us access the
current expansion function as it does because then we can simply program more
complex transformations than those supported by the classic mode without having
to program a code walker. For example, think of the program transformation that
introduces boxes [see p. 114]. In EPS, it's possible to handle them by carrying out
a preliminary inspection of the expression to find local mutable variables and then
a second walk through to transform all the references to these variables, whether
read- or write-references.

However, EPS is not all powerful; there are transformations beyond its scope.
[see p. 141] Extracting quotations is not a local transformation beause, when
we encounter a quotation, extraction obliges us to transform the quotation into a
reference to a global variable. Up to that point, there's no problem, but we must
also create that global variable (we do by inserting a **define** form in the right
place) and that is hardly a local text effect! One solution would be to enclose the
entire program in a macro (let's say, **with-quotations-extracted**) which would
return a sequence of definitions of quotations followed by the transformed program.

Other macros might need to create global variables, too, like the macro **define-
class** in MEROONET. Syntactically, it can appear inside a **let** form. Its contract
is to create a global variable containing the object representing the class. This
problem is not generally handled by macro systems, so it obliges **define-class** to
be a special form or a macro exploiting magic functions, that is, known only by
implementations.

Since EPS is so interesting, you might ask why it's not used more often. First, because of the complexity of the model, but the main reason (as we've already mentioned) is that, on the whole, macros are simple so making them all-powerful only slows down their expansion. In effect, one interesting property of the classic mode is that we never get back to the previously expanded expressions: when the macro being expanded does not begin by a macro keyword, then it's a functional application which we'll never see again. Macro expansion occurs in one sole linear pass, although the result of an expansion in EPS can always be taken up again by an embedding expander, and thus it tends to cause superfluous re-expansions.

9.5   Acceptability of an Expanded Macro

By contract, the result of a macro expansion must be a program ready to be prepared. It shouldn't contain any more abbreviations; that is, it should appear exactly like it would have been written directly. There are a few pitfalls to avoid in getting there. First, since the macro expansion is a computation, there is a possibility that it might not terminate, and as a consequence, the preparation phase would not terminate either. It doesn't happen often that a compiler loops, but when it does, it's the price we pay to have a powerful macro system that does not limit the kind of computations we can do with it.

An easy way to cause looping is to re-introduce the expression to the macro expander in the expanded macro. That could easily happen if we defined the macro `while` like this:

```
(define-abbreviation (while condition . body)                    LOOP
  '(if ,condition (begin (begin . ,body) (while ,condition . ,body))) )
```

Re-introducing the same text that we are in the process of expanding and putting it into the result of the macro expansion provokes an endless expansion in every sense of the phrase, especially if we are in the classic mode of expansion.

The same error can occur in a way that is even more surreptitious in COMMON LISP because of the keyword `&whole`. That keyword lets the macro recover the whole calling form. In the following definition, the result of the macro expansion contains the original expression.

```
(defmacro while (&whole call)                    COMMON LISP
  (let ((condition (cadr call))
        (body      (cddr call)) )
    '(if ,condition (begin (begin . ,body) ,call)) ) )
```

Many interpreters macro-expand S-expressions on the fly as they are received. To avoid expanding the same thing again and again, they could adopt a technique of *memo-izing* or *displacing* macros. That strategy consists of physically replacing the S-expression that set off the macro expansion—replacing it by the expansion that yields the macro. In that case, the preceding `while` macro would have built a cyclic structure, posing no problem for interpretation but making the compiler loop because the compiler expects to handle only DAGs (directed acyclic graphs, that is trees possibly with shared branches) [Que92a]. We can show you that variation by rewriting the `while` macro like this:

```
(defmacro while (&whole call)                    COMMON LISP
  (let ((condition (cadr call))
```

```
          (body     (cddr call)) )
    (setf (car call) 'if)
    (setf (cdr call) '(,condition (begin (begin . ,body) ,call)))
    call ) )
```

What we've just shown you about programs can also occur with quotations; they, too, can be cyclic and thus make certain compilers loop. [see p. 140]

The second pitfall, even nastier than the first, is that the expanded macro can contain values intruding from the macro expansion. The moral contract of the programmer is that the result of the macro expansion should be a program that he or she could have written directly. That implies that the program necessarily has a writable form. Scheme thus insists that quotations must be formulated with an external syntax in order to prevent the quotation of just any values.

Let's look at a particularly torturous example of a quotation with a non-writable value. The following macro builds just that by inserting a continuation into the quoted value, like this:

```
(define-abbreviation (incredible x)            BAD TASTE
    (call/cc (lambda (k) '(quote (,k ,x)))) )
```

What meaning should we give that gibberish? Let's reconsider a few of the hypotheses we've already mentioned. Writing the expanded macro in a file is impossible since we don't have a standard way of transcribing continuations. What does the invocation of a continuation taken from a different process mean anyway? Or, in C terms, what does it mean during the execution of a.out to invoke a continuation captured by cpp? In the absence of any agreement about what that means, we should just say, "No!"

That example used a continuation to highlight the strangeness of the situation. All the same, we will avoid including any value that has no written representation; likewise, we won't include primitives, closures, nor the input and output ports. Consequently, we will no longer write (',(lambda (y) car) x) nor '(',car x) nor (f ',(current-output-port)), even if in an interpreted world that would not be an error.

In short, we'll repeat the golden rule of macros: never generate a program that you could not write directly.

9.6 Defining Macros

Various forms declare global macros (with a scope that we'll analyze in the next section) and local macros. They are **define-syntax**, **letrec-syntax**, and **let-syntax** in Scheme; **defmacro** and **macrolet** in COMMON LISP; **define-abbreviation** and **let-abbreviation** in this book.

To define a macro, we build a function (the expander), and then register that expander with an appropriate name. The expander is written in the language of macros, an instance of Lisp. Now we'll analyze its consequences in the various worlds and modes that we mentioned earlier.

9.6.1   Multiple Worlds

Remember that with multiple worlds, macro expansion is a process that occurs in
a memory space separated from the final evaluation.

Endogenous Mode

According to the endogenous school, the text defining a macro (in our case, the
form **define-abbreviation**) synthesizes an expander on the fly by means of the
evaluator implementing the macro language. In that case, the keyword **define-abbreviation** can be none other than the syntactic marker that the macro expander
is searching for. The following definition presents a very naive macro expander
that implements this endogenous strategy.

```
(define *macros* '())
(define (install-macro! name expander)
  (set! *macros* (cons (cons name expander) *macros*)) )
(define (naive-endogeneous-macroexpander exps)
  (define (macro-definition? exp)
    (and (pair? exp)
         (eq? (car exp) 'define-abbreviation) ) )
  (if (pair? exps)
      (if (macro-definition? (car exps))
          (let* ((def      (car exps))
                 (name      (car (cadr def)))
                 (variables (cdr (cadr def)))
                 (body      (cddr def)) )
            (install-macro! name (macro-eval
                                  '(lambda ,variables . ,body) ))
            (naive-endogeneous-macroexpander (cdr exps)) )
          (let ((exp (expand-expression (car exps) *macros*)))
            (cons exp (naive-endogeneous-macroexpander (cdr exps))) ) )
      '() ) )
```

That macro expander takes a sequence of expressions (the set of expressions
from a file to compile) and consults the global variable ***macros***, which contains
the current macros in the form of an association-list. One by one, the expressions
are expanded by the subfunction **expand-expression** with the current macros.
When the definition of a macro is encountered, it is handled specially, on the fly,
like an evaluation inside the macro expansion. The evaluation function is represented by **macro-eval**; it might be different from native **eval**. Indeed, **macro-eval**
implements the macro language, whereas **eval** implements the language into which
we're expanding macros. This looks a little like cross-compilation. Once the expander has been built, it is inserted by **install-macro!** in the list of current
macros. You can imagine the world of difference between the definitions of macros
and the other expressions which are only expanded. The following correct example
illustrates that idea.

---

si/chap9b.scm

```
(define (fact1 n) (if (= n 0) 1 (* n (fact1 (- n 1)))))
(define-abbreviation (factorial n)
  (define (fact2 n) (if (= n 1) 1 (* n (fact2 (- n 1)))))
  (if (and (integer? n) (> n 0)) (fact2 n) '(fact1 ,n)) )
(define (some-facts)
  (list (factorial 5) (factorial (+ 3 2))) )
```

It wouldn't be healthy to confuse **fact1** and **fact2** in endogenous mode because the definition of **fact1** is merely expanded and not evaluated; it doesn't even exist yet when the macro **factorial** is defined. For that reason, the macro uses its own version—**fact2**—for its own needs. Thus expanding those three expressions leads to this:

si/chap9b.escm

```
(define (fact1 n) (if (= n 0) 1 (* n (fact1 (- n 1)))))
(define (some-facts) (list 120 (fact1 (+ 3 2))))
```

We could make that example more complicated by renaming **fact1** and **fact2** simply as **fact**. Then mentally we would have to keep track of which occurrence of the word **fact** inside the definition of **factorial** refers to which. We would also have to determine that the first occurrence refers to the value of the variable **fact** local to the macro at the time of expansion, while the second refers to the global variable **fact** at the time of execution.

There are other variations within endogenous mode. Some macro expanders make a first pass to extract the macro definitions from the set of expressions to expand. Those are then defined and serve to expand the rest of the module. This submode poses problems when macro calls define new macros because the macro expander risks not seeing them. Moreover, the fact that macros can be applied even before they are defined is disorienting enough. There again, left to right order seems mentally well adapted.

Another important variation—one that we'll see again later—is to make **define-abbreviation** a predefined macro.

Exogenous Mode

In exogenous mode, macros are no longer defined in expressions to prepare, but rather in expressions that define the macro expander. We will assume that the macro expander is modular; that is, that we can define independent macros in a separate way. The best way to define such macros is, of course, to have a macro to do so. We'll use the keyword **define-abbreviation**, and here's its metacircular definition:

```
(define-abbreviation (define-abbreviation call . body)
  '(install-macro! ',(car call) (lambda ,(cdr call) . ,body)) )
```

When the macro expander is specified by an appropriate directive, its role is to add to itself the macro just defined. We'll thus assume that the macro expansion directives specify an expansion engine that is enriched by calls to `install-macro!`. Now mastery of macro expansion is completely different since macros are defined in some modules and used in others. Let's assume that we have a preliminary module with the following contents:

---

si/chap9c.scm

```
(define (fact n) (if (= n 0) 1 (* n (fact (- n 1)))))
(define-abbreviation (factorial n)
  (if (and (integer? n) (> n 0)) (fact n) '(fact ,n)) )
```

The expansion of that module would look like this:

---

si/chap9c.escm

```
(define (fact n) (if (= n 0) 1 (* n (fact (- n 1)))))
(install-macro! 'factorial
  (lambda (n) (if (and (integer? n) (> n 0)) (fact n) '(fact ,n))) )
```

Now let's suppose we want to use the macro `factorial` for macro expansion of a module containing the definition of the function `some-facts`, like this:

---

si/chap9d.scm

```
(define (some-facts)
  (list (factorial 5) (factorial (+ 3 2))) )
```

We would get these results:

---

si/chap9d.escm

```
(define (some-facts)
  (list 120 (fact (+ 3 2))) )
```

The first occurrence of `fact` in the macro `factorial` poses no problem; it's just a reference to the global variable in the same module `si/chap9c.scm`. That's obvious if we look at its macro expansion in `si/chap9c.escm`. In contrast, the second occurrence of `fact` refers to the variable `fact` as it will exist at execution time in the module `si/chap9d.escm`. That reference is still free (in the sense of unbound) in the expanded macro, and it might very well happen that there will be no variable `fact` at execution time!

An easy solution to that problem is to add (by linking or by cutting and pasting) a module to `si/chap9d.scm`—a module from among those we have on hand: `si/chap9c.scm` defines a global variable that meets our needs. But in doing so, we will also have imported the definition of a macro, `factorial`, found in the same module, there only for the evaluation of **some-facts**, and which may introduce new errors since it invokes the function **install-macro!** which has no purpose in the generated application.

The second solution is to refine our understanding of the dependences that exist between the macros and their execution libraries, especially, *especially* the various moments of computation. The art of macros is complex because it requires a mastery of time. Let's look again at the example of **fact1**, **fact2**, and **factorial**. When we discover a site where **factorial** is used, the macro needs the function **fact2** for expansion. In contrast, its result (the macro expanded expression) needs the function **fact1** for execution. We'll say that **fact1** belongs to the *execution library* of the macro **factorial**, whereas **fact2** belongs to the *expansion library* of **factorial**. The extents of these two libraries are completely unrelated to each other. Indeed, the expansion library is needed only during macro expansion, whereas the execution library is useful only for the evaluation of the expanded macro.

Thus in exogenous mode, one solution is to define macros and their expansion library in one module, **si/libexp**, and then define their execution library in a separate module, **si/librun**. [see **Ex. 9.5**] Still working on the factorial, here's what we would write in one module:

---

si/libexp.scm

```
(define (fact2 n) (if (= n 0) 1 (* n (fact2 (- n 1)))))
(define-abbreviation (factorial n)
  (if (and (integer? n) (> n 0)) (fact2 n) '(fact1 ,n)) )
```

and in the other module:

---

si/librun.scm

```
(define (fact1 n) (if (= n 0) 1 (* n (fact1 (- n 1)))))
```

When a directive mentions the use of the macro **factorial**, the macro expander will load the module **si/libexp.scm**, and the directive language will register the fact that at execution time the library **si/librun.scm** must be linked to the application. In that way, we will be able to keep only the necessary resources at execution time, as in [DPS94b]. Figure 9.3 recapitulates these operations. It shows how we first construct the compiler adapted to compilation of the program, and then how we get the little autonomous executable that we are entitled to expect.

9.6.2   Unique World

After the preceding section, you might think that hypothesizing a unique world (rather than multiple worlds) would resolve all problems. Not so at all!

In a unique world, the evaluator reads expressions, expands the macros in them, prepares the expanded macros, and evaluates the result of the preparation. The

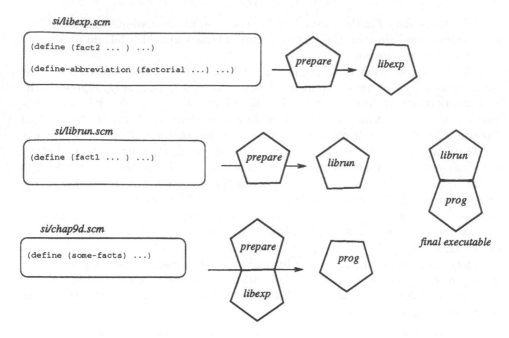

Figure 9.3 Multiple worlds: building an application

state of the macro expander is thus included in the interaction loop. According to this hypothesis, it is logical for the evaluator connected to endogenous macro expansion (the one we've called **macro-eval**) to be simply the **eval** function of the evaluator (but with all the possible variations that we saw in Chapter 8). [see p. 271] Since the world is unique, macro expansion has both read- and write-access to everything present in this world. It might seem easy then not to distinguish between the expansion library and the execution library since it suffices to submit this to the interaction loop:

```
(define (fact n) (if (= n 0) 1 (* n (fact (- n 1)))))
(define-abbreviation (factorial n)
  (if (and (integer? n) (> n 0)) (fact n) '(fact ,n)) )
```

The problem is that now we make sharing (or selling) software very difficult because it is hard and often even impossible to extract just what's needed to execute or regenerate the program that we want to share. To be sure that we've forgotten nothing, we can deliver an entire memory image, but doing so is costly. We might try a *tree-shaker* to sift out anything that's useless. (A tree-shaker is a kind of inefficient garbage collector.) Actually, as you can see in many Lisp and Scheme programs available on Internet, we should abstain from delivering programs containing macros: either we deliver everything expanded (as *macroless* programs), or we deliver only programs with local macros. And at that point, we've negated all the expressive power that macros offered us!

If you don't believe in tools for automatic extraction, there's nothing left but to do it ourselves. To do so, we must distinguish three cases: the resources useful only for macro expansion, those useful only for execution, and finally (the most problematic) those that are useful in both phases.

In order to prepare programs asynchronously, there's the function **compile-file**. Two variations oppose each other in the unique world. One might be called the *uniquely unique world*. The difference between the two concerns the macros available to prepare the module submitted to **compile-file**. Here are the three solutions that we find in nature.

1. In the uniquely unique world, there is only one macro space, and it is valid everywhere. Current macros are thus those that can use the expressions of the module being prepared. That's the case in Figure 9.4 where the macro **factorial** defined in the interaction loop is quite visible to the compiled module. Here's a subquestion then: what happens if the module being prepared defines macros itself?

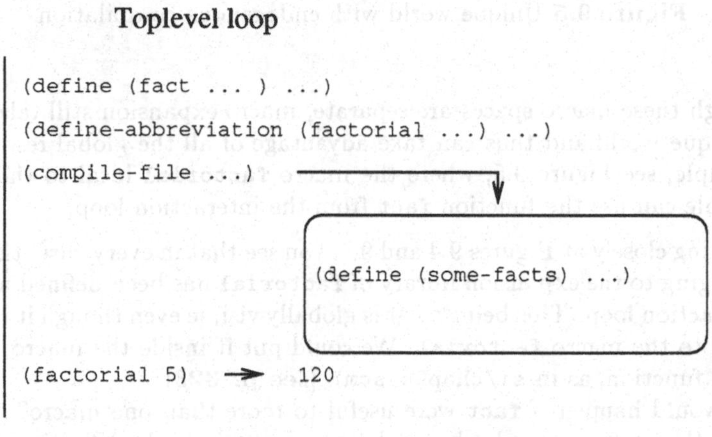

Toplevel loop

```
(define (fact ... ) ...)
(define-abbreviation (factorial ...) ...)
(compile-file ...)

                              (define (some-facts) ...)

(factorial 5)  →   120
```

Figure 9.4 Uniquely unique world

(a) In the uniquely unique world, these new macros are added to the current macros so the macro space continues to grow. (At least it does so unless we suppress macros altogether.) That's the case in Figure 9.5 if the expression (**factorial 5**) submitted to the interaction loop returns 120.

(b) Another response would be that macros defined in the module are visible only to the preparation of that module. Thus we distinguish *super global macros* from macros *only global* to the modules. In Figure 9.5, that would be the case if the expression (**factorial 5**) were submitted to the interaction loop and yielded an error.

2. Finally, if the world is not uniquely unique, then the only macros visible to the module are those that the module defines endogenously. In that case, there is a space for macros for the interaction loop, and there are initially empty spaces for macros specific to each prepared module. However, even

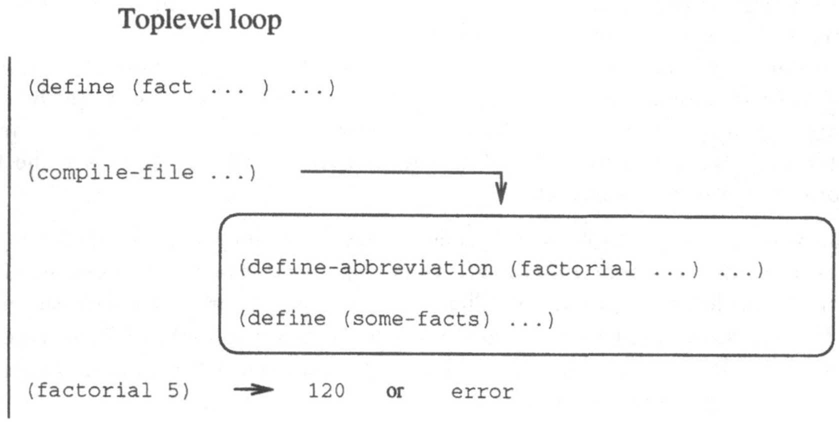

Toplevel loop

```
(define (fact ... ) ...)


(compile-file ...)


              (define-abbreviation (factorial ...) ...)

              (define (some-facts) ...)


(factorial 5)    ⟶    120    or    error
```

Figure 9.5 Unique world with endogenous compilation

though these macro spaces are separate, macro expansion still takes place in a unique world and thus can take advantage of all the global resources. For example, see Figure 9.5, where the macro **factorial** local to the compiled module can use the function **fact** from the interaction loop.

By looking closely at Figures 9.4 and 9.5, you see that in every case, the function **fact** belonging to the expansion library of **factorial** has been defined at the level of the interaction loop. This being so, it is globally visible even though it is probably useful only to the macro **factorial**. We could put it inside the macro, making it an internal function, as in **si/chap9b.scm**). [see p. 323]

What would happen if **fact** were useful to more than one macro? The problem is that the macro expander knows how to recognize only definitions of macros although we would often like to define global variables, utility functions, or various other data for the exclusive use of a set of several macros. Even though the hypothesis of multiple worlds in exogenous mode naturally insures that, that's not the case for endogenous mode nor for the unique world. Moreover, the principles of this hypothesis introduce the possibility of forcing an evaluation inside the macro expander. In COMMON LISP and other versions of Scheme, that practice is known as **eval-when**. To avoid interference, we'll name the practice **eval-in-abbreviation-world** for ourselves.

The purpose of the form **eval-in-abbreviation-world** is to make it possible to define constants, to define utility functions, to carry on any sort of computation inside and for the sole use of the macro expander. In fact, that form explicitly recognizes the need to separate that world from the exterior world of evaluation. In Figure 9.6, the function **fact** is defined in the evaluator of the macro expander, and **factorial** can thus use it to expand **some-facts**. On returning to the interaction loop, and depending on whether the worlds have "leaks" or not, **factorial** and/or **fact** can be visible and invokable again.

To program that behavior, all we have to do is ask the macro expander to recognize forms beginning with the keyword **eval-in-abbreviation-world** and

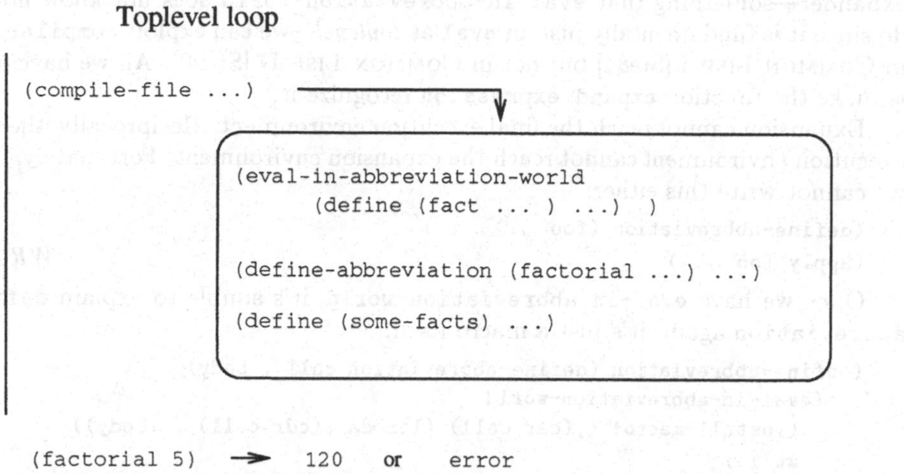

Toplevel loop

```
(compile-file ...)

                    (eval-in-abbreviation-world
                            (define (fact ... ) ...) )

                    (define-abbreviation (factorial ...) ...)

                    (define (some-facts) ...)


(factorial 5)  ➞    120   or    error
```

Figure 9.6 Endogenous evaluation

to evaluate them on the fly with the appropriate evaluator, that is, the one that
we called **macro-eval** in the function **naive-endogeneous-macroexpander**.

```
(define (expand-expression exp macroenv)
   (define (evaluation? exp)
     (and (pair? exp)
          (eq? (car exp) 'eval-in-abbreviation-world) ) )
   (define (macro-call? exp)
     (and (pair? exp) (find-expander (car exp) macroenv)) )
   (define (expand exp)
     (cond ((evaluation? exp) (macro-eval '(begin . ,(cdr exp))))
           ((macro-call? exp) (expand-macro-call exp macroenv))
           ((pair? exp)
            (let ((newcar (expand (car exp))))
              (cons newcar (expand (cdr exp))) ) )
           (else exp) ) )
   (expand exp) )
```

The function **macro-eval** is the evaluator hidden behind macro expansion. It
can be seen as an instance of the usual **eval** function, but provided with a clean
global environment, not shared with the evaluator that the interaction loop uses.
In that case, and for Figure 9.6, (**factorial 5**) and (**fact 5**) would both be in
error.

Forms appearing in **eval-in-abbreviation-world** must be considered as executable directives included in the S-expression that is being expanded. In particular, these forms can use only what will later be the current lexical environment.
We cannot write this:

```
(let ((x 33))                                               WRONG
  (eval-in-abbreviation-world (display x)) )
```

Again, if we want to introduce a variable locally for the sole benefit of the macro expander—something that `eval-in-abbreviation-world` does not know how to do since it is fundamentally just an `eval` at *toplevel*—we can exploit `compiler-let` in COMMON LISP I [Ste84] but not in COMMON LISP II [Ste90]. All we have to do is make the function `expand-expression` recognize it.

Expansion cannot reach the final execution environment. Reciprocally, the final execution environment cannot reach the expansion environment. Fortunately, then, we cannot write this either:

```
(define-abbreviation (foo ...) ... )
(apply foo ... )                                          WRONG
```

Once we have `eval-in-abbreviation-world`, it's simple to explain `define-abbreviation` again: it's just a macro itself.

```
(define-abbreviation (define-abbreviation call . body)
  '(eval-in-abbreviation-world
    (install-macro! ',(car call) (lambda ,(cdr call) . ,body))
    #t ) )
```

Now the main point is that we can place definitions of macros everywhere and not just in toplevel position. Accordingly, if we want to organize several expressions into one unique sequence, we can write this:

```
(begin (define-abbreviation (foo x) ... )
       (bar (foo 34)) )
```

However, as a question of good taste, that should not be based on a too precise expansion order, nor should it lead to such slack writing as this:

```
(if (bar) (begin (define-abbreviation (foo x) ...)      BAD TASTE
                 (hux) )
          (foo 35) )
```

Most macro expanders distinguish macros at toplevel from others. For example, that's what distinguishes internal from global instances of `define`. Macro expanders also insure that toplevel expressions are treated sequentially from left to right. For that reason, we can define a class and then its subclasses in order.

In fact, the preceding examples have hidden a few implementation details due to the fact that several evaluators co-exist so not all the preceding definitions aim at the same evaluator. In the same way as with reflective interpreters, there's a problem of accessing the data structure that defines the current macros. [see p. 271] The form `install-macro!` in the definition of `define-abbreviation` will be evaluated by `macro-eval`, but it must modify the set of current macros as scanned by the function `find-expander`. However, `find-expression` is not evaluated by `macro-eval` but by `eval`! Well, these problems are not important for the moment.

One aim of `eval-in-abbreviation-world` is to introduce definitions of global variables in the macro expander because often macros behave in a way that depends on the underlying implementation. For example, a macro that constructs a call to the function `apply` in its macro expansion can inspect its environment to know whether the function `apply` found there is binary (which is sufficient for R^2RS or n-ary (as in R^4RS). However, checking its own environment means that the macro being expanded has the same environment as its target. In the case of complicated software (and we'll look into this case in MEROON later), it is sometimes useful to expand something for another implementation, in which case it is necessary for the target implementation to be defined by *features* that can be inspected. You might see macros like this one:

```
(define-abbreviation (apply-foo x y z)
  (if (memq 'binary-apply *features*)
    '(apply foo (cons x (cons y z)))
    '(apply foo x y z) ) )
```

The variable `*features*` must be visible from the macro expander. That fact means that it must have been defined beforehand by means of `eval-in-abbreviation-world`. We can thus characterize an implementation by defining the variable `*features*` to be able to consult the macros under consideration. In the expression that follows—even though its appearance is tricky—the form `define` is at toplevel with respect to the macro language, so it is a definition of the global variable `*features*`.

```
(eval-in-abbreviation-world
  (define *features* '(31bit-fixnum binary-apply)) )
```

9.6.3 Simultaneous Evaluation

An important variation often present in any hypothesis about the unique world is evaluation occurring simultaneously with preparation. As expressions are gradually expanded, they are evaluated by the interaction loop. That's what the following definition suggests:

```
(define (simultaneous-eval-macroexpander exps)
  (define (macro-definition? exp)
    (and (pair? exp)
         (eq? (car exp) 'define-abbreviation) ) )
  (if (pair? exps)
    (if (macro-definition? (car exps))
      (let* ((def     (car exps))
             (name    (car (cadr def)))
             (variables (cdr (cadr def)))
             (body    (cddr def)) )
        (install-macro!
          name (macro-eval '(lambda ,variables . ,body)) )
        (simultaneous-eval-macroexpander (cdr exps)) )
      (let ((e (expand-expression (car exps) *macros*)))
        (eval e)
        (cons e (simultaneous-eval-macroexpander (cdr exps))) ) )
    '() ) )
```

Notice that two evaluators appear in that definition: `eval`, the evaluator in the interaction loop; and `macro-eval`, the evaluator in the macro expander. We have distinguished them from each other because they represent distinct processes occurring at distinct times.

9.6.4 Redefining Macros

The function `install-macro!` implied that macros could be redefined: if we redefine a macro, we modify the state of the macro expander thus altering the treatments that remain for it to do. When we are using an interpreter and debugging a macro, it's fine that we can redefine that macro and test it through some function that we define to contain a site where this macro is called. That means that the interpreter delays the expansion of macros as long as possible. However, most of the time, expressions are expanded only once, and certainly to insure repeatable experiments, expressions should be expanded only once. As a consequence, those expressions become independent of any possible redefinitions of macros. In that sense, macros behave in a way that we could call hyperstatic. [see p. 55]

9.6.5 Comparisons

One of the main problems with macros is that it is difficult to change them if we're not satisfied with the system that an implementation provides. In fact, that difficulty has probably vetoed the unbridled experimentation that other parts of Lisp and Scheme have taken advantage of.

The system of multiple worlds in exogenous mode seems more precise but less widely distributed. The system of multiple worlds in endogenous mode is only an instance of the exogenous mode with an expansion engine that predefines certain macros like **define-abbreviation** and others. Finally, the unique world is the most widespread, but the least easy to master in terms of delivering software. This comparison among them is a little sketchy simply because it does not take into account two new facets that we'll discuss now: compiling macros and using macros to define other macros.

Compiling Macros

In what we've covered up to now, the macro expansion of a call to a macro is most often the work of an interpreter. For that reason, its efficiency seems compromised especially if the transformation of the programs produced by the macro is long and complicated (though that is rare). In the multiple world in exogenous mode [see p. 315], we build an *ad hoc* compiler by assembling prepared (that is, compiled) modules so we get efficiency. In endogenous mode, one solution is to use a compiling function, **macro-eval**. In the unique world, we can use **compile-file** and **load**. The problem is how to compile a definition of a macro?

The question is not trivial! The macro expanders that we've presented checked the expressions to expand and did so in order to find the forms **define-abbreviation** and to define those same macros on the fly. We must thus distinguish compilation of the macro from its installation. If **define-abbreviation** is a macro that expands into the form **install-macro!**, then we're home free. In contrast, if **define-abbreviation** is a syntactic keyword, then we merely have to insure that the body of a macro is only an interpreted call to a compiled function. Once it has been compiled, we must again load the prepared program, and at that point, several problems arise: what, for example, does (**eval-in-abbreviation-world** (**load file**)) mean? The function **load** is just a wrapper around **eval**, but in the macro expansion world, we must use **macro-eval**, not **eval**! We won't even talk about an explicit call to **eval**, as in (**eval-in-abbreviation-world** (**eval '(define-abbreviation ...)))**, where, once again, **eval** must refer to `macro-eval`, rather than the evaluator in the interaction loop. This (non-)discussion clearly shows that the two global environments belonging to `eval` and `macro-eval` really are separate and provide very different entities under the same name.

We come back to the point that the macro definer has to be a macro itself; it cannot be just a syntactic marker that the macro expander searches for. Accordingly, we separate the preparation of a macro from its installation. We'll take up this point again later. [see p. 336]

Macros Defining Macros

From time to time, it's useful to define macros that generate other macros themselves. [see p. 339] This is not just some weird habit but a logical application of the principles of abstraction and freedom of expression. For example, in an object system, we might want to define the class `Point` where the accessors `Point-x` and `Point-y` should be macros instead of functions. [see p. 424] In that case, the macro `define-class` must generate those new macros.

Let's take the example of another macro, `define-alias`, which defines its first argument to be equal to its second. We'll give you two variations of it, one of them enclosing *backquotes* in *backquotes*.

```
(define-abbreviation (define-alias newname oldname)
  '(define-abbreviation (,newname . parameters)
    '(,',oldname . ,parameters) ) )
(define-abbreviation (define-alias newname oldname)
  '(define-abbreviation (,newname . parameters)
    (cons ',oldname parameters) ) )
```

Conventionally, where the result of a macro expansion is expanded again, if `define-abbreviation` is a macro, then there is no problem. In contrast, if `define-abbreviation` is merely a syntactic marker, then it's quite likely that the macro expander will not perceive this definition if it does not analyze the result of macro expansions. Consequently, we'll abandon the idea of a syntactic marker in favor of predefined and even primitives macros because we wouldn't know how to create them if they were missing.

9.7 Scope of Macros

The scope of local macros, introduced by `let-syntax` or `letrec-syntax` in Scheme, poses no problems. That's not the case, however, for macros defined by `define-syntax` because we can distinguish several cases for using macros. In this section, we'll take MEROON for discussion. It is an object system built on top of Scheme; it has already been ported to many implementations of Scheme, both interpreted and compiled. The essence of the system MEROON is in MEROONET. (See Chapter 11.) Three kinds of macros exist in that system:

1. **Type 1—occasional macros:** An occasional macro is defined in one place and used immediately afterwards. We can thus transform it into a local macro defined by a form, `let-syntax` or `macrolet`, if we have that available,

though of course that's not the case everywhere. For example, the function **make-fix-maker** in MEROONET builds a "triangle" of closures (lambda (a b c ...) (vector cn a b c ...)), but it does so "by hand." [see p. 434] The following macro does that automatically.

```
(define-abbreviation (generate-vector-of-fix-makers n)
  (let* ((numbers (iota 0 n))
         (variables (map (lambda (i) (gensym)) numbers)) )
    '(case size
       ,@(map (lambda (i)
               (let ((vars (list-tail variables (- n i))))
                 '((,i) (lambda ,vars (vector cn . ,vars))) ) )
             numbers )
       (else #f) ) ) ) )
```

An occasional macro can be abandonned, once it's been used. Its scope is greatly restricted: it does not go beyond the module where it appears.

2. **Type 2—macros local to a system**: The definition of MEROON is organized into about 25 small files. A number of abbreviations appear throughout those files, for example, the macro **when**. The scope of that macro is thus the set of files making up the source of MEROON, but no more than that, because we have no right to pollute the world exterior to MEROON.

3. **Type 3—exported macros**: MEROON exports three macros: **define-class**, **define-generic**, and **define-method**. These macros are for MEROON users but they also bootstrap MEROON. The macro **when** cannot appear in the expansion of macros of type 3 because allowing that would confer a greater scope on **when** than we planned for. The language of the macro expansion of exported macros is the user's language, not the language of MEROON itself.

Not only are there three kinds of macros; there are also three ways of using them, as illustrated in Figure 9.7. Those three ways are:

1. **To prepare MEROON sources**: This use involves expanding the source of MEROON and thus getting rid of all uses of type 1, 2, and 3. In contrast, something from the definition of macros of type 3 necessarily has to live somewhere since they are exported.

2. **To prepare a module that uses MEROON**: Preparing a module that uses MEROON means expanding MEROON macros of type 3 that this module uses.

   Consequently, in the thing that prepares this module, we have to install type 3 MEROON macros. In other words, we have to graft the expansion library of type 3 macros onto the preparer. Notice, though, that we don't actually need the expansion library of MEROON type 1 or 2.

3. **To generate an interpreter providing the user with MEROON**: In this case, we want to construct an interaction loop that provides type 3 MEROON macros. Consequently, those macros have to be installed, along with their expansion library in the macro expander connected to the interaction loop.

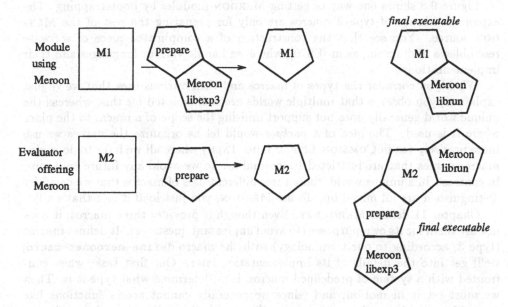

Figure 9.7 Usage of macros

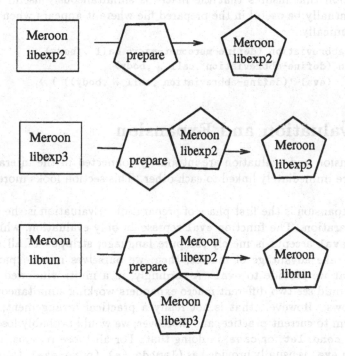

Figure 9.8 Bootstrapping MEROON

Figure 9.8 shows one way of getting Meroon modules by bootstrapping. The expansion library of type 2 macros are only for preparing the rest of the Meroon source. You see that the construction of a complicated piece of software resembles a T-diagram, as in [ES70], where we handle various languages and their implementations.

When you consider the types of macros and their various uses that we've just explained, you observe that multiple worlds are well adapted for this, whereas the unique world generally does not support limiting the scope of a macro to the place where it is used. The idea of a *package* would let us organize the names we use more precisely (as in Common Lisp or Ilog Talk) where all we have to do is give macros names that are restricted to internal use so we avoid any future collisions. In contrast, in a unique world, those three different uses of macros that we carefully distinguished are all mixed up. To use Meroon, you just load it and that's all!

Chapter 11 defines Meroonet. Even though it provides three macros, it does not use them for its own purposes (to avoid unpleasant questions). It defines macros (type 3, according to our terminology) with the macro **define-meroonet-macro**; we'll get into the details of its implementation later. Our first task, when confronted with a system of predefined macros, is to determine what type it is. Then we must set it in motion, and (since we generally cannot access functions like **install-macro!**) we have to do everything with the only macro definer in the implementation. By "everything," we mean from the simple equivalence between **define-meroonet-macro** and **define-abbreviation** up to the following convoluted definition that insures that the macro is simultaneously useful right away and will eventually be useful in the prepared file where it appears when that file is loaded dynamically.

```
(define-abbreviation (define-meroonet-macro call . body)
  '(begin (define-abbreviation ,call . ,body)
          (eval '(define-abbreviation ,call . ,body)) ) )
```

9.8 Evaluation and Expansion

Macro expansion and evaluation are intimately connected in the interaction loop since they are immediately linked to each other. This section looks more closely at that couple.

Macro expansion is the first phase of preparation. Evaluation is the phase that follows preparation. The function **eval** represents only evaluation, while the language that **eval** accepts is merely the pure language, stripped of all macros. If we want to take advantage of macros, then, we ourselves must expand the expressions that we provide to **eval**. Accordingly, in a multi-windowed evaluation system, we could see two different macro expanders working simultaneously in different windows. However, that is not really a practical arrangement; it doesn't really conform to current practice, and moreover, we would probably lose the usual macros, like **cond**, **let**, or **case**, in doing that. For all those reasons, the evaluation function **eval** is usually provided as (**lambda (e) (pure-eval (macroexpand e *macros*)))**, where **pure-eval** is the evaluator for the pure language while **macro-expand** is the public function for macro expansion and ***macros*** contains the macros known to the interaction loop.

What we've just said about **eval** is also true about **macro-eval** which has its own ***macros*** variable containing only the macros known by the preparation. A great many questions arise here about this pair, macro expansion and evaluation. We've already mentioned [see p. 277] the existence of **eval/ce** for *evaluate in the current environment*. That special form captured the entire visible lexical context. Since **eval/ce** knows how to expand the expressions it receives, does it capture the macro expansion context? In other words, if we write this:

```
(let-syntax ((foo ...))
    (eval/ce (read)) )
```

then will an expression read and containing a call to **foo** be expanded correctly by **eval/ce**? If yes, then not only must **eval/ce** keep a trace of the lexical context, but it must also save the memory state of the entire macro expander in order to keep its ability to expand **foo**. Since that seriously undermines the independence of macro expansion, we regard that practice as in seriously bad taste. However, the right solution is that evaluation should be pure and not force macro expansion right away, but then that's not practical, so etc. etc.

When we define a macro, the macro is visible for the rest of the macro expansion. Let's assume that we've defined the useful macro **when**. Then can we write this?

```
(define-abbreviation (whenever condition . corps)
    (when condition (display '(whenever is called)))
    '(when ,condition . ,corps) )
```

That macro uses the word **when** twice. The second occurrence is located in the expanded macro so it poses no problem. In contrast, the first one appears in the computation of the macro expansion and is thus evaluated by the evaluator for macro expansion, which *a priori* does not know about **when**: the macro language is not the one that we are expanding! For the macro **when** to be available for use by the definition language for macros, we should have already provided the following definition:

```
(eval-in-abbreviation-world
    (define-abbreviation (when condition . body)
    '(if ,condition (begin . ,body)) ) )
```

The problem is similar in this expression:

```
(define-abbreviation (foo)
    (define-abbreviation (bar)
    (when ...)
    (wrek) )
    (hux) )
```

The internal definition of **bar** is *a priori* destined to enrich the macro language, not the current language. The preceding expression defines the macro **bar** as the macro possible to use to write the macro. Even if the semantics seems clean, the pragmatics are a little off because we now have a problem of infinite regression. The language for defining macros and the language for defining the definition language for macros are not necessarily the same. In other words, as in the preceding example, we can't be sure that the form **when** present in the definition of **bar** is included and understood. If we had truly different languages, the problem would be even more apparent. For example, you can imagine that macros are handled by `cpp` and that for `cpp` macros themselves come from a `perl` program. Then it becomes obvious that the definition of a macro on one level has implications only on that level.

How do we resolve such a problem? One possibility is to stick to the semantics and have multiple levels of language, but (fortunately!) we rarely need to get higher than the second level. There we would again find the problems of levels of language that we saw with reflective interpreters. [see p. 302]

Another possibility would be to fuse all language levels used by the macro expander. This boils down to adopting the hypothesis of the unique world for the evaluator in macro expansion. The circle closes in on us again, and everything that we carefully separated is all mixed up once more.

A third possibility—the one adopted by R^{4}RS—is to restrain the language to express macros to only filtering and reconstructing capabilities. Macros can no longer be defined in that language!

In short, once again it's very important to distinguish the languages that come into play. In an implementation of Scheme that supports distribution and parallelism, it's probably not a good idea to make the expansion of macros distributed and parallel as well. We might even forbid the writing of macros that use non-local continuations, like this:

```
(define-abbreviation (foo x)                    BAD TASTE
  (call/cc (lambda (k)
             (set! the-k k)
             x )) )
(define-abbreviation (bar y)
  (the-k y) )
```

But how would we enforce that rule?

9.9   Using Macros

This section goes into the details of how macros are typically used. While we agree that their purpose is to transform programs, we might have many different reasons for transforming programs. Among them, we distinguish these:

- *Shortcuts* limit the number of characters a user must type (especially at toplevel or during debugging). If we want to write (`trace foo`) to make visible all the calls to the function `foo`, then we need a macro that does not evaluate `foo`.

- *Beautification* lets us mask disharmonious syntax. For example, we might use `bind-exit` rather than `call/ep` to avoid an extra `lambda`.

- *Masks* let us hide the underlying implementation—a primordial goal. We need to hide the implementation details when they are likely to change or when it's not a good idea to make them accessible for general use. As examples, consider `define-class` in MEROONET or `syntax-rules` in Scheme.

Among the masks, we also find macros whose aim is to abstract porting problems. Using a macro, like `apply-foo` [see p. 331] to hide the fact that there are two kinds of **apply**, a binary and an n-ary, is a current practice. Another porting problem crops up with the Boolean value of () in Scheme, which is True in R^{4}RS but not necessarily so in R^{3}RS. We can get around this problem by using a macro everywhere; we'll call it **meroon-if** and define it like this:

```
(define-abbreviation (meroon-if condition consequent . alternant)
  `(if (let ((tmp ,condition))
         (or tmp (null? tmp)) )
       ,consequent . ,alternant ) )
```

Of course, we can avoid that problem if our program is robust, but the fact is, some very interesting software has been written in a style that is not entirely robust, alas. Prefixing it with such a macro is one way of porting it toward another implementation.

Among the masks, we also find macros whose role is to insure that certain optimizations will be carried out independently of the target compiler. One important improvement—known as *inlining*—is to integrate functions. Some compilers offer such a directive, but inasmuch as that directive is not uniformly distributed, and its application is problematic beyond the frontiers of a given module, the simplest approach is to handle this integration ourselves. To make the calls to a function "inlinable," we associate the function with a macro of the same name. We would thus define something like this:

```
(define-abbreviation (define-inline call . body)
  (let ((name      (car call))
        (variables (cdr call)) )
    `(begin
       (define-abbreviation (,name . arguments)
         (cons (cons 'lambda (cons ',variables ',body))
               arguments ) )
       (define ,call (,name . ,variables)) ) ) )
```

That macro suffers from portability problems itself because in some dialects, it is not possible to have a macro and a function of the same name simultaneously. In other dialects, that practice is allowed, and the second definition (the function) will completely replace the first (the macro) and in consequence, the macro will no longer be accessible. Anyway, it is nearly impossible for the function to be recursive without making the macro loop (though see [Bak92b] for more detail). Finally, when a function is inlined, it's best to avoid using it as a first class value (for example, as the first argument to **apply**) since that allows you not to define the associated function.

The preceding macro is easily inlined in multiple worlds since the definition of the function is merely expanded and in fact, expanded by means of the macro that precedes it. In the resulting expanded code, only the function appears in all its uses, while all the places where the macro of the same name is called will have been expanded—just the effect we were counting on.

9.9.1 Other Characteristics

The macros in Scheme R^{4}RS have four outstanding characteristics:

1. they are hygienic; (we'll get to that idea in Section 9.10);

2. they are defined by *filtering*;

3. they build the expanded macro by substitution;

4. they have no internal state.

The advantage of defining macros by filtering is that we can then very finely control the form that the call to the macro has to respect. Moreover, in writing the definition, we do not have to write the code for checking that conformity. For example, most macros where the last argument forms an implicit **begin** don't test whether the ultimate **cdr** is really (). That's automatically verified by a filter, and an error message is sent if need be. There are efficient compilers for filters, well described in the literature, such as [Que90b, QG92, WC94].

Construction by substitution is part of *backquoting* notation but it restricts computations to only those operations that can be carried out on lists. In particular, it does not support arithmetic operations. [see Ex. 9.2]

The fact that macros have no internal state is a little more inconvenient. Because of this lack, we cannot have contextual macros, like **define-class**, which should be able to keep the hierarchy of known classes updated so that we could find necessary information there when subclasses are introduced. We would like to know the names and number of inherited fields, for example.

Even so, you can imagine a macro, like **date**, that returns a character string indicating the current date at the time it is expanded. That macro could work like Walter Tichy's RCS or Eric Allman's SCCS to maintain versions of software.

9.9.2   Code Walking

Most macros that we write take one expression and return another that they build from the subterms of the first expression. Those are rather superficial macros that don't need to frisk the input expression. However, a macro that translates an infix arithmetic expression into a Lisp expression in prefix notation, for example, needs to analyze its argument more deeply. Let's take the case, for example, of the macro **with-slots** from CLOS; we'll adapt it to a MEROONET context. The fields of an object—let's say the fields of an instance of **Point**—are handled by read- and write-functions like **Point-x** or **set-Point-y!**. It would be simpler to handle them directly by the name of their fields, **x** or **y**, for example, in the context of defining a method. Similar to Smalltalk in [GR83], we could thus write this:

```
(define-handy-method (double (o Point))
  (set! x (* 2 x))
  (set! y (* 2 y))
  o )
```

in place of this:

```
(define-method (double (o Point))
  (set-Point-x! o (* 2 (Point-x o)))
  (set-Point-y! o (* 2 (Point-y o)))
  o )
```

The new macro, **define-handy-method**, thus must now check its own body to convert the references and assignments there to variables with the name of fields of the class being discriminated upon. To access these fields, we can use accessors that do not test whether their argument belongs to the class, since the fact that the argument belongs to the class is guaranteed by discrimination. In consequence, access is simpler and increasingly more efficient.

To produce these effects, we must first recall that the body of the method is not a program but rather an S-expression before macro expansion before analysis. For that reason, we must have access to the mechanism for macro expansion. Since macro expansion can give rise to local macros, we must also have access to the expander itself, the one that takes care of the original form. Without getting tangled up in the details, we'll assume that the expander is the value of the variable (whether local or global) named `macroexpand` and that it is always visible from the body of macros.

Once the body of `define-handy-method` has been expanded, then it's a real program, and at that point it has to be analyzed. Well, we've been analyzing programs since the beginning of this book; we do it by recognizing the special forms of the language that is being analyzed. We do not go off searching for references to fields in quotations; however, we must take into account binding forms that can hide fields. It's not too complicated a task to write a code walker, as in [Cur89, Wat93] [see p. 340]; what's hard is to recognize precisely the set of special forms in the language—or rather the implementation—that we're using.

Special forms are points of reference in an implementation, but an implementation sometimes has private features, such as:

- supplementary special forms (as with `let` or `letrec`) or hidden special forms belonging to the implementation (as with `define-class`);

- special forms implemented as macros (for example, with `begin`).

In the absence of reflective information about the language, it is difficult to get out of this dilemma because we have to ask, "How do we handle `begin` forms if they've disappeared? How do we find conditionals when `if` is a macro that expands into the special form `typecase`? How do we inspect an unknown special form like `define-class` when it involves substructures (such as definitions of fields) that systematically resemble functional applications? How do we guess that `bind-exit` is a special form establishing a binding that can hide a variable of the same name?"

A good compromise would be to freeze the set of special forms and forbid any more or fewer of them. Doing that means that the implementations that use special macros would not be able to do so in any phase later than macro expansion. However, lacking reflective information about the language and its implementations, we cannot write a portable code walker in Scheme, so we have to give up writing `define-handy-method`.

9.10 Unexpected Captures

In recent years, the idea of *hygiene* with respect to macros has been carefully studied in [KFFD86, BR88, CR91a]. An expanded macro contains symbols that are in some respects "free"; that is, they are unattached and thus susceptible to interference, either capturing or being captured with the context where the macro is used. Here's an example with both effects:

```
(define-abbreviation (acons key value alist)
  '(let ((f cons)) (f (f ,key ,value) ,alist)) )
(let ((cons list)
      (f    #f) )
  (acons 'false f '()) )
```

The reference to **cons** appearing in the expanded macro **acons** referring to our familiar **cons** is going to be captured by the local variable **cons** present in the **let** form surrounding the place where **acons** is called. Conversely, the expanded macro establishes a binding for the variable **f** which will prevent the second argument of the call to **acons** from taking the value **#f** would normally have taken. In short, the macro has intercepted the variable **f**. What a mess!

When we make macros *hygienic*, we automatically escape from such problems. Let's look at how those problems are conventionally handled.

For more than thirty years, users have been solving that second problem in Lisp simply by renaming. Specifically, the variable **f** which the expanded macro introduces must not interfere at all with the lexical environment where the macro is used. For that reason, we'll carry out an α-conversion and generate a new and inimitable **gensym** in order to protect that variable. Thus, quite serenely we'll write this:

```
(define-abbreviation (acons key value alist)
  (let ((f (gensym)))
    '(let ((,f cons)) (,f (,f ,key ,value) ,alist)) ) )
```

The first problem we mentioned—producing a free reference to **cons** in the expanded macro—is more complicated to handle. In the case of the present macro, what we want is for the writer of the macro to be able to specify that the reference to **cons** is the reference to the global variable **cons** and nothing else. In fact, the global variable **cons** was the one visible from the definition of the macro **acons**. From that observation we derive the first rule of macro hygiene: the free references in the expanded macro are those that were visible from the place where the macro was defined.

In the case of **cons** and in certain Lisp or Scheme systems, there is often a method to reference a global variable independently of the context; the method is equivalent to a form like **(global cons)** or **lisp:cons**. However, the following example will show you that we may also want to associate a local binding with a variable of an expanded macro.

```
(let ((results '())
      (compose cons) )
  (let-syntax ((push (syntax-rules ()
                       ((push e) (set! results (compose e results)))) )))
    π
    results ) )
```

In the entire body π of this expression, we want the local macro **push** to compose its argument with the contents of the variable **results** and assign **results** with that result. To be hygienic, we must insure that no other internal binding to π can modify the sense of **push**. Basically, then, there are two solutions:

1. rename all the internal variables in π so that **results** and **compose** are always visible and unambiguous there;

2. rename **results** and **compose** in a consistent way; that is, in **let** bindings, in the definition of **push**, and of course in the last expression of the body of **let**.

Even though we've talked about the "capture" of bindings, there is no such thing in hygienic macros. They don't capture bindings because bindings don't yet exist in hygienic macros since there we're still in the macro expansion phase! Even more strongly, R^4RS does not reserve keywords so it's possible to define a macro with the name of a special form. As a consequence, even the word **set!** apparently free in the expanded macro of **push** could be captured by a macro local to π. Thus we don't capture bindings, we capture meanings!

Macro hygiene is a remarkable and attractive property, but we can't adopt it whole-heartedly because there are important macros that are not in fact hygienic. The most popular example is the macro **loop**. We generally get out of it by means of the function **exit**. If we were to write this:

```
(define-syntax loop                              WRONG
  (syntax-rules ()      ; should be (exit) instead
    ((loop e1 e2 ...)
     (call/cc (lambda (exit)
                (let loop () e1 e2 ... (loop)) )) ) ) )
```

then we would never get out of the loop because the variable **exit** introduced in the expanded macro cannot be captured (because of hygiene!) by a reference to **exit** in any of the forms e1, e2, ... If **exit** appeared among those expressions, its intention would be to mention what **exit** indicates at its calling site. The solution is to mention that the symbol **exit** must remain free in the expanded result. To do that, we must put it into the parentheses that follow the word **syntax-rules**. By default, it's good for everything to be hygienic. This is precisely what we wanted for the **loop** variable: to be free of any captures. However, from time to time, we have to break our own rule about hygiene.

Many competitive implementations of hygienic macros are available on the net, and they are well worth reading. Our solution will won't use filtering; it will not limit the kind of computations that can be carried out within macros; but it corresponds to a low-level implementation that we find simpler than those appearing in the literature, such as [CR91b, DHB93]. Our implementation offers a new variation where we explicitly mention the words whose meaning we want to freeze. Here's an example: the form **with-aliases** will take a set of pairs, each made up of a variable and a word, as its first argument; *for the duration of the macro expansion*, it will bind these variables to the meaning that those words have in the current context. The preserved meaning of those words is accessible from those variables, and it can be inserted in the expanded macro. The following parameters make up the body of the form **with-aliases**; their role is to compute the expanded result. Thus we would rewrite the preceding example like this:

```
(let ((results '())
      (compose cons) )
  (with-aliases ((setq set!) (r results) (c compose))
    (let-abbreviation ( ( (push e)
                          `(,setq ,r (,c ,e ,r)) ) )
π
```

```
       results ) ) )
```

In contrast, the preceding `loop` macro would be defined like this:

```
(with-aliases ((cc call/cc)(lam lambda) (ll let))
  (define-abbreviation (loop . body)
    (let ((loop (gensym)))
      '(,cc (,lam (exit) (,ll ,loop () ,@body (,loop)))) ) ) )
```

In those two examples, all the terms that we want to freeze are mentioned in a **with-aliases** which captures their meaning. They are then inserted in the expanded results and are thus independent of the context where these macros are used.

Backquote notation is not really appropriate here because the proportion of variant elements is very high. This system of macros is rather low-level because it is not automatically hygienic; rather, it merely offers the tools for being hygienic. In the next section, we'll develop this system of macros further.

9.11   A Macro System

This section describes the implementation of a system of macros with the following functions:

- **define-abbreviation** to define a global macro;
- **let-abbreviation** to define a local macro;
- **eval-in-abbreviation-world** to evaluate something in the macro world;
- **with-aliases** to preserve a given meaning.

In order to show the difference between preparation and execution more clearly, we will expand programs and then transform them into objects on the fly. The resulting objects can be handled in either of two ways: they can be evaluated by a fast interpreter, as before in Chapter 6 [see p. 183]; or they can be compiled into C by the compiler in Chapter 10, [see p. 359]. Consequently, we expand them in only one pass, and the forms are frozen into objects as soon as they are expanded.

9.11.1   Objectification—Making Objects

Reification—which we've already used in another context—is not exactly the same thing as objectification. First of all, the program being compiled is converted into an object. During its conversion, its syntax will be checked and normalized so that syntax will not be a source of any other eventual errors. This transformation resembles rapid interpretation (the two have the same goal), but this time, we're working *ad hoc*. Instead of closures without arguments to contain all the necessary ingredients for their evaluation, this time, we will make objects that can be evaluated, thus showing how robust this transformation is; additionally, these objects can be handled more generally as well.

Here is the list of classes that we need for these objects:

```
(define-class Program Object ())
(define-class Reference Program (variable))
```

```
(define-class Local-Reference Reference ())
(define-class Global-Reference Reference ())
(define-class Predefined-Reference Reference ())
(define-class Global-Assignment Program (variable form))
(define-class Local-Assignment Program (reference form))
(define-class Function Program (variables body))
(define-class Alternative Program (condition consequent alternant))
(define-class Sequence Program (first last))
(define-class Constant Program (value) )
(define-class Application Program ())
(define-class Regular-Application Application (function arguments))
(define-class Predefined-Application Application (variable arguments))
(define-class Fix-Let Program (variables arguments body))
(define-class Arguments Program (first others))
(define-class No-Argument Program ())
(define-class Variable Object (name))
(define-class Global-Variable Variable ())
(define-class Predefined-Variable Variable (description))
(define-class Local-Variable Variable (mutable? dotted?))
```

In that list, you can see several points that we've already covered. For example, closed applications are treated specially. Calls to functions are identified. The class **Program** contains only elements that can be evaluated: references and assignments are there. In contrast, instances of variables representing bindings are not programs. They are instances of the class **Variable**. There are few idiosyncracies in these definitions of classes. Generally, they have as many fields as there are syntactic components. However, the class of local variables has two Booleans: one indicating whether or not the local variable is assigned, and another indicating how it is bound. In particular, **dotted?** variables receive special treatment before they receive a list of arguments.

We assume that **read** (or some other equivalent returning the S-expression that was read) reads the expression to compile. In fact, it would be smart to read an expression by means of **cons** with five fields to store in which file, which line, and which column the expression was read so that we could get excellent warning messages in case of errors. Moreover, symbols should have a supplementary field containing any possible associated macro; then searching for such a macro would be really fast. Augmenting symbols and dotted pairs with extra arguments during macro expansion is not too costly nor cumbersome since there won't be anything left around after expansion.

Thus we walk through this S-expression, as it's being read, to convert it into an object of the class **Program**. In passing, its macros are identified and expanded. The principal function, **objectify**, takes the lexical preparation environment as its second argument. Basically, given a form, it analyzes the term in function position and starts the appropriate treatment. Treatments are not tangled up with one another any more; rather, the right ones are located in the **handler** field of objects of the class **Magic-Keyword** (according to the terminology of [SS75]). The function **objectify** itself paves the way for handling macros; we'll explain it later.

```
(define-class Magic-Keyword Object (name handler))
(define (objectify e r)
  (if (atom? e)
      (cond ((Magic-Keyword? e) e)
            ((Program? e)        e)
            ((symbol? e)         (objectify-symbol e r))
            (else                (objectify-quotation e r)) )
      (let ((m (objectify (car e) r)))
        (if (Magic-Keyword? m)
            ((Magic-Keyword-handler m) e r)
            (objectify-application m (cdr e) r)) ) ) )
```

There's nothing left to explain except the various specialized subfunctions for conversion. Most of them simply build an object where the fields are initialized with the results of the recursive inspection of the subterms of the corresponding S-expression. That's certainly the case of **objectify-alternative** and **objectify-sequence**; **objectify-sequence** analyzes the initial forms in order to normalize it in binary sequences.

```
(define (objectify-quotation value r)
  (make-Constant value) )
(define (objectify-alternative ec et ef r)
  (make-Alternative (objectify ec r)
                    (objectify et r)
                    (objectify ef r) ) )
(define (objectify-sequence e* r)
  (if (pair? e*)
      (if (pair? (cdr e*))
          (let ((a (objectify (car e*) r)))
            (make-Sequence a (objectify-sequence (cdr e*) r)) )
          (objectify (car e*) r) )
      (make-Constant 42) ) )
```

The application is a little more complex since it must analyze the initial expression and categorize it as a closed application, a call to a predefined function, or a normal application. It categorizes on the basis of its analysis of the object corresponding to the term in the function position. The only obscure point here is one we've already mentioned, [see p. 200]: whether there is a description letting us know the arity of predefined functions and how to use it to compile them better. Later, we'll cover the class **Functional-Description** when we look at how to put in the predefined environment.

```
(define (objectify-application ff e* r)
  (let ((ee* (convert2arguments (map (lambda (e) (objectify e r)) e*))) )
    (cond ((Function? ff)
           (process-closed-application ff ee*) )
          ((Predefined-Reference? ff)
           (let* ((fvf (Predefined-Reference-variable ff))
                  (desc (Predefined-Variable-description fvf)) )
             (if (Functional-Description? desc)
                 (if ((Functional-Description-comparator desc)
                      (length e*) (Functional-Description-arity desc) )
```

```
                        (make-Predefined-Application fvf ee*)
                        (objectify-error
                          "Incorrect predefined arity" ff e* ) )
                    (make-Regular-Application ff ee*) ) ) )
            (else (make-Regular-Application ff ee*)) ) ) )
    (define (process-closed-application f e*)
      (let ((v* (Function-variables f))
            (b  (Function-body f)) )
        (if (and (pair? v*) (Local-Variable-dotted? (car (last-pair v*))))
            (process-nary-closed-application f e*)
            (if (= (number-of e*) (length (Function-variables f)))
                (make-Fix-Let (Function-variables f) e* (Function-body f))
                (objectify-error "Incorrect regular arity" f e*) ) ) ) )
```

The list of arguments is translated into a unique object (an instance of the class
Arguments); the list ends with an object from the class **No-Argument**. The number
of arguments can be determined by the generic function **number-of**.

```
    (define (convert2arguments e*)
      (if (pair? e*)
          (make-Arguments (car e*) (convert2arguments (cdr e*)))
          (make-No-Argument) ) )

    (define-generic (number-of (o)))
    (define-method (number-of (o Arguments))
      (+ 1 (number-of (Arguments-others o))) )
    (define-method (number-of (o No-Argument)) 0)
```

As usual, inside closed applications, we will distinguish the particular rare and
cumbersome case of applied n-ary functions. Supplementary arguments are organized into a list; thus we modify the associated dotted variable so that it becomes
normal again. [see p. 197]

```
    (define (process-nary-closed-application f e*)
        (let* ((v* (Function-variables f))
               (b  (Function-body f))
               (o (make-Fix-Let
                    v*
                    (let gather ((e* e*) (v* v*))
                       (if (Local-Variable-dotted? (car v*))
                           (make-Arguments
                             (let pack ((e* e*))
                               (if (Arguments? e*)
                                   (make-Predefined-Application
                                     (find-variable? 'cons g.predef)
                                     (make-Arguments
                                       (Arguments-first e*)
                                       (make-Arguments
                                         (pack (Arguments-others e*))
                                         (make-No-Argument) ) ) )
                                   (make-Constant '()) ) )
                             (make-No-Argument) )
                           (if (Arguments? e*)
```

```
                    (make-Arguments (Arguments-first e*)
                                     (gather (Arguments-others e*)
                                             (cdr v*) ) )
                    (objectify-error
                      "Incorrect dotted arity" f e* ) ) ) )
          b )) )
    (set-Local-Variable-dotted?! (car (last-pair v*)) #f)
    o ) )
```

Then we analyze abstractions and transform them by means of **objectify-function**. It uses **objectify-variables-list** to handle the list of variables and thus enrich the lexical environment in which the body of the function will be treated.

```
(define (objectify-function names body r)
  (let* ((vars (objectify-variables-list names))
         (b    (objectify-sequence body (r-extend* r vars)))) )
    (make-Function vars b) ) )
(define (objectify-variables-list names)
  (if (pair? names)
      (cons (make-Local-Variable (car names) #f #f)
            (objectify-variables-list (cdr names)) )
      (if (symbol? names)
          (list (make-Local-Variable names #f #t))
          '() ) ) )
```

Finally, **objectify-symbol** carefully handles variables. It searches for them in the unique, static, current, lexical environment: **r**. If the variable is not found there, the variable is added to the mutable global environment by the function **objectify-free-global-reference**. That is, we've adopted here a way of automatically defining new variables.

```
(define (objectify-symbol variable r)
  (let ((v (find-variable? variable r)))
    (cond ((Magic-Keyword? v)        v)
          ((Local-Variable? v)       (make-Local-Reference v))
          ((Global-Variable? v)      (make-Global-Reference v))
          ((Predefined-Variable? v) (make-Predefined-Reference v))
          (else (objectify-free-global-reference variable r)) ) ) )
(define (objectify-free-global-reference name r)
  (let ((v (make-Global-Variable name)))
    (insert-global! v r)
    (make-Global-Reference v) ) )
```

The environment **r** is more or less a list of local variables followed by global variables and then the predefined variables. The static environment does not contain the values of these variables, since the values result from subsequent evaluation. This environment is represented by a list of instances of **Environment**. It's possible to extend this environment by local variables or by new global variables. New global variables are appended physically to the global part of the environment; we know how to find it again with the function **find-global-environment**.

```
(define-class Environment Object (next))
```

```
(define-class Full-Environment Environment (variable))
(define (r-extend* r vars)
  (if (pair? vars)
      (r-extend (r-extend* r (cdr vars)) (car vars))
      r ) )
(define (r-extend r var)
  (make-Full-Environment r var) )
(define (find-variable? name r)
  (if (Full-Environment? r)
      (let ((var (Full-Environment-variable r)))
        (if (eq? name
                 (cond ((Variable? var) (Variable-name var))
                       ((Magic-Keyword? var)
                        (Magic-Keyword-name var) ) ) )
            var
            (find-variable? name (Full-Environment-next r)) ) )
      (if (Environment? r)
          (find-variable? name (Environment-next r))
          #f ) ) )
(define (insert-global! variable r)
  (let ((r (find-global-environment r)))
    (set-Environment-next!
     r (make-Full-Environment (Environment-next r) variable) ) ) )
(define (mark-global-preparation-environment g)
  (make-Environment g) )
(define (find-global-environment r)
  (if (Full-Environment? r)
      (find-global-environment (Full-Environment-next r))
      r ) )
```

The way assignment is handled takes the opportunity to annotate all the local variables that will be assigned later; it sets their **mutable?** field to True. That field will be used eventually in Chapter 10. [see p. 359]

```
(define (objectify-assignment variable e r)
  (let ((ov (objectify variable r))
        (of (objectify e r)) )
    (cond ((Local-Reference? ov)
           (set-Local-Variable-mutable?!
            (Local-Reference-variable ov) #t )
           (make-Local-Assignment ov of) )
          ((Global-Reference? ov)
           (make-Global-Assignment (Global-Reference-variable ov) of) )
          (else (objectify-error
                 "Illegal mutated reference" variable )) ) ) )
```

When the initial expression is transformed into an object, it is simple to write an evaluator to interpret this object in a way that verifies the translation procedure. The evaluator resembles those presented in the preceding chapters, especially the one for objects in Chapter 3 crossed with the one for rapid interpretation in Chapter 6 [see **p. 183**].

Let's take a look at the general outline of this evaluator so that it will be more
or less transparent in what follows. Evaluation is managed by the generic function
evaluate. It takes two arguments: the first is an instance of **Program** and the
second an instance of **Environment** (a kind of A-list of pairs made up of variables
and values). The initial environment contains only predefined variables. Its static
part is the value of **g.predef** while its dynamic part is the value of **sg.predef**.
That dynamic part associates instances of **RunTime-Primitive** with predefined
functional variables. The execution environment can be extended by **sr-extend**.

9.11.2   Special Forms

The preceding translator doesn't recognize special forms, so for each one of them,
we have to indicate how to transform it into an instance of **Program**. We'll associate
an appropriate code walker with each keyword. That inspector will simply call one
of the preceding functions, all built on the same model.

```
(define special-if
  (make-Magic-Keyword
   'if (lambda (e r)
         (objectify-alternative (cadr e) (caddr e) (cadddr e) r) ) ) )
(define special-begin
  (make-Magic-Keyword
   'begin (lambda (e r)
            (objectify-sequence (cdr e) r) ) ) )
(define special-quote
  (make-Magic-Keyword
   'quote (lambda (e r)
            (objectify-quotation (cadr e) r) ) ) )
(define special-set!
  (make-Magic-Keyword
   'set! (lambda (e r)
            (objectify-assignment (cadr e) (caddr e) r) ) ) )
(define special-lambda
  (make-Magic-Keyword
   'lambda (lambda (e r)
              (objectify-function (cadr e) (cddr e) r) ) ) )
```

Of course, we could define other special forms that we would add to the preceding magic keywords to form the list ***special-form-keywords***.

```
(define *special-form-keywords*
  (list special-quote
        special-if
        special-begin
        special-set!
        special-lambda
        ;; cond, letrec, etc.
        special-let
        ) )
```

9.11.3 Evaluation Levels

We've already seen that endogenous macro expansion hides an evaluator inside. Here we need to remember that the result of objectification is not necessarily evaluated afterwards in the same memory space. In fact, Chapter 10 [see p. 359], about compiling into C, will show just that. Since we don't want to confuse these various evaluators, we'll introduce a tower of evaluators and assume the purest hypothesis, where all the evaluators are distinct: the language, the macro language, the macro language of the macro language, and so forth, will all have different global environments. These evaluators will be represented by instances of the class **Evaluator** which defines their principal characteristics.

```
(define-class Evaluator Object
  ( mother
    Preparation-Environment
    RunTime-Environment
    eval
    expand
  ) )
```

What follows is quite complex. Figure 9.9 illustrates the distinct environments that come into play. The expansion function at one level uses the evaluation function of the next level, but that one itself begins by analyzing the expressions it receives and thus by expanding them. We'll avoid infinite regression that might result from one level expanding an expansion already stripped of macros; in that case, there would be no need of the next level. Generally, two or three levels suffice. Each level has a preparation environment (for **expand**) and an execution environment (for **eval**)—except perhaps the "ground floor" where we use only the expander.

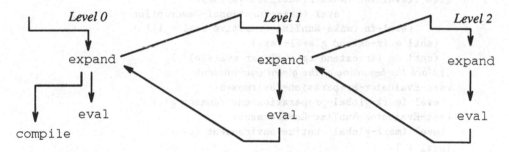

Figure 9.9 Tower of evaluators

The function **create-evaluator** builds the levels of the tower one by one on demand. It builds a new level above the one it receives as an argument. It creates a pair of functions, **expand** and **eval**, along with two environments: preparation and execution. The function **eval** systematically expands its argument before evaluating it; **eval** does that by means of an evaluation engine named **evaluate**. The only thing we have to say about **evaluate** is that it needs only the execution environment, the one saved in the field **RunTime-Environment** of the current instance of **Evaluator**, one that it modifies physically if need be. The expansion function uses the objectification engine of **objectify** with a preparation environment; that preparation environment is stored in the field **Preparation-Environment** of the current instance of **Evaluator**. To simplify our lives, the global variables discovered during expansion are *ipso facto* created in the associated execution environment by means of the function **enrich-with-new-global-variables!**. The function **eval** is installed reflectively in its own execution environment like a predefined primitive, so there is a different **eval** at each level. The preparation environment is extended by all the special forms accumulated in the variable ***special-form-keywords***. That variable must be visible at every level. The preparation environment is also extended by predefined macros that result from the call to (**make-macro-environment level**), which we'll document later.

```
(define (create-evaluator old-level)
  (let ((level 'wait)
        (g      g.predef)
        (sg     sg.predef) )
    (define (expand e)
      (let ((prg (objectify
                    e (Evaluator-Preparation-Environment level) )))
        (enrich-with-new-global-variables! level)
        prg ) )
    (define (eval e)
      (let ((prg (expand e)))
        (evaluate prg (Evaluator-RunTime-Environment level)) ) )
    ;; Create resulting evaluator instance
    (set! level (make-Evaluator old-level 'wait 'wait eval expand))
    ;; Enrich environment with eval
    (set! g (r-extend* g *special-form-keywords*))
    (set! g (r-extend* g (make-macro-environment level)))
    (let ((eval-var (make-Predefined-Variable
                       'eval (make-Functional-Description = 1 "") ))
          (eval-fn (make-RunTime-Primitive eval = 1)) )
      (set! g (r-extend g eval-var))
      (set! sg (sr-extend sg eval-var eval-fn)) )
    ;; Mark the beginning of the global environment
    (set-Evaluator-Preparation-Environment!
     level (mark-global-preparation-environment g) )
    (set-Evaluator-RunTime-Environment!
     level (mark-global-runtime-environment sg) )
    level ) )
```

If we need an expander or an evaluator, all we have to do is invoke the function **create-evaluator** and retrieve the **expand** or **eval** function we want simply by reading the fields. Careful: in contrast to a conventional expander, the function **expand** returns an instance of **Program**, not a Scheme expression. A simple conversion function will get us such an expression, if we want it. [see **Ex. 9.4**]

9.11.4 The Macros

According to our plan, predefined macros have already been added to the preparation environment. They were synthesized by the function **make-macro-environ-**

ment. The four predefined macros are `eval-in-abbreviation-world`, `define-abbreviation`, `let-abbreviation`, and `with-aliases`. They all assume the existence of an evaluator belonging to the level above that the function `make-macro-environment` has to create. However, to avoid infinite regression, creating a level above is just a promise that won't be carried out unless the associated evaluator is actually invoked. [see **Ex. 9.3**] Once a supplementary level has been created, it will not be recreated; instead, it endures and accumulates all the definitions that it receives.

```
(define (make-macro-environment current-level)
  (let ((metalevel (delay (create-evaluator current-level))))
    (list (make-Magic-Keyword 'eval-in-abbreviation-world
            (special-eval-in-abbreviation-world metalevel) )
          (make-Magic-Keyword 'define-abbreviation
            (special-define-abbreviation metalevel))
          (make-Magic-Keyword 'let-abbreviation
            (special-let-abbreviation metalevel))
          (make-Magic-Keyword 'with-aliases
            (special-with-aliases metalevel) ) ) ) )
```

The macro `eval-in-abbreviation-world` is the simplest because it merely evaluates its body with the evaluator from the level above. It demands that the level above be constructed only if need be. Like any macro, the result submitted anew to the objectification function of the current level.

```
(define (special-eval-in-abbreviation-world level)
  (lambda (e r)
    (let ((body (cdr e)))
      (objectify ((Evaluator-eval (force level))
                  `(,special-begin . ,body) )
        r ) ) ) )
```

The macro `define-abbreviation` creates and modifies global macros. The associated expander is created and then evaluated at the level above; a new magic keyword is created in the global preparation environment of the current level. The function `invoke` is a different means from `evaluate` for starting the evaluation engine. When a macro is invoked by `invoke`, it begins its calculations in the execution environment of the level above, wrapped up in the closure of the expander. The result of such a macro is, here, `#t`. We could have returned the name of the macro being defined, but that would have meant a few bytes of extra garbage (that is, a symbol).

```
(define (special-define-abbreviation level)
  (lambda (e r)
    (let* ((call     (cadr e))
           (body     (cddr e))
           (name     (car call))
           (variables (cdr call)) )
      (let ((expander ((Evaluator-eval (force level))
                       `(,special-lambda ,variables . ,body) )))
        (define (handler e r)
          (objectify (invoke expander (cdr e)) r) )
        (insert-global! (make-Magic-Keyword name handler) r)
```

```
(objectify #t r) ) ) ) )
```

We can create local macros in a similar way. The difference is that these magic keywords are inserted in front of the preparation environment at the current level in order to maintain local scope.

```
(define (special-let-abbreviation level)
  (lambda (e r)
    (let ((level  (force level))
          (macros (cadr e))
          (body   (cddr e)) )
      (define (make-macro def)
        (let* ((call      (car def))
               (body      (cdr def))
               (name      (car call))
               (variables (cdr call)) )
          (let ((expander ((Evaluator-eval level)
                            `(,special-lambda ,variables . ,body) )))
            (define (handler e r)
              (objectify (invoke expander (cdr e)) r) )
            (make-Magic-Keyword name handler) ) ) )
      (objectify `(,special-begin . ,body)
                 (r-extend* r (map make-macro macros)) ) ) ) )
```

The most complex of the four predefined macros is **with-aliases** because it has multiple effects. It must capture the meaning of a number of words in the current expander. It must bind those meanings to variables for the evaluator at the level above during the expansion of its body. This interaction among the scope, the duration, and the levels makes this one so complex.

```
(define (special-with-aliases level)
  (lambda (e current-r)
    (let* ((level   (force level))
           (oldr    (Evaluator-Preparation-Environment level))
           (oldsr   (Evaluator-RunTime-Environment level))
           (aliases (cadr e))
           (body    (cddr e)) )
      (let bind ((aliases aliases)
                 (r        oldr)
                 (sr       oldsr) )
        (if (pair? aliases)
            (let* ((variable (car (car aliases)))
                   (word     (cadr (car aliases)))
                   (var      (make-Local-Variable variable #f #f)) )
              (bind (cdr aliases)
                    (r-extend r var)
                    (sr-extend sr var (objectify word current-r)) ) )
            (let ((result 'wait))
              (set-Evaluator-Preparation-Environment! level r)
              (set-Evaluator-RunTime-Environment! level sr)
              (set! result (objectify `(,special-begin . ,body)
                                      current-r ))
              (set-Evaluator-Preparation-Environment! level oldr)
```

```
        (set-Evaluator-RunTime-Environment! level oldsr)
        result ) ) ) ) ) )
```

Modifying the execution environment of the level above would be better accommodated by a dynamic binding in order to be sure that the right execution environment will be restored after the expansion of the body of the form with-aliases.

The variables bound by with-aliases have as their values the results of the function objectify, that is, instances of Program or Magic-Keyword. Since these instances can appear in the result of a macro expansion, the function objectify must be able to recognize these cases in the expressions that it handles. For that reason, the function objectify begins by testing whether the expression it received is a magic keyword or a program already objectified. [see p. 345]

9.11.5 Limits

Following the rules of macro hygiene lets us play around statically with words and bindings, to capture a meaning and use it in contexts where it would not be visible otherwise, even in places where it should not be usable otherwise. For example, we can write this:

```
(let ((count 0))
  (with-aliases ((c count))
    (define-abbreviation (tick) c) )
  (tick) )
(let ((count 1)(c 2))
  (tick) )
```

The global macro tick refers to the local variable count which is no longer visible from the second calling site of the macro tick. Indeed, we get a new kind of error that way: a reference to a non-existing variable, even if a variable of the same name (like count) appears in the calling environment of tick! You can see the same thing again more clearly in the equivalent "de-objectified" form:

```
((LAMBDA (COUNT501)
    (BEGIN #T ;; (tick) ↝ count501
        COUNT501 ))
  0 )
((LAMBDA (COUNT502 C503) COUNT501) 1 2)
```

We have to choose the position of with-aliases carefully because it is a kind of let for the evaluator at the level above. If we wrote this:

```
(define-abbreviation (loop . body)
  (with-aliases ((cc call/cc)(lam lambda) (ll let))
    (let ((loop (gensym)))
      '(,cc (,lam (exit) (,ll ,loop () ,@body (,loop)))) ) ) )
```

then the meanings captured here are caught at the level of the macro definition, and thus they are valid only in the world of macros of macros. In practice, with-aliases appears in define-abbreviation and is thus evaluated in the world of macros when the abbreviation loop gets into the normal world. The variable cc is bound in the macro world to the meaning that the word call/cc has there. A call to the macro loop will lead to an error of the type "cc: unknown variable."

With the exception of keywords for special forms or other keywords like `else` or `=>`, the meaning of local or global variables could have been captured by first class environments and the special forms `import` and `export`. [see p. 296] However, here the mechanism we used is more powerful since it can also capture the essence of keywords for special forms and especially because it is static rather than dynamic.

The macro mechanism we've defined here allows predefined macros to be written, ones that the end user could not write, like, for example, macros creating global variables by direct use of the function `insert-global!`.

Nevertheless, this system has its imperfections. If the user wants to run through the macro expanded expressions, he or she will encounter at least two problems. First, the function `expand` has not been made visible. One way of making it visible is for `expand` at one level to be the value of a variable at the next higher level so that `(eval-in-abbreviation-world (expand '$\varepsilon$))` would be identical to ε. Second, we have to know the structure of subclasses of `Program` if we want to walk through these objects.

One of the goals of this system of macros was to show that hygienic macro expansion and compilation are tightly linked since they take advantage of an important common basis. In the preceding code, if we take out those parts connected with evaluation and with objectification strictly speaking, there is nothing left that depends specifically on macro expansion except the function `objectify`, the function `objectify-symbol`, and the functions connected to the four predefined macros. That's only about a hundred lines—very little, in fact.

A real macro system would have many other details to pin down:

1. how to program essential syntax, like `or`, `and`, `letrec`, internal `define`, etc.;

2. how to program the notation for *backquote*, intertwined as it is with expansion and objectification;

3. how to allow macro-symbols in order to resolve the problem we saw earlier in `define-handy-method`. [see p. 340]

However, we did attain the goal we first set: to introduce the idea of capturing a meaning.

9.12   Conclusions

We can summarize the problems connected to macros in two points: they are indispensible, but there are no two compatible systems. They exist in practice in many possible and divergent implementations. We've tried to survey the entire range. Few reference manuals for Lisp or Scheme indicate precisely which model for macros they provide, but in their defense we have to admit that this chapter is probably the first document to attempt to describe the immense variety of possible macro behavior.

9.13   Exercises

Exercise 9.1 : Define the macro `repeat` given at the beginning of this chapter. Make it hygienic.

Exercise 9.2 : Use `define-syntax` to define a macro taking a sequence of expressions as its argument and printing their numeric order between them. For example, (`enumerate` π_1 π_2 ... π_n) should expand into something that when evaluated will print 0, then calculate π_1, print 1, calculate π_2, etc.

Exercise 9.3 : Modify the macro system to implement the variation corresponding to a uniquely unique world.

Exercise 9.4 : Write a function to convert an instance of **Program** into an equivalent S-expression.

Exercise 9.5 : Study the programs that define MEROONET [see p. 417] to see what belongs to the expansion library, what to the execution library, what to both.

Recommended Reading

In [Gra93], you will find a very interesting apology for macros. There are more theoretical articles like [QP90]. Others, like [KFFD86, DFH88, CR91a, QP91b], focus more on the problems of hygienic expansion. There is a new and promising model of expansion in [dM95].

10
Compiling into C

O NCE again, here's a chapter about compilation, but this time, we'll look at new techniques, notably, flat environments, and we have a new target language: C. This chapter takes up a few of the problems of this odd couple. This strange marriage has certain advantages, like free optimizations of the compilation at a very low level or freely and widely available libraries of immense size. However, there are some thorns among the roses, such as the fact that we can no longer guarantee tail recursion, and we have a hard time with garbage collection.

Compiling into a high-level language like C is interesting in more ways than one. Since the target language is so rich, we can hope for a translation that is closer to the original than would be some shapeless, linear salmagundi. Since C is available on practically any machine, the code we produce has a good chance of being portable. Moreover, any optimizations that such a compiler can achieve are automatically and implicitly available to us. This fact is particularly important in the case of C, where there are compilers that carry out a great many optimizations with respect to allocating registers, laying out code, or choosing modes of address—all things that we could ignore when we focused on only one source language.

On the other hand, choosing a high-level language as the target imposes certain philosophic and pragmatic constraints as well. Such a language is typically designed for a particular style of program without supposing that such programs might be generated by other programs. In consequence, certain limits, like at most 32 arguments in function calls, or less than 16 levels of lexical blocks, and so forth, may be almost tolerable for normal users, but they are quite problematic for automatically generated programs. It is not unusual for a problem blessed with a few macros to multiple its size by 5, 10, or 20 times when it is translated into C. Such an increase can pose problems for a compiler unaccustomed to such monsters.

Moreover, the execution model of the target language may have little to do with the execution model of the source language, and that, too, can limit or complicate the translation from one to the other. C was designed as a language for writing an operating system (namely, UN*X), so by deliberate policy, it explicitly manages memory. That fact can lead to all sorts of excesses, such as pointers running amuck in the sense that the programmer loses all control over them—a situation that does not arise with Lisp, which is a safe language in that respect.

In addition, C is not particularly adapted to writing functional programs nor recursive programs either because calling a function there is notoriously expensive. Programmers generally dislike its slowness for that and consequently use it as little as possible, a practice that justifies the implementers in not trying to improve it since they know that programmers seldom use it because it's slow, etc.

Be that as it may, compiling into C is in fashion now, as witnessed by Kyoto COMMON LISP in [YH85], and refined somewhat in AKCL by William Schelter, or WCL in [Hen92b], or CLICC in [Hof93], or EcoLisp in [Att95], or Scheme→C in [Bar89], or Sqil in [Sén91], or ILOG TALK in [ILO94], or Bigloo in [Ser94].

What we'll present is no rival to those. It's just a skeleton of a compiler, but it will suffice to show you a great number of interesting points. A simple solution (some would even say a trivial one) would be to change the byte-code generator we saw in Chapter 7 [see p. 223] just enough to make it generate C. Each instruction byte could be expanded into a few appropriate C instructions. However, we're going to take a completely different path, using the technique of flat environments that we alluded to earlier. [see p. 202] This new compiler will be partitioned into passes, most of which will be produced by specialized code walkers. This technique is based on a systematic use of objects to represent and transform the code to compile. In fact, we think this systematic use of objects will make this chapter particularly elegant and easy to extend.

10.1 Objectification

We've already presented a converter from programs into objects in Section 9.11.1, [see p. 344]. It takes care of any possible macro expansions that might be found and it returns an instance of the class **Program**. To fill out that curt description, we offer the illustration in Figure 10.1 of one result of that phase of objectification. In that illustration, we'll use the following expression, which contains at least one example of every aspect we studied. For the sake of brevity, the names of classes have been abbreviated; only one part of the example appears in the figure; lists have been put into giant parentheses. We'll come back to this example in what follows.

```
(begin
  (set! index 1)
  ((lambda (cnter . tmp)
     (set! tmp (cnter (lambda (i) (lambda x (cons i x)))))
     (if cnter (cnter tmp) index) )
   (lambda (f)
     (set! index (+ 1 index))
     (f index) )
   'foo ) )    → (2 3)
```

10.2 Code Walking

Code walking, as in [Cur89, Wat93], is an important technique. It consists of traversing a tree that represents a program to compile and enriching it with various annotations to prepare the ultimate phase, that is, code generation. Depending on what we want to establish, we may favor various schemes for traversing the tree and various ways of collecting information. In short, there is no universal code walker! The evaluators in this book are rather special code walkers; so are precompilation functions like **meaning** in the chapter about fast interpretation [see p. 207].

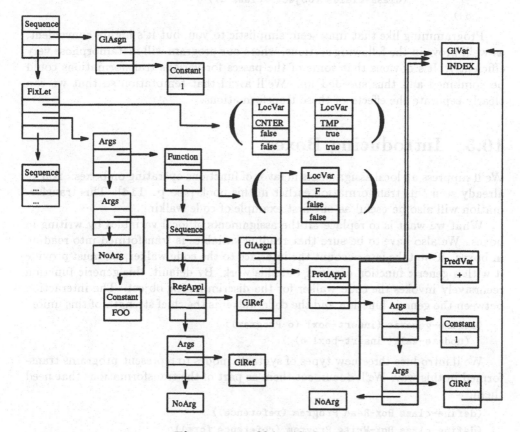

Figure 10.1 Objectified code

We're going to define only one code walker; it systematically modifies the tree that we provide it. To begin, it will be an excellent example of a *metamethod*. The function **update-walk!** takes these arguments: a generic function, an object of the class **Program**, and possibly supplementary arguments. It replaces each field of the object containing an instance of the class **Program** by the result of applying that generic function to the value of that field. Its return value is the initial object. To do all that, each object is inspected; the fields of its class are extracted one by one, verified, and recursively analyzed to see whether they belong to the class **Program**. You can see now why the class **Arguments** (which of course represents the arguments of an instance of **Application**) inherit from the class **Program**: they have to be available for inspection by a code walker.

```
(define (update-walk! g o . args)
  (for-each (lambda (field)
```

```
          (let ((vf (field-value o field)))
            (when (Program? vf)
                (let ((v (if (null? args) (g vf)
                             (apply g vf args) )))
                   (set-field-value! o v field) ) ) ) )
          (Class-fields (object->class o)) )
     o )
```

Programming like that may seem simplistic to you, but it's highly convenient, as we'll prove in the following sections, where our program will metamorphose very efficiently. It's obvious that some of the passes for various transformations could be combined and thus speeded up. We'll avoid that temptation so that we can clearly separate the effects of these transformations.

10.3   Introducing Boxes

We'll suppress all local assignments in favor of functions operating on boxes. You've already seen this transformation earlier in this book [see p. 114]. This transformation will also be useful as our first example of code walking.

What we want is to replace all the assignments of local variables by writing in boxes. We also have to be sure that reading variables is transformed into reading in boxes. If we take into account the interface to the code walker, we must provide it with a generic function carrying out this work. By default, this generic function recursively invokes the code walker for the discriminating object. The interaction between the generic function and the code walker is the chief strength of this union.

```
(define-generic (insert-box! (o Program))
  (update-walk! insert-box! o) )
```

We'll introduce three new types of syntactic nodes to represent programs transformed in this way. We'll document them as part of the transformations that need them.

```
(define-class Box-Read Program (reference))
(define-class Box-Write Program (reference form))
(define-class Box-Creation Program (variable))
```

Quite fortunately for us, during objectification, we've taken care to mark all the mutable local variables by their field **mutable?**. Consequently, transforming a read of a mutable variable into an instance of **Box-Read** is easy.

```
(define-method (insert-box! (o Local-Reference))
  (if (Local-Variable-mutable? (Local-Reference-variable o))
      (make-Box-Read o)
      o ) )
```

Transforming assignments is equally easy. A local assignment is transformed into an instance of **Box-Write**. However, we must take into account the structure of the algorithm for code walking, so we must not forget to call the code walker recursively on the form providing the new value of the assigned variable.

```
(define-method (insert-box! (o Local-Assignment))
  (make-Box-Write (Local-Assignment-reference o)
```

```
(insert-box! (Local-Assignment-form o)) ) )
```

Once every access (whether read or write) to mutable variables has been transformed to occur within boxes, the only thing left to do is to create those boxes. Local mutable variables can be created only by **lambda** or **let** forms, that is, by **Function** or **Fix-Let**[1] nodes. The technique is to insert an appropriate way to "put it in a box" in front of the body of such forms. [see p. 114] So here is how to specialize the function **insert-box!** for the two types of nodes that might introduce mutable local variables. They both depend on a subfunction to insert as many instances of **Box-Creation** in front of their body as there are mutable local variables for which boxes must be allocated.

```
(define-method (insert-box! (o Function))
  (set-Function-body!
   o (insert-box!
      (boxify-mutable-variables (Function-body o)
                                (Function-variables o) ) ) )
   o )
(define-method (insert-box! (o Fix-Let))
  (set-Fix-Let-arguments! o (insert-box! (Fix-Let-arguments o)))
  (set-Fix-Let-body!
   o (insert-box!
      (boxify-mutable-variables (Fix-Let-body o)
                                (Fix-Let-variables o) ) ) )
   o )
(define (boxify-mutable-variables form variables)
  (if (pair? variables)
      (if (Local-Variable-mutable? (car variables))
          (make-Sequence
           (make-Box-Creation (car variables))
           (boxify-mutable-variables form (cdr variables)) )
          (boxify-mutable-variables form (cdr variables)) )
      form ) )
```

With that, the transformation is complete and has been specified in only four methods, focused solely on the forms that are important for transformations. You can see the result in Figure 10.2, representing only the subparts of the previous figure that have changed.

10.4 Eliminating Nested Functions

As a language, C does not support functions inside other functions. In other words, a **lambda** inside another **lambda** cannot be translated directly. Consequently, we must eliminate these cases in a way that turns the program to compile into a simple set of closed functions, that is, functions without free variables. Once again, we're lucky to find such a natural transformation. We'll call it **lambda**-*lifting* because it makes **lambda** forms migrate toward the exterior in such a way that there are no remaining **lambda** forms in the interior. Many variations on this transformation

---

1. Even though we have not identified reducible applications, we could at least have a method to handle them.

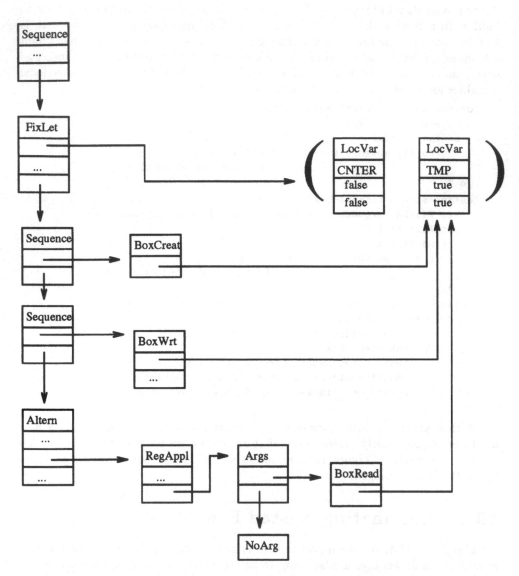

Figure 10.2 (lambda (cnter . tmp) (set! tmp ...) (if ... (...tmp) ...))

are possible, depending on the qualities we want to preserve or promote, as in [WS94, KH89, CH94].

Evaluating a `lambda` form leads to synthesizing a closure, a kind of record that encloses its definition environment. When a closure is invoked, a special function (that we have named `invoke`) knows how to evaluate the body of this closure by providing it the means to retrieve the values of free variables present in the body. In fact, only the invoker knows how to invoke closures, so we can replace these closures by records without disturbing the rest of the program on condition that every functional application passes by the generic invoker, `invoke`, the one that knows how to do this.

Let's look at an example illustrating the variation known as *OO-lifting* in [Que94]. As usual, we'll use our familiar guinea pig, the factorial function, like this:

```
(define (fact n k)
  (if (= n 0) (k 1)
      (fact (- n 1) (lambda (r) (k (* n r)))) ) )
```

We can translate it to eliminate the internal `lambda` form enclosing the variables n and k, like this:

```
(define-class Fact-Closure Object (n k))
(define-method (invoke (f Fact-Closure) r)
  (invoke (Fact-Closure-k f) (* (Fact-Closure-n f) r)) )
(define (fact n k)
  (if (= n 0) (invoke k 1)
      (fact (- n 1) (make-Fact-Closure n k)) ) )
```

The essence of the transformation is to replace the way the closure is built by an allocation of an object (`make-Fact-Closure`) containing the free variables of the body of the closure (here, n and k). A particular class is associated with this object (here, `Fact-Closure`) so that `invoke` can determine which method to use when this object is invoked.

The basis of the transformation is, for each abstraction (`Function`), to calculate the set of free variables present in its body. A new class—`Flat-Function`, refining `Function`—will store that information. The collection of free variables will be represented by instances of the class `Free-Environment` and will be ended by `No-Free`. These two classes are similar to the classes `Arguments` and `No-Argument`: they also derive from `Program`, since they also represent terms that can be evaluated. We'll also identify references to these free variables by a particular class of reference: `Free-Reference`.

```
(define-class Flat-Function Function (free))
(define-class Free-Environment Program (first others))
(define-class No-Free Program ())
(define-class Free-Reference Reference ())
```

To make this transformation work, the code walker will help out again. The function `lift!` is the interface for the entire treatment. The generic function `lift-procedures!` serves as the argument to the code walker. It takes two supplementary arguments itself: the abstraction `flatfun` in which the free variables are stored and the list of current bound variables in the variable **vars**. By default, the code walker is called recursively for all the instances of **Program**.

```
(define (lift! o)
  (lift-procedures! o #f '()) )
(define-generic (lift-procedures! (o Program) flatfun vars)
  (update-walk! lift-procedures! o flatfun vars) )
```

Only three methods are needed for the transformation. The first identifies the references to free variables, transforms them, and collects them in the current abstraction. The function **adjoin-free-variable** adds any free variable that is not yet one of the free variables already identified in the current abstraction.

```
(define-method (lift-procedures! (o Local-Reference) flatfun vars)
  (let ((v (Local-Reference-variable o)))
    (if (memq v vars)
        o (begin (adjoin-free-variable! flatfun o)
                 (make-Free-Reference v) ) ) ) )
(define (adjoin-free-variable! flatfun ref)
  (when (Flat-Function? flatfun)
    (let check ((free* (Flat-Function-free flatfun)))
      (if (No-Free? free*)
          (set-Flat-Function-free!
           flatfun (make-Free-Environment
                    ref (Flat-Function-free flatfun) ) )
          (unless (eq? (Reference-variable ref)
                       (Reference-variable
                        (Free-Environment-first free*) ) )
            (check (Free-Environment-others free*)) ) ) ) ) )
```

The form **Fix-Let** creates new bindings that might hide others. Consequently, we must add the variables of **Fix-Let** to the current bound variables before we analyze its body. At that point, it is very useful to save the reducible applications as such because it would be very costly to build these closures at execution time.

```
(define-method (lift-procedures! (o Fix-Let) flatfun vars)
  (set-Fix-Let-arguments!
   o (lift-procedures! (Fix-Let-arguments o) flatfun vars) )
  (let ((newvars (append (Fix-Let-variables o) vars)))
    (set-Fix-Let-body!
     o (lift-procedures! (Fix-Let-body o) flatfun newvars) )
    o ) )
```

Finally, the most complicated case is how to treat an abstraction. The body of the abstraction will be analyzed, and an instance of **Flat-Function** will be allocated to serve as the receptacle for any free variables discovered there. Since the free variables found there can also be free variables in the surrounding abstraction, the code walker is started again on this list of free variables which have been cleverly coded as a subclass of **Program**.

```
(define-method (lift-procedures! (o Function) flatfun vars)
  (let* ((localvars (Function-variables o))
         (body    (Function-body o))
         (newfun (make-Flat-Function localvars body (make-No-Free))) )
```

```
(set-Flat-Function-body!
 newfun (lift-procedures! body newfun localvars) )
(let ((free* (Flat-Function-free newfun)))
  (set-Flat-Function-free!
   newfun (lift-procedures! free* flatfun vars) ) )
newfun ) )
```

As usual, we'll show you the partial effect of this transformation on the current example in Figure 10.3.

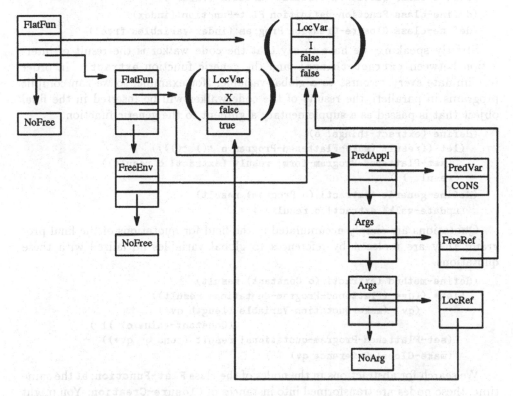

Figure 10.3 (lambda (i) (lambda x ...))

10.5 Collecting Quotations and Functions

The preceding transformation left functions in place since syntactically there were still closed **lambda** forms (that is, ones with no more free variables) inside other **lambda** forms. In doing that, however, we were merely temporizing to get a jump on the problem! The next code walker will extract quotations and definitions of functions from a program in order to put them at a higher level. We'll need only two special methods to do that.

The function **extract-things!** will transform a program into an instance of **Flattened-Program**, a specialization of the class **Program**, one provided with three supplementary fields: **form** containing the program to evaluate; **quotations**,

the list of quotations, of course; and **definitions**, the list of function definitions. Quotations will be handled by references to global variables of a new class:
Quotation-Variable. Functions will be organized by their order number, an integer, **index**. Finally, the creation of a closure will be translated by a new syntactic
node: **Closure-Creation**. (Very soon a lot of details will all become clearer at the
same time.)

```
(define-class Flattened-Program Program (form quotations definitions))
(define-class Quotation-Variable Variable (value))
(define-class Function-Definition Flat-Function (index))
(define-class Closure-Creation Program (index variables free))
```

Strictly speaking, we have to say that the code walker is the result of interaction between **extract-things!** and the generic function **extract!**. In order
to eliminate every recourse to a global variable, (for example, so we can compile
programs in parallel), the results of the code walker will be inserted in the final
object that is passed as a supplementary argument to the generic function.

```
(define (extract-things! o)
  (let ((result (make-Flattened-Program o '() '())))
    (set-Flattened-Program-form! result (extract! o result))
    result ) )
(define-generic (extract! (o Program) result)
  (update-walk! extract! o result) )
```

Quotations are simply accumulated in the field for quotations of the final program; they are replaced by references to global variables initialized with these
quotations.

```
(define-method (extract! (o Constant) result)
  (let* ((qv* (Flattened-Program-quotations result))
         (qv  (make-Quotation-Variable (length qv*)
                                       (Constant-value o) )) )
    (set-Flattened-Program-quotations! result (cons qv qv*))
    (make-Global-Reference qv) ) )
```

We search for abstractions in the nodes of the class **Flat-Function**; at the same
time, these nodes are transformed into instances of **Closure-Creation**. You might
also imagine sharing those same abstractions; that is, we could make **adjoin-def-
inition!** a memo-function. One point that might seem strange is that when we
build the closure, we save the list of variables from the original abstraction. We
will save it to make the computation of the arity of the closure easier when we
generate C.

```
(define-method (extract! (o Flat-Function) result)
  (let* ((newbody   (extract! (Flat-Function-body o) result))
         (variables (Flat-Function-variables o))
         (freevars  (let extract ((free (Flat-Function-free o)))
                      (if (Free-Environment? free)
                          (cons (Reference-variable
                                 (Free-Environment-first free) )
                                (extract
                                 (Free-Environment-others free) ) )
                          '() ) ))
```

```
            (index (adjoin-definition!
                    result variables newbody freevars )) )
        (make-Closure-Creation index variables (Flat-Function-free o)) ) ) )
    (define (adjoin-definition! result variables body free)
      (let* ((definitions (Flattened-Program-definitions result))
             (newindex (length definitions)) )
        (set-Flattened-Program-definitions!
         result (cons (make-Function-Definition
                        variables body free newindex )
                      definitions ) )
        newindex ) )
```

Again, to illustrate the results of this transformation, you can see a few choice extracts from the example in Figure 10.4.

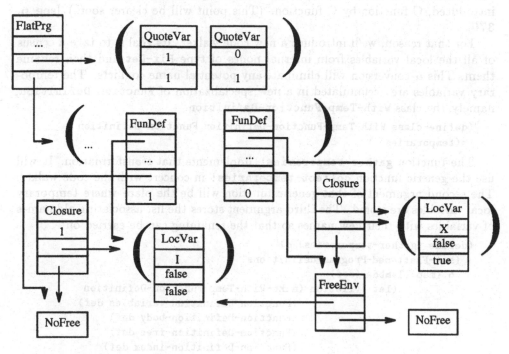

Figure 10.4 (begin (set! ...) ((lambda ...) ...))

Finally, we are going to convert the entire program into the application of a closure. That is, π will be transformed into ((lambda () π)).

```
(define (closurize-main! o)
  (let ((index (length (Flattened-Program-definitions o))))
    (set-Flattened-Program-definitions!
     o (cons (make-Function-Definition
               '() (Flattened-Program-form o) '() index )
             (Flattened-Program-definitions o) ) )
    (set-Flattened-Program-form!
     o (make-Regular-Application
        (make-Closure-Creation index '() (make-No-Free))
```

```
            (make-No-Argument) ) )
      o ) )
```

10.6   Collecting Temporary Variables

We have a decisive advantage over you, the reader, because we know already what
we want to generate. Hoping to be original, we have chosen to convert Scheme
expressions into C expressions. Deciding to do that might seem eccentric since C
is a language that involves instructions, but our choice lets us respect the structure
of Scheme. One problem then is that nodes of type **Fix-Let** cannot be translated
into C because C does not have expressions that let us introduce local[2] variables.
Our solution is to collect all the local variables from the **Fix-Let** forms that are
introduced, C function by C function. (This point will be clearer soon.) [see p.
370]

   For that reason, we'll introduce a new code walker. Its goal is to take a census
of all the local variables from internal nodes of type **Fix-Let** and then rename
them. This α-conversion will eliminate any potential name conflicts. The temporary variables are accumulated in a new specialization of **Function-Definition**,
namely, the class **With-Temp-Function-Definition**.

```
(define-class With-Temp-Function-Definition Function-Definition
   (temporaries) )
```

The function **gather-temporaries!** implements that transformation. It will
use the generic function **collect-temporaries!** in concert with the code walker.
The second argument of that generic function will be the place where temporary
local variables are stored. The third argument stores the list associating old names
of variables with their new names so that the renaming can be carried out.

```
(define (gather-temporaries! o)
  (set-Flattened-Program-definitions!
   o (map (lambda (def)
            (let ((flatfun (make-With-Temp-Function-Definition
                             (Function-Definition-variables def)
                             (Function-Definition-body def)
                             (Function-Definition-free def)
                             (Function-Definition-index def)
                             '() )))
              (collect-temporaries! flatfun flatfun '()) ) )
          (Flattened-Program-definitions o) ) )
  o )
(define-generic (collect-temporaries! (o Program) flatfun r)
  (update-walk! collect-temporaries! o flatfun r) )
```

To achieve all our wishes, we need only three more methods. Local references
are renamed, if need be, and we must not forget to rename any variables that we
put into boxes.

```
(define-method (collect-temporaries! (o Local-Reference) flatfun r)
  (let* ((variable (Local-Reference-variable o))
```

---
2. However, gcc offers such an expression in the syntactic form ({ ... }).

```
            (v (assq variable r)) )
      (if (pair? v) (make-Local-Reference (cdr v)) o) ) )
 (define-method (collect-temporaries! (o Box-Creation) flatfun r)
    (let* ((variable (Box-Creation-variable o))
           (v (assq variable r)) )
      (if (pair? v) (make-Box-Creation (cdr v)) o) ) )
```

The most complicated method, of course, is the one involved with `Fix-let`. It is recursively invoked on its arguments, and then it renames its local variables by means of the function `new-renamed-variable`. It also adds those new variables to the current function definition and is finally recursively invoked on its body in the appropriate new substitution environment.

```
(define-method (collect-temporaries! (o Fix-Let) flatfun r)
   (set-Fix-Let-arguments!
    o (collect-temporaries! (Fix-Let-arguments o) flatfun r) )
   (let* ((newvars (map new-renamed-variable
                        (Fix-Let-variables o) ))
          (newr (append (map cons (Fix-Let-variables o) newvars) r)) )
     (adjoin-temporary-variables! flatfun newvars)
     (set-Fix-Let-variables! o newvars)
     (set-Fix-Let-body!
      o (collect-temporaries! (Fix-Let-body o) flatfun newr) )
     o ) )
(define (adjoin-temporary-variables! flatfun newvars)
   (let adjoin ((temps (With-Temp-Function-Definition-temporaries
                         flatfun ))
                (vars newvars) )
     (if (pair? vars)
         (if (memq (car vars) temps)
             (adjoin temps (cdr vars))
             (adjoin (cons (car vars) temps) (cdr vars)) )
         (set-With-Temp-Function-Definition-temporaries!
          flatfun temps ) ) ) )
```

When variables are renamed, a new class of variables comes into play along with a counter to number them sequentially.

```
(define-class Renamed-Local-Variable Variable (index))
(define renaming-variables-counter 0)
(define-generic (new-renamed-variable (variable)))
(define-method (new-renamed-variable (variable Local-Variable))
   (set! renaming-variables-counter (+ renaming-variables-counter 1))
   (make-Renamed-Local-Variable
    (Variable-name variable) renaming-variables-counter ) )
```

10.7 Taking a Pause

The following Scheme expression textually suggests the final result of the metamorphoses that our example has submitted to so far. That is,

1. We introduced boxes.

2. We eliminated nested functions.

3. We collected quotations and function definitions.

4. We gathered up the temporary variables.

```
(define quote_5 'foo)                    ; collected quotation
(define-class Closure_0 Object ())       ; abstraction (lambda (f) ...)
(define-method (invoke (self Closure_0) f)
  (begin
    (set! index (+ 1 index))
    (invoke f index) ) )                 ; calculated call
(define-class Closure_1 Object (i))      ; abstraction (lambda x ...)
(define-method (invoke (self Closure_1) . x)
  (cons (Closure_1-i self)              ; closed variable i
        x ) )
(define-class Closure_2 Object ())       ; abstraction (lambda (i) ...)
(define-method (invoke (self Closure_2) i)
  (make-Closure_1 i) )                   ; allocation of a closure
(define-class Closure_3 Object ())       ; abstraction (lambda () program)
(define-method (invoke (self Closure_3))
  ((lambda (cnter_1 tmp_2)              ; renaming local variables
     (set! index 1)
     (set! cnter_1 (make-Closure_0))     ; initializing a temporary variable
     (set! tmp_2 (cons quote_5 '()))
     (set! tmp_2 (make-box tmp_2))       ; putting it into a box
     (box-write! tmp_2                   ; mutable variable
                 (invoke cnter_1 (make-Closure_2)) )
     (if cnter_1 (invoke cnter_1 (box-read tmp_2)) index) ) ) )
(invoke (make-Closure_3))                ; invocation of main program
```

10.8   Generating C

Now we've actually arrived on the enchanted shores of code generation, and as it happens, generating C. We're actually ready. There are still just a few more explanations needed. Your author does not pretend to be an expert in C, and in fact, he owes what he knows about C to careful reading in such sources as [ISO90, HS91, CEK+89]. He assumes that you've at least heard of C, but you're not encumbered by any preconceived notion of what it is exactly.

The abstract syntactic tree is complete and just waiting to be compiled, like by a *pretty-printer*, into the C language. Code generation is simple since it is so high-level. The function compile->C takes an S-expression, applies the set of transformations we just described to it in the right order, and eventually generates the equivalent program on the output port, out.

```
(define (compile->C e out)
  (set! g.current '())
  (let ((prg (extract-things! (lift! (Sexp->object e)))))
    (gather-temporaries! (closurize-main! prg))
    (generate-C-program out e prg) ) )
```

```
(define (generate-C-program out e prg)
  (generate-header          out e)
  (generate-global-environment out g.current)
  (generate-quotations      out (Flattened-Program-quotations prg))
  (generate-functions       out (Flattened-Program-definitions prg))
  (generate-main            out (Flattened-Program-form prg))
  (generate-trailer         out)
  prg )
```

Like any other C program, and more generally like some animated creature, this one has a beginning, middle, and end. So that we can have a trace, the compiled expression is printed nicely as a comment (by the function **pp** which is not standard in Scheme) A directive to the C preprocessor includes a standard header file, **scheme.h**, to define all we need for the rest of the compilation. From now on, we will also use the usual non-standard function **format** to print C code.

```
(define (generate-header out e)
  (format out "/* Compiler to C $Revision: 4.1 $ ~%")
  (pp e out)                        ; DEBUG
  (format out "  */~%~%#include \"scheme.h\"~%") )
(define (generate-trailer out)
  (format out "~%/* End of generated code. */~%") )
```

Now things get complicated. The compiled result of our current example appears on page 388. You might want to look at it before you read further.

10.8.1 Global Environment

The global variables of the program to compile fall into two categories: predefined variables, like **car** or **+**, and mutable global variables. We assume that predefined global variables cannot be changed and belong to a library of functions that will be linked to the program to make an executable. In contrast, we have to generate the global environment of variables that can be modified. In other words, we will exploit the contents of **g.current** where we accumulated the mutable global variables that appeared as free variables in the program submitted to the compiler.

The generation that we're tending towards depends on the fact that we compile an entire program, not just a fragment expecting separate compilation. (Separate compilation raises problems that we simply did not have space to cover here.) [see p. 260]

In order to simplify the C code that we generate, we will use C macros to make the code more readable. For example, we will declare a global variable in C by means of the macro **SCM_DefineGlobalVariable**. The second argument of that macro is the character string corresponding to the original name[3] in Scheme. It can be used during debugging.

```
(define (generate-global-environment out gv*)
  (when (pair? gv*)
```

---

3. The **read** function used to read the examples to compile in this chapter converts all the names of symbols in upper case.

```
          (format out "~%/* Global environment: */~%")
          (for-each (lambda (gv) (generate-global-variable out gv))
                    gv* )) )
  (define (generate-global-variable out gv)
    (let ((name (Global-Variable-name gv)))
      (format out "SCM_DefineGlobalVariable(~A,\"~A\");~%"
              (IdScheme->IdC name) name ) ) )
```

There you can see the first problem, which is that the identifiers in Scheme
are not always legal identifiers in C. The function `IdScheme->IdC` mangles legal
Scheme identifiers into legal C identifiers. In doing so, the main problem is to
eliminate illegal characters while still insuring a translation plan that keeps the
name more or less reversible so that when we encounter an identifier in C we can
reconstruct the original name of the variable in Scheme. There are many solutions
to this problem, but ours is to translate problematic characters into normal ones
and then to verify whether the name we get that way has already been used so
that we avoid name conflicts. The code for that is not particularly interesting
but, just so we hide nothing, here are the details of those functions. The variable
`Scheme->C-names-mapping` stores all the translations of names. It is predefined
with a few translations already imposed on it. Others can be added there, though
we've omitted them here.

```
  (define Scheme->C-names-mapping
    '( (*        . "TIMES")
       (<        . "LESSP")
       (pair?    . "CONSP")
       (set-cdr! . "RPLACD")
       ) )
  (define (IdScheme->IdC name)
    (let ((v (assq name Scheme->C-names-mapping)))
      (if (pair? v) (cdr v)
          (let ((str (symbol->string name)))
            (let retry ((Cname (compute-Cname str)))
              (if (Cname-clash? Cname Scheme->C-names-mapping)
                  (retry (compute-another-Cname str))
                  (begin (set! Scheme->C-names-mapping
                               (cons (cons name Cname)
                                     Scheme->C-names-mapping ) )
                         Cname ) ) ) ) ) ) )
```

When there is a conflict, we synthesize a new name by suffixing the original
name by an increasing index.

```
  (define (Cname-clash? Cname mapping)
    (let check ((mapping mapping))
      (and (pair? mapping)
           (or (string=? Cname (cdr (car mapping)))
               (check (cdr mapping)) ) ) ) )
  (define compute-another-Cname
    (let ((counter 1))
      (lambda (str)
        (set! counter (+ 1 counter))
```

```
              (compute-Cname (format #f "~A_~A" str counter)) ) ) )
    (define (compute-Cname str)
      (define (mapcan f l)
        (if (pair? l)
            (append (f (car l)) (mapcan f (cdr l)))
            '() ) )
      (define (convert-char char)
        (case char
          ((#\_)                    '(#\_ #\_))
          ((#\?)                    '(#\p))
          ((#\!)                    '(#\i))
          ((#\<)                    '(#\l))
          ((#\>)                    '(#\g))
          ((#\=)                    '(#\e))
          ((#\- #\/ #\* #\:)        '())
          (else                     (list char)) ) )
      (let ((cname (mapcan convert-char (string->list str))))
        (if (pair? cname) (list->string cname) "weird") ) )
```

An isolated underscore cannot appear in the generated names. We'll use that character, for example, in the names of temporary variables, with no risk of confusion. This translation plan cannot translate the name 1+, but since that one is not obligatorily a legal identifier in Scheme, we're not going to worry too long about it.

10.8.2 Quotations

Quotations have to be translated into a fragment of C that can be retrieved at execution time. We'll introduce an innovation here by presenting a translation plan where they will be translated only by declarations of data, excluding all executable code. We also guarantee that quotations will take the least possible space. That is, subexpressions will be identified so they can be shared.

The function generate-quotations globally insures the translation of quotations. To simplify what follows, we'll ignore the case of vectors, large integers, rationals, floating-point numbers, and any characters that can be handled without additional considerations.

```
(define (generate-quotations out qv*)
  (when (pair? qv*)
    (format out "~%/* Quotations: */~%")
    (scan-quotations out qv* (length qv*) '()) ) )
```

What's actually happening is that scan-quotations analyzes the quoted values as they appear in the instances of Quotation-Variable. Whenever possible, these values are shared. The predicate already-seen-value? detects that possibility.

```
(define (scan-quotations out qv* i results)
  (when (pair? qv*)
    (let* ((qv       (car qv*))
           (value    (Quotation-Variable-value qv))
           (other-qv (already-seen-value? value results)) )
      (cond (other-qv
```

```
            (generate-quotation-alias out qv other-qv)
            (scan-quotations out (cdr qv*) i (cons qv results)) )
          ((C-value? value)
           (generate-C-value out qv)
           (scan-quotations out (cdr qv*) i (cons qv results)) )
          ((symbol? value)
           (scan-symbol out value qv* i results) )
          ((pair? value)
           (scan-pair out value qv* i results) )
          (else (generate-error "Unhandled constant" qv)) ) ) ) )
(define (already-seen-value? value qv*)
  (and (pair? qv*)
       (if (equal? value (Quotation-Variable-value (car qv*)))
           (car qv*)
           (already-seen-value? value (cdr qv*)) ) ) )
```

All the quotations are identified in C by lexemes prefixed by **thing**. Detecting
something that can be shared is a matter of simply identifying two lexemes themselves. We do that with a C macro that implements **generate-quotation-alias**.
To make it easier to read the generated program, we comment the shared value.

```
(define (generate-quotation-alias out qv1 qv2)
  (format out "#define thing~A thing~A /* ~S */~%"
          (Quotation-Variable-name qv1)
          (Quotation-Variable-name qv2)
          (Quotation-Variable-value qv2) ) )
```

The predicate **C-value?** tests whether values are immediate. When they are,
we translate them into C with no further ado. The function **generate-C-value**
actually does that. Immediate values are the empty list, Booleans, short integers,
and character strings. All those values are translated into appropriate C objects,
and we'll assume for the moment that there are appropriate C macros to define
character strings, integers, both Booleans, and the empty list. All these C entities
are prefixed by **SCM_**. No doubt C gurus will notice that the values restricting small
numbers limit them to 16-bits in one's complement.

```
(define *maximal-fixnum* 16384)
(define *minimal-fixnum* (- *maximal-fixnum*))
(define (C-value? value)
  (or (null? value)
      (boolean? value)
      (and (integer? value)
           (< *minimal-fixnum* value)
           (< value *maximal-fixnum*) )
      (string? value) ) )
(define (generate-C-value out qv)
  (let ((value (Quotation-Variable-value qv))
        (index (Quotation-Variable-name qv)) )
    (cond ((null? value)
           (format out "#define thing~A SCM_nil /* () */~%"
                   index ) )
          ((boolean? value)
```

```
            (format out "#define thing~A ~A /* ~S */~%"
                    index (if value "SCM_true" "SCM_false") value ) )
        ((integer? value)
         (format out "#define thing~A SCM_Int2fixnum(~A)~%"
                    index value ) )
        ((string? value)
         (format out "SCM_DefineString(thing~A_object,\"~A\");~%"
                    index value )
         (format out "#define thing~A SCM_Wrap(&thing~A_object)~%"
                    index index ) ) ) ) )
```

When values are composites (that is, dotted pairs or symbols), we decompose them to determine whether sharing is possible so that we can rebuild them later from their components. A symbol is reconstructed only from the characters in its name. Strings are created prior to symbols.

```
(define (scan-symbol out value qv* i results)
   (let* ((qv    (car qv*))
          (str   (symbol->string value))
          (strqv (already-seen-value? str results)) )
      (cond (strqv (generate-symbol out qv strqv)
                   (scan-quotations out (cdr qv*) i (cons qv results)) )
            (else
             (let ((newqv (make-Quotation-Variable
                             i (symbol->string value) )))
                (scan-quotations out (cons newqv qv*)
                                 (+ i 1) results ) ) ) ) ) )
(define (generate-symbol out qv strqv)
   (format out "SCM_DefineSymbol(thing~A_object,thing~A);    /* ~S */~%"
           (Quotation-Variable-name qv)
           (Quotation-Variable-name strqv)
           (Quotation-Variable-value qv) )
   (format out "#define thing~A SCM_Wrap(&thing~A_object)~%"
           (Quotation-Variable-name qv) (Quotation-Variable-name qv) ) )
```

For dotted pairs, we begin by generating their **car** and then their **cdr**, searching for any possible shared things. Sharing might even occur between the **car** and **cdr**. The programming style by continuations inspires the function **scan-pair**, as you can see.

```
(define (scan-pair out value qv* i results)
   (let* ((qv  (car qv*))
          (d   (cdr value))
          (dqv (already-seen-value? d results)) )
      (if dqv
          (let* ((a   (car value))
                 (aqv (already-seen-value? a results)) )
             (if aqv
                 (begin
                   (generate-pair out qv aqv dqv)
                   (scan-quotations out (cdr qv*) i (cons qv results)) )
                 (let ((newaqv (make-Quotation-Variable i a)))
                   (scan-quotations out (cons newaqv qv*)
```

```
                                       (+ i 1) results ) ) ) )
              (let ((newdqv (make-Quotation-Variable i d)))
                (scan-quotations
                 out (cons newdqv qv*) (+ i 1) results ) ) ) ) )
    (define (generate-pair out qv aqv dqv)
      (format out
              "SCM_DefinePair(thing~A_object,thing~A,thing~A); /* ~S */~%"
              (Quotation-Variable-name qv)
              (Quotation-Variable-name aqv)
              (Quotation-Variable-name dqv)
              (Quotation-Variable-value qv) )
      (format out "#define thing~A SCM_Wrap(&thing~A_object)~%"
              (Quotation-Variable-name qv) (Quotation-Variable-name qv) ) )
```

Now we're going to look at an example and get into the details of data representation.

10.8.3 Declaring Data

Let's take a simple program made of a single quotation: `(quote ((#F #T) (FOO . "FOO") 33 FOO . "FOO"))`. The sort of compilation that we have just described leads to what follows here. There are a few comments to elucidate it. Enjoy!

```
/* Source expression:
 '((#F #T) (FOO . "FOO") 33 FOO . "FOO")  */

#include "scheme.h"

/* Quotations */
SCM_DefineString(thing4_object,"FOO");
#define thing4 SCM_Wrap(&thing4_object)
SCM_DefineSymbol(thing5_object,thing4);         /* FOO */
#define thing5 SCM_Wrap(&thing5_object)
SCM_DefinePair(thing3_object,thing5,thing4);  /* (FOO . "FOO") */
#define thing3 SCM_Wrap(&thing3_object)
#define thing6 SCM_Int2fixnum(33)
SCM_DefinePair(thing2_object,thing6,thing3);  /* (33 FOO . "FOO") */
#define thing2 SCM_Wrap(&thing2_object)
SCM_DefinePair(thing1_object,thing3,thing2);
                           /* ((FOO . "FOO") 33 FOO . "FOO") */
#define thing1 SCM_Wrap(&thing1_object)
#define thing9 SCM_nil                        /* () */
#define thing10 SCM_true                      /* #T */
SCM_DefinePair(thing8_object,thing10,thing9); /* (#T) */
#define thing8 SCM_Wrap(&thing8_object)
#define thing11 SCM_false                     /* #F */
SCM_DefinePair(thing7_object,thing11,thing8); /* (#F #T) */
#define thing7 SCM_Wrap(&thing7_object)
SCM_DefinePair(thing0_object,thing7,thing1);
                     /* ((#F #T) (FOO . "FOO") 33 FOO . "FOO") */
```

```
#define thing0 SCM_Wrap(&thing0_object)
          ...
```

The first thing we create is the character string "FOO". To do that, we use the macro SCM_DefineString. As its first argument, it takes the name the object will have in C. As its second argument, it takes the character string. Similarly, a symbol is created by the macro SCM_DefineSymbol. As its first argument, it also takes the name that the object will have in C, and as its second argument, it takes the character string that names this symbol. Likewise, a dotted pair is created by the macro SCM_DefinePair. As its first argument, it, too, takes the name the object will have in C, and its second and third arguments are the contents of the car and cdr.

Predefined objects like Booleans or the empty list, of course, are not created anew. Rather, they are referred to by the names SCM_true, SCM_false, and SCM_nil.

Later, [see p. 390], we'll indicate the exact representations of values in Scheme. Compilation is largely independent of the particular representation that we adopt. For the time being, it suffices to know that the creation directives like SCM_Define... allocate only objects and that we get the legal values referring to them by converting their address with SCM_Wrap. As for short integers, they are converted by SCM_Int2fixnum. For that reason, after any object is allocated, we define the C value representing it under a name beginning with thing. For example, thing4 indicates the character string "FOO" while thing6 is the short integer 33. More precisely, thing4 is the pointer to the object thing4_object, which (strictly speaking) is the character string.

The character string "FOO" is shared, as is the S-expression (FOO . "FOO"), between the objects thing4 and thing3.

10.8.4 Compiling Expressions

Compiling expressions from Scheme into C is, of course, the main task of our compiler. Here again we are innovating because we translate expressions into expressions. That way, we gain a certain clarity in the result, which respects the structure of the source program. In spite of its obvious wisdom, this choice nevertheless poses a delicate problem since it deviates slightly from the philosophy of C. C prefers instructions to expressions. This deviation is not too troublesome except when we are debugging, say, with gdb, the symbolic debugger from the *Free Software Foundation*. In single-step mode, execution occurs instruction by instruction—too gross a granularity for our choice. If we had wanted to compile into instructions (rather than into expressions), we would have adopted a technique similar to that the byte-code compiler. [see p. 223]

The actual compilation of expressions is carried out by a generic function, ->C. Its first argument is the expression to compile, of course, and its second argument is the output port on which to write the resulting C. Since we are writing to a file, we have to pay close attention to producing the code sequentially, without backtracking, in a single pass. [see p. 234]

```
(define-generic (->C (e Program) out))
```

In contrast to the preceding transformations, we're not going to use our generic code walker (because there is no default treatment here), but rather a method of generating code for each type of syntactic node. Thus there is nothing left for us to do except to enumerate the methods. They are simple enough since they systematically copy the equivalent C constructions.

As a language, C embodies very strong ideas of syntax with its precedence, variable meanings for associativity, and so forth. Since the practice is widely recommended, we are going to use parentheses throughout. For Lisp fans, this practice will add a Lisp-like flavor, though it may be distasteful for habitual C users. The parentheses will be specified by the macro `between-parentheses`.

```
(define-syntax between-parentheses
  (syntax-rules ()
    ((between-parentheses out . body)
     (let ((out out))
       (format out "(")
       (begin . body)
       (format out ")") ) ) ) )
```

Compiling References to Variables

There's more than one type of variable that we have to handle, but in general, we assimilate a Scheme variable with a C variable. The appropriate method will be subcontracted to the function `reference->C`, which will generally subcontract it immediately to the function `variable->C`. These indirections enable us to specialize their behavior more easily.

```
(define-method (->C (e Reference) out)
  (reference->C (Reference-variable e) out) )
(define-generic (reference->C (v Variable) out))
(define-method (reference->C (v Variable) out)
  (variable->C v out) )
(define-generic (variable->C (variable) out))
```

In a general way, a variable is translated by name into C, except when it has been renamed or when it indicates a quotation.

```
(define-method (variable->C (variable Variable) out)
  (format out (IdScheme->IdC (Variable-name variable))) )
(define-method (variable->C (variable Renamed-Local-Variable) out)
  (format out "~A_~A"
          (IdScheme->IdC (Variable-name variable))
          (Renamed-Local-Variable-index variable) ) )
(define-method (variable->C (variable Quotation-Variable) out)
  (format out "thing~A" (Quotation-Variable-name variable)) )
```

However, there's a particular case for non-predefined global variables—the free variables in the compiled program—because no analysis has told us whether or not they have been initialized. We thus must verify that fact explicitly by means of the macro `SCM_CheckedGlobal`. [see **Ex. 10.2**]

```
(define-method (reference->C (v Global-Variable) out)
  (format out "SCM_CheckedGlobal")
```

```
(between-parentheses out
   (variable->C v out) ) )
```

The remaining case is that of free variables for which we will once more call the appropriate macro: `SCM_Free`.

```
(define-method (->C (e Free-Reference) out)
   (format out "SCM_Free")
   (between-parentheses out
      (variable->C (Free-Reference-variable e) out) ) )
```

Compiling Assignments

Assignments are handled even more simply because there are only two kinds: assignments of global variables and assignments written in boxes. The assignment of a global variable is translated by the assignment in C of the corresponding global variable.

```
(define-method (->C (e Global-Assignment) out)
   (between-parentheses out
      (variable->C (Global-Assignment-variable e) out)
      (format out "=")
      (->C (Global-Assignment-form e) out) ) )
```

Compiling Boxes

As for boxes, there are only three operations involved. A C macro read- or write-accesses the contents of a box: `SCM_Content`. A function of the predefined library, `SCM_allocate_box`, allocates a box when needed.

```
(define-method (->C (e Box-Read) out)
   (format out "SCM_Content")
   (between-parentheses out
    (->C (Box-Read-reference e) out) ) )
(define-method (->C (e Box-Write) out)
   (between-parentheses out
      (format out "SCM_Content")
      (between-parentheses out
        (->C (Box-Write-reference e) out) )
      (format out "=")
      (->C (Box-Write-form e) out) ) )
(define-method (->C (e Box-Creation) out)
   (variable->C (Box-Creation-variable e) out)
   (format out "= SCM_allocate_box")
   (between-parentheses out
      (variable->C (Box-Creation-variable e) out) ) )
```

Compiling Alternatives

The Scheme alternative is translated into the alternative expression in C, that is, the ternary construction $\pi_0?\pi_1:\pi_2$. Since every value different from False is considered True in Scheme, we explicitly test this case. Of course, we put parentheses in everywhere!

```
(define-method (->C (e Alternative) out)
  (between-parentheses out
    (boolean->C (Alternative-condition e) out)
    (format out "~%? ")
    (->C (Alternative-consequent e) out)
    (format out "~%: ")
    (->C (Alternative-alternant e) out) ) )
(define-generic (boolean->C (e) out)
  (between-parentheses out
    (->C e out)
    (format out " != SCM_false") ) )
```

There you see one of the first sources of inefficiency in comparison to a real compiler. In the case of a predicate like (if (pair? x) ...), it is inefficient for the call to **pair?** to return a Scheme Boolean that we compare to SCM_false. It would be a better idea for **pair?** to return a C Boolean directly. We could thus specialize the function **boolean->C** to recognize and handle calls to predefined predicates. We could also unify the Booleans of C and Scheme by adopting the convention that False is represented by NULL. Then we could carry out type recovery in order to suppress these cumbersome comparisons, as in [Shi91, Ser93, WC94].

Compiling Sequences

Sequences are translated into C sequences in this notation $(\pi_1,\ldots,\pi_n)$.

```
(define-method (->C (e Sequence) out)
  (between-parentheses out
    (->C (Sequence-first e) out)
    (format out ",~%")
    (->C (Sequence-last e) out) ) )
```

10.8.5   Compiling Functional Applications

We've organized functional applications into several categories: normal functional applications, closed functional applications (where the function term is an abstraction), functional applications where the invoked function is a function value of a predefined variable. These three types of applications are produced by three classes of syntactic nodes: **Regular-Application**, **Fix-Let**, and **Predefined-Application**.

A normal functional application $(f\ x_1\ \ldots\ x_n)$ will be compiled into a C expression SCM_invoke$(f,n,x_1,\ldots\ ,x_n)$, where n is the number of arguments passed to the function and SCM_invoke is the specialized invocation function. To make the result more legible, we'll use C macros for arity of less than four, like this:

```
#define SCM_invoke0(f)       SCM_invoke(f,0)
#define SCM_invoke1(f,x)     SCM_invoke(f,1,x)
#define SCM_invoke2(f,x,y)   SCM_invoke(f,2,x,y)
#define SCM_invoke3(f,x,y,z) SCM_invoke(f,3,x,y,z)
```

For greater arity, we'll use this protocol directly:

```
(define-method (->C (e Regular-Application) out)
  (let ((n (number-of (Regular-Application-arguments e))))
    (cond ((< n 4)
           (format out "SCM_invoke~A" n)
           (between-parentheses out
             (->C (Regular-Application-function e) out)
             (->C (Regular-Application-arguments e) out) ) )
          (else (format out "SCM_invoke")
                (between-parentheses out
                  (->C (Regular-Application-function e) out)
                  (format out ",~A" n)
                  (->C (Regular-Application-arguments e) out) ) ) ) ) )
```

Closed applications will be translated into a C sequence corresponding to their body. *A posteriori*, they will justify our effort in collecting temporary variables beforehand. By the way, that collecting is equivalent to *frame coalescing*, or fusing temporary blocks, a compilation technique where we attempt to limit the number of allocations by allocating larger blocks, as in [AS94, PJ87]. If we assume that all temporary variables in the `let` forms have already been allocated, then binding these variables to their values is just an assignment. We could translate that assignment, in Lispian terms, by a rewrite rule like the following[4] where we coalesce the internal `let`s into a unique `let` surrounding all of them and associated with the local renamings. That transformation is not really legal in the general case because of this possibility: if $\ldots_1$ returns more than once, and if π_2 captures the variable x, then this x renamed as x1 will be shared. [see p. 189] Nevertheless, the transformation is correct here because x1 will not be modified; the variable is immutable, even if `set!` is present since it has been boxed; and we're using a technique of a flat environment where values are recopied.

$$
\begin{array}{ll}
(\text{begin } \ldots_1 & (\text{let } (x1 \; x2) \ldots_1 \\
\quad (\text{let } ((x \; \pi_1)) & \quad (\text{set! } x1 \; \pi_1) \\
\quad \; \pi_2 \;) & \quad \pi_2[x{\rightarrow}x1] \\
\ldots_2 & \ldots_2 \\
\quad (\text{let } ((x \; \pi_3)) & \quad (\text{set! } x2 \; \pi_3) \\
\quad \; \pi_4 \;) \;) & \quad \pi_4[x{\rightarrow}x2] \;)
\end{array}
$$

$\Rightarrow$

We only have to assign each local variable its initialization value. Since all the local variables have been identified and renamed, there's no possible confusion, nor any scope problems. A particular generic function, `bindings->C`, translates those bindings.

```
(define-method (->C (e Fix-Let) out)
  (between-parentheses out
    (bindings->C (Fix-Let-variables e) (Fix-Let-arguments e) out)
    (->C (Fix-Let-body e) out) ) )
(define-generic (bindings->C variables (arguments) out))
(define-method (bindings->C variables (e Arguments) out)
  (variable->C (car variables) out)
```

---

4. Of course, we could try to share even more of the places reserved for variables. That's the case for the variables x1 and x2 if there is no risk of confusion.

```
    (format out "=")
    (->C (Arguments-first e) out)
    (format out ",~%")
    (bindings->C (cdr variables) (Arguments-others e) out) )
  (define-method (bindings->C variables (e No-Argument) out)
    (format out "") )
```

Finally, the case of functional applications where the function is the value of a predefined variable and thus well known: they will be *inlined*. The function will be called directly without the intercession of SCM_invoke. Predefined functions are written in C and appear in the library that must be linked to the compiled program. Calling them directly is equivalent but of course more efficient than passing through SCM_invoke.

Since generating the direct call depends on how the primitive is implemented, we assume that the functional description associated with the predefined variable has a field—**generator**—that indicates the right generator to call. That generation function will receive the node corresponding to the application and will be responsible for calling ->C recursively on the arguments. It uses the generic function **arguments->C** to make those recursive calls.

```
  (define-method (->C (e Predefined-Application) out)
    ((Functional-Description-generator
       (Predefined-Variable-description
         (Predefined-Application-variable e) ) ) e out ) )
  (define-generic (arguments->C (e) out))
  (define-method (arguments->C (e Arguments) out)
    (->C (Arguments-first e) out)
    (->C (Arguments-others e) out) )
  (define-method (arguments->C (e No-Argument) out)
    #t )
```

10.8.6 Predefined Environment

When we compile applications into predefined functions, the compiler must already know those functions, so we will define a macro, **defprimitive**, for that purpose.

```
(define-class Functional-Description Object (comparator arity generator))

(define-syntax defprimitive
  (syntax-rules ()
    ((defprimitive name Cname arity)
     (let ((v (make-Predefined-Variable
                'name (make-Functional-Description
                        = arity
                        (make-predefined-application-generator 'Cname) ) )))
       (set! g.init (cons v g.init))
       'name ) ) ) )
```

Thus the definition of a primitive function is based on its name in Scheme, its name in C, and its arity. The generated calls all take the form of a function call in C, that is, a name followed by a mass of arguments within parentheses separated by commas. The function **make-predefined-application-generator** creates just such generators.

```
(define (make-predefined-application-generator Cname)
  (lambda (e out)
    (format out "~A" Cname)
    (between-parentheses out
      (arguments->C (Predefined-Application-arguments e) out) ) ) )
```

Let's look at a few examples, like the usual **cons**, **car**, +, or =.

```
(defprimitive cons "SCM_cons" 2)
(defprimitive car "SCM_car" 1)
(defprimitive + "SCM_Plus" 2)
(defprimitive = "SCM_EqnP" 2)
```

You see that **cons** is compiled into a call to the C function **SCM_cons** whereas + is compiled into a call to the C macro **SCM_Plus**. [see p. 394] Macros are distinguished from functions by capital letters in the names of the macros. Distinguishing them this way changes the speed at execution and the size of the resulting C code.

10.8.7 Compiling Functions

The preceding transformations have replaced abstractions by allocations of closures that is, nodes from the class **Closure-Creation**. These closures are all allocated by the function **SCM_close**, part of the predefined execution library. As its first argument, this function takes the address of the C function (conveniently typed by the C macro **SCM_CfunctionAddress**) corresponding to the body of the abstraction; the arity of the closure being created is its second argument; those two arguments are followed by the number of closed values, prefixing these same values. We get all those closed values simply by translating them into C from the **free** field of the description of the closure. The arity of functions that take a fixed number of arguments will be coded by that same number. In contrast, when a function has a dotted variable, it must take at least a certain number of arguments, say, i, so its arity will thus be represented by $-i - 1$. That is, the function **list** has an arity of -1.

```
(define-method (->C (e Closure-Creation) out)
  (format out "SCM_close")
  (between-parentheses out
    (format out "SCM_CfunctionAddress(function_~A),~A,~A"
      (Closure-Creation-index e)
      (generate-arity (Closure-Creation-variables e))
      (number-of (Closure-Creation-free e)) )
    (->C (Closure-Creation-free e) out) ) )
(define (generate-arity variables)
  (let count ((variables variables)(arity 0))
    (if (pair? variables)
        (if (Local-Variable-dotted? (car variables))
            (- (+ arity 1))
            (count (cdr variables) (+ 1 arity)) )
        arity ) ) )
```

```
(define-method (->C (e No-Free) out)
  #t )
(define-method (->C (e Free-Environment) out)
  (format out ",")
  (->C (Free-environment-first e) out)
  (->C (Free-environment-others e) out) )
```

Abstractions themselves have been organized into the object representing the entire program, an instance of **Flattened-Program**, as a list of functions without free variables defined by the instances of **With-Temp-Function-Definition**. Each of those functions leads to generating an equivalent function in C.

```
(define (generate-functions out definitions)
  (format out "~%/* Functions: */~%")
  (for-each (lambda (def)
              (generate-closure-structure out def)
              (generate-possibly-dotted-definition out def) )
            (reverse definitions) ) )
```

To make the generated code more legible, we will again use C macros to hide the finer details of representation. A function will be generated for each closure, along with a data structure defining where the enclosed variables are located in the object of type closure. All the names generated to represent these objects will be formed from the root function_ and an index that already appears in the **index** field of the object **Function-Definition**.[5]

The representation of the closure is defined by the macro **SCM_DefineClosure**. Its first argument is the name of the associated C function; its second argument is the list of names of captured variables, separated by semi-colons.

```
(define (generate-closure-structure out definition)
  (format out "SCM_DefineClosure(function_~A, "
          (Function-Definition-index definition) )
  (generate-local-temporaries (Function-Definition-free definition) out)
  (format out ");~%") )
```

The function **generate-possibly-dotted-definition** generates the definition of the C function by taking into account its arity. The function is defined by the macro **SCM_DeclareFunction**. It takes the name of the generated function as an argument. Its variables are defined by the macros **SCM_DeclareLocalVariable** or **SCM_DeclareLocalDottedVariable**. They take the name of the variable and its rank in the list of variables. The rank is important only for computing the list bound to a dotted variable. The body of the function does not pose a problem. We get it simply by applying the function ->C, but that is preceded by a **return**, necessary to the C functions.

```
(define (generate-possibly-dotted-definition out definition)
  (format out "~%SCM_DeclareFunction(function_~A) {~%"
          (Function-Definition-index definition) )
  (let ((vars (Function-Definition-variables definition))
        (rank -1) )
```

---

5. Since the functions are named like this: function_i, you can see that they are independent of the variables in which they are stored. Of course, it would be better if the functions associated with these non-mutable global variables were named after them, too.

```
(for-each (lambda (v)
            (set! rank (+ rank 1))
            (cond ((Local-Variable-dotted? v)
                   (format out "SCM_DeclareLocalDottedVariable(") )
                  ((Variable? v)
                   (format out "SCM_DeclareLocalVariable(") ) )
            (variable->C v out)
            (format out ",~A);~%" rank) )
          vars )
(let ((temps (With-Temp-Function-Definition-temporaries
               definition )))
  (when (pair? temps)
    (generate-local-temporaries temps out)
    (format out "~%") ) )
(format out "return ")
(->C (Function-Definition-body definition) out)
(format out ";~%}~%~%") ) )
```

Lists of variables are converted into C by means of the utility function **generate-local-temporaries**.

```
(define (generate-local-temporaries temps out)
  (when (pair? temps)
    (format out "SCM ")
    (variable->C (car temps) out)
    (format out "; ")
    (generate-local-temporaries (cdr temps) out) ) )
```

10.8.8 Initializing the Program

We have an entire Scheme program to compile now, so the only thing left for us to indicate is how to form an entire C program. For that reason, we put the initial expression into a closure during the phase of flattening out the functions. [see **p. 369**] The only major and arguable decision is that we generate a call to the function `SCM_print`, which will print the value of the compiled expression. It's not strictly necessary, and there are many interesting programs that do useful things without polluting the world with their output (cc, for example). For us, though, it is more convenient for the little programs that we compile to have printed output.

```
(define (generate-main out form)
  (format out "~%/* Expression: */~%void main(void) {~%")
  (format out "  SCM_print")
  (between-parentheses out
    (->C form out) )
  (format out ";~%  exit(0);~%}~%") )
```

Of course, we haven't yet said anything about the representation of data, nor have we defined the initial execution library. However, the compiler is complete and operational anyway, so we are going to translate our current example into C. (We manually indented the generated output to make it more legible.) Here, then, is the complete translation of our example, which by the way appears as a comment from lines 2 to 9.

[see p. 360]

---

o/chap10ex.c

```
 2 /* Compiler to C $Revision: 4.0 $
 3 (BEGIN
 4   (SET! INDEX 1)
 5   ((LAMBDA
 6     (CNTER . TMP)
 7     (SET! TMP (CNTER (LAMBDA (I) (LAMBDA X (CONS I X)))))
 8     (IF CNTER (CNTER TMP) INDEX))
 9     (LAMBDA (F) (SET! INDEX (+ 1 INDEX)) (F INDEX))
10     'FOO))  */
11
12 #include "scheme.h"
13
14 /* Global environment: */
15 SCM_DefineGlobalVariable(INDEX,"INDEX");
16
17 /* Quotations: */
18 #define thing3 SCM_nil /* () */
19 SCM_DefineString(thing4_object,"FOO");
20 #define thing4 SCM_Wrap(&thing4_object)
21 SCM_DefineSymbol(thing2_object,thing4);        /* FOO */
22 #define thing2 SCM_Wrap(&thing2_object)
23 #define thing1 SCM_Int2fixnum(1)
24 #define thing0 thing1 /* 1 */
25
26 /* Functions: */
27 SCM_DefineClosure(function_0, );
28
29 SCM_DeclareFunction(function_0) {
30   SCM_DeclareLocalVariable(F,0);
31   return ((INDEX=SCM_Plus(thing1,
32                           SCM_CheckedGlobal(INDEX))),
33         SCM_invoke1(F,
34                     SCM_CheckedGlobal(INDEX)));
35 }
36
37 SCM_DefineClosure(function_1, SCM I; );
38
39 SCM_DeclareFunction(function_1) {
40   SCM_DeclareLocalDottedVariable(X,0);
41   return SCM_cons(SCM_Free(I),
42                   X);
43 }
44
45 SCM_DefineClosure(function_2, );
46
47 SCM_DeclareFunction(function_2) {
```

```
48   SCM_DeclareLocalVariable(I,0);
49   return SCM_close(SCM_CfunctionAddress(function_1),-1,1,I);
50 }
51
52 SCM_DefineClosure(function_3, );
53
54 SCM_DeclareFunction(function_3) {
55   SCM TMP_2; SCM CNTER_1;
56   return ((INDEX=thing0),
57          (CNTER_1=SCM_close(SCM_CfunctionAddress(function_0),1,0),
58           TMP_2=SCM_cons(thing2,
59                          thing3),
60           (TMP_2= SCM_allocate_box(TMP_2),
61            ((SCM_Content(TMP_2)=
62             SCM_invoke1(CNTER_1,SCM_close(SCM_CfunctionAddress
63                                  (function_2),1,0))),
64            ((CNTER_1 != SCM_false)
65             ? SCM_invoke1(CNTER_1,
66                           SCM_Content(TMP_2))
67             : SCM_CheckedGlobal(INDEX))))));
68 }
69
70
71 /* Expression: */
72 void main(void) {
73   SCM_print(SCM_invoke0(SCM_close(SCM_CfunctionAddress(function_3),
74                                   0,0)));
75   exit(0);
76 }
77
78 /* End of generated code. */
79
```

We'll also give its expanded form, that is, one stripped of the C macros (except for **va_list**), for the functions **function_1** and **function_2**. The other expansions are from the same tap.

```
struct function_1 {
        SCM(*behavior) (void);
        long            arity;
        SCM             I;
};

SCM function_1(struct function_1 * self_,
        unsigned long size_,
        va_list arguments_)
{
        SCM             X = SCM_list(size_ - 0, arguments_);
        return SCM_cons(((*self_).I), X);
}
```

```
struct function_2 {
        SCM(*behavior) (void);
        long            arity;
};

SCM function_2(struct function_2 * self_,
        unsigned long size_,
        va_list arguments_)
{
        SCM             I = va_arg(arguments_, SCM);
        return SCM_close(((SCM(*) (void)) function_1), -1, 1, I);
}
```

If we compile it with a compiler conforming to ISO-C (one like gcc for example) with appropriate execution libraries like we've already described, then we get (a little tiny) executable that (very rapidly[6]) produces the value[7] we want.

```
% gcc -ansi -pedantic chap10ex.c scheme.o schemelib.o
% time a.out
(2 3)
0.010u 0.000s 0:00.00 0.0% 3+5k 0+0io 0pf+0w
% size a.out
text    data    bss     dec     hex
28672   4096    32      32800   8020
```

10.9 Representing Data

Now we're going to clarify the set of C macros in the file scheme.h. No need to repeat that the point of this exercise is not to deliver the most high-performance compiler possible, but rather to outline, explain, and demonstrate various techniques! We won't burden ourselves with problems like memory management; there is no garbage collector, and all allocations use the function malloc, making the adaptation of a conservative garbage collector—like the one developed by Hans Boehm in [BW88]—particularly simple.

Values in Lisp and Scheme are such that we can always inquire about their type. Consequently, it is necessary for that information about types to be associated with each value. Making the cost of this association as low as possible is the source of much torment for implementers. Values are also of variable size since they can contain an arbitrary number of values themselves. The work-around is to manipulate these values by their address, since an address has a fixed size. Objects will be allocated in memory, and their type will be encoded as the word preceding them. The inconvenience (in comparison to a statically typed language where types no longer even exist by execution time) is that simple values (like short integers might be) can no longer be handled directly since we have to follow a pointer to get one of them. There are many solutions to this problem. On many machines,

---

6. The time that appears here corresponds mostly to the time for loading the program; the part corresponding to execution is negligible. Later, you'll see how iterating the computation 10000 times gives a time of about 1 second.
7. The benchmarks were measured on a Sony News 3200 with a Mips R3000 processor.

addresses are multiples of four, leaving the two least significant bits free in an address. We can appropriate those bits, for example, to encode the kind of object being pointed to. And if the referenced value is an integer, then why not put it in place of the address? That's what we'll do for integers, making them more efficient but stripping off a bit and thus limiting their range. Other schemes have also been invented, and they are catalogued in [Gud93].

To get back to the task at hand, look at Figure 10.5. A value in Scheme will be represented by a value of C such that if its least significant bit is 1, then it is an integer coded in the remaining bits. We'll be talking about 31-bit integers for a machine of 32-bit words. If the least significant bit is 0, then we're dealing with the address of the first field of an allocated value. The type of that value appears in the word that precedes this address[8] as in [DPS94a]. Such a value appears as a real pointer in C, referring directly to the interesting values of the object. The type of Scheme values in C—what we'll be handling all the time—will be called SCM:

```
typedef union SCM_object          *SCM;
```

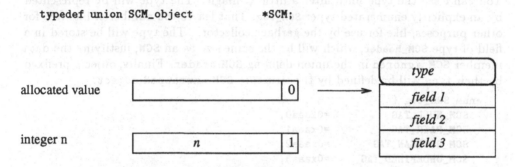

Figure 10.5 Representation of Scheme values in C

The macro `SCM_FixnumP` distinguishes a short integer from a pointer. Small integers and values can be converted back and forth by means of `SCM_Fixnum2int` and `SCM_Int2fixnum`. The integer 37 in Scheme is thus represented by the integer 75 in C.

```
#define SCM_FixnumP(x)    ((unsigned long)(x) & (unsigned long)1)
#define SCM_Fixnum2int(x) ((long)(x)>>1)
#define SCM_Int2fixnum(i) ((SCM)(((i)<<1) | 1))
```

When a value of SCM is not a short integer, it's a pointer to an object defined by `SCM_object`. That's a union of various possible types. Some types are missing, like floating-point numbers, vectors, input and output ports. However, you will find the essential types there: dotted pairs (with `cdr` in the lead to remind you that you're dealing with a list and also because `cdr` is accessed more frequently than `car`, according to [Cla79]).

---

8. The null pointer for C, **NULL**, is generally implemented as 0L. It is not a legal pointer for our compiler because there is seldom a word at the address -1.

```
union SCM_object {              struct SCM_subr {
  struct SCM_pair {               SCM (*behavior)();
    SCM cdr;                       long arity;
    SCM car;                    } subr;
  } pair;                       struct SCM_closure {
  struct SCM_string {             SCM (*behavior)();
    char Cstring[8];              long arity;
  } string;                       SCM environment[1];
  struct SCM_symbol {           } closure;
    SCM pname;                  struct SCM_escape {
  } symbol;                       struct SCM_jmp_buf *stack_address;
  struct SCM_box {              } escape;
    SCM content;              };
  } box;
```

First class objects among the variations of SCM_object are prefixed by their type.
You can't see the type until after a little C magic. The type will be represented
by an explicitly enumerated type: SCM_tag. That leaves the number of bits free for
other purposes, like for use by the garbage collector. The type will be stored in a
field of type SCM_header, which will be the same size as an SCM, justifying the data
member SCM ignored in the union defining SCM_header. Finally, objects prefixed
by their type will be defined by the structure SCM_unwrapped_object.

```
enum SCM_tag {
  SCM_NULL_TAG            =0xaaa0,
  SCM_PAIR_TAG            =0xaaa1,
  SCM_BOOLEAN_TAG         =0xaaa2,
  SCM_UNDEFINED_TAG       =0xaaa3,
  SCM_SYMBOL_TAG          =0xaaa4,
  SCM_STRING_TAG          =0xaaa5,
  SCM_SUBR_TAG            =0xaaa6,
  SCM_CLOSURE_TAG         =0xaaa7,
  SCM_ESCAPE_TAG          =0xaaa8
};
union SCM_header {
  enum SCM_tag tag;
  SCM ignored;
};
union SCM_unwrapped_object {
  struct SCM_unwrapped_immediate_object {
    union SCM_header header;
  } object;
  struct SCM_unwrapped_pair {
    union SCM_header header;
    SCM cdr;
    SCM car;
  } pair;
  struct SCM_unwrapped_string {
    union SCM_header header;
    char Cstring[8];
  } string;
```

```
struct SCM_unwrapped_symbol {
  union SCM_header header;
    SCM pname;
} symbol;
struct SCM_unwrapped_subr {
  union SCM_header header;
  SCM (*behavior)(void);
  long arity;
} subr;
struct SCM_unwrapped_closure {
  union SCM_header header;
  SCM (*behavior)(void);
  long arity;
  SCM environment[1];
} closure;
struct SCM_unwrapped_escape {
  union SCM_header header;
  struct SCM_jmp_buf
             *stack_address;
} escape;
};
```

The following macros convert references back and forth as well as extract its type from an object. In fact, only the execution library needs to distinguish SCM from SCMref.

```
typedef union SCM_unwrapped_object *SCMref;
```

```
#define SCM_Wrap(x)      ((SCM) (((union SCM_header *) x) + 1))
#define SCM_Unwrap(x)    ((SCMref) (((union SCM_header *) x) - 1))
#define SCM_2tag(x)      ((SCM_Unwrap((SCM) x))->object.header.tag)
```

Finally, the addresses of functions written in C (except when applied) are typed as returning an SCM and accepting no arguments. The macro SCM_CfunctionAddress gets this conversion for us.

```
#define SCM_CfunctionAddress(Cfunction) ((SCM (*)(void)) Cfunction)
```

10.9.1 Declaring Values

There is a set of macros to allocate Scheme values statically. Their names are prefixed by SCM_Define. To define a dotted pair, we allocate a structure defined by SCM_unwrapped_pair. Defining a symbol is similar. Each time, the object is first created; then a pointer to that object is also created and converted by SCM_Wrap into a valid reference.

```
#define SCM_DefinePair(pair,car,cdr) \
  static struct SCM_unwrapped_pair pair = {{SCM_PAIR_TAG}, cdr, car }
#define SCM_DefineSymbol(symbol,pname) \
  static struct SCM_unwrapped_symbol symbol = {{SCM_SYMBOL_TAG}, pname }
```

Defining strings is a little more complicated because C does not know how to initialize data structures of variable size. We also have to be careful in C when we handle strings not to confuse their contents with their address, and we must not neglect the null character that completes a string. Our solution is to build a definition of an appropriate structure by the defined string. Strings in Scheme will be represented by strings in C without further ado.

```
#define SCM_DefineString(Cname,string) \
  struct Cname##_struct {            \
    union SCM_header header;          \
    char Cstring[1+sizeof(string)];}; \
  static struct Cname##_struct Cname = \
    {{SCM_STRING_TAG}, string }
```

A number of predefined values have to exist. Actually, only their existence and their type (not their contents) are important to us, so they are defined by immediate objects. We call SCM_Wrap to convert an address into an SCM.

```
#define SCM_DefineImmediateObject(name,tag) \
  struct SCM_unwrapped_immediate_object name = {{tag}}
SCM_DefineImmediateObject(SCM_true_object,SCM_BOOLEAN_TAG);
SCM_DefineImmediateObject(SCM_false_object,SCM_BOOLEAN_TAG);
SCM_DefineImmediateObject(SCM_nil_object,SCM_NULL_TAG);
#define SCM_true        SCM_Wrap(&SCM_true_object)
#define SCM_false       SCM_Wrap(&SCM_false_object)
#define SCM_nil         SCM_Wrap(&SCM_nil_object)
```

Scheme Booleans are not the same as C Booleans, so we must sometimes convert a C Boolean into a Scheme Boolean. SCM_2bool does that.

```
#define SCM_2bool(i) ((i) ? SCM_true : SCM_false )
```

We'll also introduce a few supplementary macros to recognize values and and take them apart. The following predicates have names ending with P to indicate that they return a C Boolean.

```
#define SCM_Car(x)    (SCM_Unwrap(x)->pair.car)
#define SCM_Cdr(x)    (SCM_Unwrap(x)->pair.cdr)
#define SCM_NullP(x)  ((x)==SCM_nil)
#define SCM_PairP(x)  \
  ((!SCM_FixnumP(x)) && (SCM_2tag(x)==SCM_PAIR_TAG))
#define SCM_SymbolP(x) \
  ((!SCM_FixnumP(x)) && (SCM_2tag(x)==SCM_SYMBOL_TAG))
#define SCM_StringP(x) \
  ((!SCM_FixnumP(x)) && (SCM_2tag(x)==SCM_STRING_TAG))
#define SCM_EqP(x,y)  ((x)==(y))
```

Of course, macros like SCM_Car or SCM_Cdr will be used in safe situations when we know that the value is a pair. That's not the case for the following arithmetic macros, so they explicitly test whether their arguments are short integers. This style of progamming prevents removing that part of the context where we would know that the arguments are the right type since they always carry out type checking.[9] We're more interested right now in showing all variations for pedagogical reasons. Again, if we were really trying to be efficient, we would organize things quite differently.

---

9. Or then the C compiler itself takes out these superfluous tests—though that is generally not the case.

```
#define SCM_Plus(x,y)                                              \
  ( ( SCM_FixnumP(x) && SCM_FixnumP(y) )                           \
    ? SCM_Int2fixnum( SCM_Fixnum2int(x) + SCM_Fixnum2int(y) )      \
    : SCM_error(SCM_ERR_PLUS) )
#define SCM_GtP(x,y)                                               \
  ( ( SCM_FixnumP(x) && SCM_FixnumP(y) )                           \
    ? SCM_2bool( SCM_Fixnum2int(x) > SCM_Fixnum2int(y) )           \
    : SCM_error(SCM_ERR_GTP) )
            ...
```

10.9.2   Global Variables

To get the value of a mutable global variable, we use the macro `SCM_CheckedGlobal`
to verify whether the variable has been initialized or not. Consequently, we use
a C value to indicate that something has not been initialized in Scheme, namely,
`SCM_undefined`. Mutable global variables are thus simply initialized (for C) with
this value indicating that (for Scheme) they haven't yet been initialized.

```
#define SCM_CheckedGlobal(Cname) \
   ((Cname != SCM_undefined) ? Cname : SCM_error(SCM_ERR_UNINITIALIZED))
#define SCM_DefineInitializedGlobalVariable(Cname,string,value) \
   SCM Cname = SCM_Wrap(value)
#define SCM_DefineGlobalVariable(Cname,string) \
   SCM_DefineInitializedGlobalVariable(Cname,string, \
                                       &SCM_undefined_object)
#define SCM_undefined    SCM_Wrap(&SCM_undefined_object)
SCM_DefineImmediateObject(SCM_undefined_object,SCM_UNDEFINED_TAG);
```

One very important job is to bind predefined values to the global variables by
which programs can access them. For example, if we assume that the value of
the global variable `NIL` is the empty list, (), then we must bind the C variable
`NIL` to the C value `SCM_nil_object`. That's the purpose of the file `schemelib.c`
containing these definitions among others:

```
SCM_DefineInitializedGlobalVariable(NIL,"NIL",&SCM_nil_object);
SCM_DefineInitializedGlobalVariable(F,"F",&SCM_false_object);
SCM_DefineInitializedGlobalVariable(T,"T",&SCM_true_object);
```

While there is a great deal of folklore surrounding those three variables, `CAR`,
`CONS`, and others also have to be available. We get them from the macro `SCM_Def-`
`inePredefinedFunctionVariable`. Here is its definition, along with a few examples.

```
#define SCM_DefinePredefinedFunctionVariable(subr,string,\
                                      arity,Cfunction) \
   static struct SCM_unwrapped_subr subr##_object = \
     {{SCM_SUBR_TAG}, Cfunction, arity}; \
   SCM_DefineInitializedGlobalVariable(subr,string,&(subr##_object))
SCM_DefinePredefinedFunctionVariable(CAR,"CAR",1,SCM_car);
SCM_DefinePredefinedFunctionVariable(CONS,"CONS",2,SCM_cons);
SCM_DefinePredefinedFunctionVariable(EQN,"=",2,SCM_eqnp);
SCM_DefinePredefinedFunctionVariable(EQ,"EQ?",2,SCM_eqp);
```

Mutable global variables are put into boxes. Reads and writes go through the macro SCM_Content, defined like this:

```
#define SCM_Content(e) ((e)->box.content)
```

10.9.3   Defining Functions

The only thing left to explain is how functions of the program are represented. We have to study the representation of functions very carefully because the greater part of the cooperation between Scheme and C depends on it.

Primitive functions with fixed arity are represented by objects referring to C functions of the same arity. Consequently, the function **cons** could be invoked from C in the form of the simple and mnemonic SCM_cons(x,y).

First class functions in Scheme pose more serious problems. They can take any number of arguments. They can be computed. They may take their arguments in some special way if invoked by **apply**. Coming up with a way that is efficient and yet satisfies all these constraints is far from a trivial job. We'll allow ourselves a little more latitude here in showing several approaches, and for non-primitive functions, we'll adopt a way that is original and systematic (even if it's not very fast). [see **Ex. 10.1**]

Closures are represented by objects where the first field is a pointer to a C function. The second field indicates the arity of the function. The other supplementary fields contain closed variables. The macro SCM_DefineClosure defines an appropriate C structure for each type of closure.

```
#define SCM_DefineClosure(struct_name,fields) \
   struct struct_name {            \
     SCM (*behavior)(void);        \
     long arity;                   \
     fields }
```

When a closure is invoked by SCM_invoke, the closure receives itself as the first argument in order to extract its closed variables. When a function is called with an incorrect number of arguments, an error must be raised. We will assume that the function SCM_invoke takes care of this verification so that it doesn't encumber the one being called. However, when a function receives a variable number of arguments, we have to indicate to it how many to look for because there is no linguistic means of determining that in C. Thus we will assume that C functions associated with Scheme closures take the number of arguments to expect as their second argument. Those arguments come next, as **varargs** in traditional C or now renamed as **stdarg**. As we've already mentioned, this arrangement is not the best you could imagine; the one adopted for primitives is more efficient.

The names of C variables implemented afterwards (such as **self_**, **size_**, and **arguments_**) are for internal use and simply communicate with macros defining local variables. The only interesting case is that of a dotted variable which must package its arguments as a list. The function SCM_list offers the right interface for that purpose.

```
#define SCM_DeclareFunction(Cname) \
   SCM Cname (struct Cname *self_, unsigned long size_, \
```

```
                    va_list arguments_)
#define SCM_DeclareLocalVariable(Cname,rank) \
   SCM Cname = va_arg(arguments_,SCM)
#define SCM_DeclareLocalDottedVariable(Cname,rank) \
   SCM Cname = SCM_list(size_-rank,arguments_)
#define SCM_Free(Cname) ((*self_).Cname)
```

One of the beauties of this approach is that access to closed variables is expressed very simply since they name the data members of the structure associated with the closure.

10.10 Execution Library

The execution library is a set of functions written in C. Those functions must be linked to a program so that the program can get resources that it still lacks. This library is skeletal in that it doesn't contain a lot of basic utility functions like **string-ref** or **close-output-port**. We're going to describe only the major representative functions and ignore the others (notably, **SCM_print** which appears in the generated **main**).

10.10.1 Allocation

There's no memory management, so there's no garbage collector either because building one would take too long. For more about that topic, you should consult [Spi90, Wil92]. We'll leave it as an exercise to adapt Boehm's garbage collector in [BW88] to what follows.

The most obvious allocation function is **cons**. With it, we allocate an object prefixed by its type. We fill in its type the same way that we fill in its **car** and **cdr**. Finally, we convert its address into an **SCM** for the return value.

```
SCM SCM_cons (SCM x, SCM y) {
   SCMref cell = (SCMref) malloc(sizeof(struct SCM_unwrapped_pair));
   if (cell == (SCMref) NULL) SCM_error(SCM_ERR_CANT_ALLOC);
   cell->pair.header.tag = SCM_PAIR_TAG;
   cell->pair.car = x;
   cell->pair.cdr = y;
   return SCM_Wrap(cell);
}
```

Closures are allocated by the function **SCM_close**. It takes a variable number of arguments, so *a posteriori* that justifies our choice about using multiple arguments in C. Thus we need to allocate an object of type **SCM_CLOSURE_TAG** and to fill in the other fields in terms of the number of arguments received.

```
SCM
SCM_close (SCM (*Cfunction)(void), long arity, unsigned long size, ...) {
   SCMref result = (SCMref) malloc(sizeof(struct SCM_unwrapped_closure)
                                   + (size-1)*sizeof(SCM) );
   unsigned long i;
   va_list args;
   if (result == (SCMref) NULL) SCM_error(SCM_ERR_CANT_ALLOC);
```

```
result->closure.header.tag = SCM_CLOSURE_TAG;
result->closure.behavior = Cfunction;
result->closure.arity = arity;
va_start(args,size);
for ( i=0 ; i<size ; i++ ) {
  result->closure.environment[i] = va_arg(args,SCM);
}
va_end(args);
return SCM_Wrap(result);
}
```

10.10.2 Functions on Pairs

The functions **car** and **set-car!** are simple, but they must not be confused with
macros bearing similar names. These functions are safe in the sense that they
test the types of their arguments before applying them. In general, there is a safe
function and an unsafe function, and the latter should not be substituted for the
former except when the compiler can be sure that the substitution is legitimate.
Even though Lisp is not typed, its programs are such that almost two times out of
three, type testing can be suppressed, according to [Hen92a, WC94, Ser94]. The
attitude is that programmers are type-checking in their head, so a clever compiler
can take advantage of that "preprocessing."

```
SCM SCM_car (SCM x) {
  if ( SCM_PairP(x) ) {
    return SCM_Car(x);
  } else return SCM_error(SCM_ERR_CAR);
}
SCM SCM_set_cdr (SCM x, SCM y) {
  if ( SCM_PairP(x) ) {
    SCM_Unwrap(x)->pair.cdr = y;
    return x;
  } else return SCM_error(SCM_ERR_SET_CDR);
}
```

It's also a good idea to understand the function **list**. It takes a variable
number of arguments and thus receives them prefixed by that number. We have to
admit that for its internal programming, we have once again sinned by resorting
to recursion rather than iteration.

```
SCM SCM_list (unsigned long count, va_list arguments) {
  if ( count == 0 ) {
    return SCM_nil;
  } else {
    SCM arg = va_arg(arguments,SCM);
    return SCM_cons(arg,SCM_list(count-1,arguments));
  }
}
```

There is no error-trapping mechanism. We'll simply indicate errors by means
of the C macro **SCM_error**. It conveys a representative error code (customary in C),
the line number, and the file where the error occurred.

```
#define SCM_error(code) SCM_signal_error(code,__LINE__,__FILE__)
SCM SCM_signal_error (unsigned long code,
                      unsigned long line,
                      char *file ) {
  fflush(stdout);
  fprintf(stderr,"Error %u, Line %u, File %s.\n",code,line,file);
  exit(code);
}
```

10.10.3   Invocation

The two really important and subtle functions in the domain of invocations are
`SCM_invoke` and `apply`.   That's not surprising about `apply` since it has to know
the calling protocol for functions in order to conform to it.

All the function calls other than those that are integrated (that is, transformed
into a direct call to a macro or to the C function involved) pass through `SCM_invoke`.
It takes the function to call as its first argument. As its second argument, it takes
the number of arguments provided, and those arguments come next. As in the
preceding interpreters, the function `SCM_invoke` is more or less generic. It analyzes
its first argument to see that it is an invocable object: a primitive function or not
(or an escape). It then extracts the object to apply and the arity of that object.
Having extracted the arity, it compares the number of arguments it actually received. Finally, it passes these arguments to the function, following the appropriate
protocol. Here we have three different protocols. There are others, such as suffixing
the arguments by some constant such as `NULL` rather than prefixing them by their
number. (That's what Bigloo does.)

- Primitives with fixed arity (like `SCM_cons`) are called directly with their arguments. The function call can be categorized as being of the type $f(x, y)$.

- Primitives with variable arity (like `SCM_list`) must necessarily know the number of arguments provided. That number will be passed as the first argument.
  The function call is thus of the type $f(n, x_1, x_2, \ldots, x_n)$.

- Closures must not only know the number of arguments received (when they
  have variable arity) but also they have to get their closed variables, stored,
  in fact, in the closure itself. The type of function call they produce will thus
  be of the type $f(f, n, x_1, x_2, \ldots, x_n)$.

Of course, we could refine, unify, or even eliminate some of these protocols, so
here is the function `SCM_invoke`. In spite of its massive size, it is actually quite
regular in structure. (We have withheld the part about continuations. We'll get to
them in the next section.)

```
SCM SCM_invoke(SCM function, unsigned long number, ...) {
  if ( SCM_FixnumP(function) ) {
    return SCM_error(SCM_ERR_CANNOT_APPLY); /* Cannot apply a number! */
  } else {
    switch SCM_2tag(function) {
    case SCM_SUBR_TAG: {
      SCM (*behavior)(void) = (SCM_Unwrap(function)->subr).behavior;
```

```
long arity = (SCM_Unwrap(function)->subr).arity;
SCM result;
if ( arity >= 0 ) {            /* Fixed arity subr */
  if ( arity != number ) {
    return SCM_error(SCM_ERR_WRONG_ARITY); /* Wrong arity! */
  } else {
    if ( arity == 0 ) {
      result = behavior();
    } else {
      va_list args;
      va_start(args,number);
      { SCM a0 ;
        a0 = va_arg(args,SCM);
        if ( arity == 1 ) {
          result = ((SCM (*)(SCM)) *behavior)(a0);
        } else {
          SCM a1 ;
          a1 = va_arg(args,SCM);
          if ( arity == 2 ) {
            result = ((SCM (*)(SCM,SCM)) *behavior)(a0,a1);
          } else {
            SCM a2 ;
            a2 = va_arg(args,SCM);
            if ( arity == 3 ) {
              result = ((SCM (*)(SCM,SCM,SCM))
                        *behavior)(a0,a1,a2);
            } else {
              /* No fixed arity subr with more than 3 variables */
              return SCM_error(SCM_ERR_INTERNAL);
            }
          }
        }
      }
      va_end(args);
    }
    return result;
  }
} else {                       /* Nary subr */
  long min_arity = SCM_MinimalArity(arity) ;
  if ( number < min_arity ) {
    return SCM_error(SCM_ERR_MISSING_ARGS);
  } else {
    va_list args;
    SCM result;
    va_start(args,number);
    result = ((SCM (*)(unsigned long,va_list))
              *behavior)(number,args);
    va_end(args);
    return result;
  }
}
```

```
      }
      case SCM_CLOSURE_TAG: {
        SCM (*behavior)(void) = (SCM_Unwrap(function)->closure).behavior ;
        long arity = (SCM_Unwrap(function)->closure).arity ;
        SCM result;
        va_list args;
        va_start(args,number);
        if ( arity >= 0 ) {
          if ( arity != number ) { /* Wrong arity! */
            return SCM_error(SCM_ERR_WRONG_ARITY);
          } else {
            result = ((SCM (*)(SCM,unsigned long,va_list)) *behavior)
                      (function,number,args);
          }
        } else {
          long min_arity = SCM_MinimalArity(arity) ;
          if ( number < min_arity ) {
            return SCM_error(SCM_ERR_MISSING_ARGS);
          } else {
            result = ((SCM (*)(SCM,unsigned long,va_list)) *behavior)
                      (function,number,args);
          }
        }
        va_end(args);
        return result;
      }
      default: {
        SCM_error(SCM_ERR_CANNOT_APPLY);              /* Cannot apply! */
      }
    }
  }
}
```

The function **apply** is equally imposing in size. What's interesting about it is that since it is a primitive function of fixed arity, it gets its arguments as an instance of **va_list** where the last position contains a list that it must explore. The problem of interfacing multiple variables in C is that we can't construct new instances of **va_list** because it is a type that is private to the implementation of the C compiler. The only thing we can do is patiently accept this glitch and distinguish all the arities to generate all plausible calls. The boring part is that we can't enumerate all of them, so we must constrain **apply** to transmit only a limited number of arguments. That case was foreseen for COMMON LISP since there we have a constant—**call-arguments-limit**—to indicate the maximum number of arguments allowed. Its value should be at least 50. We'll restrict[10] ourselves to 14, of which only the first four possibilities are shown here.

```
SCM SCM_apply (unsigned long number, va_list arguments) {
  SCM args[31];
  SCM last_arg;
  SCM fun = va_arg(arguments,SCM);
```

---

10. If this limitation seems absurd to you, then test its value in your favorite Lisp.

```
unsigned long i;
for ( i=0 ; i<number-1 ; i++  ) {
  args[i] = va_arg(arguments,SCM);
}
last_arg = args[--i];
while ( SCM_PairP(last_arg) ) {
  args[i++] = SCM_Car(last_arg);
  last_arg = SCM_Cdr(last_arg);
}
if ( ! SCM_NullP(last_arg) ) {
  SCM_error(SCM_ERR_APPLY_ARG);
}
switch ( i ) {
case 0: return SCM_invoke(fun,0);
case 1: return SCM_invoke(fun,1,args[0]);
case 2: return SCM_invoke(fun,2,args[0],args[1]);
case 3: return SCM_invoke(fun,3,args[0],args[1],args[2]);
case 4: return SCM_invoke(fun,4,args[0],args[1],args[2],args[3]);
                    ...
default: return SCM_error(SCM_ERR_APPLY_SIZE);
}
}
```

Since C doesn't support more than 32 arguments anyway, there is no need for as many as 50. Purists will notice the (unnecessary?) test verifying whether the last **cdr** of the list containing the final arguments submitted to **apply** is really empty.

The essential problem of invocation in C is that it doesn't preserve the property imposed by Scheme that a tail call should make a constant continuation. In consequence, a program translated into C can be interrupted because of stack overflow—a situation that could not occur with any standard implementation of Scheme. Some compilers from Scheme to C (such as Scheme→C or Bigloo) use a great deal of energy to avoid such problems. They look for recursive functions, loops, and so forth, but they cannot find every case and are thus vulnerable to certain programming styles. Another solution is not to use the C stack and instead to handle Scheme continuations explicitly.

10.11   `call/cc`: To Have and Have Not

We've just finished the compilation of a significant part of Scheme into C. In spite of the fact that we still lack many functions, the essentials are present (even if not very efficient). Continuations, in contrast, are still missing. As we did for the byte-code compiler, we'll first define the function **call/ep** to provide continuations with a dynamic extent, as in Lisp, and we'll translate that by **setjmp/longjmp**.

Then in the second part of this section, we'll tackle the remaining issues about providing real continuations like in Scheme.

10.11.1 The Function call/ep

We described the function `call/ep` already in the same interface as the function `call/cc`, but the first class continuation that it synthesizes cannot legitimately be used except during its dynamic extent. [see p. 102] Here, we'll use the same implementation as in Chapter 7 to know that we've allocated an object on the heap to represent the continuation. That object will point to the `jmp_buf` in the stack, and that jump itself will refer to the continuation. Here are the functions involved:

```
SCM SCM_allocate_continuation (struct SCM_jmp_buf *address) {
  SCMref continuation =
        (SCMref) malloc(sizeof(struct SCM_unwrapped_escape));
  if (continuation == (SCMref) NULL) SCM_error(SCM_ERR_CANT_ALLOC);
  continuation->escape.header.tag = SCM_ESCAPE_TAG;
  continuation->escape.stack_address = address;
  return SCM_Wrap(continuation);
}
struct SCM_jmp_buf {
  SCM back_pointer;
  jmp_buf jb;
};
SCM SCM_callep (SCM f) {
  struct SCM_jmp_buf scmjb;
  SCM continuation = SCM_allocate_continuation(&scmjb);
  scmjb.back_pointer = continuation;
  if ( setjmp(scmjb.jb) != 0 ) {
    return jumpvalue;
  } else {
    return SCM_invoke1(f,continuation);
  }
}
```

When a continuation is invoked, the function `SCM_invoke` perceives it and verifies the arity of this call before going on to the call itself. The following fragment should be inserted in the function `SCM_invoke` as we've already defined it. To verify that the continuation is valid (and because we have no `unwind-protect` to invalidate it), we test whether it matches the `jmp_buf` in the stack and whether we really are *above* that `jmp_buf`. Unfortunately, that second verification requires us to know the direction of the C stack. That information is packaged in the macro `SCM_STACK_HIGHER`. The definition of that macro depends on the implementation, of course, but we can get information about it from a simple little program in portable C. Generally, with Un*x, the stack grows with decreasing addresses, so `SCM_STACK_HIGHER` is none other than `<=`.

```
...  case SCM_ESCAPE_TAG: {
       if ( number == 1) {
         va_list args;
         va_start(args,number);
         jumpvalue = va_arg(args,SCM);
         va_end(args);
         { struct SCM_jmp_buf *address =
             SCM_Unwrap(function)->escape.stack_address;
```

```
        if ( SCM_EqP(address->back_pointer,function)
            && ( (void *) &address
                    SCM_STACK_HIGHER (void *) address ) ) {
          longjmp(address->jb,1);
        } else {      /* surely out of dynamic extent! */
          return SCM_error(SCM_ERR_OUT_OF_EXTENT);
        }
      }
    }
  } else {
    /* Not enough arguments! */
    return SCM_error(SCM_ERR_MISSING_ARGS);
  }
} ...
```

What we said about the efficiency of **call/ep** in the context of the byte-code compiler no longer holds true here because in C **longjmp** is notoriously slow and thus enormously delays programs that use it too much. The point for us, however, is to show how well we can integrate Lisp and C, so we'll live with it.

10.11.2   The Function call/cc

Alas! if you're nostalgic for real continuations, then you are probably still longing for them at this point. We know that we can get **call/cc** as a magic function, mysterious and obscure, but unfortunately in order to *write* it, we need to know at least a little about the C stack because that stack contains what we want to capture. Unfortunately, C doesn't really offer a *portable* means of inspecting the stack so it is extremely hard to implement this type of continuation in portable C without loading ourselves down with conditional definitions. Our only choice, then, is to use CPS to transform a program so that continuations appear and then compile it all with the preceding compiler.

Making Continuations Explicit

The transformation we'll offer is equivalent to the one we presented earlier and once again uses our favorite code walker. [see p. 177] This transformation works on the initial expression, once it has been objectified. However, since the **let** forms (that is, nodes of the class **Fix-Let**) will have disappeared in this affair, we will re-introduce them by means of a second code walk to retrieve and convert closed forms. In passing, it will suppress the infamous administrative redexes. (Just after CPS, we'll explain the transformation **letify**.) Here's the new version of the compiler:

```
(define (compile->C e out)
  (set! g.current '())
  (let* ((ee (letify (cpsify (Sexp->object e)) '()))
         (prg (extract-things! (lift! ee))) )
    (gather-temporaries! (closurize-main! prg))
    (generate-C-program out e prg) ) )
```

The code walker that makes continuations explicit is called **cpsify**. It results from the interaction between the function **update-walk!** and the generic function

->CPS. Two new classes of objects are introduced: the class of continuations (serving only to mark abstractions that play the role of continuations) and the class of pseudo-variables (serving as variables for continuations).

```
(define-class Continuation Function ())
(define-class Pseudo-Variable Local-Variable ())
(define (cpsify e)
  (let ((v (new-Variable)))
    (->CPS e (make-Continuation (list v) (make-Local-Reference v))) ) )
(define new-Variable
  (let ((counter 0))
    (lambda ()
      (set! counter (+ 1 counter))
      (make-Pseudo-Variable counter #f #f) ) ) )
```

The function ->CPS takes the object to convert as its first argument and the current continuation as its second. By default, it applies the continuation to the object. The initial continuation appearing in cpsify is the objectified identity, $\lambda x.x$.

```
(define-generic (->CPS (e Program) k)
  (convert2Regular-Application k e) )
(define (convert2Regular-Application k . args)
  (make-Regular-Application k (convert2arguments args)) )
```

Now all we have to do is to articulate the appropriate methods. For sequences, that's simple: we convert the first form and relegate the second one to the continuation, like this:

```
(define-method (->CPS (e Sequence) k)
  (->CPS (Sequence-first e)
         (let ((v (new-Variable)))
           (make-Continuation
             (list v) (->CPS (Sequence-last e) k) ) ) ) )
```

For alternatives, the method is also simple, but the continuation should be duplicated in both branches of an alternative, like this:

```
(define-method (->CPS (e Alternative) k)
  (->CPS (Alternative-condition e)
         (let ((v (new-Variable)))
           (make-Continuation
             (list v) (make-Alternative
                        (make-Local-Reference v)
                        (->CPS (Alternative-consequent e) k)
                        (->CPS (Alternative-alternant e) k) ) ) ) ) )
```

Assignments are also straightforward. We convert the value to assign while being careful to make the modification in the continuation, like this:

```
(define-method (->CPS (e Box-Write) k)
  (->CPS (Box-Write-form e)
         (let ((v (new-Variable)))
           (make-Continuation
             (list v) (convert2Regular-Application
                        k (make-Box-Write
```

```
                              (Box-Write-reference e)
                              (make-Local-Reference v) ) ) ) ) ) )
(define-method (->CPS (e Global-Assignment) k)
  (->CPS (Global-Assignment-form e)
         (let ((v (new-Variable)))
           (make-Continuation
            (list v) (convert2Regular-Application
                      k (make-Global-Assignment
                         (Global-Assignment-variable e)
                         (make-Local-Reference v) ) ) ) ) ) ) )
```

To simplify our lives (and because objectification is overdoing things), we undo
closed applications in favor of an application of a closure. You recall that closed
applications generated by transformations are identified by **letify**. There will
be a great many of those by the way because the naïve CPS transformation that
we programmed generates many *administrative* redexes [SF92]. Those redexes are
not too troublesome, however, because if they are compiled correctly, they will
just naturally go away; they may be ugly to look at, but they interfere only with
interpretation.

```
(define-method (->CPS (e Fix-Let) k)
  (->CPS (make-Regular-Application
          (make-Function (Fix-Let-variables e) (Fix-Let-body e))
          (Fix-Let-arguments e) )
         k ) )
```

Functions will be burdened with another argument, one to represent the continuation of their caller.

```
(define-method (->CPS (e Function) k)
  (convert2Regular-Application
   k (let ((k (new-Variable)))
       (make-Function (cons k (Function-variables e))
                      (->CPS (Function-body e)
                             (make-Local-Reference k) ) ) ) ) ) )
```

Functional applications are more complicated forms that have to be handled
in a similar way. We must compute all the arguments, one after another, before
applying the function to them. Once again, in doing that, we've chosen left to right
order.

```
(define-method (->CPS (e Predefined-Application) k)
  (let* ((args (Predefined-Application-arguments e))
         (vars (let name ((args args))
                 (if (Arguments? args)
                     (cons (new-Variable)
                           (name (Arguments-others args)) )
                     '() ) ))
         (application
          (convert2Regular-Application
           k
           (make-Predefined-Application
            (Predefined-Application-variable e)
            (convert2arguments
```

```
                    (map make-Local-Reference vars) ) ) ) ) )
        (arguments->CPS args vars application) ) )
  (define-method (->CPS (e Regular-Application) k)
    (let* ((fun (Regular-Application-function e))
           (args (Regular-Application-arguments e))
           (varfun (new-Variable))
           (vars (let name ((args args))
                   (if (Arguments? args)
                       (cons (new-Variable)
                             (name (Arguments-others args)) )
                       '() ) ))
           (application
            (make-Regular-Application
             (make-Local-Reference varfun)
             (make-Arguments k (convert2arguments
                                (map make-Local-Reference vars) ) ) ) ) )
      (->CPS fun (make-Continuation
                  (list varfun)
                  (arguments->CPS args vars application) )) ) )
  (define (arguments->CPS args vars appl)
    (if (pair? vars)
        (->CPS (Arguments-first args)
               (make-Continuation
                (list (car vars))
                (arguments->CPS (Arguments-others args)
                                (cdr vars)
                                appl ) ) )
        appl ) )
```

Re-introducing Closed Forms

The letify transformation indicated earlier has the responsibility of identifying closed forms and translating them into appropriate let forms. However, we're going to take advantage of a little polishing here to clean up the result of ->CPS. When ->CPS handles an alternative, it will duplicate the same subtree of abstract syntax representing the continuation—by sharing it physically—in both branches of the alternative. Thus we no longer have a tree of abstract syntax, but rather a DAG (directed acyclic graph). To avoid having the eventual transformations fumble because of these hidden physical sharings, the function letify will entirely copy the DAG of abstract syntax into a pure tree of abstract syntax. We assume that we have the generic function clone available for that. [see Ex. 11.2] It should be able to duplicate any MEROONET object, and we'll adapt it to the case of variables that must be renamed. So here is that transformation. With collect-temporaries!, it has a certain resemblance to renaming local variables.

```
(define-generic (letify (o Program) env)
  (update-walk! letify (clone o) env) )
(define-method (letify (o Function) env)
  (let* ((vars (Function-variables o))
         (body (Function-body o))
```

```
                 (new-vars (map clone vars)) )
        (make-Function
         new-vars
         (letify body (append (map cons vars new-vars) env)) ) ) )
   (define-method (letify (o Local-Reference) env)
     (let* ((v (Local-Reference-variable o))
            (r (assq v env)) )
        (if (pair? r)
            (make-Local-Reference (cdr r))
            (letify-error "Disappeared variable" o) ) ) )
   (define-method (letify (o Regular-Application) env)
     (if (Function? (Regular-Application-function o))
         (letify (process-closed-application
                   (Regular-Application-function o)
                   (Regular-Application-arguments o) )
                 env )
         (make-Regular-Application
           (letify (Regular-Application-function o) env)
           (letify (Regular-Application-arguments o) env) )  ) )
   (define-method (letify (o Fix-Let) env)
     (let* ((vars (Fix-Let-variables o))
            (new-vars (map clone vars)) )
        (make-Fix-Let
         new-vars
         (letify (Fix-Let-arguments o) env)
         (letify (Fix-Let-body o)
                 (append (map cons vars new-vars) env) ) ) ) )
   (define-method (letify (o Box-Creation) env)
     (let* ((v (Box-Creation-variable o))
            (r (assq v env)) )
        (if (pair? r)
            (make-Box-Creation (cdr r))
            (letify-error "Disappeared variable" o) ) ) )
   (define-method (clone (o Pseudo-Variable))
     (new-Variable) )
```

Execution Library

It's probably hard for you to see where the preceding transformation is going.
Its goal is to make continuations apparent, that is, to make call/cc trivial to
implement. A continuation will be represented by a closure that forgets the current continuation in order to restore the one that it represents. Here's the definition of SCM_callcc. Since it is a normal function, it is called with the continuation of the caller as its first argument, so here its arity is two! The function
SCM_invoke_continuation appears first to help the C compiler, which likes to find
things in the right order.

```
SCM SCM_invoke_continuation (SCM self, unsigned long number,
                             va_list arguments) {
  SCM current_k = va_arg(arguments,SCM);
```

```
    SCM value      = va_arg(arguments,SCM);
    return SCM_invoke1(SCM_Unwrap(self)->closure.environment[0],value);
}


SCM SCM_callcc (SCM k, SCM f) {
  SCM reified_k =
    SCM_close(SCM_CfunctionAddress(SCM_invoke_continuation),
              2, 1, k);
  return SCM_invoke2(f,k,reified_k);
}
```

```
SCM_DefinePredefinedFunctionVariable(CALLCC,"CALL/CC",2,SCM_callcc);
```

The library of predefined functions in C has not changed. In contrast, their call
protocol has been modified somewhat because of these swarms of continuations. If
we write (let ((f car)) (f '(a b))), then our dumb compiler does not realize
that it is in fact equivalent to (car '(a b)) (or even directly equivalent to (quote
a) by propagating constants). It will generate a computed call to the value of the
global variable CAR, which will receive a continuation as its first argument and a
pair as its second. The new value of CAR is, in fact, merely (lambda (k p) (k
(car p))) expressed with the old function car. Consequently, we will introduce
a few C macros again here, and we will redefine the initial library with an arity
increased by one. So that we don't leave you behind here, we'll show you a few
examples. The functions prefixed by SCMq_ make up the interface to functions
prefixed by SCM_.

```
    #define SCM_DefineCPSsubr2(newname,oldname)              \
      SCM newname (SCM k, SCM x, SCM y) {                    \
        return SCM_invoke1(k,oldname(x,y));                  \
      }
    #define SCM_DefineCPSsubrN(newname,oldname)                      \
      SCM newname (unsigned long number, va_list arguments) {        \
        SCM k = va_arg(arguments,SCM);                               \
        return SCM_invoke1(k,oldname(number-1,arguments));           \
    }
    SCM_DefineCPSsubr2(SCMq_gtp,SCM_gtp)
    SCM_DefinePredefinedFunctionVariable(GREATERP,">",3,SCMq_gtp);
    SCM_DefineCPSsubrN(SCMq_list,SCM_list)
    SCM_DefinePredefinedFunctionVariable(LIST,"LIST",-2,SCMq_list);
```

One last problem is what to do with apply. We have to re-arrange its arguments
so that the continuation gets them in the right positions.

```
    SCM SCMq_apply (unsigned long number, va_list arguments) {
      SCM args[32];
      SCM last_arg;
      SCM k   = va_arg(arguments,SCM);
      SCM fun = va_arg(arguments,SCM);
      unsigned long i;
      for ( i=0 ; i<number-2 ; i++  ) {
        args[i] = va_arg(arguments,SCM);
      }
      last_arg = args[--i];
```

```
while ( SCM_PairP(last_arg) ) {
  args[i++] = SCM_Car(last_arg);
  last_arg = SCM_Cdr(last_arg);
}
if ( ! SCM_NullP(last_arg) ) {
  SCM_error(SCM_ERR_APPLY_ARG);
}
switch ( i ) {
case 0: return SCM_invoke(fun,1,k);
case 1: return SCM_invoke(fun,2,k,args[0]);
case 2: return SCM_invoke(fun,3,k,args[0],args[1]);
...
 default: return SCM_error(SCM_ERR_APPLY_SIZE);
 }
}
```

Example

Let's take our current example and look at the generated code. In spite of the C syntax, you can still see the "color" of CPS in it.

---

o/chap10kex.c

```
 2 /* Compiler to C $Revision: 4.0 $
 3 (BEGIN
 4   (SET! INDEX 1)
 5   ((LAMBDA
 6      (CNTER . TMP)
 7      (SET! TMP (CNTER (LAMBDA (I) (LAMBDA X (CONS I X)))))
 8      (IF CNTER (CNTER TMP) INDEX))
 9      (LAMBDA (F) (SET! INDEX (+ 1 INDEX)) (F INDEX))
10      'FOO)) */
11
12 #include "scheme.h"
13
14 /* Global environment: */
15 SCM_DefineGlobalVariable(INDEX,"INDEX");
16
17 /* Quotations: */
18 #define thing3 SCM_nil /* () */
19 SCM_DefineString(thing4_object,"FOO");
20 #define thing4 SCM_Wrap(&thing4_object)
21 SCM_DefineSymbol(thing2_object,thing4);        /* FOO */
22 #define thing2 SCM_Wrap(&thing2_object)
23 #define thing1 SCM_Int2fixnum(1)
24 #define thing0 thing1 /* 1 */
25
26 /* Functions: */
27 SCM_DefineClosure(function_0, SCM I; );
28
```

```
29 SCM_DeclareFunction(function_0) {
30   SCM_DeclareLocalVariable(v_25,0);
31   SCM_DeclareLocalDottedVariable(X,1);
32   SCM v_27; SCM v_26;
33   return (v_26=SCM_Free(I),
34           (v_27=X,
35            SCM_invoke1(v_25,
36                        SCM_cons(v_26,
37                                 v_27))));
38 }
39
40 SCM_DefineClosure(function_1, );
41
42 SCM_DeclareFunction(function_1) {
43   SCM_DeclareLocalVariable(v_24,0);
44   SCM_DeclareLocalVariable(I,1);
45   return SCM_invoke1(v_24,
46                      SCM_close(SCM_CfunctionAddress
47                                (function_0),-2,1,I));
48 }
49
50 SCM_DefineClosure(function_2, SCM v_15; SCM CNTER; SCM TMP; );
51
52 SCM_DeclareFunction(function_2) {
53   SCM_DeclareLocalVariable(v_21,0);
54   SCM v_20; SCM v_19; SCM v_18; SCM v_17;
55   return (v_17=(SCM_Content(SCM_Free(TMP))=v_21),
56          (v_18=SCM_Free(CNTER),
57           ((v_18 != SCM_false)
58           ? (v_19=SCM_Free(CNTER),
59             (v_20=SCM_Content(SCM_Free(TMP)),
60              SCM_invoke2(v_19,
61                          SCM_Free(v_15),
62                          v_20)))
63           : SCM_invoke1(SCM_Free(v_15),
64                         SCM_CheckedGlobal(INDEX)))));
65 }
66
67 SCM_DefineClosure(function_3, );
68
69 SCM_DeclareFunction(function_3) {
70   SCM_DeclareLocalVariable(v_15,0);
71   SCM_DeclareLocalVariable(CNTER,1);
72   SCM_DeclareLocalVariable(TMP,2);
73   SCM v_23; SCM v_22; SCM v_16;
74   return (v_16=TMP= SCM_allocate_box(TMP),
75          (v_22=CNTER,
76          (v_23=SCM_close(SCM_CfunctionAddress(function_1),2,0),
77           SCM_invoke2(v_22,
78                       SCM_close(SCM_CfunctionAddress
79                                 (function_2),1,3,v_15,CNTER,TMP),
```

```
80                       v_23))));
81 }
82
83 SCM_DefineClosure(function_4, );
84
85 SCM_DeclareFunction(function_4) {
86   SCM_DeclareLocalVariable(v_8,0);
87   SCM_DeclareLocalVariable(F,1);
88   SCM v_11; SCM v_10; SCM v_9; SCM v_12; SCM v_14; SCM v_13;
89   return (v_13=thing1,
90          (v_14=SCM_CheckedGlobal(INDEX),
91          (v_12=SCM_Plus(v_13,
92                         v_14),
93          (v_9=(INDEX=v_12),
94           (v_10=F,
95           (v_11=SCM_CheckedGlobal(INDEX),
96            SCM_invoke2(v_10,
97                        v_8,
98                        v_11)))))));
99 }
100
101 SCM_DefineClosure(function_5, );
102
103 SCM_DeclareFunction(function_5) {
104   SCM_DeclareLocalVariable(v_1,0);
105   return v_1;
106 }
107
108 SCM_DefineClosure(function_6, );
109
110 SCM_DeclareFunction(function_6) {
111   SCM v_5; SCM v_7; SCM v_6; SCM v_4; SCM v_3; SCM v_2; SCM v_28;
112   return (v_28=thing0,
113          (v_2=(INDEX=v_28),
114          (v_3=SCM_close(SCM_CfunctionAddress(function_3),3,0),
115          (v_4=SCM_close(SCM_CfunctionAddress(function_4),2,0),
116          (v_6=thing2,
117           (v_7=thing3,
118           (v_5=SCM_cons(v_6,
119                         v_7),
120            SCM_invoke3(v_3,
121                        SCM_close(SCM_CfunctionAddress
122                                  (function_5),1,0),
123                        v_4,
124                        v_5))))))));
125 }
126
127
128 /* Expression: */
129 void main(void) {
130   SCM_print(SCM_invoke0(SCM_close(SCM_CfunctionAddress
```

```
131                          (function_6),0,0)));
132   exit(0);
133 }
134
135 /* End of generated code. */
136
```

You see that the size of the file we produce grows from 76 to 130 lines. The number of functions generated by compilation also increases from 3 to 6, and the number of local variables used increases from 2 to 22. In short, the executable has fattened up a bit. The computation takes a little longer, too. (It took about 50% longer on our machine.) Afterwards, we modified **main** to repeat the computation 10 000 times (without calling **SCM_print**), and we compiled with **-O** as the optimization level. The computation then increased from 1.1 seconds to 1.7. In both cases, the computation consumes the same amount of space for continuations, but in the first case, the allocations occur on the stack (where the hardware and the C compiler provide ingenious treasures for us) whereas in the second case, allocations occur on the heap and destroy the locality of its references. As shown in [AS94], we could, of course, overcome most of these disadvantages.

```
% gcc -ansi -pedantic chap10kex.c scheme.o schemeklib.o
% time a.out
(2 3)
0.000u 0.020s 0:00.00 0.0% 3+3k 0+0io 0pf+0w
% size a.out
text    data    bss     dec     hex
32768   4096    32      36896   9020
```

The transformation that we just described does not get around the problem of stack overflow due to our not preserving the property of tail recursion. In fact, it is actually made worse by the transformation since the transformation produces more applications than before but never comes back to these applications. Functions are called but never return a result, so the C stack will overflow eventually if the computation is not completed before. One solution is to make a **longjmp** from time to time, just to lower the stack, as in [Bak].

10.12   Interface with C

Since our little compiler can represent data, and in addition, it has adopted the calling protocol for C functions, it is particularly well suited to use with C. This *foreign interface* is very important because it can take advantage of huge libraries of utilities written in C. We'll show you an example of such a foreign interface, one chosen to illustrate both its usefulness and the associated problems.

The UN*X **system** function takes a character string, hands it to the command interpreter (**sh**), and then returns an integer corresponding to its return code. We'll assume that we have a macro available—**defforeignprimitive**—to declare the interface for this **system** function to the compiler, like this:

```
(defforeignprimitive system int ("system" string) 1)
```

As planned, when the compiler sees (`system` π), the compiler will verify that its argument is a character string; then it will call the `system` function, and eventually it will convert the result (a C integer) into a Scheme integer. Since C strings and Scheme strings are coded the same way, it's easy to convert one to the other, but other conversions can pose strenuous problems, according to [RM92, DPS94a].

Of course, that conversion is not quite enough. We must again insure that the `system` function can be called by a computation or by `apply`. That condition implies that there must be a Scheme value representing the function, but we'll ignore that delicate problem.

10.13   Conclusions

This chapter presented a compiler from Scheme to C. We could adapt that compiler to the execution library of evaluators written in C, such as Bigloo [Ser94], SIOD [Car94], or SCM [Jaf94]. In this chapter, you've been able to see the problems of compilation into a high-level language, the gap that separates Scheme from C, and also the benefits of reasonable cooperation between the two languages.

We strongly urge you to compare the compiler towards C with the compiler into byte-code. We could readily marry the techniques you saw earlier with the new ones here, for example:

- changing the compilation of quotations so that they would be read by `read`;
- freeing ourselves from the C stack (and from C calling protocol) to take advantage of a stack dedicated to Scheme;
- extending the compiler to compile independent modules; and so on. **[see p. 223]**

We could also measure the cost (in the size of the execution library and in the speed of computations) of adding a function such as `load`, or more simply, `eval`. We'll leave how to incorporate them as a (strenuous) exercise. And we'll also leave as an exercise just how to bootstrap the evaluator, once it's been stuffed like that.

10.14   Exercises

Exercise 10.1 : Invoking closures could borrow the same technique as the one used for predefined functions of fixed arity; that is, it could adopt a model that could be characterized as $f(f, x, y)$. Modify whatever needs to be changed to improve the compiler in that way.

Exercise 10.2 : Access to global variables would be more efficient if we suppressed the test `SCM_CheckedGlobal` on reading. That test verifies whether the variable has been initialized. Design another analysis of initialization. In doing so, look for a way to characterize the references for which you can be sure that the variable has been initialized.

Project 10.3 : The code produced by the compiler in this chapter generates C that conforms to ISO 90 [ISO90]. Modify whatever is necessary to generate Kernighan & Ritchie C as in [KR78].

Project 10.4 : Adapt the code generator in this chapter to produce C++, as in [Str86], rather than C.

Recommended Reading

In recent years, there has been a lot of good work about compiling into C. Nitsan Séniak treats the topic excellently in his thesis [Sén91], as does Manuel Serrano in [Ser94]. If you are completely enamored of this subject, you can happily lose yourself in the source code for Bigloo [Ser94].

11

Essence of an Object System

OBJECTS! Oh, where would we be without them? This chapter defines the object system that we've used throughout this book. We deliberately restricted ourselves to a limited set of characteristics so that we would not overburden the description which will follow here. In fact, as Rabelais would say, we want to limit it to its *sustantificque mouelle*, that is, to its very essence.

This object system is called MEROON.[1] Such a system is complicated and demands considerable attention if we want it to be simultaneously efficient and portable. As a result, the system is endowed with a structure strongly influenced, maybe even distorted, by our worries about portability. To compensate for that, we're actually going to show you a reduced version of MEROON, and we'll call that reduced version[2] MEROONET.

Lisp and objects have a long history in common. It begins with one of the first object languages, Smalltalk 72, which was first implemented in Lisp. Since that time, Lisp, as an excellent development language, has served as the cradle for innumerable studies about objects. We'll mention only a couple: Flavors, developed by Symbolics for a windowing system on Lisp machines, experimented with multiple inheritance; Loops, created at Xerox Parc, introduced the idea of generic functions. Those efforts culminated in the definition of CLOS (COMMON LISP Object System) and of ΤΕΛΟΣ (the EuLISP object system). These latter two systems bring together most of the characteristics of the preceding object systems while immersing them in the typing system of the underlying language. By doing so, they satisfy the first rule of one of these systems: everything should be an object.

Compared to object systems you find in other languages, the object systems of Lisp are distinguished in two ways:

- Generic functions and their multimethods, a technique known as *multiple dispatch*.

    Sending a message, written as (*message arguments* ...), is not distinguished syntactically from calling a function, written as (*function arguments*...).

---

1. This name came from my son's teddy bear, but you may try to give a sensible meaning to that acronym.
2. Both these systems—MEROON and MEROONET—are available by anonymous ftp according to instructions on page xix.

Multimethods do not assume that the receiver of a message is unique, even though that is often the case. Rather, they determine the method as a function of the class of the significant arguments. For example, printing a number in hexadecimal on a stream is not a method for numbers, nor a method for streams, but a method working on the Cartesian product of number × stream.

- Reflection.

Reflection is the quality of systems endowed with the power to speak of themselves. These systems introduce the idea of *metaclasses*. The class of an object is itself an object and thus necessarily belongs to a class which we call a *metaclass*, which itself is also an object, and thus it goes on. The behavior of these meta-objects is known as the *meta-object protocol* or MOP. It controls the possibilities of the object system. Levels of reflection are possible, for example, from self-description to self-modification. It thus becomes possible to specify the physical representation of objects while still conserving their inherited properties so, for example, we can accomodate a persistent archiving system or a data base. Self-description is an important issue for introspection, notably for design tools to implement programs since such tools make it possible to inspect objects and to know the structure of objects so we can print them, compile them, [see p. 340], make them migrate from one machine to another, as in [Que94], and so forth.

We're extending that long history of object systems as we present MEROONET. We hope that any restrictions we imposed in building MEROONET will not overshadow the excellent qualities that it still has. Among them are the following:

- All values that can be handled in Lisp or Scheme—including vectors—can be represented by MEROONET objects without restrictions on their inheritance.

- MEROONET is self-describing because classes are objects—whole, apart, and duly available for inspection. We've avoided the trap of infinite regression as they did in ObjVlisp, according to [Coi87, BC87].

- There are generic functions, like in CLOS [BDG+88], but without multimethods.

- The code is highly efficient.

A number of implementations of object systems in Lisp or Scheme have already been described in the literature, among them [AR88, Kes88, Coi87, MNC+89, Del89, KdRB92]. However, as a system, MEROONET differs from those in several ways:

- MEROONET, as we hinted, has adopted the generic functions of Common Loops [BKK+86] but not multimethods.

- MEROONET supports classes as first class objects, as in ObjVlisp. This makes a great deal of self-description possible.

- MEROONET abhors multiple inheritance! When we know more about the semantics of multiple inheritance and when the problems posed in [DHHM92] have been resolved, then MEROONET will change its mind about this issue—maybe.

- Objects are represented as contiguous values, that is, as vectors. This representation makes it possible to define data imported from other languages and to do so by means of new field descriptors, as in [QC88, Que90a, Que95].

As we describe MEROONET, we'll also discuss the reasons for our implementation choices. Some of those choices were due to the implementation language, Scheme. Those choices, of course, might have been different if we had directly implemented MEROONET in C, for example. In trying to simplify our explanation of MEROONET, we will cover it from bottom to top, gradually introducing functions as they are needed. Documentation about how to use MEROONET is mixed in with the implementation, but you can also consult the short version of the user's manual (which we won't bother to repeat here). [see p. 87]

11.1 Foundations

The first implementation decision involves object representation in MEROONET. For that, we use sets of contiguous values. To express that in Scheme, we chose vectors. Within a vector, we reserve the first index (that is, index zero) to store the class identity, so that we can access its class from an object. That kind of relation is known as an *instantiation link*. It would be more obvious to have an object point directly to its class (that is, to the most specific class to which it belongs), but we prefer to number the classes and have each object store one such number. Printing objects by the usual means in Scheme thus becomes easier because classes are generally large[3] and unweildy data structures whose details don't mean much to most of us. They may also include circular references that make the normal way of printing with `display` cryptic or illegible. Later, when we look at the means for calling generic functions and the test for belonging to a class, you'll see other reasons for using these numbers as indices to classes.

If we number the classes, we have to be able to convert such a number into a class. All classes will consequently be archived in a vector. Since vectors cannot be extended in Scheme (in contrast to COMMON LISP) there will be a maximum number of possible classes but not explicit detection of the anomaly if the number of classes exceeds this limit. The variable `*class-number*` indicates the first free number in the vector `*classes*`. Since some classes are predefined from the moment of bootstrapping, this number will increase. Since we don't want to burden the code with overly scrupulous tests, we won't bother to test whether a number really indicates a class.

```
(define *maximal-number-of-classes* 100)
(define *classes* (make-vector *maximal-number-of-classes* #f))
(define (number->class n)
   (vector-ref *classes* n) )
(define *class-number* 0)
```

Handling classes by their numbers is somewhat laconic, so it obliges us to name all the classes. Consequently, there are no anonymous classes. Rather, classes are

---

3. For some garbage collectors, if all the values of Scheme are objects, one pointer less per object to inspect or to update might also be advantageous.

seen as static entities. That is, they are not created dynamically. The function
`->Class` converts a symbol into a class of that name. Again, not wanting to
overburden the code with superfluous tests, we make the function `->Class` return
the most recent class by the name we're looking for. That convention will help us
redefine classes without, however, giving redefinition too precise a meaning, so we
should refrain from redefining the same class many times without a good reason.

```
(define (->Class name)
  (let scan ((index (- *class-number* 1)))
    (and (>= index 0)
         (let ((c (vector-ref *classes* index)))
           (if (eq? name (Class-name c))
               c (scan (- index 1)) ) ) ) ) )
```

For generic functions, the implementation demands that they should have names
and that we can access their internal structure. For those reasons, we'll keep a list
of generic functions: `*generics*`. The function `->Generic` will convert such a
name into a generic function. (We'll come back to this point later.)

```
(define *generics* (list))
(define (->Generic name)
  (let lookup ((l *generics*))
    (if (pair? l)
        (if (eq? name (Generic-name (car l)))
            (car l)
            (lookup (cdr l)) )
        #f ) ) )
```

11.2   Representing Objects

As we've indicated, objects in MEROONET are sets of contiguous values. Since we
want every Scheme value to be assimilated by an object defined in MEROONET, we
need to take into account the idea of a vector,[4] and thus we introduce the idea of
an indexed field which contains a certain number of values, rather than containing
a unique value. That characteristic existed already in Smalltalk [GR83], but in
such a way that it was not possible to inherit a class cleanly if it had an indexed
field. MEROONET does not have this kind of limitation.

There is a problem with character strings: for reasons of efficiency, they are
usually primitives in a programming language. Nevertheless, we could represent
them by vectors of characters—not such a bad idea if we are concerned about in-
ternationalization where we might be tempted to adopt larger and larger character
sets represented by two or even four bytes. However, if we still want characters to
be only one byte, and since Scheme doesn't support data structures mixing repe-
titions of such characters (of one byte) with other values (such as pointers), then
MEROONET cannot efficiently simulate character strings.

MEROONET offers two kinds of fields: normal fields (defined by objects of the
class `Mono-Field`) and indexed fields (defined by the class `Poly-Field`). A normal

---

4. In fact, we may even want to simulate vectors by MEROONET objects, which are themselves
represented by vectors. The cost is just one coordinate to contain the instantiation link.

field will be implemented as a component of a vector, whereas an indexed field will
be represented rather like strings in Pascal, that is, by a set of indexed values. This
convention means that the representation must be prefixed by the number of its
components. To clarify these ideas, consider the class of points defined like this:

```
(define-class Point Object (x y))
```

Let's assume that the number 7 is associated with the class **Point**, so the value
as a point of (**make-Point 11 22**) will be represented by the vector **#(7 11 22)**.
A polygon could be defined as a set of points representing the various segments that
form its sides. We could make **Polygon** inherit **Point** to fix its point of reference.

```
(define-class Polygon Point ((* side)))
```

Here you see another kind of possible syntax—parenthesized—to define fields.
A normal field will be prefixed by an equal sign whereas an indexed field will be
prefixed by an asterisk.[5] If we want colored polygons, we'll create a new subclass,
like this:

```
(define-class ColoredPolygon Polygon ((= color)))
```

Every class definition gives rise to a host of functions, notably, a function for
creating objects. Its name is formed by prefixing **make-** to the name of the class.
When we create a class, we must define all its fields. In particular, we have to
define the size of each indexed field, so we will prefix the indexed values appearing
in such fields by their number. To define a triangle, that is, a three-sided polygon,
and to color it orange, we'll write it like this and then study its representation as
vectors:

```
(make-ColoredPolygon
  11                                                    ; x
  22                                                    ; y
  3 (make-Point 44 55) (make-Point 66 77) (make-Point 88 99)  ; 3 sides
  'orange )                                             ; color
→ #(9                                   ; (Class-number ColoredPolygon-class)
    11            ; x
    22            ; y
    3            ; number of sides
    #(7 44 55)   ; side[0]
    #(7 66 77)   ; side[1]
    #(7 88 99)   ; side[2]
    orange )     ; color
```

The objects of MEROONET are thus all represented by vectors where the first
component contains the number of the class of that object. To keep our terminology
straight, we'll use the word *offset* when we're talking about the offset within a vector
representing an object, and we'll say *index* when we're handling an indexed field.
Since one component is reserved for the instantiation link, the first valid offset is
given by the constant ***starting-offset***. You can find out the class of an object
by means of the function **object->class**.[6] We recognize whether a value is an

---

5. We chose the asterisk to indicate multiplicity, like Kleene used in the notation of regular
expressions.
6. That function is equivalent to the function **class-of** in COMMON LISP, EULISP, and IS-Lisp.
We named it differently to avoid introducing confusion and thus be able, for example, to mix
multiple object systems.

object of MEROONET by means of the function `Object?`. That function poses a
serious problem since Scheme does not allow the creation of new data types. The
predicate `Object?` recognizes all MEROONET objects, but unfortunately, it also
recognizes vectors of integers, etc.

To complete this prelude, here are the naming conventions for the variables
we've used:

$$o, o1, o2 \dots \quad \text{object}$$
$$v \dots \quad \text{value (integer, pair, closure, etc.)}$$
$$i \dots \quad \text{index}$$

```
(define *starting-offset* 1)
(define (object->class o)
  (vector-ref *classes* (vector-ref o 0)) )
(define (Object? o)
  (and (vector? o)
       (integer? (vector-ref o 0)) ) )
```

11.3   Defining Classes

To define a class, there is the form `define-class`, taking three successive arguments:

- the name of the class to define;

- the name of its superclass;

- the specification of its own fields.

The class that will be created will inherit fields from the definition of its superclass. That kind of inheritance is known as *field inheritance*. A class also inherits
all the behavior of its superclass with respect to existing generic functions. This
kind of inheritance is known as *method inheritance*.

Here's the syntax of the form `define-class`:

(define-class *class-name superclass-name* (*list-of-fields*))

A field appearing in the list of fields can be mentioned either directly by name
(in that case, it's a normal field) or in a list prefixed by a sign indicating whether
it is normal (equal sign) or indexed (asterisk).

Outside the class definition, a number of accompanying functions are created
automatically. (We hope you enjoy them!)

- A *predicate* recognizes objects of this class. Its name is made from the name
  of the class, suffixed as predicates usually are in Scheme with a question
  mark.

- One object *allocator* returns new instances of the class where the fields are
  not initialized. Their initial value can consequently be anything. Since the
  size of indexed fields must be specified during allocation, this allocator takes
  as many sizes as arguments as there are indexed fields in the class. The name
  of the allocator is made from the class name prefixed by `allocate-`.

- Another object *allocator* returns new instances of the class and specifies the initial values of their fields. The values constituting an indexed field are prefixed by the size of that field. The name of this allocator is made from the class name prefixed by **make-**.

- There are *selectors* for both normal and indexed fields. For each field of the class, there is a read-selector named by the class, a hyphen, and the field. The name of the corresponding write-selector is prefixed by **set-** and suffixed by the usual exclamation point, underlining the fact that it makes physical modifications. Selectors for indexed fields take a supplementary argument, an index.

- A function whose name is made from the name of the associated read-selector suffixed by **-length** accesses the size of each indexed field.

To support reflective operations, the class which is being created and which is itself an instance of the class **Class** is the value of the global variable that has the name of the class suffixed by **-class**. Here's an example of the descriptions of functions and variables[7] generated by (**define-class** ColoredPolygon Point (color)).

```
(ColoredPolygon? o)                                → a Boolean
(allocate-ColoredPolygon sides-number)             → a polygon
(make-ColoredPolygon x y sides-number sides...color) → a polygon
(ColoredPolygon-x o)                               → a value
(ColoredPolygon-y o)                               → a value
(ColoredPolygon-side o index)                      → a value
(ColoredPolygon-color o)                           → a value
(set-ColoredPolygon-x! o value)                    → unspecified
(set-ColoredPolygon-y! o value)                    → unspecified
(set-ColoredPolygon-side! o value index)           → unspecified
(set-ColoredPolygon-color! o value)                → unspecified
(ColoredPolygon-side-length o)                     → a length
ColoredPolygon-class                               → a class
```

As we indicated, classes are created by **define-class**. That special form will be implemented by a macro, unfortunately with all the problems that implies. First among those problems is that **define-class** is a macro with an internal state—its inheritance hierarchy—but the system of Scheme macros, according to [CR91b], does not allow that sort of thing. For that reason, we're going to assume that we have another macro at our disposal, **define-meroonet-macro**, and its purpose is to define macros with no restrictions on the way they are expanded. We can code **define-meroonet-macro** in any existing implementation, but not in portable Scheme.

Is that internal state of **define-class** really necessary? Yes, in MEROONET, it is, for the following reason: when a class is defined, a number of functions are created to access its fields. For example, to define the class **Point** with the

---

7. We've arbitrarily adopted the convention of naming indexed fields by singular words. We think it's natural to write (ColoredPolygon-side o i) to get the i_{th} side of a polygon and to use **side** rather than **sides** in that context.

fields **x** and **y**, the read-accessors **Point-x** and **Point-y** are created. When we define the class **Polygon**, MEROONET does not impose **Point-x** and **Point-y** as the sole accessors for the fields **x** and **y**. Instead, MEROONET creates the functions **Polygon-x** and **Polygon-y**. The definition of the class **Polygon** does not mention inherited fields; the only way of knowing about them is through the name of the superclass. Therefore, the internal state that **define-class** maintains associates the names and types of its fields with each class.

We could avoid this inconvenience by adopting another convention for naming selectors. For example, we could omit the class name from the name of the selector. To illustrate that case, let's assume that the reader for the field **x** is named **get-x**. Then the definition of the class **Polygon** would modify the value of **get-x** to indicate how to extract the field **x** from a polygon. The most simple approach then is to make **get-x** a generic function which acquires new methods as classes are defined. This is the technique that CLOS uses where it is possible during the specification of a field to mention the generic function to which a method must be added to read that field. This decision makes generic functions mutable—a situation that might prove inconvenient for static optimizations during compilation because of the difficulty then of basing anything on a value changing without restrictions.

In contrast, we have decided to make selectors pure functions, not susceptible to modifications, so we can facilitate their integration inline. Of course, that implies some subtle problems, too, like the difference that might exist between **Point-x** and **Polygon-x**. Basically, both these functions extract the same field (**x**), but more precisely, the first one extracts **x** from a point, while the second gets it from a polygon. It seems normal then for the form (**Polygon-x (make-Point 11 22)**) to raise an error and that in consequence, the selectors **Point-x** and **Polygon-x** should be different. Apart from this Byzantine situation, the greatest inconvenience of this decision is the large number of variables and global functions that it consumes. This may create a problem in computer memory but not in our own since all the names are formed systematically and the only reason for naming is for memory.

Recognizing the fields of the superclass (maintained by the internal state of **define-class**) comes into play not only in the way selectors are named: allocators need that information, too, so that their arity will be known and their compilation will be efficient. We'll get back to these ideas and elaborate them more in later sections.

In light of all these considerations, for MEROONET, we'll adopt the following solution: we define a class by constructing an object that is an instance of the class **Class** and inserting it in the hierarchy of classes. All that activity will be carried out by **register-class**. The functions accompanying that class are generated by the expansion function **Class-generate-related-names**. Conforming to the preceding description, we will temporarily define **define-class** like this:

```
(define-meroonet-macro (define-class name super-name
                                      own-field-descriptions )
  (let ((class (register-class name super-name own-field-descriptions)))
    (Class-generate-related-names class) ) )
```

That definition is problematic with respect to compilation since it mixes expansion time and evaluation time. The class is created and then inserted in the inheritance hierarchy during macro expansion, while the accompanying functions are created during the evaluation of the expanded code. Let's assume that we compile a file containing the definition of the class **Polygon**. We can see the resulting code in a file with the suffix **.o** (as with compilers into C, like KCL [YH85], Scheme→C [Bar89], or Bigloo [Ser94]) or with a suffix like **.fasl** in a lot of other compilers. But the resulting code contains only the compilation of the expansion, that is, the definition of the accompanying functions. The class has really been created in the memory state of the compiler but not at all in the memory of the Lisp or Scheme system which will be linked to this **.o** file or which will dynamically load the **.fasl** file. The class has thus evaporated and disappeared by the time the compiler has finished its work.

Consequently, the construction of a class must appear in the expansion, but if it appears only there, then we can no longer require the class to generate the accompanying functions since we need to know the fields of the superclass during macro expansion to generate[8] all the selectors. Consequently, it is necessary to know the class at macro expansion and for it to appear in macro expansion. This dual existence makes it possible to compile the definitions of a class and its subclasses in the same file, as for example, **Point** and **Polygon**. To keep MEROONET from building the same class twice[9] during interpretation—once at macro expansion and then again at the evaluation of the expanded code—we will cleverly do this: when a class is defined during macro expansion, it will be stored in the global variable ***last-defined-class***; then at evaluation, the class will be created only if ***last-defined-class*** is empty.

```
(define *last-defined-class* #f)
(define-meroonet-macro (define-class name supername
                                      own-field-descriptions )
  (set! *last-defined-class* #f)
  (let ((class (register-class name supername own-field-descriptions)))
    (set! *last-defined-class* class)
    '(begin
       (if (not *last-defined-class*)
           (register-class ',name ',supername ',own-field-descriptions) )
       ,(Class-generate-related-names class) ) ) )
```

11.4 Other Problems

Still illustrating the difficulties of macros with real-life examples (namely, from MEROONET), we note that the order in which macro are expanded is important when we use macros with an internal state, as in **define-class**. Consider the following composed form in that context:

```
(begin (define-class Point Object (x y))
       (define-class Polygon Point ((* side))) )
```

If the expansion goes from left to right, then the class **Point** is defined and is thus available for the definition of the class **Polygon**. However, in the opposite case,

---

8. Remember that there is no linguistic means in Scheme nor at execution for creating a new global variable with a computed name.
9. We've made no effort in MEROONET to give a specific meaning to the redefinition of classes, and for that reason, we avoid redefining them.

the class `Polygon` can't be constructed because its superclass is not yet known. We could get around this problem by a (more complicated) way of deferring the construction of `Polygon` as long as the definition of `Point` has not yet been expanded. The definition of `Polygon` would then be empty, whereas the definition of `Point` would contain both.

So how do we compile the definition of `ColoredPolygon` in a file different from the one containing the definitions of `Point` and `Polygon`? We have to get the fields of its superclass somehow. MEROONET doesn't trouble itself about this problem: it simply requires all classes to be compiled together. MEROON, in contrast, adopts a different strategy. A class that will be inherited must be defined either before in the same file or with the keyword `:prototype`. That keyword[10] inserts the class in the class hierarchy at the right place without generating the equivalent code. Thus we'll write this:

```
(define-class Polygon Point ((* side)) :prototype)
(define-class ColoredPolygon Polygon (color))
```

Yet another solution is to use modules with an import/export mechanism to indicate which of those modules contain information pertinent to compile which others. That solution boils down to having a kind of data base, mimetically equivalent to the internal state of the compiler projected onto the file system.

11.5   Representing Classes

Classes in MEROONET are represented by objects of MEROONET. This representation makes self-description of the system easier. It also makes it easier to write metamethods based on the structure of classes, rather than on their inheritance. For example, how to migrate from machine to machine or how to print MEROONET objects by default can be deduced from their structure, that is, from their class. Consequently, there is a class—`Object`—defining all MEROONET objects. That class serves as the root for inheritance. Classes themselves are instances of the class `Class`. Field descriptors are instances of either `Mono-Field` or `Poly-Field`, both subclasses of `Field`.

When we expand the definition of a class, we make use of a number of functions accompanying these predefined classes, such functions as `Mono-Field?` or `make-Poly-Field`, etc. Should we deduce from that that when a class exists, we can use the functions accompanying it? More specifically, once `Point` has been macro expanded, can we use the function `make-Point`? If we take account of the preceding `define-class`, we must admit that we cannot use those functions because `make-Point` is not created by expansion but by evaluation. As a result, metaclasses pose subtle compilation problems—problems that MEROONET does not address.

As a minimum, we put only what is strictly necessary into a class: its name, the associated number, the list of its fields, its superclass, the list of numbers of its subclasses. That information about subclasses will be useful when we talk about

---

10. It's actually a little more complicated in MEROON. The option `:prototype` is expanded as a test that verifies at evaluation whether the prototype conforms to the real class which must exist then.

generic functions. We register the numbers rather than the subclasses themselves in order to avoid circularity at the cost of a slight decrease in efficiency. We can summarize all that information by saying that **Class**, the class of all classes, is defined like this:

```
(define-class Class Object
    (name number fields superclass subclass-numbers) )
```

Fields themselves are defined as objects in MEROONET. Fields are characterized by their type, their name, and the class that introduces them. In that latter field, useful for the general function **field-value**, we will store the number of the class, rather than the class itself so that classes and fields can be printed. Thus we have this:

```
(define-class Field Object (name defining-class-number))
(define-class Mono-Field Field ())
(define-class Poly-Field Field ())
```

Finally, the following function will give the illusion of extracting the class that introduced it from a field without bothering about the underlying number.

```
(define (Field-defining-class field)
    (number->class (careless-Field-defining-class-number field)) )
```

Of course, before MEROONET is installed, we can't define these classes but they are needed by MEROONET itself. To get around this bootstrapping problem, we create them by hand, like this:

```
(define Object-class
    (vector 1                          ; it is a class
            'Object                    ; name
            0                          ; class-number
            '()                        ; fields
            #f                         ; no superclass
            '(1 2 3)                   ; subclass-numbers
            ) )
(define Class-class
    (vector
     1                                 ; it is also a class
     'Class                            ; name
     1                                 ; class-number
     (list                             ; fields
      (vector 4 'name             1)   ; offset= 1
      (vector 4 'number           1)   ; offset= 2
      (vector 4 'fields           1)   ; offset= 3
      (vector 4 'superclass       1)   ; offset= 4
      (vector 4 'subclass-numbers 1) ) ; offset= 5
     Object-class                      ; superclass
     '() ) )
(define Generic-class
    (vector
     1
     'Generic
     2
     (list
```

```
           (vector 4 'name              2)       ; offset= 1
           (vector 4 'default           2)       ; offset= 2
           (vector 4 'dispatch-table 2)          ; offset= 3
           (vector 4 'signature         2) )     ; offset= 4
         Object-class
         '() ) )
    (define Field-class
      (vector
       1
       'Field
       3
       (list
         (vector 4 'name                      3) ; offset= 1
         (vector 4 'defining-class-number 3) ; offset= 2
         )
       Object-class
       '(4 5) ) )
    (define Mono-Field-class
      (vector 1
              'Mono-Field
              4
              (careless-Class-fields Field-class)
              Field-class
              '() ) )
    (define Poly-Field-class
      (vector 1
              'Poly-Field
              5
              (careless-Class-fields Field-class)
              Field-class
              '() ) )
```

Afterwards, the classes are installed as they should be, like this:

```
(vector-set! *classes* 0 Object-class)
(vector-set! *classes* 1 Class-class)
(vector-set! *classes* 2 Generic-class)
(vector-set! *classes* 3 Field-class)
(vector-set! *classes* 4 Mono-Field-class)
(vector-set! *classes* 5 Poly-Field-class)
(set! *class-number* 6)
```

Since MEROONET is managed by means of the class hierarchy, which itself is represented by MEROONET objects, several functions (such as the accessors **Class-number** or **Class-fields**) are needed even before they are constructed. For that purpose, we will introduce their equivalent with a name prefixed by **careless-**. That name is justified by their definition: they don't verify the nature of their argument, so MEROONET uses them only advisedly.

```
(define (careless-Class-name class)
  (vector-ref class 1) )
(define (careless-Class-number class)
  (vector-ref class 2) )
```

```
(define (careless-Class-fields class)
  (vector-ref class 3) )
(define (careless-Class-superclass class)
  (vector-ref class 4) )
(define (careless-Field-name field)
  (vector-ref field 1) )
(define (careless-Field-defining-class-number field)
  (vector-ref field 2) )
```

11.6 Accompanying Functions

For accompanying functions, we'll use a very practical utility, **symbol-concaten-ate**, to form new names.

```
(define (symbol-concatenate . names)
  (string->symbol (apply string-append (map symbol->string names))) ) )
```

To generate accompanying functions, we have a couple of choices. The first is to generate their equivalent code directly; the second, to generate a form that will be evaluated in an appropriate closure. With the second choice, we can factor the work and thus share the text of functions for which closures are constructed, but that choice prevents fine-tuning the optimizations because there will be more calls to computed functions (rather than statically known ones) and as a consequence, they cannot be inlined. To highlight the differences between those two choices, here is how the allocator for the class **Polygon** would be defined in those two cases:

```
(define allocate-Polygon
        (lambda (size)
          (let ((o (make-vector (+ 1 2 1 size))))
            (vector-set! o 0 (careless-Class-number Polygon-class))
            (vector-set! o 3 size)
            o )
(define allocate-Polygon (make-allocator Polygon-class))
```

The first choice lets us know statically that the allocator is a unary function and that its body uses only trivial functions, like **make-vector**, for reading and writing vectors. Consequently, it can be inlined readily in a few instructions and even compiled into a C macro, if we are compiling into C. In contrast, the second definition says nothing about arity. In fact, it doesn't even tell us[11] that this is a function that will be bound to the variable **allocate-Polygon**. Even so, we'll go with the second choice because the first one is more complicated to present and requires more memory for execution and compilation, so here is how accompanying functions are generated.

```
(define (Class-generate-related-names class)
  (let* ((name (Class-name class))
         (class-variable-name (symbol-concatenate name '-class))
         (predicate-name (symbol-concatenate name '?))
         (maker-name (symbol-concatenate 'make- name))
```

---

11. In Lisp, we can't even be sure that the computation terminates, and in Scheme, we don't know whether it returns a unique value.

```
        (allocator-name (symbol-concatenate 'allocate- name)) )
  `(begin
     (define ,class-variable-name (->Class ',name))
     (define ,predicate-name (make-predicate ,class-variable-name))
     (define ,maker-name (make-maker ,class-variable-name))
     (define ,allocator-name (make-allocator ,class-variable-name))
     ,@(map (lambda (field) (Field-generate-related-names field class))
            (Class-fields class) )
     ',(Class-name class) ) ) )
```

11.6.1 Predicates

For every class in MEROONET, there is an associated predicate that responds True
about objects that are instances of that class, whether direct instances or instances
of subclasses. The speed of this predicate is important because Scheme is a language
without static typing so we are forever and again verifying the types or the classes
of the objects we are handling. At compilation, we could try to guess[12] about the
types of objects, factor the tests for types, make use of help from user declarations,
or even impose a rule that programs must be well typed, for example, by defining
methods that give information about their calling arguments.

The test about whether an object belongs to a class is thus very basic and
depends on the general predicate is-a?. To keep up its speed, is-a? assumes
that the object is an object and that the class is a class as well. Consequently,
we can't apply is-a? to just anything. In contrast, the predicate associated with
a class is less restricted. It will first test whether its argument is actually a ME-
ROONET object. Finally, we'll introduce a last predicate to use for its effect in
verifying membership and issuing an intelligible message by default. Since errors
are not standard in Scheme,[13] any errors detected by MEROONET call the function
meroonet-error, which is not defined—one portable way of getting an error!

```
(define (make-predicate class)
  (lambda (o) (and (Object? o)
                   (is-a? o class) )) )
(define (is-a? o class)
  (let up ((c (object->class o)))
    (or (eq? class c)
        (let ((sc (careless-Class-superclass c)))
          (and sc (up sc)) ) ) ) )
(define (check-class-membership o class)
  (if (not (is-a? o class))
      (meroonet-error "Wrong class" o class) ) )
```

The complexity of the predicate is-a? is linear, since we test whether the
object belongs to the target class, or whether the superclass is the target class, or
whether the superclass of the superclass is the target and so on. This strategy is
not too bad because the first try is usually right, at least in roughly one try out of
two.

---

12. The form define-method indicates the class of the discriminating variable, and we could take
advantage of that hint.
13. At least at the moment we're writing, under the reign of R^4RS [CR91b].

However, there is a potential problem of infinite regression in **is-a?**. To get the superclass, we use the function **careless-Class-superclass**, rather than the function **Class-superclass** directly. The difference between those two functions is that the careless one assumes that its first argument is a class. That assumption is safe enough in the context of **is-a?**. If we had used the other function, it would have tested whether its argument was really a class and in doing so, it would have recursively required the predicate **is-a?** and thus seriously impaired the efficiency of MEROONET.

11.6.2 Allocator without Initialization

MEROONET offers two kinds of allocators. The first creates objects whose contents may be anything; the second creates objects all of whose fields have been initialized. The same concepts exist in Lisp and in Scheme: **cons** is the allocator with initialization for dotted pairs; **vector** is the allocator with initialization for vectors. There is also a second allocator for vectors: without a second argument, **make-vector** creates vectors with unspecified contents. MEROONET supports both types of allocation.

Allocation without initialization means that the contents of an uninitialized object might be anything. There are at least two ways to understand that idea. For reasons having to do with garbage collection, (and except for garbage collectors that tolerate certain ambiguities as in [BW88]), uninitialized means generally that the object is filled with entities known to the implementation. There are two different possible semantics here, depending on whether or not those entities are first class values.

- When the entity **#<uninitialized>** appears in a field of a data structure, it explicitly marks the field as containing no value. Attempts to read such a field raise an error since there is no value associated with it.

- In implementations where there is no such entity, fields are initialized with normal values, but they might be anything. For example, in Lisp, it's often **nil**; in Le-Lisp, it's **t**; in many Scheme implementations, it's **#f**. The initial content of a field is consequently undefined, that is, unspecified, in short, anything, but it is not an error to read such a field.

There is a third interpretation—one we call "C style"—in which reading an uninitialized field has unpredictable consequences. For that reason, we strongly urge you not to try reading such a field. This interpretation is even less specific than the previous ones. For example, in this interpretation, it is not obligatory for the implementation to detect an error when there is an attempt to read such a field. Of course, since this read-procedure doesn't carry out any tests on the value it reads, it is very fast! However, when we attempt to read such a field, we may very well get the infamous but informative message "**Bus errror, core dumped**" or even worse, some result that has nothing to do with what we're trying to compute but which we might take as valid, given no warning. The proof that we never (truly never!) read an uninitialized field is left to the programmer.

The first interpretation—with the entity **#<uninitialized>**—obliges a reader to raise an error when it encounters an uninitialized field. Obviously, that costs an explicit test every time a field that might be uninitialized is read, according to [Que93b]. The second interpretation does not require such a test, so it compares favorably in this respect with C.

In terms of allocation, the C-style interpretation is even more efficient because there is no need to initialize fields nor to clear them. Paradoxically, allocation with explicit initialization is usually more efficient than allocation without initialization. In practice, allocating without initialization on the part of the user does in fact require an initialization—with **#<uninitialized>**—at a cost comparable to initialization with any value at all, like **#t**, for example. But most of the time, a field that is not initialized when it is allocated will be initialized right away anyway (and that definitely doubles the work), whereas allocation with explicit initialization fills all the constant fields definitively in one fell swoop.

According to that first interpretation, CLOS guarantees that it detects an uninitialized field. In Scheme, it's helpful to realize that variables are in fact represented by entities that can be defined in MEROONET and for which the detection of uninitialized fields is obligatory. **[see p. 60]** Since we have decided to ignore the formalists, we don't require MEROONET to handle uninitialized fields, and thus we simplify the code: uninitialized fields will be filled with **#f**.

To be useful, the idea of an allocator without initialization means that a created object must be mutable. This point is important because immutable objects are naturally closer to mathematics than are objects that have an internal state, especially so with respect to equality. **[see p. 122]** Immutable objects lend themselves well to optimization since their contents are guaranteed not to vary. Likewise, in the function **make-allocator** that we looked at earlier, we would be able to precompute the expression (**Class-number class**) (just as we do (**Class-fields class**)) if the field **number** in the **Class** were immutable. In that way, we could directly record its value rather than have to recompute it for every allocation.

An allocator without explicit initialization will be returned by the function **make-allocator**. It will take a class and return a function that accepts as arguments a list of natural integers specifying the size of each possible indexed field appearing in the definition of the class. The first computation consists of determining the size of the zone in memory (of the vector) to reserve (to allocate); to do that, we recursively run through the list of fields and their sizes. How do we know the list of fields? We extract it from the class by **Class-fields**. Once the zone in memory has been reserved, we must structure it to put the size of indexed fields there. That's the purpose of the second loop running over the fields and their sizes and maintaining a current offset inside the allocated memory zone. Finally, the object, having just acquired its "skeleton" and the instantiation link to the class where it belongs, is returned as a value.

```
(define (make-allocator class)
  (let ((fields (Class-fields class)))
    (lambda sizes
      ;; compute the size of the instance to allocate
      (let ((room (let iter ((fields fields)
                             (sizes sizes)
                             (room *starting-offset*) )
                    (if (pair? fields)
```

```
                    (cond ((Mono-Field? (car fields))
                           (iter (cdr fields) sizes (+ 1 room)) )
                          ((Poly-Field? (car fields))
                           (iter (cdr fields) (cdr sizes)
                                 (+ 1 (car sizes) room) ) ) )
                room ) )))
       (let ((o (make-vector room #f)))
         ;; setup the instantiation link and skeleton of the instance
         (vector-set! o 0 (Class-number class))
         (let iter ((fields fields)
                    (sizes sizes)
                    (offset *starting-offset*) )
           (if (pair? fields)
               (cond ((Mono-Field? (car fields))
                      (iter (cdr fields) sizes (+ 1 offset)) )
                     ((Poly-Field? (car fields))
                      (vector-set! o offset (car sizes))
                      (iter (cdr fields) (cdr sizes)
                            (+ 1 (car sizes) offset) ) ) )
               o ) ) ) ) ) ) )
```

We have a few remarks to make about that code.

1. The allocators that are created take a list of sizes as their argument. Consequently, they consume dotted pairs if they are associated with classes that have at least one indexed field. To be able to allocate, we are obliged to allocate that much! Later, we'll sketch a solution to this problem.

2. Superfluous sizes are simply ignored without generating an errror.

3. Allocation, as a procedure, runs over the list of fields in the class twice. Doing so twice is costly, especially if the list doesn't vary: we know once the class has been created whether the direct instances of the class have a fixed size or not. We'll correct this point later, too.

4. If a size is not a natural number (thus non-negative), addition will lead to a computation of the size of the memory zone to allocate that will be in error, but the error message will be very cryptic. To be more "user-friendly" in this respect, an explicit test must be carried out, and a relevant and intelligible error message should be generated.

5. Fields can be instances only of **Mono-Field** or **Poly-Field**. It's not possible to add user-defined classes of fields here.

11.6.3 Allocator with Initialization

Allocators with initialization are created in a similar way, but as we go, we'll improve the efficiency of allocators for objects of small fixed size. In Scheme, allocators without initialization (like **make-vector** or **make-string**) take the size of the object to allocate, followed by a possible value to fill in. That value will be used to initialize all components. Allocators with initialization (like **cons**, **vector**, or **string**) successively take all the initialization values. The number of initialization values becomes the size of a unique indexed field for **vector** and **string**. Since we allow multiple indexed fields simultaneously, we must know the size for each of them since we cannot infer it. Consequently, MEROONET requires the initialization values of indexed fields to be prefixed by their number. We could allocate a three-sided polygon by writing this:

```
(make-ColoredPolygon 'x 'y 3 'Point0 'Point1 'Point2 'color)
```

For allocation with intialization, we'll adopt the following technique: all the arguments are gathered into one list, **parms**; a vector is allocated with all these values and with the number of the appropriate class as its first component. Then all we have to do is to verify that the object has the correct structure for ME-ROONET, so we run through the arguments and the fields of its class to verify whether there are at least as many arguments as necessary. After this verification, the object is returned. This technique is simpler (and thus might be faster) than the one earlier that seemed more natural, the one consisting of verifying all the arguments, then allocating only after the object to be returned.

```
(define (make-maker class)
  (or (make-fix-maker class)
      (let ((fields (Class-fields class)))
        (lambda parms
          ;; create the instance
          (let ((o (apply vector (Class-number class) parms)))
            ;; check its skeleton
            (let check ((fields fields)
                        (parms parms)
                        (offset *starting-offset*) )
              (if (pair? fields)
                  (cond ((Mono-Field? (car fields))
                         (check (cdr fields) (cdr parms) (+ 1 offset)) )
                        ((Poly-Field? (car fields))
                         (check (cdr fields)
                                (list-tail (cdr parms) (car parms))
                                (+ 1 (car parms) offset) ) ) )
                  o ) ) ) ) ) ) )
```

Well, this allocator ignores superfluous arguments, but it is still not very efficient because it allocates the arguments in a list that it then converts into a vector. Since this list (the value of **parms**) is used to verify the structure of the object rather than to verify the components of the object directly, we can't even hope for a compiler sufficiently intelligent not to create that list of arguments. For that reason, we'll stick a little wart on the nose of **make-maker** to improve the case of allocators for objects that have no indexed fields.

```
(define (make-fix-maker class)
  (define (static-size? fields)
    (if (pair? fields)
        (and (Mono-Field? (car fields))
             (static-size? (cdr fields)) )
        #t ) )
  (let ((fields (Class-fields class)))
    (and (static-size? fields)
         (let ((size (length fields)))
```

```
             (cn (Class-number class)) )
        (case size
          ((0)  (lambda () (vector cn)))
          ((1)  (lambda (a) (vector cn a)))
          ((2)  (lambda (a b) (vector cn a b)))
          ((3)  (lambda (a b c) (vector cn a b c)))
          ((4)  (lambda (a b c d) (vector cn a b c d)))
          ((5)  (lambda (a b c d e) (vector cn a b c d e)))
          ((6)  (lambda (a b c d e f) (vector cn a b c d e f)))
          ((7)  (lambda (a b c d e f g) (vector cn a b c d e f g)))
          (else #f) ) ) ) ) )
```

So allocators of classes without any indexed fields and with fewer than nine normal fields are produced by closures with fixed arity. If a class has no indexed fields but more than nine normal fields, we go back to the preceding case, which verifies whether the number of initialization values is sufficient. Always hoping to minimize error detection, we'll make `cdr` or `list-tail` detect the fact when there are not enough initialization values. Those two must not truncate a list that is already empty. In the case where we're allocating small-sized objects, we'll rely on the arity check. Of course, since we are relying on various strategies to detect the same anomaly, we'll get error messages about it that are not uniform—a situation that is not the best, but the code for MEROONET would balloon by more than a fourth if we tried to be more "user-friendly" in this respect.

A native implementation of MEROONET must support efficient allocation of objects. To avoid that monstrous situation we saw earlier of allocating in order to allocate, it should probably be endowed with an internal means of building allocators of the type (`vector cn a b c ...`).

11.6.4 Accessing Fields

For every field of a class, MEROONET creates accompanying functions to read, to write, and to get the length of a field, if it is indexed. The accompanying functions related to fields (the selectors) are constructed by the subfunction of macro expansion: `Field-generate-related-names`.

```
(define (Field-generate-related-names field class)
  (let* ((fname (careless-Field-name field))
         (cname (Class-name class))
         (cname-variable (symbol-concatenate cname '-class))
         (reader-name (symbol-concatenate cname '- fname))
         (writer-name (symbol-concatenate 'set- cname '- fname '!)) )
    `(begin
       (define ,reader-name
         (make-reader
          (retrieve-named-field ,cname-variable ',fname) ) )
       (define ,writer-name
         (make-writer
          (retrieve-named-field ,cname-variable ',fname) ) )
       ,@(if (Poly-Field? field)
           `((define ,(symbol-concatenate cname '- fname '-length)
               (make-lengther
```

```
                    (retrieve-named-field ,cname-variable ',fname) ) ))
        '() ) ) ) )
```

As before, the accompanying functions are constructed by closure, not by code synthesis. The constructors are **make-reader**, **make-writer**, and **make-lengther**. As arguments, they all take a field and a class. Since the constructors have to be built at evaluation, they find these objects by the name of the global variable that contains the class and by the function **retrieve-named-field**, which gets a field in a class by name.

```
(define (retrieve-named-field class name)
  (let search ((fields (careless-Class-fields class)))
    (and (pair? fields)
         (if (eq? name (careless-Field-name (car fields)))
             (car fields)
             (search (cdr fields)) ) ) ) )
```

11.6.5   Accessors for Reading Fields

Since we have two types of fields—indexed and normal—we also have two kinds of readers with different arity. In case the implementation is not to your taste, we should point out that a constant offset accesses fields not preceded by an indexed field. The function **make-reader** for constructing readers, of course, has to take this fact into account. We'll run through the list of fields in order to determine whether that offset is constant or not. If it is, an appropriate function will be generated; otherwise, we'll resort to a general function for reading fields: **field-value**. In that way, all the fields with a constant offset (possibly indexed) are read efficiently.

Readers are safe functions in the sense that they verify whether the object to which they are applied belongs to the right class, that is, a class inheriting from the class that introduced the field in the first place. That's the role of the function **check-class-membership**, that we looked at earlier. Another reason we speak of them as safe functions is that the reader of an indexed field uses the function **check-index-range** to test whether the index is correct with respect to the size of the indexed field.

```
(define (make-reader field)
  (let ((class (Field-defining-class field)))
    (let skip ((fields (careless-Class-fields class))
               (offset *starting-offset*) )
      (if (eq? field (car fields))
          (cond ((Mono-Field? (car fields))
                 (lambda (o)
                   (check-class-membership o class)
                   (vector-ref o offset) ) )
                ((Poly-Field? (car fields))
                 (lambda (o i)
                   (check-class-membership o class)
                   (check-index-range i o offset)
                   (vector-ref o (+ offset 1 i)) ) ) )
          (cond ((Mono-Field? (car fields))
                 (skip (cdr fields) (+ 1 offset)) )
```

```
                ((Poly-Field? (car fields))
                 (cond ((Mono-Field? field)
                        (lambda (o)
                          (field-value o field) ) )
                       ((Poly-Field? field)
                        (lambda (o i)
                          (field-value o field i) ) ) ) ) ) ) ) ) ) )
     (define (check-index-range i o offset)
       (let ((size (vector-ref o offset)))
         (if (not (and (>= i 0) (< i size)))
             (meroonet-error "Out of range index" i size) ) ) )
```

For fields that are located after an indexed field, we'll make do with a mechanism that incarnates the general (not generic) function **field-value** because MEROONET does not support the creation of new types of fields. The function **field-value**, of course, is associated with the function **set-field-value!**. Computations about offsets common to both those functions are concentrated in **compute-field-offset**.

```
     (define (compute-field-offset o field)
       (let ((class (Field-defining-class field)))
         ;;(assume (check-class-membership o class))
         (let skip ((fields (careless-Class-fields class))
                    (offset *starting-offset*) )
           (if (eq? field (car fields))
               offset
               (cond ((Mono-Field? (car fields))
                      (skip (cdr fields) (+ 1 offset)) )
                     ((Poly-Field? (car fields))
                      (skip (cdr fields)
                            (+ 1 offset (vector-ref o offset)) ) ) ) ) ) ) )
     (define (field-value o field . i)
       (let ((class (Field-defining-class field)))
         (check-class-membership o class)
         (let ((fields (careless-Class-fields class))
               (offset (compute-field-offset o field)) )
           (cond ((Mono-Field? field)
                  (vector-ref o offset) )
                 ((Poly-Field? field)
                  (check-index-range (car i) o offset)
                  (vector-ref o (+ offset 1 (car i))) ) ) ) ) )
```

11.6.6 Accessors for Writing Fields

The definition of an accessor to write a field is analogous to that of a reader so it poses no difficulties. In contrast, the function **set-field-value!** has a strange signature. The signature of a writer for fields is based on the signature for a reader with the value to add at the tail of the arguments. That's the usual pattern in Scheme, for example, in **car** and **set-car!**. However, the fact that there may be

an optional index present upsets this nice pattern, so we've chosen this order[14]: (o
v field . i).

```
(define (make-writer field)
  (let ((class (Field-defining-class field)))
    (let skip ((fields (careless-Class-fields class))
               (offset *starting-offset*) )
      (if (eq? field (car fields))
          (cond ((Mono-Field? (car fields))
                 (lambda (o v)
                   (check-class-membership o class)
                   (vector-set! o offset v) ) )
                ((Poly-Field? (car fields))
                 (lambda (o i v)
                   (check-class-membership o class)
                   (check-index-range i o offset)
                   (vector-set! o (+ offset 1 i) v) )· ) )
          (cond ((Mono-Field? (car fields))
                 (skip (cdr fields) (+ 1 offset)) )
                ((Poly-Field? (car fields))
                 (cond ((Mono-Field? field)
                        (lambda (o v)
                          (set-field-value! o v field) ) )
                       ((Poly-Field? field)
                        (lambda (o i v)
                          (set-field-value! o v field i) ) ) )
                 ) ) ) ) ) )
(define (set-field-value! o v field . i)
  (let ((class (Field-defining-class field)))
    (check-class-membership o class)
    (let ((fields (careless-Class-fields class))
          (offset (compute-field-offset o field)) )
      (cond ((Mono-Field? field)
             (vector-set! o offset v) )
            ((Poly-Field? field)
             (check-index-range (car i) o offset)
             (vector-set! o (+ offset 1 (car i)) v) ) ) ) ) )
```

From a stylistic point of view, writers for fields are constructed with the prefix
set-, as in set-cdr!. We could have used the suffix -set! just as well, as in
vector-set!, but we chose the prefix to show as soon as possible that we are dealing with a modification. Visually, this choice also looks more like an assignment.

11.6.7   Accessors for Length of Fields

We can access the length of a field either by a specialized accompanying function
or by the general function field-length. Here again, we've been able to improve
access to any field that is not located after an indexed field.

```
(define (make-lengther field)
  ;; (assume (Poly-Field? field))
```

---

14. This order may remind you of putprop if you are already nostalgic about property lists.

```
         (let ((class (Field-defining-class field)))
           (let skip ((fields (careless-Class-fields class))
                      (offset *starting-offset*) )
             (if (eq? field (car fields))
                 (lambda (o)
                   (check-class-membership o class)
                   (vector-ref o offset) )
                 (cond ((Mono-Field? (car fields))
                        (skip (cdr fields) (+ 1 offset)) )
                       ((Poly-Field? (car fields))
                        (lambda (o) (field-length o field)) ) ) ) ) ) )
(define (field-length o field)
  (let* ((class (Field-defining-class field))
         (fields (careless-Class-fields class))
         (offset (compute-field-offset o field)) )
    (check-class-membership o class)
    (vector-ref o offset) ) )
```

11.7 Creating Classes

The form `define-class` does not actually create the object to represent the class
being defined. Rather, it delegates that task to the function `register-class`.
That function actually allocates the object and then calls `Class-initialize!` to
analyze the parameters of the definition of the class as well as to initialize the
various fields of the class. Once the fields have been filled in (with the help of
`parse-fields` for fields belonging to the class), the class is inserted in the class
hierarchy. Finally, the call to `update-generics` will confer all the methods that
the newly created class inherits from its superclass.

```
(define (register-class name supername own-field-descriptions)
  (Class-initialize! (allocate-Class)
                     name
                     (->Class supername)
                     own-field-descriptions ) )
(define (Class-initialize! class name superclass own-field-descriptions)
  (set-Class-number! class *class-number*)
  (set-Class-name! class name)
  (set-Class-superclass! class superclass)
  (set-Class-subclass-numbers! class '())
  (set-Class-fields!
   class (append (Class-fields superclass)
                 (parse-fields class own-field-descriptions) ) )
  ;; install definitely the class
  (set-Class-subclass-numbers!
   superclass
   (cons *class-number* (Class-subclass-numbers superclass)) )
  (vector-set! *classes* *class-number* class)
  (set! *class-number* (+ 1 *class-number*))
  ;; propagate the methods of the super to the fresh class
  (update-generics class)
```

```
class )
```

The specifications of fields belonging to the class are analyzed by the function **parse-fields**. That function analyzes the syntax of these specifications. When a specification is parenthesized, it can begin only with an equal sign or an asterisk. Any other object in that position raises an error indicated by **meroonet-error**. MEROONET does not support the redefinition of an inherited field; the function **check-conflicting-name** verifies that point. In contrast, it does not check whether the same name appears more than once among the fields of the object.

```
(define (parse-fields class own-field-descriptions)
  (define (Field-initialize! field name)
    (check-conflicting-name class name)
    (set-Field-name! field name)
    (set-Field-defining-class-number! field (Class-number class))
    field )
  (define (parse-Mono-Field name)
    (Field-initialize! (allocate-Mono-Field) name) )
  (define (parse-Poly-Field name)
    (Field-initialize! (allocate-Poly-Field) name) )
  (if (pair? own-field-descriptions)
      (cons (cond
              ((symbol? (car own-field-descriptions))
               (parse-Mono-Field (car own-field-descriptions)) )
              ((pair? (car own-field-descriptions))
               (case (caar own-field-descriptions)
                 ((=) (parse-Mono-Field
                        (cadr (car own-field-descriptions)) ))
                 ((*) (parse-Poly-Field
                        (cadr (car own-field-descriptions)) ))
                 (else (meroonet-error
                         "Erroneous field specification"
                         (car own-field-descriptions) )) ) ) )
            (parse-fields class (cdr own-field-descriptions)) )
      '() ) )
(define (check-conflicting-name class fname)
  (let check ((fields (careless-Class-fields (Class-superclass class))))
    (if (pair? fields)
        (if (eq? (careless-Field-name (car fields)) fname)
            (meroonet-error "Duplicated field name" fname)
            (check (cdr fields)) )
        #t ) ) )
```

11.8 Predefined Accompanying Functions

At this point, we've already presented the entire backbone for defining classes, but it is not yet completely operational. Indeed, we can't yet define a class because the predefined accompanying functions, like **Class**, **Field**, etc., haven't been covered yet. Well, we can't use **define-class** because those functions are missing, but the role of **define-class** is to define them, so we find ourselves stuck again with a bootstrapping problem.

With a little patience, we'll define those functions "by hand" ourselves. We'll write just the ones that are minimally necessary and we'll even simplify the code by leaving out any verifications. If everything goes well, then we will expand the definitions of predefined classes and cut-and-paste that code, as we have done before. The truth, the whole truth, and nothing but the truth, is that we have to define the predicates before the readers, the readers before the writers, and the writers before the allocators. Foremost, we have to make the accompanying functions for **Class** appear before everything else. Here, we'll show you just a synopsis of these definitions because the entire thing would be a little monotonous.

```
(define Class? (make-predicate Class-class))
(define Generic? (make-predicate Generic-class))
(define Field? (make-predicate Field-class))
(define Class-name
    (make-reader (retrieve-named-field Class-class 'name)))
(define set-Class-name!
    (make-writer (retrieve-named-field Class-class 'name)))
(define Class-number
    (make-reader (retrieve-named-field Class-class 'number)))
(define set-Class-subclass-numbers!
    (make-writer (retrieve-named-field Class-class 'subclass-numbers)))
(define make-Class (make-maker Class-class))
(define allocate-Class (make-allocator Class-class))
(define Generic-name
    (make-reader (retrieve-named-field Generic-class 'name)))
(define allocate-Poly-Field (make-allocator Poly-Field-class))
```

At this stage now, it's possible to use **define-class**. Careful: don't abuse it to redefine the predefined classes **Object**, **Class**, and all the rest. For one thing, you mustn't do so because **define-class** is not idempotent[15] so you would get twelve initial classes, among which six would be inaccessible. For another, when you compiled, you would duplicate all the accompanying functions.

11.9 Generic Functions

Generic functions are the result of adapting the idea of sending messages—important in the object world—to the functional world of Lisp. Sending a message in Smalltalk [GR83] looks like this:

```
receiver message: arguments ...
```

As people often say, everything already exists in Lisp—all you have to do is add parentheses! The first importations of message sending in Lisp used a keyword, like **send** or **=>** as in Planner [HS75], to get this:

```
(send receiver message arguments ... )
```

---

15. One work-around would be to reset ***class-number*** to zero and redefine the classes which should have the same numbers.

The receiver, of course, is the object that gets the message. It is unique in Smalltalk; that is, you can't send a message to more than one object at a time. Now, in our way of thinking that anything can be an object in Lisp, we see right away that a function like binary addition makes sense only if it knows the class of both its objects. For two integers, that is, we use binary integer addition; for two floating-point numbers, we use binary floating-point addition; and for mixed cases, we must first convert the integer argument into a floating-point number before we add them (a practice known as "floating-point contagion"). In fact, addition has methods for which there is not a unique receiver. Such methods are known as *multimethods*. The syntax for sending messages puts the receiver in a privileged position and thus undermines the idea of multimethods, so Common Loops [BKK+86] proposed changing the syntax to something more suggestive, like this:

```
(message receiver arguments ... )
```

The keyword **send** has disappeared, and the message itself appears in the function position, so it's a function. Since it inspects its arguments in order to determine which method to apply, we say it is a *generic* function. A generic function takes into account all the arguments it receives, so there are certain consequences:

1. It can treat the ones it wants to as discriminants.

2. It might not give any particular pre-eminence to the first argument (the former receiver) among the others.

3. It can take more than one argument into account as a discriminant (for example, in the case of binary addition).

In short, the idea of generic functions generalizes the idea of message-sending, and it's this idea of generic functions that MEROONET offers. However, multi-methods simply don't appear in this book. Moreover, they generally represent less than 5% of the cases in use, according to [KR90], so MEROONET doesn't even implement multimethods.

Some people interested in generic functions ask whether this generalization is still faithful to the spirit of objects. We won't attempt to respond to this delicate question. However, we will admit that generic functions completely hide the object-aspect since they are real functions that don't need a special operator like **send**. Whether or not a function should be generic and use message-sending is thus left as an implementation question and has no impact on its calling interface. On the implementation side, there is a slight surcharge due to encapsulation since the application of a generic function with a discriminating first argument (g *arguments* ...) shows that g is more or less equivalent to (**lambda args** (**apply send** (**car args**) g (**cdr args**))).

How should we represent generic functions in Scheme? Since we have to be able to apply them, in Scheme they are necessarily represented by functions. However, since we want to preserve self-description, we would like for them to be MEROONET objects belonging to the class **Generic**, so we would like for them to be simultaneously objects *and* functions, in short, functional objects, or even *funcallable objects*. CLOS and OakLisp [LP86, LP88] support such concepts.

In fact, generic functions are really objects endowed with an internal state corresponding to the set of methods that they know. Consequently, we'll adopt the following technique, even though it is largely suboptimal. A generic function will be represented simultaneously by a MEROONET object and a Scheme function, the value of the variable with the same name as the generic function. That function will contain the MEROONET object in its closure. Methods will be added to the object which will thus be visible to the Scheme function that will be applied. The generic object will be retrieved by its name (and that fact means that we cannot have anonymous generic functions) rather than by the value of the global variable bearing the same name; it will be retrieved in such a way as to be insensitive to the lexical context where generic functions and methods are defined.

The definition form for generic functions uses the following syntax:

(define-generic (*name variables* ...) [*default*...])

The first term defines the form of the call to the generic function and specifies the discriminating variable (the receiver in Smalltalk). The discriminating variable appears between parentheses. It is possible to define the default body of the generic function in the rest of the form. In a language where all values were MEROONET objects, that would be equivalent to putting a method in the class of all values, namely, Object. Since, in this implementation of Scheme, there are values that are not objects, the default body will be applied to every discriminating value which is not a MEROONET object. That property makes the integration of MEROONET and Scheme simpler; it also supports customized error trapping. One of the novelties of MEROONET is that generic functions may have any signature, even a dotted variable. In any case, the methods must have a compatible signature.

The class Generic will be defined like this:

(define-class Generic Object (name default dispatch-table signature))

We can retrieve the generic function by name with ->Generic. The field default contains the default body, either supplied by the user or synthesized automatically by default to raise an error. The signature makes it possible to judge the compatibility of methods that might be added to the generic function. This test is important, for one thing, because it would be insane to add methods of different arity: the call to a generic function is already varied enough in terms of the method that will be chosen without adding the problems presented by varying arity. For another thing, a native implementation could take advantage of the uniformity among methods to improve the call for generic functions, as in [KR90].

The internal state of a generic function is produced entirely by a vector indexed by the class numbers. The vector contains all the known methods of the generic function. This vector is known as the *dispatch table* for the generic function. Consequently, the means of calling a generic function is straightforward: the number of the class of the discriminating argument will be the index into the dispatch table to retrieve the appropriate method. This way of coding is extremely fast, but it takes up space since the set of these tables is equivalent to an $n * m$ matrix where n is the number of classes and m the total number of generic functions. There are techniques for compressing a dispatch table, as in [VH94, Que93b]. Those techniques are feasible mainly because most of the time the methods of a generic function involve only a subtree in the class hierarchy.

The methods of a generic function as well as its default body will all have the same finite arity, and that's also the case for generic functions with a dotted variable. For example, let's assume that the generic function f is defined like this:

```
(define-generic (f a (b) . c) (g b a c))
```

Then the default body will be this:

```
(lambda (a b c) (g b a c))
```

And all the methods will be represented by functions with arity comparable to
(a b c). The arity of the image of a generic function in Scheme is the same arity
specified for the generic function. For the preceding example, that will be:

```
(lambda (a b . c) ((determine-method G127 b) a b c))
```

The value of the variable G127[16] is the generic object containing the dispatch
table from which the function determine-method chooses the appropriate method.
Since not all values of Scheme are objects, we must first test whether the value of
the discriminating variable is really a MEROONET object.

```
(define (determine-method generic o)
  (if (Object? o)
      (vector-ref (Generic-dispatch-table generic)
                  (vector-ref o 0) )
      (Generic-default generic) ) )
```

So here is the definition of generic functions, finally:

```
(define-meroonet-macro (define-generic call . body)
  (parse-variable-specifications
   (cdr call)
   (lambda (discriminant variables)
     (let ((generic (gensym)))              ; make generic hygienic
       `(define ,(car call)
          (let ((,generic (register-generic
                           ',(car call)
                           (lambda ,(flat-variables variables)
                             ,(if (pair? body)
                                  `(begin . ,body)
                                  `(meroonet-error
                                    "No method" ',(car call)
                                    . ,(flat-variables variables) ) ) )
                           ',(cdr call) )))
            (lambda ,variables
              ((determine-method ,generic ,(car discriminant))
               . ,(flat-variables variables) ) ) ) ) ) ) ) )
```

The function parse-variable-specifications analyzes the list specifying the
variables in order to extract the discriminating variable and to re-organize the
list of variables to make it conform to what Scheme expects. It will be common to define-generic and define-method. It invokes its second argument on
these two results. Nonchalantly not caring a bit about dogmatism, the function
parse-variable-specifications does not verify whether there is only one discriminating variable.

---

16. To make the expansion of define-generic cleaner, the variable enclosing the generic object
has a name synthesized by gensym.

```
(define (parse-variable-specifications specifications k)
  (if (pair? specifications)
      (parse-variable-specifications
       (cdr specifications)
       (lambda (discriminant variables)
         (if (pair? (car specifications))
             (k (car specifications)
                (cons (caar specifications) variables) )
             (k discriminant (cons (car specifications) variables)) ) ) )
      (k #f specifications) ) )
```

The default body of the generic function is built then. A generic object is constructed by **register-generic** making it possible (at the level of the results of expanding of **define-generic**) to hide the coding details of generic functions, especially the variable ***generics***. Among these details, the dispatch table is constructed, so we allocate a vector that we initially fill with the default body. That default body is effectively the method which will be found if there isn't any other method around. The size of the dispatch table depends on the total number of possible classes, not on the number of actual classes. This fact means that when new classes are defined, we have to increase the size of the dispatch table for all existing generic functions.

```
(define (register-generic generic-name default signature)
  (let* ((dispatch-table (make-vector *maximal-number-of-classes*
                                      default ))
         (generic (make-Generic generic-name
                                 default
                                 dispatch-table
                                 signature )) )
    (set! *generics* (cons generic *generics*))
    generic ) )
```

The function **flat-variables** flattens a list of variables and transforms any final possible dotted variable into a normal one. That transformation occurs in the default body but will also be applied to any methods to come.

```
(define (flat-variables variables)
  (if (pair? variables)
      (cons (car variables) (flat-variables (cdr variables)))
      (if (null? variables) variables (list variables)) ) )
```

A Bit More about Class Definitions

We've already mentioned the role of the function **update-generics** when a class is defined. Its role is to propagate the methods of the superclass to this new class. If we first define the class **Point** with the method **show** to display points, and then we define the class **ColoredPoint**, it seems normal for **ColoredPoint** to inherit that method. To implement that characteristic, we need to have all the generic functions available so that we can update them.

```
(define (update-generics class)
  (let ((superclass (Class-superclass class)))
```

```
(for-each (lambda (generic)
            (vector-set! (Generic-dispatch-table generic)
                         (Class-number class)
                         (vector-ref (Generic-dispatch-table generic)
                                     (Class-number superclass) ) ) )
          *generics* ) ) )
```

11.10   Method

Methods are defined by **define-method** of course. Its syntax resembles the syntax of **define**. The list of variables is similar to the one that appears in **define-generic**: the discriminating variable occurs between parentheses as does the name of the class for which the method is installed.

   (**define-method** (*name variables* ...) *forms* ...)

The generic functions that we've already defined are objects on which we can confer new behavior or methods by means of **define-method**. Thus in MEROONET, generic functions are mutable objects, and to that degree, they make optimizations difficult, unless we freeze the class hierarchy (as with **seal** in Dylan [App92b]) and then analyze the types (or rather, the classes) a little. Making generic functions immutable would be another solution, but that requires functional objects, which we've excluded here.

We have already evoked the arity of methods for the default body in the definition of the functional image for generic functions in Scheme. Once the method has been constructed, it must be inserted in the dispatch table not only for the class for which it is defined but also for all the subclasses for which it is not redefined.

The remaining problem is the implementation of what Smalltalk calls **super** and what CLOS calls **call-next-method**; that is, the possibility for a method to invoke the method which would have been invoked if it hadn't been there. The form (**call-next-method**) can appear only in a method and corresponds to invoking the supermethod with implicitly the same[17] arguments as the method. Of course, the supermethod of the class **Object** is the default body of the generic function.

The way that the function **call-next-method** local to the body of the method searches for the supermethod is inspired by **determine-method**, but this time we need to test whether the value of the discriminating variable is indeed an object and whether the number of the class to consider for indexing is no longer the number of the direct class of the discriminating value but rather that of the superclass. Thus in order to install a method that uses **call-next-method**, we have to know the number of the superclass of the class for which we are installing the method. Careful: because of special considerations in macro expansion, this number should not be known right away but only at evaluation. For that reason, we have to resort to the following technique. The form **define-method** will build a premethod, that is, a method using as parameters the generic function and class where it will be

---

17. We haven't kept the possibility of changing these arguments as in CLOS because it would then be possible to change the contents of the discriminating variable to anything at all, and that would violate the intention of the supermethod as well as the hypotheses of the compilation, probably.

installed. In order to hide the details of this installation and to reduce the size of the macro expansion of **define-method**, we'll create the function **register-method**, like this:

```
(define-meroonet-macro (define-method call . body)
  (parse-variable-specifications
   (cdr call)
   (lambda (discriminant variables)
     (let ((g (gensym))(c (gensym)))     ; make g and c hygienic
       '(register-method
         ',(car call)
         (lambda (,g ,c)
           (lambda ,(flat-variables variables)
             (define (call-next-method)
               ((if (Class-superclass ,c)
                    (vector-ref (Generic-dispatch-table ,g)
                                (Class-number (Class-superclass ,c)) )
                    (Generic-default ,g) )
                . ,(flat-variables variables) ) )
             . ,body ) )
         ',(cadr discriminant)
         ',(cdr call) ) ) ) ) )
```

The function **register-method** determines the class and the implicated generic function, converts the premethod into a method, verifies that the signatures are compatible, and installs it in the dispatch table. To test the compatibility of signatures during macro expansion would have required **define-method** to know the signatures of generic functions. Since this verification is simple and it is done only once at installation without hampering the efficiency of calls to generic functions, we have relegated it to evaluation. Notice that there is a comparison of functions by **eq?** for propagating methods.

```
(define (register-method generic-name pre-method class-name signature)
  (let* ((generic (->Generic generic-name))
         (class (->Class class-name))
         (new-method (pre-method generic class))
         (dispatch-table (Generic-dispatch-table generic))
         (old-method (vector-ref dispatch-table (Class-number class))) )
    (check-signature-compatibility generic signature)
    (let propagate ((cn (Class-number class)))
      (let ((content (vector-ref dispatch-table cn)))
        (if (eq? content old-method)
            (begin
              (vector-set! dispatch-table cn new-method)
              (for-each
               propagate
               (Class-subclass-numbers (number->class cn)) ) ) ) ) ) ) )
(define (check-signature-compatibility generic signature)
  (define (coherent-signatures? la lb)
    (if (pair? la)
        (if (pair? lb)
            (and (or ;;similar discriminating variable
```

```
                    (and (pair? (car la)) (pair? (car lb)))
                    ;;similar regular variable
                    (and (symbol? (car la)) (symbol? (car lb))) )
                (coherent-signatures? (cdr la) (cdr lb)) )
          #f )
      (or (and (null? la) (null? lb))
          ;;similar dotted variable
          (and (symbol? la) (symbol? lb)) ) ) )
  (if (not (coherent-signatures? (Generic-signature generic) signature))
    (meroonet-error "Incompatible signatures" generic signature) ) )
```

11.11   Conclusions

In the programs you've just seen, there are a lot of points that could be improved
to increase the speed of MEROONET in Scheme or to heighten its reflective qualities.
You can also imagine other improvements in a native implementation where every
value would be a MEROONET object. For that reason, EULISP, ILOG TALK, and
CLtL2 all integrate the concepts of objects in their basic foundations.

11.12   Exercises

Exercise 11.1 : Design a better, less approximate version of Object?.

Exercise 11.2 : Design a generic function, clone, to copy a MEROONET object.
Make that a shallow copy.

Exercise 11.3 : We could create new types of classes, subclasses of Class, that
we call metaclasses. Write a metaclass where the instances are classes that count
the number of objects that they have created.

Exercise 11.4 : In order to heighten the reflective qualities of MEROONET, classes
and fields could have supplementary fields to refer to the accompanying functions
(predicate and allocators for classes; reader, writer, and length-getter for fields)
that are associated with them. Extend MEROONET to do that.

Exercise 11.5 : CLOS does not demand that a generic function should already
exist in order to add a new method to it. Modify define-method to create the
generic function on the fly, if it doesn't exist already.

Exercise 11.6 : In some object systems like CLOS or EULISP, it is possible,
conjointly with call-next-method, to know whether there is a method that follows,
by means of next-method?. This reflective capacity makes it possible to reel off all
the supermethods without error. The "method" that follows the one for Object
corresponds to the default body, but next-method? replies False when there is no
method other than that one. Modify define-method to get next-method?.

Recommended Reading

Another approach to objects in Scheme is inspired by that of T in [AR88]. For the fans of meta-objects, there is the historic article defining ObjVlisp, [Coi87] or the self-description of CLOS in [KdRB92].

Answers to Exercises

Exercise 1.1 : All you have to do is put trace commands in the right places, like this:

```
(define (tracing.evaluate exp env)
   (if ... ...
       (case (car exp) ...
           (else (let ((fn        (evaluate (car e) env))
                       (arguments (evlis (cdr e) env)) )x
                   (display '(calling ,(car e) with . ,arguments)
                            *trace-port* )
                   (let ((result (invoke fn arguments)))
                     (display '(returning from ,(car e) with ,result)
                              *trace-port* )
                     result ) )) ) ) )
```

Notice two points. First, the *name* of a function is printed, rather than its value. That convention is usually more informative. Second, print statements are sent out on a particular stream so that they can be more easily redirected to a window or log-file or even mixed in with the usual output stream.

Exercise 1.2 : In [Wan80b], that optimization is attributed to Friedman and Wise. The optimization lets us overlook the fact that there is still another (**evlis '() env**) to carry out when we evaluate the last term in a list. In practice, since the result is independent of **env**, there is no point in storing this call along with the value of **env**. Since lists of arguments are usually on the order of three or four terms, and since this optimization can always be carried out at the end of a list, it becomes a very useful one. Notice the local function that saves a test, too.

```
(define (evlis exps env)
   (define (evlis exps)
   ;;(assume (pair? exps))
     (if (pair? (cdr exps))
         (cons (evaluate (car exps) env)
               (evlis (cdr exps)) )
         (list (evaluate (car exps) env)) ) )
   (if (pair? exps)
       (evlis exps)
       '() ) )
```

Exercise 1.3 : This representation is known as the *rib cage* because of its obvious resemblance to that part of the body. It lowers the cost of a function call in the

number of pairs consumed, but it increases the cost for searching and for modifying
the value of variables. Moreover, verifying the arity of the function is no longer so
safe because we can no longer detect superfluous arguments this way. To do so, we
have to modify **extend**.

```
(define (lookup id env)
  (if (pair? env)
      (let look ((names (caar env))
                 (values (cdar env)) )
        (cond ((symbol? names)
               (if (eq? names id) values
                   (lookup id (cdr env)) ) )
              ((null? names) (lookup id (cdr env)))
              ((eq? (car names) id)
               (if (pair? values)
                   (car values)
                   (wrong "Too less values") ) )
              (else (if (pair? values)
                        (look (cdr names) (cdr values))
                        (wrong "Too less values") )) ) )
      (wrong "No such binding" id) ) )
```

You can deduce the function **update!** straightforwardly from **lookup**.

Exercise 1.4 :

```
(define (s.make-function variables body env)
  (lambda (values current.env)
    (for-each (lambda (var val)
                (putprop var 'apval (cons val (getprop var 'apval))) )
              variables values )
    (let ((result (eprogn body current.env)))
      (for-each (lambda (var)
                  (putprop var 'apval (cdr (getprop var 'apval))) )
                variables )
      result ) ) )
(define (s.lookup id env)
  (car (getprop id 'apval)) )
(define (s.update! id env value)
  (set-car! (getprop id 'apval) value) )
```


Exercise 1.5 : Since there are many other predicates in the same predicament,
just define a macro to define them. Notice that the value of **the-false-value** is
True for the definition Lisp.

```
(define-syntax defpredicate
  (syntax-rules ()
    ((defpredicate name value arity)
     (defprimitive name
       (lambda values (or (apply value values) the-false-value))
       arity ) ) ) )
(defpredicate > > 2)
```

Exercise 1.6 : The hard part of this exercise is due to the fact that the arity of `list` is so variable. For that reason, you should define it directly by `definitial`, like this:

```
(definitial list
   (lambda (values) values) )
```

Exercise 1.7 : Well, of course, the obvious way to define `call/cc` is to use `call/cc`. The trick is to convert the underlying Lisp functions into functions in the Lisp being defined.

```
(defprimitive call/cc
   (lambda (f)
      (call/cc (lambda (g)
                  (invoke
                   f (list (lambda (values)
                              (if (= (length values) 1)
                                  (g (car values))
                                  (wrong "Incorrect arity" g) ) ))) ) )
      1 )
```

Exercise 1.8 : Here we have very much the same problem as in the definition of `call/cc`: you have to do the work between the abstractions of the underlying definition Lisp and the Lisp being defined. The function `apply` has variable arity, by the way, and it must transform its list of arguments (especially its last one) into an authentic list of values.

```
(definitial apply
   (lambda (values)
      (if (>= (length values) 2)
          (let ((f (car values))
                (args (let flat ((args (cdr values)))
                        (if (null? (cdr args))
                            (car args)
                            (cons (car args) (flat (cdr args))) ) )) )
             (invoke f args) )
          (wrong "Incorrect arity" 'apply) ) ) )
```

Exercise 1.9 : Just store the call continuation to the interpreter and bind this escape (conveniently adapted to the function calling protocol) to the variable `end`.

```
(define (chapter1d-scheme)
   (define (toplevel)
      (display (evaluate (read) env.global))
      (toplevel) )
   (display "Welcome to Scheme")(newline)
   (call/cc (lambda (end)
               (defprimitive end end 1)
               (toplevel) )) )
```

Exercise 1.10 : Of course, these comparisons depend simultaneously on at least two factors: the implementation that you are using and the programs that you are benchmarking. Normally, the comparisons show a ratio on the order of 5 to 15, according to [ITW86].

Even so, this exercise is useful to make you aware of the fact that the definition of **evaluate** is written in a fundamental Lisp, and it can be evaluated simulataneously by Scheme or by the language that **evaluate** defines.

Exercise 1.11 : Since you can always take sequences back to binary sequences, all you have to do here is to show how to rewrite them. The idea is to encapsulate expressions that risk inducing hooks inside *thunks*.

```
(begin expression₁ expression₂)
≡   ((lambda (void other) (other))
         expression₁
         (lambda () expression₂) )
```

Exercise 2.1 : It's straightforwardly translated as (**cons 1 2**). For compatibility, you could also define this:

```
(define (funcall f . args) (apply f args))
(define (function f) f)
```

Or, again, you could define it with macros, like this:

```
(define-syntax funcall
  (syntax-rules ()
     ((funcall f arg ...) (f arg ...)) ) )
(define-syntax function
  (syntax-rules ()
     ((function f) f) ) )
```

Exercise 2.2 : The problem here is to know:

1. whether it is legal to talk about the function **bar** although it has not yet been defined;

2. in the case where **bar** has been defined before the result of (**function bar**) has been applied, whether you're going to get an error or the new function that has just been defined.

The difference is in the special form, **function**: are we talking about *the* function **bar** or about the value instantly associated with it in the name space for functions?

Exercise 2.3 : All you have to do is to modify **invoke** so that it recognizes numbers and lists in the function position. Do it like this:

```
(define (invoke fn args)
  (cond ((procedure? fn) (fn args))
        ((number? fn)
          (if (= (length args) 1)
              (if (>= fn 0) (list-ref (car args) fn)
                  (list-tail (car args) (- fn)) )
              (wrong "Incorrect arity" fn) ) )
```

```
((pair? fn)
 (map (lambda (f) (invoke f args))
       fn ) )
(else (wrong "Cannot apply" fn)) ) )
```

Exercise 2.4 : The difficulty is that the function being passed belongs to the Lisp being defined, not to the definition Lisp.

```
(definitial new-assoc/de
  (lambda (values current.denv)
    (if (= 3 (length values))
        (let ((tag        (car values))
              (default    (cadr values))
              (comparator (caddr values)) )
          (let look ((denv current.denv))
            (if (pair? denv)
                (if (eq? the-false-value
                         (invoke comparator (list tag (caar denv))
                                            current.denv ) )
                    (look (cdr denv))
                    (cdar denv) )
                (invoke default (list tag) current.denv) ) ) )
        (wrong "Incorrect arity" 'assoc/de) ) ) )
```

Exercise 2.5 : Here again you have to adapt the function **specific-error** to the underlying exception system.

```
(define-syntax dynamic-let
  (syntax-rules ()
    ((dynamic-let () . body)
     (begin . body) )
    ((dynamic-let ((variable value) others ...) . body)
     (bind/de 'variable (list value)
              (lambda () (dynamic-let (others ...) . body)) ) ) ) )
(define-syntax dynamic
  (syntax-rules ()
    ((dynamic variable)
     (car (assoc/de 'variable specific-error)) ) ) )
(define-syntax dynamic-set!
  (syntax-rules ()
    ((dynamic-set! variable value)
     (set-car! (assoc/de 'variable specific-error) value) ) ) )
```

Exercise 2.6 : A private variable, **properties**, common to the two functions, contains the lists of properties for all the symbols.

```
(let ((properties '()))
  (set! putprop
        (lambda (symbol key value)
          (let ((plist (assq symbol properties)))
            (if (pair? plist)
```

```
                    (let ((couple (assq key (cdr plist))))
                       (if (pair? couple)
                           (set-cdr! couple value)
                           (set-cdr! plist (cons (cons key value)
                                                  (cdr plist) )) ) )
                    (let ((plist (list symbol (cons key value))))
                       (set! properties (cons plist properties)) ) ) )
             value ) )
        (set! getprop
             (lambda (symbol key)
                (let ((plist (assq symbol properties)))
                   (if (pair? plist)
                       (let ((couple (assq key (cdr plist))))
                          (if (pair? couple)
                              (cdr couple)
                              #f ) )
                       #f ) ) ) ) )
```

Exercise 2.7 : Just add the following clause to the interpreter, `evaluate`.

```
. . .
((label)   ;Syntax: (label name (lambda (variables) body))
 (let* ((name     (cadr e))
        (new-env (extend env (list name) (list 'void)))
        (def      (caddr e))
        (fun      (make-function (cadr def) (cddr def) new-env)) )
    (update! name new-env fun)
    fun ) )
```

Exercise 2.8 : Just add the following clause to `f.evaluate`. Notice the resemblance to `flet` except with respect to the function environment where local functions are created.

```
. . .
((labels)
 (let ((new-fenv (extend fenv
                          (map car (cadr e))
                          (map (lambda (def) 'void) (cadr e)) )))
    (for-each (lambda (def)
                 (update! (car def)
                          new-fenv
                          (f.make-function (cadr def) (cddr def)
                                            env new-fenv ) ) )
              (cadr e) )
    (f.eprogn (cddr e) env new-fenv ) ) )
```

Exercise 2.9 : Since a `let` form preserves indetermination, you have to make sure not to sequence the computation of initialization forms and thus organize them into a `let`, which must however be in the right environment. You could do that using a hygienic expansion or a whole lot of **gensyms** for the temporary variables, $temp_i$.

```
(let ((variable₁ 'void)
      ...
      (variableₙ 'void) )
  (let ((temp₁ expression₁)
        ...
        (tempₙ expressionₙ) )
    (set! variable₁ temp₁)
    ...
    (set! variableₙ tempₙ)
    corps ) )
```

Exercise 2.10 : Here's a binary version. The η-conversion has been modified to take a binary function into account.

```
(define fix2
  (let ((d (lambda (w)
             (lambda (f)
               (f (lambda (x y) (((w w) f) x y))) ))))
    (d d) ) )
```

Last but not least, here is an n-ary version.

```
(define fixN
  (let ((d (lambda (w)
             (lambda (f)
               (f (lambda args (apply ((w w) f) args))) ))))
    (d d) ) )
```

Exercise 2.11 : Perhaps a little intuition is enough to see that the preceding definition for fixN can be extended, like this:

```
(define NfixN
  (let ((d (lambda (w)
             (lambda (f*)
               (list ((car f*)
                      (lambda a (apply (car ((w w) f*)) a))
                      (lambda a (apply (cadr ((w w) f*)) a)) )
                     ((cadr f*)
                      (lambda a (apply (car ((w w) f*)) a))
                      (lambda a (apply (cadr ((w w) f*)) a)) ) ) ) )))
    (d d) ) )
```

Now be careful to prevent ((w w) f) being evaluated too hastily, and then generalize the extension in this way:

```
(define NfixN2
  (let ((d (lambda (w)
             (lambda (f*)
               (map (lambda (f)
                      (apply f (map (lambda (i)
                                      (lambda a (apply
                                                 (list-ref ((w w) f*) i)
                                                 a )) )
                                    (iota 0 (length f*)) )) )
```

```
                            f* ) ) )))
            (d d) ) )
```

Careful: the order of the functions for which you take the fixed point must always be the same. Consequently, the definition of **odd?** must be first in the list and the functional that defines it must have **odd?** as its first variable.

The function **iota** is thus defined in a way that recalls APL, like this:

```
    (define (iota start end)
      (if (< start end)
          (cons start (iota (+ 1 start) end))
          '() ) )
```

Exercise 2.12 : That function is attributed to Klop in [Bar84]. You can verify that ((**klop meta-fact**) 5) really does compute 120.

Since all the internal variables **s**, **c**, **h**, **e**, and **m** are bound to **r**, their order does not matter much in the application (**m e c h e s**). It is sufficient for the arity to be respected. You can even add or cut back on variables. If you reduce **s**, **c**, **h**, **e**, and **m** to nothing more than **w**, then you get **Y**.

Exercise 2.13 : The answer is 120. Isn't it nice that auto-application makes recursion possible here? Another possibility would have been to modify the code for the factorial to that it takes itself as an argument. That would lead to this:

```
    (define (factfact n)
      (define (internal-fact f n)
        (if (= n 1) 1
            (* n (f f (- n 1))) ) )
      (internal-fact internal-fact n) )
```

Exercise 3.1 : That form could be named (**the-current-continuation**) because it returns its own continuation. There we see the point of **call/cc** with respect to **the-continuation** since **the-continuation** brings back only its continuation, a poor thing of no interest to us. Let's look at the details of a computation, and as we do so, let's index the continuations and functions that come into play; we'll abbreviate the abbreviation **call/cc** as just **cc** here. Continuations will prefix expressions as an index, so we'll calculate $_{k_0}$(**call/cc**$_1$ **call/cc**$_2$); k_0 is the continuation with which to calculate (**cc**$_1$ **cc**$_2$). Remember that the definition of **call/cc** is this:

$$_k(\text{call/cc } \phi) \quad \rightarrow \quad _k(\phi \ k)$$

Thus we have that $_{k_0}(\text{cc}_1 \ \text{cc}_2)$ is rewritten as $_{k_0}(\text{cc}_2 \ k_0)$, which in turn is rewritten as $_{k_0}(k_0 \ k_0)$, which returns the value k_0.

Exercise 3.2 : We'll use the same conventions as the preceding exercise and index this expression like this: $_{k_0}((\text{cc}_1 \ \text{cc}_2) \ (\text{cc}_3 \ \text{cc}_4))$. For simplicity, let's assume that the terms of a functional application are evaluated from left to right. Then the original expression becomes this: $_{k_0}(_{k_1}(\text{cc}_1 \ \text{cc}_2) \ (\text{cc}_3 \ \text{cc}_4))$ where k_1 is $\lambda\phi._{k_0}(\phi \ _{k_2}(\text{cc}_3 \ \text{cc}_4))$ and k_2 is $\lambda\epsilon._{k_0}(k_1 \ \epsilon)$. The initial form is rewritten as $_{k_0}(k_1 \ k_2)$, that is, $_{k_0}(k_2 \ _{k_2'}(\text{cc}_3 \ \text{cc}_4))$ where k_2' is $\lambda\epsilon._{k_0}(k_2 \ \epsilon)$. That leads to $_{k_0}(k_1 \ k_2')$

and then to $k_0(k_1' \; k_2'')$ ... So you see that the calculation loops indefinitely. You can verify that this looping does not depend on the order of evaluation of the terms of the functional application. This may very well be the shortest possible program, measured in number of terms, that will loop indefinitely.

Exercise 3.3 : Each computation prefixed by a *label* will be transformed into a local function within a huge form, `labels`. The `go`s are translated into calls to those functions, but they are associated with a dynamic escape to insure that the `go` forms have the right continuation. The expansion looks like this:

```
(block EXIT
  (let (LABEL (TAG (list 'tagbody)))
    (labels ((INIT () expressions_0... (label_1))
             (label_1 () expressions_1... (label_2))
             ...
             (label_n () expressions_n... (return-from EXIT nil))) )
      (setq LABEL (function INIT))
      (while #t
        (setq LABEL (catch TAG (funcall LABEL))) ) ) ) )
```

The forms (go *label*) are translated into (`throw` TAG *label*); (`return` *value*) will become (`return-from` EXIT *value*). In the preceding lines, those names are written in all capital letters to avoid conflicts.

A fairly complicated translation of `go` insures the right continuation of the branching, and in (`bar` (`go` L)), it prevents `bar` from being called when (`go` L) returns a value. That unfortunately would have happened if we had carelessly written this, for example:

```
(tagbody  A (return (+ 1 (catch 'foo (go B))))
          B (* 2 (throw 'foo 5)) )
```

See also [Bak92c].

Exercise 3.4 : Introduce a new subclass of functions:

```
(define-class function-with-arity function (arity))
```

Then redefine the evaluation of `lambda` forms so that they now create one such instance:

```
(define (evaluate-lambda n* e* r k)
  (resume k (make-function-with-arity n* e* r (length n*))) )
```

Now adapt the invocation protocol for these new functions, like this:

```
(define-method (invoke (f function-with-arity) v* r k)
  (if (= (function-with-arity-arity f) (length v*))
    (let ((env (extend-env (function-env f)
                           (function-variables f)
                           v* )))
      (evaluate-begin (function-body f) env k) )
    (wrong "Incorrect arity" (function-variables f) v*) ) )
```

Exercise 3.5 :

```
(definitial apply
  (make-primitive
   'apply
   (lambda (v* r k)
     (if (>= (length v*) 2)
         (let ((f (car v*))
               (args (let flat ((args (cdr v*)))
                       (if (null? (cdr args))
                           (car args)
                           (cons (car args) (flat (cdr args))) ) )) )
           (invoke f args r k) )
         (wrong "Incorrect arity" 'apply) ) ) ) )
```

Exercise 3.6 : Take a little inspiration from the preceding exercise and define a new type of function, like this:

```
(define-class function-nadic function (arity))
(define (evaluate-lambda n* e* r k)
  (resume k (make-function-with-arity n* e* r (length n*))) )
(define-method (invoke (f function-nadic) v* r k)
  (define (extend-env env names values)
    (if (pair? names)
        (make-variable-env
         (extend-env env (cdr names) (cdr values))
         (car names)
         (car values) )
        (make-variable-env env names values) ) )
  (if (>= (length v*) (function-nadic-arity f))
      (let ((env (extend-env (function-env f)
                             (function-variables f)
                             v* )))
        (evaluate-begin (function-body f) env k) )
      (wrong "Incorrect arity" (function-variables f) v*) ) )
```

Exercise 3.7 : Put the interaction loop in the initial continuation. For example, you could write this:

```
(define (chap3j-interpreter)
  (letrec ((k.init (make-bottom-cont
                    'void (lambda (v) (display v)
                                     (toplevel) ) ))
           (toplevel (lambda () (evaluate (read) r.init k.init))) )
    (toplevel) ) )
```

Exercise 3.8 : Define the class of reified continuations; all it does is encapsulate three things: an internal continuation (an instance of **continuation**), the function **call/cc** to build such an object, and the right method of invocation.

```
(define-class reified-continuation value (k))
(definitial call/cc
```

```
(make-primitive 'call/cc
                (lambda (v* r k)
                  (if (= 1 (length v*))
                      (invoke (car v*)
                              (list (make-reified-continuation k))
                              r
                              k )
                      (wrong "Incorrect arity" 'call/cc v*) ) ) ) )
(define-method (invoke (f reified-continuation) v* r k)
  (if (= 1 (length v*))
      (resume (reified-continuation-k f) (car v*))
      (wrong "Continuations expect one argument" v* r k) ) )
```

Exercise 3.9 : This point of this function is never to return.

```
(defun eternal-return (thunk)                            COMMON LISP
  (labels ((loop ()
             (unwind-protect (thunk)
               (loop) ) ))
    (loop) ) )
```

Exercise 3.10 : The values of those expressions are 33 and 44. The function **make-box** simulates a box with no apparent assignment nor function side effects. We get this effect by combining **call/cc** and **letrec**. If you think of the expansion of **letrec** in terms of **let** and **set!**, then it is easier to see how we get that. However, it makes life much more difficult for partisans of the special form **letrec** in the presence of first class continuations that can be invoked more than once.

Exercise 3.11 : First, rewrite **evaluate** simply as a generic function, like this:

```
(define-generic (evaluate (e) r k)
  (wrong "Not a program" e r k) )
```

Then take the existing functions to ornament **evaluate**, like this:

```
(define-method (evaluate (e quotation) r k)
  (evaluate-quote (quotation-value e) r k) )
(define-method (evaluate (e assignment) r k)
  (evaluate-set! (assignment-name e)
                 (assignment-form e)
                 r k ) )
...
```

Then you still have to define classes corresponding to the various possible syntactic forms, like this:

```
(define-class program Object ())
(define-class quotation program (value))
(define-class assignment program (name form))
...
```

Now the only thing left to do is to define an appropriate reader that knows how to read a program and build an instance of **program**. That's the purpose of the function **objectify** that you'll see in Section 9.11.1.

Exercise 3.12 : To define **throw** as a function, do this:

```
(definitial throw
  (make-primitive
   'throw
   (lambda (v* r k)
     (if (= 2 (length v*))
         (catch-lookup k (car v*)
                       (make-throw-cont k '(quote ,(cadr v*)) r) )
         (wrong "Incorrect arity" 'throw v*) ) ) ) )
```

So that we didn't simply define a variation on **catch-lookup**, we fabricated a false instance of **throw-cont** to trick the interpreter. The only important value there is the one to transmit.

Exercise 3.13 : Code translated into CPS is slower because it creates many closures to simulate continuation. By the way, a transformation into CPS is not idempotent. That is, translating code into CPS and then translating that result into CPS does not yield the identity. That's obvious when we consider the factorial in CPS. The continuation **k** can be any function at all and may also have side effects on control. For example, we could write this:

```
(define (cps-fact n k)
  (if (= n 0) (k 1) (cps-fact (- n 1) (lambda (v) (k (* n v)))))) )
```

The function **cps-fact** can be invoked with a rather special continuation, as in this example:

```
(call/cc (lambda (k) (* 2 (cps-fact 4 k)))) → 24
```

Exercise 3.14 : The function **the-current-continuation** could also be defined as in Exercise 3.1, like this:

```
(define (cc f)
  (let ((reified? #f))
    (let ((k (the-current-continuation)))
      (if reified? k (begin (set! reified? #t) (f k))) ) ) )
```

Special thanks to Luc Moreau, who suggested this exercise in [Mor94].

Exercise 4.1 : Many techniques exist; among them, return partial results or use continuations. Here are two solutions:

```
(define (min-max1 tree)
  (define (mm tree)
    (if (pair? tree)
        (let ((a (mm (car tree)))
              (d (mm (cdr tree))) )
          (list (min (car a) (car d))
                (max (cadr a) (cadr d)) ) )
        (list tree tree) ) )
  (mm tree) )
(define (min-max2 tree)
  (define (mm tree k)
    (if (pair? tree)
```

```
        (mm (car tree)
            (lambda (mina maxa)
              (mm (cdr tree)
                  (lambda (mind maxd)
                    (k (min mina mind)
                       (max maxa maxd) ) ) ) ) )
        (k tree tree) ) )
   (mm tree list) )
```

That first solution consumes a lot of lists that are promptly forgotten. For this kind of algorithm, you can imagine carrying out transformations that eliminate this kind of abusive consummation; those transformations are known in [Wad88] as *deforestation* The second solution consumes a lot of closures. The version in this book is much more efficient, in spite of its side effects (though the side effects might make it intolerable to certain people).

Exercise 4.2 : The following functions are prefixed by **q** to distinguish them from the corresponding primitive functions.

```
(define (qons a d) (lambda (msg) (msg a d)))
(define (qar pair) (pair (lambda (a d) a)))
(define (qdr pair) (pair (lambda (a d) d)))
```

Exercise 4.3 : Use the idea that two dotted pairs are the same if a modification of one is visible in the other.

```
(define (pair-eq? a b)
  (let ((tag (list 'tag))
        (original-car (car a)) )
    (set-car! a tag)
    (let ((result (eq? (car b) tag)))
      (set-car! a original-car)
      result ) ) )
```

Exercise 4.4 : Assuming you've already added a clause to **evaluate** to recognize the special form **or**,

```
...
((or) (evaluate-or (cadr e) (caddr e) r s k)) ...
```

then do something like this:

```
(define (evaluate-or e1 e2 r s k)
  (evaluate e1 r s (lambda (v ss)
                     (((v 'boolify)
                       (lambda () (k v ss))
                       (lambda () (evaluate e2 r s k)) ) )) ) )
```

Notice that β is evaluated with the memory **s** not **ss**.

Exercise 4.5 : Actually that exercise is a little ambiguous. Here are two solutions; one returns the value that the variable had before the calculation of the value to assign; the other, after that calculation.

```
(define (new1-evaluate-set! n e r s k)
  (evaluate e r s
    (lambda (v ss)
      (k (ss (r n)) (update ss (r n) v)) ) ) )
(define (new2-evaluate-set! n e r s k)
  (evaluate e r s
    (lambda (v ss)
      (k (s (r n)) (update ss (r n) v)) ) ) )
```

Those two programs give different results for the following expression:

```
(let ((x 1))
  (set! x (set! x 2)) )
```

Exercise 4.6 : The only problem with `apply` is that the last argument is a list of the Scheme interpreter that we have to decode into values. -11 is a label to help us identify the primitive `apply`.

```
(definitial apply
  (create-function
    -11 (lambda (v* s k)
          (define (first-pairs v*)
            ;; (assume (pair? v*))
            (if (pair? (cdr v*))
                (cons (car v*) (first-pairs (cdr v*)))
                '() ) )
          (define (terms-of v s)
            (if (eq? (v 'type) 'pair)
                (cons (s (v 'car)) (terms-of (s (v 'cdr)) s))
                '() ) )
          (if (>= (length v*) 2)
              (if (eq? ((car v*) 'type) 'function)
                  (((car v*) 'behavior)
                   (append (first-pairs (cdr v*))
                           (terms-of (car (last-pair (cdr v*))) s) )
                   s k )
                  (wrong "First argument not a function") )
              (wrong "Incorrect arity for apply") ) ) ) )
```

For `call/cc`, we allocate a label for each continuation to make it unique.

```
(definitial call/cc
  (create-function
    -13 (lambda (v* s k)
          (if (= 1 (length v*))
              (if (eq? ((car v*) 'type) 'function)
                  (allocate 1 s
                    (lambda (a* ss)
                      (((car v*) 'behavior)
                       (list (create-function
                               (car a*)
                               (lambda (vv* sss kk)
                                 (if (= 1 (length vv*))
                                     (k (car vv*) sss)
```

```
                              (wrong "Incorrect arity") ) ) ) )
                ss k ) ) )
           (wrong "Non functional argument for call/cc") )
        (wrong "Incorrect arity for call/cc") ) ) ) )
```

Exercise 4.7 : The difficulty is to test the compatibility of the arity and to change a list (of the Scheme interpreter) into a list of values of the Scheme being interpreted.

```
(define (evaluate-nlambda n* e* r s k)
  (define (arity n*)
    (cond ((pair? n*) (+ 1 (arity (cdr n*))))
          ((null? n*) 0)
          (else     1) ) )
  (define (update-environment r n* a*)
    (cond ((pair? n*) (update-environment
                          (update r (car n*) (car a*)) (cdr n*) (cdr a*) ))
          ((null? n*) r)
          (else (update r n* (car a*))) ) )
  (define (update-store s a* v* n*)
    (cond ((pair? n*) (update-store (update s (car a*) (car v*))
                                    (cdr a*) (cdr v*) (cdr n*) ))
          ((null? n*) s)
          (else (allocate-list v* s (lambda (v ss)
                                      (update ss (car a*) v) ))) ) )
  (allocate 1 s
    (lambda (a* ss)
      (k (create-function
          (car a*)
          (lambda (v* s k)
            (if (compatible-arity? n* v*)
                (allocate (arity n*) s
                  (lambda (a* ss)
                    (evaluate-begin e*
                                    (update-environment r n* a*)
                                    (update-store ss a* v* n*)
                                    k ) ) )
                (wrong "Incorrect arity") ) ) )
         ss ) ) ) )
(define (compatible-arity? n* v*)
  (cond ((pair? n*) (and (pair? v*)
                         (compatible-arity? (cdr n*) (cdr v*)) ))
        ((null? n*) (null? v*))
        ((symbol? n*) #t) ) )
```

Exercise 5.1 : Prove it by induction on the number of terms in the application.

Exercise 5.2 :

$$\mathcal{L}[\![(\text{label } \nu \ \pi)]\!]\rho = (\mathbf{Y} \ \lambda\varepsilon.(\mathcal{L}[\![\pi]\!] \ \rho[\nu \to \varepsilon]))$$

Exercise 5.3 :

$\mathcal{E}[\![(\text{dynamic } \nu)]\!]\rho\delta\kappa\sigma =$
  $\text{let } \varepsilon = (\delta\ \nu)$
  $\text{in}\quad \text{if } \varepsilon = \textit{no-such-dynamic-variable}$
      $\text{then}\quad \text{let } \alpha = (\gamma\ \nu)$
            $\text{in}\quad \text{if } \alpha = \textit{no-such-global-variable}$
                $\text{then } \textit{wrong}\ \text{``No such variable''}$
                $\text{else } (\kappa\ (\sigma\ \alpha)\ \sigma)$
                endif
      $\text{else } (\kappa\ \varepsilon\ \sigma)$
      endif

Exercise 5.4 : The macro will transform the application into a series of thunks that we evaluate in a non-prescribed order implemented by the function `determine!`.

```
(define-syntax unordered
  (syntax-rules ()
    ((unordered f) (f))
    ((unordered f arg ...)
     (determine! (lambda () f) (lambda () arg) ... ) ) ) )
(define (determine! . thunks)
  (let ((results (iota 0 (length thunks))))
    (let loop ((permut (random-permutation (length thunks))))
      (if (pair? permut)
          (begin (set-car! (list-tail results (car permut))
                           (force (list-ref thunks (car permut))) )
                 (loop (cdr permut)) )
          (apply (car results) (cdr results)) ) ) ) )
```

Notice that the choice of the permutation is made at the beginning, so this solution is not really as good as the denotation used in this chapter. If the function **random-permutation** is defined like this:

```
(define (random-permutation n)
  (shuffle (iota 0 n)) )
```

then we could make the choice of the permutation dynamic by means of **d.determine!**.

```
(define (d.determine! . thunks)
  (let ((results (iota 0 (length thunks))))
    (let loop ((permut (shuffle (iota 0 (length thunks)))))
      (if (pair? permut)
          (begin (set-car! (list-tail results (car permut))
                           (force (list-ref thunks (car permut))) )
                 (loop (shuffle (cdr permut))) )
          (apply (car results) (cdr results)) ) ) ) )
```

Exercise 6.1 : A simple way of doing that is to add a supplementary argument to the combinator to indicate which variable (either a symbol or simply its name), like this:

```
(define (CHECKED-GLOBAL-REF- i n)
  (lambda ()
    (let ((v (global-fetch i)))
      (if (eq? v undefined-value)
          (wrong "Uninitialized variable" n)
          v ) ) ) )
```

However, that solution increases the overall size of the code generated. A better solution is to generate a symbol table so that the name of the faulty variable would be there.

```
(define sg.current.names (list 'foo))
(define (stand-alone-producer e)
  (set! g.current (original.g.current))
  (let* ((m (meaning e r.init #t))
         (size (length g.current))
         (global-names (map car (reverse g.current))) )
    (lambda ()
      (set! sg.current (make-vector size undefined-value))
      (set! sg.current.names global-names)
      (set! *env* sr.init)
      (m) ) ) )
(define (CHECKED-GLOBAL-REF+ i)
  (lambda ()
    (let ((v (global-fetch i)))
      (if (eq? v undefined-value)
          (wrong "Uninitialized variable" (list-ref sg.current.names i))
          v ) ) ) )
```

Exercise 6.2 : The function `list` is, of course, just `(lambda l l)`, so all you have to do is use this definition and play around with the combinators, like this:

```
(definitial list ((NARY-CLOSURE (SHALLOW-ARGUMENT-REF 0) 0)))
```

Exercise 6.3 : First, you can redefine every combinator c as `(lambda args '(c . ,args))`. Then all you have to do is print the results of pretreatment.

Exercise 6.4 : The most direct way to get there is to modify the evaluation order for arguments of applications and thus adopt right to left order.

```
(define (FROM-RIGHT-STORE-ARGUMENT m m* rank)
  (lambda ()
    (let* ((v* (m*))
           (v (m)) )
      (set-activation-frame-argument! v* rank v)
      v* ) ) )
(define (FROM-RIGHT-CONS-ARGUMENT m m* arity)
  (lambda ()
    (let* ((v* (m*))
           (v (m)) )
      (set-activation-frame-argument!
       v* arity (cons v (activation-frame-argument v* arity))) )
```

```
v* ) ) )
```

You could also modify **meaning*** to preserve the evaluation order but to allocate the record before computing the arguments. By the way, computing the function term before computing the arguments (regardless of the order in which they are evaluated) lets you look at the closure you get, for example, to allocate an activation record adapted to the number of temporary variables required. Then there will be only one allocation, not two.

Exercise 6.5 : Insert the following line as a special form in **meaning**:

```
... ((redefine) (meaning-redefine (cadr e))) ...
```

Then redefine its effect, like this:

```
(define (meaning-redefine n)
  (let ((kind1 (global-variable? g.init n)))
    (if kind1
        (let ((value (vector-ref sg.init (cdr kind1))))
          (let ((kind2 (global-variable? g.current n)))
            (if kind2
                (static-wrong "Already redefined variable" n)
                (let ((index (g.current-extend! n)))
                  (vector-set! sg.current index value) ) ) ) )
        (static-wrong "No such variable to redefine" n) )
    (lambda () 2001) ) )
```

That redefinition occurs during pretreatment, not during execution. The form **redefine** returns just any value.

Exercise 6.6 : A function without variables does not need to extend the current environment. Extending the current environment slowed down access to deep variables. Change **meaning-fix-abstraction** so that it detects thunks, and define a new combinator to do that.

```
(define (meaning-fix-abstraction n* e+ r tail?)
  (let ((arity (length n*)))
    (if (= arity 0)
        (let ((m+ (meaning-sequence e+ r #t)))
          (THUNK-CLOSURE m+) )
        (let* ((r2 (r-extend* r n*))
               (m+ (meaning-sequence e+ r2 #t)) )
          (FIX-CLOSURE m+ arity) ) ) ) )
(define (THUNK-CLOSURE m+)
  (let ((arity+1 (+ 0 1)))
    (lambda ()
      (define (the-function v* sr)
        (if (= (activation-frame-argument-length v*) arity+1)
            (begin (set! *env* sr)
                   (m+) )
            (wrong "Incorrect arity") ) )
      (make-closure the-function *env*) ) ) )
```

Exercise 7.1 : First, create the register, like this:

```
(define *dynenv* -1)
```

Then modify the functions that preserve the environment, like this:

```
(define (preserve-environment)
  (stack-push *dynenv*)
  (stack-push *env*) )
(define (restore-environment)
  (set! *env* (stack-pop))
  (set! *dynenv* (stack-pop)) )
```

There's hardly anything left to do as far as finding the dynamic environment now, but the way to handle the stack has changed.

```
(define (search-dynenv-index)
  *dynenv* )
(define (pop-dynamic-binding)
  (stack-pop)
  (stack-pop)
  (set! *dynenv* (stack-pop)) )
(define (push-dynamic-binding index value)
  (stack-push *dynenv*)
  (stack-push value)
  (stack-push index)
  (set! *dynenv* (- *stack-index* 1)) )
```

Exercise 7.2 : The function is simple:

```
(definitial load
  (let* ((arity 1)
         (arity+1 (+ arity 1)) )
    (make-primitive
     (lambda ()
       (if (= arity+1 (activation-frame-argument-length *val*))
           (let ((filename (activation-frame-argument *val* 0)))
             (set! *pc* (install-object-file! filename)) )
           (signal-exception
            #t (list "Incorrect arity" 'load) ) ) ) ) ) )
```

However, that definition poses a few problems. Analyze, for example, how a captured continuation returns and restarts when a file is being loaded. For example,

```
(display 'attention)
(call/cc (lambda (k) (set! *k* k)))
(display 'caution)
```

After this file has been loaded, will invoking the continuation *k* reprint the symbol **caution**? Yes, with this implementation!

Also notice that if we load the compiled file defining a global variable, say, **bar**, which was unknown to the application, it will remain unknown to the application.

Exercise 7.3 : Here's the function:

```
(definitial global-value
  (let* ((arity 1)
         (arity+1 (+ arity 1)) )
    (define (get-index name)
      (let ((where (memq name sg.current.names)))
        (if where (- (length where) 1)
            (signal-exception
             #f (list "Undefined global variable" name) ) ) ) )
    (make-primitive
     (lambda ()
       (if (= arity+1 (activation-frame-argument-length *val*))
           (let* ((name (activation-frame-argument *val* 0))
                  (i (get-index name)) )
             (set! *val* (global-fetch i))
             (when (eq? *val* undefined-value)
               (signal-exception #f (list "Uninitialized variable" i)) )
             (set! *pc* (stack-pop)) )
           (signal-exception
            #t (list "Incorrect arity" 'global-value) ) ) ) ) ) )
```

Since we have re-introduced the possibility of an non-existing variable, of course, we have to test whether the variable has been initialized.

Exercise 7.4 : First, add the allocation of a vector to the function `run-machine` to store the current value of dynamic variables.

```
... (set! *dynamics* (make-vector (+ 1 (length dynamics))
                                  undefined-value )) ;NEW
```

Then redefine the appropriate access functions, like this:

```
(define (find-dynamic-value index)
  (let ((v (vector-ref *dynamics* index)))
    (if (eq? v undefined-value)
        (signal-exception #f (list "No such dynamic binding" index))
        v ) ) )
(define (push-dynamic-binding index value)
  (stack-push (vector-ref *dynamics* index))
  (stack-push index)
  (vector-set! *dynamics* index value) )
(define (pop-dynamic-binding)
  (let* ((index (stack-pop))
         (old-value (stack-pop)) )
    (vector-set! *dynamics* index old-value) ) )
```

Alas! that implementation is unfortunately incorrect because immediate access takes advantage of the fact that saved values are now found on the stack. A continuation capture gets only the values to restore, not the current values. When an escape suppresses a slice of the stack, it fails to restore the dynamic variables to what they were when the form `bind-exit` began to be evaluated. To correct all that, we must have a form like `unwind-protect` or more simply we must abandon superficial implementation for a deeper implementation that doesn't pose that kind of problem and can be extended naturally in parallel.

Exercise 7.5 : With the following renamer, you can even interchange two variables by writing a list of substitutions such as ((fact fib) (fib fact)), but look out: this is a dangerous game to play!

```
(define (build-application-renaming-variables
          new-application-name application-name substitutions )
  (if (probe-file application-name)
      (call-with-input-file application-name
        (lambda (in)
          (let* ((dynamics     (read in))
                 (global-names (read in))
                 (constants    (read in))
                 (code         (read in))
                 (entries      (read in)) )
            (close-input-port in)
            (write-result-file
             new-application-name
             (list ";;;renamed variables from " application-name)
             dynamics
             (let sublis ((global-names global-names))
               (if (pair? global-names)
                   (cons (let ((s (assq (car global-names)
                                        substitutions )))
                           (if (pair? s) (cadr s)
                               (car global-names) ) )
                         (sublis (cdr global-names)) )
                   global-names ) )
             constants
             code
             entries ) ) ) )
      (signal #f (list "No such file" application-name)) ) )
```

Exercise 7.6 : Be careful to modify the right instruction!

```
(define-instruction (CHECKED-GLOBAL-REF i) 8
  (set! *val* (global-fetch i))
  (if (eq? *val* undefined-value)
      (signal-exception #t (list "Uninitialized variable" i))
      (vector-set! *code* (- *pc* 2) 7) ) )
```

Exercise 8.1 : The test is not necessary because it doesn't recognize two variables by the same name. That convention prevents a list of variables from being cyclic.

Exercise 8.2 : Here's the hint:

```
(define (prepare e)
  (eval/ce `(lambda () ,e)) )
```

Exercise 8.3 :

```
(define (eval/at e)
  (let ((g (gensym)))
    (eval/ce '(lambda (,g) (eval/ce ,g))) ) )
```

Exercise 8.4 : Yes, by programming an appropriate error handler, like this:

```
(set! variable-defined?
      (lambda (env name)
        (bind-exit (return)
          (monitor (lambda (c ex) (return #f))
            (eval/b name env)
            #t ) ) ) )
```

Exercise 8.5 : We will quietly skip over how to handle the special form `monitor`, which appears in the definition of the reflective interpreter. After all, if we don't make any mistakes, `monitor` behaves just like `begin`. What follows here does not exactly conform to Scheme because the definition of special forms requires their names to be used as variables (not exactly legal, we know). However, that works in many implementations of Scheme. For the form `the-environment`, we will define it to capture the necessary bindings.

```
(define-syntax the-environment
  (syntax-rules ()
    ((the-environment)
     (capture-the-environment make-toplevel make-flambda flambda?
       flambda-behavior prompt-in prompt-out exit it extend error
       global-env toplevel eval evlis eprogn reference quote if set!
       lambda flambda monitor ) ) ) )
(define-syntax capture-the-environment
  (syntax-rules ()
    ((capture-the-environment word ...)
     (lambda (name . value)
       (case name
         ((word) ((handle-location word) value)) ...
         ((display) (if (pair? value)
                        (wrong "Immutable" 'display)
                        show ))
         (else (if (pair? value)
                   (set-top-level-value! name (car value))
                   (top-level-value name) )) ) ) ) ) )
(define-syntax handle-location
  (syntax-rules ()
    ((handle-location name)
     (lambda (value)
       (if (pair? value)
           (set! name (car value))
           name ) ) ) ) )
```

Finally we'll define the functions to handle the first class environment; they are `variable-defined?`, `variable-value`, and `set-variable-value!`.

```
(define undefined (cons 'un 'defined))
(define-class Envir Object
  ( name value next ) )
(define (enrich env . names)
  (let enrich ((env env)(names names))
    (if (pair? names)
        (enrich (make-Envir (car names) undefined env) (cdr names))
        env ) ) )
(define (variable-defined? name env)
  (if (Envir? env)
      (or (eq? name (Envir-name env))
          (variable-defined? name (Envir-next env)) )
      #t ) )
(define (variable-value name env)
  (if (Envir? env)
      (if (eq? name (Envir-name env))
          (let ((value (Envir-value env)))
            (if (eq? value undefined)
                (error "Uninitialized variable" name)
                value ) )
          (variable-value name (Envir-next env)) )
      (env name) ) )
```

As you see, the environment is a linked list of nodes ending with a closure. Now the reflective interpreter can run!

Exercise 9.1 : Use the hygienic macros of Scheme to write this:

```
(define-syntax repeat1
  (syntax-rules (:while :unless :do)
    ((_ :while p :unless q :do body ...)
     (let loop ()
       (if p (begin (if (not q) (begin body ...))
                    (loop) )) ) ) ) )
```

You could also use **define-abbreviation** directly to write this instead:

```
(with-aliases ((+let let) (+begin begin) (+when when) (+not not))
  (define-abbreviation (repeat2 . parms)
    (let ((p    (list-ref parms 1))
          (q    (list-ref parms 3))
          (body (list-tail parms 5))
          (loop (gensym)) )
      `(,+let ,loop ()
          (,+when ,p (,+begin (,+when (,+not ,q) . ,body)
                              (,loop) )) ) ) ) )
```

Exercise 9.2 : The difficulty here is to do arithmetic with the macro language of Scheme. One approach is to generate calls at execution to the function **length** on lists of selected lengths.

```
(define-syntax enumerate
  (syntax-rules ()
```

```
       ((enumerate) (display 0))
       ((enumerate e1 e2 ...)
        (begin (display 0) (enumerate-aux e1 (e1) e2 ...) ) ) ) )
  (define-syntax enumerate-aux
    (syntax-rules ()
      ((enumerate-aux e1 len) (begin e1 (display (length 'len))))
      ((enumerate-aux e1 len e2 e3 ...)
       (begin e1 (display (length 'len))
              (enumerate-aux e2 (e2 . len) e3 ...) ) ) ) )
```

Exercise 9.3 : All you have to do is modify the function `make-macro-envi-ronment` so that all the levels are melded into one, like this:

```
(define (make-macro-environment current-level)
  (let ((metalevel (delay current-level)))
    (list (make-Magic-Keyword 'eval-in-abbreviation-world
            (special-eval-in-abbreviation-world metalevel) )
          (make-Magic-Keyword 'define-abbreviation
            (special-define-abbreviation metalevel))
          (make-Magic-Keyword 'let-abbreviation
            (special-let-abbreviation metalevel))
          (make-Magic-Keyword 'with-aliases
            (special-with-aliases metalevel) ) ) ) )
```

Exercise 9.4 : Writing the converter is a cake-walk. The only real point of interest is how to rename the variables. We'll keep an A-list to store the correspondances.

```
(define-generic (->Scheme (e) r))
(define-method (->Scheme (e Alternative) r)
  '(if ,(->Scheme (Alternative-condition e) r)
       ,(->Scheme (Alternative-consequent e) r)
       ,(->Scheme (Alternative-alternant e) r) ) )
(define-method (->Scheme (e Local-Assignment) r)
  '(set! ,(->Scheme (Local-Assignment-reference e) r)
         ,(->Scheme (Local-Assignment-form e) r) ) )
(define-method (->Scheme (e Reference) r)
  (variable->Scheme (Reference-variable e) r) )
(define-method (->Scheme (e Function) r)
  (define (renamings-extend r variables names)
    (if (pair? names)
        (renamings-extend (cons (cons (car variables) (car names)) r)
                          (cdr variables) (cdr names) )
        r ) )
  (define (pack variables names)
    (if (pair? variables)
        (if (Local-Variable-dotted? (car variables))
            (car names)
            (cons (car names) (pack (cdr variables) (cdr names))) )
        '() ) )
  (let* ((variables (Function-variables e))
```

```
        (new-names (map (lambda (v) (gensym))
                        variables ))
        (newr (renamings-extend r variables new-names)) )
    '(lambda ,(pack variables new-names)
       ,(->Scheme (Function-body e) newr)) ) )
  (define-generic (variable->Scheme (e) r))
```

Exercise 9.5 : As it's written, MEROONET mixes the two worlds of expansion and execution; several resources belong to both worlds simultaneously. For example, `register-class` is invoked at expansion and when a file is loaded.

Exercise 10.1 : All you have to change is the function SCM_invoke and the calling protocol for closures of minor fixed arity. It suffices to take the one for primitives of fixed arity—just don't forget to provide the object representing the closure as the first argument. You must also change the interface for generated C functions to make them adopt the signature you've just adopted.

Exercise 10.2 : Refine global variables so that they have a supplementary field indicating whether they have really been intialized or not. In consequence of that design change, you'll have to change how free global variables are detected.

```
(define-class Global-Variable Variable (initialized?))
(define (objectify-free-global-reference name r)
  (let ((v (make-Global-Variable name #f)))
    (set! g.current (cons v g.current))
    (make-Global-Reference v) ) )
```

Then insert the analysis in the compiler. It involves the interaction between the generic inspector and the generic function inian!.

```
(define (compile->C e out)
  (set! g.current '())
  (let ((prg (extract-things!
               (lift! (initialization-analyze! (Sexp->object e)))  )))
    (gather-temporaries! (closurize-main! prg))
    (generate-C-program out e prg) ) )
(define (initialization-analyze! e)
  (call/cc (lambda (exit) (inian! e (lambda () (exit 'finished)))))
  e )
(define-generic (inian! (e) exit)
  (update-walk! inian! e exit) )
```

Now the problem is to follow the flow of computation and to determine the global variables that will surely be written before they are read. Rather than develop a specific and complicated analysis for that, why not try to determine a subset of variables that have surely been initialized? That's what the following five methods do.

```
(define-method (inian! (e Global-Assignment) exit)
  (call-next-method)
  (let ((gv (Global-Assignment-variable e)))
    (set-Global-Variable-initialized?! gv #t)
```

```
        (inian-warning "Surely initialized variable" gv)
        e ) )
  (define-method (inian! (e Global-Reference) exit)
    (let ((gv (Global-Reference-variable e)))
      (cond ((Predefined-Variable? gv) e)
            ((Global-Variable-initialized? gv) e)
            (else (inian-error "Surely uninitialized variable" gv)
              (exit) ) ) ) )
  (define-method (inian! (e Alternative) exit)
    (inian! (Alternative-condition e) exit)
    (exit) )
  (define-method (inian! (e Application) exit)
    (call-next-method)
    (exit) )
  (define-method (inian! (e Function) exit)
    e )
```

That analysis follows the computation, determines assignments, and stops once the
computation becomes too complicated to follow; that is, once a function is applied
or once an alternative appears. In contrast, it is not necessary to look at the body
of abstractions since a closure is calculated in finite time and without any errors.

Exercise 11.1 : The predicate `Object?` can be re-enforced and made less error-
prone if you reserve another component in the vectors representing objects to contain a label. After creating this label, you should modify the predicate `Object?`
as well as all the places where there is an allocation that should add this label,
especially during bootstrapping, that is, when the predefined classes are defined.

```
(define *starting-offset* 2)
(define meroonet-tag (cons 'meroonet 'tag))
(define (Object? o)
  (and (vector? o)
       (>= (vector-length o) *starting-offset*)
       (eq? (vector-ref o 1) meroonet-tag) ) )
```

This modification will make the predicate more robust, but it does not increase
the speed. However, the predicate can still be fooled if the label on an object is
extracted by `vector-ref` and inserted in some other vector.

Exercise 11.2 : Since the function is generic, you can specialize it for certain
classes. The following version gobbles up too many dotted pairs.

```
(define-generic (clone (o))
  (list->vector (vector->list o)) )
```

Exercise 11.3 : Define a new type of class, the metaclass `CountingClass`, with
a supplementary field to count the allocations that will occur.

```
(define-class CountingClass Class (counter))
```

The code in MEROONET was written so that any modifications you make should
not put everything else in jeopardy. It should be possible to define a class with
that metaclass, like this:

```
(define-meroonet-macro (define-CountingClass name super-name
                                              own-field-descriptions )
  (let ((class (register-CountingClass
                name super-name own-field-descriptions )))
    (generate-related-names class) ) )
(define (register-CountingClass name super-name own-field-descriptions)
  (initialize! (allocate-CountingClass)
               name
               (->Class super-name)
               own-field-descriptions ) )
```

However, a better way of doing it would be to extend the syntax of `define-class` to accept an option indicating the metaclass to use, making `Class` the default. Then you must make several functions generic, like:

```
(define-generic (generate-related-names (class)))
(define-method (generate-related-names (class Class))
  (Class-generate-related-names class) )
(define-generic (initialize! (o) . args))
(define-method (initialize! (o Class) . args)
  (apply Class-initialize! o args) )
(define-method (initialize! (class CountingClass) . args)
  (set-CountingClass-counter! class 0)
  (call-next-method) )
```

The allocators in the accompanying functions should be modified to maintain the counter, like this:

```
(define-method (generate-related-names (class CountingClass))
  (let ((cname (symbol-append (Class-name class) '-class))
        (alloc-name (symbol-append 'allocate- (Class-name class)))
        (make-name (symbol-append 'make- (Class-name class))) )
    '(begin ,(call-next-method)
            (set! ,alloc-name              ;patch the allocator
                  (let ((old ,alloc-name))
                    (lambda sizes
                      (set-CountingClass-counter!
                       ,cname (+ 1 (CountingClass-counter ,cname)) )
                      (apply old sizes) ) ) )
            (set! ,make-name               ;patch the maker
                  (let ((old ,make-name))
                    (lambda args
                      (set-CountingClass-counter!
                       ,cname (+ 1 (CountingClass-counter ,cname)) )
                      (apply old args) ) ) ) ) ) )
```

To complete the exercise, here's an example of how to use it to count points:

```
(define-CountingClass CountedPoint Object (x y))
(unless (and (= 0 (CountingClass-counter CountedPoint-class))
             (allocate-CountedPoint)
             (= 1 (CountingClass-counter CountedPoint-class))
             (make-CountedPoint 11 22)
             (= 2 (CountingClass-counter CountedPoint-class)) )
```

```
;; should not be evaluated if everything is OK
(meroonet-error "Failed test on CountedPoint") )
```

Exercise 11.4 : Create a new metaclass, **ReflectiveClass**, with the supplementary fields, **predicate**, **allocator**, and **maker**. Then modify the way accompanying functions are generated so that these fields will be filled during the definition of the class. Do the same for the fields.

```
(define-class ReflectiveClass Class (predicate allocator maker))
(define-method (generate-related-names (class ReflectiveClass))
  (let ((cname (symbol-append (Class-name class) '-class))
        (predicate-name (symbol-append (Class-name class) '?))
        (allocator-name (symbol-append 'allocate- (Class-name class)))
        (maker-name (symbol-append 'make- (Class-name class))) )
   `(begin ,(call-next-method)
           (set-ReflectiveClass-predicate! ,cname ,predicate-name)
           (set-ReflectiveClass-allocator! ,cname ,allocator-name)
           (set-ReflectiveClass-maker! ,cname ,maker-name) ) ) )
```

Exercise 11.5 : The essential problem is to detect whether a generic function exists. In Scheme, it is not possible to know whether or not a global variable exists, so you'll have to consult the list ***generics***. Fortunately, it contains all the known generic functions.

```
(define-meroonet-macro (define-method call . body)
  (parse-variable-specifications
   (cdr call)
   (lambda (discriminant variables)
     (let ((g (gensym))(c (gensym)))        ; make g and c hygienic
      `(begin
        (unless (->Generic ',(car call)) (define-generic ,call)) ;new
        (register-method
         ',(car call)
         (lambda (,g ,c)
           (lambda ,(flat-variables variables)
             (define (call-next-method)
               ((if (Class-superclass ,c)
                    (vector-ref (Generic-dispatch-table ,g)
                                (Class-number (Class-superclass ,c)) )
                    (Generic-default ,g) )
                . ,(flat-variables variables) ) )
             . ,body ) )
         ',(cadr discriminant)
         ',(cdr call) ) ) ) ) ) )
```

Exercise 11.6 : Every method now has two local functions, **call-next-method** and **next-method?**. It would be clever not to generate them unless the body of the method contains calls to these functions.

```
(define-meroonet-macro (define-method call . body)
  (parse-variable-specifications
```

```
      (cdr call)
      (lambda (discriminant variables)
        (let ((g (gensym))(c (gensym)))      ; make g and c hygienic
         `(register-method
           ',(car call)
           (lambda (,g ,c)
             (lambda ,(flat-variables variables)
               ,@(generate-next-method-functions g c variables)
               . ,body ) )
           ',(cadr discriminant)
           ',(cdr call) ) ) ) ) )
```

The function `next-method?` is inspired by `call-next-method`, but it merely verifies whether a method exists; it doesn't bother to invoke one.

```
    (define (generate-next-method-functions g c variables)
      (let ((get-next-method (gensym)))
       `((define (,get-next-method)
           (if (Class-superclass ,c)
               (vector-ref (Generic-dispatch-table ,g)
                           (Class-number (Class-superclass ,c)) )
               (Generic-default ,g) ) )
         (define (call-next-method)
           ((,get-next-method) . ,(flat-variables variables)) )
         (define (next-method?)
           (not (eq? (,get-next-method) (Generic-default ,g)))) ) ) ) )
```

Bibliography

[85M85]   *Macscheme Reference Manual.* Semantic Microsystems, Sausalito, California, 1985.

[All78]   John Allen. *Anatomy of Lisp.* Computer Science Series. McGraw-Hill, 1978.

[ALQ95]   Sophie Anglade, Jean-Jacques Lacrampe, and Christian Queinnec. Semantics of combinations in scheme. *Lisp Pointers, ACM SIGPLAN Special Interest Publication on Lisp,* 7(4):15–20, October–December 1995.

[App87]   Andrew Appel. Garbage Collection can be faster than Stack Allocation. *Information Processing Letters,* 25(4):275–279, June 1987.

[App92a]   Andrew Appel. *Compiling with continuations.* Cambridge Press, 1992.

[App92b]   Apple Computer, Eastern Research and Technology. *Dylan, An object-oriented dynamic language.* Apple Computer, Inc., April 1992.

[AR88]   Norman Adams and Jonathan Rees. Object-oriented programming in Scheme. In *Conference Record of the 1988 ACM Conference on Lisp and Functional Programming,* pages 277–288, August 1988.

[AS85]   Harold Abelson and Gerald Jay with Julie Sussman Sussman. *Structure and Interpretation of Computer Programs.* MIT Press, Cambridge, Mass., 1985.

[AS94]   Andrew W Appel and Zhong Shao. An empirical and analytic study of stack vs heap cost for languages with closures. Technical Report CS-TR-450-94, Princeton University, Department of Computer Science, Princeton (New-Jersey USA), March 1994.

[Att95]   Giuseppe Attardi. The embeddable common Lisp. *Lisp Pointers, ACM SIG-PLAN Special Interest Publication on Lisp,* 8(1):30–41, January–April 1995. LUV-94, Fourth International LISP Users and Vendors Conference.

[Bak]   Henry G Baker. Cons should not cons its arguments, part ii: Cheney on the m.t.a. ftp://ftp.netcom.com/pub/hb/hbaker/CheneyMTA.ps.

[Bak78]   Henry G Baker. List processing in real time on a serial computer. *Communications of the ACM,* 21(4):280–294, April 1978.

[Bak92a]   Henry G Baker. The buried binding and dead binding problems of Lisp 1.5. *Lisp Pointers, ACM SIGPLAN Special Interest Publication on Lisp,* 5(2):11–19, April–June 1992.

[Bak92b]   Henry G Baker. Inlining semantics for subroutines which are recursive. *SIGPLAN Notices,* 27(12):39–46, December 1992.

[Bak92c]   Henry G Baker. Metacircular semantics for common Lisp special forms. *Lisp Pointers,* 5(4):11–20, 1992.

[Bak93]   Henry G Baker. Equal rights for functional objects or, the more things change, the more they are the same. *OOPS Messenger*, 4(4):2–27, October 1993.

[Bar84]   H P Barendregt. *The Lambda Calculus*. Number 103 in Studies in Logic. North Holland, Amsterdam, 1984.

[Bar89]   Joel F. Bartlett. Scheme->c a portable scheme-to-c compiler. Research Report 89 1, DEC Western Research Laboratory, Palo Alto, California, January 1989.

[Baw88]   Alan Bawden. Reification without evaluation. In *Conference Record of the 1988 ACM Symposium on LISP and Functional Programming*, pages 342–351, Snowbird, Utah, July 1988. ACM Press.

[BC87]   Jean-Pierre Briot and Pierre Cointe. A uniform model for object-oriented languages using the class abstraction. In *IJCAI '87*, pages 40–43, 1987.

[BCSJ86]   Jean-Pierre Briot, Pierre Cointe, and Emmanuel Saint-James. Réécriture et récursion dans une fermeture, étude dans un Lisp à liaison superficielle et application aux objets. In Pierre Cointe and Jean Bézivin, editors, 3èmes journées *LOO/AFCET*, number 48 in Revue Bigre+Globule, pages 90–100, IRCAM, Paris (France), January 1986.

[BDG$^+$88] Daniel G. Bobrow, Linda G. DeMichiel, Richard P. Gabriel, Sonya E. Keene, Gregor Kiczales, and David A. Moon. Common Lisp object system specification. *SIGPLAN Notices*, 23, September 1988. special issue.

[Bel73]   James R Bell. Threaded code. *Communications of the ACM*, 16(6):370–372, June 1973.

[Bet91]   David Michael Betz. *XSCHEME: An Object-oriented Scheme*. P.O. Box 144, Peterborough, NH 03458 (USA), July 1991. version 0.28.

[BG94]   Henri E Bal and Dick Grune. *Programming Language Essentials*. Addison Wesley, 1994.

[BHY87]   Adrienne Bloss, Paul Hudak, and Jonathan Young. Code optimizations for lazy evaluation. *International journal on Lisp and Symbolic Computation*, 1(2):147–164, 1987.

[BJ86]   David H Bartley and John C Jensen. The implementation of pc Scheme. In *Conference Record of the 1986 ACM Symposium on LISP and Functional Programming*, pages 86–93, Cambridge, Massachusetts, August 1986. ACM Press.

[BKK$^+$86] D G Bobrow, K Kahn, G Kiczales, L Masinter, M Stefik, and F Zdybel. Commonloops: Merging Lisp and object oriented programming. In *OOPSLA '86 — Object-Oriented Programming Systems and LAnguages*, pages 17–29, Portland (Oregon, USA), 1986.

[BM82]   Robert S. Boyer and J. Strother Moore. A mechanical proof of the unsolvability of the halting problem. Technical Report ICSCA-CMP-28, July 1982.

[BR88]   Alan Bawden and Jonathan Rees. Syntactic closures. In *Proceedings of the 1988 ACM Symposium on LISP and Functional Programming*, Salt Lake City, Utah., July 1988.

[BW88]   Hans J Boehm and M Weiser. Garbage collection in an uncooperative environment. *Software — Practice and Experience*, 18(9), September 1988.

[Car93]   Luca Cardelli. An implementation of F$_<$. Research Report 97, DEC-SRC, February 1993.

[Car94]   George J. Carrette. *Siod, Scheme In One Defun*. PARADIGM Associates Incorporated, 29 Putnam Ave, Suite 6, Cambridge, MA 02138, USA, 1994.

[Cay83]   Michel Cayrol. *Le Langage Lisp*. Cepadues Editions, Toulouse (France), 1983.

[CC77]   P. Cousot and R. Cousot. Abstract interpretation: a unified lattice model for static analysis of programs by construction or approximation of fixpoints. In *POPL'77 — 4th ACM SIGPLAN-SIGACT Symposium on Principles of Programming Languages*, pages 238–252, Los Angeles, CA, January 1977. ACM Press.

[CDD+91]   J. Chailloux, M. Devin, F. Dupont, J.-M. Hullot, B. Serpette, and J. Vuillemin. *Le-Lisp version 15.24, le manuel de référence*. INRIA, May 1991.

[CEK+89]   L W Cannon, R A Elliott, L W Kirchhoff, J H Miller, J M Milner, R W Mitze, E P Schan, N O Whittington, H Spencer, and D Keppel. *Recommended C Style and Coding Standards*, November 1989.

[CG77]   Douglas W. Clark and C. Cordell Green. An empirical study of list structure in LISP. *Communications of the ACM*, 20(2):78–87, February 1977.

[CH94]   William D Clinger and Lars Thomas Hansen. Lambda, the ultimate label, or a simple optimizing compiler for Scheme. In *Proceedings of the 1994 ACM Conference on Lisp and Functional Programmming* [lfp94], pages 128–139.

[Cha80]   Jérôme Chailloux. *Le modèle VLISP : description, implémentation et évaluation*. Thèse de troisième cycle, Université de Vincennes, April 1980. Rapport LITP 80-20, Paris (France).

[Cha94]   Gregory J Chaitin. The limits of mathematics. IBM PO Box 704, Yorktown Heights, NY 10598 (USA), July 1994.

[CHO88]   William D. Clinger, Anne H. Hartheimer, and Eric M. Ost. Implementation strategies for continuations. In *Conference Record of the 1988 ACM Conference on Lisp and Functional Programming*, pages 124–131, August 1988.

[Chr95]   Christophe. *La Famille Fenouillard*. Armand Colin, 1895.

[Cla79]   Douglas W. Clark. Measurements of dynamic list structure use in Lisp. *IEEE Transactions on Software Engineering*, 5(1):51–59, January 1979.

[Cli84]   William Clinger. The Scheme 311 compiler: an exercise in denotational semantics. In *Conference Record of the 1984 ACM Symposium on Lisp and Functional Programming*, pages 356–364, 1984.

[Coi87]   Pierre Cointe. The ObjVlisp kernel: a reflexive architecture to define a uniform object oriented system. In P. Maes and D. Nardi, editors, *Workshop on MetaLevel Architectures and Reflection*, Alghiero, Sardinia (Italy), October 1987. North Holland.

[Com84]   Douglas Comer. *Operating System Design: The XINU Approach*. Prentice-Hall, 1984.

[CR91a]   William Clinger and Jonathan Rees. Macros that work. In *POPL '91 – Eighteenth Annual ACM symposium on Principles of Programming Languages*, pages 155–162, Orlando, (Florida USA), January 1991.

[CR91b]   William Clinger and Jonathan A Rees. The revised[4] report on the algorithmic language Scheme. *Lisp Pointer*, 4(3), 1991.

[Cur89]   Pavel Curtis. (algorithms). *Lisp Pointers, ACM SIGPLAN Special Interest Publication on Lisp*, 3(1):48–61, July 1989.

[Dan87]   Olivier Danvy. Memory allocation and higher-order functions. In *Proceedings of the ACM SIGPLAN'87 Symposium on Interpreters and Interpretive Techniques*, SIGPLAN Notices, Vol. 22, No 7, pages 241–252, Saint-Paul, Minnesota, June 1987. ACM, ACM Press.

[Del89]   Vincent Delacour. Picolo expresso. *Revue Bigre+Globule*, (65):30–42, July
           1989.

[Deu80]   L Peter Deutsch. Bytelisp and its alto implementation. In *Conference Record
           of the 1980 LISP Conference* [lfp80], pages 231–242.

[Deu89]   Alain Deutsch. Génération automatique d'interprèteurs et compilation à partir
           de spécifications dénotationnelles. Rapport de DEA-LAP 1988 LITP-RXF 89-
           17, LITP, January 1989.

[Dev85]   Matthieu Devin. Le portage du système Le-Lisp. Rapport technique 50,
           INRIA-Rocquencourt, May 1985.

[DF90]   Olivier Danvy and Andrzej Filinski. Abstracting control. In *LFP '90 –
           ACM Symposium on Lisp and Functional Programming*, pages 151–160, Nice
           (France), June 1990.

[DFH86]   R. Kent Dybvig, Daniel P. Friedman, and Christopher T. Haynes. Expansion-
           passing style: Beyond conventional macros. In *Conference Record of the 1986
           ACM Conference on Lisp and Functional Programming*, pages 143–150, 1986.

[DFH88]   R. Kent Dybvig, Daniel P. Friedman, and Christopher T. Haynes. Expansion-
           passing style: a general macro mechanism. *International journal on Lisp and
           Symbolic Computation*, 1(1):53–76, June 1988.

[DH92]   Olivier Danvy and John Hatcliff. Thunks (continued). In *Proceedings of the
           Workshop on Static Analysis WSA'92*, volume 81-82 of *Bigre Journal*, pages
           3–11, Bordeaux, France, September 1992. IRISA, Rennes, France. Extended
           version available as Technical Report CIS-92-28, Kansas State University.

[DHB93]   R. Kent Dybvig, Robert Hieb, and Carl Bruggeman. Syntactic abstraction in
           Scheme. *International journal on Lisp and Symbolic Computation*, 5(4):295–
           326, 1993.

[DHHM92]   R Ducournau, M Habib, M Huchard, and M L Mugnier. Monotonic conflict
           resolution mechanisms for inheritance. In *OOPSLA '92 — Object-Oriented
           Programming Systems and LAnguages*, pages 16–4, 1992.

[Dil88]   Antoni Diller. *Compiling Functional Languages*. John Wiley and sons, 1988.

[DM88]   Olivier Danvy and Karoline Malmkjær. A Blond primer. DIKU report 88/21,
           University of Copenhagen, Copenhagen, Denmark, 1988.

[dM95]   Antoine Dumesnil de Maricourt. *Macro-expansion en Lisp, sémantique et réal-
           isation*. Thèse d'université, Université Paris 7, Paris (France), June 1995.

[DPS94a]   Harley Davis, Pierre Parquier, and Nitsan Séniak. Sweet harmony: the
           talk/c++ connection. In *Proceedings of the 1994 ACM Conference on Lisp
           and Functional Programmming* [lfp94], pages 121–127.

[DPS94b]   Harley Davis, Pierre Parquier, and Nitsan Séniak. Talking about modules and
           delivery. In *Proceedings of the 1994 ACM Conference on Lisp and Functional
           Programmming* [lfp94], pages 113–120.

[dR87]   Jim des Rivières. Control-related meta-level facilities in Lisp. In P. Maes
           and D. Nardi, editors, *Workshop on Meta-Level Architecture and Reflection*,
           Alghiero, Sardinia (Italy), October 1987. North Holland.

[dRS84]   Jim des Rivières and Brian Cantwell Smith. The implementation of procedu-
           rally reflective languages. In *Conference Record of the 1984 ACM Symposium
           on LISP and Functional Programming*, pages 331–347, Austin, Texas, August
           1984. ACM Press.

[Dyb87]   R. Kent Dybvig. *The Scheme Programming Language*. Prentice-Hall, Inc., Englewood Cliffs, New Jersey, 1987.

[ES70]   Jay Earley and Howard Sturgis. A formalism for translator interactions. *Communications of the ACM*, 13(10):607–617, October 1970.

[Fel88]   Matthias Felleisen. The theory and practice of first-class prompts. In *POPL '88 – Fifteenth Annual ACM symposium on Principles of Programming Languages*, pages 180–190, San Diego (California USA), January 1988.

[Fel90]   Matthias Felleisen. On the expressive power of programming languages. In Neil Jones, editor, *ESOP '90 – European Symposium on Programming*, volume 432 of *Lecture Notes in Computer Science*, pages 134–151, Copehaguen (Danmark), 1990. Springer-Verlag.

[FF87]   Matthias Felleisen and Daniel P. Friedman. A reduction semantics for imperative higher-order languages. *Parallel Architectures and Languages Europe*, 259:206–223, 1987.

[FF89]   Matthias Felleisen and Daniel P Friedman. A syntactic theory of sequential state. *Theoretical Computer Science*, 69(3):243–287, 1989. Preliminary version in: *Proc. 14th ACM Symposium on Principles of Programming Languages*, 1987, 314-325.

[FFDM87] Matthias Felleisen, Daniel P. Friedman, Bruce Duba, and John Merrill. Beyond continuations. Computer Science Dept. Technical Report 216, Indiana University, Bloomington, Indiana, February 1987.

[FH89]   Matthias Felleisen and Robert Hieb. The revised report on the syntactic theories of sequential control and state. Computer Science Technical Report No. 100, Rice University, June 1989.

[FL87]   Marc Feeley and Guy LaPalme. Using closures for code generation. *Journal of Computer Languages*, 12(1):47–66, 1987.

[FM90]   Marc Feeley and James S. Miller. A parallel virtual machine for efficient Scheme compilation. In *Proceedings of the 1990 ACM Conference on Lisp and Functional Programming*, Nice, France, June 1990.

[FW76]   D.P. Friedman and D.S. Wise. Cons should not evaluate its arguments. In Michaelson and Milner, editors, *Proceedings of the 3rd International Colloquium on "Automata, Languages and Programming"*, pages 257–284. Edinburgh University Press, July 1976.

[FW84]   Daniel P. Friedman and Mitchell Wand. Reification: Reflection without metaphysics. In *Conference Record of the 1984 ACM Symposium on LISP and Functional Programming*, pages 348–355, Austin, TX., August 1984.

[FWFD88] Matthias Felleisen, Mitchell Wand, Daniel P. Friedman, and Bruce Duba. Abstract continuations: a mathematical semantics for handling functional jumps. In *Proceedings of the 1988 ACM Symposium on LISP and Functional Programming*, Salt Lake City, Utah., July 1988.

[FWH92] Daniel P Friedman, Mitchell Wand, and Christopher Haynes. *Essentials of Programming Languages*. MIT Press, Cambridge MA and McGraw-Hill, 1992.

[Gab88]   Richard P Gabriel. The why of y. *Lisp Pointers, ACM SIGPLAN Special Interest Publication on Lisp*, 2(2):15–25, 1988.

[GBM82] Martin L. Griss, Eric Benson, and Gerald Q Maguire. Psl: A portable LISP system. In *Conference Record of the 1982 ACM Symposium on LISP and Functional Programming*, pages 88–97, Pittsburgh, Pennsylvania, August 1982. ACM Press.

[Gor75]   Michael J C Gordon. Operational reasoning and denotational semantics. In G. Huet and G. Kahn, editors, *Actes du Colloque IRIA "Constructions et Justifications de Programmes"*, pages 83–98, Arc et Senans, July 1975.

[Gor88]   Michael J C Gordon. *Programming Language Theory and its Implementation.* International Series in Computer Science. Prentice-Hall, 1988.

[GP88]   Richard P Gabriel and Kent M Pitman. Technical issues of separation in function cells and value cells. *International journal on Lisp and Symbolic Computation*, 1(1):81–101, June 1988.

[GR83]   Adèle Goldberg and David Robson. *Smalltalk-80, The Language and its Implementation.* Addison Wesley, 1983.

[Gra93]   Paul Graham. *On Lisp, Advanced Techniques for Common Lisp.* Prentice-Hall, 1993.

[Gre77]   Patrick Greussay. *Contribution à la définition interprétative et à l'implémentation des Lambda-langages.* Thèse d'état, Université Paris VI, November 1977. Rapport LITP 78-2.

[Gud93]   David Gudeman. Representing type information in dynamically typed languages. Technical Report 93–27, Department of Computer Science, University of Arizona, Tucson, AZ 85721, USA, October 1993.

[Han90]   Chris Hanson. Efficient stack allocation for tail-recursive languages. In *Proceedings of the 1990 ACM Conference on Lisp and Functional Programming*, Nice, France, June 1990.

[HD90]   Robert Hieb and R. Kent Dybvig. Continuations and concurrency. In *PPOPP '90 – ACM SIGPLAN Symposium on Principles and Practices of Parallel Programming*, pages 128–136, Seattle (Washington US), March 1990.

[HDB90]   Robert Hieb, R. Kent Dybvig, and Carl Bruggeman. Representing control in the presence of first-class continuations. In *Proceedings of the SIGPLAN '90 Conference on Programming Language Design and Implementation*, pages 66–77, White Plains, New York, June 1990.

[Hen80]   Peter Henderson. *Functional Programming, Application and Implementation.* International Series in Computer Science. Prentice-Hall, 1980.

[Hen92a] Fritz Henglein. Global tagging optimization by type inference. In *Proceedings of the 1992 ACM Conference on Lisp and Functional Programming*, pages 205–215, San Francisco, USA, June 1992.

[Hen92b] Wade Hennessey. Wcl: Delivering efficient COMMON LISP applications under UN⋆X. In *Conference Record of the 1992 ACM Symposium on LISP and Functional Programming*, pages 260–269, San Francisco, California, June 1992. ACM Press.

[HFW84]   Christopher T. Haynes, Daniel P. Friedman, and Mitchell Wand. Continuations and coroutines. In *Conference Record of the 1984 ACM Symposium on Lisp and Functional Programming*, pages 293–298, Austin, TX., 1984.

[Hof93]   Ulrich Hoffmann. Using c as target code for translating highlevel programming languages. Technical Report APPLY/CAU/IV.4/2, Christian-Albrechts-Universitey of Kiel, 1993.

[Hon93]   P. Joseph Hong. Threaded code designs for forth interpreters. *SIG FORTH, Newsletter of the ACM's Special Interest Group on FORTH*, 4(2):11–18, fall 1993.

[HS75]   Carl Hewitt and Brian Smith. Towards a programming apprentice. *IEEE Transactions on Software Engineering*, 1(1):26–45, March 1975.

[HS91]   Samuel P Harbison and Guy L Steele, Jr. *C: A Reference Manual*. Prentice-Hall, 1991.

[IEE91]   IEEE Std 1178-1990. *IEEE Standard for the Scheme Programming Language*. Institute of Electrical and Electronic Engineers, Inc., New York, NY, 1991.

[ILO94]   ILOG, 2 Avenue Galliéni, BP 85, 94253 Gentilly, France. *Ilog-Talk Reference Manual*, 1994.

[IM89]   Takayasu Ito and Manabu Matsui. A parallel lisp language PaiLisp and its kernel specification. In Takayasu Ito and Robert H Halstead, Jr., editors, *Proceedings of the US/Japan Workshop on Parallel Lisp*, volume Lecture Notes in Computer Science 441, pages 58–100, Sendai (Japan), June 1989. Springer-Verlag.

[IMY92]   Yuuji Ichisugi, Satoshi Matsuoka, and Akinori Yonezawa. RbCL: A reflective object-oriented concurrent language without a run-time kernel. In Yonezawa and Smith [YS92], pages 24–35.

[ISO90]   ISO/IEC 9899:1990. Programmming language — c. Technical report, Information Technology, 1990.

[ISO94]   ISO-IEC/JTC1/SC22/WG16. Programming language ISLISP, CD 13816. Technical report, ISO-IEC/JTC1/SC22/WG16, 1994.

[ITW86]   Takayasu Ito, Takashi Tamura, and Shin-ichi Wada. Theoretical comparisons of interpreted/compiled executions of Lisp on sequential and parallel machine models. In H J Kugler, editor, *Proceedings of the IFIP 10th World Computer Congress*, Dublin (Ireland), September 1986. North Holland.

[Jaf94]   Aubrey Jaffer. *Reference Manual for scm*, 1994.

[JF92]   Stanley Jefferson and Daniel P Friedman. A simple reflective interpreter. In Yonezawa and Smith [YS92], pages 48–58.

[JGS93]   Neil D Jones, C Karsten Gomard, and Peter Sestoft. *Partial Evaluation and Automatic Program Generation*. Prentice Hall International, 1993. With chapters by L.O. Andersen and T. Mogensen.

[Kah87]   Gilles Kahn. Natural semantics. In *Proc. of STACS 1987, Lecture Notes in Computer Science*, chapter 247. Springer–Verlag, March 1987.

[Kam90]   Samuel Kamin. *Programming Languages: an Interpreter-Based Approach*. Addison-Wesley, Reading, Mass., 1990.

[KdRB92] Gregor Kiczales, Jim des Rivières, and Daniel G Bobrow. *The Art of the Metaobject Protocol*. MIT Press, Cambridge MA, 1992.

[Kes88]   Robert R. Kessler. *Lisp, Objects, and Symbolic Programming*. Scott, Foreman/Little, Brown College Division, Glenview, Illinois, 1988.

[KFFD86] Eugene E. Kohlbecker, Daniel P. Friedman, Matthias Felleisen, and Bruce Duba. Hygienic macro expansion. *Symposium on LISP and Functional Programming*, pages 151–161, August 1986.

[KH89]   Richard Kelsey and Paul Hudak. Realistic compilation by program transformation. In *POPL'89 — 16th ACM SIGPLAN-SIGACT Symposium on Principles of Programming Languages*, pages 281–292, Austin (Texas, USA), January 1989. ACM Press.

[Knu84]   Donald Ervin Knuth. *The TEX Book*. Addison Wesley, 1984.

[KR78]   Brian W Kernighan and Dennis Ritchie. *The C Programming Language*. Prentice-Hall, Englewood Cliffs, New Jersey, 1978.

[KR90]   Gregor Kiczales and Luis Rodriguez. Efficient method dispatch in pcl. In *LFP '90 – ACM Symposium on Lisp and Functional Programming*, pages 99–1052, Nice (France), June 1990.

[KW90]   Morry Katz and Daniel Weise. Continuing into the future: on the interaction of futures and first-class continuations. In *Proceedings of the 1990 ACM Conference on Lisp and Functional Programming*, Nice, France, June 1990.

[Lak80]   Fred H. Lakin. Computing with text-graphic forms. In *Conference Record of the 1980 Lisp Conference*, pages 100–105, 1980.

[Lan65]   P J Landin. A Correspondence between algol 60 and Church's Lambda-notation. *Communications of the ACM*, 8:89–101 and 158–165, February 1965.

[Leb05]   Maurice Leblanc. *813*. Éditions Pierre Lafitte, 1905.

[LF88]   Henry Lieberman and Christopher Fry. Common eval. *Lisp Pointers*, 2(1):23–33, July 1988.

[LF93]   Shinn-Der Lee and Daniel P Friedman. Quasi-static scoping: Sharing variable bindings across multiple lexical scopes. In *POPL '93 – Twentieth Annual ACM symposium on Principles of Programming Languages*, pages 479–492, Charleston (South Carolina, USA), January 1993. ACM Press.

[lfp80]   *Conference Record of the 1980 LISP Conference*, Stanford (California USA), August 1980. The LISP Conference.

[lfp94]   *Proceedings of the 1994 ACM Conference on Lisp and Functional Programming*, Orlando (Florida USA), June 1994. ACM Press.

[Lie87]   Henry Lieberman. Reversible object-oriented interpreters. In *ECOOP '87 – European Conference on Object-Oriented Programming*, volume Special issue of Bigre 54, pages 13–22, Paris (France), June 1987. AFCET.

[LLSt93]   Bil Lewis, Dan LaLiberte, Richard Stallman, and the GNU Manual Group. Gnu emacs Lisp reference manual. Technical report, Free Software Foundation, 675 Massachusetts Avenue, Cambridge MA 02139 USA, Edition 2.0 1993.

[LP86]   Kevin J. Lang and Barak A. Pearlmutter. Oaklisp: an object-oriented Scheme with first class types. In *ACM Conference on Object-Oriented Systems, Programming, Languages and Applications*, pages 30–37, September 1986.

[LP88]   Kevin J. Lang and Barak A. Pearlmutter. Oaklisp: an object-oriented dialect of Scheme. *International journal on Lisp and Symbolic Computation*, 1(1):39–51, May 1988.

[LW93]   Xavier Leroy and Pierre Weis. *Manuel de référence du langage Caml*. InterÉditions, 1993.

[MAE+62]   John McCarthy, Paul W. Abrahams, Daniel J. Edwards, Timothy P. Hart, and Michael I. Levin. Lisp 1.5 programmer's manual. Technical report, MIT Press, Cambridge, MA (USA), 1962.

[Man74]   Zohar Manna. *Mathematical Theory of Computation*. Computer Science Series. McGraw-Hill, 1974.

[Mas86]   Ian A Mason. *The Semantics of Destructive Lisp*. CSLI Lecture Notes, Leland Stanford Junior University, California USA, 1986.

[Mat92]   Luis Mateu. Efficient implementation of coroutines. In Yves Bekkers and Jacques Cohen, editors, *International Workshop on Memory Management*, number 637 in Lecture Notes in Computer Science, pages 230–247, Saint-Malo (France), September 1992. Springer-Verlag.

[MB93]   Luis Mateu-Brule. *Stratégies avancées de gestion de blocs de contrôle.* Thèse de doctorat d'université, Université Pierre et Marie Curie (Paris 6), Paris (France), February 1993.

[McC60]   John McCarthy. Recursive functions of symbolic expressions and their computation by machine – part i. *Communications of the ACM*, 3(1):184–195, 1960.

[McC78a] John McCarthy. Lisp history. In *Proc. SIGPLAN History of Programming Languages Conference*, pages 217–223, 1978. Also Sigplan Notices 13(8).

[McC78b] John McCarthy. A micro-manual for Lisp - not the whole truth. In *Proc. SIGPLAN History of Programming Languages Conference*, pages 215–216, 1978. Also Sigplan Notices 13(8).

[McD93]   Raymond C McDowell. The relatedness and comparative utility of various approaches to operational semantics. Technical Report MS-CIS-93-16, LINC LAB 246, University of Pennsylvania, February 1993.

[MNC⁺89] Gérald Masini, Amedeo Napoli, Dominique Colnet, Daniel Léonard, and Karl Tombre. *Les langages à objets.* InterÉditions, 1989.

[Mor92]   Luc Moreau. An operational semantics for a parallel functional language with continuations. In D. Etiemble and J-C. Syre, editors, *PARLE '92 – Parallel Architectures and Languages Europe*, pages 415–430, Paris (France), June 1992. Lecture Notes in Computer Science 605, Springer-Verlag.

[Mor94]   Luc Moreau. *Sound Evaluation of Parallel Functional Programs with First-Class Continuations.* Thèse de docteur en sciences apppliquées, Université de Liège (Belgique), avril 1994.

[Mos70]   Joel Moses. The function of FUNCTION in LISP. *SIGSAM Bulletin*, 15:13–27, July 1970.

[Moz87]   Wolfgang A Mozart. Don Giovanni, 1787.

[MP80]   Steven S. Muchnick and Uwe F. Pleban. A semantic comparison of lisp and Scheme. In *Conference Record of the 1980 Lisp Conference*, pages 56–65. The Lisp Conference, P.O. Box 487, Redwood Estates CA., 1980.

[MQ94]   Luc Moreau and Christian Queinnec. Partial continuations as the difference of continuations, a duumvirate of control operators. In Manuel Hermenegildo and Jaan Penjam, editors, *Lecture Notes in Computer Science 844*, pages 182–197, Madrid (Spain), September 1994. International Workshop PLILP '94 – Programming Language Implementation and Logic Programming, Springer-Verlag.

[MR91]   James S Miller and Guillermo J Rozas. Free variables and first-class environments. *International journal on Lisp and Symbolic Computation*, 4(2):107–141, 1991.

[MS80]   F Lockwood Morris and Jerald S Schwarz. Computing cyclic list structures. In *Conference Record of the 1980 Lisp Conference*, pages 144–153. The Lisp Conference, 1980.

[Mul92]   Robert Muller. M-lisp: A representation-independent dialect of lisp with reduction semantics. *ACM Transactions on Programming Languages and Systems*, 14(4):589–615, October 1992.

[Nei84]   Eugen Neidl. *Étude des relations avec l'interprète dans la compilation de Lisp*. Thèse de troisième cycle, Université Paris 6, Paris (France), 1984.

[Nor72]   Eric Norman. 1100 Lisp reference manual. Technical report, University of Wisconsin, 1972.

[NQ89]   Greg Nuyens and Christian Queinnec. Identifier Semantics: a Matter of References. Technical Report LIX RR 89 02, 67–80, Laboratoire d'Informatique de l'École Polytechnique, May 1989.

[PE92]   Julian Padget and Greg Nuyens (Editors). The eulisp definition. Technical report, University of Bath, 1992.

[Per79]   Jean-François Perrot. Lisp et λ-calcul. In Bernard Robinet (ed), editor, λ-*calcul et sémantique formelle des langages de programmation*, La Châtre (France), 1979. AFCET-GROPLAN, LITP-ENSTA, Paris.

[Pit80]   Kent Pitman. Special forms in Lisp. In *Conference Record of the 1980 LISP Conference* [lfp80], pages 179–187.

[PJ87]   Simon L. Peyton-Jones. *The Implementation of Functional Programming Languages*. International Series in Computer Science. Prentice-Hall, 1987.

[PNB93]   Padget, J.A., Nuyens, G., and Bretthauer, H. An overview of EuLisp. *Lisp and Symbolic Computation*, 6(1/2):9–98, 1993.

[QC88]   Christian Queinnec and Pierre Cointe. An open-ended Data Representation Model for Eu-Lisp. In *LFP '88 – ACM Symposium on Lisp and Functional Programming*, pages 298–308, Snowbird (Utah, USA), 1988.

[QD93]   Christian Queinnec and David De Roure. Design of a concurrent and distributed language. In Robert H Halstead Jr and Takayasu Ito, editors, *Parallel Symbolic Computing: Languages, Systems, and Applications, (US/Japan Workshop Proceedings)*, volume Lecture Notes in Computer Science 748, pages 234–259, Boston (Massachussetts USA), October 1993.

[QD96]   Christian Queinnec and David De Roure. Sharing code through first-class environments. In *Proceedings of ICFP'96 — ACM SIGPLAN International Conference on Functional Programming*, pages ??–??, Philadelphia (Pennsylvania, USA), May 1996.

[QG92]   Christian Queinnec and Jean-Marie Geffroy. Partial evaluation applied to symbolic pattern matching with intelligent backtrack. In M Billaud, P Castéran, MM Corsini, K Musumbu, and A Rauzy, editors, *WSA '92—Workshop on Static Analysis*, number 81-82 in Revue Bigre+Globule, pages 109–117, Bordeaux (France), September 1992.

[QP90]   Christian Queinnec and Julian Padget. A deterministic model for modules and macros. Bath Computing Group Technical Report 90-36, University of Bath, Bath (UK), 1990.

[QP91a]   Christian Queinnec and Julian Padget. A proposal for a modular Lisp with macros and dynamic evaluation. In *Journées de Travail sur l'Analyse Statique en Programmation Équationnelle, Fonctionnelle et Logique*, pages 1–8, Bordeaux (France), October 1991. Revue Bigre+Globule 74.

[QP91b]   Christian Queinnec and Julian Padget. Modules, macros and Lisp. In *Eleventh International Conference of the Chilean Computer Science Society*, pages 111–123, Santiago (Chile), October 1991. Plenum Publishing Corporation, New York NY (USA).

[QS91]   Christian Queinnec and Bernard Serpette. A Dynamic Extent Control Operator for Partial Continuations. In *POPL '91 – Eighteenth Annual ACM symposium on Principles of Programming Languages*, pages 174–184, Orlando (Florida USA), January 1991.

[Que82]   Christian Queinnec. *Langage d'un autre type : Lisp*. Eyrolles, Paris (France), 1982.

[Que89]   Christian Queinnec. Lisp – Almost a whole Truth. Technical Report LIX/RR/89/03, 79–106, Laboratoire d'Informatique de l'École Polytechnique, December 1989.

[Que90a] Christian Queinnec. A Framework for Data Aggregates. In Pierre Cointe, Philippe Gautron, and Christian Queinnec, editors, *Actes des JFLA 90 – Journées Francophones des Langages Applicatifs*, pages 21–32, La Rochelle (France), January 1990. Revue Bigre+Globule 69.

[Que90b] Christian Queinnec. *Le filtrage : une application de (et pour) Lisp*. InterÉditions, Paris (France), 1990. ISBN 2-7296-0332-8.

[Que90c] Christian Queinnec. PolyScheme : A Semantics for a Concurrent Scheme. In *Workshop on High Performance and Parallel Computing in Lisp*, Twickenham (UK), November 1990. European Conference on Lisp and its Practical Applications.

[Que92a] Christian Queinnec. Compiling syntactically recursive programs. *Lisp Pointers, ACM SIGPLAN Special Interest Publication on Lisp*, 5(4):2–10, October-December 1992.

[Que92b] Christian Queinnec. A concurrent and distributed extension to scheme. In D. Etiemble and J-C. Syre, editors, *PARLE '92 – Parallel Architectures and Languages Europe*, pages 431–446, Paris (France), June 1992. Lecture Notes in Computer Science 605, Springer-Verlag.

[Que93a] Christian Queinnec. Continuation conscious compilation. *Lisp Pointers, ACM SIGPLAN Special Interest Publication on Lisp*, 6(1):2–14, January 1993.

[Que93b] Christian Queinnec. Designing MEROON v3. In Christian Rathke, Jürgen Kopp, Hubertus Hohl, and Harry Bretthauer, editors, *Object-Oriented Programming in Lisp: Languages and Applications. A Report on the ECOOP'93 Workshop*, number 788, Sankt Augustin (Germany), September 1993.

[Que93c] Christian Queinnec. A library of high-level control operators. *Lisp Pointers, ACM SIGPLAN Special Interest Publication on Lisp*, 6(4):11–26, October 1993.

[Que93d] Christian Queinnec. Literate programming from scheme to TEX. Research Report LIX RR 93.05, Laboratoire d'Informatique de l'École Polytechnique, 91128 Palaiseau Cedex, France, November 1993.

[Que94]   Christian Queinnec. Locality, causality and continuations. In *LFP '94 – ACM Symposium on Lisp and Functional Programming*, pages 91–102, Orlando (Florida, USA), June 1994. ACM Press.

[Que95]   Christian Queinnec. Dmeroon overview of a distributed class-based causally-coherent data model. In T. Ito, R. Halstead, and C. Queinnec, editors, *PSLS 95 – Parallel Symbolic Langages and Systems*, Beaune (France), October 1995.

[R3R86]   Revised[3] report on the algorithmic language scheme. *ACM Sigplan Notices*, 21(12), December 1986.

[RA82]   Jonathan A. Rees and Norman I. Adams. T: a dialect of lisp or, lambda: the ultimate software tool. In *Conference Record of the 1982 ACM Symposium on Lisp and Functional Programming*, pages 114–122, 1982.

[RAM84]   Jonathan A. Rees, Norman I. Adams, and James R. Meehan. *The T Manual, Fourth Edition*. Yale University Computer Science Department, January 1984.

[Ray91]   Eric Raymond. *The New Hacker's Dictionary*. MIT Press, Cambridge MA, 1991. With assistance and illustrations by Guy L. Steele Jr.

[Rey72]   John Reynolds. Definitional interpreters for higher order programming languages. In *ACM Conference Proceedings*, pages 717–740. ACM, 1972.

[Rib69]   Daniel Ribbens. *Programmation non numérique : Lisp 1.5*. Monographies d'Informatique, AFCET, Dunod, Paris, 1969.

[RM92]   John R Rose and Hans Muller. Integrating the Scheme and c languages. In *LFP '92 – ACM Symposium on Lisp and Functional Programming*, pages 247–259, San Francisco (California USA), June 1992. ACM Press. Lisp Pointers V(1).

[Row90]   William Rowan. A Lisp compiler producing compact code. In *Conference Record of the 1980 Lisp Conference* [lfp80], pages 216–222.

[Roz92]   Guillermo Juan Rozas. Taming the y operator. In *LFP '92 – ACM Symposium on Lisp and Functional Programming*, pages 226–234, San Francisco (California USA), June 1992. ACM Press. Lisp Pointers V(1).

[Sam79]   Hanan Sammet. Deep and shallow binding: The assignment operation. *Computer Languages*, 4:187–198, 1979.

[Sch86]   David A Schmidt. *Denotational Semantics, a Methodology for Language Development*. Allyn and Bacon, 1986.

[Sco76]   Dana Scott. Data types as lattices. *Siam J. Computing*, 5(3):522–587, 1976.

[Sén89]   Nitsan Séniak. Compilation de Scheme par spécialisation explicite. *Revue Bigre+Globule*, (65):160–170, July 1989.

[Sén91]   Nitsan Séniak. *Théorie et pratique de Sqil, un langage intermédiaire pour la compilation des langages fonctionnels*. Thèse de doctorat d'université, Université Pierre et Marie Curie (Paris 6), Paris (France), October 1991.

[Ser93]   Manuel Serrano. De l'utilisation des analyses de flot de contrôle dans la compilation des langages fonctionnels. In Pierre Lescanne, editor, *Actes des journées du GDR de Programmation*, 1993.

[Ser94]   Manuel Serrano. *Bigloo User's Manual*, 1994. available on `ftp://ftp.inria.fr/INRIA/Projects/icsla/Implementations`.

[SF89]   George Springer and Daniel P. Friedman. *Scheme and the Art of Programming*. MIT Press and McGraw-Hill, 1989.

[SF92]   Amr Sabry and Matthias Felleisen. Reasoning about continuation-passing style programs. In *LFP '92 – ACM Symposium on Lisp and Functional Programming*, pages 288–298, San Francisco (California USA), June 1992. ACM Press. Lisp Pointers V(1).

[SG93]   Guy L. Steele, Jr. and Richard P Gabriel. The evolution of Lisp. In *The Second ACM SIGPLAN History of Proramming Languages Conference (HOPL-II)*, pages 231–270, Cambridge (Massachusetts, USA), April 1993. ACM SIGPLAN Notices 8, 3.

[Shi91]   Olin Shivers. Data-flow analysis and type recovery in Scheme. In Peter Lee, editor, *Topics in Advanced Language Implementation*. The MIT Press, Cambridge, MASS, 1991.

[SJ87]   Emmanuel Saint-James. *De la Méta-Récursivité comme Outil d'Implémentation*. Thèse d'état, Université Paris VI, December 1987.

[SJ93]   Emmanuel Saint-James. *La programmation appplicative (de LISP à la machine en passant par le lambda-calcul)*. Hermès, 1993.

[Sla61]   J R Slagle. *A Heuristic Program that Solves Symbolic Integration Problems in Freshman Calculees, Symbolic Automatic Integration (SAINT)*. PhD thesis, MIT, Lincoln Lab, 1961.

[Spi90]   Éric Spir. *Gestion dynamique de la mémoire dans les langages de programmation, application à Lisp*. Science informatique. InterÉditions, Paris (France), 1990.

[SS75]   Gerald Jay Sussman and Guy Lewis Steele Jr. Scheme: an interpreter for extended lambda calculus. MIT AI Memo 349, Massachusetts Institute of Technology, Cambridge, Mass., December 1975.

[SS78a]   Guy Lewis Steele Jr. and Gerald Jay Sussman. The art of the interpreter, or the modularity complex (parts zero, one, and two). MIT AI Memo 453, Massachusetts Institute of Technology, Cambridge, Mass., May 1978.

[SS78b]   Guy Lewis Steele Jr. and Gerald Jay Sussman. The revised report on Scheme, a dialect of lisp. MIT AI Memo 452, Massachusetts Institute of Technology, Cambridge, Mass., January 1978.

[SS80]   Guy Lewis Steele Jr. and Gerald Jay Sussman. The dream of a lifetime: a lazy variable extent mechanism. In *Conference Record of the 1980 Lisp Conference*, pages 163–172. The Lisp Conference, 1980.

[Ste78]   Guy Lewis Steele Jr. Rabbit: a compiler for Scheme. MIT AI Memo 474, Massachusetts Institute of Technology, Cambridge, Mass., May 1978.

[Ste84]   Guy L. Steele, Jr. *Common Lisp, the Language*. Digital Press, Burlington MA (USA), 1984.

[Ste90]   Guy L. Steele, Jr. *Common Lisp, the Language*. Digital Press, Burlington MA (USA), 2nd edition, 1990.

[Sto77]   Joseph E Stoy. *Denotational Semantics: The Scott-Strachey Approach to Programming Language Theory*. MIT Press, Cambridge Massachussetts USA, 1977.

[Str86]   Bjarne Stroustrup. *The C++ Programming Language*. Addison Wesley, 1986. ou "Le langage C++", InterÉditions 1989.

[SW94]   Manuel Serrano and Pierre Weis. 1+1=1: An optimizing caml compiler. In *Record of the 1994 ACM SIGPLAN Workshop on ML and its Applications*, pages 101–111, Orlando (Florida, USA), June 1994. INRIA RR 2265.

[Tak88]   M. Takeichi. Lambda-hoisting: A transformation technique for fully lazy evaluation of functional programs. *New Generation Computing*, (5):377–391, 1988.

[Tei74]   Warren Teitelman. *InterLISP Reference Manual*. Xerox Palo Alto Research Center, Palo Alto (California, USA), 1974.

[Tei76]   Warren Teitelman. Clisp: Conversational LISP. *IEEE Trans. on Computers*, C-25(4):354–357, April 1976.

[VH94]   Jan Vitek and R Nigel Horspool. Taming message passing: Efficient method
          look-up for dynamically typed languages. In *ECOOP '94 — 8th European
          Conference on Object-Oriented Programming*, Bologna (Italy), 1994.

[Wad88]   Philip Wadler. Deforestation: Transforming programs to eliminate trees. In
          H Ganzinger, editor, *ESOP '88 – European Symposium on Programming*, vol-
          ume 300 of *Lecture Notes in Computer Science*, pages 344–358, 1988.

[Wan80a] Mitchell Wand. Continuation-based multiprocessing. In *Conference Record of
          the 1980 Lisp Conference*, pages 19–28. The Lisp Conference, 1980.

[Wan80b] Mitchell Wand. Continuation-based program transformation strategies. *Jour-
          nal of the ACM*, 27(1):164–180, 1980.

[Wan84]   Mitchell Wand. A semantic prototyping system. In *Proceedings ACM SIG-
          PLAN '84 Compiler Construction Conference*, pages 213–221, 1984.

[Wan86]   Mitchell Wand. The mystery of the tower revealed: a non-reflective description
          of the reflective tower. In *Proceedings of the 1986 ACM Symposium on LISP
          and Functional Programming*, pages 298–307, August 1986.

[Wat93]   Richard C Waters. Macroexpand-all: An example of a simple Lisp code walker.
          Lisp Pointers, ACM SIGPLAN Special Interest Publication on Lisp, 6(1):25–32,
          January 1993.

[WC94]   Andrew K Wright and Robert Cartwright. A practical soft typing system for
          Scheme. In *Proceedings of the 1994 ACM Conference on Lisp and Functional
          Programmming* [lfp94], pages 250–262.

[WH88]   Patrick H Winston and Berthold K Horn. *Lisp*. Addison Wesley, third edition,
          1988.

[Wil92]   Paul R. Wilson. Uniprocessor garbage collection techniques. In Yves Bekkers
          and Jacques Cohen, editors, *International Workshop on Memory Management*,
          number 637 in Lecture Notes in Computer Science, pages 1–42, St. Malo,
          France, September 1992. Springer-Verlag.

[WL93]   Pierre Weis and Xavier Leroy. *Le langage Caml*. InterÉditions, 1993.

[WS90]   Larry Wall and Randal L Schwartz. *Programming perl*. O'Reilly & Associates,
          Inc., 1990.

[WS94]   Mitchell Wand and Paul Steckler. Selective and lightweight closure conversion.
          In *POPL'94 — 21st ACM SIGPLAN-SIGACT Symposium on Principles of
          Programming Languages*, pages 435–445, Portland (Oregon, USA), January
          1994. ACM Press.

[YH85]   Taiichi Yuasa and Masami Hagiya. Kyoto common Lisp report. Technical
          report, Kyoto University, Japan, 1985.

[YS92]   Akinori Yonezawa and Brian C. Smith, editors. *Reflection and Meta-Level
          Architecture: Proceedings of the International Workshop on New Models for
          Software Architecture '92*, Tokyo, Japan, November 1992. Research Institute of
          Software Engineering (RISE) and Information-Technology Promotion Agency,
          Japan (IPA), in cooperation with ACM SIGPLAN, JSST, IPSJ.

Index

F

N